SUSTAINABLE CORPORATIONS

ASPEN COURSEBOOK SERIES

SUSTAINABLE CORPORATIONS

Alan R. Palmiter
William T. Wilson, III, Presidential Chair for Business Law
Wake Forest University

ASPEN PUBLISHING

Cover image: Enrique Palacio Sansegu/iStock.com

To contact Customer Service, e-mail customer.service@aspenpublishing.com, call 1-800-950-5259, or mail correspondence to:

Aspen Publishing
Attn: Order Department
PO Box 990
Frederick, MD 21705

Printed in the United States of America.

1 2 3 4 5 6 7 8 9 0

ISBN 978-1-5438-4900-4

Library of Congress Cataloging-in-Publication Data application is in process.

About Aspen Publishing

Aspen Publishing is a leading provider of educational content and digital learning solutions to law schools in the U.S. and around the world. Aspen provides best-in-class solutions for legal education through authoritative textbooks, written by renowned authors, and breakthrough products such as Connected eBooks, Connected Quizzing, and PracticePerfect.

The Aspen Casebook Series (famously known among law faculty and students as the "red and black" casebooks) encompasses hundreds of highly regarded textbooks in more than eighty disciplines, from large enrollment courses, such as Torts and Contracts to emerging electives such as Sustainability and the Law of Policing. Study aids such as the *Examples & Explanations* and the *Emanuel Law Outlines* series, both highly popular collections, help law students master complex subject matter.

Major products, programs, and initiatives include:

- **Connected eBooks** are enhanced digital textbooks and study aids that come with a suite of online content and learning tools designed to maximize student success. Designed in collaboration with hundreds of faculty and students, the Connected eBook is a significant leap forward in the legal education learning tools available to students.
- **Connected Quizzing** is an easy-to-use formative assessment tool that tests law students' understanding and provides timely feedback to improve learning outcomes. Delivered through CasebookConnect.com, the learning platform already used by students to access their Aspen casebooks, Connected Quizzing is simple to implement and integrates seamlessly with law school course curricula.
- **PracticePerfect** is a visually engaging, interactive study aid to explain commonly encountered legal doctrines through easy-to-understand animated videos, illustrative examples, and numerous practice questions. Developed by a team of experts, PracticePerfect is the ideal study companion for today's law students.
- The **Aspen Learning Library** enables law schools to provide their students with access to the most popular study aids on the market across all of their courses. Available through an annual subscription, the online library consists of study aids in e-book, audio, and video formats with full text search, note-taking, and highlighting capabilities.
- Aspen's **Digital Bookshelf** is an institutional-level online education bookshelf, consolidating everything students and professors need to ensure success. This program ensures that every student has access to affordable course materials from day one.
- **Leading Edge** is a community centered on thinking differently about legal education and putting those thoughts into actionable strategies. At the core of the program is the Leading Edge Conference, an annual gathering of legal education thought leaders looking to pool ideas and identify promising directions of exploration.

To my Dad, who taught me to read with purpose and to write with care
To my Mom, who taught me to question most everything
and to respect the answers of others
To our Lina Jo, who teaches me to be intrepid and to love

Summary of Contents

Table of Contents

Preface

This book is obsolete. This book is timeless. This book is both.

The book is obsolete because changes in the modern corporation are happening at an exponential rate in ways that seem unlikely, often unpredictable. The book is timeless because it deals with themes that are as old as humanity, and the corporation as it evolves continues to draw from our inherent human nature. The book is both obsolete and timeless because it weaves together contemporary accounts of the corporation in transition, reminding us that who we are is what we make.

The Sustainable Corporation

> The book's cover, as well as each unit and chapter heading, includes an image of the Pantheon in Rome. It is the most remarkable edifice. More visited than any other Roman monument, it has survived intact for nearly two millennia. Its oculus, perhaps its defining feature, represents three interconnected ideas. First, beauty is eternal, not just everlasting. Second, our planetary existence depends on the sun, and we human beings cannot exist without the natural world the sun makes possible. Third, we human beings have the capacity to manipulate nature—to create eternal adaptations using the sun.

Origins

This book happened over time. It began as a tutorial in 2012 when three Wake Law students helped me prepare reading materials for a comparative company law course that I was to teach at the University of Bergamo (Italy). Using materials from a 2011 symposium at Wake Forest on "The Sustainable Corporation," the course laid out a roadmap in search of what seemed then a mythical creature.

Over the years, as I repeated the course in Bergamo and later Padua, as well as at Wake Forest and Brooklyn, the readings evolved to become a coherent textbook for a course that has included both undergraduate and professional law students. There have also been students pursuing degrees in economics, management, and sustainability.

Sequential Nature

The book, unlike many law texts, is meant to be absorbed in a sequential fell swoop. Whether a concentrated four-week course (the typical schedule in Bergamo), an eight-week course (the schedule in Padua), or a typical 14-week course (at Wake Forest and Brooklyn), the concepts introduced in the book build on each other. The book is meant to take students and professors on a journey from point A to point Z—just like the Amazon logo.

Thus, the textbook begins with a look at the corporation's current design, then the unsustainable nature of this design, next the current voluntary responses to make the corporation more sustainable (the "triple bottom line"), then proposals to re-design the corporation, and finally an inside-out rethinking of the corporation as moral actor. Though a bit idiosyncratic, it's a roadmap that has resonated with professors who have co-taught the course with me and with our students.

Readings

The book is mostly a series of readings from a variety of sources. There are law and management articles, Internet blogs, law cases, policy statements, news stories, book excerpts—written by law and management professors, by policy thinkers, by journalists, by scientists, even by religious leaders.

Book's animating principles

In writing this book, I have sought to follow three principles. The first identified by Thomas Piketty, an economist from France who studies wealth distribution: "Knowing the facts . . . can allow us to have a more informed discussion." That is, data matter. The second identified by Mahatma Gandhi, a Cambridge-trained lawyer from India: "An ounce of practice is worth a thousand words." That is, actions count more than words. The third identified by Joanna Macy, a former CIA spy and wise Buddhist teacher of environmental and human systems from the United States: "The heart that breaks open can contain the whole universe."

That is, I have sought to be attentive, to be present, and to be kind.

Each chapter begins with a "chapter's focus"—offering suggestions on what to focus on as you read the chapter, and thus an overview of the chapter. Each chapter concludes with "concluding thoughts"—setting out stories, fables, essays, and poems that seek to provide an understanding of the chapter that suggests the integrative nature of corporate sustainability.

Many of the readings include excerpts of material that reflect my own evolutionary thinking on the topics of the book. There are excerpts from my student books on Corporations and Securities Regulation, providing a "Newtonian physics" exposition of the corporate world, which is often explained as a set of relatively straightforward concepts and incentive structures.

But the contemporary corporation is far more subtle and complex. It is better explained by "quantum mechanics," where one thing can exist in two places at once. For example, the corporation can be seen as both a shareholder wealth maximizing machine and the world's most dominant social institution seeking to satisfy a host of stakeholders. This "non-duality thinking" informs the evolving corporation, I believe, as we transition from what some describe as shareholder Capitalism to stakeholder Capitalism. I wonder whether "awakening capitalism" is a more apt way to describe this epochal change.

Editing and Citation Form

This book is meant as a teaching resource, not a research tool. Toward this end, the readings are heavily edited, generally without adding ellipses or brackets to signal the edits. Citations and footnotes are omitted, along with whole paragraphs and sections, without any identifying notations. Often readings are redacted and paraphrased, again without anything more than a signal to this effect at the beginning of the reading.

In short, you should use caution when quoting primary materials from this book. The full text of the readings is available in all instances in the online version of the book, with hyperlinks to the complete version of most of the readings.

In particular, most of the scholarly articles (both law and management) do not reference the journal in which they have been published. That is, the book has almost no citations! Instead, the online version of the book includes hyperlinks to where the referenced articles can be found, typically the Social Science Research Network (SSRN). My purpose has been not only to improve readability, but to democratize the law and management scholarship. Rather than signal an article's merits by indicating where it was published, I invite you to consider the article's merits based on the idea it advances. Of course, the online version of the book has hyperlinks to the article, thus indicating whether and where it was published.

Online Companion

This book has its own online companion: check the Resources tab in Casebook Connect.

On the online companion, you can find supplemental readings and other materials, including suggested videos, scavenger hunts, group projects, even student papers. And for professors there are PPTs, a teacher's manual, sample syllabi, and suggestions for reviewing student submissions.

The online companion suggests videos that cover topics related to each chapter. For example, the online companion for the Overview (Roadmap for Our Journey) suggests two videos:

(1) A short video by Thomas Piketty (a French economist who has gained international fame for his number crunching on the question of wealth and income inequality over time) and James Heckman (a Nobel laureate economist at the University of Chicago, whose work links the quality of early childhood development and health, economic, and social outcomes). *Why Economics Needs Facts* [2:13].

(2) A longer video that you may have heard about, or maybe even already watched, by Steven Pinker (a famous psych professor at Yale). *Is the World Getting Better or Worse? A Look at the Numbers*, TED Talk (2018) [18:23]. The video summarizes the main findings of Pinker's book *Enlightenment Now: The Case for Reason, Science, Humanism, and Progress* (2018). One thing Pinker doesn't mention in the video is the important role of the corporation in human progress over the past two centuries. See Transcript of Talk. But then, he's a psychologist—not a corporate law/management type! That is, Pinker is a person with a hammer who mostly sees nails.

The online companion also suggests music videos for each chapter. For example, the online companion for the Overview (Roadmap for Our Journey) suggests you watch—or simply listen to—Yusuf/Cat Stevens: *The Wind* [1:47] / *The Wind (Original)* [1:57]:

I listen to the wind, to the wind of my soul
Where I'll end up, well, I think only God really knows . . .
I listen to my words but they fall far below
I let my music take me where my heart wants to go. . . .

Acknowledgments

I am grateful to my students over the years for their comments and enthusiasm about this book. Many of the readings in the book are those that students in their reflection papers identified as capturing well the topics of the different chapters. I am especially thankful for the many research papers written by students for the course. These papers were a primary research tool for me, as well as supplying useful excerpts in many of the chapters.

As the book went into final production, several students provided valuable input on the book's format and content: Hannah Neff (Wake Law '22); Emily Solley (Wake Law '22); Amalia Llano (Amsterdam MS Ecosystem Science '20). In particular, I appreciate the work of Noelle Henry (Wake Law '23) on the teacher's manual for the book, which includes answers to the pop-quiz questions in the class PPTs. Finally, I am indebted to Jordan Mock (Wake Law '22), who reviewed the entire manuscript, offering many thoughts and suggestions that improved the final product.

The book began with the support of Professor Enrico Ginevra (Bergamo Law), who accepted in 2012 that my course on Comparative Company Law would be about the avant-garde topic of "sustainable corporations." I am grateful for the decanal encouragement that I teach the course in the United States: Suzanne Reynolds (Wake Law—2017) and Christina Mulligan (Brooklyn Law—2019). I also wish to recognize two friends from Italy, who opened doors for me to teach the course (and the book) at their law schools: Maurizio Bianchini (Padova Law) and Edgardo Ricciardiello (Bologna Law).

In addition, I gratefully acknowledge the following sources for permission to reprint portions of their work:

Text

"Big business is beginning to accept broader social responsibilities." The Economist (August 24, 2019). Copyright © The Economist Newspaper Limited 2022. All rights reserved.

Anabtawi, Iman and Lynn Stout. "Fiduciary Duties for Activist Shareholders." Stanford Law Review, vol. 60, no. 5 (2008). Reprinted with permission.

Beale, Sara Sun. "The Development and Evolution of the U.S. Law of Corporate Criminal Liability" (January 6, 2014). A version of this paper was presented at the German Conference on Comparative Law, Marburg Germany, September 2013, and a German version will be published in Zeitschrift für die gesamte Strafrechtswissenschaf, 2014 Forthcoming. Available at SSRN: https://ssrn.com/abstract=2375318.

Bellifanti, Tamara and Lynn A. Stout. "Contested Visions: The Value of Systems Theory for Corporate Law," 166 U. Pa. L. Rev. 579 (2018). Reprinted with permission.

Bloom, Neil. "Boardroom coup at ExxonMobil is a global governance earthquake" (June 17, 2021), boardagenda.com. Reprinted with permission. Available at https://boardagenda.com/2021/06/17/boardroom-coup-at-exxonmobil-is-a-global-governance-earthquake/.

Conference Board, The. *Corporate Board Practices in the Russell 3000 and S&P 500.* Copyright © 2019 The Conference Board, Inc. All rights reserved.

Dennehy, Kevin. Interview with Daniel Esty, "New Values: Online Yale Summit to Explore Shift in Corporate Sustainability" (April 24, 2020). Available at https://environment.yale.edu/news/article/yale-business-sustainability-summit. Reprinted with permission from the Yale School of the Environment.

Erickson, Emily PG. "The Cocktail Party in Your Head," medium.com blog post dated January 27, 2022. Reprinted with permission. Available at https://elemental.medium.com/the-cocktail-party-in-your-head-bdeeb394349a.

Fancy, Tariq. "Financial world greenwashing the public with deadly distraction in sustainable investing practices," USA Today (March 16, 2021). Reprinted with permission from the author.

Filli, Christian. "Human Evolution and the Rise of the Corporate Super-Organisms," blog from 2018 originally posted on medium.com. Reprinted with permission.

Georgiev, George S. "The Human Capital Management Movement in U.S. Corporate Law" (March 1, 2021). 95 Tulane Law Review 639 (2021), Emory Legal Studies Research Paper No. 21-11. Reprinted with permission.

Greenfield, Kent. "The Puzzle of Short-Termism," Wake Forest Law Review, Vol. 46, No. 3 (October 3, 2011). Boston College Law School Legal Studies Research Paper. Available at SSRN: https://ssrn.com/abstract=2221956.

Hanauer, Nick. "The dirty secret of capitalism—and a new way forward." Transcript from July 2019 TED Talk. Reprinted with permisison. Available at https://www.ted.com/talks/nick_hanauer_the_dirty_secret_of_capitalism_and_a_new_way_forward/transcript?language=en.

Henisz, Witold. Tim Koller, and Robin Nuttall. "Getting your ESG proposition right. Here's why" (November 14, 2019). This article was originally published by McKinsey & Company, www.mckinsey.com. Copyright © 2022 All rights reserved. Reprinted by permission.

Karmel, Richard. "Why companies should use the UNGP Reporting Framework to demonstrate that they respect human rights," www.business-humanrights.org (March 3, 2015). Reprinted with permission.

Kuti, Dr. Ojuolape. "Why do we often blame someone else?" Medium.com (Jul 31, 2021). Available at https://medium.com/@lapekuti/why-do-we-often-blame-someone-else-b8cf895c9ae5. Reprinted with permission from the author.

Langelaar. Lotte. "The dangers of greenwashing," blog post dated May 4, 2021 from one-handed-economist.com. Reprinted with permission. Available at https://one-handed-economist.com/?p=2714.

LawShelf/Educational Media. Module 1: Overview of Securities Law. Reprinted with permission from National Paralegal College. Available at https://lawshelf.com/videocoursesmoduleview/overview-of-securities-law-module-1-of-5.

Macey, Jonathan R. and Leo Strine. "Citizens United As Bad Corporate Law" (August 16, 2018). U of Penn, Inst for Law & Econ Research Paper No. 18-28, Harvard Law School, John M. Olin Institute for Law, Economics, and Business Discussion Paper No. 972, Yale Law & Economics Research Paper No. 598. Reprinted with permission from Leo Strine.

Millon, David. "Two Models of Corporate Social Responsibility," 46 Wake Forest L. Rev. 523 (2011). Available at http://www.wakeforestlawreview.com/2011/10/two-models-of-corporate-social-responsibility/. Reprinted with permission from the author.

Oh, Peter B. "Veil-Piercing," 89 Texas Law Review 81 (2010). Reprinted with permission from the author. Available at: https://scholarship.law.pitt.edu/fac_articles/130.

Palmiter, Alan R. *Examples and Explanations for Corporations*, 9th edition (2020). Aspen Publishing. Copyright © 2020.

Palmiter, Alan and Frank Partnoy. *Corporations: A Contemporary Approach* (2nd ed. 2014). West Publishers. Copyright © 2014.

Ramsay, Ian and Belinda Sandonato. "An Analysis of the Business Objectives of the Largest Listed Companies in Australia, the United Kingdom and the United States." This article was first published by Thomson Reuters in Company and Securites Law Journal, Vol. 36, No. 1 (2018). Reproduced with permission of Thomson Reuters (Professional) Australia Limited, legal.thomsonreuters.com.au.

Reiser, Dana Brakman. "Benefit Corporations—A Sustainable Form of Organization?" (September 2012). 46 Wake Forest L. Rev. 591 (2011) and Brooklyn Law School, Legal Studies Paper No. 293. Reprinted with permission. Available at SSRN: https://ssrn.com/abstract=2144795.

Roe, Mark J. "Stock Market Short-Termism's Impact" (October 22, 2018). European Corporate Governance Institute (ECGI) – Law Working Paper No. 426/2018, Harvard Public Law Working Paper No. 18-28. Available at SSRN: https://ssrn.com/abstract=3171090 or http://dx.doi.org/10.2139/ssrn.3171090.

Sneirson, Judd F. "Shareholder Primacy and Corporate Compliance" (February 23, 2015). Fordham Environmental Law Journal, Vol. 26, p. 450, 2015. Reprinted with permission.

Strine. Leo. "Corporate Power Ratchet: The Courts' Role in Eroding 'We the People's' Ability to Constrain Our Corporate Creations" (2016). Harvard Civil Rights-Civil Liberties Law Review (CR-CL), Vol. 51, p. 423, 2016 and U. of Penn. Inst. for Law & Econ Research Paper No. 15-37. Reprinted with permission from Leo Strine.

Strine, Leo E. Jr. "Our Continuing Struggle With the Idea That For-Profit Corporations Seek Profit," 47 Wake Forest L. Rev. 135 (2012). Reprinted with permission from the author. Available at: http://www.wakeforestlawreview.com/2012/04/our-continuing-struggle-with-the-idea-that-for-profit-corporations-seek-profit/.

Tunjic, Peter. "A Copernican Revolution In Corporate Governance," LinkedIn blog post dated April 7, 2016. Retrieved from https://www.linkedin.com/pulse/copernican-revolution-corporate-governance-peter-tunjic/?trk=mp-reader-card. Reprinted with permission.

Wagner, Wendy E. "Imagining Corporate Sustainability As A Public Good Rather Than A Corporate Bad," 47 Wake Forest L. Rev. 561 (2011). Reprinted with permission from the author.

White, James Boyd. "How Should We Talk about Corporations? The Languages of Economics and of Citizenship." Yale L.J. 94 (1985): 1416-25. Copyright © 1985 Yale Law Journal.

Williams, Cynthia A. "Corporate Social Responsibility and Corporate Governance" from Oxford Handbook of Corporate Law and Governance (Jeff Gordon & Georg Ringe, editors). Reprinted with permission from the author.

Winter, Jaap W. "Corporate Governance Going Astray: Executive Remuneration Built to Fail" (March 22, 2011). Festschrift for Professor Klaus Hopt, pp. 1521-1535, Walter de Gruyter Duisenberg School of Finance Policy Paper No. 5. Available at SSRN: https://ssrn.com/abstract=1792483. Reprinted with permission.

Images

Diagrams of the liberal, conservative, and libertarian moral matrices. From *The Righteous Mind* (2013) courtesy of Knopf Doubleday/Penguin Random House. Copyright © Jonathan Haidt.

Infographics from *Corporate Progress on the Ceres Roadmap for Sustainability* (2018). Reprinted with permission from Ceres.

Illustration: comparison of selection between groups, between individuals within a group, and between genes within an individual. *American Scientist*, vol. 96 (September 2008). Copyright © 2008 American Scientist.

Overview

Roadmap of Our Journey

What is old becomes new, what is new becomes old. So much of what we know is being rethought, moving us from a sense of order to one of disorder to the discovery of a new order. From every corner of human inquiry, our paradigms are shifting. We are in transition.

This book invites you to join me in considering the emerging possibilities of the sustainable corporation. At first blush, it would seem a quixotic undertaking. For many the term "sustainable corporation" is an oxymoron. How can a corporation possibly be sustainable? Yet, this undertaking represents the great hope of our time: that an emergent sustainable corporation might arise from the ashes of the traditional unsustainable corporation. In fact, I believe this is now beginning to happen.

So, as you'll discover as you read this book I often splatter myself on the pages. The book presents a series of questions, and you will notice that often the questions are left open. When the book offers answers, many are tentative. The nature of the sustainable corporation is shifting. But I do not mean to hide the ball. When something seems true, I say so. When it seems false, I also point this out and attempt to explain why.

Above all, I invite you to invest yourself in the readings. It is inevitable that you will confront questions that are challenging, even uncomfortable. And your answers may often be different from mine.

For the climate: it's now or never

The Intergovernmental Panel on Climate Change, the world's leader on climate research, issued a report in April 2022. The report makes clear that reducing CHG emissions—swiftly enough to meet the goals of the 2015 Paris Agreement—will require a colossal, coordinated effort.

Simply stated, we must change nearly all aspects of human life: (1) how we produce electricity and power transportation; (2) how we build cities, manufacture goods, grow our food; (3) how we protect (and replenish) our forests and wetlands. GHG emissions must peak by 2025, no later. Then we must begin to reduce emissions fast—while drawing down carbon from the atmosphere. Climate stability is within reach, but only if we act. Now.

We have the technology—already! We have business and financial capacity—more than enough! We just lack the spine, the guts, the will. This book is both a journey and a roadmap toward reclaiming modernity, saving humanity, and finding ourselves. Nominally, it's about corporations.

Book's Focus

This book asks you to join me in considering the *possibility* of the "sustainable corporation." In the first unit, you will want to focus on the essential design of what I consider the most dominant institution in our modern world—the corporation. A sustainable future, I believe, depends on us addressing the nature of the corporation.

In the second unit, the book's focus shifts to appreciating the corporation's design flaws—through the prism of its legal structure. The book looks at the corporation's limited liability, short-termism, inward-focused decision-making, and political personhood.

In the third unit, the book considers how the corporate world has lately been responding to these flaws—namely, a remarkable new and growing focus on the triple-bottom line of "people, planet, profits" or sometimes referred to as the "environment, social, governance" (ESG) movement.

In the fourth unit, the book identifies recent attempts to re-design the corporation—and thus the roles of shareholders and executives. The book looks at new hybrid business forms, repurposed corporate disclosure, and a consortium (Ceres) of sustainability-minded institutional shareholders and corporate executives.

Finally, in the fifth unit, the book considers the corporation as a moral system, undergoing systemic change. This leads to an undergirding question: is stakeholder Capitalism a delusion? Perhaps the key to the corporation's future may not be simply modifying its DNA but rethinking our own roles in the corporation—as workers, consumers, investors. Maybe this is already happening.

0.1 The Journey Ahead

Book's Abstract

I am hoping you will see this book as a journey. So, for the first reading I offer you an overview of the readings that follow. Here is the abstract that I submitted to Aspen Publishing when I proposed (successfully) that the book be published.

Sustainable Corporations

Abstract

Nobody has ever seen a corporation. It is a legal, cultural construct—a figment of the human imagination. This is what makes it so powerful.

Today, the corporation is presented in business schools and law schools as an entity imbued with various characteristics that minimize conflicts between its principal constituents: risk capitalists (the corporation's shareholders) and management (the corporation's top executives). In this construct, employees, customers, suppliers, and society at large are along for the ride. We teach the corporation as a kind of Newtonian physics: it's the gravity of our transactional curriculum.

But the corporation has not been what it seems. It has not been an entity responsible for its own dealings—but instead has been an externalizing machine designed to push social and environmental costs onto others. It has not been a mediator of conflicting stakeholder interests—but instead has been a profit-making apparatus designed to maximize short-term financial gains for its shareholders. It has not been a reflection of societal priorities—but instead has been a plutocracy run by an inward-looking cadre of self-perpetuating executives. And it has not been a creature of law—but instead has been a political person empowered (long before *Citizens United*) to shape the regulatory landscape in which it operates.

But there are anti-gravity forces at work. The corporation is being rethought—its purpose and its responsibilities toward people, planet, and profits. There is a new triple bottom line. Voluntary corporate compliance with environmental norms, recent studies reveal, goes beyond what Newtonian physics would predict. The emergence of human capital management, likewise, is not just about shareholder profits. Further, the environmental/social/governance movement (so-called ESG) is inexplicable and real. The leading institutional shareholder Blackrock refuses to invest any of its $3.6 trillion in discretionary assets in any company that fails to articulate a social purpose that is both measured and managed. The country's leading CEOs in the Business Roundtable a couple years ago declared that the purpose of the corporation is to promote the interests of customers, employees, suppliers, communities, and shareholders—in that order. The Business Roundtable said it was compelled to redefine the corporation's purpose because government has become dysfunctional.

Hmmm. Maybe the corporation is better explained by quantum mechanics—accepting that something can exist in two places at once. We must come to terms with the anti-gravity nature of the corporation; our assumptions about *homo economicus* are deeply flawed. For example, there are now benefit corporations that mandate a social purpose specified in their corporate charters. There are mandates—some governmental and some imposed by private groups—that compel companies to measure and disclose their ESG performance. Lately, various firms are ranking corporate ESG performance—thus, to guide investment decisions and shareholder voting. Coca-Cola is said to be thinking of discontinuing its sale of toxic sugar water, including its eponymous beverage. And there's a new corporate engagement dance between institutional shareholders and corporate managers, even at ExxonMobil.

But maybe all of this is just high-level greenwashing—the deceptive appearance of caring about the environment, our atmosphere, consumers, company employees, and other workers in the supply chain. There certainly is evidence that stakeholder Capitalism is a delusion or cynical business as usual. Yet, maybe we are entering a new phase of Capitalism. Maybe Capitalism can save itself from itself. Perhaps we are witness to the corporation re-conceiving itself as a moral system—after all, real responses to the "me too" movement have come from business, not from government. There are glimmers that the corporation—long a super-organism, a beehive of jaw-dropping human collaboration—is morphing from a destructive caterpillar to a transcendent butterfly. Even more, perhaps we are seeing individuals in the corporation recognizing and rethinking their own internal dissonances, revealing the possibility of real humanity in business.

The book's mission is a simple one: to have every US law school offer as an upper-level course—one sequenced after the basic Corporations course—that would be named Sustainable Corporations. First, corporate law professors teach gravity, then we teach anti-gravity. That is, first we teach the incentive structure of the orthodox corporation, and then we teach the incentive structure of this new organic, human version of the corporation. Toward that end, the book offers a synthesis of writings from law, management, philosophy, psychology, sociology, even biology—by academics, journalists, business people, poets, bloggers, scientists, even religious leaders.

The book starts by quoting Pope Francis's encyclical *Laudato Si* and concludes by describing the wisdom of trees.

Early Reviews

The book was published in the Fall 2022. Even before publication, early drafts received good reviews from law professors who write and teach on corporate law. Here are some excerpts from their reviews:

> *I'm generally excited about the proposal. . . . It's very well written, timely, and . . . engaging [with] multimedia material. . . . I would be interested in adopting it for a short course following the regular Business Associations course.*
>
> *The proposal is highly provocative. . . . The book is comprehensive and modular enough that adopters who don't completely agree with Palmiter's perspective can still easily adapt it for their courses. I like the boxes drawing student's attention to the main questions and themes as they review the materials. In addition, I like the non-textual items, like the videos and especially the [group projects].*
>
> *I really like the proposed substance and coverage. It strikes me as comprehensive and well organized. I like the breadth of the proposed solutions/changes in how corporations are managed.*
>
> *If Prof. Palmiter can pull off the combination of topical, up-to-date business materials with the full range of interdisciplinary materials he suggests, it will be a strong offering. I would definitely think about adopting for a class or seminar on the topic.*

There you have it. Did I pull it off? You'll decide.

0.2 Meaning of "Sustainability"

But before beginning on this journey, it is useful to pause and consider what makes something sustainable—whether a corporation, a coffee maker, or a crypto-currency. There are many answers to this question, and this book is meant to present the question again and again—though without necessarily offering a clear answer.

UN Definition of Sustainability

A widely-used definition of "sustainability" comes from the United Nations: sustainable development is simply that which meets current social needs while ensuring that future generations can meet their needs. See General Assembly of the United Nations, *Our Common Future: Sustainable Development* (Brundtland Report 1987). Notice, however, that the definition does not take into account the survival of non-human species or the health of biodiverse ecosystems. That is, if humans somehow survive the Sixth Extinction, but many other species don't, so be it! Or maybe thriving biodiversity is essential to human survival.

Doughnut Definition

Other definitions are more specific and more inclusive. For example, economist Kate Raworth describes sustainable development as "human prosperity in a flourishing web of life." *Doughnut Economics: Seven Ways to Think Like a 21st Century Economist* (2017). The goal is for us to somehow learn to flourish by staying within the doughnut of planetary resources and human needs. If we fail to attend to things inside the doughnut hole, we fall short of meeting our essential human needs (food, housing, healthcare, political voice). If we extend beyond the doughnut, we overshoot and exhaust Earth's life-sustaining systems (stable climate, fertile soils, fresh water, protective ozone). The goal: stay within both the social and planetary boundaries of the doughnut.

For the climate: it's now or never

Sustainability and the environmental movement are kissing cousins. Both have a lineage that respects our planetary biome. The environmental movement is said to have originated with Aldo Leopold (a Forest Service/wildlife management professor) who noticed that ethical obligations toward land were absent in our thinking about land. In his foundational text *A Sand County Almanac* (1949), he wrote, "A thing is right when it tends to preserve the integrity, stability, and beauty of the biotic community. It is wrong when it tends otherwise."

Sustainability, however, is in some sense broader. It encompasses how the human community (society) is affected by something or some action. For example, an environmental program that preserved the integrity, stability, and beauty of a biotic community—but at the expense of people living in poor neighborhoods—might meet the environmental test, but not the sustainability test. For this reason, many have added "social justice" to the environmental test—thus, to align the environmental movement more closely with the sustainability movement.

Ancient Texts

But perhaps these definitions are insufficient. Ancient texts may well speak more clearly to us. For example, Genesis 1:1-2:4 (translated from the Hebrew) says:

> In the beginning God created the heaven and the earth.
>
> And God said, Let the earth bring forth grass, the herb yielding seed, and the fruit tree yielding fruit after his kind, whose seed is in itself, upon the earth: and it was so.
>
> And God said, Let the waters bring forth abundantly the moving creature that hath life, and fowl that may fly above the earth in the open firmament of heaven.
>
> And God said, Let the earth bring forth the living creature after his kind, cattle, and creeping thing, and beast of the earth after his kind: and it was so.
>
> And God said, Let us make man in our image, after our likeness: and . . . God said unto them, Be fruitful, and multiply, and *replenish* the earth, and *be responsible* to it: be *stewards* of the fish of the sea, and of the fowl of the air, and of every living thing that moveth upon the earth.
>
> And on the seventh day God ended his work which he had made; and he rested on the seventh day from all his work which he had made.

As you move through the readings, you will surely come to an even broader, more useful understanding of sustainability. My further guess is that your understanding will further evolve, long after you have put this book aside.

0.3 Seismic Change Coming to Capitalism?

What Is Capitalism?

Many have observed the success of Capitalism in creating wealth. Robert Gilpin (a political science professor at Princeton) in his book *The Challenge of Global Capitalism: The World Economy in the 21st Century* (2000) wrote:

> Capitalism is the most successful wealth-creating economic system that the world has ever known; no other system, as the distinguished economist Joseph Schumpeter pointed out, has benefited "the common people" as much. Capitalism, he observed, creates wealth through advancing continuously to ever higher levels of productivity and technological sophistication; this process requires that the "old" be destroyed before the "new" can take over. Technological progress, the ultimate driving force of Capitalism, requires the continuous discarding of obsolete factories, economic sectors, and even human skills. The system rewards the adaptable and the efficient; it punishes the redundant and the less productive.

Gilpin identified Capitalism as having gone through two great phases: the first during the Eighteenth Century's industrial revolution; and the second after the collapse of Soviet Union and during the globalization that led to the rise of China. Thus, modern Capitalism has been built on the international trading system, which despite its economic benefits paradoxically is "constantly being threatened by protectionism." Likewise, the international monetary system affects the welfare of people around the world, yet the importance of monetary stability and global economic well-being is hardly recognized.

A central actor in our modern Capitalism have been multi-national corporations, with which we have a love-hate relationship. We generally approve of the role of these corporations in the economy and our lives. We certainly buy their products and services, and accept employment in them. But, at the same time, we view their size and power as a threat to our social and economic well-being. The corporations, in turn, engage in lobbying and media campaigns to convince us that they actually increase exports, jobs, and wages.

As globalization has led to different strategies—such as the regional integration of Europe, the parochial (even xenophobic) politics of the United States, and the phenomenal growth of the Asian economies—it has also attracted its nay-sayers, some of whom believe unregulated international finance poses a serious threat to the world economy. Yet most economists view Capitalism (and its globalized free markets) as promising increasing prosperity and international cooperation.

Is Big Business Becoming Socially Responsible?

But prosperity may not be enough. The challenges we face—a climate crisis, rising social inequality, lately a pandemic, all accompanied by a sense of doom—call for Capitalism to look in the mirror. Next is a recent article from The Economist. It addresses Capitalism's look into the mirror and touches on many of the themes of this book.

Big Business Is Beginning To Accept Broader Social Responsibilities
Pursuing shareholder value is no longer enough, it seems

Briefing (Aug. 22, 2019)
The Economist

At a recent dinner in London, a chief executive promised that his airline would soon offer electric flights. A credit provider enthused about increasing financial inclusion in the developing world; a luxury-car executive promised to replace the leather in her vehicles' opulent interiors with pineapple matting and mushroom-based *faux* leather. They seemed to think such things made the companies they run sound more attractive. They probably felt that they were doing good.

Businesspeople, being people, like to feel they are doing good. Until the financial crisis, though, for a generation or so most had been happy to think that they did good simply by doing well. They subscribed to the view that treating their shareholders' need for profit as paramount represented their highest purpose. Economists, business gurus and blue-chip CEOs like those who make up America's Business Roundtable confirmed them in their view. In a free market, pursuing shareholder value would in and of itself deliver the best goods and services to the public, optimise employment, and create the most wealth—wealth which could then be put to all sorts of good uses. It is a view of the world at the same time bracing in its simple rigour and comforting in the lack of social burdens it places on corporate backs.

It is also one which has faced increasing pressure over the past decade. Environmental, social and governance (ESG) criteria have come to play a role in more and more decisions about how to allocate financial investment. The assets managed under such criteria in Europe, America, Canada, Japan, Australia, and New Zealand rose from $22.9trn in 2016 to $30.7trn at the start of 2018, according to the Global Sustainable Investment Alliance. According to Colin Mayer at the University of Oxford, whose recent book "Prosperity" is an attack on the concept of shareholder primacy, ESG has shot yet further up investors' agendas since. Some of the world's biggest asset managers, such as BlackRock, an indexation giant, are strongly in favour of this turn in events. The firm's boss, Larry Fink, has repeatedly backed the notion that corporations should pursue a purpose as well as, or beyond, simple profits.

The discontent does not end with investors. Bright young workers of the sort businesses most desire expect to work in a place that reflects their values much more than their parents' generation did. And the public at large sees a world with daunting problems—most notably climate change and economic inequality—that governments aren't solving. It also sees companies which it holds partially responsible for these dire straits using their ever greater profits (see chart 1) to funnel cash to stockholders, rather than investing them in ways that make everyone's life better. The lollygaggers should be pulling their weight.

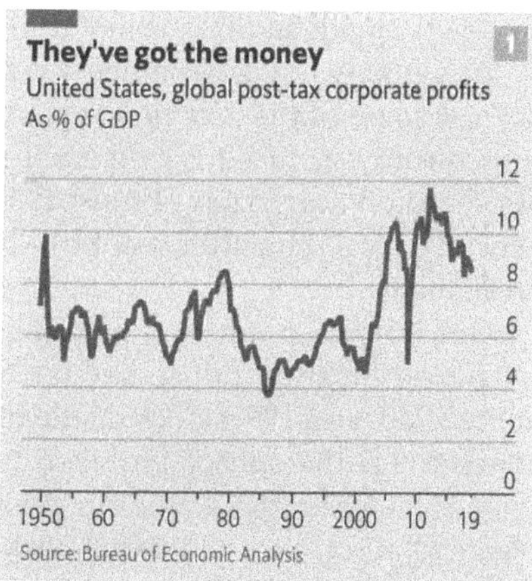

The Economist

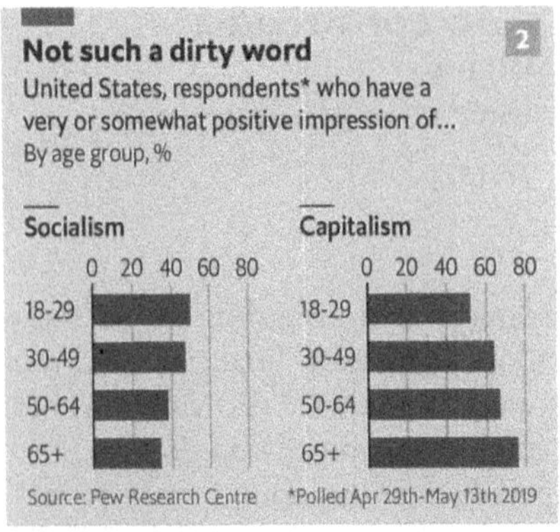

The Economist

If they won't do so willingly, perhaps they should be forced. Senator Elizabeth Warren, one of the leading contenders for the Democratic presidential nomination, says that being a big company is a privilege, not a right. She wants big American companies to apply for charters that would oblige them to look after stakeholders, especially local ones. Those who let the side down would have their charters revoked. Ms Warren talks of herself as a defender of capitalism; many see her plans as bordering on the socialist. But that may not matter. Among young Americans, socialism is ever less of a boo word (see chart 2).

In the face of this rising tide, the Business Roundtable has either seen the light or caved in, depending on whom you ask. On August 19th the great and good of CEO-land announced a change of heart about what public companies are for. They now believe that firms should indeed serve stakeholders as well as shareholders. They should offer good value to customers; support their workers with training; be inclusive in matters of gender and race; deal fairly and ethically with all their suppliers; support the communities in which they work; and protect the environment.

There was an immediate backlash. The Council of Institutional Investors, a non-profit group of asset managers, swiftly denounced it. Others railed against it as "appeasement" of politicians like Ms Warren, and a decisive step towards the death of capitalism. This might seem extreme: at first glance, the roundtable's recommendations border on the anodyne. But if the purpose of the company slips its shareholder-value moorings, who knows where it might end up?

Whose Company Is It Anyway?

The most quoted assertion of the primacy of shareholder value comes from Milton Friedman, an economist. In 1962 he wrote that "there is one and only one social responsibility of business—to use its resources and engage in activities designed to increase its profits so long as it stays within the rules of the game, which is to say, engages in open and free competition without deception or fraud."

At a time when governments expected companies to be patriotic and communities saw some of them as vital resources his forthrightness shocked many. But though subsequently traduced as extreme, Friedman's position had a fair amount of give in it. He called on companies not just to stay within the law but to honour society's more general ethical standards, too; he did not equate shareholder interests with short-term profitability.

But that was not how it felt. The way that business schools and management consultants in America, Britain and continental Europe proselytised for shareholder value in the 1980s and 1990s offered little by way of nuance. The biggest corporate-governance concern was the agency problem: how to align managers with the interests of the value-seeking shareholders. "Any chief executive who went against [that] orthodoxy was regarded as soft and told to get back on the pitch," recalls Rick Haythornthwaite, the chairman of Mastercard.

Such heretics can now hold their heads up again. This is not simply because of the political climate or the public mood. Some economists argue that Friedman's position belongs to a simpler time. Oliver Hart of Harvard University and Luigi Zingales of the University of Chicago see his argument as principally motivated by a form of the agency problem; he didn't like managers being charitable with shareholders' money, even if it was ostensibly in the firm's interests. The shareholders could, after all, lavish their profits on such good causes themselves.

True, perhaps, back then, say Mr Hart and Mr Zingales. Now, they argue, the externalities that businesses impose on society are sometimes impossible for shareholders to mitigate as individuals, particularly if the political and legal system is a barrier to change. Individual shareholders cannot do much in law to prohibit weapons in America, for example. But they can exercise their rights as owners to influence the firms that sell guns. Thus, companies can have purposes—but owners must provide them, not managers.

Others argue that the idea of shareholder value, while still central, needs some modifications. Raghuram Rajan, an economist at the University of Chicago and former head of India's central bank, advocates taking note of the non-financial investments workers and suppliers make in a company with a new measure of "firm value" which explicitly takes note of a specified set of such stakeholdings.

Some companies have taken on board the idea that their increased power puts new demands on them. Satya Nadella, chief executive of Microsoft, says that a sense of purpose—together with a mission that is "aligned with what the world needs"—is a powerful way for his company to earn public trust. And because trust matters, this puts purpose at the core of Microsoft's business model. "As technology becomes so pervasive in our lives and society, we as platform companies have more responsibility, whether it's ethics around artificial intelligence, cyber-security or privacy," he says. "There is a moral obligation."

Firms in other industries are having similar thoughts. In each business, says Mr Haythornthwaite of MasterCard, a wave of digitisation is likely to lead to one company pulling ahead. Because of that concentration of power, he says, the winning platform will need to forge a close link with society to maintain trust.

Climate change is perhaps the most obvious example of companies doing more than they have to in a good cause. Twenty-five big American companies, including four tech giants, campaigned against America's withdrawal from the Paris agreement in 2017. Globally, 232 firms that are collectively worth over $6trn have committed to cut their carbon emissions in line with the accord's goal of limiting global warming to less than 2°C.

Some 1,400 companies around the world either already use internal carbon prices or soon will. Many big firms now aim for carbon neutrality in their operations. Some have made big investments to that end. Apple has a renewable energy capacity equivalent to its total energy use.

Laudable as some of this is, it is hardly a response commensurate to the climate crisis.

Companies going carbon-neutral are mostly consumer-facing ones, rather than intensive emitters. Money for coal may now be scarce, at least in the rich world, but big institutional investors own a sizeable chunk of the world's major oil companies—many of which apply a theoretical price of carbon to investment analysis but still keep pumping fossil fuel. And net-zero pledges may reinforce the misapprehension that the best way of fighting climate change is through the choices of individual companies and consumers, rather than a thoroughgoing economy-wide transition.

Companies are also backing liberal social causes. In 2015 Marc Benioff of Salesforce, a software firm, led other bosses, including Apple's Tim Cook, into opposing a bill in Indiana that would have allowed discrimination against gay people. After President Donald Trump's election in November 2016, bosses mounted the barricades over his ban on travel to America from Muslim-majority countries. In 2018 Nike created an advertisement featuring Colin Kaepernick, a quarterback fired after kneeling during America's national anthem in protest against police racism. PayPal has blocked some groups, including white nationalists, from using its services.

The firm's boss, Dan Schulman, says PayPal's aim is to broadcast its broader purpose. Others might deride it as "virtue signalling". But that modish phrase does not quite capture what is going on. In economics and evolutionary biology, where the idea of signalling grew up, a valid signal needs to be costly—otherwise it can be easily faked. These corporate positions do not look costly; indeed, they may well be profitable. A stand in favour of Colin Kaepernick fits Nike's brand, which celebrates the goal-oriented individual and has keen black fans. Nike's stock dipped a tad when the controversy hit: but its sales rose immediately, and its shares soon recovered.

There are risks to such strategies. Nike had little to fear from red-staters calling for boycotts. Others may be more susceptible. Backlash can come from the other side, too; corporate sponsorship of Pride marches in London and New York has led some LGBTQ activists to organise alternative events from which business is excluded.

From Each According to Their Abilities

There is also the problem of setting yourself up for a fall. Salesforce stumbled last year when its software turned out to be being used by US Border Patrol to deal with illegal immigration. Ben & Jerry's, which sprinkles its ice cream with a do-the-right-thing anti-capitalist vibe, found itself scolded by Britain's advertising regulator this summer for plastering ads for fatty frozen calories around schools in London.

The politics of the consumer are not the only ones that firms need to consider; in tech, particularly, the politics of the workforce matter. It was the company's employees who complained about Salesforce's links to immigration control. Last year, employees at Google forced the firm to stop providing the Pentagon with AI technology for drone strikes and to drop out of the procurement process for JEDI, a cloud-computing facility for the armed forces. Google depends, perhaps more than any of its peers, on a smallish number of cutting-edge data scientists and software engineers; their views carry weight. Microsoft, despite similar misgivings from its employees, is still in the running for the JEDI contract. Amazon, for its part, is facing employee pressure over contracts with oil and gas companies.

If corporate political stances can be justified in terms of keeping workers or consumers happy it does not mean that they are insincere—simply that they may be overdetermined. This can be irksome for the right. Companies rarely make a stand for the rights of the unborn, or for border security. But this is the market at work. Companies tend to have a preference for both consumers and employees who are young, educated, and affluent—which is to say, who can be expected to embrace socially liberal politics.

What the world has not yet seen is a situation where ESG issues come into material, systemic conflict with profits. Purpose is flavour of the month, says Stephen Bainbridge, professor of law at the University of California, Los Angeles, "but are companies really going to give shareholders a 10% haircut for the sake of stakeholders?"

Such issues become particularly clear when it comes to increasing spending on the poorer parts of the workforce. Relentless downsizing makes little sense. "There are diminishing returns from firing people over and over again," says Jeff Ubben of ValueAct Capital, a hedge fund. "It is not the right strategy for the future". Some firms have lifted minimum wages and are spending more on retraining workers to cope with future automation. But profits are very sensitive to labour costs. According to Darren Walker, president of the Ford Foundation, one of America's biggest charitable endowments, plenty of chief executives are having conversations about how to spend more on workers and benefits, but feel they cannot do so alone. "They will need cover," he says; a broader shift towards corporate purpose could provide it.

Many influential investors and bosses imagine a return to something like the "managerial capitalism" of earlier times, when some CEOs, their interests presumably insufficiently aligned with those of shareholders, paid more attention to stakeholders and local communities. Not all are enthusiastic. Paul Singer, founder of Elliott Management, the world's biggest activist hedge fund, says that the current debate over corporate purpose "risks obscuring the fact that earning a rate of return for pension plans, retirement accounts, universities, hospitals, charitable endowments and so on is itself a social good—a very high one". What is more, he notes, this social good is one that no entity other than the corporation can sustainably provide.

There is also a problem of accountability. "Once the corporation decides that earning returns is no longer its primary purpose, to whom will it be accountable?" says Mr Singer. The answer, he thinks, is "the loudest and most passionate political activists"—though others might hope the settled convictions of the shareholders would come into play.

One answer to these criticisms could be to devise a framework that would allow companies and bosses to state clearly that they want to do more besides make a profit. Almost 3,000 companies worldwide have been certified "B corporations" in the past decade, which means that their ethical, social, and environmental practices have been certified by independent monitors to meet the standards laid down by B Lab, a non-profit group in Pennsylvania. But not many big companies have applied. Those which have are mostly consumer brands.

An alternative to this approach would be to have companies say what purpose they had beyond shareholder value and then hold them to it. This is the approach Mr Mayer of Oxford recommends for Britain: a legal requirement for companies to have a purpose in their articles of association and provide measures to prove it is being fulfilled. Stating the purpose in such a way as to make it open to such measurement, though, would prove hard.

As capitalism takes flak from all sides, it is hard for those in the business and investing class to object to firms voluntarily doing their bit to tweak the system. But when reliable returns are put at risk, things can change. Last year Jason Perez, a police sergeant in Corona, California, had enough. His state could no longer afford wage increases for police and other public servants partly because Calpers, one of the world's biggest pension funds, was underfunded. It had also been an early standard bearer for ESG investing. In 2001 it dumped tobacco stocks—which then outperformed.

By 2017, Calpers was underfunded to the tune of $139bn. Its ESG strategy had cost only about $2bn. But Mr Perez took the reasonable view that a couple of billion was real money. "Eleven people in my family are in law enforcement and I had to make sure their pensions were protected," he says. To that end he campaigned for a board seat at Calpers on the basis of letting the fund invest in law-abiding, profit-maximising companies purely on the basis of potential returns. Pitted against the fund's chief ESG guru, Priya Mathur, he won. However companies reset and refine their purposes in the years to come, they will still need to perform for people like Mr Perez.

0.4 Some Preliminary Thoughts

Relationship to Corporate Law

Some of my students have commented that this book goes well beyond corporate law. Some say this as a criticism, others say it with delight. The book and the topics it raises are meant to be iconoclastic. Neither the book's approach nor its style is intended to be ho-hum—or comfortable. The book raises many uncomfortable topics, such as the externalities that the corporation has visited (some might say wreaked) on society. Think of the corporation's role in CO2 emissions, in our obesity crisis, in income and wealth disparities, and in perpetuating stereotypes and biases. The book also deals with the corporation as a political actor and its remaking of the regulatory landscape to suit itself.

That said, this is a book that also engages with many tenets of US corporate law, seeking to put them into broader contexts. Understanding limited liability, board decision-making and the business judgment rule, the process for choosing directors to the board, and the ways in which the corporation engages in politics—each very much about corporate law—is essential to considering whether and how the corporation can be sustainable.

Glossary

OK. I knew you couldn't wait. Here are some of the terms and where they first show up:

BJR—business judgment rule [1.2]
SWM—shareholder wealth maximization [1.3]
IAD—internal affairs doctrine [1.2]
SEC—US Securities & Exchange Commission [1.3]
PHC—publicly-held corporation [1.2]
SME—small- or medium-sized enterprise [1.2]
LCA—life-cycle analysis [3.1]
CSR—corporate social responsibility [3.2]
SRI—socially responsible investing [3.3]
PRI—UN Principles of Responsible Investing [3.3]
ESG—environment / social / governance [3.1]
MPT—modern portfolio theory [3.3]
PBC—public benefit corporation [4.1]
SDG—UN Sustainable Development Goals [4.3]

New Terminology

It's a daunting undertaking—this search for the sustainable corporation. And humanity's very future hangs in the balance. There will be times you will feel overwhelmed. The topics will be new and technical. There will be lots of abbreviations, like BJR, SWM, IAD, SEC, PHC, SME, LCA, CSR, SRI, PRI, ESG, MPT, PBC, SDG. (Please, don't bother to look them up—you'll soon encounter each one soon enough, and they'll each make perfect sense.). In short, not only will this be a journey, but it will also be an adventure.

* * *

Concluding Thoughts

We Each Have a Role

You will discover that throughout the book I will be asking you to think about your role in corporate sustainability. How can we embark on such an important journey without also thinking about where we fit in? In this regard, I am reminded of an Aztec fable:

> Once upon a time in ancient Mexico, there was a great fire. The animals gathered at the fire's edge confused and unsure how to deal with the great conflagration. Then, the resplendent quetzal bird flew to a nearby stream, filled his beak with water, flew back over the burning landscape, and emptied the water from his beak on the fire. He then flew back toward the stream. When the owl saw this, he cried out and said, "Quetzal bird, what are you doing? You can't put out the fire!" Unperturbed, the quetzal bird answered, "That may be true. But it's the best I can do." And off the quetzal flew toward the stream to refill his beak with water.

And off we fly, too.

UNIT 1

INTRODUCTION

Our journey begins. We start with a look at the basics of US law, then an introduction to US corporate law, next a look at US publicly traded corporations, and finally a primer on US securities regulation.

For some of you, this introductory look at US law and the US corporation will be new-through for many of you this unit will be a refresher. That said, my goal is to help you see both the US legal system and US corporate law through new eyes.

A look ahead down the road. This unit sets you up for the second unit, where we consider the corporation's unsustainable design. The third unit then offers a hopeful look at recent corporate adaptations to this design—the so-called "triple bottom line." The fourth unit invites you to consider more fundamental changes in the redesign of the corporation. And, finally, the fifth unit concludes with a rethinking of the corporation itself–and ourselves.

Unit 1 **Intro to corporation**	Unit 2 **Unsustainable design**	Unit 3 **Triple bottom line**	Unit 4 **Redesign corporation**	Unit 5 **Rethink corporation**
1.1 US law 1.2 US corporation 1.3 US public corp 1.4 US securities reg	2.1 Limited liability 2.2 Short-termism 2.3 Board mono-culture 2.4 Corp in politics	3.1 Planet: environ 3.2 People: CSR 3.3 Profits: SRI	4.1 Benefit corp 4.2 ESG disclosure 4.3 Consortium: Ceres	5.1 Corp as moral system 5.2 Stakeholder capitalism–delusion? 5.3 Personal integrity

Chapter 1.1

US Law

We look first at US law, the undergirding of US corporate law and US securities regulation. In this introduction to the basics of US law, you will notice that the animating theme is how and whether US law is legitimate. As we will later see, the US corporation shares many features of the US legal system, such as its separation of functions, its dependence on judge-made law, and its interesting straddling of the US federal system. Thus, it's useful to begin thinking about how US law has sought to be legitimate—in this way to inform our inquiry into how the corporation can be made sustainable and thus legitimate.

Chapter's Focus

You should focus on what makes the various structures of US law legitimate. Although most of you already have been introduced to today's topics in your studies, you'll want to re-consider how law seeks to achieve social justice and thus legitimacy.

For example, what explains the separation of powers between our governmental bodies, how is power divided between the states and the federal government, and why do minority/individual civil rights exist in a system of majority rule? This chapter will serve as a foundation for the question of how the corporation might be restructured to achieve social justice and legitimacy.

As you go through the readings, consider how the US common law system (in this modern age of statutes) compares to the civil law system (built on Roman law) prevalent in the rest of the world. Which is more legitimate? Then consider how legislative enactments (statutes) have become an important part of US law.

You'll also want to consider whether US democracy is legitimate. As you'll see, although US democracy has in theory many attributes that suggest political legitimacy, the functioning of our federal government in practice raises questions about its true nature. For example, you'll discover that no US law or policy has been enacted in the last couple decades when that law or policy was supported only by poor and middle-class Americans. Only if the elites and corporations supported the law or policy did it happen. Maybe what we have is not a democracy, but instead market capitalism.

If so, our search for the sustainable corporation takes on a special immediacy and meaning.

1.1.1 Nature of US Law

This chapter's main reading introduces (or likely re-introduces) you to US law—in broad strokes. It's from a book written by two political science professors for US college (non-law) students. The book offers an overview of US law—its purposes, history, principal institutions, structure, and methodology.

An Introduction to the American Legal System

(5th ed. 2020)

John M. Scheb II & Hemant Sharma

Introduction

US society is very much preoccupied with law. We have an elaborate system to make and enforce the law. A large professional class is engaged in the practice of law. Numerous academic institutions are devoted to teaching the law. Our mass media and popular culture reflect the social preoccupation with law, in that we are exposed to a steady barrage of books, films, newspaper articles, television shows; and web sites dealing with the law.

What is "law"? Here's a simple formulation: law is a set of rules promulgated and enforced by government—positive law. That is, "the command of the sovereign" that takes the form of a rule, a principle, or a directive that applies with equal force to everyone. To be legitimate, the law must be perceived as rational, fair, and just and, some would say, must conform to a higher law.

Chapter 1: Development of US Law

Higher Law

Natural law is said to flow from man's "natural" condition—that is, the social condition existing prior to the emergence of government. Natural law thus refers to universal principles of morality and justice. In De Republica, the Roman orator Cicero (106-43 B.C.) defined natural law as "right reason in agreement with nature." In his influential Commentaries on the Laws of England (1769), William Blackstone asserted the primacy of natural law.

Our Declaration of Independence (1776) asserts that "all men are created equal, that they are endowed by their Creator with certain unalienable rights, that among these are Life, Liberty, and the pursuit of Happiness."

But natural law is not enforceable. It is a philosophical concept—it is the idea that morality and justice transcend positive law. Natural law provides a basis to criticize and sometimes disobey positive law.

Legitimacy of Law in a Democratic Society

The legitimacy of law in a democratic society depends on how the law is made. In a representative democracy, law is made by elected representatives serving in a legislature. All members of the legislature have the right to introduce legislation; a majority is required to enact a law. In a democracy, legislators are elected through free and fair elections in which all adult citizens have the right to participate.

The United States relies on representative democracy, but not simple representative democracy. Rather, majority rule in our constitutional republic is tempered by minority rights. And lawmaking power is vested not only in the legislature, but also the executive (regulatory agencies), and the courts.

How these bodies make law is key to whether their legal pronouncements are regarded as legitimate—both in their substantive and procedure. Do people believe the law's content is fair, just, and reasonable? Do people regard how it is enacted, applied, and enforced to be fair, just, and reasonable?

Forms and Sources of Positive Law

In the US legal system, the law is the sum of the following complex, dynamic, and sometimes contradictory elements:

- Constitution. The fundamental law. It sets forth the structure and powers of government as well as the rights of citizens vis-a-vis that government.
- Statute (or ordinance). A law enacted by a legislature (or local government) that is generally applicable within the jurisdiction of that legislature (or government).
- Executive order (or regulation). An order issued by a President, governor, county executive, or mayor (or a rule promulgated by a regulatory agency) on matters over which the executive (or agency) has authority.
- Judicial decision. A decision by a court of law enunciating a principle of law—which decisions are usually followed by other courts.
- Treaty. A legally binding agreement between countries.

The Functions of Law in Society

Law promotes social order and stability, but can be a force for change. Law seeks to establish justice, but offers no guarantees. Law specifies how government operates, but cannot ensure good government.

Fundamentally, law protects people and their property. For some, this is the primary purpose of law. Without the coercive power of the state, people must protect themselves, their families, and their property by force. Law, at least ideally, protects the weak and the strong.

Law, Liberty, and Morality

Classical liberals like Thomas Jefferson saw law as a way to protect not only life and property but also liberty. Thus, freedom of speech and freedom of religion were as important as the right to own property and to engage in private enterprise.

Conservatives, on the other hand, see law and morality as inextricably intertwined. Thus, the preservation of societal morality is one of the essential functions of law—to prevent disintegration of the society.

Law and Economic Life

A society's economic system affects its law, and vice versa. As the social theorist Max Weber recognized, a capitalist economy requires a highly developed legal system capable of enforcing contracts and property claims and providing a predictable climate in which business can take place. Uncertainty in the law regarding property, contracts, and commercial transactions impedes voluntary economic activity. But when too many conflicting demands are placed on the law, it becomes excessively complex, bureaucratic, redundant, and inscrutable, which frustrates economic activity.

Others, including Marxists of various persuasions, see law in capitalist societies as a tool of oppression and a protector of inequality. Thus, law in a capitalist society merely cloaks the power of the elites.

Social Control

Law is a means of social control. So are informal, unwritten rules transmitted and enforced by social groups, including families, peers, and colleagues. And our individual conscience develops and enforces moral principles. Religious institutions develop, transmit, and reinforce their own precepts. Together social norms, moral principles, and religious precepts also constrain human behavior.

Resolution of Conflict

Law is a means of conflict resolution. Individuals, groups, families, corporations, and governments usually can work out their differences informally through discussion, negotiation, and compromise. The law serves as a framework and provides mechanisms for peaceful resolution of conflicts.

Do we need more law or less law? As society becomes more diverse, impersonal, complex, and specialized, this question becomes more important. With increasing social, economic, and political diversity, a social consensus is difficult to maintain.

[The authors then describe informal tribal law, monarchical rule, Roman Law, the Napoleonic Code, and the Civil Law Tradition.]

The Common-Law Tradition

US law is derived largely from the English common law, which dates from the Norman Conquest of 1066. Seeking to replace the patchwork of local laws and customs, often applied by feudal courts, and church law enforced by ecclesiastical courts. William the Conqueror (the first Norman king of England) strengthened the royal courts, and later his successors dispatched royal judges and expanded their role in county Courts—taking jurisdiction in cases formerly decided by feudal and local courts.

The King's judges settled disputes based on the customs of the Anglo-Saxon people and the well-established principles of feudal society. They grew increasingly popular given their reliance on trial by jury. From their decisions grew a law common to the entire kingdom, hence the term "common law."

The Doctrine of Stare Decisis

In 1292 court clerks began recording the rulings of the common-law courts. By the fourteenth century these decisions served as precedents to guide judges in similar cases. As the centuries passed, coherent principles of law emerged from the decisions of the judges. Thus, unlike Roman law, which was based writings of legal scholars, the common law arose from judicial decisions.

The common-law doctrine of following precedent, known as stare decisis (meaning "to stand by that which is decided"), took hold with the printing press in the fifteenth century. Today, it remains an important component of both the English and US legal systems. Under the doctrine, courts should follow relevant principles of law enunciated in previous decisions by the highest court within the jurisdiction.

Civil and Criminal Law

Early on, the common law developed a distinction between civil law and criminal law. The criminal law sought to punish people for offenses against the Crown (and prosecuted by the Crown); the civil law provided remedies for essentially private wrongs involving property, contracts, or personal injury (in cases between private parties).

Juries

One key to the success of the common law was the jury trial. Before the common law, trials in England often happened by ordeal. The defendant was tortured by fire or water. If a defendant survived the ordeal, God had intervened to prove the defendant's innocence before the law.

The common-law courts substituted a kinder process of fact-finding. The judges would hear testimony from witnesses, and neighbors of the accused or of the litigants (the jury) would serve as fact-finders.

Equity

At first, the common law was flexible, but by the fourteenth century, it had become highly technical and rigid. So, aggrieved parties unable to secure a remedy at common law would appeal to the King directly for justice. The King often delegated these matters to his Chancellor, a cleric and a member of the King's court seen as the "keeper of the King's conscience." Eventually, a secular tribunal called the Court of Chancery arose, and it developed its own set of legal principles called equity.

"Equity" comes from the Latin aequitas, which means justice or equality. When existing legal rules and procedures are insufficient to remedy injustice, a court should rely on general principles of fairness in granting relief. The Court of Chancery did not follow the writ system [specialized form documents necessary for bringing a case in the King's courts] nor did it utilize juries. Instead, chancellors determined the facts and fashioned equitable remedies.

Reception of the Common Law in America

As England became a colonial power, the common-law tradition was exported throughout the Empire—to Australia, New Zealand, Canada (with the exception of Quebec), and to same extent India.

In the United States, after independence was declared, some new US states adopted statutes or constitutional provisions that followed the English common law, provided it did not conflict with the new state and federal constitutions. Other states adopted the common law, in whole or in part, through judicial decisions. Today, the legal system of Louisiana (based on the Napoleonic Code) is the only one not based essentially on the common law.

The US Constitution

By the spring of 1776, most Americans saw that independence from England was both necessary and desirable. On July 4, the Continental Congress adopted the Declaration of Independence. Authored by Thomas Jefferson, the Declaration outlined the colonies' grievances against the King and asserted the right of revolution. Many of the ideas expressed in the Declaration had been articulated a century earlier by John Locke, who had identified the natural rights of "life, liberty and property."

The Articles of Confederation

After the US Revolution, the United States was a confederation of sovereign states held together (barely) by an agreement called the Articles of Confederation. Congress had no power to tax and no power to regulate interstate commerce. There was no presidency to provide leadership and speak for the new nation. Nor was there a national court system to settle disputes between states or parties residing in different states. And the Articles of Confederation could not be amended except by unanimous consent of the states. In early 1787, Congress called for a federal convention to meet in Philadelphia "for the sole and express purpose of revising the Articles of Confederation."

Adoption of the Constitution

The delegates to the Philadelphia Convention decided to scrap the Articles of Confederation and draft a new constitution. The Framers accepted the states as sovereign political entities, but understood that without a strong national government, interstate rivalries would seriously undermine economic growth and political stability.

The delegates faced a number of contentious issues. The two greatest were (1) a disagreement between the small and large states over representation in Congress and (2) the conflict between northern and southern states over slavery. Ultimately, the Convention reached agreement on September 17, 1787, when 39 delegates representing twelve states placed their signatures on what would become the Nation's new fundamental law. Although ratification of the Constitution was in some states a close question, by 1790 all thirteen of the original states had ratified the document.

The Constitution corrected the major deficiencies of the Articles of Confederation: (1) it strengthened the national government; (2) it gave Congress ample legislative powers; (3) it established an executive branch; and (4) it provided for a national court system. And it provided a blueprint for a workable Government, one that could adapt to social, economic, and technological change.

Separation of Powers

The Framers of the Constitution had no interest in creating a parliamentary system, which could be manipulated by monarchs or captured by impassioned, short-lived majorities. So, the Constitution distributes the three basic functions of government among Congress (Article I), the President (Article II), and the Judiciary (Article III).

The Framers of the Constitution believed in a system of checks and balances. Thus, the Constitution contains a number of "auxiliary precautions." The President can veto bills passed by Congress, but Congress can override the President's veto by a two-thirds majority in both houses. The President can appoint judges, ambassadors, and other high government officials, but the Senate must consent to these appointments. The President is commander-in-chief, but Congress has the authority to declare war, raise and support an army and a navy, and make rules governing the armed forces. The idea was that no one institution can permanently dominate the others.

The Framers said much less about the judiciary, which Alexander Hamilton described as "the least dangerous branch" of the new national government. The

President and the Senate are given the shared power to appoint federal judges, but these appointments are for life. Congress is authorized to establish lower federal courts and determine their jurisdiction. The only way to remove judges from office is through a cumbersome impeachment process, requiring proof the judge committed "high crimes or misdemeanors." The Framers wanted an independent federal judiciary.

Judicial Review

The text of the Constitution is silent on how the judiciary can oversee the other branches. In Marbury v. Madison (1803), the single most important case in US constitutional history, the Supreme Court asserted the power to review acts of Congress and declare them null and void if found to be contrary to the Constitution. Later the Court extended this power to review state laws under the Federal Constitution.

"Judicial review"—the power of the federal courts to rule on the constitutionality of legislation—is nowhere explicitly provided for in the Constitution. However, many Framers of the Constitution supported the concept of judicial review and probably expected it. Today, judicial review is well established.

The Bill of Rights

There is no question that the protection of the liberty and property of the individual was one of the Framers'' highest goals. Yet the original Constitution had little to say about individual rights. The Framers assumed the limited national government they were creating would not threaten individual liberty and property. State governments would do this.

But not everyone agreed. So, a "gentlemen's agreement" was worked out. Key states agreed to ratify the Constitution on the condition that Congress would immediately take up creating a bill of rights. The first Congress in 1789 adopted ten amendments to the Constitution, known collectively as the Bill of Rights. They were ratified by the requisite nine states in 1791. The Bill of Rights address the threat of abuse by government officials and perceived inadequacies of the common law in curtailing such abuses.

The First Amendment Freedoms

The First Amendment recognizes the fundamental freedoms of religion, speech, press, and assembly as well as the right to petition government for a redress of grievances.

Rights of Persons Accused of Crimes

The Fifth, Sixth, and Eighth Amendments protect the right to a speedy and public trial by an impartial jury, the right to counsel, the right to confront prosecution witnesses, and the right to compel the testimony of witnesses for the defense. They also protect against compulsory self-incrimination, double jeopardy, excessive bail, excessive fines, and cruel and unusual punishments.

Other Notable Constitutional Amendments

Since ratification of the Bill of Rights, the Constitution has been amended only seventeen times. The most important are the post-Civil War amendments, which abolished slavery (Thirteenth Amendment, 1865), prohibited states from denying equal protection and due process of law to all citizens, including newly freed slaves (Fourteenth Amendment, 1868), and forbade the denial of voting rights on the basis of race (Fifteenth Amendment, 1870).

Incorporation of the Bill of Rights

The Bill of Rights limits the power of the national government, thus originally leaving citizens of states to look to their state constitutions for protection from abuse by state or local officials. But the Supreme Court has come to understand that the Fourteenth Amendment makes the Bill of Rights enforceable against state and local governments as well as the national government. Under the incorporation doctrine, the Court has held that most of the Bill of Rights is embraced within the terms "liberty" or "due process" and are thus applicable to the states.

Modern Statutes and Codification

Although the US legal system is based on English common law, Congress and the fifty state legislatures have become extremely active in adopting statutes to meet modem conditions. Once adopted, a statute supersedes the common law within that jurisdiction. Many modem statutes deal with subjects unknown to the common law, such as civil rights, public health, antitrust law, environmental protection, and social welfare. Although Congress doesn't have general statutory power under the Constitution, it has relied upon its broad Commerce Clause authority (Article 1, Section 8) to legislate in many areas only indirectly related to commerce.

Statutory Construction

Although basic common-law concepts remain today defined essentially as they were centuries ago, the law has now been codified. Thus, to answer questions of law, lawyers and judges now look first to the relevant statutes. Of course, the meaning of statutory provisions is not always plain or obvious. Thus, a principal function of contemporary courts is statutory construction—that is, giving concrete meaning to statutory provisions open to different interpretations.

Codification

An important development in the US legal system has been the codification of the common law—the legislative transformation (especially by state legislatures) of law in a given area into a clear, systematic code of laws. This has happened mostly through the diffusion of uniform codes. Consider commercial law, which covers sales of goods, leases, negotiable instruments, insurance, brokerage, shipping, and other matters pertaining to business. The common law—the product of a rural, agrarian, pre-industrialized society—was not very relevant to modem commercial practices. States have enacted statutes in this area, though before the 1950s with little uniformity. In 1952, the Uniform Commercial Code (UCC) was developed by legal scholars and business practitioners. It spread rapidly among the states, as state legislators saw the wisdom of uniformity in business law. Today, all 50 states have adopted the UCC, in whole or in part, thus greatly facilitating interstate commerce.

Administrative Regulation

The role of government has changed dramatically in the two centuries since the US nation was founded. In the early days of the republic, government essentially followed the dictum that "that government is best which governs least." For the most part, the national government left such functions as social welfare and education to state and local governments and concerned itself with the regulation of foreign trade, internal improvements such as canals and post roads, and the protection of the national security. State and local governments, in turn, tended to leave matters of social welfare and education to neighborhoods, churches, and families.

In the wake of post-Civil War industrialization and the emergence of an economy dominated by giant corporations, the limited role of government began to change. A new ethos emerged, one in which government assumed primary responsibility for solving social problems. With the passage of the Interstate Commerce Act in 1887 and the concomitant establishment of the Interstate Commerce Commission, the relatively unobtrusive government envisaged by the Founders became ever more complex and intrusive. The era of Progressive reform in the early twentieth century and the subsequent New Deal fostered by President Franklin D. Roosevelt in the 1930s expanded such regulation, as did the New Frontier and Great Society of the 1960s.

The expansive role now played by the national government renders the legislative task of Congress considerably more difficult. Consequently, Congress has come to rely more and more on "experts" for the development as well as the implementation of regulations. The Food and Drug Administration (FDA), the Federal Aviation Administration (FAA), the Environmental Protection Agency (EPA), and the Securities and Exchange Commission (SEC) are just a few of the government agencies to which Congress has delegated broad authority to make public policy.

The Decisional Law

Although federal and state statutes often modify substantive law and procedural law, courts play an equally important role in the development of law. Trial courts mostly make factual determinations, apply settled law to established facts, and impose sanctions. In reviewing the decisions of trial courts, appellate courts interpret federal and state constitutions and statutes—including such majestic phrases as "equal protection of the laws."

Likewise, federal and state statutes often use vague language like "affecting commerce" or "reasonable likelihood." Courts must assign meaning to these and a multitude of other terms often following precedent under the common-law doctrine of stare decisis. When there is no applicable precedent, appellate courts can fill gaps and make new law.

Chapter 2: Structure of the US Law

Federalism

Federalism is a hallmark of the US constitutional system: the fundamental division of authority between the national government in Washington, D.C. and the 50 state governments. Of course, state law is subordinate the U.S. Constitution and federal law.

There are significant legal differences between the national government and that of the states. The authority of the federal government extends throughout the United States and its territories, whereas state authority is confined within state borders. The national government has sole authority to make treaties with other nations, enact laws governing the high seas, coin money, regulate standards of weights and measures, regulate international trade, regulate immigration and naturalization, and provide for the national defense. The national government also has primary, although not exclusive, authority to regulate interstate commerce, which is a major source of federal legislative power.

The states, on the other hand, have exclusive authority over their own machinery of government. They have exclusive power to establish and control local governments (cities, counties, and townships). States have sole responsibility for conducting elections and apportioning electoral districts, although in exercising these functions they must comply with federal constitutional standards. States are the primary locus of the police power—the power to make laws in furtherance of the public health, safety, welfare, and morality. States also have primary (though no longer exclusive) authority over commerce within their borders.

The federal government and the states also possess a number of concurrent powers, that is, powers vested in both levels of government. These powers include the power to tax, to spend and borrow money, to enact legislation, to charter and regulate banks, and to establish courts of law and administrative and regulatory agencies. The national government and the states also both possess the power of eminent domain, which is the power to take private property for public use, as long as property owners are compensated for the taking.

Legislatures

All governments make laws, or legislation. In a democracy, the governmental institution with primary responsibility for enacting legislation is the legislature. Legislatures in the United States and other democratic countries are composed of the people's elected representatives chosen through free and fair elections. The members of these assemblies are known as legislators. In the lawmaking process, legislators follow either the preferences of their constituents or their own best judgment, depending on whether they consider themselves to be delegates or trustees.

Judicial Systems

Law also evolves through a process of judicial interpretation in particular cases. These cases may arise in either federal or state courts. The federal government and each of the fifty state governments maintain their own systems of courts. These systems include both trial courts and appellate courts. Trial courts conduct civil and criminal trials and various types of hearings. Trial courts make factual determinations and are the primary settlers of legal disputes. Appellate courts hear appeals from the trial courts. The appellate courts are not fact-finding bodies. Rather, their role is to review the proceedings of lower courts, correct errors, and settle unresolved legal issues.

The Chief Executive

Chief executives at all levels of government, that is, mayors, governors, and presidents, play an important role in the US legal system. Chief executives can issue executive orders based on statutory provisions and, in some instances, direct constitutional authority. Executive orders have the force of law—they must be obeyed in the same way that statutes and court decisions command obedience.

Presidents and most governors can also veto bills enacted by their respective legislatures. For the U.S. Congress and most state legislatures to override a veto, more than a simple majority vote is required. This ensures that controversial legislation will not be enacted without a sufficiently strong consensus in the government.

Executives also perform a critical function in the enforcement of the law. Legislation and judicial decisions are not self-enforcing. Oftentimes the chief executive or other officials within the executive branch are called upon to carry out the will of courts and legislatures. Of course, in deciding how to implement statutes and court decisions, executive officials shape the laws it is applied in concrete circumstances.

Regulatory and Administrative Agencies

The modem chief executive sits atop a massive bureaucracy—a panoply of departments, boards, commissions, and other agencies. These agencies have various functions. Some are law enforcement agencies that serve to investigate crimes, apprehend offenders, and assist in their prosecution. Others are purely administrative agencies—their job is to carry out government programs like social security, Medicaid, or public housing programs. Still others are regulatory agencies, whose role is to create and enforce regulations in specific policy areas. They do this by invoking authority granted to them by the legislature, which has delegated power to agencies to act as, in effect, miniature legislatures. For example, Congress has created the Environmental Protection Agency and vested it with the authority to make and enforce regulations to give specific content to the Nation's environmental laws. In making these regulations, EPA and other regulatory agencies follow a rulemaking procedure outlined by Congress.

Agencies vary not only in their functions but also in their relationship to the chief executive. Most agencies are located within the major departments of the executive branch, which means that the President or governor has a good deal of control over them, Others, called independent agencies, are freestanding entities over which presidents and governors have less control. These agencies are typically directed by boards whose members are appointed for set terms of office and can only be removed for good cause.

The Legal Profession

The US legal profession has its roots in English common-law practice. In England, trial lawyers were (and are) called "barristers," while attorneys who provided other legal services were (and are) known as "solicitors." In the United States, we do not use that nomenclature. We only have "lawyers," although the distinction between "trial lawyers" and "transactional lawyers" remains relevant. Indeed, lawyers in the United States have become extremely specialized. As in medicine, the general practitioner is becoming increasingly rare. Lawyers today specialize in torts, estate planning, corporate law, taxation, civil rights, contracts, real estate, criminal defense work, and every other conceivable area of the law.

Legal Education and Admission to the Bar

About half the Framers of the U.S. Constitution were lawyers who "read laws" and held apprenticeships with those who practiced law. Today the predominant path to becoming a lawyer is to successfully complete a three-year JD degree from one of the 184 law schools accredited by the US Bar Association. Indeed, all but a few states now require that to take a bar examination for admission to the practice of law after completing the JD degree.

The number of applicants who annually seek admission to law schools grew in the 1960s and 1970s, a time of social upheaval when many students were inspired to channel social and economic changes through law. Lately applications to law school have declined after the 2008 Financial Crisis. A prospective law student must have a four-year college degree and generally score well on a Law School Aptitude Test (LSAT) and have a credible grade point average (CPA). Law schools are selective but do not demand that pre-legal education be in a particular field. Business, history, political science, and economics have been popular undergraduate majors. Admission committees often employ various criteria beyond LSAT and GPA scores to enroll a diverse group. Prior to 1960 women and minority students represented a very small percentage of law students. Today, they represent a substantial percentage of the enrollment in most law schools.

Law schools usually require completion of basic courses in contracts, property, torts, criminal law, civil procedure, constitutional law, legal research and writing, evidence, and professional responsibility. Electives are available in fields such as corporations, estates and trusts, taxation, administrative law, and commercial law and often include skills courses in trial and appellate advocacy and clinical training in client counseling.

Since first introduced at the Harvard Law School in the 1870s the "case method" has been the principal method of instruction in law school. Casebooks today contain not only reported appellate court cases but also related materials. Professors frequently employ the "Socratic method," with students reciting cases and responding to in-depth questions posed concerning analysis of a case and its implications in the law. Most basic law courses culminate in a written examination requiring a detailed analysis of hypothetical factual situations with discussion of applicable rules of law.

The Organized Bar

State laws govern the admission requirements to be a licensed attorney in the state and require passage of a written bar examination. Usually, the highest court in the state has oversight of the bar admission policies and requires a thorough check of the applicant's background. Successful applicants take an oath to support the federal and state constitution and adhere to the ethical requirements of being a lawyer.

Being admitted to the bar in one state does not permit a lawyer to practice in another state. Nevertheless, a lawyer can usually be admitted to practice in another state on a limited basis when accompanied by a lawyer admitted in that state. Admission to the practice of law in a state does not carry with it admission to practice in a federal court. Instead, each federal trial and appellate court has its own requirements.

Legal Assistance for Indigent Persons

In most areas bar associations have established legal aid offices to assist persons of limited means in obtaining legal advice. Assistance is often provided for persons of limited income. Congress has provided limited federal funds, and state and local agencies, including bar associations, often assist in funding these offices. These offices often employ staff lawyers, and in many areas law students assist as interns. In many instances a legal aid office will refer a case to a practicing attorney who agrees to handle a case on a pro bona (for benefit of the public) basis without charge to the client. Of course, indigent criminal defendants are furnished legal counsel.

Professional Responsibility
Professional responsibility of lawyers has become a major topic. Lawyers are regulated by codes of professional conduct often patterned after the Model Code of Professional Conduct promulgated by the US Bar Association (ABA), a voluntary association of lawyers. The Model Code has no legal effect because the ABA is a private organization, but many state legislatures and the highest court of the states have adopted the ABA Model Code with some variations. Because lawyers are deemed to be "officers of the court,' judges exercise inherent power to discipline them and even hold them in contempt of court for violations of ethical standards in the conduct of litigation.

The Adversarial System of Justice

The US court system follows the historic adversarial system this nation inherited from the English common law. Unlike the system that prevails in civil law countries, the adversarial system separates the function of gathering evidence from the judge's role in pretrial and trial processes. The theory of the common-law approach is that because a judge has not participated in the investigative process the parties are assured their case will be heard by a neutral decision-maker.

In the adversary process the competing parties develop the evidence through investigation. Parties, usually through their lawyers, present their evidence and arguments in support of their positions and seek to demonstrate the weakness of the other side of the case. This affords each party an opportunity to have a lawyer-conducted examination and cross-examination of witnesses, and challenges to the evidence and argument presented by the opposing sides. An important aspect of the adversarial system is the development of detailed procedural rules that a judge must apply impartially irrespective of the merits of a party's 'case.

Juries
In the United States juries are a vital component of the adversarial system and deeply rooted in Anglo-US tradition. In the late eighteenth century, William Blackstone called the jury a "strong barrier between the liberties of the people and the prerogative of the crown." Today, Americans continue to regard the jury as an important check on government.

In America juries are selected from a cross-section of the adult community without regard to educational attainments. Thus, a college professor may be seated next to an elementary school dropout. To ensure an impartial jury, parties have the right to challenge jurors as to their basic qualifications to render a fair and impartial verdict. Although a prospective juror is not usually disqualified by having heard or read about a case, a juror who has formed an opinion about a pending case or who may have an interest in the litigation will be disqualified from serving. Juries decide the facts in a case and must apply the law as instructed by the presiding judge.

Conclusion

The US legal system is extremely complicated, due in large part to federalism: the division of political and legal authority among one national government and fifty state governments. No two sets of state laws are identical. Even where states have emulated laws of other states, there are likely to be nuances. No two state court systems are exactly alike. Even those that are superficially similar are likely to have significant jurisdictional, procedural, and administrative differences. And of course, the federal system is quite unique in many respects.

The US legal system depends on the contributions of many different actors, most notably the legislators who write statutes, the chief executives and other executive officials who enforce them, and the judges who apply them to specific cases. The system also depends on litigants, people who are willing to subject their disputes to courts of law for orderly and peaceful resolution, as well as the lawyers who help litigants navigate a legal maze that can be at times maddening. Ultimately, though, the US legal system depends on the faith and support of average Americans who are asked to believe that our legal system represents a sincere effort to achieve the rule of law in this country.

1.1.2 Nature (and Legitimacy) of US Democracy

What Makes Democracy Legitimate

In reading Scheb and Sharma's introduction to US law, notice the many ways that US law seeks to achieve social justice and legitimacy, two important concerns also shared implicitly by corporate law.

Robert Dahl, a political theorist, describes various attributes of a democratic constitution that contribute to its legitimacy—that is, its acceptance by both the citizenry and elites.

(1) Stable institutions. The constitution should provide for stable democratic institutions—namely, elected officials; free, fair, and frequent elections; freedom of expression; alternative sources of information; associational autonomy; and inclusive citizenship.
(2) Fundamental rights. The constitution should protect both majority and minority rights—these basic rights and duties are subsumed in many of the democratic institutions.
(3) Neutrality. The constitution should be neutral, neither favoring nor penalizing the views or legitimate interests of any group of citizens.
(4) Accountability. The constitution should enable citizens to hold political leaders accountable for their decisions and conduct, within a reasonable amount of time.

(5) Fair representation. The constitution should create a sense that the views of the citizens are represented in the development of law and policies.
(6) Informed consensus. The constitution should facilitate the "conciliation of diverse interests" in the development of law and policies.
(7) Effective government. The constitution should ensure that government confronts the major issues and problems that citizens themselves confront without deadlock or delay.
(8) Competent decisions. The constitution should encourage political leaders to draw on the best knowledge available to make wise, not necessarily decisive, policy.
(9) Transparency. The constitution should ensure that the operation of the government is open to public view so that citizens can understand how and what it is doing.
(10) Resiliency. The constitution should not be rigid or immutable, but instead should be adaptable to novel situations.

Robert A. Dahl, *On Democracy* 124-127 (1998). Does the US Constitution fit these parameters? Surely, it does in some ways. But, just as surely, we are still in search of a "more perfect union"—no?

Is US Democracy Legitimate?

Given Dahl's checklist of what makes a democracy legitimate, you may be thinking to yourself, "Well, the Scheb and Sharma reading addresses this question and presents a stylized version of US law, but there's more beneath the surface." For example, the reading says that courts "interpret the law"—even though it's been quite clear that courts have broad leeway to "make law." Think about how the US Constitution's commerce clause, without any mention of state laws that impede commerce, has been interpreted to forbid states from discriminating against interstate commerce—that is, a court-created ban on state protectionism.

Further, though this might surprise you, the notion that law reflects the public will is widely questioned. An influential study by Martin Gilens (a political science professor at Princeton) examined the extent to which voter preferences (such as raising the minimum wage or requiring employers to provide health insurance) are linked to federal policies and law:

> [Based on] two thousand survey questions on proposed policy changes between 1981 and 2002, I find a moderately strong relationship between what the public wants and what the government does, albeit with a strong bias toward the status quo. But I also find that when Americans with different income levels differ in their policy preferences, actual policy outcomes strongly reflect the preferences of the most

> affluent but bear virtually no relationship to the preferences of poor or middle-income Americans. Representational biases of this magnitude call into question the very democratic character of our society.

Martin Gilens, *Inequality and Democratic Responsiveness* (2005) [available at scholar.princeton]. A subsequent follow-up study by Gilens and Benjamin Page (a Northwestern sociologist) came to an even more stark conclusion:

> Multivariate analysis indicates that economic elites and organized groups representing business interests have substantial independent impacts on U.S. government policy, while average citizens and mass-based interest groups have little or no independent influence.
>
> Further, we find the nearly total failure of "median voter" theory. When the preferences of economic elites and the stands of organized interest groups are controlled for, the preferences of the average American appear to have only a minuscule, near-zero, statistically non-significant impact upon public policy.
>
> Nor do organized interest groups substitute for direct citizen influence, by embodying citizens' will and ensuring that their [collective] wishes prevail. Interest groups do have substantial independent impacts on policy, and a few groups (particularly labor unions) represent average citizens' views reasonably well. But the interest-group system as a whole does not. For example, the net alignments of the most influential, business-oriented groups are negatively related to the average citizen's wishes.
>
> What do our findings say about democracy in America? They certainly constitute troubling news for advocates of "populistic" democracy, who want governments to respond primarily or exclusively to the policy preferences of their citizens. In the United States, our findings indicate, the majority does not rule—at least not in the causal sense of actually determining policy outcomes. When a majority of citizens disagrees with economic elites or with organized interests, they generally lose. Moreover, because of the strong status quo bias built into the U.S. political system, even when fairly large majorities of Americans favor policy change, they generally do not get it.

Gilens & Page, *Testing Theories of American Politics: Elites, Interest Groups, and Average Citizens* (2014) [available at Cambridge University Press].

How does a bill really become law?

So much of this may be disquieting. The public will does not necessarily lead to public laws. You may remember the quite famous. Schoolhouse Rock, How a Bill Becomes a Law (2010). Its premise is that laws arise from public concern about a problem. Is this too simplistic? Is it even misleading?

Are things really this grim? Perhaps, average citizens are inattentive to politics and ignorant about public policy, and thus populist democracy is a panacea. If so, we shouldn't worry if popular, but poorly informed preferences fail to influence policy making. Don't economic elites and interest-group leaders have more policy expertise than the average citizen and thus know better which policies will benefit everyone?

Gilens and Page address this argument:

> We tend to doubt that the elites know more. We believe instead that—collectively—ordinary citizens generally know their own values and interests pretty well, and that their expressed policy preferences are worthy of respect. Moreover, we are not so sure about the informational advantages of elites. Yes, detailed policy knowledge tends to rise with income and status. Surely wealthy Americans and corporate executives tend to know a lot about tax and regulatory policies that directly affect them. But how much do they know about the human impact of Social Security, Medicare, food stamps, or unemployment insurance, none of which is likely to be crucial to their own well-being? Most important, we see no reason to think that informational expertise is always accompanied by an inclination to transcend one's own interests or a determination to work for the common good.

This is big stuff. Our democracy is not what the textbook said it is. What do you think?

1.1.3 Comparison to "Blockchain"

So, this is supposed to be a book for a law course, and we will be studying corporations mostly from a legal perspective. But you'll notice that the corporation is an "institution" that is meant to engender trust. That is, in many ways the corporation exists beyond law.

With this in mind, I invite you to think about the most recent "institution" in modern life meant to endanger trust: blockchain technology. IBM offers a "blockchain for dummies" definition:

> Blockchain is a shared, immutable [computer-stored] ledger that facilitates the process of recording transactions and tracking assets in a business network. An asset can be tangible (a house, car, cash, land) or intangible (intellectual property, patents, copyrights, branding). Virtually anything of value can be tracked and traded on a blockchain network, reducing risk and cutting costs for all involved.
>
> Blockchain is important because business runs on information. The faster it's received and the more accurate it is, the better. Blockchain is ideal for delivering that information because it provides immediate, shared and completely transparent information stored on an immutable ledger that can be accessed only by permissioned network members. A blockchain network can track orders, payments, accounts, production and much more. And because members share a single view of the truth, you can see all details of a transaction end to end, giving you greater confidence, as well as new efficiencies and opportunities.

As you can see, the technology is meant to facilitate human trust and reduce uncertainty (just like the corporation). For example, blockchain can be used to test whether a coffee shop's coffee is really fair-trade, sustainably-sourced coffee. My purpose for introducing blockchain is to get you thinking about both its applicability in ensuring sustainable business practices and what makes a human institution/organization legitimate–in particular, how it engenders trust.

Limits of blockchain. Blockchain is not a panacea. For example, it has been pointed out that blockchain systems are hard to create, because the good data entry on which blockchain relies is expensive. See Jimmy Song, *Why Blockchain Is Hard* (5/14/18) [available on Medium.com]:

> The main thing distinguishing a blockchain from a normal database is that there are specific rules about how to put data into the database. That is, it cannot conflict with some other data that's already in the database (consistent), it's append-only (immutable), and the data itself is locked to an owner (ownable), it's replicable and available. Finally, everyone agrees on what the state of the things in the database are (canonical) without a central party (decentralized).

Blockchain and the corporation. Despite its shortfalls, blockchain in the corporation has gained a good deal of traction, particularly with respect to the coordination of shareholders and their voting at annual meetings. For example, some have argued that blockchain could lower shareholder voting costs and facilitate fast and efficient involvement of shareholders in the company—by replacing the current chains of intermediaries and remote voting systems with the transparency, verification and identification offered by blockchain technology. Anne LaFarre & Christoph Van der Elst, *Blockchain Technology for Corporate Governance and Shareholder Activism* (2018) [available on SSRN].

Others have pointed out that blockchain can be (and actually is already being) used to create Decentralized Autonomous Organizations (DAOs). These DAOs represent a radical rethinking of how organizations, such as corporations, can be structured and run, including changes in ownership, governance, decision-making and profit distribution. DAOs are designed to be automated and decentralized, placing decision-making (such as the allocation of capital to particular projects or in different investments) in the hands in an automated system, subject to voting rights on possible projects/investments by owners of DAO tokens. DAOs not only lower transaction costs dramatically—and transaction costs are said by many

What are DAOs?

Here's an explanation from The Economist (4/19/22):

DAOs are collectives that use automation and crowdsourcing to make decisions. They do not rely on a single central authority, like a boss. Instead, DAO members typically use cryptocurrency to buy tokens, granting them voting rights. Jonah Erlich, a member of ConstitutionDAO, which tried to buy one of the original copies of the US Constitution at auction, has likened a DAO to a group chat with a bank account. They use "smart contracts"—rules encoded in programs that execute themselves automatically under certain conditions—to carry out their business. Funds are only transferred, for example, if the majority of token-holders have digitally signed off on a transaction.

The first DAO (known as such) was created in 2016 by users on the Ethereum blockchain. It was intended to work like a venture-capital fund, allowing users to invest using cryptocurrency, pitch projects, and potentially receive financial returns, following a vote by its members to invest or take out money. It quickly raised the equivalent of nearly $150 million to invest in startups. But things turned sour. Barely two months after it launched, a hacker took advantage of a loophole in the code to steal 3.6 million ether, then worth around $70 million.

to be the reason for a firm's existence—through their use of smart contracts that can prevent laws and other rules from being broken. It's been pointed out that business structures have evolved over the centuries and DAOs are simply another evolution and that DAOs require us to rethink organizational law, including the granting of legal personality to DAOs and limited liability to DAO token holders. See Alexandra Sims, *Blockchain and Decentralised Autonomous Organisations (DAOs): The Evolution of Companies?* (2020) [available on SSRN].

* * *

Concluding Thoughts

A Buddhist Kaon

A young man, looking to find the meaning of life, came to a wise sage. "Dear, sage, what is the meaning of life?" asked the young man.

The sage looked at him and then asked, "Do you have a child?" "Yes, I have a daughter," answered the young man. "How would you feel if she were to die?" asked the sage. "I would be devastated. I would not be able to go on living. I don't know what I would do without her," the young man answered.

"Do you have any siblings?" asked the sage. "Yes. I have a sister, and she has a son," answered the young man. "And how would you feel if her son died?" asked the sage. "I would be very sad for her. It would be so difficult to see her suffering. And I would miss my young nephew," answered the young man.

"And what if a neighbor's child died?" asked the sage. "That would be terrible. I would feel for them. Though not as much as I would for my sister."

"And what if the child of a person across town were to die?" asked the sage. "That would be sad news. I would hope the family would be able to go on. But I would probably not pay much attention," answered the young man.

"And a stranger in a faraway land. What if they lost a child?" asked the sage. "Oh, I probably wouldn't notice," answered the young man. "After all, that's life."

The sage then said, " You already know the meaning of life."

* * *

So, this story about the meaning of life is expressed in other ways, such as the saying that "all politics is local" and the survey finding that 35% of Americans would not spend $1 of their own money to fight climate change.

Yet, we live in an inter-connected world. The death of a child on the other side of the globe should be relevant to us—to each of us. How do we make it so that our politics are not just local, that collectively we care about the climate crisis, and that together we seek social justice for all?

Is the corporation capable of recognizing and responding to our interconnected world? That is the question that animates our journey. Read on, fellow traveler.

Chapter 1.2

US Corporate Law

What is corporate law? What is the corporation? What makes the corporation so useful and so powerful?

This chapter introduces you to US corporate law. As you will see, the US corporation is grafted onto the root structure of US law—namely, the common law, our unique US federalism, and a division of labor between the legislature, the executive branch (administrative agencies), and the courts. An animating question, one that continues from our look at US law, is what makes the US corporation legitimate.

Our look at the US corporation is a segue to the US public corporation—the large, dominant business form whose ownership interests (shares) are traded on public stock trading markets. Our search for the sustainable corporation is mostly a search for the sustainable public corporation. The idea—and the hope—is that once we find the sustainable publicly traded corporation, we will also have found the sustainable closely held corporation (one whose ownership interests are not traded on public stock markets, but instead owned by a small group, often a family).

Chapter's Focus

You will want to focus on the sources of US corporate law (namely, state statutory rules and decisional law) and how they interact.

You'll discover that the corporation is generally understood as the "inside" relationship between shareholders and management (directors and officers). You'll want to focus on the five key attributes of this relationship: (1) how the relationship is created and how long it lasts; (2) how business management is allocated within the corporation; (3) how cash flow and profits are distributed in the corporation; (4) how shareholders can get out of the corporation; and (5) the responsibilities of shareholders and managers to others "outside" the corporation.

You'll then want to focus on some of the remarkable, even unique, aspects of the US corporation. You'll discover that US corporations are creatures of state law—though federal law is important for publicly traded corporations. You'll also learn that US corporate law is mostly enabling, not mandatory—thus, its many default terms are subject to modification. You'll want to focus on Delaware, the pre-eminent US state for corporate law, and ask yourself why Delaware has come to have this special role in US corporate federalism.

1.2.1 Nature of US Corporation

What is a corporation? It is a framework by which people conduct modern business. It is a convenient legal entity that can enter into contracts, own property, and be a party in court. It comes in assorted sizes, from a publicly held multinational conglomerate to a one-person business.

The corporation is a creature of law—a legal construct. Nobody (not even your professor) has ever seen one. The corporation's existence and attributes arise from state enabling statutes, which give business participants significant freedom to choose their own customized relationships. But the statutory framework is incomplete, and judicial norms fill the many gaps left by the statutes. Other gaps, particularly those involving disclosure to investors, are filled by federal securities law.

Ultimately, the corporation is an investment vehicle for the pooling of money and labor—a grand capitalist tool. ***Money capital*** comes from shareholders and creditors; ***human capital*** comes from executives and employees. Both money and labor expect a return on their investment. The corporation defines their legal relationships and mediates their conflicting interests.

Essential Corporate Attributes

What are the essential attributes of the US business corporation—the elements that undergird all business organization forms in the world?

Suppose you are asked to invest in a business. What would be your questions? The paradigm business corporation answers five basic questions that arise in every investment relationship:

- **How long does the investment last?** The corporation has an independent, perpetual existence. It is an entity distinct from those who contribute capital (shareholders and lenders) and those who manage the business (directors and officers). The persons who constitute the corporation may come and go, but the corporate entity remains. It owns the business assets and is liable for any business debts.
- **Who manages the investment?** The locus of corporate power is the board of directors, which manages and supervises the business. (The board often delegates its power to officers to act for and bind the corporation.) In exercising their management powers, the directors are subject to fiduciary duties. Shareholders have only a limited governance role. They can vote to elect directors, approve fundamental corporate changes, and initiate limited reforms, but have no power to act on behalf of the corporation.
- **What is the return on the investment?** The corporation establishes a hierarchy to the financial returns generated by the business. Creditors (including bank lenders, bondholders, trade creditors, and employees) are first in line and receive a return based on their contracts. Shareholders are last in line and receive dividends as declared at the discretion of the board of directors. If the business dissolves, creditors' claims have priority, and shareholders are residual claimants.

- **How can investors get out?** Ownership interests (shares) are freely transferable. Shareholders can realize the value of their investment by selling to other investors interested in acquiring their financial rights. The corporation entity, however, has no obligation to repurchase these ownership interests. Managers (directors and officers) cannot transfer their positions but can resign at any time.
- **What are investors' responsibilities to others?** The corporation is liable for its own obligations, but otherwise creates a "nonrecourse" structure. Corporate insiders (directors, officers, and shareholders) are not personally liable to outsiders on corporate obligations. Outsiders (such as contract creditors and tort victims) bear the risk of corporate insolvency. Corporate investors and managers risk only their investment.

Thus, the corporation combines five attributes: (1) separate, perpetual legal personality; (2) centralized management under a board structure; (3) shared ownership interests tied to residual earnings and assets; (4) transferability of ownership interests; and (5) limited liability for all participants.

Of course, there are exceptions. For example, shareholders in closely held corporations can agree to manage the business, pay themselves specified dividends, and limit their ability to transfer their shares. In some circumstances, courts use equitable principles to hold shareholders personally liable for corporate debts beyond their investment, or lenders may require shareholders to personally guarantee the corporation's obligations. The corporation is mostly a malleable set of *default rules* that specifies the terms of the parties' relationship unless they agree otherwise. This places a premium on the lawyer's role as creative planner.

Note on Corporate Nomenclature

There is some confusion about what is meant by private corporation and public corporation. A "private corporation" generally refers to a ***nongovernmental, for-profit business*** that has been incorporated under a state statute. If the private corporation is owned by a few shareholders, it is referred to as a "closely held corporation" or "close corporation." Or, when the private corporation is owned by many shareholders whose shares trade on public trading markets such as the New York Stock Exchange, it is referred to as a "publicly held corporation" or "public corporation." See MBCA §1.40 (Definition 18A). Thus, Apple Inc. is a private corporation that is also a public corporation. And Mom & Pop Grocery Corp. is a private corporation that is also a close corporation. To keep things simple, this book avoids the term "private corporation."

Some corporations are ***governmental***, such as the Federal Deposit Insurance Corporation. The FDIC, a government agency established to insure bank deposits, was created by an act of Congress, and is governed by a board of governors whose members are appointed by the president. Although some people might call the FDIC a public corporation, it's much clearer to call it a governmental agency.

Inside and Outside the Corporation

Historically, the US corporation has drawn a line around its shareholders and managers (directors and officers), all of whom are "inside" the corporation. All others are mostly left "outside" the corporation. Although these outsiders have a stake in the corporation, they are not regarded as within the special relationship between shareholders and managers.

Consider the many persons that participate in the joint economic activities that constitute the corporation. Shareholders—whether individual investors or institutions that invest for their beneficiaries (pension funds, mutual funds, insurance companies, endowments)—provide money capital. Managers (directors and officers) oversee the business and its employees. Lenders supply additional money capital as secured bank loans, unsecured bonds, short-term notes, and suppliers' trade credit. Suppliers provide inputs for the business under long-term contracts and in market transactions. Customers are essential—without them, the business cannot exist. Those injured by the business (whether as employees, customers, or strangers) have claims on the business directly or through governmental enforcement such as antitrust, banking, environmental, health, product safety, and workplace safety. As an economic actor in society, the corporation pays federal, state, and local taxes.

US corporate law, however, focuses on the relationship between shareholders and managers—the two constituent groups understood to be "inside" the corporation. "Outside" the corporation are creditors, suppliers, customers, employees, and government authorities, which usually are subject to legal norms that treat the corporation as a person—for example, the laws of contract, debtor-creditor, antitrust, labor, and tax. These outsiders are often described as "stakeholders."

Theory of the Firm

In the paradigm for-profit corporation, shareholders delegate control over their investment to managers. By separating the finance and management functions, the corporation creates an investment vehicle for raising large amounts of capital and operating large enterprises. This separation between shareholders and managers, however, makes the corporation a breeding ground for conflicting interests and opportunism.

Shareholders and managers often have different agendas. Once shareholders have invested, managers may become lazy, extract exorbitant perquisites (or worse), or be reluctant to take business risks that threaten their job security. Once managers have committed their human capital, shareholders may demand immediate returns, want managers to take high risks, or seek intrusive control powers. Despite these conflicts, the premise of the corporation is that neither shareholders nor managers can exist without the other—the corporation allows them to coexist and collaborate.

Corporate law seeks to minimize shareholder-manager conflicts and to maximize the firm's overall success. Besides creating a structure for business activities, corporate law is supposed to reduce internal conflicts of interest—often referred to as "agency problems" since they mimic the conflicts in the principal-agent relationship. Sometimes corporate law assumes legal intervention is too costly and leaves risk with shareholders. For example, the judicially created *business judgment rule gives* directors broad discretion to run the business without judicial second-guessing. In other contexts, corporate law regulates conflicts. Shareholders, for example, must approve the board's decision to merge the corporation into another corporation.

Over the last few decades, some legal theorists (and occasionally courts) have described the corporation as a "nexus of contracts." Contractarians view the corporation as a set of voluntary relationships among corporate constituents bound together by formal contracts, statutory norms, implicit understandings, and market constraints. The corporation serves as an organizing tool for their relationships. Corporate law, a collection of rules and mechanisms for specifying the roles of the corporate constituents, reflects the bargain the parties would have struck had they negotiated.

This vision of the corporation contrasts with the traditional notion of the corporation as "creature of state law"—that is, a regulatory device. To traditionalists, the corporation creates dangerous opportunities for managers to exploit shareholders and other constituents. Traditionalists maintain that in a public corporation active managers often exercise "control" at the expense of passive shareholder "owners." In close corporations where no market exists for shareholder interests, the majority can unfairly exploit the minority. Corporate law, particularly corporate fiduciary duties, serves to protect shareholders.

Traditionalists thus place great emphasis on corporate law as a means to control manager opportunism. They urge greater shareholder voting powers, broad disclosure rights, and strong fiduciary protection. On the other hand, contractarians believe that corporate law embodies the terms the parties have chosen, which when combined with market forces, efficiently restrain manager opportunism. For example, contractarians argue that if managers in public corporations act opportunistically, investors can sell their shares; falling market prices of corporate shares will make it harder for the corporation to raise capital and to compete in product and service markets; and, eventually, any corporation in which managers disregard shareholders will become a takeover target or go bankrupt.

Traditionalists	**Contractarians**
The corporation is a creature of law; no real bargaining occurs in the modern public corporation.	The corporation (like a contract) is a legal device chosen by the parties to organize business activities.
Managers can use "control" to exploit shareholders and other corporate constituents.	Managers cannot exploit "control" because market constraints align their interests with those of the shareholders.
Shareholders can be exploited because they are unsophisticated, uniformed, and non-collectivized.	Public shareholders act in sophisticated markets; close corporation participants can protect themselves by contract.
Capital (and other) markets are not always efficient; markets act slowly and unevenly to discipline poor managers.	Capital markets operate efficiently so stock prices of public corporations reflect all available public information.

Traditionalists	Contractarians
Corporate law should mandate rules to promote fairness and efficiency.	Corporate law should infer the parties' bargain, whether explicit or implicit.
Judges should actively enforce managers' fiduciary duties to the corporation and shareholders.	Judges should intervene with caution, only to fill gaps in the parties' bargain and protect markets.
Managers will abuse incentives, such as by manipulating financials or taking excessive compensation.	Managers can be given incentives, such as stock options, to motivate them to make the business more productive.

1.2.2 Sources of US Corporate Law

Historical Sketch of Corporation

The modern corporation did not happen in one blazing moment of inspiration. Instead, we can trace its current attributes to various earlier times and forms. The idea of an amalgamation of persons forming a separate juridical personality moved from Greece to Rome, to the Continent, and to England. Originally, perpetual separate existence in England was reserved for ecclesiastical, municipal, and charitable bodies whose existence was conferred by sovereign grant. The idea of common ownership by a body of passive investors originates from joint-stock trading companies, such as the East India Company (a monopoly franchise) in the early 1600s. A combination of continuity of life, centralized management, financial interests in profits, transferability of shares, and limited liability for private business existed in the 1700s in the form of complex deeds of settlement—an *unincorporated* association!

These concepts came to the American colonies. At first corporations, like political municipalities, had to receive a special charter from the state legislature. Legislatures granted charters on a case-by-case basis to noncommercial associations (such as churches, universities, and charities) that wanted the convenience of perpetual existence and to commercial associations (such as banks, navigation companies, canals, and turnpikes) with special public purposes and large capital needs. As the needs for capital (and thus incorporation) increased during the early 1800s, states began to enact general incorporation statutes for specified, usually capital-intensive, businesses. From the beginning, many feared the concentrated economic power inherent in the corporate device and early charters limited the amount of capital corporations could raise or the activities in which they could engage. Eventually, the US corporation evolved in the mid-1800s into a legal form available to all, though subject to significant statutory restrictions.

During the late 1800s two major trends, leading in opposite directions, shaped modern US corporate law. The first trend led to restraints on business activities. In the 1880s, Congress created the Interstate Commerce Commission to regulate the railroad monopolies. In 1890 and 1916, Congress passed antitrust legislation (the Sherman and Clayton Acts) to combat concentrations of corporate economic power. In the early 1900s, states enacted "blue sky" laws to deal with fraud in the sale of corporate securities. In the 1930s, Congress passed a series of securities laws aimed at abusive management practices in national securities markets.

The other trend led to a liberalization of state corporation statutes. In the late 1800s, to attract incorporation revenues, some states amended their statutes to lift limits on the amount of capital that a corporation could raise, to permit corporate ownership of other corporations, and generally to increase the flexibility available to corporate management. Eventually Delaware won this race of laxity, which some have called a scurrilous "race to the bottom" and others an efficiency-producing "race to the top." Today, most large, publicly traded US corporations are incorporated in Delaware.

Erosion of Limitations on Corporate Power

In looking at the history of the US corporation, it's useful to consider the evolution of corporate powers. In the early nineteenth century, as state legislatures chartered corporations for narrow purposes and with limited powers, courts fashioned the "ultra vires doctrine" to invalidate corporate transactions beyond the powers stated in the corporation's charter. Thus, both to protect investors in such capital-intensive businesses as canals, railroads, and banks and reflecting the popular concern about corporate power, early courts applied the ultra vires doctrine with vigor. Whenever a transaction was beyond the corporation's limited purposes or powers, either party to the contract could disaffirm it, even after the other party's full or partial performance. The ultra vires doctrine thus invited parties to weasel out of contracts entered into by corporations whenever a deal went sour—thus limiting the attractiveness of the corporate form.

Around the turn of the last century, however, courts confronted the commercial uncertainty created by the ultra vires doctrine and modified it in three respects. First, courts permitted an ultra vires defense only if the contract was still *executory* and had not yet been performed. Second, courts interpreted charter provisions flexibly to authorize transactions reasonably incidental to the business. Third, most courts held that the ultra vires defense could be barred by unanimous shareholder approval, unless a creditor would be injured.

At about the same time, state legislatures passed "general incorporation" statutes that authorized a wide variety of corporate purposes and powers. Drafters of corporate articles accepted the invitation, enumerating multiple business purposes and specifying powers for virtually every imaginable business transaction.

Later, legislatures passed modern enabling statutes that authorized "general purpose" clauses and specified a long laundry list of corporate powers. Today detailed drafting is no longer necessary. In many jurisdictions, the articles need not recite even that the corporation has the purpose of engaging in any lawful business or the power to engage in any lawful transaction—both are implicit. MBCA §§3.01, 3.02; cf. Del. GCL §102(a)(3) (requiring articles to set forth "nature of the business or purposes to be conducted or promoted").

Modern State Business Corporation Statutes

The corporation statutes of each state describe the basic corporate attributes. The Model Business Corporation Act (adopted in about 35 states) is typical and specifies:

- how to form a corporation (MBCA Chapters 1, 2, 3, 4, 5)
- the financial rights of shareholders (MBCA Chapter 6)
- the governance roles of shareholders, directors, and officers (MBCA Chapters 7, 8)
- the transferability rights of shareholders (MBCA §6.27)
- limited liability for shareholders (MBCA §6.22)
- structural changes such as charter amendments, mergers, and dissolution (MBCA Chapters 10, 11, 12, 13, 14)

Some of the statutory terms are mandatory, such as limit on the payment of dividends. Others, such as the removal of directors without cause or shareholder action without a meeting, are default terms that apply unless the parties choose different terms. Contractarians often view corporate statutes as providing standardized "off-the-rack" terms that apply unless the parties (usually in the charter) choose different, firm-specific terms. Under the internal affairs doctrine, the law of the state of incorporation governs all shareholder-manager matters in multistate corporations (see MBCA §3.2.1).

Although no two state corporation statutes are identical, there has been a trend toward greater uniformity and modernization. In 1950, the American Bar Association's invitation-only committee on corporate laws published the first model business corporation act. This model act, and its many revisions, served as the basis for corporation statutes in most states. In 1984, the ABA committee substantially reorganized and rewrote the model act, which follows the enabling structure of Delaware's corporate statute. The model act has since been revised on a number of occasions, including a major (though mostly cosmetic) revision in 2016.

Not all states, however, have enacted a corporate statute based on the model act. In fact, the most prominent corporate law states—Delaware, California, and New York—have their own idiosyncratic corporation statutes. Delaware's statute is particularly important in US corporate law because of the leadership of its legislature in being the first to enact corporate law reforms, the sophistication of the state's corporate bar, and the expertise and influence of its judiciary—and especially because most large, public corporations are incorporated in Delaware.

One thing to notice is that state corporation statutes generally treat all corporations the same. Corporations with numerous, widely dispersed shareholders (publicly held corporations) generally are subject to the same statutory rules as corporations with a small group of shareholders who do not have a public market for their shares (closely held corporations).

Role of Judge-Made Law

Corporation statutes are not all-encompassing; court decisions clarify and fill in the gaps of the statutes and the corporation's constitutive documents.

The most important judicial gap-filling involves the fiduciary duties of directors, officers, and controlling shareholders. Common-law fiduciary principles that regulate abuse by those who control the corporation's decision-making machinery lie at the heart of corporate law. See Chapter 11 (introduction to fiduciary duties). Lately, many fiduciary rules have turned on the disinterestedness and independence of outside (nonmanagement) directors in making corporate decisions.

ALI Principles of Corporate Governance

In 1977, the American Law Institute embarked on a long-term project to describe and unify the basic standards of corporate governance and structure, particularly in those areas not addressed by state corporation statutes. The project was controversial, often pitting contractarians against traditionalists. In 1993, after more than 15 years, the project came to a conclusion when the ALI approved a final version of the Principles of Corporate Governance. The ALI Principles—which (among other things) lay out the fundamental objectives of the business corporation, the legal functions (and duties) of directors, officers, and controlling shareholders, and the procedures for enforcing these duties—have not received the same reception as other ALI documents, such as the ALI restatements. Although some courts have embraced portions of the ALI Principles as useful statements of corporate law, other courts have given them little attention, and some have openly rejected them.

Federal Law

There is no federal corporation statute, despite regular calls for a uniform national law applicable to some or all aspects of publicly traded corporations. Despite the absence of a federal law of corporations, federal statutes add a significant layer of corporate regulation. The Securities Act of 1933 regulates the disclosure when corporations raise capital in public markets, whether by selling stock or taking on debt. The Securities Exchange Act of 1934 imposes periodic reporting requirements and proxy (shareholder voting) disclosure rules on corporations whose stock is publicly traded. In addition, the Exchange Act regulates the trading of securities in public and private markets, including insider trading—that is, the use of material, nonpublic corporate information to buy or sell stock.

Nonetheless, the landscape of corporate governance (the relationship between corporate managers and shareholders) has been significantly altered by two important pieces of federal legislation. In 2002, responding to a spate of corporate and accounting scandals, Congress passed the Sarbanes-Oxley Act—sweeping legislation that federalizes specific aspects of corporate law for public corporations. Among the Act's reforms are limits on corporations hiring their audit firms to do non-audit work for the corporation, rules governing the composition and functions of the board's audit committee, provisions requiring forfeiture of executive pay when companies correct their financials, bars on individuals from holding corporate office if they have committed securities fraud, prohibitions on companies making personal loans to their executives, mandates for companies to institute and disclose systems of internal controls, and SEC rules governing professional conduct of corporate/securities lawyers.

In 2010, responding to the financial crisis of September 2008 and perceived gaps in financial regulation, Congress passed the Dodd-Frank Act—massive legislation principally concerned with banking reform and securities regulation, but also having major implications for public corporations. Among other things, the Act mandates that compensation committees be composed entirely of independent directors, requires that shareholders have a "say on executive pay," requires corporations to adopt "clawback" policies when executives profit on false financial disclosures, mandates a new SEC program for employees who report securities violations to receive "whistleblower" bounties, and authorizes the SEC to pass rules giving shareholders the ability (at corporate expense) to nominate directors to the board.

1.2.3 Corporation as Constitutional Person

The corporation as "person" is a powerful metaphor. Corporate personality facilitates the aggregation of capital and labor with the attributes of a single entity capable of contracting, owning property, and being a party in court—just like a natural person. For commercial purposes, state and federal law largely respects the corporation-as-person metaphor. Most commercial statutes either specifically define corporations to be persons under the statute or have been so interpreted.

But there are many noncommercial contexts in which the law does not treat the corporation as a natural person, such as laws on intestacy, adoption, and political voting. This makes perfect sense. It would seem ludicrous if a corporation could be an adoptive parent (except in the movies) or if the political rule were "one corporation, one vote." Thus, the corporation sometimes has rights under the US Constitution that are normally associated with those of natural persons and sometimes not.

Broad Commercial Rights

According to the Supreme Court, the constitutional status of the corporation varies depending on the constitutional right at issue. The Supreme Court has had no trouble treating the corporation as a constitutional "person" when constitutional provisions can be seen as protecting *commercial interests* of the business.

Corporations are protected against state restrictions that burden interstate commerce. *Allenberg Cotton Co., Inc. v. Pittman*, 419 U.S. 20 (1974). Corporate property is protected against governmental deprivation under the Due Process Clauses of the Fifth and Fourteenth Amendments. *Oklahoma Press Publishing Co. v. Walling*, 327 U.S. 186 (1946). Corporations are "persons" entitled to equal protection under the Fourteenth Amendment, thus protecting them from state regulation aimed only at corporations. *Santa Clara County v. Southern Pac. Ry.*, 118 U.S. 394 (1886).

Corporations have First Amendment rights to express themselves as to commercial matters such as advertising their products. *Virginia State Board of Pharmacy v. Virginia Citizens Consumer Council*, 425 U.S. 748 (1976). And corporations have a First Amendment right to *not* be associated with certain speech, thus permitting them to refuse to distribute state-mandated information to customers. *Pacific Gas & Electric Co. v. Public Utilities Commission*, 475 U.S. 1 (1986).

The one (and largely superseded) exception to the commercial-interest analysis was the Supreme Court's refusal to treat corporations as "citizens" protected by the Privileges and Immunities Clause of Article IV. *Paul v. Virginia*, 75 U.S. (8 Wall.) 168 (1868). In theory, this allows states to regulate "foreign" corporations (those incorporated in another state) doing in-state business differently from their own "domestic" corporations, though in practice the differences in regulation have been minor and the equal protection afforded corporations under the Fourteenth Amendment essentially ensures nondiscrimination against foreign corporations.

Limited Noncommercial Rights

As to the corporation's *noncommercial interests*, the Supreme Court has been less willing to extend constitutional protection. For example, corporations cannot claim a Fifth Amendment privilege against self-incrimination. *Bellis v. United States*, 417 U.S. 85 (1974). Yet when the corporation's interests are closely linked to an individual's interests, such as in a one-person corporation, some lower courts have suggested that the individual's privilege against self-incrimination may extend to the corporation. And corporations have only a limited Fourth Amendment right to be free from unreasonable searches and seizures since business privacy is less compelling than personal privacy. *G.M. Leasing Corp. v. United States*, 429 U.S. 338 (1977).

Nonetheless, a corporation has significant free-speech protection under the First Amendment—even as to noncommercial political matters. For example, a state cannot forbid a corporation from expressing its views on a state referendum involving individual tax rates, even when the referendum did not materially affect the corporation's business. *First National Bank of Boston v. Bellotti*, 435 U.S. 765 (1978). Corporations can communicate with the legislative and executive branches by lobbying and commenting on proposed laws and rulemakings and can seek to sway the legislative branch in *amicus* briefs. Corporations can also set up their own political action committees (PACs) funded by voluntary contributions from their shareholders, managers, and employees—thus to speak on political issues and to contribute (subject to limits) to candidates and political parties.

In 2010, the Supreme Court held in a controversial 5-4 decision that a corporation cannot be prohibited from spending its own money to support or oppose a candidate for political office. *Citizens United v. Federal Election Comm'n*, 558 U.S. 310 (2010). Central to its analysis, the Court in *Citizens United* overruled an earlier 1990 decision that held a state could prohibit corporations from making campaign contributions to state candidates. *Austin v. Michigan Chamber of Commerce*, 494 U.S. 652 (1990). The Court in *Citizens United* rejected that there were compelling justifications to ban political expenditures by corporations that had "amassed" resources in the marketplace because wealthy individuals could not be banned from spending their money to speak out for or against candidates. Thus, although corporations (like individuals) can be limited with respect to their direct *contributions* to political candidates, corporations (like individuals) cannot be limited with respect to *expenditures*— on their own or through independent PACs—for speech that supports or opposes political candidates.

1.2.4 Private Nature of US Corporation

Corporate Formation

In the United States a corporation can be formed in any state, no matter where it does business. That is, the parties can choose the governing law for their corporate relationship. The question of where to incorporate requires balancing the benefits of incorporating in a state that provides flexibility in managing the business against the costs of incorporating elsewhere and then qualifying to do business as a *foreign corporation* in other states where business is to be conducted. The decision often comes down to a choice between the business's home state and Delaware.

The incorporation choice will determine how much in franchise taxes the corporation pays to the incorporating state. See Del. GCL §503 (based on authorized shares or capital). But business taxes will depend on where the corporation actually conducts business.

Internal Affairs Doctrine

In the United States, the law of the state of incorporation, with limited exceptions, governs the relationships among the parties in the corporation. This choice of law rule, known as the "internal affairs doctrine," permits the parties through the incorporation process to fix the law that applies to their corporate relationship, wherever litigation is brought. The corporation's "internal affairs" are those that relate to the legal relationships between the traditionally regarded corporate participants, including the rights of shareholders, the fiduciary duties of directors, and the procedures for corporate action.

Under the internal affairs doctrine, state courts are bound to accept the corporate law rules of the incorporating state, even when those rules are different or inconsistent with rules of the forum state. See *McDermott v. Lewis,* 558 U.S. 310 (Del. 1987) (applying Panamanian law that permitted parent corporation to vote shares of subsidiary, even though such voting is prohibited under corporate law of Delaware and all other US states).

Qualification of Foreign Corporations

A business incorporated in one state may conduct *intrastate* operations in another state (such as manufacturing or other regular business activities) if "qualified" to do business in the other state. To "qualify" the corporation must simply file a certified copy of its articles, pay a filing fee, and appoint a local agent to receive service of process in that state. MBCA §15.01; Del. GCL §371.

What are the penalties for doing business without being qualified? Some states fine the corporation and its officers for failing to qualify. Others treat the business as unincorporated, thus subjecting corporate officers to individual liability for contracts made in that state. Until a foreign corporation is qualified, it generally cannot bring lawsuits in local court. MBCA §15.02; cf. Del. GCL §383 (Court of Chancery can enjoin nonqualified foreign corporation from transacting business in state).

Delaware's Preeminence for National and Multinational Businesses

Generally, a business that will operate locally will be incorporated locally because doing so is easier and less costly. If the business will operate throughout the United States, the corporation will be incorporated in one state and qualified as a foreign corporation elsewhere.

Most large publicly held corporations (and nearly three-fourths of companies that become public in an initial public offering) have chosen Delaware as their state of incorporation. There are a number of explanations for this:

- Delaware's statute is designed to give management flexibility in structuring and running the business
- the Delaware courts and corporate bar are highly experienced and sophisticated in corporate law matters
- a large body of case law interprets the Delaware statute, thus providing certainty to corporate planners
- the Delaware legislature is a leader in corporate law reform and regularly amends the Delaware corporation's statute as new needs and problems arise

Some academics have criticized Delaware for having a pro-management slant and engaging in a chartering "race to the bottom." Cary, *Federalism and Corporate Law: Reflections upon Delaware,* 88 Yale L.J. 663 (1974). Others, observing the prevalence of Delaware corporations and the willingness of shareholders to invest in them, have argued that Delaware is engaged in a "race to the top." Winter, *State Law, Shareholder Protection, and the Theory of the Corporation,* 6 J. Legal Stud. 251 (1977). Empirical studies suggest that reincorporating in Delaware does not adversely affect (and may even raise) a corporation's stock prices. Moreover, the many Delaware court decisions favoring shareholder interests cast doubt on a "race to the bottom" thesis.

Nonetheless, the Cary/Winter debate continues—on new fronts. Recent scholarship has questioned whether a "market for corporate charters" produces optimal corporate law. Although nearly 60 percent of publicly traded US corporations are incorporated in Delaware, whose antitakeover statutes are less protective of management than other states, many public corporations remain incorporated in their home states. This home-state protection suggests that states compete to insulate management from financially beneficial corporate takeovers, at the expense of shareholders. In fact, non-Delaware corporations are more likely to incorporate and remain incorporated in their home state when the state offers relatively greater antitakeover protections.

You may be wondering whether large businesses choose Delaware because of perceived efficiencies or simply to follow the crowd. A recent study considers this question. Using the incorporation histories of over 22,000 public companies from 1930 to 2010, the study finds that firms are more influenced by changes in others' incorporation decisions than by changes in the law. That is, Delaware's popularity seems to be about "following the crowd." The study considers an unexpected legal shock—namely, a 1985 Delaware statute that permits exculpation clauses absolving directors of personal liability for negligence. Coinciding with the statute's enactment, Delaware increased its long-run share of the US chartering market from 30 percent to 74 percent. The study attributes most of this change to a cascading effect in which the decisions of past firms successively influenced future firms. Delaware corporations also enjoyed abnormal returns precisely during those years in which the Delaware network grew the most. See Sarath Sanga, *Network Effects in Corporate Governance* (2017) [available on SSRN].

Unique Aspects of US Corporation

What are civil law notaries?

Notaries public in the United States have the limited role of administering oaths and attesting to signatures on certain documents. Civil law notaries, on the other hand, are highly-trained, licensed legal practitioners who after earning a law degree must go through years of additional formal education and training. Civil law notaries have expansive roles of drafting, preparing, and recording legal instruments, including those dealing with company formation. They are vested with authentication power of the State over property conveyancing, company transactions, successions and estate planning, and powers of attorney.

As you may be noticing, the US corporation and US corporate law are peculiar—even unique. Unlike corporate law in most of the world, which imposes on the corporation various responsibilities to stakeholders (such as creditors, employees, even society), US corporate law creates a largely enabling structure for the corporation's shareholders and managers (directors and officers). That is, US corporate law focuses on the "internal" relationship between shareholders and managers, leaving other legal regimes to regulate the "external" relationships between the corporation and everyone else.

The next reading is drawn from a talk I gave at the opening convocations of two notarial schools in Italy. As a talk, you might notice, it was way too long! But the text, I hope, is a readable description of some of the peculiar and important aspects of US corporations, which I describe as a "corporate elephant":

(1) US corporations are creatures of state (not federal) law
(2) US corporate law is mostly enabling, not mandatory
(3) Delaware is the pre-eminent US state for corporate law
(4) US corporate law focuses on shareholders, not creditors

(5) The nature of US corporate law is fiduciary duties
(6) US corporate law is dynamic.

My hope is that upon reflecting on these specific aspects of the US corporation, you'll discern the whole.

The US Corporate Elephant

(2005)

Alan R. Palmiter

[available on SSRN]

Drawn from a speech at the opening convocations for notarial schools in Milan and Bologna, Italy, this is a story of modern US corporate law. Unlike the statist nature of the corporation in many other countries, the nature of the US corporation is essentially private. It is based on state corporate law, chosen by the parties. Federal law, though regulating disclosure to public investors, mostly avoids a role in the management of the corporation.

The corporation rules of state law are largely enabling, not mandatory. The parties have wide latitude in choosing their own structures. The preeminent provider of state law is Delaware, whose preeminence comes from offering a balanced package of legislative responsiveness, legal expertise, judicial expertise and efficiency, comprehensive case law, and assurances of being non-political.

Corporate law in the United States provides only basic creditor protections, assuming that most protections will come through markets and contracts. Significant emphasis is placed on fiduciary duties of corporate directors—to the corporation and shareholders. Fiduciary duties are dynamic, adapting to new governance and market circumstances. Also dynamic are other aspects of corporate law, as illustrated by the legislative, administrative, and judicial responses to recent corporate and accounting scandals.

Some aspects of corporate law, fundamental to the legitimacy of the corporation, remain unaddressed. The role of the corporation in politics, the place of institutional investors in corporate governance, the responsibility of the corporation for social and environmental practices not mandated by law. These are the current questions for corporate law. Will the corporation be up to the task?

Introduction

Company law is everywhere in tumult. Reforms in Italy. High-level reports and EC communications in Europe. Enron and Sarbanes-Oxley in the United States. What does it mean? My purpose is to offer some perspective—an American perspective—on corporate law and corporate reform.

In thinking about how to tell the story of US corporate law, I am reminded of the parable of the six blind men and the elephant. The story is told, perhaps by the Buddha, that six wise men of Indostan went from their village to observe an Elephant. Though blind, each wanted to satisfy his curiosity, to understand the nature of the strange being so much discussed.

The First approached the Elephant and came on his broad and sturdy side. "Oh, my," he said, "The Elephant is a wall!" The Second, feeling the tusk, said, "So round, smooth and sharp, this Elephant is a spear!" The Third approached and found the moving trunk in his hands, "I now know the Elephant. It is a snake!" The Fourth felt about and found the leg. "It is plain, the Elephant is a tree!" The Fifth touched the wide ear, "This marvelous Elephant is a fan." The Sixth grabbed the swinging tail, "The Elephant is a rope!"

The six wise men of Indostan then returned to their village and began to discuss the nature of the Elephant, each from his own observation. You can imagine the debate. Although each was right, each was wrong.

Now all parables have a moral. In one version of the story, the one I prefer, the parable ends with another, a seventh blind man, who listens to his six friends and discerns from them the whole and true nature of the Elephant. Observation is not enough; there must also be objectivity and synthesis.

This I see as my task. To describe the US corporation—the Elephant of the American economy, if not the global economy. This is a daunting task since US corporate law has so many dimensions.

One approach might be to describe our corporate law's resolution of specific problems, problems common to developed company law systems everywhere—such as how US corporations are capitalized, how powers are allocated between our monistic board and shareholders, when corporate actors have the authority to represent the corporation, how creditors are protected by judicial doctrines that disregard limited liability, what the role is of institutional shareholders in US public corporations, what the status is of shareholder agreements in our close corporations, and so on.

These would be the details. And just as the majesty of any company law lies in the details, this is the case of the Elephant—of our US corporate law. But I fear that in describing the details, some of them esoteric to even us American lawyers, I would create an incomplete impression. I would be both right and wrong.

Instead, I propose to describe the basic aspects, or characteristics, of US corporate law. Like the blind men of Indostan, I make six fundamental observations. I invite you to synthesize them and "see" the organic whole.

1 US corporate law is (mainly) state law, not federal law

In the United States, corporate law is fundamentally a matter of state law. From the beginning, this has been true. In 1819, our first and perhaps greatest Supreme Court Chief Justice, John Marshall, made clear: "Corporations are creatures of [state] law."

Each state has its own corporate legislation, which specifies the essential rules of the corporation: how the corporation is formed, its purposes and powers, its registered agent, how it is capitalized, the limitations on distributions to shareholders, the meetings of shareholders and their voting rights, the management authority of the board of directors and officers, the annual disclosure of company finances, the procedures for amending the articles and the bylaws, the merger into another corporation (or other entities), the process of dissolution, the treatment of corporations incorporated outside the state. The essential topics and language of state corporate statutes would be very familiar to any Italian lawyer or notary.

But what state's corporate law applies when a business operates throughout our national economy? The system of state corporate law is made coherent by the US choice of law rule: the internal affairs of every corporation are governed by the law of the state of its incorporation. This is a judicial doctrine with more than 150 years of uniform adherence. What is the internal affairs doctrine? According to the case law of every US jurisdiction and now embodied in state statutes, any questions involving shareholder rights, management duties, and perhaps creditor protections (to the extent these are specified by corporate law) are resolved by only one law: the corporate law of the state of incorporation. Why do state courts accede to other states' law? Early in the history because of the legislative nature of the corporation; later because of the commercial importance of certainty in corporate law; today because of long habit that has assumed constitutional dimensions. In 1987, our US Supreme Court explained, "No principle of corporation law and practice is more firmly established than a State's authority to regulate domestic corporations."

This system gives great weight, and respect, to the parties' choice of where to incorporate. Philosophically and practically, choice is at the heart of the system. There is choice at the time of the corporation's original formation by the initial investors and entrepreneurs. There is choice each time that new investors, new creditors, and new managers join the firm—they implicitly accept that the operative rules will be based on the state of incorporation. There is choice whenever the parties reincorporate—this is accomplished by merging into or converting to a corporation in another state, upon the initiation by the corporation's board and approval by a majority of its shareholders.

Lately choice in US corporate law has mushroomed to encompass the type of business entity that parties (advised by their lawyers) can select. Lawyers are usually involved but need not be. Notaries, as known in the civil law tradition, have no role. The array is breathtaking. Where only a generation ago the choice was between a partnership and corporation (your società in nome colletiva and società per azioni), today there are limited partnerships, limited liability companies, limited liability partnerships, limited liability limited partnerships—all sharing some level of corporate-type limited liability but modifying one or more aspects of the governance rules. Like corporations, all of this new alphabet soup of entities is subject to the parties' agreement, along with a perfunctory filing with the state. For my purposes and that of most US corporate lawyers, I treat these entities as part of our US corporate law.

These corporate forms—all arising under state law—offer great flexibility. They are each a malleable vessel into which can be poured the world's largest private organizations—corporations like Exxon/Mobil and Microsoft, or the humblest ones (but collectively the most important in our economy) such as corporations that run a family-owned corner gas station or software companies whose only assets are an idea and a PC connected to the Internet.

State corporation statutes make almost no distinction between the rules governing corporations whose shares trade on public stock markets—public corporations, as we call them—and corporations that have no trading market—close corporations. The text of the statutory rules on incorporation, capital formation, shareholder voting, and management authority is the same whether a public or close corporation. Instead, the differences arise in how courts interpret the statutory rules and apply the judge-made law of fiduciary duties. Let me give an example. Public corporation shareholders have no right generally to demand that the corporation buy back their shares—their only liquidity is to sell in public stock markets. The statutes are clear. But minority shareholders in a close corporation who claim that their fiduciary rights or reasonable expectations have been violated by an oppressive majority can in most state courts insist on a corporate buyout or even a court-imposed dissolution. Same statute—two different results.

What is the role of federal, national law? Federal law, which applies uniformly and with supremacy, has only a supportive role. There is no federal law of corporations, and the practice of federal courts to articulate principles of corporate law ended in 1938 with the demise of federal common law. Historically, federal securities laws passed in the 1930s only specify the informational rights of investors, and the concomitant disclosure duties of managers, in companies whose securities are listed on national stock markets or whose size suggests that public trading is occurring.

These public companies are subject to a set of mandatory rules administered by our Securities and Exchange Commission when companies sell securities to public investors, when they seek shareholder votes through our American proxy voting, and when bidders seek to acquire corporate control through mergers or tender offers. And public companies must periodically—and today almost continuously—inform public markets and investors of their ongoing business and its prospects.

Failure to disclose honestly triggers governmental enforcement and, more important, private litigation under our famous antifraud rule 10b-5. The rule, which forbids the making of materially false or misleading statements in connection with securities trading, is the basis for a monumental body of judge-made law in private securities enforcement cases. Best known are our terrifying securities class actions brought against public companies and their executives (both in the US and abroad) for issuing false press releases, misleading SEC filings or manipulated financials.

In short, in the United States, state corporate law defines corporate structure and governance; and federal law requires disclosure to public shareholders. Federal cases abjure any desire to use disclosure rules to create standards of fair conduct. State corporate law, until now, has mostly acceded to this bifurcation of roles. The most disclosure that state statutes require is the filing of an uninformative annual statement stating the corporation's business and the names of its principal officers. And state courts require disclosure, in shareholder voting cases, along the same lines as their federal counterparts under Rule 10b-5.

2 US corporate law is enabling, not mandatory

The word "law" to describe US corporate law is somewhat of a misnomer. US corporate law is not law in the sense we are accustomed to thinking of positive law—that is, state-created and enforced rules that dictate private behavior. Instead, US corporate law is mostly a series of default rules—that is, background rules that apply unless the parties specify otherwise. It is an enabling system that fosters private choice, private rules, and private relationships.

For example, corporate statutes specify that shares normally carry voting rights, but the articles of incorporation can create non-voting shares. Or in a close corporation, parties can agree to assign their voting rights in an irrevocable proxy to another person. Another example. The full board of directors is normally elected each year, but the articles can specify staggered terms in which only one-third of the board is elected annually. Or again in a close corporation, the corporate statutes permit agreements among all the shareholders on board composition. Such shareholder agreements can even do away with the board of directors.

That is, voting rights and annual board elections (and most corporate law rules) are default terms. In its enabling character US corporate law specifies the rules that seem to fit most corporations, what most corporate parties would choose, but the parties have broad flexibility to make their own arrangements.

The remarkable result is that only a handful of our corporate law rules, at least in the statute books, are mandatory in the sense that the rules are ones on which the parties cannot come to a different agreement. For example, each public corporation must have a board of directors with authority over the business; there must always exist a class of shareholders with voting power; shareholder meetings must occur annually; distributions to shareholders cannot occur if the business is insolvent; the board must propose (and the shareholders must agree) to amend the articles or merge with another corporation. Most everything else is subject to agreement.

In a study comparing the company law rules of the EC directives (which I have the impression cover a good deal of company law in Europe) and US corporate statutes of the 50 states, Professor William Carney (at Emory law school) compared the nature of European and American company rules. He counted a total of 131 EC rules, of which 67 were mandatory—no possibility for the parties to agree otherwise. He then searched US corporate law and found only 14 of these 131 rules existed in all the US states, he found that another 22 of these EC rules existed in some states, and (quite remarkable) he found that 95 EC rules existed nowhere in the United States—at least in the statutes. He then looked at the 67 mandatory rules in the EC. Only 4 of these 67 mandatory provisions existed in all US states, 9 others had been adopted in some states, and the remaining 54 mandatory rules had not been adopted in any US state.

Let me give you an example of this non-mandatory nature of US corporate law. There is no requirement that US corporations file or give public notice of who may act as representative on behalf of the corporation. Imagine a furniture business in my home state of North Carolina. The business plans to purchase 1000 sofas from an Italian manufacturer. Is the president of the North Carolina corporation authorized to make the purchase? No statute, no corporate filing, no corporate rule will answer your question. Instead, corporate authority is a private matter for the corporation's board of directors to decide. Any outsider will have to ask for internal documentation from the corporation—the articles of incorporation (to confirm the board's powers have not been changed), bylaws that specify the general powers of the corporate president, a resolution of the board authorizing the president to make the purchase, and a certificate of the corporate secretary verifying the authenticity of these internal documents.

Who stands behind this private system of law? In the example of corporate authority, the Italian buyer could request that the North Carolina seller provide it with an opinion from a reputable (and one would hope well insured) US law firm. The law firm would identify the corporate documents studied and state that the papers appear to be authentic and valid, would confirm that the person who purports to be the corporate president is in fact that person, and would opine that the president has been authorized by the board to enter into the sales agreement. What if it is a fraud? The third-party buyer could claim the corporation created the appearance of authority—appearances that themselves become binding according to US judge-made law. And the private law firm—assuming the function of a notary in Italy—would be responsible for the conclusions in its private opinion concerning the corporation's internal delegation of authority.

3 Delaware is preeminent

Observers of US corporate law, particularly in Europe, are immediately struck by the importance of Delaware, a tiny state on the Atlantic coast bordered by New Jersey, Pennsylvania, and Maryland. In 1787, it was the first state to ratify the US Constitution, recognizing immediately the value of being part of a larger commercial union.

Today more than 50 percent of our largest US corporations are incorporated in Delaware; more than 80 percent of new public corporations choose Delaware when they sell stock to the public. And both numbers continue to grow. When policy makers debate issues of corporate law—for example, whether state corporate law provides adequate corporate governance—they focus on Delaware law. Not only do public corporations (and their legal and financial advisers) choose Delaware, a large number of sophisticated closely-held businesses choose Delaware for its corporation, limited partnership, and limited liability company statutes.

Delaware has not always had this leading role as incorporator for the United States. In the late 1800s, the role was assumed by New Jersey. It had an early enabling statute, which among other things permitted corporations to own the shares of other corporations—hus making possible the famous monopolistic holding company structures known as "trusts." But in the early 1900s, New Jersey committed a grievous competitive error. Its governor, the idealistic Woodrow Wilson, urged the New Jersey legislature to reform the state's corporate law to make it more regulatory. Less flexibility for unscrupulous corporate actors. The result was that businesses re-incorporated in Delaware, which had in 1899 borrowed much of the earlier New Jersey statute as its own.

But other states, you might think, could copy the Delaware statute. How has Delaware achieved its prominence? How might an EU member, after the *Centros* and *Uberseering* decisions, mimic Delaware's success? There is no one answer. Instead, there is a blend of explanations for Delaware's preeminence:

First, Delaware is a leader, a first mover, in revising its statute to reflect technological and business innovations. For example, its statute was the first to allow shareholders to act (without a meeting) by mailing their written consents, the first to permit boards of directors to meet by telephonic communication, the first to permit shareholder voting on the Internet, the first to permit corporate charters that exculpate directors who make good faith errors. Statutory reform is a constant, ongoing process in Delaware. Proposed legislation comes from the Delaware corporate bar association - composed of the state's prominent corporate lawyers, in theory representatives of management and investor viewpoints. Although the Delaware constitution requires that any corporate legislation pass by a two-thirds vote, the legislature readily and quickly adopts revisions proposed by the state bar association.

Second, Delaware has an experienced and expert group of corporate lawyers. It is a learned, proud, and insular community. In such a small state, everyone knows everyone else. Law review articles and practical treatises by senior members of the corporate bar, as well as judges, constitute what you would call the "doctrine" of Delaware law.

Third, Delaware has a court system designed to respond quickly, efficiently, and expertly to corporate litigation. All corporate law cases are brought before the Delaware Court of Chancery, which hears cases without a jury. The Chancery Court judges, appointed by the state governor for 12-year terms, are selected on the basis of their corporate law expertise—typically mid-career stars of the Delaware bar. Appeals from Chancery Court decisions are made directly and as of right to the Delaware Supreme Court, whose 5 members are also appointed for 12-year terms on the basis (in part) of their corporate law credentials. It is an efficient court system. Important corporate cases—particularly involving takeovers—can be heard and decided by the Chancery Court, then appealed to the Supreme Court, in less than a month. Most Chancery Court decisions that are appealed are affirmed; most decisions are not appealed. To avoid any political tensions, the ten members of the Chancery and Supreme Courts must include an equal number of Democrats and Republicans.

Fourth, the Delaware judges have created a deep and broad body of case law—what you would call "jurisprudence." Delaware decisions cover all of the interstices of the Delaware statute: what constitutes a quorum for a shareholders' meeting? what are the liquidity rights of shareholders in a close corporation? what are the standards for reviewing parent-subsidiary dealings and mergers? what are the responsibilities of a board seeking to protect a negotiated merger agreement? what are the methods to value corporate shares in appraisal? what are the responsibilities of directors defending against an unwanted takeover? In great detail, Delaware cases answer (and update earlier answers) to the questions. On most corporate law topics, there are more Delaware court decisions than all of the decisions from other states combined. Lawyers and state courts outside of Delaware regularly refer to Delaware decisions for guidance.

Fifth, Delaware is a small state. A significant part of its public budget (about 20 percent) comes from filing and franchise fees. Even more comes indirectly from the business generated by transaction services, litigation and counseling performed by Delaware law firms. This means that Delaware cannot lightly change its corporate law to prefer a particular company, a particular management agenda, or a particular investor movement. Its financial dependence on being an independent provider of corporate law keeps Delaware from acting impulsively. For example, on the difficult question of takeovers, while other states quickly adopted antitakeover statutes in the 1980s when requested by local managers, Delaware deliberated for more than three years before adopting one, one of the mildest antitakeover statutes adopted by any state.

What about competition from other states? There really is none. The other states have been content to provide corporate law for their closely-held businesses and preferential rules for the public corporations that have stayed home. In the 1980s Kansas and Nevada sought to make corporate law a new business—by copying the Delaware statute and even formally adopting its case law—but hardly anybody was interested. Even though more expensive, Delaware offered a better product.

But Delaware has competition, not from other states, but instead from the looming federal government that periodically threatens to intervene and supersede Delaware law if the state fails in its unique role. In fact, two of the periods of greatest activism in the Delaware courts, which resulted in an expansion of shareholder protections in takeovers and the strengthening of accountability for corporate boards, coincided with heightened federal awareness. The first in the mid-1980s when Congress debated whether to intervene in the explosive takeover market. And more recently last year, as Congress rushed forward with the Sarbanes-Oxley law to respond to the corporate scandals of Enron, WorldCom, and other major US companies.

The US corporate law landscape, however, is not an expansive Delaware surrounded by a chaotic array of other states. States have chosen relative uniformity in their corporate law rules, without any federal direction. Most states (about 38) have adopted a version of the Model Business Corporation Act. Others, such as New York and California, have statutes with mostly standard provisions, only a few surprises. The MBCA is a model statute prepared by the Business Law Committee of the American Bar Association. Many of its provisions are adaptations of Delaware provisions—though often better organized and more clearly written.

Revised with some regularity, the MBCA was first promulgated in 1949. Its most significant revision was in 1984. Like Delaware, states that have adopted the MBCA rely on their state bar associations to draft and propose revisions. There are some differences between the Delaware statute and the MBCA, but they are few. In some respects, the differences only highlight the many similarities and uniformity of US corporate law. For example, the MBCA has much simpler legal capital rules on proper payment for corporate shares and on distributions to shareholders—although the Delaware scheme in this area is easily manipulated and is no more intrusive than the MBCA. Another example are the procedures for shareholders to bring litigation, but in the end both Delaware and the MBCA permit independent directors, under some circumstances, to terminate an unwanted shareholder suit.

But there is a growing divergence between Delaware and the MBCA today. Delaware's leadership as corporate law reformer has been brought into question. Two recent MBCA reforms offer innovative and challenging steps forward—away from Delaware law. Changes that may impose greater corporate discipline and rebalance corporate governance. One set of MBCA amendments creates statutory standards of conduct and liability for corporate directors—particularly concerning independence and monitoring of corporate legal compliance. They thus seek to codify through statute the contours of fiduciary duties of corporate directors. Another set of MBCA amendments deals with the voting and appraisal rights of shareholders in fundamental transactions, such as mergers, sales of assets, and tender offers. The MBCA amendments impose uniform treatment, regardless how a transaction is structured, thus rejecting the formalism of Delaware law in which artful planning can be used to alter and even eliminate shareholder rights.

Will states adopt these innovative MBCA provisions? How will Delaware respond? Time will tell.

4 US corporate statutes are thin on creditor protection

Creditor protection, a centerpiece of European company law, is largely absent from the mandatory structure of US corporate law. By and large, we have no minimum capital requirements for beginning an incorporated business, no fixed requirements of capital reserves, only porous (almost empty) rules on accounting limits for making shareholder distributions, no liability for directors whose good faith actions cause their company to become insolvent.

This has not always been the case. During our early corporate history and through the middle half of the twentieth century, creditor protection was important to US state legislatures. Minimum capital requirements were a basic aspect of US corporate law. So were rules on par value and capital reserves, which were seen as creating an inviolate trust fund or equity cushion for the protection of creditors. Directors, particularly of banks and other savings institutions, who made risky decisions for a bank in financial trouble faced the threat of personal liability. And shareholders of banks were liable for up to three times their investment if the bank failed—a de facto insurance fund for bank depositors.

Over the last half of the twentieth century these formal protections have been dismantled, not because of a conscious reform movement, but through a slow process of attrition. Today it is possible to incorporate a business without any capital, rewrite assets and capital accounts on the balance sheet, gamble on the business while the company faces insolvency—all in the name of maximizing shareholder returns. The statutory rules of corporate law generally only mandate that distributions to shareholders, whether the payment of dividends or repurchase of shares, occur when the corporation is solvent, based on a manipulable balance sheet and the business's ability to pay its existing, foreseeable debts. Rules that prohibit corporate loans to finance the purchase of company shares or rules that prohibit promises of future services to acquire company shares each year disappear, even more, from the statute books. That is, the ex-ante rules imposed by corporate law for the protection of creditors are few and each year fewer.

This may seem appalling, even barbaric. What happens if corporate actors, through risky undertakings or sloppy (or corrupt) handling of cash, leave a business insolvent—unable to pay legitimate creditor claims? The American answer is peculiarly American. We leave the matter to private protection through ex ante contracts and markets. And for those understandings that did not find their way into a contract, we rely on courts to protect ex post reasonable expectations. Ultimately, our reluctance to aggrandize creditor rights comes from our enthusiasm for shareholder primacy. After all, we Americans are capitalists.

First, we expect voluntary creditors who are concerned about corporate transactions or activities that might undermine their claims to insist on contractual protections. For example, banks that extend credit to an incorporated business often demand personal guarantees from the corporate owners. The banks also impose contractual stipulations on business activities –choice of manager, size of salaries, timing of distributions, accounting ratios for new debt, and so on. That is, the banks write their own creditor protections. Another example. Corporations that issue bonds, another form of lending, make various creditor protection promises in an indenture—a set of corporate promises whose terms offer bondholders standardized protections. Less strong creditors, such as suppliers or employees, will insist on frequent payment schedules or will increase their prices to take into account the risk of corporate insolvency. As for involuntary creditors, such as tort victims injured by corporate activities, we require insurance for certain business activities and otherwise (at least for now) we assume involuntary creditors will have their own insurance.

Second, we rely on courts to impose ex post relief against abusive corporate actors. Under a metaphoric and purposefully vague judicial doctrine, "piercing the corporate veil," creditors can obtain direct, personal recovery from corporate shareholders and managers who abused the corporate privilege. If creditors (either voluntary and involuntary) identify that a corporate insider misrepresented the corporation's solvency or business size, or that the insider de-capitalized the business at the expense of creditor claims, courts will disregard the rule of limited liability. In fact, piercing the corporate veil—though it occurs only in close corporations—s the most frequent type of corporate litigation in the United States. In the end, this ex-post doctrine (applied case by case) imposes a set of corporate obligations for the protection of creditors.

An example of a piercing case illustrates. An owner of a fleet of taxis in New York City incorporated 10 separate corporations, each owning two cabs. Operating without any minimum capital requirements, the companies maintained only the insurance required by state law. When one of the cabs injured a pedestrian, the New York state court decided that separate incorporation and under-insurance were not reasons for imposing individual liability on the owner. That is, corporate law imposed no ex-ante creditor protections. But the court decided there was ex post protection. In post-insolvency litigation, the owner could be individually liable if there was evidence he had taken cash (through dividends or otherwise) from the companies, leaving them insolvent or near insolvency.

5 Fiduciary duties are the binding cement

Power in the US corporation resides in the board of directors –not the shareholders' annual meeting. This, the Delaware judges frequently remind us, is THE fundamental principle of US corporate law. The board, in reliance on the corporation's officers, has authority over the business and affairs of the corporation—whether publicly traded or closely held. The board chooses the corporate executives, sets dividends, initiates mergers, and makes changes to the business. The shareholders? They elect the directors and can veto only specified fundamental transactions.

With power comes responsibility, accountability. The main legal accountability in the corporation arises not in legislated corporate rules, which we have seen are largely enabling not regulatory, but from fiduciary duties enforced by courts. Shareholders have rights to bring lawsuits to enforce these fiduciary duties, subject to significant procedural controls.

The animating principle of US fiduciary law is that the business judgment of directors (and those to whom they delegate corporate authority) should not be questioned. The business judgment rule. A famous case involving the early Ford Motor Co. stated this principle clearly: "Judges are not business men." In our 150-year history of corporate fiduciary duties, no more than a handful of cases have imposed liability on directors who made good faith, well-meaning business decisions, no matter how flawed or unfortunate the outcome. Given the business judgment rule, the directors' "duty of care" is symbolic, aspirational.

Courts intervene only when directors' ignorance is outrageous or inexcusable given the circumstances of an important decision—a violation of the "duty to be informed." Or when directors fail completely to supervise corruption in the corporation (private or public)—a violation of the "duty to monitor." Or when directors act in their own self-interest contrary to corporate interests—a violating of the "duty of loyalty."

In fact, if one were to observe the most significant matters addressed by corporate law in the United States over the last 25 years—they all involve court cases that interpret (and sometimes reformulate) corporate fiduciary duties. Let me give some examples.

Corporate groups. The transactions between companies in a corporate group—stock issuances, payments of dividends, intra-group contracts, even mergers—are regulated mostly by fiduciary law. Although the parent has power over the subsidiary, fiduciary law limits that power. Some complain that the fiduciary rules are too lax in this area, but their existence affects (if not dictates) how corporate groups allocate profit centers, choose dividend policy, engage in intra-group transactions, and structure intra-group buyouts and mergers.

Takeovers. The defenses that incumbent corporate executives may use to prevent shareholders from selling to an unwanted, outside bidder are regulated mostly by fiduciary law. Federal law imposes some inconvenient disclosure and timing impediments; and state antitakeover statutes (outside of Delaware) sometimes present difficult, but usually, surmountable obstacles. But any lawyer advising on what can and can't be done in a takeover (particularly of a Delaware corporation) refers to a venerable line of fiduciary cases dating from 1985.

Compensation of executives. The methods by which executives are compensated (and the strong, lately perverse incentives that some stock-based compensation can create) are regulated by fiduciary standards. Federal tax law has a minor role; federal securities regulation requires that the compensation be disclosed; state statutes are almost completely enabling. Only courts using process-based fiduciary rules, with Delaware once indifferent and now taking a harder look at the issue, create a potential limit.

Internal controls and corporate monitoring. The principal rules on how boards monitor financial disclosure systems, construct legal compliance programs, and approve executive loans are all derived from fiduciary principles. That US public boards are composed of independent directors, and what constitutes independence, largely derives from principles articulated in fiduciary duty cases.

In some areas, fiduciary law is silent—and thus corporate law is silent. Our fiduciary standards are largely empty with respect to the duties of institutional shareholders when they vote shares. Our fiduciary law does not regulate corporate political activities or contributions, or charitable giving. Our fiduciary law accepts, but does not require, that corporations voluntarily promote social and environmental practices not mandated by law. In these sensitive areas, without meaningful fiduciary standards or parameters, there is a legal vacuum.

6 US corporate law is dynamic

The last, and perhaps most revealing, characteristic of US corporate law is its dynamism. With reforms coming in a regular stream from state and federal legislatures, state and federal courts, federal regulators, and capital markets, change in US corporate law is inescapable. This has been particularly true during the last 20 years.

The questions today sweeping through Europe have been asked, many of them answered, by the US corporate law system since the mid-1980s: the relationship of shareholders and other corporate constituencies; the possibilities for mergers and takeovers; the role of institutional shareholders; the functions and relevance of outside directors. Some were answered by Delaware courts applying state fiduciary law, some by state legislatures that passed antitakeover statutes (these, a bizarre exception to the enabling nature of US corporate law), some came from new SEC rules that empower shareholder communications, some by federal courts that imposed duties of transparency on corporate executives, some by practices (new norms) among directors on corporate boards.

Then over the last two years, the collapse of Enron and the series of corporate scandals that resulted in a 35 percent overall decline in the US stock markets—a 7 trillion-dollar loss from the markets' height—presented a wake-up call. The corporate scandals, which we have come to refer to simply as "Enron," exposed inadequacies, maybe fundamental flaws, in the US corporate law system. And certainly, with our corporate governance. How could Enron, the company voted by Fortune Magazine for five years in a row as "the most innovative company in America," have gone bankrupt in less than six months? What was its board doing waiving the company's ethics code to allow insider profiteering? There were other companies. How could Tyco agree to pay an executive an extra multi-million-dollar severance if convicted of a felony? How could WorldCom treat its purchases of telecommunications capacity as an asset, rather than an expense—ultimately forcing it to restate earnings by 11 billion dollars, and causing shareholder losses of $200 billion?

Overnight our magnificent corporate law system suddenly seemed terribly wrong. Enron was not an isolated abnormality. Across the system, corporate managers driven by the promise of stock option wealth greedily and dishonestly had abused the confidence of investors and the market. Accountability had collapsed. Auditors, taking on new roles as consultants urging their corporate clients to take risks, abandoned their role as certifiers of financial truth. Wall Street analysts were paid to create an atmosphere of ebullience, whatever their better judgment said. Corporate lawyers had become transactional engineers, no longer voices of wisdom and conscience. Regulators had become complacent, happy to boast that US stock markets (and the roaring economy) were the envy of the world.

The US Congress response to Enron was Pavlovian—bell rings, dog salivates. Congress heard stories of an inept, passive auditing committee at Enron, and mandated that audit committees of public corporations be composed exclusively of outside directors, tasked them with selecting and supervising the company's outside auditor, and required at least one member be a financial expert. Congress heard stories of auditor complicity, and mandated a new accounting board to supervise the auditing profession. Congress heard stories of conflicts in accounting firms between auditing and consulting functions, and barred such dual service. Congress heard stories of excessive loans to corporate insiders and forbade them. Congress heard stories of lawyers assisting company misbehavior and mandated new SEC rules on lawyer whistleblowing. Congress heard stories of executives dumping their company stock, while employees in the company pension plan were frozen, and banned the practice. Congress heard stories of oblivious, witless corporate executives, and mandated that CEOs and CFOs certify their company's financials and internal reporting systems. And, as you know, Congress extended many of these new rules to companies outside the United States, including in Europe, if their stock is traded on US markets.

Today, after Enron, US corporate law is at a crossroads. The Sarbanes-Oxley Act, by federally codifying a new set of best practices in public corporations, raises questions about the centrality of state corporate law. In addition, new rules by the stock exchanges and norms urged by institutional investors create a set of new guidelines—apart from state corporate law—for the independence and role of outside directors, such as committee composition, multiple service on boards, and executive sessions of the board without management present. The SEC has proposed new rules requiring companies to disclose how directors are nominated to the board, as well as a new rule that the corporation-funded nomination process be opened to long-term 5 percent shareholders. The increase in securities fraud lawsuits in federal courts, lately settled by companies that promise corporate governance reform, make state courts seem less important. Where have the states been? Somewhat late, but now present, state courts have begun to articulate a reformed corporate fiduciary law, particularly in Delaware.

In speeches and remarkably candid scholarly articles, and now in a wave of new court opinions, the Delaware judges have begun to signal that they believe themselves up to the task. According to the latest cases, takeover protections are to be scrutinized more carefully; excessive executive compensation is no longer an open-ended game; the independence of outside directors and their good faith are under intense new scrutiny. Formalism is out; substance seems to be in. And human motivations have retaken center state in the judicial calculus. As Chief Justice Norman Veasey of the Delaware Supreme Court recently stated, "We did not just fall off the turnip truck ... we can tell whether somebody is acting independently." With a poetic flourish, Veasey went on, "Directors who are supposed to be independent should have the guts to be a pain in the neck."

But the post-Enron world is hardly revolutionary. The essentially private structure of US corporate law remains intact. Shareholders are still the focus of our corporate law. The board of directors, composed of a majority of independent members, remains at the helm of our public corporations. Outside auditors constitute the principal check on management financial reporting. Reforms by Congress, the stock exchanges, and the SEC only reinforce these central theses. States continue in their primary role, as enablers of this private structure. Even as the new Sarbanes-Oxley rules mandate changes, many already in progress, US corporate law remains largely a matter of state-based private choice, tempered by fiduciary duties molded and enforced by Delaware judges. Is this a legitimate system, one deserving of our confidence and trust? Will our corporate law be up to the task? We will see.

Conclusion

So that is the Elephant—the six fundamental defining characteristics of US corporate law. First, state corporation law provides the framework, with federal law in a supporting role. Second, private choice is the engine of state corporate law, which is mostly facilitative, not mandatory. Third, Delaware is the preeminent leader of this incorporation-based system of private ordering. Fourth, US corporate law's animating philosophy of shareholder primacy means that creditors (and other outsiders) must rely on other systems of protection. Fifth, meanwhile, shareholders find their protection not in corporate statutes, but in a set of judicially-created rules that balance managerial discretion and accountability—fiduciary duties, we call them. Finally, sixth, US corporate law is subject to constant change, the latest corporate scandals resulting in a cacophony of voices and reforms. And today that dialogue—the debate about the Elephant—reaches beyond our village.

1.2.5 New Directions for US Corporate Law

As you'll notice, the corporation typically has been viewed as a somewhat static vessel into which is poured a business—sometimes a business with a handful of investors and a limited business plan, and sometimes a large business with many investors and a broad range of operations. But lately, the corporation is being used to network many businesses—think about Airbnb, Lyft, and Amazon. For example, today Airbnb offers travelers the most "hotel rooms" in the world, without itself owning any hotels. Likewise, Lyft and Uber have more "taxis" in their fleets than any taxi company, without owning any cars or employing any drivers (though this last point has been subject to litigation). And Amazon sells more products than any other retailer in the world, without having (or having very few) "stores"—remember those places of brick and mortar where we once did all our shopping.

In the process, the corporation is undergoing change—as it is designed to do. As many of the largest and most successful businesses now operate as "platforms" to connect people, transfer information and facilitate economic transactions, a team of international law professors recently asserted that corporate law must adapt to accommodate these "platform companies" that are disrupting retail, hotels, and taxis—and soon financial services. While the "classic" corporation focuses on the relationship between shareholders and managers, this team of professors argued that corporate law should respond by providing for more "community-driven" organizational forms (away from the current hierarchical shareholder-dominated structure), by creating a more "open and accessible platform culture" (different from the shareholder-focused disclosure regime), and by facilitating "the creation, curation and consumption of meaningful content" (unlike the current corporate form that is meant to deliver products and services on a "take it or leave it" basis). See Mark Fenwick, Joseph A. McCahery & Eric Vermeulen, *The End of "Corporate" Governance: Hello "Platform Governance"* (2018) [available on SSRN].

The corporation is dynamic. We already saw this in our look at how some business forms today aren't even run by humans—decentralized autonomous organizations—and we will be seeing how the corporation (the business undertaking still run by humans) is in the throes of change. This is exciting!

* * *

Concluding Thoughts

The Individual and the Collective

Every year I say the following to my Corporations students:

> Are there any among you who could make a pencil? Imagine you're on a deserted island for a lifetime. Could you make one? You know what it's supposed to be. But do you know how to make graphite? How to saw wood into a hexagonal rod? Or how to concoct yellow

paint—probably using fancy petrochemicals? Or the rubber for the eraser? Or the metal that holds the rubber eraser in place? Do you know metallurgy? Or, by the way, do you know how to extract latex from a tree? And then boil it down to make rubber?

All of this to make the point that corporations are quite useful because they allow for human collaboration and specialization in amazing ways!

Well, it turns out that an economist asked similar questions in an essay called *I, Pencil*. (I did not know about this essay when I first posed my pencil questions, having noticed a pencil sitting on the podium where I was lecturing.) The economist, Lawrence Read, wrote his essay in 1948 to extol the virtues of capitalism (and individual entrepreneurship) over socialism (and state control of the economy).

But I find him to be so wrong about corporations and Capitalism. They are not private matters. Government has an important role to make sure the toxic chemicals used in the pencil's yellow paint don't harm workers or people living near the chemical plant. And we need government to limit the deforestation of the Amazon by rubber plantations—a terrible price of rubber erasers before we figured out how to make synthetic rubber. And we need government (for example, in China, the leading manufacturer of lead pencils) to ensure that labor conditions do not lead to human suffering or to global economic instability. And so on.

Ironically, Read did not acknowledge how interconnected the world is. His essay does not mention "regulation" at all, though it does mention "markets" three times and "individuals" thirteen times. His nine mentions of "government" are all pejorative. Strangely, in celebrating the individual, Read failed to see how a pencil is actually a non-individual, highly interconnected event.

So, too, is the corporation!

Chapter 1.3

US Public Corporation

Now that you understand the peculiar structure of the US corporation and its incorporation-based private ordering, you are ready to consider the specific case of the US public corporation. Although there is much variation among public corporations (for example, ExxonMobil vs. Google), you will discover there are unifying legal and structural themes.

This chapter, the penultimate in our introduction to the US corporation, is meant as a springboard for the final chapter on US securities regulation—the disclosure rules that apply to US public corporations.

Chapter's Focus

You'll want to first focus on corporate governance in the US public corporation—the relationship between management (especially the board of directors) and shareholders (whose investment interests are traded on public stock markets). How do shareholders exercise their rights to sell, vote, and sue? And, in what ways has federal law come to regulate corporate governance in US public corporations?

Next, you'll want to consider the fiduciary duties of "care, loyalty, and good faith" that directors are said to owe to the corporation and how these duties are diluted by the famous "business judgment rule" (BJR). Given the BJR, you'll want to think about the "self-regulatory" nature of US corporate law.

Finally, you'll discover that the *stated* animating purpose of the US corporation is shareholder wealth maximization (SWM). You'll want to consider how this purpose defines the contours of the BJR and corporate fiduciary duties. You will want to consider whether a sustainable corporation can co-exist with SWM.

After this chapter, you'll be ready to consider the final chapter of this unit, one that looks at how US securities regulation—mostly a federal body of law—requires US public corporations to disclose information to investors and markets, and the ways in which it disciplines corporations (and others) who make false and misleading statements that affect stock prices in those markets.

1.3.1 Corporate Governance in US Public Corporation

Corporate law creates a framework for the relationship between shareholders and management (directors and officers). This framework is called "corporate governance"—a set of rules and practices by which corporations are controlled and operated. Corporate governance includes shareholder oversight of the corporation's board of directors and the duties that directors owe to the corporation and its shareholders.

US corporate governance arises from four key sources:

- state corporate law (predominantly Delaware, where most US publicly traded corporations are incorporated)
- the federal Securities Act of 1933 and Securities Exchange Act of 1934, and the regulations of the Securities and Exchange Commission (SEC) (governing disclosure by public companies)
- stock exchange listing rules (predominantly the New York Stock Exchange (NYSE) and the NASDAQ) (specifying certain best practices for listed companies)
- federal statutes covering particular areas of corporate practice (such as Federal Reserve regulations with respect to banks and other financial institutions, and similar regulatory schemes on communications, transportation and other regulated fields).

See Adam O Emmerich, William Savvit, Sebastian Niles & Kathleen I Tatum, *The Corporate Governance Review: United States* (10th ed. 2020) [available on SSRN] (corporate lawyers from leading US corporate law firm, Wachtell Lipton, describing sources of US corporate governance as "varied and interrelated . . . and not always harmonized . . . [making] for an environment of frequent change and evolution").

To understand the US public corporation is to understand two related forces that shape corporate governance. The first is state corporate law and its structure of shareholder voting and board decision-making, moderated by judge-created fiduciary duties that corporate directors owe to the corporation and its shareholders. Second is the largely mandatory set of disclosure rules of federal securities law. Corporate governance is largely molded by the interplay of these two forces.

Next is an overview of the state and federal norms that shape corporate governance in the publicly traded corporation. For some of you, it will be a refresher. For those of you who have not taken Corporations or Business Associations, you'll find interesting the framework of the public corporation, one that we'll return to regularly in our search for the sustainable corporation.

Corporations: Examples & Explanations

(9th ed. 2020)

Alan R. Palmiter

[Aspen Publishing]

Chapter 11

Corporate Fiduciary Duties—An Introduction

At the heart of corporate law lie duties of trust and confidence—fiduciary duties—owed by those who conduct and manage the corporation's business and affairs to the body of constituents known as the "corporation." Directors, officers, and controlling shareholders are obligated to act in the corporation's best interests, which traditionally has meant primarily for the benefit of shareholders—the owners of the corporation's residual financial rights.

State courts, not legislatures, have been the primary shapers of corporate fiduciary duties. Judicial rules balance management flexibility and accountability, producing often vague and shifting standards. The American Law Institute has contributed the Principles of Corporate Governance (see §1.2.4) to articulate and provide guidance on corporate fiduciary duties and the standards of judicial review they entail. Fiduciary duties fuel the ongoing debate over the function and responsibility of the corporation in society.

This chapter introduces the theory and nature of corporate fiduciary duties (§11.1), gives an overview of the duties of care and loyalty (§11.2), and describes the reality of fiduciary duties in modern corporations (§11.3), particularly as they relate to independent directors (§11.4). The chapter also offers an overview of recent federal legislation—the Sarbanes-Oxley Act of 2002 and the Dodd-Frank Act of 2010—that introduce a variety of corporate governance reforms in public corporations and thus federalize some corporate fiduciary duties (§11.5).

§11.1 The Corporate Fiduciary—A Unique Relationship

§11.1.1 Analogies to Trusts and Partnerships

What is the corporate fiduciary's relationship to the corporation? Early courts analogized the corporation to a trust, the directors to trustees, and the shareholders to trust beneficiaries. But modern courts recognize that the analogy is flawed because trustees have limited discretion compared to directors.

Sometimes the corporation, particularly when closely held, has also been analogized to a partnership. But corporate fiduciaries operate in a system that prizes corporate permanence, as well as centralized management and the discretion specialization entails. Although some cases have implied partner-like duties for participants in close corporations (see §27.2.2), the cases are exceptions to the broad discretion afforded corporate directors.

In the end, the most that can be said is that directors have a unique relationship to the corporation. The relationship arises from the broad authority delegated directors to manage and supervise the corporation's business and affairs, subject to the rights of shareholders to elect directors.

Note on Duties of Other Corporate Insiders

Courts have generally imposed fiduciary duties on corporate officers similar to those imposed on directors. MBCA §8.41. Non-officer employees have traditional duties of care, loyalty, and obedience as agents of the corporation. In addition, corporate officers and employees have a duty of candor that requires them to give the corporation (the board of directors or a supervisor) information relevant to their corporate position.

In general, persons retained by the corporation do not have corporate fiduciary duties. For example, an attorney who advises a majority shareholder in an unfair squeezeout of minority shareholders is not bound by fiduciary duties to the corporation, though the attorney can be liable for tortious aiding and abetting of the majority's breach.

§11.1.2 Theory of Corporate Fiduciary Duties

The genius of the U.S. corporation lies in its specialization of function. For example, the corporation separates the risk taking of investors and the decision making of specialized managers. This separation creates an inevitable tension.

- **Management discretion.** The efficiency of specialized management suggests that managers should have broad discretion. Giving shareholders (and courts) significant oversight would undermine this premise of the corporate form. In cases of normal business decision making, judicial abstention is appropriate.
- **Management accountability.** Entrusting management to nonowners suggests a need for substantial accountability. Nonowners managers have natural incentives to be lazy or faithless. Although shareholder voting constrains management abuse, voting is episodic. Without supplemental limits, management discretion would ultimately cause investors to lose confidence in the corporate form. In cases of management opportunism, judicial intervention is the norm.

Corporate fiduciary law seeks to resolve this tension by identifying when courts should abstain and when courts should intervene in corporate decision-making and other actions by those who exercise control authority in the corporation.

§11.1.3 To Whom Are Fiduciary Duties Owed?

Corporate directors are said to owe fiduciary duties to the "corporation," not the individual shareholders who elected them. Some courts and many commentators assert that fiduciary rules thus proceed from a theory of maximizing corporate financial well-being by focusing on *shareholder wealth maximization*. The theory posits that any fiduciary rule—whether governing boardroom behavior or use of inside information—must maximize the value of shareholders' interests in the corporation. As residual claimants of the corporation's income stream, shareholders are the most interested in effective management. Under this theory, the corporation's other constituents such as bondholders, creditors, employees, and communities where the business operates are limited to their contractual rights and other legal protections. See *Equity-Linked Investors, LP v. Adams*, 705 A.2d 1040 (Del. Ch. 1997) (finding that new borrowing by financially troubled firm did not violate rights of preferred shareholders, which "are contractual in nature"). To the extent other constituents have unprotected interests inconsistent with those of shareholders, the interests of shareholders prevail—a *shareholder primacy* approach.

In most instances, courts have said that corporate fiduciary duties run to the corporation and the body of equity shareholders. When the business is insolvent, however, these duties run to the corporation's creditors—who become the corporation's new residual claimants. See *Geyer v. Ingersoll Publications Co.*, 621 A.2d 784 (Del. Ch. 1992). When the corporation is on the verge of insolvency, the question arises whether directors should be allowed to take risks to return to solvency (for the benefit of shareholders) or avoid risks to preserve assets (for the benefit of creditors). Although some cases suggest that fiduciary duties shift on the "lip of insolvency," most courts have rejected this notion. Even when the corporation is in trouble, directors owe duties to the corporation and its future.

* * *

Note on Corporate Purpose

Lately, the theory of shareholder primacy has come into question. Commentators point out that courts regularly defer to board decisions that recognize long-term shareholder interests and thus the interests of other corporate stakeholders, such as employees, customers, suppliers, and communities. Others point out that the single-minded pursuit of shareholder wealth is actually harmful to investors, corporations, and society at large. A myopic shareholder focus undermines business resiliency, may harm employees and customers, and often leads to reckless behavior that hurts society.

In fact, the Business Roundtable in 2019 issued a statement that redefines the purpose of the US corporation. The statement's signatories—CEOs of many of the largest corporations in the world, including Apple, JP Morgan, and Walmart—committed themselves and their companies to "deliver value to customers, to invest in our employees, to deal fairly and ethically with our suppliers, to support the communities in which we work, and to generate long term value for shareholders." Whether the statement is more than "greenwashing" (creating a false impression of corporate social responsibility (CSR)) and whether it leads to actual changes in corporate culture and legal rules has yet to be seen. See, e.g., Hester M. Pierce, "Statement on Proposed Amendments to Modernize and Enhance Financial Disclosures" (Jan. 30, 2020) (statement by SEC commissioner supporting proposals before the SEC for rules requiring more complete and consistent disclosure on environmental/social/governance (ESG) matters).

§11.2 Fiduciary Duties of Care and Loyalty

According to traditional fiduciary analysis, corporate managers owe two duties to the corporation: care and loyalty. Each duty describes standards for judicial review of corporate decision-making and fiduciary activities.

Note on Duty of Good Faith

Delaware courts have recently articulated a duty of "good faith" that applies when directors act *intentionally* to violate positive law, with a purpose other than to advance the corporation's best interests, or with a conscious disregard for their duties to act. *Walt Disney Co. Deriv. Litig.*, 906 A.2d 27 (2006). The courts have said that the duty of good faith is breached when directors fail to consider the financial ramifications of an executive's contingent pay package, fail to establish an oversight system to monitor the corporation's legal compliance, or act as "stooges" for a controlling shareholder. The courts have explained the good faith duty as a subset of the duty of loyalty and, as such, a duty that cannot be exculpated. See Del. GCL §102(b)(7) (see §15.1).

§11.2.1 Duty of Care

The duty of care addresses the attentiveness and prudence of managers in performing their decision-making and oversight functions. The famous "BJR" presumes that directors (and officers) carry out their functions in good faith, after sufficient investigation, and for acceptable reasons. Unless this presumption is overcome, courts abstain from second-guessing well-meaning business decisions even when they are flops. This is a risk that shareholders take when they make a corporate investment. See Chapter 12.

To encourage directors to take business risks without fear of personal liability, corporate law protects well-meaning directors through exculpation provisions in the corporation's articles (see §12.5), statutory and contractual indemnification (see §15.1), and directors' and officers' insurance (see §15.2).

§11.2.2 Duty of Loyalty

The duty of loyalty addresses fiduciaries' conflicts of interest and requires fiduciaries to put the corporation's interests ahead of their own—that is, fiduciaries cannot serve two masters. Corporate fiduciaries breach their duty of loyalty when they divert corporate assets, business opportunities, or proprietary information for personal gain.

Flagrant Diversion Diversion can be as simple, and as reprehensible, as a corporate official stealing tangible corporate assets. This is a plain breach of the fiduciary's duty of loyalty since the diversion was unauthorized and the corporation received no benefit in the transaction. Besides disaffirming the transaction as unauthorized (see §3.3.3), the corporation can sue for breach of fiduciary duty and in tort.

Self-Dealing Diversion can be masked in a self-dealing transaction. When a fiduciary enters into a transaction with the corporation on unfair terms, the effect (from the corporation's standpoint) is the same as if he had appropriated the difference between the transaction's fair value and the transaction's price. Courts, as well as statutes, address when a self-dealing transaction is unfair. See Chapter 13.

A parent corporation that controls a partially owned subsidiary can breach its duty to the minority shareholders of the subsidiary if the parent prefers itself at the expense of the minority. See §17.2. The ultimate form of preferential dealing occurs when the parent squeezes out the minority (in a merger or other transaction) and forces the minority to accept unfair consideration for their shares. See §17.3.

Executive Compensation When a director or officer sells his executive services to the corporation, diversion can occur if the executive's compensation exceeds the fair value of his services. See Chapter 14.

Usurping Corporate Opportunity When a corporate fiduciary seizes for herself a desirable business opportunity that the corporation may have taken and profited from, diversion occurs if the fiduciary denies the corporation the opportunity to expand profitably. See Chapter 16.

Disclosure to Shareholders Corporate officials who provide shareholders false or deceptive information, on which the shareholders rely to their detriment, not only undermine corporate credibility and transparency, but frustrate shareholders' expectations of fiduciary honesty and accountability. Duties of disclosure arise when directors seek a shareholder vote (see Chapter 8—state law; Chapter 10—federal proxy fraud) and when corporate officials communicate to stock trading markets (see §21.1—state law; Chapter 22—federal Rule 10b-5).

Trading on Inside Information When a fiduciary is aware of confidential corporate information—such as the impending takeover of another company—and he buys the target's stock, diversion can occur if the fiduciary's trading interferes with the corporation's takeover plans. By the same logic, when the fiduciary trades with the company's shareholders using inside information, the fiduciary diverts to himself information belonging to the corporation. See Chapter 23.

Selling Out A corporate official who accepts a bribe to sell her corporate office breaches a duty to the corporation. Likewise, a controlling shareholder who sells his controlling interest to a new owner who then diverts corporate assets to herself exposes the remaining shareholders to the new owner's looting. See §20.2.

Entrenchment A manager who uses the corporate governance machinery to protect his incumbency effectively diverts control from the shareholders to himself. Besides preventing shareholders from exercising their control rights—whether by voting or selling to a new owner—management entrenchment undermines the disciplining effect on management of a robust market in corporate control. See Chapter 8 (voting manipulation); §39.2 (takeover defenses).

There is no uniform standard for judging these conflict-of-interest transactions. Some are flatly prohibited (insider trading), others receive searching judicial fairness review (squeezeouts), and others are subject to internal corporate safeguards (executive compensation).

§11.2.3 Judicial Enforcement of Fiduciary Duties

Fiduciary duties generally are said to be owed to the corporation and not to particular shareholders, and must be enforced in the name of the corporation. This reflects the practical and conceptual danger of one shareholder purporting to speak for the body of shareholders. Rarely, however, are fiduciary breaches challenged by the corporation, because those who abused their control are unlikely to sue themselves. Instead, fiduciary breaches usually are challenged by shareholders in derivative litigation brought on behalf of the corporation (see Chapter 18).

§11.3 Fiduciary Duties—Corporate and Market Realities

§11.3.1 Fiduciary Duties in Closely Held Corporations

In closely held corporations (those that do not have a trading market for their shares) the corporate participants often have a relationship of special trust. No market exists for their shares. Some courts have implied a duty among participants akin to that of partners. Other courts have used statutory protections against "oppression" to intervene on behalf of minority shareholders. See Chapter 27.

A frequent issue in close corporations is whether fiduciary duties can be modified by agreement. Although modern partnership law permits partners to waive fiduciary rights, courts have been less willing to see corporate fiduciary duties as default terms. Compare RUPA §103(b) (permitting partners to reduce duty of care, if not unreasonable, and to waive duty of loyalty as to categories of activities, if not manifestly unreasonable). Rather, corporate fiduciary duties have been viewed as immutable aspects of the corporate relationship.

§11.3.2 Fiduciary Duties in Modern Public Corporations

In public corporations, management has three principal functions. First, directors and senior executives make "enterprise" decisions concerning operational and business matters—such as where to locate a new facility or whether to discontinue a product line. The board establishes the strategic plan; senior executives carry it out. Directors rely on the senior executives for information in establishing and monitoring the business plan. Shareholder and management interests typically overlap as to these enterprise decisions, as reflected in the deferential BJR.

Second, directors act on "ownership" issues—such as initiating a merger with another company or constructing takeover defenses. Outside directors (that is, directors who are not employed by the corporation) have assumed special prominence on these issues, as courts often defer to the independent judgment of outside directors when corporate control is at stake. Although directors in public corporations once were criticized for acting as "rubber stamps" for management, directors lately have become more forceful. Spurred by activist institutional investors and the clamor after Sarbanes-Oxley, outside directors have asserted themselves by replacing CEOs, negotiating takeovers, and making themselves more accountable. Outside directors, sometimes acting in special committees, often turn to their own legal and investment advisors.

Third, directors are responsible for "oversight" of the corporation—such as reviewing senior executives' performance and ensuring corporate compliance with legal norms. In public corporations the board often establishes compliance programs and receives regular management reports. As corporate responsibility has grown in such areas as regulatory compliance and foreign bribery, courts have increasingly insisted on higher levels of board oversight. In addition, disclosure by the company to public trading markets allows shareholders to gauge how well management is overseeing the corporation.

Management in public corporations lives under the watchful eye of the securities markets. When the market detects mismanagement, the trading price of the company's stock falls. This makes it attractive for outside bidders or shareholder insurgents to acquire control and oust the ineffective management. In extreme cases, a collapse in the stock price signals to creditors that the company is insolvent and should be put in the hands of a bankruptcy court. Fiduciary norms take these corrective mechanisms into account, relaxing scrutiny when control markets are available to discipline poor management and tightening scrutiny when the board attempts to insulate itself from these markets.

11.4 Independent Directors

Over the last several years, directors who do not have an employment relationship with the corporation—so-called independent directors—have assumed increased prominence in U.S. public corporations. The accounting and financial scandals that came to light in the early 2000s focused attention on the failures of outside directors to monitor and oversee corporate management. Paradoxically, the response has been to assign even greater importance to independent directors. Empirical studies are mixed on whether outside directors increase company profitability and whether they have an effect on controlling management excesses.

Sarbanes-Oxley The Sarbanes-Oxley Act of 2002 specifies the responsibilities of independent directors on the audit committees of public corporations. As required by Sarbanes-Oxley, stock exchanges have adopted listing standards that specify the composition and functions of the audit committees of listed companies (including foreign issuers and small business issuers). Under these standards, audit committees must be composed entirely of independent directors, as defined by the SEC.

In addition, all reporting companies must disclose whether at least one member of the audit committee is a financial expert. Sarbanes-Oxley §407, Reg. S-K, Item 401 (defining "audit committee financial expert" as one with significant auditing, accounting, financial, or comparable experience).

In addition, the exchanges' governance listing standards must also specify that the audit committee of listed companies be responsible for appointing, compensating, and overseeing the company's independent audit firm—a curtailment of the power of the full board and shareholders over outside accountants. The audit committee (not the board) must have the authority to hire independent counsel and other advisors, their fees to be paid by the listed company. Rule 10A-3; Exchange Act Rel. No. 47,654 (2003).

Dodd-Frank The Dodd-Frank Act of 2010 also intrudes into the boardroom of public corporations, requiring the stock exchanges to adopt listing standards that require all the directors on the corporation's compensation committee to be independent. Dodd-Frank §952. The committee must also have the authority to hire independent compensation consultants.

Delaware State courts, particularly in Delaware, have increasingly deferred to independent directors in various contexts. Delaware courts review deferentially corporate transactions in which management has a conflicting interest if a majority of the board is composed of directors who are ***disinterested*** (no conflicting financial interest in the transaction) and ***independent*** (neither beholden to interested party because of financial or business relationships, nor dominated by interested party through family or social relationships). See *Orman v. Cullman*, 794 A.2d 5 (Del. Ch. 2002) (distinguishing between "interest" and "independence" of directors).

Delaware courts focus on director independence in deciding whether

- to shift the burden to the challenging shareholder in transactions involving management conflicts. See §13.3.3 (director self-dealing transactions), §17.3.3 (squeeze-out mergers).
- to review executive pay under a waste standard, rather than the more burdensome fairness standard. See §14.2.3 (executive compensation).
- to indemnify corporate officials who become liable or settle claims arising from their corporate position. See §15.1.2 (permissive indemnification).
- to approve settlement of derivative litigation. See *Kahn v. Sullivan*, 594 A.2d 48 (Del. 1991) (approving settlement of claim that company had wasted corporate assets in donating money for art museum to house CEO's personal art collection).
- to dismiss shareholder derivative litigation, either on the basis of "demand futility" or recommendations of a special litigation committee. See §18.5.3 (demand requirement), §18.5.4 (special litigation committee).
- to uphold antitakeover measures (whether in anticipation of unwanted bids or in response to particular threats) and deal protection measures. See §8.2.2 (shark repellents), §39.2.3 (takeover defenses), §39.2.4 (deal protections).

Delaware courts have recently shown more willingness to inquire into the social and business relationships between outside directors and management—to test whether there exists implicit directorial bias. For example, the Delaware Chancery Court questioned the independence of a tenured Stanford law professor, who as a member of a special litigation committee was asked to determine whether suit should be brought against various corporate executives who allegedly had engaged in insider trading. The court concluded the professor's and executives' close and overlapping ties to Stanford—as large donors, fellow professors, and members of a university policy institute—suggested an institutional context in which motives of "friendship and collegiality" could not be ignored. *In re Oracle Corp. Derivative Litig.*, 824 A.2d 917

(Del. Ch. 2003). The Delaware Supreme Court has recently signaled its willingness also to inquire into social and business ties in evaluating directorial independence. See *Marchand v. Barnhill*, 212 A.3d 805 (Del. 2019) (finding that director lacked "independence" in demand-futility case when family of director being sued had mentored the director throughout his business career, even making sizable donation to local college so that campus facility was named after director); cf. *Beam v. Stewart*, 845 A.2d 1040 (Del. 2004) (finding directors sufficiently "independent" in demand-futility case, despite longstanding personal friendships and close business relationships to CEO, who held 94 percent of the company's voting power).

The MBCA goes one step further and makes lack of independence a basis for imposing liability on directors in an interested-party transaction. See MBCA §8.31(a)(2)(iii) (stating that director violates standard of liability if director's judgment is affected because of a lack of objectivity due to director's familial, financial, or business relationship with interested person or a lack of independence due to director's domination or control by interested person). Upon such a showing, the director has the burden to prove that he reasonably believed the challenged conduct was in the best interests of the corporation. MBCA §8.31(a)(2)(iii)(B).

Corporate Governance in Stock Listing Standards The New York Stock Exchange and the NASDAQ have adopted listing standards—many of them mandated by Sarbanes-Oxley and Dodd-Frank (see below)—that compel listed companies to adopt corporate governance structures that emphasize oversight by "independent directors." Among the governance listing standards are requirements that listed companies (1) have a majority of independent directors (with independence specifically defined), (2) permit independent directors to meet in executive session without management present, (3) have specific board committee (audit, nominating, and compensation) composed solely of independent directors, (4) have codes of conduct, and (5) have corporate governance guidelines specifying director qualifications, compensation, education, responsibilities, succession, evaluation, and access to management. Exceptions are provided for foreign companies whose securities are listed in the United States.

§11.5 Federalization of Corporate Governance

Although corporate fiduciary duties arise mostly under state law, federal law has come to play an important role in corporate governance of public corporations. Since the 1930s, federal securities regulation has imposed disclosure requirements that compel corporate fiduciaries in public corporations to reveal information about the operational and financial details of the business as well as the roles of the fiduciaries in the corporation. Thus, corporate fiduciaries in public companies must disclose information to new public shareholders (see Chapter 5) when shareholders vote (see Chapter 9) and when shareholders tender their shares (see Chapter 38). Corporate fiduciaries also face restrictions on their ability to trade in company shares while in the possession of nonpublic material information (see Chapter 23). But, with rare exceptions, the federal regulatory scheme has been premised on disclosure to shareholders.

Over the past two decades, however, federal law has expanded beyond requiring corporate disclosures. The corporate scandals of the early 2000s and the financial crisis of 2008 led Congress to rethink the place of federal law in corporate governance of public corporations. In 2002 Congress responded to the misdeeds at companies like Enron and WorldCom by enacting the Sarbanes-Oxley Act, which revamped the regulation of the accounting profession and imposed a variety of new rules on the boards of directors and officers of public companies. In 2010 Congress responded to the financial crisis in the banking sector by enacting the Dodd-Frank Act, not only to reregulate the financial markets but also to add new rules on corporate governance and executive compensation in all public companies.

Fiduciary Duties and BJR

As you can see, fiduciary duties are at the heart of corporate law—their heartbeat modulated by the business judgment rule (BJR). In the end, the BJR is a doctrine of "judicial abstention" that relieves directors of personal liability for their decisions—absent fraud, corruption, illegality, or complete disregard of their duties. It thus represents an important policy choice by state corporate law that decision-making in the private corporation should not be subject to public scrutiny.

Enabling State Law Versus Mandatory Federal Law

As you may have noticed, the federal reforms of corporate/securities law under the Sarbanes-Oxley Act of 2002 and the Dodd-Frank Act of 2020 (and some stock market rules) have displaced state law on corporate governance for US public corporations. This displacement raises the question that surfaces regularly about the US public corporation and whether corporate arrangements should be mandated by public law or "privately ordered" by corporations themselves. State corporate law generally accepts and facilitates private ordering, but a significant and growing number of arrangements are governed by "corporate regulations" mandated by federal securities law administered by the US Securities and Exchange Commission (SEC).

Which is optimal: mandatory or privately-ordered rules? A recent article argues that the answer to this question depends on the nature of investors and their incentives in choosing corporate arrangements. Although the rise of institutional shareholders means market pricing will reflect investor perceptions about corporate governance arrangements, perhaps it would be better if these shareholders could simply choose which SEC rules they find valuable and which they'd prefer the corporation not follow. Among other things, if investors could choose which SEC rules apply to their corporations, SEC rulemaking would not need to engage in a cost-benefit analysis, but instead leave this to shareholders and the markets they inhabit. Investor ordering, the author asserts, would allow for a more dynamic regulatory system. The SEC would simply set "default" rules and shareholder voting, informed by the stock markets, would determine whether to implement them or not. See Scott Hirst, *The Case for Investor Ordering* (2018) [available on SSRN]. Its a remarkable idea—law as optional!

The Importance of "Corporate Culture"

So, we've been imbedded in the world of law. But is law—corporate law and securities regulation—really what determines the behavior of people in a corporation? Many have observed that corporate governance has lately become less about complying with legal rules—expounded by state judges interpreting corporate fiduciary law and federal courts interpreting securities disclosure rules—and more about behavioral norms, which are increasingly created and enforced by shareholders. See Zohar Goshen & Sharon Hanes, *The Death of Corporate Law* (2018) [available on SSRN]. Here's their interesting thesis:

> For decades, corporate law played a pivotal role in regulating corporations across the United States. Consequently, Delaware, the leading state of incorporation, and its courts came to occupy a central and influential position in corporate law and governance. This, however, is no longer the case: The compositional shift in equity markets from retail to institutional ownership has relocated regulatory power over corporations from courts to markets. Corporate law has, as a result, and as illustrated by the decline of the Delaware courts, lost its pride of place and is now largely a dead letter.
>
> What explains the connection between the rise of institutional ownership and the death of corporate law? We answer this question by unpacking the relationship between market dynamics and the role of corporate law. Our analysis uncovers a critical, yet hitherto unnoticed, insight: The more competent shareholders become, the less important corporate law will be. Increases in shareholder competence reduce management agency costs, intensify market actors' preference for private ordering outside of courts, and, ultimately, drive corporate law into oblivion.

Corporate Governance as Myth

Corporate governance includes a variegated set of norms—sometimes referred to as "corporate culture" or "soft law"—that, blowing in the wind, determine the relationship within the corporation between shareholders and management. These norms are much more pliable and amorphous than the usual rules one encounters in "hard law." Thus, there is a certain "shadows on the wall" quality about the corporation. In fact, a leading corporate law professor has suggested that corporate law is actually based on myths:

> Various fundamental rules of corporate law are based on myths. These myths play an important role in attracting public acceptance and support for what otherwise would be unpopular and controversial regulations. Thus, the role played by myth in corporate law can have either positive or negative social effects depending on one's opinion of the social value of the underlying legal rule the myth buttresses or affirms.
>
> Four political and sociological myths play important roles in law: (1) the myth that corporations are owned by their shareholders and represent ownership interests in businesses rather than mere financial claims on the cash flows of those businesses, coupled with certain political (voting) rights that protect those claims; (2) the "shareholder value myth," that corporate officers and directors are legally required to maximize firm value; (3) that subsidiary companies are independent from and not subject to the control of their parent companies and must remain so in order for the parent company to avoid liability for the contract and tort debts of the subsidiary under various alter ego and piercing the corporate veil theories of corporate law; and (4) the legal regulation of insider trading is justified because of the necessity of creating a "level playing field" among participants in financial markets.

Jonathan R. Macey, *The Central Role of Political Myth in Corporate Law* (2020) [available on SSRN]. Yes, the corporation is a bit like what Alice found when she went down the rabbit's hole.

1.3.2 First Look: What Is the Public Corporation's Purpose?

As you may be noticing, our search for the sustainable corporation turns again and again to the question of the corporation's purpose—and specifically, the purpose of the US public corporation. There is a continuum of views. Some say the corporation's purpose is to maximize the financial returns to shareholders, subject to applicable legal norms. Others say that this understanding is too narrow, and the corporation's purpose must be seen as serving social interests and thus the interests of all corporate constituents, including creditors, employees, customers, suppliers, even communities. What is your view? (And, let's see if it evolves as you continue through this book.)

Milton Friedman's View on SWM

So, it turns out, a 1970 *Time* essay titled "The Social Responsibility of Business Is to Increase Its Profits" by University of Chicago economist Milton Friedman has achieved the status of rock lyrics: "Born in the USA, I was born in the USA." In his essay, Friedman (who would later win a Nobel Prize in Economics) said this:

> [T]here is one and only one social responsibility of business—to use its resources and engage in activities designed to increase its profits so long as it stays within the rules of the game, which is to say, engages in open and free competition without deception [or] fraud.

Is he saying that the only responsibility of corporate managers is to maximize shareholder profits? Certainly, not. A business that sold baby formula laced with melamine would not pass his test of "staying within the rules of the game." And do these rules only include those imposed by government? That is, if it's legal, then it's OK.

Lots of ink (and lately bytes) have been spilled on this question. In the end, who cares? Corporate managers will do what they will do. Sometimes they will see themselves as limited by legal rules, such as the antifraud rules of the securities laws. Sometimes they will be limited by what the markets in which they operate allow them to do and not to do—remember "open and free competition." And sometimes they will be limited by what they think is right and wrong. For example, deception that is neither intentional nor reckless is not actually prohibited by the securities laws, and sometimes tolerated by the financial markets. Yet many people in business believe it's wrong to say something that you're not sure about because it might turn out to be false. Call it "reputational incentives"—or just doing the right thing.

Shareholder Wealth Maximization (and Its Limits)

To give you a sense for the ongoing debate on the corporate purpose, I ask you to read an interesting article by Leo Strine, who wrote it when he was the Chief Justice of the Delaware Supreme Court. (Today, he is an influential and still-prolific "senior statesman" on US corporate law.) He asserts that the "for-profit corporation" in the United States is designed to make profits for its shareholders, unless government regulation makes clear that the corporation is to seek other ends. You'll notice that Strine has a somewhat irreverent view of the corporation, suggesting that when left to its own (at least, current) devices, it may not serve the social ends we intended for it.

But, as you read the article, you may want to ask whether Strine is correct that courts actually require directors to maximize shareholder profits? A "progressive law" scholar, Professor Lyman Johnson, questions this assertion. Lyman Johnson, *Unsettledness in Delaware Corporate Law: Business Judgment Rule and Corporate Purpose* (2013) [available on SSRN]. Johnson argues that the famous BJR assumes too much about corporate actors—and that courts should abandon it in favor of fiduciary duties. He also asserts that the corporation should be broadly conceived as an enterprise in which the sum is greater than the parts. One implication of this broad understanding is that for-profit corporations need not be about maximizing wealth for their shareholders (or really for anyone), but instead about pursuing goals agreed to by those who compose the corporation. That is, a for-profit corporation could be about maximizing community, religious fervor or even happiness, along with shareholder returns.

Others are coming to similar conclusions—namely, that the corporation is not merely about a set of state-created assumptions, but rather a much more organic set of ambitions and constraints. Recently, a management/law professor from Erasmus University and Hebrew University proposed a pluralist conception of the corporation (an amalgam of general and private law) using social systems theory and the framework of complexity. Seeing the corporation as rooted in the natural sciences, not necessarily the political sciences, we should understand the "heterogeneity and firm-specific power relations" in the corporation as courts and jurists grapple with fiduciary duties and corporate objective. In short, one-size-fits-all is a poor actual or theoretical account of the corporation. Leon Lejuda Anidjar, *From the Law of Corporations to the Law of Corporate* (2020) [available on SSRN].

Our Continuing Struggle with the Idea that For-Profit Corporations Seek Profit

(2012)

Leo E. Strine, Jr.

[available on SSRN]

This Essay addresses an issue that, to be candid, perplexes me. That issue is the continuing dismay evidenced in Western, capitalist nations when public corporations that pursue profit for their stockholders take actions that adversely affect the nation's economic stability, the corporation's employees, or the environment.

When a corporation's ardor for profits leads it to take excessive risks that endanger the firm's solvency, commentators react with shock and dismay. How can corporate managers be so blinded by the immediate prospect of profit that they would ignore what, in hindsight, seem like such obvious risks? Likewise, we rent our garments in anger and chagrin when energy companies take environmental shortcuts in drilling for oil or mining coal, surprised that profit-maximizing firms have been less than optimally protective of the environment and their workers, that they did not go beyond what was simply necessary to ensure that regulators allowed them to operate. Similarly, we anguish when the board of a venerable homeland corporate icon reacts receptively to a premium takeover bid from a foreign acquirer. How could the board sell out and undermine the traditional values the firm stands for? It cannot be that the long-term stockholders would put their desire for a one-time, short-term profit ahead of the continued independence of a nationally important institution?

In this Essay, I identify some recent instances that reflect our continued inability to view the for-profit corporation with a gimlet eye. These examples track recurrent patterns. I begin with a couple stories in the headlines of corporate greed at BP in connection with the Deepwater disaster in the Gulf of Mexico and at the U.S. banks that were bailed out by the federal government. I then proceed to less obvious stories where courts have affirmed the preeminence of stockholders in the for-profit corporation, the first in an older case challenging Henry Ford's stated preference for employees over stockholders and the second in a recent one challenging Craigslist's attempt to protect its online community from stockholders selling in a takeover. Next, I consider how stockholders have fared in other capitalist countries, looking at Kraft's successful takeover of Cadbury in the United Kingdom and BHP Billiton's failed bid to acquire the Potash Corporation of Saskatchewan. In the end, policy makers should not delude themselves about the corporation's ability to police itself; government still has a critical role in setting the rules of the game.

I. Oil Spills and Bailed Out Banks: Relearning Obvious Lessons of History

The first situations I address exemplify the tendency to underestimate the extent to which firms subject to pressures to deliver short-term profits for their stockholders pose a serious risk of generating societally destructive externalities. I will only briefly discuss these examples because they are, at least in my estimation, so obvious.

A. Risk Taking with Underwater Drilling

The first story is the BP oil spill disaster in the Gulf. In the wake of the spill, there was widespread outrage about corporate callousness. How could a corporation drill so deep with no reliable plans as to how to address a leak in the well? How could so many safety features be inoperable? To me, it is to be expected that a corporation that stands to gain large profits from aggressive drilling activity would less than optimally consider the environmental risks and occupational hazards that novel drilling activity posed. BP, after all, stood to gain all the profits from its activities, while the risks to the environment would be borne largely by others.

Not only do corporations have incentives to disregard risks for the sake of profits, but there is a natural tendency to pay attention to short-term profits over long-term risks. In fact, most of us place a higher value on immediate satisfaction than on the long-term risks created by such satisfaction. If we can get all the benefits of the immediate satisfaction for ourselves, and know that the longer-term costs will be shared with a lot of others, we go for today over tomorrow even more. And, when an industry is among the leaders in having lobbyists precisely for the purpose of minimizing governmental regulation of its activity, trusting that industry to balance environmental concerns and worker safety responsibly against the prospect of immediate profit would seem even more naïve.

B. Risk Taking with Now Underwater Mortgages

The other rather obvious example of silly surprise is the recent financial crisis. This crisis was in no small measure caused by the signing of trillions of dollars in risk-shifting transactions, the bulk of which had at their root packages containing subprime mortgages. The parties who wrote these mortgages did not act or think as typical lenders. They did not expect the borrowers to pay off the mortgage contracts as written. Instead, the idea was that the mortgages would be refinanced again as already inflated real estate prices continued to rise. Even better, of course, the loans were securitized so the underwriters—the first-instance "lenders"—could pass the risk down the line. Buyers of these securities were plentiful. Most of these transactions were motivated by a desire to make speculative trading profits, not to hedge risks. And the willingness of rating agencies to give the packages a triple-A rating allowed fiduciaries—so-called "sophisticated investors"—to buy them for pension funds.

As Professor Lynn Stout has recently pointed out, there was an even bigger warning sign. In 2008, the $67 trillion credit default swap market was made up almost exclusively of credit default swaps written on mortgage-backed bonds in a market in which the total value of all underlying asset-backed and corporate bonds in the United States that year was a mere $15 trillion. Rank speculation was thus the rule, not the exception.

The mismatch between immediate reward and the bearing of ultimate risk could not have been more extreme, as speculation ran wild in the wake of the erosion of key legal barriers to gambling of this kind. But legislators and regulators had become drunk on their own cocktails, having naïvely (or worse) assumed that markets would "price" these risks. So, indeed, had many academics, such as many of my law and economics scholar-friends in the academy who confidently told me in the years before the meltdown that my worries over the credit bubble and increased leverage in the financial sector reflected my inadequate appreciation of the keen ability of current financial and capital markets to price risks accurately.

Nor, of course, did one need worry that financial institutions that had regularly received government bailouts because of their systemic importance would be less than optimally incentivized to prudently assess risks. And the growing complexity of financial institutions themselves was no worry, again, for the same reasons. Markets would take care of it and price it, ignoring of course that the capital markets themselves had grown in complexity and churned like a meth-fueled gerbil's wheel. Whatever these capital markets were driven by, a deep examination of the long-term risks of transactions generating large short-term profits did not, in the end, turn out to be high on the list.

And when it all crashed down, the first to receive treatment were those who had profited most. No doubt they felt pain, but not enough that one can confidently believe they are worse off today than if they had not behaved recklessly. Most obviously, though, the importance of these institutions to our economies made it impossible not to bail them out. And bailed out they were, given huge subsidies, partly comprised of free money to borrow in order to make profitable trades and return to health.

The borrowers, who share a good deal of responsibility, too, but whose need to take risks was perhaps easier to rationalize as moral—a house to live in and bills paid off versus the ability to buy an even cooler sports car—got a rawer deal. Rawest of all, though, was the deal for millions of hard working people who were paying their bills until the calamity destroyed economic growth and resulted in double-digit, persistent unemployment. They continue to suffer as do many others who have retained their jobs but endured furloughs, benefit cuts and pay freezes, and seen their local taxes increase as services by budget-crunched governments diminish.

For now, however, the important lesson is simple. For-profit businesses have incentives toward current profit-maximization that make them poorly positioned to evaluate risk and be safe regulators. The environmental wreckage in the Gulf of Mexico and the global human wreckage caused by the financial sector's imprudence should be rather plain evidence of that truth.

II. "Community Values" on the Assembly Line and in Online Classifieds: Recognizing the Incentives in the Stockholder-Financed Corporation

Another enduring myth is that there exist "special" for-profit corporations, ones that will behave differently from others over the long-run because they are controlled by visionaries who will place some idea of the public good ahead of profit. In saying this is a myth, I don't mean to imply that there are not very talented entrepreneurs who figure out how to do well by doing good. There are, thankfully, a number of businesses that do pay good wages, provide safe working environments and livable weekly hours, treat the environment with respect, and play the competitive game fairly. Instead, my point is that managers in stockholder-financed corporations are inevitably answerable to the stockholders, whatever the "community values" articulated by the corporation's founders or others, which is why regulations designed to protect against the externality risks inherent in profit-seeking are critical.

A. A Taste of History: Henry Ford's Social Vision for Ford Motor Company

Ultimately, any for-profit corporation that sells shares to others has to be accountable to its stockholders for delivering a financial return. This is not a new notion. An American entrepreneur by the name of Henry Ford tested that proposition and lost some ninety-three years ago in a famous case. In that case, Ford brazenly proclaimed that he was not managing Ford Motor Company to generate the best sustainable return for its stockholders. Rather, he announced that the stockholders should be content with the relatively small dividend they were getting and that Ford Motor Company would focus more on helping its consumers by lowering prices and on bettering the lives of its workers and society at large by raising wages and creating more jobs

To simplify, the Michigan Supreme Court held that Ford could not justify his actions that way, and that although he could help other constituencies such as workers and consumers, as an instrument to the end of benefiting stockholders, he could not subordinate the stockholders" best interest. This holding was central, in my view, to the court's embrace of what we call the BJR. Under that rule, the judiciary does not second-guess the decision of a well-motivated, non-conflicted fiduciary. Fundamental to the rule, however, is that the fiduciary be motivated by a desire to increase the value of the corporation for the benefit of the stockholders. By confessing that he was placing his altruistic interest in helping workers and consumers over his duty to stockholders, Henry Ford made it impossible for the court to afford him business judgment deference.

B. History Repeats Itself: Craigslist as an Attempted "Community" Corporation

In 2010, Chancellor Chandler decided a case in Delaware with some striking similarities to *Dodge v. Ford Motor*. The case pitted the founder of Craigslist, the online classifieds firm, against eBay, the well-known online auction giant. As with the Dodge brothers and Ford, eBay (the suing stockholder) was also a competitor of the firm being sued. Also, as in Dodge v. Ford Motor, the firm being sued had a leader who openly argued that he was running the firm primarily to the end of something other than stockholder wealth, subordinating stockholders" financial well-being to his own unique social perspective. At Craigslist, according to this argument, the superior interest was the supposed community of users of its services, services the firm had been selling cheaply or giving away, when higher prices seemed to be readily attainable.

But that core issue was not the subject of eBay's lawsuit, which instead focused on the measures Craigslist's founder took to ensure that he and his heirs would control Craigslist and to cement his vision that Craigslist be a community-oriented and community-driven corporation, not a cold-blooded profit machine. To that end, Craig Newmark (the Craigslist founder, controlling stockholder, and director) and Jim Buckmaster (the other controlling stockholder and director on Craigslist's three-member board) implemented actions aimed at stopping or slowing eBay's ability to acquire Craigslist, or otherwise disrupt what Craig and Jim called Craigslist's "corporate culture."

The most important antitakeover measure was the adoption of a shareholder rights plan that would have diluted eBay's ownership of Craigslist upon even a minor increase in eBay's minority stockholding position. In defending their decision in court, Jim and Craig did not argue that they employed the poison pill to protect the economic interests of the company's stockholders. No, instead Jim and Craig argued that the pill was justified by their heartfelt desire to protect Craigslist's coveted social values and community-centered culture from the disruption an eBay acquisition might have on those values and culture.

Echoing what I view as a standard notion behind the BJR, Chancellor Chandler rejected Jim and Craig's argument. In so ruling, he stated, "Directors for a for-profit Delaware corporation cannot deploy a rights plan to defend a business strategy that openly eschews stockholder wealth maximization—at least not consistently with the directors'' fiduciary duty under Delaware law." This, to my view, rather expected statement, drew fire from both ends of our corporate law political spectrum, if there be such a thing.

A group promoting a new form of for-profit corporation, the charter of which indicates that other ends, such as philanthropic or community-aimed ends, can be put ahead of profit, reacted with hyperbole, urging corporations to leave Delaware. If, they said, you remain incorporated in Delaware, your stockholders will be able to hold you accountable for putting their interests first. You must go elsewhere, to a fictional land where you can take other people's money, use it as you wish, and ignore the best interests of those with the only right to vote. In this fictional land, I suppose a fictional accountability mechanism will exist whereby the fiduciaries, if they are a controlling interest, will be held accountable for responsibly balancing all these interests. Of course, a very distinguished mind of the political left, Adolph Berle, believed that when corporate fiduciaries were allowed to consider all interests without legally binding constraints, they were freed of accountability to any. Equally unrealistic is the idea that corporations authorized to consider other interests will be able to do so at the expense of stockholder profits if voting control of the corporation remains in the stock market. Just how long will hedge funds and mutual funds subordinate their desire for returns to the desire of a founder to do good?

From a different political perspective come those who seem to take umbrage at plain statements like the Chancellor's for unmasking the face of capitalism. These commentators seem dismayed when anyone starkly recognizes that as a matter of corporate law, the object of the corporation is to produce profits for the stockholders and that the social beliefs of the managers, no more than their own financial interests, cannot be their end in managing the corporation. Maxwell Kennerly, in his review of the eBay decision, noted what he perceived to be a triad of conservative academic commentators who were unhappy with Senator Al Franken's statement that "it is literally malfeasance for a corporation not to do everything it legally can to maximize its profits"—a statement, that in Kennerly's view, encapsulates a material portion of the holding in the eBay opinion.

The consternation at Chancellor Chandler's eBay decision is surprising for another related reason. The whole design of corporate law in the United States is built around the relationship between corporate managers and stockholders, not relationships with other constituencies. In the corporate republic, only stockholders get to vote and only stockholders get to sue to enforce directors'' fiduciary duties. The natural focus of the managers in such a system is therefore supposed to be on advancing the best interests of the stockholders, subject to the legal constraints within which the firm operates. Precisely because it is ultimately the equity market that is the primary accountability system for public firms, efforts to tinker around with the margins of corporate law through initiatives like constituency statutes, the so-called Corporate Social Responsibility movement, and antitakeover provisions have been of very little utility in insulating corporate boards from stockholder and stock market pressures.

The public interest, in the end, depends on protection by the public's elected representatives in the form of law. The well-intentioned efforts of many entrepreneurs and company managers, who have a duty to their investors to deliver a profit, to be responsible employers and corporate citizens is undoubtedly socially valuable. But it is no adequate substitute for a sound legally determined baseline. By so stating, I do not mean to imply that the corporate law requires directors to maximize short-term profits for stockholders. Rather, I simply indicate that the corporate law requires directors, as a matter of their duty of loyalty, to pursue a good faith strategy to maximize profits for the stockholders. The directors, of course, retain substantial discretion, outside the context of a change of control, to decide how best to achieve that goal and the appropriate time frame for delivering those returns.

III. National Interests Community Icons: Some Instructive Lessons from Abroad

The power of stockholders'' ardor for profits shows up especially in corporate takeovers, where the benefits to stockholders are on full display and the costs to other corporate constituencies can be stark. The tension revealed in a takeover is highlighted when the corporation is an icon with a long history of presence and responsibility in a community. How does corporate and takeover law choose? An interesting answer comes from outside the United States. In Kraft's takeover of the iconic Cadbury, long-standing U.K. law tilted decidedly in favor of stockholder interests, but U.K. politicians found the logical consequences of their own settled law dismaying. By contrast, when the Australian mining firm BHP Billiton sought to acquire the Potash Corporation of Saskatchewan, the Canadian government had the legal authority to express its objection in full conformity with the law, and did so. It turns out that even in capitalist societies whose economies are premised on profit-seeking, the full implications of giving stockholders the power to make societally-important decisions remains controversial.

A. Frustrations of Nonfrustration: Lessons from the Odd Case of Cadbury

Perhaps the most surprising manifestation of political naïveté about the nature of the corporation comes from England and the controversy over Kraft's acquisition of Cadbury, the maker of very sweet, nearly chocolate products. The idea that the maker of Dairy Milk would be acquired by a maker of boxed macaroni and cheese was seen as a threat to a British icon, and to British jobs, rather than as a natural alliance of culinary co-travelers. Despite the fact that Kraft was already an employer of many in England and had a good reputation as a quality employer responsive to environmental and free trade concerns, opposition to a Kraft takeover was widespread in the United Kingdom.

A wide range of commentators, the British public, and Members of Parliament from not just the Labour party, but also the Tory and Liberal Democrat parties, voiced objection to the idea that an English icon would be owned by an American company. Even though the current British ownership was already well on its way to shutting down some of the company's most historic operations and shipping production to lower wage Poland, U.S. ownership was thought to make the prospect of even more moves of this kind possible. Despite the fact that Cadbury was itself a company that had prospered by buying up other nation's icons—remember A&W Root Beer, or Dr. Pepper, or Canada Dry Ginger Ale—its Chairman, Sir Roger Carr, was aghast that so-called short-term stockholders had taken shares from the company's long-term investors when Kraft made its bid public. How could these long-term stockholders have abandoned the company, and why should these new short-termers decide the fate of a 200 year old British treasure?

It is hardly surprising that Kraft eventually succeeded in its bid. The whole focus of the U.K. approach is that if the stockholders like the price of a takeover bid, they get to take it. The U.K. regime leaves no real room for a board to block a financed bid except by convincing its stockholders that the price is too low. If the stockholders believe the price is right, they get to accept the bid. And all market evidence has long made clear that, absent board or government interposition, stockholders will sell out into any bid offering a substantial premium. What was more surprising was to see politicians of all the major parties in the United Kingdom bemoan the foreordained result that followed from the United Kingdom's long-standing approach, especially given that Cadbury could have had a lot of suitors less savory than Kraft. The Cadbury takeover confirms how deeply rooted the power of the stockholder profit motive is in the for-profit corporation.

It is revealing to consider the aftermath of the Cadbury takeover. After the Code of the Takeover Panel rejected all three of Carr's proposals, it instead offered its own proposals as to how the Takeover Code might be amended to prevent future Cadbury-like hostile takeovers. I offer a couple of the most material proposals as examples. First, the Code Committee recommended that the formal offer period—the period in which an interested acquirer may make an offer or bid for the target—be shortened by requiring a potential offeror to make a bid within twenty-eight days of announcing its interest to make a bid. Second, the Code Committee proposed a prohibition of certain deal protection devices currently legal under the Code--very limited termination fees and matching rights.

Upon a preliminary inspection of the Code Committee's proposals, however, it appears that were the Takeover Code modified as proposed, it might actually make hostile takeovers more, not less, likely, at least insofar as the proposed changes would make it more difficult for U.K. target companies to negotiate and secure a friendly acquisition over a hostile one. For instance, take the proposal that would truncate the put-up or shut-up time period and require that target companies make public the identity of any potential offeror that has expressed an interest in making a bid. Although the purpose of this change is to dissuade the practice of making so-called "virtual bids"—ones where a would-be hostile acquirer announces that it is interested in making a bid well before that potential acquirer has any intention of doing so—the Committee's proposal to make mandatory the reporting and public disclosure of the interested bidder's identity might have the unintended consequence of dissuading overtures from would-be friendly acquirers, particularly friendly strategic acquirers, who would rather remain anonymous and maintain the confidentiality of merger negotiations with the target until a binding contract is inked.

The Code Committee's second material proposed modification, the prohibition of termination fees and matching rights, poses a similar deterrent to would-be friendly acquirers. A friendly bidder is less likely to negotiate an acquisition with a target if it is unable to secure assurances from the target that the target is serious about doing a deal, and more crucially to the friendly bidder, serious about doing the deal proposed by the friendly bidder. Without the availability of modest deal protection devices, friendly acquisition partners may be even more reluctant to emerge than now, where the current regime already leaves strategic partners and private equity funds with very little compensation if they get topped.

For an American, the Cadbury situation is, as our philosopher Yogi Berra put it, like déjà vu all over again. For over thirty years in the United States, a variety of palliatives, such as state constituency statutes allowing boards to block bids harmful to other constituencies, and the infamous poison pill, have done little but give target boards some room to get a better deal from a so-called white knight if a hostile bid loomed. The pressures boards faced from their stockholders to accept lucrative bids made resistance in most cases futile. As a result, U.S. communities have seen icon after icon fall into foreign hands, and our own major stock exchange may soon be a subsidiary of a merger vehicle formed by the owners of the German Boerse.

B. Candid Canada: The Refreshing Honesty of the Potash Decision

By comparison, I come now to the Canadian government's decision to block the $40 billion bid of an Australian corporation, BHP Billiton, Ltd. ("BHP"), to acquire the Potash Corporation of Saskatchewan. As I have learned, potash is not an illicit admixture to add to brownies, but a valuable crop nutrient and with a capital letter, for our purposes, a company. And Saskatchewan is the Saudi Arabia of potash with a little "p" and the current home of Potash with a capital "P." As I have further learned, the province has an economic strategy to leverage its advantage in potash (and the resulting stream of governmental royalties) into a better overall economic position. Potash

Corporation was already managed from the United States and BHP made certain assurances that it would protect provincial interests. But the provincial government was dubious that under BHP's ownership, Potash would maintain its commitment to the province's version of OPEC, Canpotex. Canpotex is an industry-wide marketing initiative fostered by the province. Rather, the provincial government concluded that BHP's commercial interests as a profit-maximizing firm might lead it to cut prices, reduce royalties to the province, and otherwise be less likely to generate royalties and jobs for the province than if Potash remained independent.

The Investment Canada Act was the tool used by the province to get its way. Under that statute, the Canadian government can block any transaction above C$312 million if the transaction does not promise "net benefits" to Canada. After extensive advocacy by the Provincial government, Canadian Industry Minister Tony Clement blocked BHP's bid, finding that it would not produce a net benefit for Canada. That this action was taken by a conservative government that generally advocates for a more open form of capitalism had special resonance.

For present purposes, however, I wish to focus only on one refreshing aspect of the application of the Investment Canada Act to the Potash situation, which is its total lack of pretense or sham. The statute is a naked grant of power to the national government to block a takeover when it believes Canada will be better off without it. Obviously, there are legitimate questions to be asked about the overall utility of such a statute and I do not intend to comment one way or the other on the wisdom of the decision to use the statute to block the BHP bid. But I do think that the statute's candor deserves applause because it forces Canadian society to ask genuine questions about what is in the public interest. In other analogous situations, governments have twisted their antitrust rules, come up with situation-specific corporate law rules, or taken a strained view of what was a national security (i.e., military-terrorist) threat in order to find a basis to block transactions that were, in reality, feared to be economically injurious to the target company's nation.

Although Australians may have been chagrined by the Canadian government's blockage of BHP's bid, Aussies could not claim shock because their nation has a similar statute. Moreover, the reality that another possible bidder for Potash was a Chinese-government-owned firm highlights the difficult reality of the so-called global market. Canada faced a situation in which a corporation that controlled an important national resource could pass into the hands of owners who either (in the case of BHP) were deemed more likely to be driven by market forces to reduce the benefits to Saskatchewan of the company's operations or (in the case of a potential Chinese-government-owned bidder) would have been free to take actions not directed primarily at producing benefits for stockholders, but rather for advancing the self-interest of another nation.

C. Globalized Capital and Product Markets Make Regulation in the Public Interest More, Not Less, Vital

The most critical issue before us is that we have globalized capital markets. These capital markets put more intense pressure than ever on corporations to deliver short term profits. In almost all the Organization for Economic Cooperation and Development ("OECD") nations, only capital has a vote on who comprises the board of directors.

With increasing institutional ownership and greatly decreased holding periods, corporate electorates are more demanding than ever and unlikely to give serious thought to the long-term, given that few stockholders hold their shares for longer than a year at a time.

Although we have globalized capital markets and have opened our product markets to exports, we have done little to effectively globalize the regulatory structures that ensure that for-profit corporations do not generate unacceptable levels of harm to others in their pursuit of profit. Although the World Trade Organization does in fact at times act as an effective club in keeping nations from preventing exports from entering their markets, no similarly powerful international body ensures that all corporations participating in international commerce must meet minimally decent standards of labor treatment or environmental safety and respect. Likewise, although financial institutions can and do take actions that affect the stability of all nations, their safety and soundness is remitted to a patchwork of national regulation. Nations fear that if they require fair treatment of workers, protection of the environment, the payment of taxes to support the nation's needs, and sound capital requirements for financial institutions, corporate activity will flee to other nations where there is little or no regulation.

The examples I have discussed above are not designed to convince you that any particular level of regulation is optimal. But they are designed to point out this reality: if, as I do, you believe that the temptations of profit can lead to corporate behavior that can harm society, you should be skeptical about claims that corporations are better-positioned to regulate themselves now than they used to be.

In many ways, the opposite is in fact true. Corporations increasingly have no genuine connection to any particular community or even nation. A huge disconnect has arisen between the wealth, lifestyle, daily experiences, and interests of the top corporate managers and that of most of the employees in the various nations in which their corporations have operations. Corporate managers are increasingly subject to removal at the instance of highly aggressive institutional investors who do not hold shares or think long-term. The actual long-term providers of capital are more and more divorced from the ownership of the shares of particular companies, and have largely yielded their votes to money managers compensated largely on short-term metrics. Providers of debt are also less well positioned to act as monitors, as corporate debt is syndicated and trades largely like equity capital, leading to far less stable lender-borrower relationships and less intensive, long-term monitoring of corporate risk-taking.

To deliver profits, corporations must endure competition from competitors willing to locate jobs in nations without labor or environmental protection. That creates incentives to reduce wage rolls and pay, particularly in the European Union or in nations like Canada and the United States that have responsible regulatory standards, and to take fewer product safety and environmental precautions. When their competitors seem to be making large, short-term profits by suspect means that have substantial long-term risk--see the subprime debacle discussed above—corporate managers face strong pressure from the capital markets to get in the game, regardless of whether they personally believe the game to be just another form of gambling.

Concluding Thoughts: Rules for the Global Game

Milton Friedman is a person who has written a lot of things I don't necessarily agree with. But he wrote a famous article in which he said that "there is one and only one social responsibility of business—to use its resources and engage in activities designed to increase its profits so long as it stays within the rules of the game. . . ." When the pressure to deliver profits becomes, as it has, more intense, the rules of the game become even more important. Human nature, the founders of my nation teach, should be taken into account in designing those rules, and we should not assume that men and women of commerce are somehow better than average.

To ensure that for-profit corporations do not generate excessive externalities, strong boundaries remain critical. To address externality risk and fundamental concerns about appropriate protection of workers and the environment in globalized capital and product markets, the rules of the game must ultimately become global, too. But in the meantime, enlightened societies must resist the temptation to roll back the societal protections that spread the blessings of capitalism more broadly, ended child labor, gave workers safe places to work, protected consumers from harmful products, provided decent wages and humane working hours, and ensured that the pursuit of profit would not pollute the world in which we live. After all, it was speedy national, not international, action that kept the financial crisis from being even worse. We cannot dispense with the protections provided by the nation-state until we come up with an effective replacement.

Emerging Views on Corporate Purpose

In his article urging a greater focus on the implicit nature of each corporation, Professor Johnson mentioned that the Craigslist approach to "shareholder profits" was similar to that of Facebook. When Facebook went public in 2012, it included in its SEC filing a "letter to shareholders" written by the company's founder, CEO and principal shareholder, Mark Zuckerberg.

Facebook Prospectus

(February 1, 2012)
PAGE 68

Our Mission and Our Business

As I said above, Facebook was not originally founded to be a company. We've always cared primarily about our social mission, the services we're building and the people who use them. This is a different approach for a public company to take, so I want to explain why I think it works.

I started off by writing the first version of Facebook myself because it was something I wanted to exist. Since then, most of the ideas and code that have gone into Facebook have come from the great people we've attracted to our team.

Most great people care primarily about building and being a part of great things, but they also want to make money. Through the process of building a team—and also building a developer community, advertising market and investor base—I've developed a deep appreciation for how building a strong company with a strong economic engine and strong growth can be the best way to align many people to solve important problems.

Simply put: we don't build services to make money; we make money to build better services.

And we think this is a good way to build something. These days I think more and more people want to use services from companies that believe in something beyond simply maximizing profits

By focusing on our mission and building great services, we believe we will create the most value for our shareholders and partners over the long term—and this in turn will enable us to keep attracting the best people and building more great services. We don't wake up in the morning with the primary goal of making money, but we understand that the best way to achieve our mission is to build a strong and valuable company.

This is how we think about our IPO as well. We're going public for our employees and our investors. We made a commitment to them when we gave them equity that we'd work hard to make it worth a lot and make it liquid, and this IPO is fulfilling our commitment. As we become a public company, we're making a similar commitment to our new investors and we will work just as hard to fulfill it.

Mark Zuckerberg

What is your impression of Zuckerberg's statement that "we make money to build [a better company]"? Is this just a way for Facebook to attract more users and for Zuckerberg to make more money? Facebook, Inc. is incorporated in Delaware. Does his statement—assuming its intention is shared by the Facebook board of directors—violate Delaware law? Or have shareholders in Facebook, by investing in the company, implicitly bought into and ratified Zuckerberg's vision of the company? Or do investors regard these statements about "social mission" as window-dressing—sometimes known as "greenwashing—and thus not to be taken seriously?

Could you imagine the SEC saying that this statement was false and misleading, and thus should have been excluded from the company's IPO prospectus? Or, even more outlandish, imagine a shareholders' securities fraud lawsuit claiming that Zuckerberg deceived them. In the next chapter, we turn to how federal securities regulation mandates disclosure (and regulates false statements) by publicly traded corporations.

* * *

Concluding Thoughts

Business Versus Commerce

One day you take a drive in the countryside. You notice a pottery shop in a quaint little town. So, you stop to check it out. The ceramic pots are beautiful. You ask the woman at the counter, "Who makes these pots?" She answers, "I throw them, my son paints them, and then we fire them in the kiln in the studio out back." You decide to buy one.

As you leave the shop with your pot, you think to yourself, "Did I just engage in a business transaction or a commercial transaction? The pottery shop is a business, but then my purchase was in commerce."

The etymology of "business" is interesting. The word comes from "busy-ness"—the state of being busy. And "busy" in old English means "anxiety" or "concerned." That is, business can be understood as the state of being anxious.

The etymology of "commerce" is also interesting. The word comes from the Latin "com" and "merx," where "com" means bringing together—think combine, commingle –and "merx" means something of value—think merchant, mercantile, market. So, commerce is bringing together things of value. But "merx" is also the root for the old French "merci"—or grace or mercy. That is, commerce can be understood as the bringing together of mercy.

"Hmmm," you think to yourself. "The transaction in which I bought the pot felt more like an exchange of things of value, even of mercy, than an exchange of anxiety. Of course, sometimes shopping is an exchange of anxiety. Spending money (made at a job I don't much like) for the plastic bowls from a store (made and sold by those who don't much like their jobs, either)—that's business. But the pot? Well, that was an exchange of mercy. The potter and her son made something of beauty, with their hands, minds, and hearts. And I hope they felt the money I gave them was of equivalent value."

But now the hard question. Would your purchase of the ceramic pot be less an exchange of mercy if the potter had voted for a candidate in the last election different from the one you voted for?

Chapter 1.4

US Securities Regulation

As we've seen, the US public corporation is simply a corporation whose stock is traded on public securities markets. The US public corporation, although a creature of state law, is very much defined by the disclosure requirements (and even corporate governance rules) of the US securities laws. Therefore, we finish our look at the US corporation with an exploration—actually a primer—of US securities regulation.

A look forward on our roadmap. This unit's introduction to the US corporation sets us on our journey in search of the sustainable corporation. The next unit identifies ways in which the US corporation—particularly the public corporation—is designed to be unsustainable. Then in the third unit we look at the voluntary steps taken by many US public corporations to engage with the Triple Bottom Line—planet, people, and profits. (This sometimes goes by the label ESG, meaning environment, social, governance.) The fourth unit considers some proposals to redesign the corporation, such as benefit corporations, mandatory environment/social/governance (ESG) disclosure, and consortia of institutional shareholders and corporate managers. And, finally, the fifth unit invites you to rethink the corporation as a moral system and how we each fit in this system.

Chapter's Focus

Before looking at US securities regulation, you'll want to notice how the structure of the US public corporation is comparable to the US constitutional structure—that is, how the US public corporation is a private constitution. This should not be surprising, given that human institutions arise from "analogous" thinking. In particular, you'll notice that the fundamental rights of shareholders in US public corporations (voice, exit and loyalty)—all protected by US securities regulation—are similar to the basic rights of citizens in our democracy (political voting, citizen mobility, and expectations of fair treatment).

Next, you'll become acquainted with the basics of US securities regulation—the disclosure rules that apply to public corporations whose stock is traded on public stock markets (so-called listed companies). You'll want to focus on how there are essentially two regulatory schemes, one (under the Securities Act of 1933) that seeks to ensure full disclosure when companies raise capital from investors by offering their securities on public trading markets and another (under the Securities Exchange Act of 1934) that seeks to ensure that companies whose shares are traded on public stock markets provide investors with ongoing full disclosure, thus to ensure that stock prices reflect business realities.

We'll conclude our look at securities regulation by considering the antifraud rules that arise when corporations raise money from public investors and when corporations (and insiders) communicate to investors in public stock markets.

You'll notice that both the '33 and '34 Acts, along with the antifraud rules, seek to assist securities markets (and those who inhabit them) to move information into price. Sometimes the stock markets need a lot of help, such as when a new company engages in an initial public offering (IPO)—investors get SEC registration, mandated prospectus disclosures, and heightened antifraud protections. Sometimes the stock markets can fend for themselves, such as when a startup company engages in a private placement with sophisticated investors or when a seasoned public company seeks debt financing from institutional investors.

You'll then be ready for the rest of the book, as we return again and again to the structural elements of the US corporation—especially the US public corporation and thus US securities regulation.

1.4.1 Public Corporation as Private Constitution

As you might have been noticing, the US public corporation shares many attributes of republican government—it's essentially a "small republic." Both the publicly traded US corporation and the US Constitution create hierarchical structures in which the principals have delegated authority to agents. And in both structures the principals retain important exit, voice, and loyalty prerogatives. Over time, those who define the contours of the corporation have drawn from constitutional norms and language. And, somewhat surprisingly, the constitutional structure may have originally been drawn from notions about the early US corporation. That is, the US public corporation and the US Constitution have been feeding on each other conceptually since their beginnings.

Next is a comparison of the "private" US corporation and the "public" US constitutional structure. This comparison poses an animating question of this introductory unit—namely, what makes human organizations legitimate? The comparison should both help you become more comfortable thinking about the corporation and also open your imagination to how the corporation might be made . . . sustainable.

Public Corporation as Private Constitution

Rivista Diritto Societario (2008)
[available at SSRN]

Alan R. Palmiter

The large publicly traded corporation in the United States derives its essential structure and metaphoric language from the republican form of government laid out in the US Constitution. Public shareholders elect a decision-making body that formulates and supervises an executive bureaucracy, subject to review by a judiciary (typically, in Delaware) that balances shareholder interests and management prerogatives.

The analogy to the republican government structure found in the federal Constitution and replicated in all 50 states is unavoidable. Both "specialized hierarchies" create a principal-agent model of separated powers that contains similar sets of voting rights, nearly identical standards of judicial review, and generally parallel recognition of exit opportunities.Thus, an understanding of US corporate governance inevitably compels an understanding and appreciation of the structures of US political governance—and vice versa. Metaphorically, the public corporation is private constitution.

***

"It may be that universal history is the history of a handful of metaphors."

Jorge Luis Borges
Labyrinths (1962)

Human society depends on human institutions. In fact, human institutions are at the root of civilization. Our institutional instincts may be genetic, deeply rooted as we are in human hierarchies. Even casual observation of primate societies reveals our attachment to specialized structures. No doubt some of our hierarchies are also learned. Human organizations vary from society to society, and within society.

My inquiry is simple to state: how and why is our US Constitution (political governance) similar to our large business organizations (corporate governance)? At a superficial level, the analogies have long been recognized. In the eighteenth century, Blackstone observed in his Commentaries on the Law of England that the corporation is a "little republic." He described—as generations of corporate commentators have since—their formation, powers and privileges, the composition and decision-making prerogatives of their governing board, their answerability to interested persons, and ultimately their dissolution.

At a rhetorical level, corporate governance borrows freely from political governance—and, to some extent, vice versa. Consider a handful of linguistic counterparts from constitutional and corporate court decisions:

(1) "One person, one vote" becomes "one share, one vote."
(2) "Government serves the will of the people" finds its analogy in "the Board cannot impose its will on the stockholders."

(3) The "rational basis test" (judicial deference to legislative policy) is mirrored in the "business judgment rule" (judicial deference to board policy decisions).
(4) The dictum that political "voting is clearly a fundamental right" is echoed in the dictum that the "stockholder's vote is a fundamental right of owning stock."
(5) "The people are masters and all officials of the state are servants of the people" takes wing with "directors are agents of shareholders, not their Platonic masters."

Beyond rhetoric, the texts and structures of our Constitution and corporate statutes bear remarkable similarities—powerfully suggesting a common source. The US Constitution begins with a preamble declaring prerogatives of "the people" and the formation of a new nation, followed by specification of the powers of the legislature, the responsibilities of the executive, and the jurisdiction of the judiciary, and concluding with provisions specifying rights of citizenship, expansion into new territories, and the process of amendment. Of course, personal liberties are guaranteed in the first set of amendments—the Bill of Rights.

The typical US corporate statute follows a similar schematic. It first describes the process for formation of the corporation, followed by a statement of corporate powers, the powers and operation of the board of directors, the titles and duties of officers, the various rights and prerogatives of shareholders (particularly voting rights), and concluding with the processes for corporate expansion through merger, for corporate change through amendment of the articles, and for corporate death through dissolution. Implicit (and sometimes explicit) is judicial oversight of the corporate structure.

Noticing these similarities Albert Hirschman—in 1970—pointed out that organizational answerability and thus legitimacy is achieved through a confluence of voice, exit and loyalty. This, he said happened in many human organizational spheres, including the corporate and the political. But my inquiry, I believe, involves more than reciting and specifying Hirschman's insight. For example, partnerships and families can be usefully compared—offering an interesting and fruitful line of inquiry. Or imperial CEOs could well be compared to political emperors. My thesis is that our notions of republican government (and its democratic ideals and practices) inform our notions of corporate governance. And thus to understand the modern public corporation—and to set its agenda—compels us to understand and dissect its republican impetus.

As we consider the calls for governance reform of public corporations, the dramatic and recent arrival of institutional investors in corporate governance, as well as the internationalization of corporate ownership and thus governance, it is useful to bear in mind the Japanese proverb, "Vision without action is a daydream; action without vision is a nightmare." To contemplate the public corporation merely as an economic phenomenon or as a set of historical financial adventures fails to see its essentially borrowed and political character, to see its animating metaphors. And just as republican government shows its inherent limitations—the Arrow Theorem perhaps only grazing the surface—we cannot afford not to regard the political constitutional underpinnings, both rhetorical and theoretical, of the modern corporation.

That we have borrowed from the political sphere to structure the private/economic sphere is not new. The constitutional/corporate borrowing is a relative newcomer to a long history of human reference to and reliance on one organizational mode to inform another. We operate on analogies, on metaphors. Consider how the business partnership draws its egalitarian principles from the family structure—and how family precepts and vocabulary in turn dominate discussion of the partnership. Consider how the patriarchal business model draws from its imperial counterpart—for example, the Roman economic unit is cast from the same mold as the Roman political empire.

The US Constitution precedes the US public corporation by a few years, and thus the structuring vocabulary and doctrinal formulas seem to flow from the political to the economic. Recent scholarship, however, suggests that constitutional structures may actually have been drawn from British stock companies. Whoever inspired the other, each offers us a wealth of lessons about how we have constituted (and should constitute) the other. And each presents a host of open questions for which answers, theoretical and practical, can be found in the literature and scholarship of each. That this dialogue across disciplines has not been formalized is perhaps evidence of how deep the distrust government has had of the corporation, and the corporation of government. Or how little constitutional study (by political scientists) and corporate law scholarship (by legal economists) mix.

I begin my inquiry by sketching the emergence of the corporation as the dominant social institution in modern society. I then draw the obvious parallels between the US constitutional structure (focusing on the federal level, which is replicated in every state) and the US public corporation (looking at the Delaware phenomenon, which is largely duplicated in all other states). I then turn to consider the essential protective prerogatives of citizens and shareholders—voice, loyalty, and exit—the techniques identified by Hirschman to oversee and discipline wayward governance.

If nothing else, this exercise suggests that an understanding of the US public corporation depends on an understanding of the US constitutional structure—our corporate metaphor. And any argument that the modern corporation has a manifest global destiny fails to confront and acknowledge the variety of constitutional notions that still inhabit the globe. That is, metaphorical variations may well supply different visions for the corporation.

1. The emergence of the pubic corporation

Significant to my thesis is the modern movement, well underway, from a US society dominated by political institutions and public norms (republican government) to one dominated by private institutions and private norms (public corporations). The transformation in the United States has received much attention—both from an adoring right and from an appalled left.

Consider the most obvious measure of any society's most important institution: its tallest structures. The pyramids of Ancient Egypt; the Parthenon of Ancient Greece; the Towers of Babel; the Temple in Jerusalem; the Gothic churches of medieval Europe; the Mayan temples; the majestic legislative houses of the Nineteenth Century; and the Twin Towers of our time. The exceptions—like the Capitol in Washington, DC or the Duomo in Florence—prove the rule.

Or consider for a moment the power of the modern corporation in our private lives. The essential elements of human existence (food, shelter, movement, belonging, sex) are lately functions assumed or, at least, fomented by the corporation. What (no longer "who") supplies our livelihood? our food? our agriculture? our transportation? our acquaintances? our energy? our communication? our health care? Nearly compartmentalized in a public sphere—at least in the United States—are our collective defense, our transportation system, our water supply. Our education system moves inexorably away from the public to the private.

In fact, when one looks at the most important public concerns in the United States as revealed in contemporary public surveys (the following from recent Gallup polls), the problems and thus the solutions rest nearly as much with government as with the corporation.

	Government	Corporation
1 Iraq	**✓**	✓
2 Economy / jobs	✓	**✓**
3 Health care	✓	**✓**
4 Immigration	**✓**	✓
5 Fix government	**✓**	✓
6 Energy	**✓**	**✓**
7 Terrorism	**✓**	✓
8 Education	**✓**	✓
9 Morality / ethics	✓	✓
10 Environment	**✓**	**✓**

Curiously, some of the problems (such as the Iraq war, the immigration dilemma, and climate chaos) are popularly perceived as more the brainchild of the corporation than of government. And *political* depravity and *corporate* perfidy vie for the top target of public vilification. Whether the perceptions have substance, our collective perception becomes reality. Whether assumed or imposed, the public corporation's economic, social and political roles are not about to go away.

So, my inquiry becomes as much a window into two overlapping legal regimes as one into US society and how we allocate power. It is at once a study of the history and jurisprudence of the US Constitution, and a study of the history and jurisprudence of the public corporation. It is a story of political powers and individual rights, of corporate powers and shareholder rights. Ultimately, it sketches our shared conception of what a "specialized hierarchy" should look like.

Curiously, it was this inquiry that animated the ground-breaking study in the 1930s of the modern US corporation by Adolf Berle, a Wall Street lawyer and law professor, whose data was collected by an economist colleague Gardiner Means. Berle and Means decried that the modern US corporation (really, professional corporate executives) had assumed so much power in American life, without adequate systems of answerability. They identified the separation of ownership and control essentially as a *political* problem, borrowing from the logic and rhetoric of political discourse. That Berle and Means are now identified with having identified an *economic* problem—the agency costs in the public corporation—is a testament of how effectively the government/corporate parallelism is (or has been) hidden from view.

2. The parallels—two specialized hierarchies

The principals in the US Constitution are "the people" and in the US corporation "the shareholders"—at least, rhetorically. Both are described as masters and owners of their collective hierarchical enterprise. Both are described as the principal beneficiaries of their enterprise—all those forming the body politic to enjoy inalienable rights of life, liberty, and the pursuit of happiness, and all common equity shareholders in the corporation to have their wealth maximized.

Of course, in both organizations, deep and ongoing questions exist about the contours of membership. Does membership extend to other constituencies, such as black men and women and immigrants under the US Constitution, or to creditors and employees and communities in the public corporation? The failure of the political constitution to adequately resolve these questions has resulted in a history of regular and continuing episodes of turmoil and violence. The ability of the economic sphere to adequately define and re-draw the corporation's boundaries will test its legitimacy.

Both sets of principals—though dispersed, quite heterogeneous and suffering from collective action deficits—have the power to elect the organization's law-making bodies. The citizens vote for congressional representatives to the Congress for fixed terms; the shareholders vote for the board of directors, also for fixed terms. The Congress (a decision-making body) has the power to make laws, sharing it in only limited circumstances with the executive and judiciary. The board of directors (required to act as a body) has the power to direct all corporate business and affairs, sharing this power in only limited circumstances with shareholders.

The delegation of power to the executive is the hallmark (and a controversial one) of the modern US government and the modern US corporation. In theory, the executive branch in each case operates only with respect to delegated power, except in the special carveouts. In practice, the executive branch operates with significant prerogatives, given its numerical superiority, the power to spend, the power to set the organizational agenda, and the power over information. The label "imperial presidency" and "imperial CEO" are rhetorical devices used to bemoan the lack of oversight, on the one hand by the Congress and the other by the board of directors.

The executive—at least in the United States—is chosen through different mechanisms under the US Constitution and in the public corporation. The US President, sometimes called the "chief executive," is chosen by citizens through a bizarre intermediated process (the Electoral College) meant to provide a buffer against popular willfulness. The cabinet and other senior executive officers then must be vetted by the legislature (specifically, the consent of the Senate). The corporate CEO, formerly called the "corporate president," is selected (along with the other executive officers) by the board, despite calls for a direct shareholder vote on executive pay, if not more.

Removal of government/corporate officials also turns out to be difficult in both organizational structures. Under the US Constitution, to remove the president or any federal judge, the official must be charged by the House of Representatives, and tried and convicted by the Senate, subject to a super-majority vote. No US president has ever been formally removed from office; federal judges have fared nearly as well. The removal of directors by shareholders follows a similar pattern—with charges, a chance to defend, and a vote whose expense is borne in most cases by the complaining shareholder. By comparison, the CEO can be removed by the board at will, though this is a rare occurrence.

The judiciary, which oversees the exercise of organizational power for the protection of the principals, is constituted in similar ways. Federal judges serve for life; Delaware judges for renewable 12-year terms. Judicial appointment is supposed to be non-political: federal judges by practice and law are prevented from political activities; Delaware judges are appointed to maintain a political balance on the state's bench, and must be scrupulously independent of corporate officials. In fact, Delaware courts (especially the Court of Chancery) can be seen as a system of alternative dispute resolution that is part of the overall organizational package offered to corporations that choose a Delaware incorporation.

Central to the judicial function under both regimes is respect for re-composition of the structure. Amendments to the corporate articles and bylaws receive special judicial attention and deference. Amendments to the US Constitution, as well as changed societal conceptions over time, constitute the bulk of the Supreme Court's agenda. In addition, both regimes pay special attention to process, sometimes over substance. Harsh administrative rules are acceptable if procedurally sound; harsh corporate decisions are acceptable if vetted by informed, independent directors.

One curiosity of these two parallel "specialized hierarchies" has been how each contemplates the other. The constitutional structure has long viewed with a jaundiced (even fearful) eye the corporate structure and its power. Corporations were originally permitted by legislative grant only for limited purposes and powers, with limited capital, and with limited duration. For the past century, corporations have been specifically forbidden to participate in political elections—though their money, like water flowing downstream, has found its way. Lobbying and commercial/investment speech by corporations is tolerated, but subject to sometimes heavy regulation. [Note: this was before *Citizens United* in 2010, which strengthened the political clout of corporations.]

And just as corporations are not supposed to cross into government, government in the United States is forbidden from owning private corporations. In fact, to ensure broad ownership (and thus to guard against concentrated ownership) institutional shareholders such as mutual funds and insurance companies are prohibited from owning more than 5-10 percent of any corporation's voting power. Likewise, US banks are prevented from the role assumed in other countries of holding voting corporate securities for their own account. [Another note: both *Citizens United* and the bank bailouts of the Financial Crisis of 2008 make clear that the separating line between government and the corporation is a porous one.]

3. Protective devices in specialized hierarchies

a. Voice

Hirschman identifies voice as an effective, and socially desirable, way of avoiding decline in an organization. Rather than exiting in disgust or loyally accepting organizational apathy, members can express their views and thus foment change.

In the US Constitution, voice is enshrined as the fundamental right to vote. Voting in political elections receives special recognition in many ways. Regular voting is specified. The state cannot interfere with each citizen's right to vote. Discrimination is prohibited on a variety of grounds—both the usual (race, gender, national origin) and the unusual (economic, place of residence, party affiliation). Thus, while taxes on virtually all other activities are permitted, poll taxes are not. Nonetheless, effective access to the ballot is limited, typically requiring party nomination or not insubstantial signatures.

In the public corporation, voting is also viewed as fundamental. Although voting is not inherent, shareholders who do not receive voting rights heavily discount their shares. For voting shareholders, voting for directors (as well as on fundamental corporate transactions and shareholder resolutions) is treated as a mandatory and non-waivable cornerstone of corporate law. Regular director elections are specified; judicial intervention, often on an expedited basis, applies in cases of voting irregularities. Discrimination (through such devices as high-voting and non-voting shares) is permitted, but viewed with disfavor. That said, access to the ballot, though theoretically open, is limited in practice by the expensive proxy mechanism.

In the political sphere, votes cannot be sold—though money can be spent lavishly to educate, convince, and cajole voters. Public funding of candidate campaigns is seen with favor, though disregarded in practice. In the corporate sphere, votes can be sold, but only under limited circumstances. The political rhetoric against vote-selling permeates (and once permeated even more) corporate doctrine on the subject. While shareholders have nearly unlimited freedom to slice and dice their economic rights, their attempts to treat voting rights as they do cash-flow rights have met stolid resistance.

Curiously, political voting did not originally contemplate that citizens would vote beyond electing Representatives, with the President and the Senators buffered from direct elections. At most, the US Constitution contemplated the possibility of amendments through a vague convention process, which has never been exercised. Nonetheless, the tendency has been toward more direct voting. The Senate came to be elected directly in 1913, Western states added voter-initiated referenda to their constitutions, and primary voting became the norm after Watergate.

Similarly, voting in US public corporations traditionally has expected that shareholders would elect a board slate selected by the incumbent board or would vote on board-initiated mergers and article amendments. Rubber-stamping was the norm. Lately, with the emergence of institutional shareholders, voting in the corporation has taken new directions. The shareholders' dormant power to initiate bylaw amendments has found new life; the potency of shareholder-initiated resolutions has been proved; and shareholders have even sought to have access to the corporation-funded nomination process. At each step, shareholder activists—both self-styled and derided as a political movement—have borrowed the forms and rhetoric of political activism. Whether shareholder activism "works" has led to debates that pit reformers against traditionalists.

The US Constitution contemplates that political voting will be supported by information rights—the First Amendment enshrining the freedom of speech (especially political speech), the freedom of the press (especially when covering political matters and persons), and the right to assemble (particularly for political purposes). Although electoral fraud is not regulated—candidates can say and promise what they please—it is often punished politically. Beyond these freedoms, which protect against government interference, citizens have access to internal government information under the Freedom of Information Act—a stated purpose for which was to facilitate informed voting.

In like manner, the public corporation since its christening in the New Deal also carries information rights that support corporate suffrage. In particular, federal securities laws require that shareholders receive specified information when they vote (proxy statements), regulated ballots (proxy cards), and updates on the corporation (annual reports). Proxy fraud is heavily regulated, both at the federal and state level. And for information that is not made available through the proxy process, state law has its own FOIA in the form of inspection rights—with voting specifically recognized as a "proper purpose" for shareholder information requests.

Voting follows wealth in both systems. Although money is not supposed to buy political elections, the recognized truth is that a federal campaign (whether to Congress or for the Presidency) requires the support of the wealthy. And the Supreme Court has enshrined the ability of candidates to spend as they choose. Likewise, attempts to limit corporate voting rights on a "per shareholder" basis have failed. Although some institutional shareholders face statutory (populist) caps on the voting power they may hold, many do not. For example, takeover firms and hedge funds exercise unrestricted corporate voting rights—sometimes through naked vote buying—and are celebrated in some circles, denounced in others.

In a departure (though with historic antecedents) from political voting, corporate voting contemplates that intermediaries will vote on behalf of the ultimate beneficial shareholders. Institutional shareholding, with its recent ascendance and with similarities to old-time voting along party lines, creates a new voting dynamic that the metaphorical tools borrowed from political voting are ill-suited given the new face of corporate governance. For example, it remains unclear whether institutional investors (whose portfolio turnover is legion) should have voting rights, at all. Possible reforms include broader voting transparency, requirements to survey beneficial owners, duties of care and loyalty akin to those of corporate managers. As to these issues, the regulatory apparatus that molds the corporation, particularly judicial review, will have to forge new approaches, no doubt drawn from existing metaphors.

b. Loyalty

Hirschman understands "loyalty" as the adherence of members to the organization. The more loyalty, the less often are voice and exit necessary as disciplining strategies. But loyalty, like trust, is earned. For purposes of thinking about the overlap between political and corporate governance, I regard loyalty as the rights that social members have to demand respect for their organizational position—that is, the judicially-enforceable norms that inhere in the organizational structure.

Under the US Constitution, the loyalty owed by the government is reflected in the Bill of Rights (and its extension to the states through the Fourteenth Amendment). These rights, particularly as measured against legislative prerogatives, have led to classifications that guide judicial review. Similarly, the officials of public corporations owe fiduciary duties—classified as loyalty and care—to shareholders, with the shades of judicial review varying according to the extent of conflicts between shareholder and manager interests. Remarkably, the levels of review in each context—and their justifications—are nearly identical in wording and substance.

Legislative action is subject to minimal review ("rational basis") when the legislature is not seen as intruding on personal liberties, such as in the area of commercial regulation; in these areas, the political process, with voting as its backstop, is seen as sufficiently protective. Legislative action that touches on categories that the political process is seen as defective—race, national origin, religion—are subject to intrusive review ("strict scrutiny") because of the danger of majority tyranny. In between, legislative action that raises questions about majority overreaching, subject to some political pressure—such as gender—is subject to balanced review ("intermediate scrutiny").

Board decisions are subject to essentially the same three tiers of review, each varying according to the perceived level of conflict between managerial (whether the board or the majority shareholder) and non-managerial owner interests. Board decisions dealing with corporate operations are presumed to be consonant with general corporate interests and receive minimal review ("duty of care" and "BJR"). Board decisions that involve clear financial conflicts between decision-makers and shareholder interests—director self-dealing transactions, squeeze-out mergers, and manipulation of shareholder voting—receive extensive and intrusive review ("duty of loyalty"). Board decisions that combine elements of business as usual and managerial self-interest are subject to a careful balancing ("proportionate review").

In looking at these review standards, courts and academic observers sometimes characterize the approach as "abstention"—that is, when matters are either "too political" or "too business" for judicial competence. Similarly, notions of standing—complex topics both in Delaware and before the US Supreme Court—define the limits of judicial involvement. Whether a shareholder or citizen can claim rights, and thus a day in court, tends in both cases to turn on the directness of his pecuniary injury. Standing doctrine, which measures individual injury against collective harm, follows the money both under the US Constitution and in the corporation.

While political governance has long sought space for human rights, as reflected in venerable doctrines such as due process, free expression, right to privacy, even human dignity, corporate governance is only lately called upon to identify and act upon that space. Although (cynical) non-shareholder constituency statutes purport to abjure judicial interference when boards act on behalf of creditors, employees, suppliers, customers and communities, the "corporate social responsibility" movement has largely been one carried on outside of the judicial sphere. That is, the powerful political metaphors of respecting other's humanity increasingly find expression in director surveys, corporate codes of conduct, and as a marketing device—though not yet fully in the legal structure of the corporation.

While corporate organization has as one of its main attributes the externalization of risk (both through limited-liability rules against flow-through of corporate liability to participants and through "separate entity" rules against flow-back of participant liability to the corporation), the externalities of government action are less studied—as such. Corporate law has developed elaborate rules for internalizing risk in limited circumstances under the "piercing the corporate veil" doctrine. But, by and large, corporate externalization of risk is one of its great and catastrophic characteristics.

Political organization under the US Constitution recognizes the dangers of externalization in some contexts. The Contract Clause prevents the government from reneging on its debt obligations; the Third Amendment prohibits the forced quartering of soldiers; the Fifth Amendment requires payment of just compensation in cases of government property takings. Curiously, the morphing of the US Constitution into the vessel for a modern social state has meant that the government's taxing and regulatory powers have assumed a broad scope. That is, externalities have come to be viewed as the price we citizens pay.

c. Exit

Hirschman sees exit as the option of last resort for disaffected social members. The rise of stock markets in the corporation and the disciplining effect that mass exit (selling, followed by hostile takeovers) has on corporate governance is now orthodoxy. The tension between voice and exit in this context has been much debated, with voice seeming to be currently more popular (and available) in the public corporation.

Public corporations are built on, and defined by, exit rights. The availability of liquidity through stock markets distinguishes the public corporation and the privately-held one. Exit rights (as share liquidity) are jealously guarded under corporate law. For example, shareholders in a public corporation can sell without restriction; although management has latitude to discourage hostile bids by adopting poison pills, it cannot formally squelch the shareholders' right to sell.

In the process, the stock markets facilitate (and perhaps necessitate) the specialized structure of the public corporation. An iterative loop pushes corporation governance to adopt modalities to conform to stock market expectations, and market expectations are then molded by governance structures. Exit (and entry) becomes the clearest form of expression of shareholder interests; and governance mechanisms compel executives (through stock-based compensation) to become fluent in the market's language.

The US Constitution recognizes exit, though more subtly. The brilliance of the US federal system, it is often said, resides in the ability for migration from state to state. Each state serves as a social laboratory, whose failings and successes are tested through the protected exit and entry rights of the country's citizenry. In fact, the Privileges and Immunities Clause can be seen as essentially designed to ensure free and unimpaired exercise of the ability to exit one state and enter another.

Not surprisingly, the US Constitution does not formally recognize a right of exit. This proved costly. A bloody civil war was fought over the nature and extent of the exit rights of states from the Union. Nonetheless, exit rights have been assumed. While immigration is regulated (even cruelly), emigration is not. Moreover, loyalty oaths are no longer permitted, while flag burning is. In fact, violent exit from the constitutional structure, if it were to go awry, is specifically preserved in the Second Amendment and its right of state militias (and perhaps citizens) to bear arms. The notion that the right to bear arms constitutes and supports an exit right is deeply held by many.

Moreover, free trade—a matter left in the US Constitution to the political process—serves as a sort of exit right. If US laws and regulations become too burdensome, or if US government services become too inadequate, it is possible to take umbrage elsewhere. Exit to avoid heavy environmental regulation, labor standards, taxation, even substandard health care lately animate a central part of the political dialogue. That is, just as corporate exit communicates about the adequacy of corporate management, political exit communicates about the viability of government competence.

Conclusion

Perhaps this game of analogies is trite, revealing little insight. Maybe it is overdrawn, failing to recognize the inherent differences between political and economic activity. Or perhaps, when the details are flattened and the edges softened, it reveals an ineluctable, common conceptual source for republican government and the public corporation. Their genetic makeup establishes their co-fraternity.

Thus, the language of private choice, contract, and markets (still in vogue) may actually mislead us about the true nature of the corporation. For example, contemplations about what the corporation would be if contractual, drafted from scratch, fails to appreciate that there is no *tabula rasa*. The private corporation is an iteration, built on a set of metaphors, of the public constitution. In fact, when corporations have been drafted as contracts—whether 17th Century British deeds of settlement or 19th Century Sardinian banks—their specialized hierarchy has been that of republican constitution.

The constitutional form—with specialization built into its separation of powers, with group decision-making to foster wisdom, with voting to ensure its legitimacy, with judicial supervision as a necessary protection, and with exit always available-has enjoyed a powerful place in the American mind. And today, just as important as these republican notions and their metaphors are to our body politic, they are essential to understanding the public corporation and molding it to our collective will.

1.4.2 Overview of US Securities Regulation

As we have seen, the defining characteristic of the public corporation is that its ownership interests—its common stock—are traded on public stock markets. A "public listing" (as it's known in other parts of the world) means that the publicly traded corporation is subject to the disclosure rules of the federal securities laws. As we will discover later on—for example, when we look at how corporate voting happens in US public corporations and how US public corporations are lately more focused on ESG matters—one of the recurring questions is how much should public corporations be asked to disclose both to their shareholders and also to the public at large.

The next reading, part of an online course for securities paralegals, is meant to introduce you to the structure and vocabulary of US securities regulation. Again, as with our earlier look at corporate governance in the public corporation, this reading is something that should be quite familiar if you've taken Business Organizations or Securities Regulation. But, if you have not, it will introduce you to the essential nature of federal securities regulation and the terminology that you will be encountering throughout this book. It's critical to our search for the sustainable corporation.

LawShelf/Educational Media

Module 1: Overview of Securities Law

Overview

The word "security" is a term of art that describes an ownership or economic interest in a company. This term includes common investments, like stocks and bonds, but it can also refer to more complex investments, like promissory notes and "call" and "put" options.

The United States is home to the largest and most sophisticated financial markets in the world. Each year, stock markets like the New York Stock Exchange and the Nasdaq, and equity derivatives markets such as the Chicago Board Options Exchange and Chicago Mercantile Exchange, collectively draw trillions of investment dollars from investors across the world as they trade securities.

One explanation for the fact that the United States serves as a global investment center is its robust system of "securities regulation." In our first module, we'll explore the regulatory framework of securities law by learning about what is meant by securities regulation. We'll introduce key terms in the field, the most important topics in securities regulation and finally, we'll learn about the entities that enforce these laws.

Important terms

A basic understanding of terminology related to securities regulation is necessary before exploring the field.

> We'll begin by defining the term **investor**, who is someone who buys or sells securities. The term "retail investor" typically refers to one who buys securities from a broker. Someone who purchases small amounts of stock from time to time would likely be considered a retail investor. On the other hand, an "institutional investor" typically refers to a large entity, such as an insurance company, union, bank or mutual fund, that invests large sums of money to purchase securities.
>
> Next is the **broker-dealer**, which is a company that is in the business of buying and selling securities for others. Their customers call them to buy or sell stock. For example, investment firms such as JP Morgan and Merrill Lynch are broker-dealers. People who work for broker dealers are typically called "brokers."
>
> On the other side of a securities transaction is an **issuer** of securities, which is a company that has created, or "issued", the securities. It can be a corpora-

tion, a limited liability company or other business entity. For example, Apple, Inc., is an issuer.

An **underwriter** is a company that buys securities from issuers with the goal of reselling them to other investors. For example, in an initial public offering, the issuer will sell securities to the underwriter, who will then sell them to the public at-large. Large investment banks like Goldman Sachs often act as underwriters.

A company that issues publicly traded securities must have a **board of directors**, who are responsible for appointing the officers of the company. Officers are the senior-most personnel at a company. Some examples of officers include: the chief executive officer (CEO); the chief financial officer (CFO); the general counsel or chief legal officer (CLO); the chief compliance officer; and the chief risk officer, sometimes the chief sustainability officer.

Finally, there is an **outside auditor**. This is typically an accounting firm that reviews the company's financial records to ensure that information provided to the public is accurate and compliant with Generally Accepted Accounting Principles. Outside auditors, as opposed to inside accountants employed by the company, bring objective expertise to a critical aspect of public reporting-the financial condition of the company.

Prior to the Great Depression, the United States did not have a robust federal system of securities regulation. In the 1920s, states had lackadaisical approaches to regulating securities. As a result, many companies and promoters were not truthful or forthcoming regarding negative company information.

Investors were tempted by promises of rags to riches transformations. Approximately $50 billion in new securities were offered during the decade. Due in large part to overselling and fraudulent practices, however, half of these securities ultimately became valueless or almost valueless. In October 1929, the stock market crashed and public confidence in the United States capital markets plummeted.

The federal government enacted a new regulatory regime to restore investor confidence in legitimate companies and to prevent misconduct. We'll begin with the first major law, the Securities Act of 1933.

The Securities Act of 1933

The Securities Act of 1933 is typically referred to as the "Securities Act" or the "'33 Act." The overarching goal of the Securities Act is to enable investors to make informed investment decisions by requiring full disclosure of all important information concerning the issuer and its business. It accomplishes this goal in several ways.

First, the Securities Act broadly defines "securities" to include all forms of ownership in a company. It also broadly defines "selling" and "offering to sell" securities to include any means by which someone might try to get an investor to buy a security.

Second, the Securities Act requires the issuer of securities to affirmatively disclose important financial information through registration statements and prospectuses. These documents are filed with the Securities and Exchange Commission and made public once they are final. Investors, analysts and the market at large can then absorb and analyze this information before making investment decisions. Additionally, the

Securities Act prohibits the sale of securities unless they have been properly registered and the required disclosures have been made.

Finally, the Securities Act prohibits misrepresentations in registration statements and prospectuses used when offering securities to the public, and it holds issuers, underwriters and others who are responsible for these documents accountable to investors for any misrepresentations.

Despite its breadth, the law doesn't require the registration of all securities. For example, private offerings to a limited number of people or institutions or certain "small" offerings and bonds issued by federal, state or municipal governments do not have to be registered.

The Securities Exchange Act of 1934

The second law we'll introduce is The Securities Exchange Act of 1934, known as the "Exchange Act" or "'34 Act." Congress designed it to complement the Securities Act of 1933. The Exchange Act embodies two primary purposes. First, it ensures that securities transactions are regulated uniformly throughout the United States. Second, it fosters transparent, fair and orderly markets. The Exchange Act accomplishes these goals in several ways.

First, the Exchange Act created the Securities and Exchange Commission. The SEC is the primary regulator of securities transactions in the United States. The Exchange Act endows the SEC with broad authority over all aspects of the securities industry. This includes the power to register, regulate and oversee issuers, brokerage firms and exchanges. It also includes the power, when authorized by Congress, to enact specific, technical rules to accomplish Congress' broader objectives.

Second, The Exchange Act requires public companies to issue annual reports (called "Form 10-Ks") and quarterly reports (called "Form 10-Qs") to keep the investing public informed as to the current state of the company. These reports must disclose the company's current financial status, business outlook and major risks as they exist at the time.

Third, the Exchange Act broadly prohibits fraud in connection with any purchase or sale of securities. The anti-fraud provisions in the Securities Act are limited to the initial public offering stage and the actors involved in bringing a security to the public. The Exchange Act, by contrast, prohibits fraud in subsequent "secondary market" transactions, such as those that occur on an exchange. For example, if a company was truthful in its initial public offering documents, several years pass, and then the company misrepresents its revenues in an annual report, the Exchange Act antifraud provisions would apply.

Fourth, the Exchange Act prohibits company insiders and those who gain access to confidential information from trading on that "inside information," also known as "insider trading." The purpose of this prohibition is to ensure broad investor confidence and mitigate fear that the other side is buying or selling the stock due to access to nonpublic information.

Finally, the Exchange Act prohibits certain officers, directors, large shareholders and other "insiders" from engaging in "round trip" transactions (e.g., buying and then selling a stock) within a short time period, including the "short swing profit" rule, which prohibits stock sales by insiders for profit within certain time ranges of important corporate announcements. These provisions assume that the insider has access to superior information and may consciously-or subconsciously-desire to take advantage of that information.

Securities industry regulators

There are several entities involved in the regulation of securities. First and foremost is the Securities Exchange Commission, the primary securities regulator in the United States. It consists of five presidentially-appointed Commissioners who serve staggered five-year terms. The mission of the Securities and Exchange Commission is to protect investors, maintain fair, orderly, and efficient markets, and facilitate capital formation. To help the Commissioners, the SEC has several departments and offices.

- The Division of Corporate Finance: ensures compliance with the registration and prospectus requirements for newly-issued securities as well as the periodic reporting requirements of publicly traded companies.
- The Division of Investment Management: oversees investment companies, financial advisers, and other specific investment products. Investments such as mutual funds, electronically traded funds ("ETFs"), and variable insurance products fall under this division's auspices.
- The Division of Enforcement: investigates potential violations of the federal securities laws. When the Division of Enforcement believes that a violation has occurred, it will prosecute a civil action to recover fines, penalties and disgorgement of profits.

If the SEC believes that a violation of the securities laws has occurred, it may prosecute a civil matter in one of two forums. It may proceed in a United States District Court, in which case the alleged violation is decided by a jury in proceedings overseen by a federal judge. The SEC may also proceed in an "in-house" forum before an Administrative Law Judge, who can make decisions for the agency. The ALJ's decision may be appealed to the Commissioners. The decision of the Commission may be appealed to a United States Court of Appeals and ultimately to the Supreme Court.

The second enforcer of securities regulations laws is the United States Department of Justice, which handles criminal prosecution for securities violations. The DOJ has created a "Securities and Financial Fraud Unit" that addresses these criminal matters. Criminal prosecutions under the federal securities laws are brought in the federal courts.

In addition to federal regulation, there is a patchwork of state regulators that govern securities transactions that occur within the state. State securities laws are often referred to as "blue sky laws." This term is believed to have been coined in the early 1900s for stocks that had "as much value as a patch of blue sky."

Private industry groups also engage in regulatory oversight. These are often referred to as "self-regulatory organizations." For example, the Financial Industry Regulatory Authority (often referred to as "FINRA") oversees the relationship between brokers and investors.

1.4.3 Liability for Securities Fraud

Section 10(b) of the Exchange Act authorizes the SEC to promulgate rules to prohibit "manipulative or deceptive devices or contrivances." In 1942, the SEC promulgated Rule 10b-5 to prohibit not only fraudulent *sales* of securities, but also fraudulent *purchases* of securities.

Rule 10b-5 has proved to be the mainstay for private claims of securities fraud (often in securities fraud class actions). And it is also a potent tool in SEC enforcement, when the agency seeks injunctions and other equitable remedies against fraudulent securities transactions. The SEC can also recommend that the US Justice Department institute a 10b-5 criminal action, a common occurrence in insider-trading cases.

Elements of 10b-5 Case

Over time the US Supreme Court has elucidated the elements of a private 10b-5 case:

(1) Materially false or misleading statement. The 10b-5 plaintiff must identify a statement that contained a false statement of fact or that omitted material information that rendered the statement misleading. Thus, a corporate press release that falsely stated the company's earnings or omitted key information about product safety, resulting in stock analysts to revise their views of the company's stock price, would meet this element.

(2) Scienter. The 10b-5 plaintiff must show that the maker of the statement knew it was false or lacked a reasonable basis. Thus, if the corporate executives issuing this materially false or misleading press release were aware that the earnings had been misstated or that there was a likelihood of expensive products liability lawsuits, their awareness (or reckless disregard of these facts) would meet this element.

(3) Reliance. To recover, the 10b-5 plaintiff must show that they actually and justifiably relied on the false or misleading statement. Importantly, in a securities fraud class action, there is a presumption of reliance if the statement was made into an established securities market, where a price effect establishes "market reliance." (This is known as the "fraud on the market" theory of reliance.)

(4) Causation. To recover, the 10b-5 plaintiff must show that their purchase or sale of securities arose from the false or misleading statement (transaction causation) and that they suffered pecuniary losses because of the statement (loss causation). An investor that did not actually purchase or sale securities cannot recover.

(5) Damages. The 10b-5 plaintiff typically will claim "out of pocket" damages—that is, the difference between the "true value" of the securities that the plaintiff bought or sold and the actual transaction

price. Often, the market price of the securities after corrective disclosure will provide a guide for what the true value of the securities absent the fraud.

Typical Private 10b-5 Cases

There are five basic patterns for private Rule 10b-5 actions. The underlying constant is that securities trades arise out of an informational asymmetry involving deception or other unfairness. Rule 10b-5 liability serves as an equalizer.

Securities Trading. A party to a securities transaction gives false or misleading information to induce the other party to enter into the transaction—or remains silent when he has a duty to disclose. The dupe sues the swindler.

Corporate Trading. A corporate manager induces her corporation to enter into a disadvantageous securities transaction. The corporation (or a shareholder or other representative on behalf of the corporation) sues the venal manager.

Corporate Disclosures. A corporation (without trading) issues false or misleading information to the public about its securities, or it remains silent when it has a duty to disclose. Contemporaneous purchasers or sellers (often in a class action) sue the corporation for their trading losses, which often run into the millions of dollars. (Perceived abuses in this kind of litigation, such as the routine filing of lawsuits following unexpected fluctuations in an issuer's stock price, motivated special pleading requirements and other procedural hurdles in the Private Securities Reform Litigation Act of 1995.)

Insider Trading. Corporate insiders either use confidential corporate information to enter into securities transactions or tip the information to others who, though knowing it is confidential, trade on the tip. Contemporaneous traders sue the insiders and their tippees.In addition, outsiders with no relationship to the corporation use confidential information about the company entrusted to them by others (such as corporate raiders) and trade on this information. Contemporaneous traders, as well as the holders of the confidential information, sue the outsiders and their tippees.

Customer-Broker Disputes. Securities professionals engage in deceptive or other unprofessional conduct in connection with securities trading by or for their customers. The customers bring claims against the brokers and their firms, often in arbitration proceedings.

Securities Fraud Class Actions

One of the principal uses of Rule 10b-5 has been in private securities fraud class actions in which defrauded shareholders seek money damages for trading losses caused by false or misleading statements made by corporate management. The number of securities class actions has recently been on the rise—with 300-400 cases per year since 2017, up from 150-200 per year from 1995 to 2016. As discussed throughout this chapter, the substantive and procedural rules introduced by the PSLRA shape the procedures and claims of 10b-5 class actions. See http://securities.stanford.edu (collecting all securities fraud class action filings since 1995, along with studies and comprehensive graphic summaries).

* * *

Concluding Thoughts

Full Disclosure on Becoming a Father

Adapted and translated from
"Los efectos secundarios de ser un padre"

Doctor: Mr. Jones?

Man: Yes, that's me.

Doctor: Let me introduce myself. I am Dr. Smith. I have just taken care of your wife. And, first of all, I want to ask you to stay calm.

Man: OK.

Doctor: Everything went well. Your baby boy weighs seven pounds, nine ounces. He is healthy, and your wife is resting.

Man: Thank goodness. That's great to hear.

Doctor: Have you read the prospectus?

Man: What prospectus?

Doctor: The one that we left you with? "The side effects and risk factors of having a child."

Man: Side effects? Risk factors?

Doctor: Here, look at the first page where it says "side effects" and then on the second page are the "risk factors." If you look closely, you'll see that it says the following: "During the first months the child can cause insomnia, exhaustion, decrease in the frequency of sexual relations with the partner, visits and stays of the mother-in-law at the home, and dislocations of your back leaning over the cradle."

Man: Oh, my.

Doctor: The risk factors include the following: "In 90% of the cases, it has been observed that during the next 14 years after birth there is usually euphoria, along with moments of joy of high and medium intensity. These feelings alternate with school worries and an increase of the conjugal discussions about the child's origin."

Man: And does that improve?

Doctor: The pharmaceutical studies go in the direction of demonstrating that from the age of 15, the child usually produces bad headaches, progressive paternal disorientation, a decrease in authority, and an increase in isolation from the parents, accompanied (of course) by slamming of doors and moderate to strong quarrels.

Man: My goodness. Anything else?

Doctor: If the child becomes chronic — that is to say, if the child reaches the age of 35 and returns to their parents' home — there is encampment on the sofa, the lack of a job or other benefits. The child then begins to live in the parents' refrigerator and off the parents' checking account due to massive ingestion of soup and other foods.

[Man faints]

Doctor [to nurse]: We let them be parents without their ever reading the prospectus. And then comes the "oh-my's" and the "my goodness's" – and the fainting.

UNIT 2

UNSUSTAINABLE DESIGN

This second unit looks at the fundamental design elements that many perceive make the US corporation unsustainable. These elements, part of the corporate DNA, impede the corporation's usefulness as an instrument to provide for current social needs while also ensuring that future generations can meet their needs—a widely used definition of sustainability.

Chapter 2.1 focuses on corporate limited liability, the corporate law rule that codifies the attitude "let someone else deal with it" and thus fosters the firm's externalization of harm on those seen as outside the firm. Chapter 2.2 looks at the corporation's need for "instant gratification" (short-termism) and its natural ally, the business judgment rule. Chapter 2.3 looks at the engrained "mono-culture" of corporate management and specifically how the selection process for corporate directors inculcates a myopic groupthink, especially in public corporations. Finally, chapter 2.4 considers the corporation as "political person" and the ways the corporation uses its political clout to avoid regulation—thus to preserve its status as an externalizing, short-termist, myopic machine.

A look ahead down the road. Unit 2 is a precursor to our look in Unit 3 at how corporations are voluntarily addressing the Triple Bottom Line: environmental stewardship (Planet), attention to workers and customers (People), and leadership in response to pressure from socially responsible investors (Profits)—that is, a growing awareness of Environmental/Social/Governance (ESG). Unit 4 describes ways the corporation is being redesigned: hybrid-purpose benefit corporations, mandatory ESG disclosure, and consortia between institutional shareholders and corporate management (Ceres). Unit 5 concludes with an invitation for you to rethink the corporation—as a system, as a moral actor, and as a place for personal integrity and trust (being true to ourselves).

Unit 1 Intro to corporation	Unit 2 Unsustainable design	Unit 3 Triple bottom line	Unit 4 Redesign corporation	Unit 5 Rethink corporation
1.1 US law 1.2 US corporation 1.3 US public corp 1.4 US securities reg	2.1 Limited liability 2.2 Short-termism 2.3 Board mono-culture 2.4 Corp in politics	3.1 Planet: environ 3.2 People: CSR 3.3 Profits: SRI	4.1 Benefit corp 4.2 ESG disclosure 4.3 Consortium: Ceres	5.1 Corp as moral system 5.2 Stakeholder capitalism–delusion? 5.3 Personal integrity

Chapter 2.1

Corporate Limited Liability

Corporate limited liability is widely seen as one of the fundamental characteristics of the corporation. By allowing corporate investors to separate business assets from their personal assets, the corporation ensures that investors stand to lose only what they have invested in the business. This is also the rule for managers and others who work in the corporation—that is, those who have invested their human capital. They, too, generally stand only to lose the work they've put into the business if the business fails.

Although the term in English is "limited liability," other languages are more forthright about this corporate characteristic. For example, in Spanish, Italian, and French, it's called "limited responsibility." That is, investors and others who contribute to the corporation are assured they are not responsible for the environmental and social harm caused by their investment—at least not beyond what they put in.

The idea behind limited liability is that it promotes investment in the corporation and encourages corporate managers to take risks on behalf of investors. Further, by assuring investors limited liability no matter how many corporations they invest in, the rule fosters diversification and even the operation of securities trading markets. Limited liability is thus a bedrock of Capitalism.

The general understanding is that if society wants those in the corporation to "internalize" the harm that the corporation otherwise "externalizes" onto others, then society should regulate the corporation. This can happen through government rules that compel the corporation to pay for the harm it causes or that force investors and even managers to compensate those harmed or be subject to fines beyond their investment. That is, government decides how much corporate externalization of harm is OK.

Chapter's Focus

The corporation is said to be an "externalizing machine." You will want to focus on the nature of corporate limited liability, including its history and justifications. Also, consider the factors underlying the "piercing the corporate veil" doctrine, a judge-made exception to corporate limited liability. When does piercing happen?

After considering the contours of corporate limited liability, you will want to focus on: (1) different regimes that seek to have those who manage the corporation "internalize" corporate costs; (2) a proposal for *unlimited* shareholder liability, even in public corporations, in cases where the corporation incurs tort liability beyond its ability to pay; (3) the ramifications of expanding corporate criminal liability, so the corporation becomes criminally liable for criminal activities by corporate insiders; and (4) the possibilities and implications of revoking corporate charters for corporations engaged in patterns of lawless behavior. Do these different responses solve the problem of corporate externalization of social and environmental harm?

This chapter invites you to think about how the corporation's externalization of harm fits with the remaining topics in this unit—specifically, the corporation's short-termism, the often clubbish nature of boards of directors, and the corporation's untoward role in politics.

2.1.1 Corporation as Expression of Modern Capitalism

Before we explore corporate limited liability, it's useful to contextualize the corporation in Capitalism. The corporation—particularly the large, multinational corporation that dominates the US and global economy—is an expression of the essentially extractive, responsibility-avoiding, short-term focused, inward-looking, and politically-manipulative philosophy that we call Capitalism. The corporation's relationship to labor and capital, to production and the environment, to current desires and long-term needs, and to democracy and elitism are all relationships implicit in modern Capitalism.

There have been many recent calls to Save Capitalism! Slowly, it is dawning on us that Capitalism (a relatively recent human construct) and the corporation (its principal instrument) are non-sustainable in their current forms. The call has gone out to reform Capitalism, beginning with the corporation. That is the animating inquiry of our journey: Can the corporation be reformed, restructured, even re-conceptualized so that Capitalism can save itself from itself? This book invites you to think about this question.

Consider the following strident indictment of Capitalism by a blogger with 180,000 followers. The essay proposes a solution that calls on business to become small, meaningful, and human. Whether the essay's solution is realistic, it's clearly and poignantly presented. But more important, the essay provides a roadmap for the remainder of this unit and the book. What design elements make the modern corporation unsustainable? What are the repercussions of its unsustainable design? Where do we go from here?

It's Not Capitalism We Have To Save – It's Everything Else (Capitalism's Obsolete – So Why Don't We Let Go?)

(Feb. 7, 2019)

Umair Haque

Eudomonia/Medium

[redacted/paraphrased]

Various leading financial publications have declared, "We have to save Capitalism!!" Really? Capitalism doesn't need saving, it's everything else that needs saving: Democracy, the planet, a peaceful and prosperous world.

Let me tell you a story—indulge me.

My friend Jake quit his job as a banker to pursue his dream—to be a microbrewer. From banker to capitalist? Not at all. He's not exploiting his coworkers and customers. He's not maximizing profits. He works 20 hours a day, alongside his employees.

Jake isn't living off anyone else's hard work and kicking back on a superyacht. He's just sharing his love of a good brew And even though he's a small business "owner," he employs people and makes things for sale—he's not a capitalist.

> Capitalism is Evil Jake who churns out a vile, commercial brew, cuts corners, treat his workers like dirt. Evil Jake would love his workers on food stamps—more profit for him.
>
> Evil Jake's modus operandi? Maximize profits for shareholders by exploiting everyone and everything while dumping business costs on society. That's Capitalism, my friends.
>
> America is the greatest experiment in Capitalism, a system in which profits are maximized in the shortest timeframes possible, by exploiting as much as possible, so that "owners" can grow obscenely rich.
>
> What happens when we apply this system? First, the planet implodes because exploiting it is totally free.
>
> Second, economies implode. For example, 80% of Americans live paycheck to paycheck, 70% can't come up with $1000 for an emergency, and 50% have no retirement savings. That's American Capitalism.
>
> Third, society implodes. The middle class—without social investment in such things as high-speed trains or affordable education—starts to shrink. American middle-class incomes have stagnated for half a century, even as capitalists charge more for essentials like medicine, school, and decent housing.
>
> Fourth, democracy implodes. The capitalists buy Congresses whole—so they and their trophy mistresses become a new nobility. We saw this in America beginning in the 1980s—as lobbying, corruption, and bribery all rose. We're more like a feudal society where people are born into, and then remain in, strata of power and privilege.
>
> "Saving Capitalism" means the end of democracy, the planet, modern societies, and prosperity. Which do we want to save?
>
> But business, commerce, enterprise, and trade don't have to disappear. There are avenues besides Capitalism: "corporations" with purposes besides maximizing profits; "jobs" that aren't based on exploitation; "profits" earned through means other than abuse, negligence, and corruption. All these things we need to reimagine.
>
> Capitalism is badly obsolete. We have run out of things to exploit—from water to air to minds and bodies. If we eke out a living the old way, the price will be increasingly severe backlash—climate change, fanaticism, inequality.
>
> Other forms of political economy had their day. Tribalism. Feudalism. Colonialism. Empire. The end of Capitalism is finally here. We should let it go.
>
> Nothing made Jake happier than letting go his foolish dream that he would be a capitalist-banker, living off the work of others. Only after he embraced—with wisdom, courage, and grace—what moved him (making good beer for others) did his life begin to overflow with meaning.
>
> Letting go of what we're familiar with and what we've been taught to admire and cherish—that's hard. And so here we are, my friends. We should celebrate the end of Capitalism, knowing it will mean more freedom, more life, more possibility.
>
> If your house was engulfed by flames, would you cry out, "Save the fire!!"?

2.1.2 Limited Liability and Externalization of Corporation's Harm

Extractive Nature of the Corporation

Nearly from the beginning, the corporation's design has been extractive. Its engrained principle of limited liability—the principle that shareholders are not responsible for obligations of the corporation—purposely pushes many of the corporation's costs onto those who often share in its benefits only indirectly, if at all. It might surprise you that limited liability was ***not always*** part of the corporate design, with many businesses and sectors able to thrive without it, at least until about 100 years ago. But limited liability is now the norm, extended to non-corporate forms with mindless enthusiasm.

The limited-liability principle and her close cousin, shareholder wealth maximization, were addressed by Pope Francis in his Encyclical Letter, *Laudato Sí*:

> 195. The principle of the maximization of profits, frequently isolated from other considerations, reflects a misunderstanding of the very concept of the economy. As long as production is increased, little concern is given to whether it is at the cost of future resources or the health of the environment; as long as the clearing of a forest increases production, no one calculates the losses entailed in the desertification of the land, the harm done to biodiversity or the increased pollution. In a word, businesses profit by calculating and paying only a fraction of the costs involved. Yet only when "the economic and social costs of using up shared environmental resources are recognized with transparency and fully borne by those who incur them, not by other peoples or future generations," [BENEDICT XVI, Encyclical Letter Caritas in Veritate (29 June 2009), 50: AAS 101 (2009), 686] can those actions be considered ethical. An instrumental way of reasoning, which provides a purely static analysis of realities in the service of present needs, is at work whether resources are allocated by the market or by state central planning.

Pope Francis, Encyclical Letter on the Care for Our Common Home, *Laudato Sí* (May 24, 2015). In short, the design of profit-maximizing business (including the profit-maximizing corporation) is to externalize its many social and environmental costs on current and future generations.

History of US Corporate Limited Liability

Corporate limited liability in the United States was not part of the original design of the corporation. The idea that shareholders and other investors stand only to lose their investment, without further responsibility for business losses, came about half a century after the first business corporations were chartered. Instead, shareholders in the earliest corporations were treated like partners in a partnership—at least for liability purposes. That is, each shareholder had full personal liability for corporate obligations if the corporation was unable to pay its debts when they came due.

Over time, limited liability became part of the corporate form—though "call regimes" existed through the 1930s particularly for banks, so that depositors of a failed bank could call on shareholders to put in 3 to 5 times their initial investment. It was a kind of bank deposit insurance—and it mostly worked! About 50.8 percent of the calls made to bank shareholders were actually paid. But, today, all major businesses (including accounting firms and law firms) operate with limited liability.

Justifications for Limited Liability

Limited liability has been justified on many grounds: it encourages investment, it fosters diversification by shareholders, it reduces the need for (costly) shareholder monitoring of management, and it even permits stock trading markets to exist given that no shareholder (no matter what their wealth) has to figure in the risk of liability for corporate insolvency. In short, many economists conclude that limited liability is what third parties dealing with the corporations would agree to—given the value of limited liability to the corporation and presumably society.

2.1.3 Piercing the Corporate Veil

Over time courts created an exception to limited liability under a doctrine poetically called "piercing the corporate veil" (PCV). This doctrine permits courts to disregard limited liability and impose personal liability on shareholders to "achieve justice and prevent fraud" when a corporation is insolvent (unable to pay its bills as they come due) and creditors look to shareholders or other insiders for payment of the corporation's obligations

A comprehensive academic study by Professor Peter Oh (Pitt Law) of almost 3,000 cases in which corporate creditors sought to pierce the corporate veil and hold insiders liable for the corporation's obligations is interesting at a number of levels. First, it's remarkable that somebody would read and analyze 3,000 court decisions to find judicial patterns and tendencies—a quite unique method of "common law" scholarship, no? Second, misrepresentations made to outsiders and the siphoning of corporate assets by insiders seem to be nearly determinative factors in whether a court imposes shareholder liability. Third, piercing has never happened in a US public corporation—ever! See also Robert K. Thompson, *Piercing the Corporate Veil: An Empirical Study* (1991) [available on Cornell.edu] (analyzing 1,600 PCV cases through 1985, and finding no cases of piercing the corporate veil in publicly traded corporations).

Choice of Law

Corporate limited liability and the PCV exception are relatively uniform across US jurisdictions. Nonetheless, the issue sometimes arises: What state law provides the rules that govern insiders' liability to outsiders? There is no clear consensus. Generally, courts assume that limited liability and PCV are internal affairs. Governed by the law of the state of incorporation.

This approach may make sense in contracts cases, where creditors dissatisfied with the incorporating state's limited liability regime, can negotiate different terms. In tort cases, however, it can be argued that the state law with the most significant relationship to the parties and the occurrence should balance the policies of limited liability and tort compensation and deterrence. In the end, given that courts usually decide piercing cases on the basis of whether insiders were acting "badly," the actual piercing test may be irrelevant.

Veil-Piercing

(2010)

Peter B. Oh

[available on SSRN]

From its inception veil-piercing has been a scourge on corporate law. Exactly when the veil of limited liability can and will be circumvented to reach into a shareholder's own assets has befuddled courts, litigants, and scholars alike. And the doctrine has been bedeviled by empirical evidence of a chasm between the theory and practice of veil-piercing; notably, veil-piercing claims inexplicably seem to prevail more often in Contract than Tort, a finding that flouts the engrained distinction between voluntary and involuntary creditors.

With a dataset of 2908 cases from 1658 to 2006, this study presents the most comprehensive portrait of veil-piercing decisions yet. Unlike predecessors, this study examines Fraud, a long-suspected accessory to veil-piercing, as well as specific sub-claims in Contract, Tort, and Fraud to provide a fine-grained portrait of voluntary and involuntary creditors. And this study analyzes the rationales instrumental to a piercing decision.

The findings largely comport with our legal intuitions. The most successful civil veil-piercing claims lie in Fraud or involve specific evidence of fraud or misrepresentation. Further, claims not only prevail more often in Tort than Contract, but adhere to the voluntary-involuntary creditor distinction. Surprisingly, though, veil-piercing presents a greater risk to individual shareholders than corporate groups.

* * *

For as long as limited liability has existed, courts have disregarded the form of malfeasant corporate entities to access a shareholder's own assets. With characteristic flair, Wormser declared that "the refusal of the courts to allow quiddits and quillets to stand in the way of justice is nowhere better exemplified [than by veil-piercing]—Our Lady of the Common Law."

Lady Justice has worked with metaphors. At the turn of the last century, courts borrowing from agency law used imagery of a corporate "alter ego" and "instrumentality" to adjudicate veil-piercing claims. Justice Cardozo cautioned that "metaphors in law are to be narrowly watched, for starting as devices to liberate thought, they end often by enslaving it."

Cardozo's fear has proven to be prophetic. The inherent imprecision in metaphors has resulted in a doctrinal mess. Courts have resorted to compiling ever-expanding lists of fact-specific factors: domination and control, failure to observe corporate formalities, the presence of an involuntary creditor, the commingling of assets, confusion of affairs, perpetuation of a fraud, and so on.

Almost two decades ago, Robert Thompson conducted a pioneering content analysis of approximately 1,600 federal and state veil-piercing cases. Despite the oft-expressed judicial presumption respecting the separation between a corporation and its shareholders, Thompson found that veil-piercing claims succeeded 40.2% of the time, and exclusively in close corporations. Further, veil-piercing occurred far less often against corporate parents than individual shareholders. Surprisingly, success was not highly correlated with evidence of shareholder domination, a failure to observe corporate formalities—such as conducting meetings or keeping records—or inadequate capitalization. Most notably, Thompson found that veil-piercing claims arose and prevailed more often in Contract than Tort cases—even though nearly "every commentator" has concluded the inability of involuntary creditors to bargain or insure themselves against risk makes veil-piercing more compelling in Tort than Contract cases.

The discrepancy Contract and Tort cases may arise from a factor omitted in the Thompson study: Fraud. How does Fraud affect Contract or Tort cases? The present study seeks to answer the question. Using a dataset constructed from 1658 through 2006, thus adding twenty-one years to the time frame examined by Thompson, this study looks at 2,908 federal and state cases

The results largely confirm our legal intuitions about veil-piercing. Federal and state courts pierce almost 50% of the time and only the veil of close corporations. As expected, the most successful civil veil-piercing claims are grounded in Fraud or supported by specific evidence of fraud or misrepresentation. Moreover, veil-piercing claims prevail more often in Tort than Contract, reversing the counterintuitive asymmetry found by Thompson's study – thus confirming what commentators, courts, and practitioners have long believed. Similarly, quite predictable suspects comprise the most common instrumental factors: commingling, control or domination, injustice or unfairness, fraud or misrepresentation, and inadequate capitalization.

* * *

[The following are charts from Professor Oh's article.]

Veil-piercing claims prevail exclusively against close corporations.

Table 3. Veil-Piercing by Corporation Type

Corporation	*n*	V-P Rate (%)
Close	2925	48.58
Public	4	0.00

Table 4. Veil-Piercing by Shareholder Type and Jurisdiction

Shareholder	*n*	V-P Rate (%)
Entity	889	**41.17**
Federal	377	37.14
State	512	44.14
Person	2047	**51.69**
Federal	482	**55.60**
State	1565	**50.48**

Table 7. Veil-Piercing by Claim and Jurisdiction

Claim	*n*	V-P Rate (%)
Contract	1730	**46.24**
Federal	408	42.65
State	1322	47.35
Criminal	48	**66.67**
Federal	**10**	**50.00**
State	38	**71.05**
Fraud	400	**61.00**
Federal	157	**53.50**

Claim	*n*	V-P Rate (%)
State	243	**65.84**
Statute	897	**49.50**
Federal	383	**50.65**
State	514	**48.64**
Tort	377	47.75
Federal	129	48.06
State	248	47.58

Table 15. Veil-Piercing by Creditor and Shareholder Type

Claim	*n*	V-P Rate (%)
Voluntary	1933.5	47.50
Entity	511.5	41.35
Person	1420	**49.82**
Involuntary	627.5	**52.83**
Entity	171.5	41.45
Person	456	**57.22**

PCV Takeaways

As you can see, piercing happens only in close corporations, and at a quite low rate compared to the hundreds of thousands of businesses that fail every year in the United States. In the more than 200 years of piercing cases, Professor Oh identified only 2,925 reported cases in which a piercing claim made its way into a published court opinion. Although plaintiffs have had a relatively good success rate in piercing cases (about 49 percent), it's clear that piercing is a nearly infinitesimal exception to the rule of limited liability. When a corporation fails, creditors typically swallow their losses, perhaps recovering a portion in bankruptcy, and then move on.

Of particular interest in the Oh study is that piercing happens more often when the plaintiff-creditor seeks to hold an ***individual*** shareholder personally liable, as opposed to a ***corporate*** shareholder (parent corporation or other affiliate). This means corporations can separate assets and risks ***within*** the corporation by creating a wholly-owned subsidiary. And this separation is respected whether the plaintiff is a tort victim (an involuntary creditor) or a contract creditor (a voluntary creditor). That is, courts seem to respect the corporate form even when confronted by a tort victim who had no chance to negotiate for an exception to limited liability!

Expressive Function of Corporate Law

Notice that the piercing doctrine proceeds on the assumption that corporate creditors are outside the corporation, with insiders owing them responsibilities only when the parties negotiated for it or the insiders seriously abused creditor expectations (commingling of assets, injustice or unfairness, fraud or misrepresentation, and inadequate capitalization).

But there's an interesting segment of the inside-outside line of the corporation where corporate creditors (like banks, trade lenders, even employees) are viewed as being inside the corporation. This happens when the corporation is in financial distress and bankruptcy looms. In bankruptcy—the point when the corporation cannot pay its debts as they come due—shareholders lose their place in line and instead access to the corporation's cash flow and assets is handed over to creditors. Further, in bankruptcy the duties of directors shift from maximizing shareholder wealth to ensuring fair treatment of creditors. This shift of emphasis—at least in US courts—happens at the point of bankruptcy, not simply when the corporation is in financial distress.

When courts articulate the duties that directors owe to creditors when the corporation is in financial distress, their judicial pronouncements serve an important expressive function—basically, reminding directors that they represent the "corporation" not just shareholders. Jonathan C. Lipton, *The Expressive Function of Directors' Duties to Creditors* (2007) [available on SSRN] (explaining Delaware cases stating directors owe duties to corporate creditors when the corporation is "in distress" as educating directors on the limits on directorial discretion, the boundaries of acceptable conduct towards creditors, and the importance of contract).

In fact, piercing doctrine serves a similar expressive function—reminding insiders (particularly in close corporations) that they have responsibilities to those who have reposed trust in the corporation, including the trust by creditors that the corporation's insiders will take their responsibilities to creditors seriously.

2.1.4 Limited Liability in Action

Next is a case decided by the US Supreme Court. The issue before the Court was straightforward: Are corporate parents liable under the federal Superfund statute for the costs of cleaning up toxic waste sites created by their wholly-owned subsidiaries? You would assume the answer is yes. How can a corporation avoid responsibility for environmental harm under a *federal* environmental statute simply by using *state* corporate law to put its environmentally harmful operations in a subsidiary—that is, by filing a piece of paper with a state agency? Certainly, the federal policy calling on responsible parties to pay to clean up their environmental messes (specifically, Superfund sites) should supersede any state corporate policy allowing business firms to choose limited liability. Read on!

BUSINESS ORGANIZATIONS: A CONTEMPORARY APPROACH

(3d ed. 2019)

Alan Palmiter, Frank Partnoy & Elizabeth Pollman

[West Publishers]

CHAPTER 13 CORPORATE ENVIRONMENTAL LIABILITY

A. Environmental Liability of Corporate Actors

Comprehensive Environmental Response, Compensation and Liability Act (CERCLA)

§ 107 (42 U.S.C. § 9607)

(a) (2) Covered persons; scope; recoverable costs and damages

Any person who at the time of disposal of any hazardous substance owned or operated any facility at which such hazardous substances were disposed of . . . shall be liable for . . . all costs of removal or remedial action incurred by the United States Government or a State.

The Comprehensive Environmental Response, Compensation and Liability Act (CERCLA or "Superfund" statute) imposes liability for the costs of cleaning up toxic waste sites on the "owners" and "operators" of facilities where hazardous chemicals have been dumped. It was adopted in 1980 in response to the serious environmental and health risks posed by industrial pollution.

CERCLA defines the term "person" to include corporations and other business organizations. But the phrase "owner or operator" is defined only by tautology as "any person owning or operating" a facility. This circular definition generates more questions than it answers. For example, a significant question under the statute, given that many companies that actually owned and operated these facilities have gone bankrupt or were sold before Superfund claims were made, has been whether parent corporations can be liable for the clean-up costs.

Normal rules of limited liability would say no. That is, corporate parents can place risks in separately-incorporated subsidiaries without incurring liability, except when exceptional circumstances call for piercing the corporate veil. But over the first two decades of CE\ RCLA enforcement, federal courts often interpreted "owner" and "operator" expansively to impose liability on parent corporations for toxic waste sites created by their subsidiaries.

United States v. Bestfoods involved a suit brought by the federal government to recover the costs of cleaning up industrial waste generated by a chemical plant in Muskegon, Michigan. The plant had begun dumping hazardous chemicals in 1957.

The company that owned the plant then was sold in 1965 to CPC International, Inc., the original defendant in the case. CPC had operated the business as a wholly-owned subsidiary, keeping many of the original managers who performed duties for both corporations. The dumping continued under CPC's ownership until 1972, when the subsidiary was sold to another company that eventually went bankrupt.

In 1981, the Environmental Protection Agency began to clean up the site, with a remedial plan costing tens of millions of dollars. To recover some of that money, the United States filed an action under § 107 against CPC and others. After a bench trial, the District Court held that CPC, as parent of the subsidiary engaged in the hazardous dumping, had "owned or operated" the facility under CERCLA.

A divided panel of the Sixth Circuit reversed, concluding that a parent corporation can be liable as an operator "only when the requirements necessary to pierce the corporate veil under state law are met." Applying Michigan veil-piercing law, the Court of Appeals decided that CPC was not liable for the actions of its subsidiary, since the parent and subsidiary maintained separate personalities and the parent did not use the corporate form to perpetrate fraud or subvert justice.

Food for Thought

Does a company's market reputation suffer when it becomes liable for environmental violations? A comprehensive study of corporate environmental liability between 1980 and 2000 found declines in share prices of companies held liable, but the declines did not exceed the amount paid in fines and compliance costs. Of the 478 cases studied, only 28 involved criminal claims, compared to 197 civil suits and 146 regulatory actions.

Of the 148 firms for which information about legal penalties was available, the study found average (median) fines of $13.2 million ($1.52 million) and average (median) compliance costs of $93.6 million ($13.5 million). Average costs were higher given the handful of companies that incurred extraordinarily high penalties (such as the $5.3 billion *Exxon Valdez* settlement).

The issue before the Supreme Court was whether under CERCLA a parent corporation that actively participated in, and exercised control over, the operations of a subsidiary may, without more, be held liable as an "owner" or "operator" of a polluting facility owned or operated by its subsidiary. The Supreme Court answered that the corporate parent could not be held *indirectly* (or *derivatively*) liable, unless the corporate veil could be pierced. But the Court also held that a corporate parent that actively participated in, and exercised control over, the operations of the facility itself could be held *directly* liable in its own right as an "operator" of the facility.

In other words, the Court rejected the more expansive readings of "owner" and "operator" used by some lower courts. It held instead that "owner" or "operator" liability under CERCLA had to conform to corporate law norms of limited liability. As you read the case, notice the pervasive presence of state corporate law in interpreting the reach of federal environmental regulation.

Unites States v. Bestfoods
524 U.S. 51 (1998)

Justice Souter delivered the opinion of the Court.

It is a general principle of corporate law deeply "ingrained in our economic and legal systems" that a parent corporation (so-called because of control through ownership of another corporation's stock) is not liable for the acts of its subsidiaries. Thus it is hornbook law that "the exercise of the 'control' which stock ownership gives to the stockholders will not create liability beyond the assets of the subsidiary. That 'control' includes the election of directors, the making of by-laws and the doing of all other acts incident to the legal status of stockholders. Nor will a duplication of some or all of the directors or executive officers be fatal." Although this respect for corporate distinctions when the subsidiary is a polluter has been severely criticized in the literature, nothing in CERCLA purports to reject this bedrock principle, and against this venerable common-law backdrop, the congressional silence is audible.

But there is an equally fundamental principle of corporate law, applicable to the parent-subsidiary relationship as well as generally, that the corporate veil may be pierced and the shareholder held liable for the corporation's conduct when, inter alia, the corporate form would otherwise be misused to accomplish certain wrongful purposes, most notably fraud, on the shareholder's behalf. Nothing in CERCLA purports to rewrite this well-settled rule, either. CERCLA is thus like many another congressional enactment in giving no indication that "the entire corpus of state corporation law is to be replaced simply because a plaintiff's cause of action is based upon a federal statute," and the failure of the statute to speak to a matter as fundamental as the liability implications of corporate ownership demands application of the rule that "in order to abrogate a common-law principle, the statute must speak directly to the question addressed by the common law." The Court of Appeals was accordingly correct in holding that when (but only when) the corporate veil may be pierced, may a parent corporation be charged with derivative CERCLA liability for its subsidiary's actions.[10]

If the Act rested liability entirely on ownership of a polluting facility, this opinion might end here; but CERCLA liability may turn on operation as well as ownership, and nothing in the statute's terms bars a parent corporation from direct liability for its own actions in operating a facility owned by its subsidiary. The fact that a corporate subsidiary happens to own a polluting facility operated by its parent does nothing to displace the rule that the parent "corporation is itself responsible for the wrongs committed by its agents in the course of its business," and whereas the rules of veil piercing limit derivative liability for the actions of another corporation, CERCLA's "operator" provision is concerned primarily with direct liability for one's own actions. It is this direct liability that is properly seen as being at issue here.

Under the plain language of the statute, any person who operates a polluting facility is directly liable for the costs of cleaning up the pollution. This is so regardless of whether that person is the facility's owner, the owner's parent corporation, or even a saboteur who sneaks into the facility at night to discharge its poisons out of malice. If any such act of operating a corporate subsidiary's facility is done on behalf of a parent corporation, the existence of the parent-subsidiary relationship under state corporate law is simply irrelevant to the issue of direct liability.

This much is easy to say: the difficulty comes in defining actions sufficient to constitute direct parental "operation." Here of course we may again rue the uselessness of CERCLA's definition of a facility's "operator" as "any person operating" the facility. In the organizational sense, the word ordinarily means "to conduct the affairs of; manage: operate a business." So, under CERCLA, an operator must manage, direct, or conduct operations specifically related to pollution, that is, operations having to do with the leakage or disposal of hazardous waste, or decisions about compliance with environmental regulations.

10. Some courts and commentators have suggested that this indirect, veil-piercing approach can subject a parent corporation to liability only as an owner, and not as an operator. We think it is otherwise, however. If a subsidiary that operates, but does not own, a facility is so pervasively controlled by its parent for a sufficiently improper purpose to warrant veil piercing, the parent may be held derivatively liable for the subsidiary's acts as an operator.

With this understanding, we think that the appeals court erred in limiting direct liability under the statute to a parent's sole operation, so as to eliminate any possible finding that CPC is liable as an operator on the facts of this case.

By emphasizing that "CPC is directly liable under section 107(a)(2) as an operator because CPC actively participated in and exerted significant control over the subsidiary's business and decision-making," the District Court applied the "actual control" test of whether the parent "actually operated the business of its subsidiary," as several Circuits have employed it.

The well-taken objection to the actual control test, however, is its fusion of direct and indirect liability. If direct liability for the parent's operation of the facility is to be kept distinct from derivative liability for the subsidiary's own operation, the focus of the enquiry must necessarily be different under the two tests. "The question is not whether the parent operates the subsidiary, but rather whether it operates the facility, and that operation is evidenced by participation in the activities of the facility, not the subsidiary." The analysis should rest on the relationship between CPC and the Muskegon facility itself.

In imposing direct liability, the District Court failed to recognize that "it is entirely appropriate for directors of a parent corporation to serve as directors of its subsidiary, and that fact alone may not serve to expose the parent corporation to liability for its subsidiary's acts."

This recognition that the corporate personalities remain distinct has its corollary in the "well established principle [of corporate law] that directors and officers holding positions with a parent and its subsidiary can and do 'change hats' to represent the two corporations separately, despite their common ownership." It cannot be enough to establish liability here that dual officers and directors made policy decisions and supervised activities at the facility. The Government would have to show that, despite the general presumption to the contrary, the officers and directors were acting in their capacities as CPC officers and directors, and not as subsidiary officers and directors, when they committed those acts.

Indeed, if common corporate personnel acting at management and directorial levels were enough to support a finding of a parent corporation's direct operator liability under CERCLA, then the resort to veil piercing to establish indirect, derivative liability for the subsidiary's violations would be academic. There would in essence be a relaxed, CERCLA-specific rule of derivative liability that would banish traditional standards and expectations from the law of CERCLA liability. But, such a rule does not arise from congressional silence, and CERCLA's silence is dispositive.

Again norms of corporate behavior (undisturbed by any CERCLA provision) are crucial reference points. "Activities that involve the facility but which are consistent with the parent's investor status, such as monitoring of the subsidiary's performance, supervision of the subsidiary's finance and capital budget decisions, and articulation of general policies and procedures, should not give rise to direct liability." The critical question is whether, in degree and detail, actions directed to the facility by an agent of the parent alone are eccentric under accepted norms of parental oversight of a subsidiary's facility.

There is, in fact, some evidence that CPC engaged in just this type and degree of activity at the Muskegon plant. The District Court's opinion speaks of an agent of CPC alone who played a conspicuous part in dealing with the toxic risks emanating from the operation of the plant. Williams worked only for CPC; he was not an employee, officer, or director of [the subsidiary], and thus, his actions were of necessity taken only on behalf of CPC. The District Court found that "Williams . . . actively participated in and exerted control over a variety of [the subsidiary's] environmental matters," and he "issued directives regarding [the subsidiary's] responses to regulatory inquiries."

We think that these findings are enough to raise an issue of CPC's operation of the facility through Williams's actions, though we would draw no ultimate conclusion from these findings at this point.

POINTS FOR DISCUSSION

1. "Owner" or "operator" liability.

As *Bestfoods* makes clear, CERCLA liability turns on whether a corporation is the "owner" or "operator" of a polluting facility. Because the purpose of the statute is to identify responsible persons so they can pay for remediation, doesn't it make sense to interpret these words so that any corporation that conducts its for-profit operations through a subsidiary, and controls the subsidiary's board and its operations, should be deemed both the owner and operator of the subsidiary's facilities? If the purpose of the statute is remediation, why should taxpayers foot the bill to clean up toxic waste sites, rather than the business entities that profited from and had the power to prevent the pollution?

Why did the Supreme Court decide that, in the "normal" parent-subsidiary situation, the parent corporation was neither the owner nor the operator of the polluting facilities?

2. Derivative vs. direct liability.

The Supreme Court identified two types of CERCLA liability for parent corporations whose subsidiaries owned or operated a polluting facility. The Court held that the parent's *derivative* liability could arise only under traditional veil-piercing standards—that is, when the parent had "misused [the corporate form] to accomplish certain wrongful purposes." And the Court held that the parent's *direct* liability could arise if the parent operated the facility, "evidenced by participation in the activities of the facility"—noting that "norms of corporate behavior are crucial reference points."

Given that both derivative and direct liability require a showing of abnormal corporate behavior, what's the difference between the two standards?

3. Deference to corporate norms.

In articulating the standards for parent liability under CERCLA, the Court refers to corporate limited liability as a "bedrock principle," though without mentioning that it arises under state law. Why this oversight? Why should *state* limited liability norms govern a *federal* regulatory regime, whose purpose is to have parties pay for clean-up costs of toxic waste sites for which they were responsible? Isn't federal law and policy supreme?

In short, aren't federally-mandated environmental policies more important than state-based capital formation?

4. Rewarding laxity?

Notice that the Court's standards for parent liability under CERCLA are more solicitous of corporations that put their environmentally-sensitive operations in a wholly-owned subsidiary and then make no effort to oversee the subsidiary's environmental compliance and handling of toxic chemicals, compared to corporations that seek to direct and manage the subsidiary's environmental practices. Does this make sense?

Impact of Limited Liability

How does limited liability affect corporate behavior? A recent study by two finance professors looked at how the Supreme Court's decision in *United States v. Bestfoods* to reduce the liability exposure of corporate parents for subsidiary environmental cleanup costs affected actual corporate behavior—here, industrial pollution. Pat Akey & Ian Appel, *The Limits of Limited Liability: Evidence from Industrial Pollution* (2017) [available on SSRN].

The study focused on subsidiary environmental operations in jurisdictions where courts had previously adopted veil-piercing standards that created parent liability more readily. Using a difference-in-differences framework, the study found that increased liability protection for parent corporations led to a 10 percent increase in toxic emissions by subsidiaries—a result not linked to increased production. Rather, after the Supreme Court decision, subsidiaries were 12 to 25 percent less likely to engage in pollution abatement activities related to production. The study found these effects were driven by less-solvent subsidiaries and by parents that are closer to financial distress, findings consistent with risk-shifting behavior. The authors concluded, "our results highlight moral hazard problems associated with limited liability." That is, limited liability—by design—makes people less responsible.

The impact of limited liability on actual corporate behavior shows up in other industries, including the shipping industry. According to a recent article, the maritime shipping industry (which handles more than 80 percent of global trade flows) "has evolved over the past decades to systematically evade corporate responsibilities." See Guillaume Vuillemey, *Evading Corporate Responsibilities: Evidence from the Shipping Industry* (2021) [available on SSRN]. According to Professor Vuillemey (a finance professor at HEC Paris), shipping firms often fail to comply with regulatory standards and avoid potential tort liabilities through a number of stratagems that include "dissociating legal and ultimate ownership, fragmenting assets in one-ship subsidiaries, using flags of convenience, and evading end-of-life responsibilities with 'last-voyage flags.'" Professor Vuillemey concludes, based on various intra-firm "microeconomic tests," that "responsibility evasion, amidst global competition, is a dominant motive behind these patterns"—a dark side of globalization.

Make the Connection

As you will discover when we look at corporate fiduciary duties, corporate directors have oversight responsibilities – and what's sometimes described as a "duty of obedience" – that requires that they ensure the corporation complies with internal and external norms. See Alan R. Palmiter, *Duty of Obedience: The Forgotten Duty* (2010) [available on SSRN]. This means, among other things, that directors must implement legal compliance programs that ensure the corporation abides by relevant legal requirements, such as money-laundering rules for banks and pollution-abatement requirements for industrial companies. Further, corporate directors and officers cannot choose to disregard external norms on a cost-benefit analysis based on a calculation that expected profitability exceeds the likelihood of detection and costs of getting caught. Knowing non-compliance with legal norms is not only a breach of fiduciary duty, but also unprotected by the business judgment rule and director-exculpation charter provisions. Thus, directors can be held personally liable for illegal acts committed by the corporation "even though committed to benefit the corporation." *Miller v. Am. Tel. & Telegraph Co.*, 507 F.2d, 759, 761 (3d Cir. 1974). Isn't it curious that even though *environmental law* may not require parent corporations to ensure environmental compliance by their subsidiaries, *corporate law* may compel corporate directors and officers to ensure such compliance?

2.1.5 Alternatives to Limited Liability

Pro Rata Shareholder Liability (Public Corporations)

Although there have been calls to reform limited liability, they have fallen on deaf ears. For example, a 1990s law review article by two highly-regarded Harvard law professors proposed that shareholders in US public corporations should pay when the corporation is unable to pay the claims of the corporation's involuntary creditors. Henry Hansmann & Reinier Kraakman, *Toward Unlimited Shareholder Liability for Corporate Torts* (1991) [available on openYLS].

The authors offered an array of arguments for how pro rata shareholder liability would induce corporate management to be more responsible in managing risks that might lead to corporate tort liability. They explained that this would create a compensation scheme in the case of mass torts, where the corporate tortfeasor had become insolvent. They argued that a liability rule would not induce investors to abandon share ownership—after all, individuals drive cars and accept that they might become responsible (unlimited personal liability) if they cause an accident that hurts others.

Here's how Hansmann and Kraakman concluded their article:

> Our analysis indicates that the most common arguments offered on behalf of limited liability—arguments that turn on characteristics that are specific to corporate tortfeasors and the special concerns of corporate law—are largely unpersuasive. There is no reason to suppose that unlimited liability would discourage shareholder investment except in firms that, under the prevailing norms of tort law, impose net costs on society. Even in the case of publicly-held corporations, unlimited liability would not burden the capital markets except, again, to the extent that it would lower share prices to reflect the full social costs of corporate activities. Moreover, nothing about the ownership structure of the corporation, including the larger publicly-held corporation, presents insurmountable obstacles to the judicial administration of an unlimited liability rule. Although a workable rule would call for a number of refinements to accommodate the exigencies of freely-trading shares, our preliminary sketch of a regime of unlimited liability suggests many of the appropriate adaptations.

Their proposal went nowhere. No court ever cited the article, and other articles on corporate limited liability have given it short shrift. In fact, after a few years, it disappeared from view. The idea of piercing liability in public corporations was simply too much!

Why is this not surprising? Let's try a mind game. Assume, for a moment, that BP lacked the financial resources to pay for the clean-up costs and to compensate the people and communities harmed by the company's Deepwater Horizons oil spill. Now assume that BP shareholders were then compelled to pay these costs on some sort of pro rata basis. That means that shareholders who thought owning BP stock was an investment (an asset) discover that their stock is now going to result in a bill in the mail (a liability)! Given that most BP shareholders are institutional shareholders, this would mean that these shareholders would be compelled to compensate the victims of the oil spill from their investment portfolios.

Wouldn't that lead these institutional shareholders, as well as people who entrusted their money to these firms, to become worried about their investments suddenly becoming a financial liability? Wouldn't that be an affront to capitalism? Isn't compensation—when an oil spill is beyond the ability of a company to pay—the responsibility of government? You can imagine the boatload of arguments against BP shareholders being held liable. The very temerity of this mind game may suggest, also, why the proposal by Professors Hansmann & Kraakman for pro rata shareholder liability for corporate torts did not gain any support. It's hard to imagine a modern capitalist system in which the capitalists are held directly and unlimitedly responsible for the costs that they impose on society. What fun would capitalism be without limited liability?

In fact, far from pro rata shareholder liability, what we find are corporations shedding mass tort liability. Here's a quick exposé on how corporations avoid such liability:

> Modern mass tort defendants—including Johnson & Johnson, Purdue Pharma, USA Gymnastics, and Boy Scouts of America—have developed unprecedented techniques for resolving mass tort cases. They combine innovation with exploitation. Before a mass-tort lawsuit is filed, corporate defendants use divisive mergers to access bankruptcy on their terms. Once in a bankruptcy court of their choosing, the corporations take advantage of the Bankruptcy Code to craft their own ad hoc resolution mechanisms implemented through plans of reorganization—such as third-party releases of the Sackler family. These maneuvers may also allow culpable parties to sequester funds outside of the bankruptcy court's purview and then rely on statutory loopholes to suppress victim recoveries. In addition, mass restructuring debtors often pursue victim balkanization—thus to pit current victims against future victims and facilitate settlements that create disparate treatment across victim classes.

Samir D. Parikh, *Mass Exploitation* (2021) [available on SSRN]. You were wondering what bankruptcy lawyers in big law firms do?

Corporate Criminal Liability

Another idea to have corporate insiders "internalize" the externalities created by the corporation is corporate criminal liability, which in the United States has happened primarily at the federal level. By imposing liability on the corporation when individuals in the corporation commit criminal acts, criminal corporate liability is in some ways the apotheosis of limited liability. Corporations that are found criminally liable are punished by means of fines payable by the corporation to the government—and, lately, the corporation is also sanctioned under agreements with prosecutors to change its behavior. These penalties arguably impose liability on those who *benefit* from corporate criminality (namely, shareholders) and compel behavioral changes by those responsible for the criminality (namely, management).

In the United States, corporate criminal liability developed in the early 1900s in response to "the unprecedented concentration of economic power in corporations, as well as new hazards to public health and safety." Sara Sun Beale, *The Development and Evolution of the U.S. Law of Corporate Criminal Liability* (2013) [available on SSRN].

Ease of prosecuting corporations

Interestingly, the Supreme Court has created a procedural framework that eases the government's burden in enforcing corporate criminality. Under the Fourth Amendment, prosecutors can gather information with broadly worded subpoenas, thus avoiding the costs of seeking and defending search warrants. And under the Fifth Amendment, corporations cannot claim the privilege of self-incrimination. Further, the federal sentencing guidelines create incentives for corporations to institute internal compliance programs meant to police company employees and inculcate pro-social norms. The overall effect is that government prosecutors face few procedural roadblocks in prosecuting corporate criminality, but face the substantive defense by the corporation that it has privately undertaken the compliance function—thus displacing the public prosecutor. See Miriam H. Baer, *Personhood, Procedure and the Endurance of Corporate Compliance* (2020) [available on SSRN].

Today, corporate criminality continues to arise mostly under federal law. Over the years, enforcement of corporate criminal liability has evolved, with penalties usually adjusted to reflect corporate culpability. Under modern criminal sentencing guidelines, corporations that perform their own internal investigations, cooperate with both regulators and prosecutors, and actively pursue settlement of claims of misconduct can reduce penalties. And, to avoid criminal liability, corporations often enter into deferred prosecution agreements that require changes in corporate business practices and governance, as well as monitoring to ensure compliance.

In the United States, the seminal case on corporate criminality was *New York Central & Hudson River Railroad Co. v. United States*, decided by the Supreme Court in 1909. The case arose under legislation enacted during the post-Civil War era when Congress enlarged the reach of federal criminal law, because of the dramatic postwar economic expansion and the growth in interstate commerce fueled by the national rail system.

Professor Sun-Beale tells the story:

> At first, the federal criminal statutes were quite narrow. For example, Congress made it a federal crime to transport explosives and cattle with contagious diseases in interstate commerce. But toward the end of the 1800s, Congress enacted sweeping legislation aimed at monopolistic activity that interfered with interstate commerce. The Interstate Commerce Commission Act of 1887, the first federal law to regulate private industry, prohibited price discrimination against smaller market participants, such as farmers, and it created the Interstate Commerce Commission (ICC).
>
> In 1903, after calls on Congress by both the ICC and President Theodore Roosevelt to strengthen the restrictions on the railroads and other industries, Congress enacted the Elkins Act of 1903, which created corporate criminal liability for railroads. The reasons to impose criminal fines directly on the railroads were various. First, when violations benefitted only the railroad, but not its officers and agents, the public—and jurors—were likely to disfavor convicting individual defendants regardless of the strength of the evidence. Second, when the corporation, the real beneficiary of a criminal violation "not only goes unpunished, the law is effectively nullified and brought into "general discredit." Finally, in some cases individual prosecutions were infeasible because of the difficulty of identifying any particular employee who was responsible.
>
> The Elkins Act provided:
>
>> That anything done * * * by a corporation common carrier, * * * which, if done or omitted to be done by any director or officer thereof, or person acting for or employed by such corporation, would constitute a misdemeanor under this Act shall also be held to be a misdemeanor committed by such corporation, and upon conviction thereof it shall be subject to like penalties as are prescribed in this Act. * * * * In construing and enforcing the provisions of this section the act, omission, or failure of any officer, agent, or other person acting within the scope of his employment

> shall in every case be also deemed to be the act, omission, or failure of such carrier as well as that of the person.

The prosecution that gave rise to the *New York Central* case involved the payment of illegal rebates to the railroad on sugar shipped from New York to Detroit in violation of the requirement that railroads charge all shippers the same published rate. The Supreme Court unanimously rejected New York Central's claim that criminal liability was unconstitutional because it punished innocent shareholders without due process. Acknowledging an early statement by Blackstone that a corporation cannot commit a crime, the Court quoted with approval the following passage from an American criminal law treatise:

> Since a corporation acts by its officers and agents, their purposes, motives, and intent are just as much those of the corporation as are the things done. If, for example, the invisible, intangible essence or air which we term a corporation can level mountains, fill up valleys, lay down iron tracks, and run railroad cars on them, it can intend to do it, and can act therein as well viciously as virtuously.

The Court stated that imposing corporate criminal liability was critical to the regulation of rates. The opinion noted that before the legislation was enacted the ICC had published multiple reports stating that "statutes against rebates could not be effectually enforced so long as individuals only were subject to punishment for violation of the law, when the giving of rebates or concessions inured to the benefit of the corporations of which the individuals were but the instruments." Given that almost all interstate commerce was in the hands of corporations, the Court concluded that giving corporations immunity from criminal punishment because of "the old and exploded doctrine that a corporation cannot commit a crime" would effectively "take away the only means of effectually controlling the subject-matter and correcting the abuses aimed at."

The opinion also established the federal standard for corporate criminal liability, extending the tort concept of *respondeat superior*. As in tort law, the corporation may be held responsible for acts of the agent in the course of his employment when the act is done in whole or part for the benefit of the principal, here the corporation. Thus, because fixing rates was within the scope of authority of the corporation's general freight manager, New York Central was held liable for his acts.

Step away for a moment. Aren't penalties imposed on the corporation actually borne by innocent shareholders, creditors, employees, and others? Does corporate criminality, and its threat, really lead corporate decision makers to internalize social norms—when it's the shareholders who actually pay? For example, did the heavy criminal fines imposed on BP after the Deepwater Horizons oil spill change the company's previous indifference to oil drilling safety? Or maybe the fines were seen—by management and even by shareholders—simply as a cost of doing business and taking risks?

As criminal law is used more and more to accomplish corporate governance "reforms," its use has been brought further into question. Some assert that non-prosecution and deferred-prosecution agreements—in which prosecutors extract corporate governance concessions from corporate wrong-doers—may be illegitimate. That is, such agreements allow prosecutors to impose their views on "proper corporate governance" without going through the regular law-making process, something at odds with the rule of law. See Jennifer Arlen, *Prosecuting Beyond the Rule of Law: Corporate Mandates Imposed Through Deferred Prosecution Agreements* (2016) [available on SSRN] (unlike formal agency rule-making, prosecutors who use deferred and non-prosecution agreements to create and impose new corporate duties face few limitations on the scope of their authority or through judicial review).

US law courses on corporate criminality

Whatever you may think about corporate criminality, the subject is getting more and more attention. Not only are criminal prosecutions of the corporation on the rise—especially with respect to foreign bribery under the Foreign Corrupt Practices Act—but so are courses in US law schools. See Samuel W. Buell, Corporate Crime: An Introduction to the Law and Its Enforcement, Open-Source Textbook (2021) [described on SSRN] (materials drawn from intersection of corporate and criminal law, as well as contemporary developments in enforcement practice—corporate fraud, obstruction of justice, FCPA, insider trading, health care crimes, securities enforcement).

Yet others see possibilities to "incapacitate" criminal corporations—that is, accepting that the corporation can't be "kicked or locked up," maybe it can be denied engaging in certain activities when it engages in criminal conduct. See William Robert Thomas, *Incapacitating Criminal Corporations* (2019) [available on SSRN]. That is, rather than working to deter or rehabilitate a corporation that has gone astray by imposing compliance and governance reforms, the corporation can be prevented through various means (such as deferred prosecution agreements or even injunctions) from undertaking or continuing specified activities. The solution aims to treat the corporation more like an individual—tie 'em up, figuratively!

Another question is whether it makes sense to impose criminal sanctions on a corporation that itself is suffering from "organizational dysfunction." Punishing such corporations might be at odds with the deterrence and retribution goals of criminal law, particularly by leaving victim interests unaddressed and being unfair to corporate stakeholders. Maybe corporate criminal defendants should be allowed to raise an insanity defense! When a corporate criminal defendant's "mind" is sufficiently disordered, the corporation may be seen as a "victim" of evil-minded employees. Treatment—rather than punishment—should be the way of dealing with dysfunctional corporations, thus to reduce the chance that others will be harmed and innocent stakeholders not punished. Mihailis Diamantis, *The Corporate Insanity Defense* (2020) [available on SSRN].

Or maybe the way to deal with corporate criminality—something urged by law and economics scholars—is to simply throw the ***individual*** miscreants in jail. Recently, this is what happened when France Telecom was accused of having a corporate culture so toxic that 35 of the company's employees were driven to suicide in the mid-2000s. Just last year, three executives of the company were convicted of ***harcelement moral institutionnel*** (or "institutional moral harassment"). The ruling by a Paris criminal court capped a months-long trial and years-long saga that spurred protests and highlighted issues of labor relations and workplace conditions in a country with a contentious relationship to capitalism. In addition, France Telecom was fined $120,000, the maximum penalty. Its ex-CEO, Didier Lombard, was sentenced to four months in prison and fined $23,000, along with his former second-in-command and head of human resources. A trade union that represents the company's workers, has been tracking employee suicides since 2007, and its leaders said they welcomed the court's decision. The union shop's president said in a statement, "We hope that this judgment will serve as an example so that this type of situation never happens again." Reis Thebault, *"Three French Executives Convicted in the Suicides of 35 of Their Workers,"* Sydney Morning Herald (Dec 22, 2019).

Finally, there is the problem that corporate criminality may miss the "bad apple" corporation. Although many observers have concluded that there may too much corporate criminality, there is also the problem that there may be too little. Consider the doctrine of respondeat superior, which exposes the corporation to criminal liability if a corporate actor (such as a low-level employee) commits a criminal act on behalf of the corporation. Although this doctrine catches corporations that may never have wanted their corporate actors to act criminally—and thus may be too broad—it also may be too narrow. By focusing only on individual corporate actors acting on behalf of the corporation, the law misses corporations that have a criminal culture. That is, corporate criminality does not capture the conduct across many individuals in the corporation, none of which satisfy the actus reas and mens reas required for individual criminality, but when combined this collective conduct is something that warrants punishment and deterrence. That is, under-breadth may be a bigger problem than over-breadth. As Will Thomas (a management professor at Michigan) explains:

> There are several reasons to worry about underbreadth more. First, because respondeat superior treats an individual employee's liability as a predicate to corporate liability, the doctrine reliably excludes from the criminal law predictable swaths of cases where, in our ordinary lives, we would be disposed to attribute responsibility to an organization rather than to any individual. Second, respondeat superior is not generically underinclusive—that is, it is not failing to capture just any random instances of wrongdoing. Rather, the stronger the normative basis is for assigning responsibility to an organization, the less well-equipped the doctrine is to assign it. As a result, respondeat superior risks focusing corporate criminal law on peripheral cases of organizational wrongdoing while excluding paradigmatic ones. Third, this disconnect between normative practice and legal doctrine is poised to grow ever starker as machine learning and other algorithmic decisionmaking processes further confound the criminal law's attempts to trace corporate misconduct to a single, predicate offender. Finally, the past three decades have seen laudable, successful efforts to mitigate the risks associated with respondeat superior's overbreadth. However, those mechanisms ameliorating the problems associated with overbreadth do nothing to manage underbreadth—and, if anything, are likely to make the aforementioned problems with underbreadth even worse.

W. Robert (Will) Thomas, *Corporate Criminal Law Is Too Broad—Worse, It's Too Narrow* (2021) [available on SSRN].

Although criminalizing corporate misdeeds might seem like a great way to focus the corporation's attention on the social harms it causes, it may not be a very useful solution in practice. Not only does it often leave corporate executives (the decision makers) off the hook, but it often misses miscreant corporate cultures. It's no wonder that Delaware—the most corporation-friendly state—was the first state to legislate corporate criminality. Remember that what's good for corporations is good for Delaware.

Revocation of Corporate Charter

Recently, some have urged another (quite ancient) solution to corporate irresponsibility or illegality—namely, the revocation of the corporate charter. See Mitchell F. Crusto, *Green Business: Should We Revoke Corporate Charters for Environmental Violations?* (2003) [available on SSRN]. State corporate statutes have long provided for the state to revoke a corporate charter for wrongful or illegal conduct—typically, in an action initiated by the state's attorney general. See MBCA §14.30(a)(1) (action by attorney general seeking judicial dissolution of corporation that has "continued to exceed authority"). Although administrative dissolution of corporations is common when the corporation fails to pay annual franchise fees or file the required annual report, revocation of corporate charters for criminal activity is far less frequent. But sometimes it happens. For example, Delaware's attorney general recently obtained a consent judgment cancelling the certificates of formation of several LLCs allegedly involved in criminal activities—for "abusing LLC powers and privileges." See Consent Decree, Del. Ch. (June 11, 2019).

So, what would be the effect of revocation of a corporate charter when a corporation's culture becomes lawless? Think about the Wells Fargo fraudulent-accounts scandal, Volkswagen's Dieselgate, or the unaddressed sexual harassment claims at Fox News and CBS. See Jennifer Hill, *Legal Personhood and Liability for Flawed Corporate Cultures* (2018) [available on SSRN] (considering entity criminal liability and personal liability of directors and officers for breach of duties to their companies). If the corporate charter were revoked, shareholders (including public shareholders) would presumably be exposed to joint and several liability in what would become a massive "business partnership." Although corporate law generally does not impose individual liability on passive shareholders when the corporation is dissolved administratively, it's unclear whether the typical institutional shareholder should be seen as passive—and innocent—when a charter is revoked because of a culture of corporate criminality or lawlessness.

Recently, Senator Elizabeth Warren proposed legislation that would require large US public corporations (with more than $1 billion in annual revenue) to be federally chartered—an idea first floated in the 1970s as a way to deal with corporate irresponsibility. Besides calling for employee participation on corporate boards and restrictions on corporate political expenditures, the proposal (the "Accountable Capitalism Act") would also authorize state attorneys general to petition a new Office of United States Corporations to revoke the federal charter of any corporation with a "history of egregious and repeated illegal conduct" where the corporation failed to take "meaningful steps" to address the problems. The liability of directors, officers, and shareholders upon such revocation is not addressed.

Is the death penalty for errant corporations really a good idea? Maybe "killing corporations" is needed to "save humanity." Given the growing frustration with corporations—such as for complicity in human rights violations—there is increasing discussion about the "corporate death penalty." Stefan J. Padfield, *Killing Corporations to Save Humans: How Corporate Personhood, Human Rights, and the Corporate Death Penalty Intersect* (2020) [available on SSRN]. Despite concerns that the corporate death penalty could harm corporate constituents (employees, customers, suppliers, even shareholders), the corporate death penalty would actually seem to be consistent both with pro-rights corporate personality theories and with anti-accountability concerns. In short, if the corporation is to have personhood, it and those who depend on it should accept responsibility—no?

* * *

Concluding Thoughts

A Short History of Western Civilization

The inside-outside nature of the corporation has deep roots in Western civilization. In the sixth century BCE, two philosophical traditions in Greece took on the question of the nature of reality—and thus the distribution of power in society. Heraclitus was of the view that reality is dynamic, always changing, a unity of opposites: "No man ever steps into the same river twice." Parmenides, on the other hand, was of the view that there is one reality, change is impossible, existence is timeless and uniform: "Whatever is is, and whatever is not cannot be."

The classic Greek philosophers, and then Western civilization, largely opted for Parmenides—consider the "categorization project" of Aristotle. The so-called Enlightenment, as well. One modern expression of this is that the corporation is seen as a duality: inside and outside. Those inside have no responsibilities to those outside, unless there is a contract or some government regulation that imposes duties on insiders. For example, unless regulated, environmental pollution occasioned by those inside the corporation generally is viewed as someone else's concern.

According to the long-dominant paradigm of commerce, this means that the interconnectedness between business insiders and those outside the business is understood to be bounded by the "nature" of the corporation. That's the way things are, say many. But Heraclitus might point out that this disconnect—that is, the notion that the corporation draws a line between inside and outside—is not borne out by experience. Parmenides would be of the view that interconnectedness is not inherent in reality. Non-duality thinking—for example, the notion that the corporation can be understood as both inside and outside the line at the same time—simply cannot be according to Parmenides. Or according to the dominant paradigmatic understanding of the corporation, which has held so many in a mental vice.

Isn't it time for us to face reality and begin to work at non-duality thinking?

Chapter 2.2

Corporate Short-Termism

We continue our look at the unsustainable design of the US public corporation, this time focusing on how corporate management (goaded by shareholders) often seeks to maximize financial returns only in the short-term, thus failing to address longer-term risks such as social injustice and climate change. The public corporation—forged today mostly by the expectations of institutional shareholders—is infused with short-termism. Corporate dogma extols the maximization of shareholder wealth in the present, as reflected in current stock prices.

Thus, management decisions—bolstered by the "super wickedness" of financial markets—reflect at most a five- to seven-year time horizon, often less. Longer-term, cross-generational decision-making is anathema to the corporate design. Even decisions with potential longer-term cataclysmic results like climate collapse often seem to have had negligible impact on present decisions, based as they are on financial "net present value." And the courts accept this short-termism, given the judicial abstention principle supplied by the business judgment rule.

Chapter's Focus

You will want to focus on how short-term "shareholder wealth maximization" pervades corporate decision-making, as well as the attitudes of many shareholders, including most institutional shareholders.

You will want to focus on why short-termism can be seen as a "future externality"—that is, the imposition of costs on the future—and how it exists across different kinds of business firms.

You will want to consider how short-termism operated to induce both financial firms to disregard the risks leading up to the Financial Crisis of 2008 and operating companies to promote short-term results over longer-term projects. You will also notice how the post-Crisis legislative reforms, particularly the Dodd-Frank Act of 2010, sought to increase shareholder power—potentially exacerbating the problem that much of shareholder power is exercised by short-term (indifferent) intermediaries.

Finally, you will want to consider whether these claims that companies are actually engaged in short-term thinking are true. Does the data support the idea that US corporations have in fact cut back on longer-term research and development (R&D) and other capital investments, even as they continue to buyback corporate shares (thus sending cash to shareholders)? In fact, there is evidence that short-term stock pricing is actually sensitive to whether corporations are planning for the future. What about confronting the risks of social upheaval and climate chaos?

2.2.1 Nature of Corporate Short-Termism

Contemporary observers, following in the footsteps of Karl Marx, have identified short-termism as being at the heart of Capitalism's (ineluctable) pattern of periodic crises and collapses. Financiers just can't seem to get enough of "pump and dump." See Matt Taibbi, *The Great American Bubble Machine*, Rolling Stone (Jan. 16, 2015). Even staunch advocates of our Capitalism have found that the corporate system has serious flaws. For example, executive pay has been and still is structured to encourage short-term attitudes, risking the whole financial system. See Richard Posner, *The Crisis of Capitalist Democracy* (2011).

Pressures Toward Short-Termism

SWM as a Schelling point

SWM and short-termism are kissing cousins. Perhaps SWM is inevitable in the corporation. Imagine shareholders and corporate managers bargaining over their relationship. The managers want the shareholders' capital, but without strings attached—discretion to do with it as they choose, limited accountability for mistakes, and control over free cash flow. If shareholders accede to this, given that managers likely know better how to put the capital to productive use, the shareholders are likely then to insist on managers maximizing what shareholders are promised in return—"surplus value." Martin Edwards, *Shareholder Wealth Maximization: A Schelling Point* (2021) [available at SSRN] (asserting SWM is "persistent" because it's the outcome one would expect when shareholder/manager bargainers coordinate based on how they each expect the other to act—a Schelling point).

One of the principal attributes of share ownership in US corporations is voting rights. Over time, the "rationally apathetic" shareholder has been replaced by a more "activist institutional" shareholder. But voting remains the exception, rather than the rule, for how shareholders express their preferences in the corporation. Most of the time investors vote with their feet—buying and selling stock. It's called "the Wall Street rule."

Studies on investment time horizons in US and UK corporations find that short-termism exists across all corporations, whether closely-held or publicly-held and whether institutional or individual investors. See McCahery & Vermeulen, *"Ignored" Third Dimension of Corporate Governance* (2014) [available on SSRN]. Shareholder activism, particularly by hedge funds, has made the pressure in the boardroom toward short-termism even stronger. Jain, et al, *Optimal Balance in Public Corporations* (2014) [available on SSRN].

One observer, speaking from personal experience with corporate boards, concludes that the result of shareholders pressuring corporate management for short-term results has been the phenomenon of increasing stock buybacks, making it "extremely difficult for companies to recapture their focus on innovation, growth and wealth creation." Eric P. M. Vermeulen, *New Metrics for Corporate Governance: Shifting Strategies of 'Activist' Investors in an Aging IPO Market* (2015) [available on SSRN] (pointing to examples from the private and the public markets, and finding a "slow but sure" shift in corporate governance thinking). Further, stock buybacks have the effect of leaving firms with less financial resilience to weather business and economic downturns. See J.B. Heaton, *The Social Costs of Dividends and Share Repurchases*, Harvard Bankruptcy Roundtable (2019) (asserting that stock buybacks "dramatically" increase the risk of corporate debt, shifting the risk of corporate bankruptcy to involuntary and unsophisticated creditors).

Culture of Short-Termism

The Sustainable Companies Project—a joint effort spearheaded by an academic center in Norway, with 40 law scholars across 26 different countries—has identified the legal and attitudinal cornerstones of corporate short-termism: the (questionable) norm that the animating corporate purpose is "shareholder wealth maximization," the centrality of the business judgment rule across many jurisdictions, the power of shareholders to reframe corporate purposes, and the *role of law* in re-directing management attention toward systems of risk management and "sustainability due diligence"—that is, toward a new corporate system. Basically, the law has created a pernicious space in which the assumption of short-termism as a legal and social norm has flourished.

What is short-termism? Perhaps it's investing in the present (which pressures corporate managers to manage in the present) and thus putting off the harm that a particular strategy occasions on other investors in the future—a "temporal externality," according to the prominent progressive law scholar, Professor Kent Greenfield (Boston College).

The Puzzle of Short-Termism

((2011)

Kent Greenfield

[available on SSRN]

When pondering the question of the "sustainable corporation," one of the intractable problems is the nature of the corporation to produce externalities. By noting this characteristic, I am not making a moral point but an economic one. The nature of the firm is to create financial wealth by producing goods and services for profit; without regulatory or contractual limits, the firm has every incentive to externalize costs onto those whose interests are not included in the firm's current financial calculus. In fact, because of the corporation's tendency to create benefits for itself by pushing costs onto others, the corporation could aptly be called an "externality machine."

The obvious, routine kind of externality is the one that happens in the same time frame as the benefits gained. These current externalities take a number of forms and are subject to some push-back from stakeholders and regulators. A company might refuse to provide health benefits to its employees, leaving Medicare or Medicaid to pick up the tab. The company might save on production costs by skirting environmental laws, thereby forcing communities, neighbors, or employees to suffer risks of harm that do not need to be accounted for on the company's financial statements. Alternatively, the company could sell shoddy products to one-time purchasers, produce goods in sweatshops, or underfund employees' pension funds.

The more difficult kind of externality to address—especially if our focus is on the sustainability of the corporation—is the future externality. What I mean here is the kind of cost that a corporation's management can externalize to the future. From management's perspective, the future is a much more attractive place to push off costs. Stakeholders who must bear such future costs will be less aware of those costs than current costs, and even if they do learn of such future costs, they will be less able to gain the attention of regulators.

Let me ask about one particular kind of future externality: future costs to shareholders. I recognize that shareholders are not usually the focus in a discussion of externalities. In the present, their interests are sufficiently (even if not perfectly) aligned with those of management that we need not concern ourselves with externalities borne by shareholders other than through the usual corporate governance tools. But in the case of future externalities, the analysis is more complex. Current shareholders may prioritize present returns over future returns, and current shareholders may not expect to be future shareholders at all. This means that corporate managers have incentives not only to externalize costs to current and future stakeholders whose interests they can ignore but also to future shareholders as well. This means that corporations will, by their very natures, be fixated on the short term.

If one is worried about the sustainability of corporations from an environmental, social, or political perspective, the problem of "short-termism" has to be a central worry. This is because in the long run the interests of corporations conflate with those of society as a whole. Short-termism is a problem whether we focus our attention on the sustainability of the corporation or the ethics of its management.

Short-termism is also costly economically, since the economy as a whole benefits when companies have a long-term strategy. The economy is a summation of the fortunes of the millions of companies and individuals that make it up; if most companies make decisions that prioritize the short-term at the expense of the long-term, we all suffer. A nation's wealth grows more over time when companies invest for the future and maintain their viability as a going concern.

Despite some naysayers, the problem of short-termism is very real. Shareholders hold their stocks, on average, for less than a year, and even less for small companies. Institutional investors have been said to be particularly bad on this front, acting "more as traders, seeking short-term gain." Managers admit that they make decisions that harm the company in the long-term in order to meet short-term earnings expectations. In 2006, both the Conference Board and the Business Roundtable, two of the nation's most prominent business organizations, issued reports "decrying the short-term focus of the stock market and its dominance over American business behavior." And, let's remember, that was two years before the collapse.

But there is a puzzle. In contrast to the others who suffer the costs of future externalities, future shareholders have a way to communicate with present-day managers and shareholders. They "communicate" with the present by way of the market. What I mean is that in a well-functioning, efficient market, present-day decisions that exact a future cost will affect present-day stock price. Current stock price will be affected by future losses because current stock price is a function (in part) of future profitability of the firm. With that truth in mind, why do managers focus on the short term? Why would a company benefit from short-term management? If short-termism is a problem because it falsely inflates the company's stock price, how does that occur? That is, why would share prices be inflated rather than depressed for such a company?

The Short-Term Puzzle

So here we get to the nub of the problem: if by definition short-termism is costly to companies in the long run and to the economy as a whole because the economy is a summation of the well-being of everyone--then why do we see the short-term management tactics?

Puzzling Out the Puzzle

One possible answer lies in the nature of management. To state the obvious, companies are controlled by managers, and some managers intend to be at the company for a long period of time and therefore look toward the long-term. Other managers want to make their money and get out. This would explain why some managers would want to manage their companies for the short term. But it does not explain why the market does not consistently punish such behavior. If managers make decisions that will hurt the company in the long-term for selfish reasons, why does the share price not fall?

Another answer might be that that some investors, too, focus on the short-term, so that they buy stock of companies so oriented. But even that does not fully answer the question, since short-term-oriented shareholders should not be able to realize any benefit from owning shares in a short-term-oriented company. If dividends are inflated in the short-term at the cost of the long-term fortunes of the company, whatever benefit realized from the short-term dividends will be more than set-off by the decline in the stock price brought about by the decline in the real value of the company. No benefit should be gained from such a strategy if indeed it is known to the investing public. As the costs of the short-term strategy become clearer, the stock price will plummet, and those holding the shares of such a company will find fewer willing buyers.

The Information Fallacy

Of course, this argument depends on an unreasonable and simplistic assumption — that the market is perfectly informed. In fact, investors are not perfectly informed, and it is often costly or impossible to determine whether companies are being managed for the long- or short-term. That is, it is often costly or impossible to determine whether an increase in quarterly earnings is evidence of a short-term orientation that will be costly to the company in the long-term, or if the increase is due to the realization of returns from a successful long-term strategy.

This fact poses a significant difficulty for public policy. Profits and earnings for a long-term-oriented company may be indistinguishable from profits and earnings for a short-term-oriented company. It is easy to show the numbers; it is rather difficult for most investors to determine the reason for such numbers. In fact, a company that is utilizing short-term managerial strategies may show profits and earnings that are greater than companies with a long-term focus. And capital markets may not "punish" such short-term management if it is not clear that the inflated earnings are based on strategies that are costly in the long-term.

The existence and extent of this lag time between the establishment of a long- or short- time horizon and the recognition of the costs or benefits thereof in the stock price will depend on a number of factors. The most prominent of these will be how obvious the strategy is to investors in the market. The more obvious the strategy, the more efficient the capital markets will be in "pricing" the securities issued by the company. If a company that is pursuing a short-term strategy is able to camouflage it as a long-term strategy, the stock price will be falsely inflated until the strategy becomes sufficiently clear to the investing public that they recognize that it is overpriced. Only then will the share price fall to a level that correctly reflects the company's value.

Most investors will not invest the time to distinguish between the long-term companies that are not yet making money and the companies that are simply floundering. Instead, they will look toward companies that are showing profits and earnings. The problem here is that some of these companies are realizing the benefits of successful long-term strategies, while others are simply exchanging long-term benefits for short-term profits at the cost of the company's long-term prospects.

Sophisticated Investors in an Uninformed Market
Note that nothing I have said so far will be unknown to sophisticated investors. They know 'that earnings and profits in the short-term do not necessarily translate into long-term success. They know that a failure to show short-term earnings does not necessarily mean that the company is destined to fail. But they also know that it is costly to figure out which is which, and that what counts to them is the value of their portfolio as a whole over time, not the profits from a single investment.

Making a Short-term Strategy Work in an Uninformed Market
What if an investor could time their investments? The gains from the short-term strategy could be immense. The long-term value of their portfolios would be the summation of a series of above-market, short-term gains. And the strategy could be maintained as long as there are enough investment opportunities available so that the money investors pull out of one company can find a place to land elsewhere. But how could such timing be accomplished? How would they do that? The answer is by taking over management of the company or by buying enough stock in a company that the management is forced to listen to you.

Obviously, such a tactic would be available only to investors with significant capital to invest. But if investors are successful in doing so then the company can be made to do the things that shift future company value to the present. For example, the company can buy back stock, increasing immediate returns to investors; pay management exorbitant compensation, in effect taking present and future earnings of the company as individual compensation; sell off portions of the company for cash, distributing the cash as a dividend; or leverage the company highly, multiplying the return on equity at the cost of increased risk for the firm in the long-term. Moreover, while the investors themselves are managing the company in such a way, they need not make the true implications of their decisions clear to the investing public.

What to Expect in a Short-Term Market
So that's the story of how short-term-oriented investors could collude with, or become, short-term-oriented management to cause businesses to manage for the short-term without being punished by the market in the short term. Such a strategy will hurt the company in the long term and impose external costs onto company shareholders and stakeholders with long-term interests--as well as society and the economy in general.

But such costs will not be borne in the short term by the investors or managers. As long as they "get out" in time, they will be able to enjoy above-market returns. And as long as they can continue to find companies that are susceptible to the same strategy, they can maintain above-market returns for the duration. But of course such returns are not truly a reflection of anything other than being a winner in a zero-sum game. The returns are not a reflection of excellent management, or product innovation, or the creation of value. They are only, in economists' terminology, the "extraction of rents," the shifting of financial gain from someone who is losing at least as much. The fact that those who are losing exist mostly in the future does not make the losses any less real.

Kinda bleak, no? But is Greenfield right to think that to solve the paradox of short-termism (which hurts shareholders in the long term) shareholders just need to do a better job of understanding what's in their best interests—and identify and reward long-term companies, while shunning short-term companies? Seems simple enough. But for institutional shareholders, this is a particularly tricky problem—their incentives are a bit murky, given that they are investing other people's money. Studies indicate that the "cultural norm" of short-term SWM is pervasive among institutional shareholders and mostly beyond "market" control mechanisms. See Bavoso, *Resilience of Shareholder Value* (2013) [available on SSRN].

Human Nature to Focus on the Short-Term

Interestingly, the "super-wicked" problem—that of discounting future losses so that they become trivial in making calculations and decisions today—may be deeply ingrained in us. And it may be even more potent than imagined. The economics literature reports a tendency that future losses are discounted less than future gains, the so-called "sign effect in intertemporal decision-making." Thus, if future losses are discounted more than are future gains, there is even more reason for decision makers to take chances on "mixed lotteries" involving both gains and losses, given that the losses are discounted away. Referred to as Hyperopic Loss Aversion, one of the behavioral effects is for investors to prefer equity—leading to a widely observed "equity premium" in which investors seek high-risk equity investments over lower-risk debt investments. In short, decision-making disregards the potential high costs of choosing high-risk projects for the future—it's in our human nature! See Jan Krause, Patrick Ring & Ulrich Schmidt, *Hyperopic Loss Aversion* (2020) [available on SSRN].

Regulation as short-termist driver?

A recent paper postulates that short-termism in financial markets could come from regulation itself. Christian Pierre Walter, *Regulation Risk: The Case of Insolvency II* (2021) [available on SSRN]. Leibniz observed that change is continuous. But is this so? Neo-classic economics assumes so—consider "fair value valuation" and the "absence of opportunity of arbitrage." But maybe reality is different. Maybe change, including in financial markets, happens in unexpected ways. Removing the Leibniz assumption could make financial regulation "more sustainable for long horizons and uncertain risks."

And it's not enough that people have a desire to cooperate and act for the longer-term. We are driven to be myopic and thus to cooperate less than might be optimal. The solution may lie in institutional arrangements, such as corporate culture, to guide and minimize our short-term selfish tendencies. See Marco Persichina, *Cascading Defections from Cooperation Triggered by Present-Biased Behaviors in the Commons* (2021) [available on SSRN] (finding that "defective behaviors from the cooperative equilibrium in the management of common resources can be fueled and triggered by the presence of agents with myopic behaviors").

One driver of short-termism—at least in financial matters—is the motivating influence of a current perception that we are relatively worse off. A recent study finds that people who are led to believe that they are poorer than others are more likely to take financial risks—that is, to seek big financial returns now. They will play the lottery, hoping to win big, because they often believe that life is beyond their control. Dietmar Fehr & Yannick Reichlin, *Perceived Relative Wealth and Risk Taking* (2021) [available on SSRN] (commenting that economic analysis can be improved by looking at people's personality traits). The upshot of this, perhaps, is that we might be able to cool the fires of financial short-termism by having people feel they are more in control of their lives and that they are relatively financially OK.

2.2.2 Manifestations of Corporate Short-Termism

What do business people think about the objectives and time horizon of their firms? The following study by an Australian law school professor (University of Melbourne) and a member of the Australian Securities and Investment Commission looked at the business objectives of the largest public traded companies in Australian, the United Kingdom, and the United States – three countries where shareholder primacy holds sway.

An Analysis of the Business Objectives of the Largest Listed Companies in Australia, the United Kingdom and the United States

(2018)

Ian Ramsay and Belinda Sandonato

[available on SSRN]

Introduction

In this research note the authors analyse the business objectives of the top 100 companies listed on each of the Australian Securities Exchange (the S&P/ASX 100), the London Stock Exchange (the FTSE 100) and the New York Stock Exchange (the NYSE 100) to determine to what extent stakeholder interests are taken into account in the objectives. We classify the objectives according to whether the company prioritises the interests of shareholders, prioritises the interests of shareholders but takes into account the interests of other stakeholders, or prioritises the interests of stakeholders. For those companies that prioritise the interests of shareholders, we examine how this objective is described.

The objective of this article is to provide a comparison of the business objectives of the largest listed companies in three countries. The rationale for the research is the ongoing debate regarding in whose interests companies are managed. Because we expect the board of directors to approve the company's business objective, the objective represents the view of the board and is therefore a useful way of determining to what extent the interests of stakeholders are taken into account.

Location of business objectives statement

For all companies reviewed in each jurisdiction, a statement of business objectives was identifiable in publicly available documents published on the company website. In determining the business objective for each company, the most recent annual report for each company was first reviewed.

Table 3—Location of statements of business objectives for S&P/ASX 100, FTSE 100 and NYSE 100 companies

	Corporate governance statement	Board charter	Business overview/ strategy section of website	Values statement	Annual report
S&P/ASX 100	9	18	4	1	68
FTSE 100	2	0	8	2	89
NYSE 100	44	2	4	2	48

Business objectives Australia—S&P/ASX 100

Our review of the business objectives of the S&P/ASX 100 companies revealed that the largest Australian companies by market capitalisation are primarily focussed on the interests of their shareholders.

Table 4—Analysis of business objectives for the S&P/ASX 100 companies

Prioritise interests of shareholders only	Prioritise interests, of share-holders but take into account the interests of other (unnamed) stake-holders	Prioritise interests of shareholders but take into account the interests of other specified stakeholders	Prioritise interests of a specified list of stakeholders	Prioritise the interests of stakeholders generally
48	15	20	14	3

UK—FTSE 100

Our review of the business objectives of the FTSE 100 companies revealed that a majority of the largest UK listed companies by market capitalisation prioritise share-holder interests ahead of other stakeholders.

Table 6—Analysis of business objectives for the FTSE 100 companies

Prioritise interests of shareholders only	Prioritise interests of shareholders but take into account the interests of other (unnamed) stakeholders	Prioritise interests of shareholders but take into account the interests of other specified stakeholders	Prioritise interests of a specified list of stakeholders	Prioritise the interests of stakeholders generally
17	11	41	26	5

US—NYSE 100

Our review of the business objectives of the NYSE 100 companies shows that the majority of the largest companies on the NYSE by market capitalisation prioritise the interests of their shareholders above other stakeholders.

Table 8—Analysis of business objectives for the NYSE 100 companies

Prioritise interests of shareholders only	Prioritise interests of shareholders but take into account the interests of other (unnamed) stakeholders	Prioritise interests of shareholders but take into account the interests of other specified stakeholders	Prioritise interests of a specified list of stakeholders	Prioritise the interest of stakeholders generally
43	9	27	17	4

Forty-three of the 100 companies reviewed prioritise shareholders exclusively in setting their business objectives. For example, Johnson & Johnson Inc. states:

> The fundamental responsibility of the Directors is to exercise their business judgment on matters of critical and long-term significance to the Company in furtherance of what they reasonably believe to be in the best interest of the Company, and therefore its shareholders.

The companies that prioritise shareholder interests but take into account other, named stakeholders often list employees, customers and clients as other stakeholders whose interests they consider. For example, Citigroup Inc. states in its Corporate Governance Guidelines:

> The Board of Directors' primary responsibility is to provide effective governance over Citi's affairs for the benefit of its stockholders, and to consider the interests of its diverse constituencies around the world, including its customers, employees, suppliers and local communities.

Bristol-Myers Squibb Company states:

> The basic responsibility of the directors is to exercise their business judgment to act in the best interests of the Company and its stockholders. In carrying out this responsibility, the Board also considers the concerns of its other stakeholders and interested parties, including its employees, customers, suppliers, partners, local communities, and the public at large.

Nine companies prioritise shareholders while taking into account the interests of other, unnamed stakeholders. For example, Merck & Company states:

> The primary mission of our Board is to represent and protect the long-term interests of the company's shareholders . . . As such, our objective is to balance fiduciary duty and accountability to generate longterm shareholder value, while also considering, in a transparent manner, the concerns of other stakeholders.

Table 10—Comparison of the business objectives for the S&P/ASX 100, FTSE 100 and NYSE 100 companies

Business objective	Number of companies		
	Australia—S&P/ ASX 100	United Kingdom— FTSE 100	United States— NYSE 100
Prioritise interests of shareholders only	48	17	43
Prioritise interests of shareholders but take into account the interests of other (unnamed) stakeholders	15	11	9
Prioritise interests of shareholders but rake into account the interests of other specified stakeholders	20	41	27
Prioritise interests of a specified list of stakeholders	14	26	17
Prioritise the interests of stake-holders generally	3	5	4

Which shareholder interests?

While 79 of the NYSE 100 companies prioritise shareholders in their statement of business objectives, the particular shareholder interests they focus on differs. Table 9 sets out how the companies describe their objective in relation to shareholders. As previously noted, companies often cite more than one objective and are therefore counted in more than one category.

Table 9—How the NYSE 100 companies describe their objectives in relation to shareholders

Objective	Number of companies
Maximise/improve/enhance shareholders' returns/value	27
Provide sustainable or risk-adjusted returns for shareholders	12
Protect or enhance the interests of shareholders	5
Provide long-term returns for shareholders	30
Provide satisfactory returns for shareholders	2
Manage for or in the interests of shareholders	30

Table 9 shows that the majority of companies that prioritise the interests of shareholders are concerned with providing long term returns for shareholders or managing for or in the interests of shareholders. An example of a company in the first category is Time Warner Inc. which states in its Corporate Governance Guidelines:

> The Board's primary responsibility is to maximize long-term stockholder value for the Corporation's stockholders.

An example of a company in the second category is the Walt Disney Company which states in its Corporate Governance Guidelines:

> [T]he responsibility of the Board of Directors is to supervise and direct the management of the Company in the interest and for the benefit of the Company's shareholders.

Table 11—Comparison of how the S&P/ASX 100, FTSE 100 and NYSE 100 companies describe their objectives in relation to shareholders

Objective	Number of companies		
	Australia—S&P/ASX 100	United Kingdom—FTSE 100	United States—NYSE 100
Maximise/improve/enhance shareholders' returns/value	54	43	27
Provide sustainable or risk-adjusted returns for shareholders	31	32	12
Protect or enhance the interests of shareholders	15	3	5
Provide long-term returns for shareholders	28	25	30
Provide satisfactory returns for shareholders	4	2	2
Manage for or in the interests of shareholders	15	3	30

Conclusion

The majority of companies in all three jurisdictions prioritise the interests of shareholders (83 of the S&P/ASX 100 companies, 79 of the NYSE 100 companies and 69 of the FTSE 100 companies). However, an important difference is that fewer of the FTSE 100 companies prioritise the interests of shareholders only and the FTSE 100 companies were more likely than either the S&P/ASX 100 or the NYSE 100 companies to prioritise shareholders but consider the interests of other named stakeholders such as employees, customers and suppliers. This might be a result of the effect of s 172(1) of the Companies Act 2006 (UK) that requires directors to promote the success of the company for the benefit of shareholders, but in doing so, to have regard to other stakeholders such as employees, customers and suppliers. There were also differences across the three jurisdictions in how companies describe the interests of shareholders when they prioritise their interests. Although the companies in all three jurisdictions emphasised returns to shareholders, this was more of an emphasis for the S&P/ASX 100 and FTSE 100 companies while the NYSE 100 companies consider managing for or in the interests of shareholders far more of a priority than the S&P/ASX 100 and FTSE 100 companies.

Short-Termism in the Financial Crisis

Many perceive that short-termism drove the causes of the Financial Crisis of 2008. For example, Professor Lynne Dalla identified that short-termism dominated both the thinking and actions of financial firms (such as the banks at the epicenter of the 2008 Financial Crisis) and also the non-financial firms that depended on financing (and stock valuations) from the financial firms. Lynne L. Dallas, *Short-Termism, the Financial Crisis, and Corporate Governance*, (2012) [available on SSRN]. She observed that financial firms (such as the big banks) engaged in risky sub-prime lending and investments, driven by the expectations of their short-term shareholders. In turn, executives in non-financial firms often "managed earnings"—that is, engaged in deceit about the amount and timing of company profits—driven by the expectations of their short-term shareholders. And some financial firms—particularly, hedge funds—used shareholder voting to force even more short-term activities in non-financial firms, whose executives she described as being subject to "herd behavior."

Comparative hedge fund activism

While some studies of hedge fund activism in US corporations suggest that such activism actually awakens management from their stupor, thus benefitting shareholders short-term and longer-term, the value of hedge fund activism (and attitudes about short-term management fixes) may be different in other countries. For example, a recent study finds that hedge fund activism in Japan does not necessarily improve management effectiveness, managerial decisions, labor management, or market perception. Looking at financial data in Japan, the study found "no enduring changes" in the first three areas and that market perception of hedge-fund activism was consistently unfavorable—that is, the value placed on short-termism varies depending on the country and its corporate culture. John Buchanan, and Dominic Heesang Chai, *Unexpected Corporate Outcomes from Hedge Fund Activism in Japan*(2018) [available on SSRN].

Hedge Fund Activism

In recent years, academic attention has focused on hedge fund activism as the principal driver of short-termism in US corporations. A leading scholar on US corporate governance, Professor Jack Coffee (Columbia Law School), said the following:

> Few doubt that hedge fund activism has radically changed corporate governance in the United States—for better or for worse. Proponents see activists as desirable agents of change who intentionally invest in underperforming companies to organize (democratize) more passive shareholders to support their proposals to change the target's business model and/or management.
>
> Skeptics respond that things do not work this simply. Actual proxy contests are few, and most activist engagements are resolved through private settlement

> between the activists, who rarely hold 10% or more of the stock, and corporate management. As a result, activists holding often only a small percentage of the stock are imposing their agenda on other shareholders who hold much more. Increasingly, large (and longer-term) indexed shareholders—BlackRock, State Street and Vanguard in particular—are objecting that this pattern of private settlements excludes them.
>
> Besides thwarting the will of the "silent majority" of long-term investors and their intermediaries, these activists often have short-term "private" agendas at odds with such longer-term "public goals" of most institutional shareholders—such as greater gender diversity on the board and a shift from "dirty" to "clean" energy. Thus, the activists have constrained the ability of public companies to behave in a manner consistent with the public morality.

John C. Coffee, *The Agency Costs of Activism: Information Leakage, Thwarted Majorities, and the Public Morality* (2017) [available on SSRN].

2.2.3 Evaluations of Shareholder Activism/Empowerment

Counter-Productivity of Shareholder Empowerment

So how has short-termism been addressed? Strangely, by calls for more shareholder empowerment. Consider the legislative reforms following the Financial Crisis of 2008—particularly, the Dodd-Frank Act of 2010. These reforms aimed at increasing shareholder power in the corporation, but failed to address (and may have exacerbated) the problem that shareholders focused on short-term results may have been the drivers of the financial myopia that resulted in a near collapse of the financial system. According to Professor Usha Rodrigues (Georgia Law), such mechanisms as say-on-pay and proxy access give shareholders a greater corporate voice, but this only exacerbates the problem that this voice calls for quick returns, rather than long-term corporate thinking and planning. Usha Rodrigues, *Corporate Governance in Age of Separation of Ownership* (2011) [available on SSRN].

Echoing Professor Rodrigues's criticism of Dodd-Frank's counter-productive empowerment of shareholders is the observation that the current securities laws—and their requirement of quarterly financial reporting by public companies—also promote short-termism. See John R. Graham, Campbell R. Harvey & Shivaram Rajgopal, *The Economic Implications of Corporate Financial Reporting* (2005) [available on SSRN] (surveying 401 financial executives and finding that most would cancel or delay profitable business plans if the plans would cause expected quarterly results to fall short). As a result, there are regular calls to move from quarterly to semi-annual or even annual reporting. But others doubt that such a move would actually quell management short-termism. See John C. Coffee, *What Really Drives "Short-*

Termism"?, CLS Blue Sky Blog (2018) (arguing that semi-annual reporting would make management even more driven to show short-term results, every six months); *see also* James J. Park, *Do the Securities Laws Promote Short-Termism?* [available on SSRN] (arguing that projections by research analysts, not quarterly reporting, fuels management's obsession with short-term results; recommending that company disclosures address projections).

Short-Termism and Risk-Taking

After the Financial Crisis of 2008, which revealed the risk-taking behavior of large financial institutions, there were widespread demands to recognize the "publicness" of these firms and to reform their internal decision-making. The Dodd-Frank Act of 2010, seeking to protect the interests of non-shareholder stakeholders in financial firms, gave shareholders a greater role in the corporate governance of these firms. Professor Jill Fisch (Pennsylvania Law School) has criticized the effort to enlist shareholders as agents of public values. Jill F. Fisch, *The Mess at Morgan: Risk, Incentives and Shareholder Empowerment* (2015) [available on SSRN]. Professor Fisch argues that "incorporation of publicness" into corporate governance mistakenly assumes that shareholders' interests are aligned with those of non-shareholder stakeholders.

Further, some limits on shareholder activism may actually enhance firm value. A recent study (looking at the period from 1978 to 2008) finds that *shareholder-approved* protective arrangements—such as staggered boards and supermajority requirements in the corporate charter—are actually associated with increased firm value. That is, limiting shareholder rights (and the ineluctable pressure toward short-termism) may enable management to exploit competitive private information and pursue long-term wealth maximization. Cremers, Masconale & Sepe, *Commitment and Entrenchment in Corporate Governance* (2016) [available on SSRN] (but finding protective arrangements *not requiring shareholder approval*, such as poison pills and golden parachutes, are associated with decreased firm value).

2.2.4 Proposed Solutions to Short-Termism

In 2015, Leo Strine (while Chief Justice of the Delaware Supreme Court) laid out what he called a "sensible, nonpartisan agenda" to increase long-termism in US corporations:

> These days it has become fashionable to talk about whether the incentive system for the governance of American corporations optimally encourages long-term investment, sustainable policies, and therefore creates the most long-term economic and social benefit for American workers and investors.

> Many have come to the conclusion that the answer to that question is no. As these commentators note, the investment horizon of the ultimate source of most equity capital—human beings who must give their money to institutional investors to save for retirement and college for their kids—is long. That horizon is much more aligned with what it takes to run a real business than that of the direct stockholders, who are money managers and are under strong pressure to deliver immediate returns at all times. Americans want corporations that are focused on sustainable wealth and job creation.
>
> But, there is too little talk accompanied by a specific policy agenda to address that incentive system. This paper proposes a genuine, realistic agenda that would better promote a sustainable, long-term commitment to economic growth in the United States. This agenda should not divide Americans along party lines. Indeed, most of the elements have substantial bipartisan support. Nor does this agenda involve freeing corporate managers from accountability to investors for delivering profitable returns. Rather, it makes all those who represent human investors more accountable, but for delivering on what most counts for ordinary investors, which is the creation of durable wealth by socially responsible means.
>
> The fundamental elements of this strategy to promote long-term American competitiveness include:
>
> (i) tax policy that discourages counterproductive behavior and encourages investment and work
> (ii) investment policies to revitalize our infrastructure, address climate change, create jobs, and close our deficit
> (iii) reforming the incentives of and enhancing the fiduciary accountability of institutional investors
> (iv) reducing the focus on quarterly earnings estimates and improving the quality of information provided to investors
> (v) an American commitment to an international level playing field to reduce incentives to offshore jobs, erode the social safety net, and pollute the planet.

Leo E. Strine, *Securing Our Nation's Economic Future: A Sensible, Nonpartisan Agenda to Increase Long-Term Investment and Job Creation in the United States* (2015) [available on SSRN].

This all sounds wonderful—a rousing political speech. But seven years later, none of the proposals have been seriously considered, much less implemented. Remember that federal law and policy don't happen without the support of the elites and corporations—and, lately, big investors. But even if these things did happen, isn't the problem that short-termism is "ingrained in business practices"? Can changes to tax policy change this? Further, consider the big infrastructure bill in Congress. Will it lead corporations to see that we must de-carbonize in much the way we went to war in WWII after the country was attacked? That is, can short-termism be dealt with by changing some tax and other incentives?

Promoting Long-Term Shareholding

An interesting proposal to solve short-termism in US corporations is to give more voting power to longer-term shareholders—such as indexed mutual funds that on behalf of their long-term investors are "in it" for the long run. Thus, there have been proposals from various quarters would to vary voting rights, board nomination rights, and other levers of governance by "looking back" at the length of time investors have continuously held securities in the past. For example, to make a shareholder's proposal, a shareholder must have held a certain amount of shares for a given period (one to three years), with fewer shares required to make a proposal the longer the holding period. That is, the SEC's shareholder proposal rule trusts longer-holding shareholders than shorter-holding shareholders to act consistent with the corporation's best interests.

Along the lines of encouraging long-term shareholders is the proposal by Professor Larry Cunningham to focus on and promote "quality shareholders." He views this as a solution to our increasingly fragmented pool of shareholders—including activist short-termists (like hedge funds) and passive long-termists (like indexed funds). The concept of quality shareholders, invented by Warren Buffett, recognizes that shareholders with a long-term investment horizon provide special value to a company and should be rewarded with special voting rights. This idea is already imbedded in some companies' voting structures, such as the dual-class shares of Google, which give to founders greater voting rights than public shareholders on the theory that the founders will know better how to achieve the company's long-term goals—in Google's case "to organize the world's information and to make in universally accessible and useful." To address "myopic short-termism and ignorant indexing," Cunningham proposes a variety of ways for companies to increase the voting power of long-term quality shareholders. Lawrence A. Cunningham, *The Case for Empowering Quality Shareholders* (2020) [available on SSRN]. The move to quality shareholders, however, is not assured. For example, why would short-termists and indexers be willing to concede greater voting rights to self-defined quality shareholders? Perhaps, instead of changing corporate voting, the goal might be to help the dominant indexers (which hold at least 60 percent of most companies' voting shares) become more refined, more involved—leading to more quality!

The idea of giving long-holding shareholders more rights than short-holding shareholders has been criticized on the ground that the relevant inquiry should be on the "future investment horizons" of particular shareholders. A recent study, using a database of thousands of institutional investors and hundreds of thousands of individual investments, finds (1) that future investment horizon does indeed lengthen as past holding period increases, and (2) most institutional shareholders have relatively long holding periods.

Based on these findings, the authors argue for a "forward looking" approach in which shareholders (especially institutions) that commit to taking long-term investment horizons would have greater voting rights. Robert Anderson IV & George Dent, Jr. *Institutional Investors, Investment Horizons, and Corporate Governance* (2018) [available on SSRN].

2.2.5 Critique of Short-Termism Alarmists

As you can see, short-termism has gotten a bad name among many academics. But perhaps it's not as bad as they say. Recently, Professor Mark Roe (Harvard Law School) offered a more measured view of short-termism:

> Stock-market-driven short-termism is crippling the American economy, according to legal, judicial, and media analyses. Firms are forgoing the R&D they need, cutting capital spending, and buying back their own stock so feverishly that they starve themselves of cash. The stock market is the primary cause: directors and executives cannot manage for the long-term when their shareholders furiously trade their company's stock, they cannot make long-term investments when stockholders demand to see profits on this quarter's financial statements, they cannot even strategize about the long-term when shareholder activists demand immediate results, and they cannot keep the cash to invest in their future when stock market pressure drains away that cash in stock buybacks.
>
> This doomsday version of the stock-market-driven short-termism argument embeds economy-wide predictions that have not been well-examined. Examining them allows us to judge how severe these problems are: if the scenario is correct and strong, we should first see sharp increases in stock trading in recent decades and more frequent activist interventions, and these increases should be accompanied by (1) economy-wide R&D spending declining from what it should be, (2) buybacks bleeding cash out from the corporate sector, and (3) sharply declining investment spending in the U.S., where large firms depend on stock markets and where activists are important, as compared to advanced economies that do not depend as much on stock markets.
>
> But these predicted economy-wide outcomes either are untrue or have not been shown to be true. Corporate R&D is not declining, corporate cash is not bleeding out, and the world's developed nations with neither American-style quarterly-oriented stock markets nor aggressive activist investors are investing no more in capital equipment than the U.S. The economy-wide picture is more one of capital markets moving capital from larger, older firms to smaller, younger ones. It is more a picture of a post-industrial economy doing more R&D than before, often in venture capital start-ups, and whose investment intensity depends on overall economic activity, not stock market trading or hedge fund activism. The economy-wide data could hide stock-market hits to R&D and America-specific declining capi-

tal spending, but if so, these have not been uncovered. Hence, the calamitous form of the stock-market-driven short-termist argument needs to be reconsidered, recalibrated, and, quite plausibly, rejected.

Public firms can be too bureaucratic for entrepreneurial-driven innovation; innovation may best be done in private, venture capital firms and then later routinized and monetized in public firms. Moreover, even if some public firms suffer from stock-market-driven short-termism, the overall economy need not, because venture capital firms and private equity firms can pick up the slack from public firms. Lastly comes the broadest question: why has a view that thus far lacks strong economy-wide evidentiary support become one of the few corporate governance issues that is widely accepted as true, and that attracts attention from the media, political players, policymakers, and the public.

A simple explanation is that the firm-by-firm, micro-data showing short-termism not to be a problem, and to often be an economic benefit, may be correct. Perhaps the short-termist idea is overblown, pushed rhetorically by corporate executives and their representatives as justifying according executives and boards yet more autonomy from shareholders. Executives have self-interested reasons to push the short-termism story, as it justifies more executive autonomy and less power for shareholders.

Short-termism theory also serves executives in deflecting blame. The polity distrusts large corporations, seeing them as not run for the average person and as means to perpetuate a wealthy elite, while often stifling employees, customers, and society overall. The short-termist argument allows executives to deflect those charges and point a finger at Wall Street: "We're not the problem," they can say. "It's the short-term traders and the activist shareholders that prevent us from being the good guys we'd really otherwise be. Our hands are tied."

Another but subtle self-interested channel is in play. The ideology of short-termism gives believing executives a coherent world view. They are not being selfish when seeking power to elide shareholders and diminish shareholder authority inside the corporation; they are doing the right thing for the economy and society. It is not self-aggrandizement. Ideological coherence—the banishment of self-doubt—provides its own source of managerial power.

A more insidious and destabilizing version of this political thesis has not been vividly raised. Stock markets could have become efficiently more short-term because product cycles are shortening, technology is changing more rapidly than ever, and the impact of that technological change is wider, deeper, and more disruptive than before. These market forces are channeled into and through the corporation, which cannot or at least does not provide security for its constituents. But even if this efficiency dynamic is true—and I believe it to be largely true—understanding that truth will not end the problem: whether it's efficient or not, people whose working lives, personal lives, and sense of self are disrupted by workplace change and employment disruption will react. They often blame markets, financial and otherwise. This short-termist criticism is accurate: markets caused the disruption, irrespective of whether markets were efficiently or inefficiently short-

> term. Those affected react politically and can conveniently, even if inaccurately, call the problem stock market "short-termism."
>
> But this possibility would mean that the truth or falsity of the stock market short-termist idea is politically and socially unimportant. Even if change brings about economic progress overall, that overall progress fails to comfort those who lose from the transformed economy. We thus have more than a simple interpretive problem at hand—does the evidence support short-termism as perniciously coming from excessive stock-market trading?—but serious conflict. And it may well be serious conflict that will not abate.

Mark J. Roe, *Stock Market Short-Termism's Impact* (2018) [available on SSRN]. In a follow-up study, Roe points out that if short-termism really existed, one would expect (1) investment spending in the United States to be declining faster than in Europe and Japan, where large companies depend less on stock markets for capital and where shareholder activists are less influential; (2) cash from large share buybacks inducing a bleeding out of cash from the U.S. corporate sector; and (3) economy-wide declines in corporate R&D spending. Mark Roe, *Looking for the Economy-Wide Effects of Stock Market Short-Termism* (2021) [available on SSRN]. In this more recent study, Roe finds that:

> U.S. corporate R&D spending, far from falling, has been rising since the 1970, and is rising faster than the economy is growing. And corporate cash holdings (as a percentage of total assets), are at near record high levels. More telling is that the pattern of net payouts by S&P 500 companies tracks new investment into smaller public companies.
>
> While critics see short-termism as damaging American R&D, the numbers show corporate R&D spending to be rising, while government support for innovation and R&D has been falling since the financial crisis. If innovation needs more support, it's the government cutbacks that would first seem to need to be addressed.

In the end, Roe seems to regard financial short-termism in the United States as at most a modest problem. But what about the business community's failure to notice and act on the terrible ecological and human storms on the horizon? Here, Roe offers a useful way of seeing the problem:

> What precisely is stock market short-termism? Stock markets that overemphasize immediate results and discount long-term results too heavily are too short-term. Critics say this affliction is severe and the distorted time horizon leads too many public firms to stop investing in good projects, to shut down work on viable R&D, and to use up cash by buying back stock when the firm has good ways to invest that cash.
>
> Some readers will balk at this view. "That's Type-A short-termism, yes—it's focused on low investment, declining R&D, and stock buybacks.
>
> But that's not the only kind of short-termism. And it's not even the worst kind. Due to stock market short-term pressure, firms also degrade their workforce, pollute the environment, skirt sound regulation to damage stakeholders, cause financial crises, and risk climate catastrophe.
>
> Recent rhetoric on corporate social responsibility, corporate purpose, and corporate respect for ESG issues has become inextricably

> intertwined with stock-market short-termism. But the two should be untangled. Distorted financial time horizons (Type A financial short-termism) has little to do with corporate responsibility and purpose issues (Type B social short-termism). Although linking the two is widely accepted and some advocate for big corporations to be controlled by long-term shareholders who better appreciate the environment and social issues, Type B problems are not primarily time-horizon problems.
>
> In fact, in talking about Type B social problems, we should strike the "short-term" modifier. Corporate indifference to environmental and social problems is to be condemned, but it's generally due to truncated corporate time horizons. For example, no one would say that a corporation that leaks toxins into an aquifer year-after-year or that exploits employees decade-after-decade is sound because the malfeasance is long-term. It's the nature of the malfeasance that's objectionable, not its duration. And its long-term nature makes it more objectionable, not less.

Mark J. Roe, Missing the Target: Why Stock Market Short-Termism Is Not the Problem (2022 Oxford University Press) (Chapter 3 – Social Costs from Stock Market Driven Corporate Short-Termism).

Glimmers of Hope

If short-termism is a "temporal externality," the question becomes how to overcome our natural inclination to discount future costs (risks). One way is to change our vocabulary. This is happening in business, which over the last couple decades has become aware of the risk of disregarding risk. Accounting risk, which was at the heart of the accounting scandals of 2000, was addressed by more attention to manipulated financial statements. Management risk, which was at the heart of the subprime mortgage crisis of 2008, was addressed by more attention to bank lending practices and valuation of financial assets. Human capital management, which has increasingly been recognized as a core part of the modern networked business, is being addressed by more attention to employee well-being and thus productivity. And climate risk, which has been seen as too far in the future to deserve current attention, is showing itself to be more present and thus more in need of attention.

Along these lines, it has been argued that large, diversified institutional shareholders should be focused on the risks to their overall portfolio, not the risks of specific companies—and this is now beginning to happen. For example, suppose the manager of an investment fund concludes that if ExxonMobil (one of its portfolio companies) generates an extra $10 billion of revenues from its oil and gas business, that will result in climate-change losses of more than $10 billion in other portfolio companies—what should the manager do? According to modern portfolio theory, the fund should then take measures (sell ExxonMobil or use engagement) to prevent ExxonMobil from generating these portfolio losses, given that its current oil and gas activities hurt the fund's overall returns.

Professor Jeffrey Gordon (Columbia Law School) has noticed this and has argued that asset managers of large diversified funds "should seek to mitigate systematic risk, which most notably would include climate change risk, financial stability risk, and social stability risk." Jeffrey N. Gordon, *Systematic Stewardship* (2021) [available on SSRN]. Professor Gordon notes that this "portfolio approach follows the already-established pattern of assets managers' pursuit of corporate governance measures that may increase returns across the portfolio if even not maximizing for particular firms." Systematic risk reduction, Gordon argues, both improves risk-adjusted portfolio returns and avoids harm across the entire economy—harm that would damage the interests of employees and consumers, as well as shareholders.

All of this adds up to corporate intermediaries—namely, institutional shareholders and corporate boards—paying more attention to systematic risks. The days that "it's somebody else's problem" may be beginning to recede.

* * *

Concluding Thoughts

How Do We Count?

The problem of short-termism is a counting problem. How do we count things happening now and the same things in the future? Do we count the future things less, the same, maybe more?

Here's a counting question for you to consider.
How many words are there in blue berries?

A. One
B. Two
C. Three
D. More than three
E. Please, let's move to the next chapter on "board myopia"

A is the answer that most people give. Most everyone, including my very best law students, when asked the question say there is only one word in "blueberries." Sadly, this is what law school does to you.

B is a plausible answer. When I ask the question orally, I pause between "blue" and "berries." And, for this written question, if you look carefully, you'll notice that there is a tiny space in the text between the two words. That is, sometimes it's important to pay close attention.

C is also a good answer. Think about it. "Blue" is a word. And "berries" is a word. But "berries" is plural. How can you count something that's plural as one? Plural denotes two or more. That means "berries" has to be at least two. Thus, there have to be least three words in "blue berries."

D is the correct answer. If you think a bit more deeply, you'll realize that the question was really, how many words can be formed from the letters B-L-U-E-B-E-R-R-I-E-S. That, as you know, is something many game books ask—the something people work on when they fly in an airplane. Let's see. B-L-U-E / B-L-U-R-B / L-U-B-E / B-U-R-I-E-S. And so on. (Do you feel like I threw you under the B-U-S?)

E is an acceptable answer. Because we'll next consider how nonduality thinking—the type that led so many of my students to answer A—is endemic in the corporation. In particular, it's almost hard-wired in the public corporation's board of directors. This has been one of the driving forces behind the Great Unraveling, the failure of humanity to live within the "sustainability doughnut."

Chapter 2.3

Board Mono-Culture

We next consider another unsustainable aspect of the US public corporation—namely, its tendency to have boards of directors composed of like-minded corporate executives, rather than a more representative set of corporate constituents.

This non-egalitarian, inward-looking feature of the US public corporation is not necessarily part of its legal design, but instead is cultural—though fostered by legal rules that place in the hands of incumbent directors the decision of who is nominated to the board and judicial acceptance of the resulting board myopia.

Thus, the design of the modern corporation—specifically, the US-based multinational—has come to be self-referential. The cookie-cutter composition and interlocked nature of many boards of US public corporations reinforce the tendency toward inward-focused (and often externalizing and short-termist) decision-making. The modern public corporation's reliance on a relatively small cadre of like-minded business leaders generates a "club" mentality, sometimes referred to as *groupthink*.

This club mentality finds expression in the regulatory capture of government by corporations, through corporate lobbying, social posturing, and spending on political elections—the subject of the next chapter.

Chapter's Focus

You will want to focus on the composition of boards of directors in US public corporations and what kinds of persons become directors. You will also want to understand the nomination and election process for directors, and how reform efforts have fared, especially the story of proxy access.

You will want to focus on how and why corporate executives tend to be inward-focused, given the "corporate culture" in which they live and how courts defer to this culture and the "structural bias" that arises from board membership—that is, the tendency of directors to "go along to get along."

You will want to consider the debate on whether "insulated boards" (especially, staggered boards) take a longer-term perspective (and thus arguably produce greater social value) or whether they create a tendency to disregard shareholder value (and thus arguably diminish social value). You will also find interesting the studies on "sociopathies" among top corporate executives, the feeder population for corporate boards of US public corporations.

What we face. Mono-cultures are pervasive. They are imbedded in the human condition. Tinkering with law at the margins is unlikely to do much unless we address the dynamics of the underlying social phenomena.

> She asked for a raise. They almost fired her.
>
> It wasn't what she expected. One of our administrative assistants simply explained what it was like to work full-time, making barely ten bucks an hour. She walked right into the provost's office, catching him off guard. He listened patiently for a few minutes and then launched into this whole bit about how he "knew what it was like" to "feel like you don't have enough money," but "there's nothing I can do."
>
> That's when she interrupted him. She said he couldn't possibly understand what it was like, because he'd been working in administration for decades now, making well above $100,000 a year.
>
> His little tricks weren't going to work this time. No, this time she was going to explain the facts. She couldn't afford groceries. She'd fallen and fractured her wrist last year. The ER doctor had recommended surgery, but she couldn't afford it, so it just healed "however it was going to." She'd lost partial function in that hand now. She couldn't afford to go to the dentist. She couldn't afford to fix her car, or her appliances. Her life was one hula-hoop of bills and debt, and more bills.
>
> How did the provost respond? He decided to file a disciplinary action report on her, for being disruptive. That's how much he truly understood what she was going through. That's how much he cared.
>
> So, no raise.
>
> Recently, I found out that our HR department routinely steers full-time employees at my university to our campus food pantry. Teachers like me have been donating to it for years now. We were under the impression it was for our students, not our staff.
>
> Imagine how that feels.

Amy Wildfire, *We Can't Keep Going Like This*, Medium (June 13, 2021).

2.3.1 Snapshot of Current Board Composition

Before exploring some of the specifics of board composition, it's useful to get an overarching picture. Here is a description from the Conference Board (an independent corporate research group) on the current status of who sits on the corporate boards of US public corporations:

> Despite the demand for refreshment and more diversity, the makeup of many public company boards remains unchanged.

Corporate governance has undergone a profound transformation in the last two decades, as a result of the legislative and regulatory changes that have expanded director responsibilities as well as the rise of more vocal shareholders. Yet the composition of the board of directors has not changed as rapidly as other governance practices, and to this day many public company boards do not see any turnover that is not the result of retirement at the end of a fairly long tenure.

According to a comprehensive review of SEC filings made in 2018, 50.4% of Russell 3000 companies and 42.5% of S&P 500 companies disclosed no change whatsoever in the composition of their board of directors.

Directors are in for a long ride: their average tenure exceeds 10 years. About one-fourth of Russell 3000 directors who step down do so after more than 15 years of service. The longest average board member tenures are seen in the financials (13.2 years), consumer staples (11.1 years), and real estate (11 years) industries.

Despite calls for more inclusiveness and diverse skills, companies continue to value prior board experience in their director selection. Only a quarter of firms select directors who have never served on a public company board before. Further, corporate boards remain inaccessible to younger generations of business leaders, with the directors under age 60 mostly only in new-economy sectors such as IT and communications. Only 10% of Russell 3000 directors and 6.3% of S&P 500 directors are younger than 50, and in both indexes about one-fifth of board members are older than 70.

While there has been some progress on gender diversity, a staggering 20% of firms in the Russell 3000 still have no female representatives on their boards. Moreover, even though women are elected as corporate directors in larger numbers than before, almost all board chair positions remain held by men (only 4.1% of Russell 3000 companies have a female board chair).

Board knowledge about climate change

Research reveals a disconnect between what corporate directors say about the significance of climate change and their actual knowledge. Gavin Hinks, *Boards Lack the Right Knowledge Set for Effective Climate Policies*, Board Agenda (Dec. 15, 2021) (describing study by executive search firm that many UK boards "have yet to obtain the right knowledge for handling their climate policies, while others have yet to define the appropriate targets to ensure they're on track to meet the needs of a net zero world").

One way to find out if somebody knows the basics of climate change is to ask, "Can you explain how the following words are connected? Gulf stream, Greenland, salinity." Here's the answer, if you're curious: Heather Murphy, *A Crucial System of Ocean Currents Is Faltering, Research Suggests*, NYT (Aug. 5, 2021). Kinda chilling—no?

Periodically evaluating director performance is critical to a more meritocratic and dynamic boardroom. However, even though many board members consider the performance of at least one fellow director as suboptimal, in the Russell 3000, only 14.2% of companies disclose that the contribution of individual directors is reviewed annually.

Among smaller companies, staggered board structures also stand in the way of change. Almost 60%of firms with revenue under $1 billion continue to retain a classified board and hold annual elections only for one class of their directors, not all. And while just 9.5% of financial institutions with asset value of $100 billion or higher have director classes, it rises to 44.1% for those with asset values under $10 billion.

Though declining in popularity, a simple plurality-voting standard remains prevalent. This voting standard allows incumbents in uncontested elections to be reelected to the board even if a majority of the shares were voted against them. In the Russell 3000, 51.5% of boards retain plurality voting.

Finally, only 15.5% of the Russell 3000 companies have adopted some type of proxy access bylaws. Such bylaws allow qualified shareholders to include their own director nominees on the proxy ballot, alongside candidates proposed by management. In all other companies, shareholders that want to bring forward a different slate of nominees must pay to circulate their own proxy materials.

The Conference Board, *Corporate Board Practices in the Russell 3000 and S&P 500* (2019).

Corporate elites

Professor Stephen Bainbridge (UCLA Law), an astute observer of Corporate America offered the following take on who now inhabit corporate C-suites:

> In 1995 Christopher Lasch in his *The Revolt of the Elites* identified an emergent split between the New Elites and the rest of society. In particular, Lasch explained that "the new elites . . . regard the masses with mingled scorn and apprehension." They dismissed the masses' values as "mindless patriotism, religious fundamentalism, racism, homophobia, and retrograde views of women." These changes became trends that accelerated in subsequent years.
>
> A quarter-century later, Lasch's new elites have risen to the top of corporate hierarchies. They brought their values into the C-suite. CEOs increasingly reflect the values of the Blue state coastal bubbles in which they are embedded, especially on environmental and social issues. No Fortune 100 CEOs contributed to Donald Trump's 2016 presidential campaign, for example, but eleven gave to Hillary Clinton [and 89 did not]. More generally, "liberal groups accounted for eight of the top ten ideological causes of the ultra-rich, and seven of the ten congressional candidates most dependent on money from such people were Democrats."
>
> As a result, as a Slate essay observed, "Fortune 500 companies today are socially liberal, especially on areas surrounding diversity, gay rights, and immigration; they are unabashedly in favor of free trade and globalization, express concern about climate change, and embrace renewable energy." In doing so, they are simply reflecting the changing values of their CEOs.

2.3.2 Process of Director Nomination and Election

The nomination process in the US public corporation, as a practical matter, rests almost exclusively in the hands of the board of directors. Generally, shareholders can nominate their own slate of directors, but must bear the costs of sending proxy materials to fellow shareholders –which in a public corporation is usually prohibitively expensive given that election related expenses are reimbursable only if the insurgent slate wins.

Even though boards of directors have largely insulated themselves from shareholder nominations, boards have not been immune from shareholder pressures to be more "democratic." In the 1980s there was a movement to have directors serve three-year terms, with only one-third of the board up for election each year. These "staggered boards" proved to be a powerful antitakeover mechanism, but have been on the decline as shareholders have pressured corporate management to "declassify" the board so that all directors are up for election annually.

There are other winds of change. A recent reform movement called "proxy access"—now prevalent in the largest US corporations—gives shareholders access to the company's proxy ballot to nominate their own director candidates.

Corporations Examples and Explanations

(9th ed. 2021)

Alan R. Palmiter

§9.4.3 Proxy Access

Over the last couple decades U.S. corporate governance has grappled with whether to open the board nomination process in public companies so shareholders can place their nominees in the company's proxy materials *at company expense*. The history of "proxy access" has been convoluted and interesting. Nearly all the actors in modern corporate governance have played a role: activist and institutional shareholders, corporate management, the SEC, the federal courts, the U.S. Congress, the Delaware legislature, the Delaware courts, and even corporate law professors.

Proposed Rule 14a-11 (2003). Proxy access began in 2003 when the SEC proposed a new Rule 14a-11 that would have permitted shareholders (or a group of shareholders) holding five percent of a company's voting shares to nominate one to three directors to the company's board—provided a majority of shareholders had authorized such a vote in the previous election cycle or 35 percent had withheld their vote from a particular board nominee. See Exchange Act Rel. No. 48,626 (2003) (proposing release). The proposal met a firestorm of opposition from corporate management. At first the SEC dithered and then eventually decided not to pursue the rulemaking.

AFSCME proposal (2005). In response to the SEC's inaction, activist shareholders (supported by corporate law professors) began a company-by-company movement proposing amendments to company bylaws to create a process for shareholders to use the company's proxy mechanism to nominate a "short slate" constituting fewer than a majority of directors. Eventually, the SEC took the position that such proposals were excludable as "related to an election" under the then-applicable Rule 14a-8 exclusion, but the Second Circuit held that the exclusion did not cover share-

One person

New York City Comptroller Scott Stringer announced his "Boardroom Accountability Project" in November 2014. Frustrated by the inability to nominate directors to the board—and troubled by stories of dysfunctional boards at many companies—Stringer headed a coalition of large institutional shareholders that targeted 75 corporations for proxy access bylaws. The companies were chosen because of the known risks to which they had exposed shareholders: 33 were in carbon-intensive industries; 24 had little or no gender, racial, or ethnic diversity on their boards; and 25 had other problems. As a result of this announcement, shareholders celebrated—the stock price in those 75 companies rising 0.53 percent on just the announcement. As proxy access spread in the following years, researchers estimated that company-by-company proxy access had added at least $132 billion in value to US listed companies. Just one person!

holder proposals seeking to create proxy access. See *AFSCME v. AIG, Inc.*, 462 F.3d 121 (2d. Cir. 2006). In response, the SEC amended Rule 14a-8 to overrule the court's decision, allowing companies to exclude such shareholder proposals. Exchange Act Rel. No. 56,914 (2007).

Dodd-Frank and re-promulgated Rule 14a-11 (2010). Without a proxy access rule and faced with a revised Rule 14a-8 that limited shareholder-initiated proxy access, institutional shareholders turned to Congress. In 2010 Congress put proxy access back on the corporate governance agenda when it passed the Dodd-Frank Act and specifically authorized the SEC to promulgate a proxy access rule. Dodd-Frank §971. Within months, the SEC accepted the Dodd-Frank invitation and re-promulgated Rule 14a-11 in even stronger form than before. Exchange Act Rel. No. 62,674 (2010) (permitting nomination of directors constituting at most one-fourth of the board by shareholders, or groups of shareholders, that had held 1, 3, or 5 percent of company's voting shares for at least three years, the percentage varying with company size).

***Business Roundtable* case (2011).** The plot thickened, however, when corporate management (through the Business Roundtable and U.S. Chamber of Commerce) challenged the reincarnated Rule 14a-11 in federal court for failing to adequately consider the costs and benefits of the new governance rights granted to shareholders. The D.C. Circuit agreed and held that the SEC had failed to consider the rule's effect on "efficiency, competition and capital formation." *Business Roundtable v. SEC*, 647 F.3d 1144 (D.C. Cir. 2011) (vacating rule). Even though Dodd-Frank seemed to have authorized the SEC to make this cost-benefit determination, the SEC decided not to appeal the decision to the Supreme Court and not to propose the rule again, apparently worried it could not meet the (unusually) high standard of review set by the D.C. Circuit.

Company-by-company bylaws. Despite the failure of proxy access to become an SEC rule, many shareholder activists decided to take matters into their own hands and returned to the

Palace coup at ExxonMobil

In April 2021, a hedge fund named Engine No. 1 executed a soft coup against one of the world's most powerful companies, ExxonMobil. Although it controlled only 0.02 percent of the company's shares, the "little engine that could" was able to place two renewable energy experts on the oil company's board of directors.

Major institutional shareholders, which have lately goaded oil companies to do more about climate change, had started to punish executives over their inaction. ExxonMobil, the biggest of Big Oil, was their first target.

Exxon had gotten plenty of warning before the coup. But Darren Woods, Exxon's CEO, had brushed off the possibility. Then when Exxon's board slate started to lose in the proxy count, Woods paused the shareholders' meeting for an hour and made pleading calls to major shareholders. He lost anyway.

company-by-company approach. The SEC had reopened this door in 2010 when it revised Rule 14a-8 (as part of its Rule 14a-11 rulemaking) to permit shareholders to propose bylaw changes to establish procedures for nominating directors in the company's proxy materials. Shareholder activists were further emboldened by changes to the Delaware corporate statute, added by the Delaware legislature in 2009, which made clear that shareholders can amend company bylaws to provide for proxy access as well as mandatory reimbursement of proxy expenses incurred by shareholders in director elections. See Del. GCL §§112, 113; see also MBCA §2.06(c).

Widespread adoption of proxy access. In the past few years, proxy access has gone from being virtually nonexistent in U.S. public corporations to a mainstay of U.S. corporate governance. After a successful campaign in 2014 by the NY Comptroller to create proxy access at 68 different public companies—successful in xx of them—proxy access became one of the most widespread and successful shareholder proposals.

Palace coup at ExxonMobil (cont'd)

Engine No. 1 prevailed because it won the votes of both old and new institutional shareholders. Older state-pension funds sought to protect their interests in the overall stock market. And newer financial firms (like State Street and BlackRock) used their single-digit percentages of Exxon stock to advance the long-term interests of their indexed funds in the broader market. Working together, these funds brought Exxon to heel.

Many noticed that this was weird. When have shareholders seen capitalism as incompatible with solving climate change? Yet, Exxon's shareholders—that is, the owners of capital—were recruited to join the fight against climate change. Wall Street battled Big Oil. Government watched from the sidelines.

See Robinson Meyer, *Wall Street's Skirmish with Exxon Is "Monumental,"* The Atlantic (June 1, 2021).

As of 2021, two-thirds of large public companies and 90 percent of the Fortune 100 have adopted proxy access. In many instances, proxy access bylaws were added not by shareholder vote, but instead by corporate boards in response to shareholder proposals or to stave off shareholder activism.

Use of proxy access. As of 2022, no institutional shareholder or group of shareholders has used a company's proxy-access mechanism to nominate their own candidates to the board.

2.3.3 Corporate Director Networks and Interlocks

So how do board networks work? One important piece of early research into corporate networks examined them in ten countries, finding (as a starting point) that the corporation was a dominant force in the American economy and served in a leadership function across many realms of society including technology and growth. Stokman, Ziegler & Scott, *Networks of Corporate Power* (1985). Specifically, the book looked at director interlocks, defined as the relationship that results when one board member serves on multiple boards of different companies. The authors found that the United States had "a more densely connected" corporate network than countries like Britain. Additionally, their research (based on board composition in the early 1980s) suggested that a substantial percentage of the interlocks consisted of directors who held at least four board seats.

There have been some changes in the past couple decades. For example, recent studies have found a decline in "over-boarding"—that is, a decline in the phenomenon of directors serving on multiple boards and thus diluting firm value. For example, in 2012, about half of all directors on the boards of US public companies served on only one board. Further, on average, corporate directors who served on multiple boards served on 1.7 additional boards:

Directorships held	All firms: Directors	S&P 500 directors		Non-S&P 500 directors		
1	5449	47.41%	1205	35.47%	4244	52.41%
2	3255	28.32%	1034	30.44%	2221	27.43%
3	1701	14.80%	677	19.93%	1024	12.65%
4	701	6.10%	296	8.71%	405	5.00%
5	245	2.13%	116	3.41%	129	1.59%
6	78	0.68%	37	1.09%	41	0.51%
7	46	0.40%	20	0.59%	26	0.32%
8	17	0.15%	11	0.32%	6	0.07%
10	2	0.02%	1	0.03%	1	0.01%
Total directors	11,494		3397		8097	
Number of firms	2077		532		1545	

A recent study from 2016 summarized current research on the question of director over-boarding:

> The literature disagrees on the link between so-called busy boards (where many independent directors hold multiple board seats) and firm performance. On balance, however, the results suggest a negative association between board busyness and firm performance.

Why does a director with many directorships undermine firm value? Shouldn't a well-connected director increase the value of the (many) firms on which he serves? A finance article from a few years ago describes the close personal and professional connections between directors in US public corporations. Director interlocks are regulated by antitrust law, which prohibits directors in the same industry from sitting on competitors' boards, but the antitrust rules do not apply when directors are from different industries. When directors serve on interlocked boards—that is, when two directors on one board also serve together on another board—they tend to "go along to get along." In fact, studies show directors' desire to be invited to other boards makes them even more mono-cultural, more willing to please the dominant "group paradigm." Shareholder interests (and more broadly society's interests in pluralism) are thus disserved.

2.3.4 Responses to Insulated Corporate Boards

Judicial Attitudes Toward Structural Bias

By and large, courts have accepted the clubbish nature of corporate boards. The Delaware Supreme Court, for example, has accepted that corporate boards can be composed of like-minded people while directors somehow still retain their "independence." Even when directors are professional and social friends, the courts in Delaware have found the directors to be "independent" and thus capable of objectivity in the face of directorial conflicts of interest. That is, Delaware judges accept that the "structural bias" prevalent on US corporate boards is a way of life.

The case below illustrates this judicial willingness to accept structural bias. But first some background. In Delaware, judicial review of board decisions often turns on whether the decision was by independent directors—that is, nonmanagement, outside directors.

Studying corporate governance

Lately, a good deal of law and management scholarship has turned to the question: What kind of corporate governance improves shareholder value? See Offer Eldar, *A Lawyer's Guide to Empirical Corporate Governance* (2021) [available on SSRN] (pointing out that most studies: (1) compare firms with and without the governance provisions under study, (2) evaluate the value of firms before and after such provisions, and (3) evaluate the effect on shareholder value). Does this seem right? Aren't there societal values—such as diversity, ecological sensitivity, and social equality—that shareholder value does not capture?

(1) Pre-suit demand: Delaware courts require that shareholders (before filing a derivative suit) must first make a demand for action by the board; if the board is composed of a majority of independent and disinterested directors, the suit will be dismissed.
(2) Dismissal of shareholder litigation: Delaware courts give deference to a board committee composed of independent and disinterested directors after shareholder derivative litigation has been filed; if the independent and disinterested committee requests dismissal of the litigation on an informed and reasonable basis, the court will (after an independent review) dismiss the litigation.
(3) Takeovers: Delaware courts will defer to a board committee composed of independent directors in negotiating the terms of a merger or other acquisition, even when there are conflicts of interest (such as with a parent company having a controlling interest in the company).

In the following case, the Delaware Supreme Court decided that general allegations of social/professional ties and friendship were not sufficient to question the independence of directors who were tasked with deciding whether pre-suit demand would be futile.

The plaintiff alleged that Martha Stewart (a famous TV celebrity and entrepreneur) breached her duties of loyalty and care by selling stock of another company (ImClone) and then making misleading statements to the media about the sale. The shareholder plaintiff contended that demand on the board would be futile because social and business connections created a reasonable doubt as to the independence of a majority of the board of directors. The Court of Chancery held that demand was required—and thus dismissed the suit—because the plaintiff had not alleged specific facts to demonstrate a lack of independence, and the Delaware Supreme Court affirmed.

Beam ex. rel. Martha Stewart Living Omnimedia, Inc. v. Stewart

(Del. 2004)

The plaintiff, Monica A. Beam, owns shares of Martha Stewart Living Omnimedia, Inc. (MSO). Beam filed a derivative action in the Court of Chancery against Martha Stewart, the five other members of MSO's board of directors, and former board member L. John Doerr. In four counts, Beam's complaint alleged that Stewart breached her fiduciary duties of loyalty and care by illegally selling ImClone stock in December of 2001 and by mishandling the media attention that followed, thereby jeopardizing the financial future of MSO. The Court of Chancery dismissed the complaint because Beam failed to plead particularized facts demonstrating presuit demand futility.

When Beam filed the complaint in the Court of Chancery, the MSO board of directors consisted of six members: Stewart, Sharon L. Patrick, Arthur C. Martinez, Darla D. Moore, Naomi O. Seligman, and Jeffrey W. Ubben. The Chancellor concluded that the complaint alleged sufficient facts to support the conclusion that two of the directors, Stewart and Patrick, were not disinterested or independent for purposes of considering a presuit demand.

The Court of Chancery found that Stewart's potential civil and criminal liability for the acts underlying Beam's claim rendered Stewart an interested party and therefore unable to consider demand. The Court also found that Patrick's position as president and chief operating officer of MSO and inside director, together with the substantial compensation she receives from the company, raised a reasonable doubt as to her ability objectively to consider demand. The defendants do not challenge the Court's conclusions with respect to Patrick and Stewart.

We now address the plaintiff's allegations concerning the independence of the other board members. We must determine if the following allegations of the complaint, and the reasonable inferences that may flow from them, create a reasonable doubt of the independence of either Martinez, Moore or Seligman:

[The court quotes, from the Plaintiffs' complaint, allegations regarding Martinez, Moore and Seligman.]

Decision of the Court of Chancery

The Chancellor found that Beam had not alleged sufficient facts to support the conclusion that demand was futile because he determined that the complaint failed to raise a reasonable doubt that these outside directors are independent of Stewart. Because Patrick and Stewart herself are not independent for demand purposes, all the plaintiff need show is that one of the remaining directors is not independent, there being only six board members.

As to these three directors, it is appropriate here to quote the Chancellor's analysis of the allegations regarding these directors:

> **Martinez.** The factual allegations regarding Stewart's friendship with Martinez are inadequate to raise a reasonable doubt of his independence. While employed by Sears, Martinez developed business ties to MSO due to Sears' marketing of a substantial quantity of MSO products. Martinez was recruited to serve on MSO's board of directors by Beers, who is described as Stewart's longtime personal friend and confidante and who was at that time

an MSO director. Shortly after Martinez joined MSO's board, Patrick was quoted in a magazine article saying, "Arthur [Martinez] is an old friend to both me and Martha [Stewart]."

Weighing against these factors, the amended complaint discloses that Martinez has been an executive and director for major corporations since at least 1990. At present he serves as a director for four prominent corporations, including MSO, and is the chairman of the Federal Reserve Bank of Chicago. One might say that Martinez's reputation for acting as a careful fiduciary is essential to his career – a matter in which he would surely have a material interest. Furthermore, the complaint does not give a single example of any action by Martinez that might be construed as evidence of even a slight inclination to disregard his duties as a fiduciary for any reason. In this context, I cannot reasonably infer that the friendship between Stewart and Martinez raises a reasonable doubt of Martinez's ability to evaluate demand independently of Stewart's personal interests.

Moore. The allegations regarding the friendship between Moore and Stewart are somewhat more detailed, yet still fall short of raising a reasonable doubt about Moore's ability properly to consider the demand. In 1995, Stewart's lawyer, Allen Grubman, hosted a wedding reception for his daughter. Among those in attendance at the reception were Moore, Stewart, and Waksal. In addition, Fortune magazine published an article in 1996 that focused on the close personal friendships among Moore, Stewart, and Beers. In September 2001, when Beers resigned from MSO's board of directors, Moore was selected to replace her. Although the amended complaint lists fewer positions of fiduciary responsibility for Moore than were listed for Martinez, it is clear that Moore's professional reputation similarly would be harmed if she failed to fulfill her fiduciary obligations.

To my mind, this is quite a close call. Perhaps the balance could have been tipped by additional, more detailed allegations about the closeness or nature of the friendship, details of the business and social interactions between the two, or allegations raising additional considerations that might inappropriately affect Moore's ability to impartially consider pursuit of a lawsuit against Stewart. On the facts pled, however, I cannot say that I have a reasonable doubt of Moore's ability to properly consider demand.

Seligman. No particular felicity is alleged to exist between Stewart and Seligman. The amended complaint reports in ominous tones, however, that Seligman, who is a director both for MSO and for John Wiley Sons [a book publisher], contacted JWS's chief executive officer about an unflattering biography of Stewart slated for publication. From this, the Court is asked to infer that Seligman acted in a way that preferred the protection of Stewart over her fiduciary duties to one or both of these companies. Without details about the nature of the contact, other than Seligman's wish to "express concern," it is impossible reasonably to make this inference. Stewart's public image, as plaintiff persistently asserts, is critical to the fortunes of MSO and its shareholders. As a fiduciary of MSO, Seligman may have felt obligated to express concern and seek additional information about the publication before its release. As a fiduciary of JWS, she could well have anticipated some risk of liability if any of the unflattering characterizations of Stewart proved to be insufficiently researched or made carelessly.

There is no allegation that Seligman made any inappropriate attempt to prevent the publication of the biography. Nor does the amended complaint indicate whether the biography was ultimately published and, if so, whether Seligman's inquiry is believed to have resulted in any changes to the content of the book. As alleged, this matter does not serve to raise a reasonable doubt of Seligman's independence or ability to consider demand on the complaint.

* * *

In sum, plaintiff offers various theories to suggest reasons that the outside directors might be inappropriately swayed by Stewart's wishes or interests, but fails to plead sufficient facts that could permit the Court reasonably to infer that one or more of the theories could be accurate.

Demand Futility and Director Independence

The issue in this case is the quantum of doubt about a director's independence that is "reasonable" in order to excuse a pre-suit demand. The parties argue opposite sides of that issue.

The key principle upon which this area of our jurisprudence is based is that the directors are entitled to a presumption that they were faithful to their fiduciary duties.

A director will be considered unable to act objectively with respect to a pre-suit demand if he or she is interested in the outcome of the litigation or is otherwise not independent. A director's interest may be shown by demonstrating a potential personal benefit or detriment to the director as a result of the decision. The primary basis upon which a director's independence must be measured is whether the director's decision is based on the corporate merits of the subject before the board, rather than extraneous considerations or influences.

Independence Is a Contextual Inquiry

Independence is a fact-specific determination made in the context of a particular case. In order to show lack of independence, the complaint of a stockholder-plaintiff must create a reasonable doubt that a director is not so "beholden" to an interested director (in this case Stewart) that his or her "discretion would be sterilized."

Personal Friendship

A variety of motivations, including friendship, may influence the demand futility inquiry. But, to render a director unable to consider demand, a relationship must be of a bias-producing nature. Allegations of mere personal friendship or a mere outside business relationship, standing alone, are insufficient to raise a reasonable doubt about a director's independence.

The facts alleged by Beam regarding the relationships between Stewart and these other members of MSO's board of directors largely boil down to a "structural bias" argument, which presupposes that the professional and social relationships that naturally develop among members of a board impede independent decision-making.

In the present case, the plaintiff attempted to plead affinity beyond mere friendship between Stewart and the other directors, but her attempt is not sufficient to demonstrate demand futility. Even if the alleged friendships may have preceded the directors' membership on MSO's board and did not necessarily arise out of that membership, these relationships are of the same nature as those giving rise to the structural bias argument.

Allegations that Stewart and the other directors moved in the same social circles, attended the same weddings, developed business relationships before joining the board, and described each other as "friends," even when coupled with Stewart's 94% voting power, are insufficient, without more, to rebut the presumption of independence. They do not provide a sufficient basis from which reasonably to infer that Martinez, Moore and Seligman may have been beholden to Stewart.

1. Seligman

Beam's allegations concerning Seligman's lack of independence raise an additional issue not present in the Moore and Martinez relationships. Those allegations are not necessarily based on a purported friendship between Seligman and Stewart. Rather, they are based on a specific past act by Seligman that, Beam claims, indicates Seligman's lack of independence from Stewart.

The bare fact that Seligman contacted JWS, on whose board Seligman also served, to dissuade JWS from publishing unfavorable references to Stewart, even if done at Stewart's request, is insufficient to create a reasonable doubt that Seligman is capable of considering pre-suit demand free of Stewart's influence.

Indeed, the reasonable inference is that Seligman's purported intervention on Stewart's behalf was of benefit to MSO and its reputation, which is allegedly tied to Stewart's reputation, as the Chancellor noted.

1. Moore

The Court of Chancery concluded that the plaintiff's allegations with respect to Moore's social relationship with Stewart presented "quite a close call." We do not agree that the facts as alleged present a "close call" with respect to Moore's independence. These allegations center on: (a) Moore's attendance at a wedding reception for the daughter of Stewart's lawyer where Stewart and Waksal were also present; (b) a *Fortune* magazine article focusing on the close personal relationships among Moore, Stewart and Beers; and (c) the fact that Moore replaced Beers on the MSO board. In our view, these bare social relationships clearly do not create a reasonable doubt of independence.

3. Stewart's 94% Stock Ownership

Beam attempts to bolster her allegations regarding the relationships between Stewart and Seligman and Moore by emphasizing Stewart's overwhelming voting control of MSO. That attempt also fails to create a reasonable doubt of independence. A stockholder's control of a corporation does not excuse presuit demand on the board without particularized allegations of relationships between the directors and the controlling stockholder demonstrating that the directors are beholden to the stockholder.

Debate on Staggered Boards

Do "chummy" boards—such as staggered boards where directors serve three-year terms and thus are somewhat insulated from outside pressures—produce good or poor results for shareholders? This question has gotten a lot of attention. Some argue that such boards are too insulated from shareholder pressures, and thus fail to focus on the long-term. See Lucian Bebchuk, The Myth that Insulating Boards Serves Long-Term Value (2013) [available on SSRN]. Others argue precisely the opposite—that insulating directors from shareholder pressure serves the corporation's long-term interests. See Martin Lipton, *Some Thoughts for Boards of Directors in 2015* (Dec. 2, 2014).

A recent study in Massachusetts-incorporated firms, all covered by a 1990 law requiring staggered boards, suggests that sometimes such boards improve shareholder value:

> We find that relative to a matched control group of companies, for treated companies the law led to an increase in [the much-criticized] Tobin's Q, investment in CAPEX and R&D, patents, higher-quality patented innovations, and resulted in higher profitability. These effects are concentrated in innovating firms, especially those facing greater Wall Street scrutiny. An increase in institutional and dedicated investors also accompanied the imposition of SBs, facilitating a longer-term orientation.

Robert Daines, Shelley Xin Li & Charles C.Y. Wang, *Can Staggered Boards Improve Value? Causal Evidence from* Massachusetts (2020) [available on SSRN]. Especially among start-ups with business plans that stock markets might have trouble understanding, staggered boards seem to allow the managers to focus on innovations and long-term plans. This illustrates that the debate on staggered boards yields not a single "yes or no" answer, but instead an "it depends."

Perhaps the staggered-board debate is too narrow. Isn't the better question not whether corporate boards serve shareholder interests, but whether they serve broader corporate and societal interests? For one, even if corporate boards serve "shareholder" interests, they may fail to serve the interests of the true "owners" of the corporation. Leo Strine has pointed out that because boards face short-term pressures from financial intermediaries (particularly from hedge funds and other institutional shareholders), these pressures may lead to results that do not reflect the interests of the "real" owners—the ultimate, long-term investors (pensioners, college savers, retirement savers, insured, and even citizens whose wealth is invested by sovereign wealth funds). See Leo Strine, *Can We Do Better by Ordinary Investors?* (2014) [available on SSRN].

Independent Chair

For the last decade, investors and scholars have assumed independent boards of directors serve as a robust check on management's power, thus ensuring the corporation does no harm. It is therefore not surprising that in addition to monitoring by external corporate gatekeepers (such as auditors, analysts and credit ratings), a new breed of internal gatekeepers has emerged: board gatekeepers.

Indeed, over the last decade, investors have pushed companies to install an independent chair on their board, or alternately, nominate a director as the Lead Independent Director. In both cases, these roles are meant to serve an independent gatekeeping function—a necessary guardrail against managements' ability to exert undue control over the boardroom. But a closer look at board gatekeepers' independence paints a concerning reality—they are often deprived of the powers necessary to rebalance the boardroom dynamic, and in many cases, their own independence is questionable at best.

2.3.5 Corporate "Groupthink"

Groupthink arises when a group of people desiring harmony or conformity engage in irrational or dysfunctional decision-making. Derived from the "doublethink" of George Orwell's *1984*, "groupthink" describes something more than our human tendency to conform, but extends to "rationalized conformity" where we explain group values as not only expedient, but also right and good. According to the psychologist Irving Janis, who in the 1970s pioneered research on the subject, the desire for cohesion becomes so powerful that we override "realistic appraisal" of the alternatives, resulting in a "moral deterioration" and sometimes "dehumanized action against outgroups."

Groupthink in business

Although groupthink often happens in political contexts—think Nazi Germany's decision to invade Russia, Watergate, and media predictions that Hillary Clinton would win in 2016—it can come up in other contexts, including business. The collapse of Swissair offers a case study. Swissair was an airline thought to be so financially stable it was called the "Flying Bank." Its board, composed of members with similar backgrounds and lacking in airline industry expertise, came to believe the company was invulnerable and unquestionably moral—two common symptoms of groupthink. One poor decision after another in the late 1990s eventually doomed the airline, which went bankrupt in 2002.

Corporate Groupthink in the Food Industry

The inward-looking nature of corporate boards, a "tone at the top" that permeates the US corporation is revealed in many ways. Below is a story of how executives in the food industry, though recognizing how junk food has led to an obesity epidemic in the United States, were unable to take effective action because of the corporate culture of "making profits." Rather than focusing outward on how unhealthy (though tasty) foods may harm consumers, not to mention the population, the focus of food companies is inward—on sales, competitive position, and the financial bottom line.

The Extraordinary Science of Addictive Junk Food

New York Times, February 20, 2013

Michael Moss

[redacted/paraphrased]

Michael Moss is an investigative reporter for The Times. He won a Pulitzer Prize in 2010 for his reporting on the meat industry.

On the evening of April 8, 1999, a long line of Town Cars and taxis pulled up to the Minneapolis headquarters of Pillsbury and discharged 11 men who controlled America's largest food companies. Nestlé was in attendance, as were Kraft and Nabisco, General Mills and Procter & Gamble, Coca-Cola and Mars. Rivals any other day, the CEOs and company presidents had come together for a rare, private meeting. On the agenda was one item: the emerging US obesity epidemic and how to deal with it. While the atmosphere was cordial, the men assembled were hardly friends. Their stature was defined by their skill in fighting one another for what they called "stomach share"—the amount of digestive space that any one company's brand can grab from the competition.

The meeting had been carefully scripted by James Behnke, the 55-year-old CEO of Pillsbury, who was "anxious but also hopeful" about the plan to have the country's leading food-company executives address America's growing obesity problem. There was concern also about the possibility of sugar taxes or other government action.

Behnke, a chemist with a PhD in food science, had been Pillsbury's chief technical officer and helped create a number of successful products, including microwaveable popcorn. Although he admired Pillsbury, he had become troubled by images of obese children who suffered from diabetes and exhibited early signs of hypertension and heart disease. Food-science experts had been painting an increasingly grim picture of the public's ability to cope with the industry's formulations—from the body's fragile controls on overeating to the hidden power of some processed foods to make people feel hungrier still. Behnke had decided the time had come to warn the other CEOs that his company and theirs might have over-designed and over-marketed products that raised health concerns.

The meeting took place in Pillsbury's auditorium. The VP of Kraft, Michael Mudd, was the first to speak. "Let me say right at the start, obesity among children is not an easy subject. There are no easy answers—for what the public health community must do to bring this problem under control or for what the industry should do. But this much is clear: For those of us who've looked hard at this issue, whether they're public health professionals or staff specialists in your own companies, we feel sure that the one thing we shouldn't do is nothing."

Mudd clicked through 114 slides projected on a screen behind him. As of 1999, most American adults were now considered overweight, with nearly one-quarter—40 million adults—defined as clinically obese. Obesity rates among children had more than doubled since 1980, with the number of kids considered obese above 12 million. (The nation's obesity rates would climb much higher.) Academia, the Centers for Disease Control and Prevention, the American Heart Association, and the American Cancer Society were all blaming the food companies. The secretary of agriculture had described obesity as a "national epidemic."

Recent obesity statistics

According to the Centers for Disease Control, obesity prevalence among American adults increased from 30.5 percent in 1999 to 42.4 percent in 2018, with severe obesity increasing from 4.7 percent to 9.2 percent during this period. And obesity rates were higher among non-Hispanic Black adults (49.6 percent) and Hispanic adults (44.8 percent). As of 2018, one in five kids in the United States was considered to be obese.

Mudd then did the unthinkable. He drew a connection to the last thing the CEOs wanted linked to their products: cigarettes. He quoted a Yale psychology/public health professor who said the processed-food industry should be seen as a public health menace: "As a culture, we've become upset by the tobacco companies advertising to children, but we sit idly by while the food companies do the very same thing. The toll taken on the public health by a poor diet rivals that taken by tobacco."

What to do? Mudd presented a plan in which food companies would first acknowledge some culpability. The industry would rely on the expertise of scientists—its own and others—to better understand what drove Americans to overeat. Then, acknowledging the role that packaged foods and drinks play in overeating, the industry would cut back on the use of salt, sugar and fat. Advertising would be critical with a new industrywide code on food marketing, especially to children.

When Mudd stopped talking, Stephen Sanger (the head of General Mills) stood up. His company had the most to lose in a fight against obesity. Under Sanger's leadership, General Mills had not only come to control the cereal aisle but also other parts of the grocery store. The company's Yoplait brand had made sweetened breakfast yogurt into "a veritable dessert" with twice as much sugar per serving as the company's marshmallow cereal Lucky Charms. But because of yogurt's image as wholesome, Yoplait's sales were soaring. And a Yoplait variation from a squeezable tube was aimed at kids.

According to those at the meeting, Sanger reminded the group that consumers were "fickle"—worried sometimes about sugar, other times about fat. General Mills, he said, offered products to dieters and other concerned shoppers, from low-sugar options to whole grains. But "people bought what they liked, and they liked what tasted good."

Sanger said that General Mills would not pull back. The company had a responsibility to the public and its shareholders. He would push onward, and he urged the others to do the same. Sanger's response effectively ended the meeting.

The meeting had been remarkable: that insiders would admit guilt, that the organizers had anticipated that the obesity epidemic was only starting, and that the imperative to satisfy the public's demand for unhealthy foods in the name of shareholder returns would be decisive.

What I found, over four years of research and reporting, was a conscious effort—taking place in labs and marketing meetings and grocery-store aisles—to get people hooked on foods that are convenient and inexpensive. I talked to more than 300 people in or formerly employed by the processed-food industry, from scientists to marketers to CEOs. Some were willing whistle-blowers, while others spoke reluctantly when presented with some of the thousands of pages of secret memos that I obtained from inside the food industry's operations.

[The remainder of the article describes "case studies . . . on how the foods are created and sold to people who, while not powerless, are extremely vulnerable to the intensity of these companies' industrial formulations and selling campaigns."]

The debate over whether government should dictate consumer choice—such as by taxing sugary drinks—can be highly controversial. New York City was forced to withdraw its proposal to tax larger sugary-drink bottles after the sugary drink industry threatened to sue, including on the basis of the constitutional rights of companies to advertise and sell what they choose. Instead, the city ended up relying on a media campaign that resulted in lower consumption of sugary drinks by adults and highschool students. See Kansagra, et al, *Reducing Sugar Drink Consumption: New York City's Approach*, Am J. Public Health (2015).

Elsewhere, attempts by government to tax sugary drinks have turned into a ferocious global policy brawl. In Colombia, for example, proponents of a sugary-drink tax faced intimidation and censorship. The woman who led an advocacy group in the country urging a 20 percent tax on sugary drinks was silenced by intimidation (men on motorcycles pounding on her car saying, "you know what will happen if you continue") and after a government agency ordered the group's TV commercials off the air, under threat of a $250,000 fine. NYT, *She Took on the Soda Industry. Then She Was Silenced* (Nov. 13, 2017). The industry's response: "Slapping a tax on our products and walking away won't do anything about obesity in this country or globally," said William Dermody, spokesman for the American Beverage Association, an industry trade group.

But pressure on companies to answer for their sugary drinks has not gone away. Lately some shareholders have taken up the cause. For example, Coca-Cola received a proposal from an activist shareholder (owning 100 shares) to have the company report on the financial and reputational risks to the company stemming from sugar's ties to obesity, diabetes, and other health issues. See Christopher Lee, Bloomberg, *Cola-Cola Faces Shareholder Activism on Sugar's Health Risks* (Feb. 11, 2019). Coca-Cola sought to exclude the proposal saying the company had already cut back on sugar in more than 500 drinks globally, and sells more than 1,100 low- or no-sugar drinks, including increasingly popular sparkling water brands.

Inward-focused politicians

It's interesting to notice that the phenomenon of inward-focused directors is shared by national politicians, who tend to be "microscopic rather than telescopic." See Simon Anholt, *Which Country does the Most Good for the World?* TED Talk (July 2, 2014). Politicians—like corporate directors—face pressures from their constituents to focus on their own political unit's wealth, competitiveness, and growth. National politicians—like corporate directors—view other countries as being competitors, not part of their internal "solution set." This tendency, however, may be counter-productive. Countries perceived as "good" (those that are outward-looking) also tend to be wealthy, competitive, and often growing. That is, the prevalent "cultural pathology" exhibited by politicians and their countries to be inward-focused may be counter-productive in a globalized world. Perhaps this is true for corporations also.

On the question of Food Inc. (as a famous documentary describes the modern food business), you might be interested in the thoughts Vandana Shiva, a deep thinker on our modern food systems and the role of business. In an interview Shiva said: "We are living the final stages of a very deceitful system that has made everything that is very costly for the planet, costly for the producer, look cheap for the consumer. So very high-cost production with GMOs and patents and royalties and fossil fuel is made to look like cheap food." She highlighted a new way of understanding the externalities of our food (and consumer) habits. "Every young person should recognize that working with their hands and their hearts and their minds—and they're interconnected—is the highest evolution of our species. Working with our hands is not a degradation. It's our real humanity."

Board Groupthink and SWM

A provocative essay by an Australian corporate-governance observer identifies that the dominant "shareholder wealth" paradigm has the tell-tale signs of groupthink. The essay identifies the eight signs of groupthink and explains how shareholder primacy is protected by the corporate governance/industrial complex.

Shareholder Primacy: Paradigm or Groupthink

(Oct. 29, 2013)

Peter Tunjic

[redacted/paraphrased]

In 1972, the psychologist Irving Janis documented and described eight signs of groupthink. Most of his cases arose in politics and the military—Pearl Harbor, Bay of Pigs invasion, space shuttle Challenger disaster, and more recently the 2016 presidential election. But they have also been extended to the corporate world—Swissair, Marks & Spencer, and British Airways. They all involve instances in which a group of people, seeking harmony and conformity, engage in a dysfunctional decision-making outcome. Here are the signs of groupthink applied by Tunjic to SWM:

- **Illusion of invulnerability:** Members ignore obvious danger, take extreme risk, and are overly optimistic. [Example: Professor Lucian Bebchuk of Harvard promotes hedge fund activism despite evidence that hedge funds promote short-termist outcomes that hurt long-term shareholder value]
- **Illusion of morality:** Members believe their decisions are morally correct, ignoring the ethical consequences of their decisions. [Example: Milton Friedman took the view that the morally right thing for business to do is make as much money for shareholders as possible, "so long as it stays within the rules of the game."]
- **Collective rationalization:** Members discredit and explain away warning contrary to group thinking. [Example: the push by corporate governance reformers is for more independent directors, more shareholder influence, and more monitoring – despite a lack of evidence that this "good" corporate governance produces results.]
- **Out-group stereotyping:** Members construct negative stereotypes of rivals outside the group. [Example: Lynn Stout, a law academic who has questioned shareholder primacy, is stereo-typed by Carl Icahn and others as "wrongheaded, a [coddled] tenured professor, pompous, silly, and laughable."]
- **Pressure to conform:** Members pressure any in the group who express arguments against the group's stereotypes, illusions, or commitments, viewing such opposition as disloyalty. [Example: those who question the value of independent directors are called on to explain their "deviation" from an unvalidated norm.]
- **Self-censorship:** Members withhold their dissenting views and counter-arguments. [Example: Tunjic offers none, but suggests, "This is for you to decide."]
- **Illusion of unanimity:** Members perceive falsely that everyone agrees with them. [Example: Both McKinsey and Yale law professor Jonathan Macey both proclaim "SWM is universally accepted as management's paramount goal."]
- **Appearance of mindguards:** Some members appoint themselves to the role of protecting the group from adverse information that might threaten the group. [Example: when Tunjic posted an essay comparing modern corporate governance to pre-Copernican astronomy on a LinkedIn corporate governance group, it was removed days after being posted.]

An interesting TED Talk describes how the founder and CEO of Bridgewater—perhaps the most successful hedge fund in an industry littered with hubris and failures—creates a corporate culture (and environment for group meetings) in which ideas are discussed and then voted on—an antidote to groupthink. See *TED Talk: How To Build A Company Where the Best Ideas Win* (2017). The process seeks to value accountability, conflict, and efficiency—that is, to replace groupthink with a meritocracy of ideas.

How does boardroom psychology affect corporate culture, which in turn affects corporate performance? Professor Don Langevoort (Georgetown Law Center) explores this three-link causal chain, which is also relevant to enhanced corporate criminal and civil liability when corporate cultures are judged to be deficient. Donald C. Langevoort, *The Effects of Shareholder Primacy, Publicness, and 'Privateness' on Corporate Cultures* (2019) [available on SSRN]. The first link (the "contestation about primacy in corporate governance") has assumed a boardroom mindset of shareholder primary, though managers' protestations of shareholder primacy may simply mask a self-centered managerialism. The second link identifies the place of corporate culture in the "overarching canopy of social culture"—that is, much of who we are arises from how we see ourselves in the workplace and business. Langevoort then wonders if "managerialism" triumphs over shareholder or even stakeholder primacy, thus assuring managers a "desired level of autonomy" from shareholders and stakeholders, will managers become more or less honest? With nobody to guard the guards, we resort (as did Greek philosophers) to *noblesse oblige*.

Cultural attitudes create a gravitational pull in a business, often forcing decisions and outcomes toward an unseen center. In an important longitudinal study on how five large businesses in Australia, each a leader in their sector, committed to decarbonization and then over a decade slowly lost their way, the authors suggest the nearly intractable power of the shareholder short-term profit norm in private business. Christopher Wright & Daniel Nyberg, *An Inconvenient Truth: How Organizations Translate Climate Change into Business as Usual* (2016) [available on Journal of Academic Management] [summary].

An Inconvenient Truth: How Organizations Translate Climate Change into Business as Usual

(2016)

Christopher Wright & Daniel Nyberg

[full article and summary available on Academy of Management/summarized below]

The authors explained their study:

> Based on five in-depth case studies of major Australian corporations over a 10-year period (2005–2015), we identify three key stages in the corporate

translation of climate change: framing, localizing, and normalizing. We develop a grounded model that explains how the revolutionary import of grand challenges is converted into the mundane and comfortable concerns of "business as usual." Specifically, we highlight the policy limitations of a reliance on business and market responses to the climate crisis.

All five corporations—each a leader in their industry—initially committed to making environmentally responsible changes in their practices, products, or services, but returned to "business as usual" by the end the of decade-long study period.

Here are the five corporations studied over the decade of the study:

The first chart below describes the five corporations that were studied. The next chart shows how the businesses moved from what the researchers call "framing" (executives presenting climate change as urgent and strategic) to "localizing" (implementing eco-efficient practices and green products and services) to "normalizing" (returning to business as usual after criticism from shareholders, politicians, the media and other business leaders).

Case	Industry	Employees	Climate change engagement
EnergyCo	Electricity and gas	1,500	• One of country's largest GHG emitters • Rebranded itself in 2005 as a "green" energy company • Invested in renewable energy generation (hydro, wind, and solar) to supplement aging coal-fired power stations • Began to advocate strongly for ETS and redesigned company for carbon pricing in 2009
FinanceCo	Banking	36,000	• One of Australia's largest financial institutions • Focused on environmental reporting since the mid-1990s • Began to advocate strongly for climate science and government pricing of carbon emissions in 2006 • Established carbon trading and began to price carbon risk in institutional lending in 2009
GlobalCo	Manufacturing	5,600	• New global CEO launched a focus on eco-innovation in 2004 • Established targets for eco-innovation R&D, sales from eco-products, and reductions in carbon emissions and water usage • Developed eco-innovation challenges with partner organizations • In 2001, a new CEO focused corporate strategy on sustainability and climate change

Case	Industry	Employees	Climate change engagement
InsureCo	Insurance	15,000	• Operationalized through R&D into climate change and extreme weather events in terms of insured risk • Began to advocate strongly for government action on climate change and carbon pricing in 2006
MediaCo	Media/communications	8,000	• CEO launched focus on climate change in 2007 • Emphasized reducing the company's carbon footprint and improving energy efficiency • Implemented a culture change initiative aimed at achieving carbon neutral status

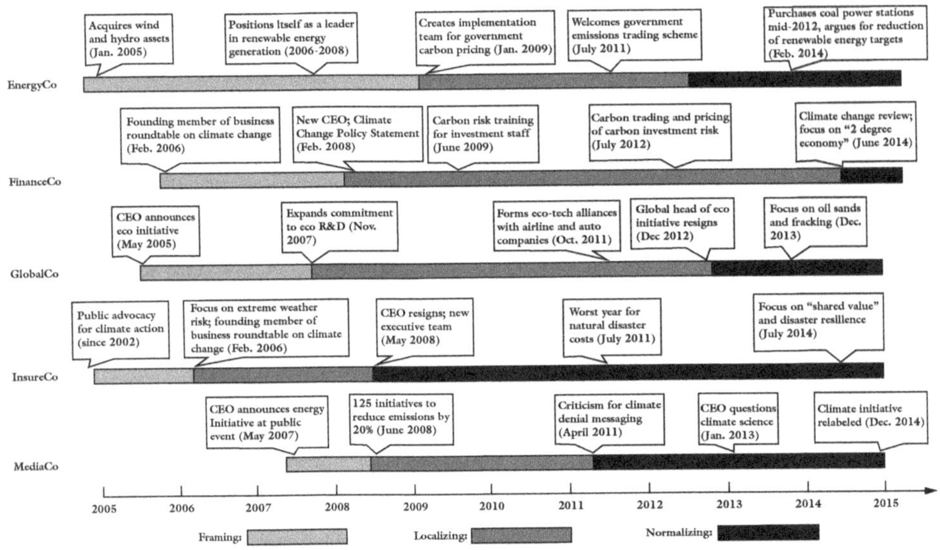

What led to this back-tracking? The authors identified three forces at work in each of the companies:

- Corporations' prioritization of short-term goals and results—"most evident in the focus on quarterly and semi-annual reporting and the shrinking tenure of executive managers"—make them "inherently unsuited to deal with issues that play out over the medium to long term.
- Even though companies' technological innovations are touted as solutions to environmental problems, "corporate reliance on economic growth and fossil fuel–based energy is the central contributor to escalating carbon emissions." Fixes needed in the energy, transportation, and manufacturing industries conflict with profit goals. "Among the corporations we studied, even firms that were relatively progressive on this issue explicitly discounted the idea that

responding to climate change should involve activities that threaten growth and existing business activities."

- "Meaningfully responding to many of the grand challenges facing the world requires systemic intervention based around central authority," such as a government agency or multinational organization.

One manager summarized what happened:

> The problem [of staying focused on decarbonization] is that governments to some extent have been loath to intervene in a mandatory way, to prescribe and regulate economies and companies. So, we've fallen back on a consensus that the way to respond to this is through cap and trade or pricing mechanisms, or even hope that companies will self-regulate and do the right thing. But publicly listed companies have a fiduciary duty, a prime objective, to maximize shareholder value. So, there's a fundamental disconnect between the problem and the preferred response. To rely on companies to save us from climate change simply isn't going to happen.

The authors commented that companies seeking to create markets for renewable energy, such as solar and wind power, "have a major role to play, no doubt about that. Examples like Tesla and Elon Musk are quite a good thing. The problem is that it's one company pushing against a momentum of significant vested interests that will fight tooth and nail."

The authors concluded their study by identifying how people seem more moral when acting individually than when they act collectively:

> Managers need to break out of that short-term thinking and think about "What is the world going to look like in 50 years?" and "What sort of world am I leaving for my children?" Some have had that epiphany, thinking, "I'm a powerful person, I run a large company, and I've realized that beyond short-term shareholder value, I've got to think about the legacy I'm leaving."
>
> The managers we interviewed were, for the most part, emotionally invested and morally concerned about the social and environmental consequences of climate change. However, they were also well aware of their limited room to maneuver, and that, if they did not fulfill market demands, they would be replaced. These managers were pragmatic, rather than cynical or naive. They recognized the tension between meaningful engagement with the grand challenge of climate change and an organizational focus on short-term profitability.

2.3.6 Corporate CEOs (and Directors) as Sociopaths

So, *who* are the persons who sit on public corporation boards in the United States? One clear answer is that they are primarily corporate executives in other companies and firms that serve large corporations. Are these execs

Separating the wheat from the chaff

A recent Hulu documentary focused on WeWork, a company started by Adam Neumann that created office space for small, mostly startups, in various high-tech cities. In 2019, the company had an unsuccessful IPO and later collapsed. The documentary included interviews with former employees, who all talked about how WeWork had given them a sense of fulfillment that no other corporate job had given them. Neumann had stressed building a culture of "we" that focused on community rather than the individual. He invented "Community Adjust EBITDA," an accounting metric rejected by the NYSE and NASDAQ. In the end, WeWork became detached from reality and failed.

Was WeWork a complete scam or a failed experiment in reinventing capitalism? The moral of the story seems to be that in trying to reinvent the corporation, its participants cannot disregard data. Realism generally works better than utopianism. If so, how does one identify when a corporate culture is workable or an illusion?

normal people? Or are they, as some have observed, prone to sociopathy? For example, the question came up after the Financial Crisis of 2008 whether CEOs (particularly of banks) who had seemed indifferent to putting the financial system at existential risk were some sort of special human breed.

The evidence suggests that they might be. One recent study analyzed the CEO letters to shareholders at a particular bank and found evidence of a mix of narcissism, hubris/overconfidence, and CEO-attribution. The study found that over half the sentences analyzed contained narcissistic-speak; very few sentences (only 2 percent) contained bad news; and half of the good news was attributed to the CEO, with all the bad news attributed externally.

In fact, psychopaths (people who are pathologically indifferent to others) seem to be prevalent in the C-suite. According to another recent study, Seductive Operational Bullies (SOBs) can be found wherever power, status, or money is at stake. The study concludes, "Outwardly normal, apparently successful and charming, their inner lack of empathy, shame, guilt, or remorse, has serious interpersonal repercussions, and can destroy organizations. Their great adaptive qualities mean they often reach top executive positions, especially in organizations that appreciate impression management, corporate gamesmanship, risk taking, coolness under pressure, domination, competitiveness, and assertiveness. The ease with which SOBs rise to the top raises the question whether the design of some organizations makes them a natural home for psychopathic individuals."

A recent book came to the conclusion that the incidence of sociopaths among CEOs is about 4 percent, which is four times the rate in society at large. The author concludes, "Capitalism is structured really as a physical manifestation of the brain anomaly known as psychopathy." And perhaps in some corporations a psychopath CEO's traits are highly useful for the organization—a coolness under fire, an absence of empathy (such as when down-sizing is necessary), and a ruthlessness to get things done. But, over time, the business may suffer with somebody so self-centered at the helm.

How do CEOs become sociopaths? Is it in their nature and they simply rise to the top in corporate organizations? Or do big corporations enable this kind of person and nurture sociopathic behavior? Some speculate that runaway executive pay is part of the problem. CEOs of large businesses regularly make decisions that impact, often negatively, the lives of others. But they live in "private jet and limousine" worlds insulated from the impact of their decisions. They believe that their wealth is a measure of their goodness, and their goodness justifies more wealth. Or maybe they live in deep internal dissonance, with money a salve.

2.3.7 Women in the Boardroom

One of the most telling symptoms of board mono-culture is the relative absence of women on US corporate boards. Beginning in the 1990s, corporate law scholars pointed out that women on corporate boards had a positive impact on corporate performance—particularly in monitoring and responding to corporate misbehavior. One reason, according to a study from several years ago, is that women directors seem to be more attentive to the company's legal compliance and so are often tasked with monitoring compliance programs. See Renee B. Adams & Daniel Ferreira, *Women in the Boardroom and Their Impact on Governance and Performance* (2008) [available on SSRN] (finding that women directors have better attendance records and are often placed on board monitoring committees, resulting in significant impact on board inputs and outcomes). In addition, the study found that in firms with more gender-diverse boards, CEO turnover is more sensitive to stock performance and directors receive more equity-based compensation. Other studies suggest women are more "other focused" than men, thus resulting in decisions by boards with a critical number of women that are more sensitive to legal compliance and moral (pro-social) corporate decisions.

A recent study considers specifically the relationship between gender diversity on boards and corporate scandals:

> The relationship between women on boards and corporate scandals is plagued with a reverse causality issue, as more women on boards may reduce the propensity of corporations to be exposed to scandals, while the occurrence of scandals may have led corporations to appoint more women. To address this, we propose a Granger-style reverse causality minimization procedure. This procedure involves three regression steps [which I've edited out]. Applying our Granger-style reverse causality minimization procedure to 2,880 U.S. firms between 2007 and 2016, we find that boards with higher diversity, for reasons other than scandals, were better than their lower diversity counterparts in reducing scandals once encountering them.

Chris Godfrey & Andreas G.F. Hoepner, Ming-Tsung Lin & Ser-Huang Poon, *Women on Boards and Corporate Scandals: Evidence from a Granger Style Reverse Causality Minimization Procedure* (2020) [available on SSRN].

Because of political pressure and indications that women enhance corporate social value, sixteen countries now impose quotas for women's representation on boards, and many more have voluntary quotas in corporate governance codes. In the United States, support for diversity has grown in principle, but progress has lagged in practice. As one recent study noted, "the stakes in this debate are substantial. Corporate boards affect the lives of millions of employees and consumers, and the policies and practices of the global marketplace. As recent scandals demonstrate, failures in board governance can carry an enormous cost; Enron [and the Financial Crisis are] notorious examples. Who gains access to these boards is therefore an issue of broad social importance." Deborah Rhode & Amanda K. Packel, *Diversity on Corporate Boards: How Much Difference Does Difference Make?* (2014) [available on SSRN]. Although studies continue to show mixed results on whether women directors contribute to the financial "bottom line" of companies, more recent studies make clear that the real value of women on corporate boards may be "rooted in social justice, equal opportunity, and corporate reputation."

Further, greater gender diversity on corporate boards also leads to greater awareness of the full dimensions of a board decision—that is, women seem to think more holistically than men. As Professor Peter Huang (Colorado Law School) has pointed out, mindfulness and diversity go hand in hand:

> Many important decisions can be difficult; require focused, cognitive attention; produce delayed, noisy feedback; benefit from careful and clear thinking; and quite often trigger anxiety, stress, and other strong, negative emotions. Much empirical, experimental, and field research finds that we often make decisions leading to outcomes we judge as suboptimal.
>
> This Article advocates "boosts" to improve mindfulness, thinking, and diversity. Mindfulness involves paying attention in an intentional way to life as it unfolds moment to moment. Mindfulness improves decision-making through many pathways, including by reducing stress and negative affect. Thinking boosts include thinking technologies and diversity. Thinking technologies involve computer or digital technologies to assist people in their thinking. Examples of novel, fun thinking technologies include a financial entertainment computer video game where a player is a vampire managing a blood bar and planning for retirement and video adventure games designed to teach players to recognize and mitigate their cognitive biases. Diversity creates bonuses for organizations by improving decision-making, creativity, innovation, prediction, problem-solving, and productivity.

Professor Huang, *Boost: Improving Mindfulness, Thinking, and Diversity* (2018) [available on SSRN]. Others have pointed out the value of vocal, clear-thinking minorities in group decision-making. See McAllister, Blay & Kadous, *Fraud Brainstorming Group Composition: The Persuasive Power of a Skeptical Minority* (2018) [available on SSRN] (experiment finding that groups with a minority of "professional skeptics" provide higher group fraud risk assessments than control groups, with these effects persisting to group members' individual, post-brainstorming fraud risk assessments).

Pointing to these and other studies, California recently enacted a measure (SB 826), which requires that all public corporations incorporated or headquartered in California have at least one woman director (by 2019) and at least three women directors on boards of more than six directors (by 2021). Although the new law has been challenged as unconstitutional—by creating the potential for inconsistent state corporate standards for board composition—the law's immediate effect was a decline in the value of California-headquartered companies. See Sunwoo Hwang, Anil Shivadsani & Elena Simintzi, *Mandating Women on Boards: Evidence from the United States* (2019) [available on SSRN] (finding significant decline in stock prices of California-headquartered companies, with the decline directly related to the number of new women directors the legislation would require). The authors of the study speculate that perhaps the problem is that the pool of qualified women directors is small. Or perhaps the problem is that shareholders don't like being told who will be on their boards, because shareholders are active enablers of board mono-culture.

Of course, the under-representation of women on the corporate boards of US companies could well be a symptom of the relative under-representation of women as corporate CEOs. Recent studies, however, show that the number of women CEOs is on the rise and that there is a correlation between a company's board structure and whether its CEO is a woman. Melissa B. Frye & Duong Pham, *CEO Gender and Corporate Board Structures* (2018) [available on SSRN] (finding a "remarkable" increase in the number of female executives, and "evidence that female CEOs are associated with smaller boards that are more independent, more gender diversified, have a lower ratio of inside to outside directors, a broader director network, and younger directors"). These findings are consistent with the notion that women representation in the boardroom increases board monitoring.

Another explanation of the under-representation of women in leadership roles in US corporations is the politics of corporate CEOs. A recent study found that when companies are led by Democratic CEOs (those whose political giving was mostly to Democrats) the company had more and better-compensated women in the company's C-suite compared to companies led by Republican CEOs. See Alma Cohen, Moshe Hazan & David Weiss, *Politics and Gender in the Executive Suite* (2020) [available on SSRN]. To show causality, the study looked at the effect of replacing a Republican CEO with a Democratic CEO and, sure enough, the switch leads to more and equally-compensated women in the C-suite. Interestingly, though, the CEO's politics does not affect boardroom gender composition—suggesting that board composition marches to a different cultural/political drum than C-suite composition.

This leads to another thought. If board culture drives board composition, then a key to board diversity is the director search process. As Professor Omari Simmons (Wake Forest Law) has pointed out, executive search firms (ESFs) are a key mechanism of corporate governance—specifically in the "elite labor market" of corporate directors. See Omari Scott Simmons, *Forgotten Gatekeepers: Executive Search Firms and Corporate Governance* (2019) [available on SSRN]. Whatever may be happening to corporate governance reform legislatively and judicially, ESFs provide a variety of private solutions to governance problems, and any regulatory response should understand where the rubber actually meets the road.

A student in this course summarized the problem of women in corporate leadership in one of her reflection papers as one of groupthink:

> The solution to dismantling board groupthink is diversification of boardroom populations. However, diversification is hard to achieve because groupthink perpetuates homogeneity. Increased gender representation in boardrooms has been particularly difficult to accomplish, as evidenced by the fact that women remain relatively absent on US corporate boards. I believe one significant obstacle to achieving increased representation of gender in boardroom is the widespread perception of the female identity as fragile, emotional, and inept. Scholars, Anne Fausto-Sterling and Susan Bordo, illustrate that societies' normalized use of binaries constructs this problematic perception of the female identity because such binaries associate the feminine identity with negative connotations. Anne Fausto-Sterling, *Dualisms Denied in Sexing the Body*, Perseus Book Group, 20, 21 (2000). Fausto-Sterling claims that in the Euro-American tradition, from the earliest literature down to modern media of present day, dualisms, "pairs of opposing concepts, objects, or belief systems" have been employed to compartmentalize and understand the world. The common use of dualisms "makes invisible the interdependencies of each pair . . . enabling sets of pairs to map onto each other." For instance, consider:

Male	**Female**
Reason	Nature
Mind	Body
Master	Slave
Civilized	Primitive
Production	Reproduction
Self	Other

2.3.8 Artificial Intelligence in the Boardroom

Perhaps you're thinking, if directors are subject to so many psychological foibles and preconceptions—with *groupthink* just the tip of the iceberg—maybe we should root out these human biases and introduce "artificial intelligence" in the boardroom. Certainly, AI would have noticed that Enron was a financial house of cards (as did a group of MBA students at Cornell two years before the company's financial weakness was exposed) and that subprime mortgages were built on the false assumption that real estate prices would never fall (the valuation models for mortgage-backed securities only looked back to 20 years of experience in the US real estate markets).

Perhaps human directors should be encouraged—even required—to use AI. See Florian Moslein, ***Robots in the Boardroom: Artificial Intelligence and Corporate Law*** (2017/18) [available on SSRN]. In fact, some functions (such as estimating the consumer demand for a new product or identifying a prospective CEO's propensity to be mendacious) may be better performed by AI, which can be freed of human psychological biases—such as the anchoring/priming/availability heuristics that underlie groupthink. See Daniel Kahneman, ***Thinking Fast and Slow*** (2011). At present, however, corporate directors by law must be human individuals—one of the few mandatory rules of US corporate law.

Do markets mitigate self-delusion?

Self-delusion and informational biases, it turns out, far from being mitigated by markets may well be more pronounced in the presence of markets. See Shimon Kogan, Florian Schneider, and Roberto A. Weber, ***Self-serving Biases in Beliefs about Collective Action*** (2021) [available on SSRN] (finding that beliefs about collective outcomes, such as economic growth or firm profitability, are subject to self-serving biases among individuals, and even more so when mediated by markets).

But will AI have a sense of humor? A recent study finds that humor used in "earnings" calls (a corporate ritual in which stock analysts ask questions of company executives about the company's financial performance) rewards humor. Analysts who use humor in asking questions are more successful in eliciting information, and company executives who use humor are more successful in engendering analyst goodwill—and thus higher stock prices. See Andrew C. Call, Rachel W. Flam, Joshua A. Lee & Nathan Y. Sharp, ***Analysts and Managers Use of Humor on Public Earnings Calls*** (2019) [available on SSRN] (study of 85,000 earnings calls from 2003-2016, finding that analysts who use humor to soften tough questions get more information, and that stock recommendations and the market reaction following an earnings call are positive when executives use humor). In short, law school should be teaching you the skill of being funny. Have you heard a good joke lately?

* * *

Concluding Thoughts

How Does One Change Groupthink?

Here's a classic story.

In early 1942, just months after the United States formally entered World War II, the US government faced a big problem. American men leaving for active duty had created a shortage of six million workers. Predictions were that the country's productivity would come to a halt by the end of 1943. The solution: bring women into the workforce.

President Roosevelt tasked the Office of War Information (OWI), a newly formed federal propaganda agency, with selling the idea of women workers to the country. The OWI reported, "The importance of women to a nation engaged in total war must be convincingly presented." Private industry and the American media joined in to generate some of the era's most enduring and well-known images.

You've probably seen the rest of the story. Freelance artist J. Howard Miller (and later Normal Rockwell for *The Saturday Evening Post*) painted Rosie the Riveter:

J. Howard William, *Rosie the Riveter* (1943)

The OWI's recruitment campaign was a success. "There are practically no jobs, it has been found, that cannot be adapted for women workers," Newsweek reported in August 1943. "They are in the shipyards, lumber mills, steel mills, foundries. They are welders, electricians, mechanics and even boilermakers. They operate streetcars, buses, cranes and tractors." In March 1941, 10.8 million American women were employed; by August 1944, that number had risen to 18 million.

Further, the US Treasury used Rockwell's art to advertise war bonds, thus ensuring that Americans would identify with Rosie the Riveter throughout the war. And although no posters depicted the hundreds of thousands of Black women who joined White Rosie on the factory floors, the Rosie the Riveter propaganda was pivotal in the war effort, and later undergirded the US feminist movement.

Kirstin Butler, ***Rosie the Riveter Isn't Who You Think She Is***, PBS: American Experience (Dec. 16, 2021).

Chapter 2.4

Corporations in Politics

Corporate personhood permits corporations to participate in our economy and public life. It also makes the modern US corporation unsustainable. Under *Citizens United*, corporations have the constitutionally-protected right to use corporate funds to speak for or against candidates in political elections. Beyond this, corporations can also engage in corporate lobbying, support political actions committees (PACs), affiliate with political groups that seek particular legislative outcomes (such as ALEC), and spend corporate funds on "public issue" campaigns. In many respects, *Citizens United* is just the tip of corporations in politics.

Corporate political activities—increasingly permitted and protected by law—raise the question whether corporations can be instruments that respond to present and future social needs when the corporation has been given the tools to insulate itself from social oversight expressed through governmental regulation. That is, even if there were a broad societal desire to revisit the rules of limited liability, to impose measures to counter-act short-termism or to open corporate boards to broader membership and perspectives, the corporation's "political persona" allows it to mold public opinion and sway government action, thus undermining society's ability to bend the corporation to meet our collective needs.

Chapter's Focus

You will want to notice that corporate personhood is not a recent phenomenon, but has been part of the corporation since its inception—at least with respect to the corporation's economic activities. Meanwhile corporations in politics, through corporate lobbying, is a relatively recent phenomenon that began in earnest only in the 1970s, as corporations sought to use government to protect and advance corporate business interests.

You will learn about the history of the regulation of corporate participation in politics, beginning with a ban in 1907 on both corporate expenditures and corporate contributions in federal election campaigns. You will also discover that the Supreme Court has taken different views on whether corporate expenditures in political referenda and elections can be regulated. You will want to focus on the Supreme Court's decision in *Citizens United*, which upheld the right of all corporations (non-profit and for-profit) to spend money to influence political elections.

You will discover a wide set of views on the Supreme Court about the nature of the corporation—as having rights of a natural person, being subject to government control as a "creature of law," and representing a "contract" between its shareholders and managers.

You will notice that the *Citizens United* logic that corporations are persons with expressive rights has been used lately to diminish the regulatory reach of government outside the context of political elections.

Finally, you will want to consider whether corporations, which are products of markets, should be subject only to market constraints with respect to their political activities. You will find interesting that Judge Guido Calabresi views corporate speech as privileged speech by those with access to the wealth of corporation and thus something that both distorts what is heard by the public and squelches contrary viewpoints, even when intensely held.

2.4.1 Corporations in Democracy?

Before we consider the specific ways in which US corporations participate in our political life, it is useful to consider whether corporations should participate at all. Is the corporation's "political persona" consistent with democratic theory, given the corporation's functioning in markets? In his 2001 book *The Meaning of Markets*, Charles Lindblom (a Yale economics professor) questioned the corporation's political personhood and touched upon many of the themes in this chapter:

> Market systems do not make a place for individuals' collective compulsions and wishes. Although *individual* choices are reflected in the market system, the market system does not assimilate *collective* free choices. The market system gives "we the people" no freedom, for example, to take a company's land for a highway or to impose an elementary education on every child. Only the democratic state gives people this kind of collective choice.
>
> Further, we should not confuse the freedoms of individual persons (generally to be prized) with freedoms of institutions (not to be prized). Societies would make a disastrous mistake in granting general or broad freedom to such an institution as a police force or a tax office—it would be a nightmare! Institutions, whether governmental or private (for-profit or non-profit), have to be put under controls to hold them to their responsibilities, to limit powers that could otherwise be irresponsibly and dangerously exercised.
>
> Thus, business organizations need supervisory controls and are entitled to no general freedom. Market systems work only because enterprises are controlled by their customers, employees, and suppliers through the interactions of the market system, as well as through government controls.
>
> Set aside the mom-and-pop grocery and other small enterprises whose prerogatives in a democratic political system are hardly distinguishable

from those of individual persons. It is the large enterprises that pose obstructions to political democracy. Through their spending and their relations with government officials they exercise much more power than do citizens.

If an enterprise incorporates, it then enjoys certain additional rights. Limited liability, for example, limits losses to stockholders if the enterprise fails. Investors thus protected, corporate executives can acquire from them—and then spend—funds far larger than possible for wealthy individual persons, even larger than possible for some nation-states. The corporation plays the role of an oversized greatly empowered citizen. The role constitutes a mammoth violation of the political equality ordinarily deemed necessary for genuine democracy.

More familiar examples of corporate activity inconsistent with political equality are corporate spending on election campaigns or to cultivate close relations with government officials. Corporations can draw on "public" funds that are drawn from the receipts of the enterprise, thus from customers and stockholders rather than from the personal income of enterprise executives. The individual citizen is on his own. Laws sometimes limit executive use of "public" funds, but it takes little ingenuity to escape them.

Although the law varies from one country to another, it generally grants corporations as legally fictitious persons many of the rights, including right of political participation, that one might think appropriate in a democracy only for living, breathing persons. Corporations are legally entitled to engage heavily in political activity, even if they cannot vote or run for office. Theirs, too, are legal right of free speech and of communication with political elites.

I do not see how it is possible to reconcile democracy with the practice of conferring on institutions the rights and powers of real persons. The rationale for democracy is rights and powers for living, hurting, and aspiring persons whose assigned rights and powers give them protection as well as opportunities to pursue their aspirations. It makes no sense to assign such rights and powers to fire hydrants or computers—they neither suffer or aspire. Neither does a corporation suffer or aspire.

For the performance of the functions that societies assign to corporations—to organize air transport, for example, or extract ore—corporations need certain rights and powers such as to buy and sell and to manage a workforce. I see no necessary obstacle to democracy when corporations hold those rights and powers. Every society minimally recognizes such a principle—but I do not know of any society that permits, say, a corporation to run for and hold political office.

Unlike individual persons, organizations are presumably servants of society, neither fellow citizens nor masters. Consider Unilever, which like all large corporations, in some respects acts more like a state than like a person or servant. Only with a legal status and a set of rules appropriate to its functions will it and other corporations meet the requirements of political democracy.

2.4.2 History of Corporations in Politics

Corporation as Commercial Person

One of the principal attributes of the corporation—perhaps its most important—is that it creates a permanent, enduring structure. Shareholders, directors, and officers may come and go, but the corporation perdures. It has its own perpetual existence. And part of its being is that it can own property, enter into contracts, commit and answer for wrongs, and sue and be sued. From the beginning, the corporation was meant to be a "commercial person."

In addition, the US corporation has been a member of the body politic, its political nature inherent from the start. US corporations, as you may remember from our look at their history, were originally seen as having a public interest and existed by virtue of special state (and even federal) legislative chartering. These early corporations were often given monopolies to engage in public functions, such as water supply, bridges, banking, and railroads. Early corporations were viewed with caution, their specific purposes and powers circumscribed in their state-granted charters.

But, over time, for-profit business corporations became more and more insinuated in public life. Corporations demanded "freedom" from protectionist state legislation, which they were able to claim using the Civil War Amendments to the US Constitution. For example, the early Supreme Court cases interpreting the Equal Protection Clause of the Fourteenth Amendment were mostly brought by out-of-state corporations with multistate operations that sought to insulate themselves (usually successfully) from discriminatory state laws aimed at protecting local business from competition by often better-financed national firms.

Corporations and "Other People's Money"

Concerns about the political clout of corporations reached a bit of a crescendo during the Progressive Era when people—including famously Louis Brandeis—noticed that corporations were using "other people's money" to advance the personal (sometimes political) agendas of corporate managers. In 1907, Congress passed the Tillman Act to prohibit, with criminal sanctions for non-complying corporate executives, any corporation or bank from spending corporate funds on federal elections. Thus, Wall Street (the "investor class") sought to protect itself from Main Street (the rising "managerial class") using corporate profits to pay for management's political agendas. (The legislation was also justified as a way of keeping the corrosive influence of moneyed corporations out of politics.)

In the end, corporations—that is, the executives who make corporate decisions—are spending "other people's money" when the corporation engages in political speech. There's an interesting story of how after the Supreme Court in *Bellotti* decided that banks in Massachusetts could oppose a state referendum to increase tax rates on high-wealth individuals (including bankers) that the then-mayor of Boston decided to use municipal funds (Boston is organized as a "municipal corporation") to support the referendum.

Townsfolk were upset because it was municipal spending without representation. The incident made clear that spending by corporations—of all ilk—depends on the legitimacy of "corporate democracy." Nikolas Bowie, *Corporate Democracy: How Corporations Justified Their Right to Speak in 1970s Boston* (2018) [available on SSRN].

Corporation and Lobbying

But the corporation was not to be subdued. Corporations continued to be involved in politics at the federal and state level, regularly getting their way through "lobbying"—a highly effective way for corporate management to use corporate clout to advance the corporation's agenda. Especially with the formation of the Business Roundtable in the 1970s, lobbying proved highly successful as a way for corporations to exert influence in Washington and state capitols.

Because lobbying in the United States is subject to a high degree of transparency, researchers have used lobbying data to assess the effectiveness of corporate lobbying. Generally, the consensus is that corporate lobbying pays. The return on each dollar spent on lobbying ranges from a few dollars to hundreds of dollars, depending on the methodology employed. Similarly, lobbying activity positively correlates with firm performance as measured using a variety of metrics, including a portfolio-based approach. Although corporations do not always get what they want from the government, studies indicate that when corporations do not want federal legislation Congress rarely takes it up.

A recent study finds synergistic corruption in companies that engage in lobbying. CEOs of such companies engage in insider trading after sponsored bills are introduced and passed by Congress. Meanwhile, lobbying also leads to such companies receiving more government contracts, thus increasing the company's stock price. Everyone wins—the company, the CEO, and the shareholders—at the expense (perhaps) of the public. Jennifer Brodmann, Omer Unsal & M. Kabir Hassan, *Political Lobbying, Insider Trading, and CEO Compensation* (2019) [available at SSRN].

Lobbying is made effective when corporate executives promise to support (or threaten the withdrawal of support from) government officials. Clout. Although corporate funds could not be used for and against candidates to political office, executives could use their own personal funds, derived from their corporate positions, to advance their own political agendas. And, after the Watergate, Congress permitted corporation-specific PACs to spend money on political campaigns, which had been collected from corporate executives, employees, and shareholders to support and oppose political candidates—subject to reporting and contribution limits.

Corporations and Think Tanks

Corporations have many arrows in their political quiver. In addition to lobbying—which essentially tells legislators, "Let us tell you our side of the story. And now do as we ask, or act at your own peril!"—corporations can influence public opinion and thus mold legislative views by supporting "think tanks." The story of how the oil and gas industry used various think tanks to engage in a campaign of climate denial is telling.

How Big Oil Lost Control of Its Climate Misinformation Machine

InsideClimate News (Dec. 17, 2017)

Neela Banerjee

The Heartland Institute, a conservative think tank, launched a billboard campaign in 2012 to compare believers in global warming to "murderers and madmen" such as the Unabomber, Charles Manson, and Osama bin Laden. The backlash was so severe that Heartland pulled the plug within 24 hours, but it still lost major donors and political allies and faced criticism that its fight against climate science was beyond extreme.

Five years later, on June 1, 2017, the group's chief executive, Joseph Bast, was a guest of Donald Trump in the White House Rose Garden as the president announced the withdrawal of the United States from the Paris climate agreement.

"We are winning in the global warming war," Bast declared later in an email to supporters.

Heartland's rebound is striking. Its ascent into the Trump administration's orbit, where it now advises the Environmental Protection Agency on climate change issues, marks the most dramatic success yet in a decades-long crusade, first funded by fossil fuel money, against the mainstream scientific conclusion that human activity is warming the planet and inviting disastrous consequences.

Hundreds of millions of dollars from corporations such as ExxonMobil and wealthy individuals such as the billionaires Charles and David Koch have supported the development of a sprawling network, which includes Heartland and other think tanks, advocacy groups and political operatives. They have cast doubt on consensus science, confused public opinion and forestalled passage of laws and regulations that would address the global environmental crisis. It is one of the largest, longest, and most consequential misinformation efforts mounted against mainstream science by an industry. Climate denial, thanks to the network's influence, has become a core message of the Republican Party, now in control of the White House and Congress.

"This didn't come out of nowhere. Trump was taught to say these things on climate by Heartland, the Competitive Enterprise Institute and other think tanks. They maintained this denial space in public policy dialogue," said Kert Davies, director of the Climate Investigations Center, a watchdog group. "And you can definitely credit Exxon and Koch brothers' money for giving the think tanks the megaphone to keep climate science denial in the world."

But now, just like the Republican upstarts that threaten the party establishment, Heartland is taking climate denial farther than many fossil fuel companies can support. While ExxonMobil today publicly accepts the reality of human-caused climate change and says the problem should be addressed, Heartland has continued arguing the benefits of a warming world. The group is pushing the EPA to overturn its official conclusion—known as the endangerment finding—that excessive carbon dioxide is a danger to human health and welfare. The finding, affirmed by the Supreme Court, is what empowers the agency to regulate carbon dioxide and other greenhouse gases.

You might have noticed that even though the Heartland Institute went off the deep end in denying climiate change, ExxonMobil now says that climate change should be addressed. But, before you take comfort, it turns out that ExxonMobil does not actually support any meaningful regulation that would cut into its oil and gas business. Although the company has said that it supports a carbon tax as a way to transition from fossil fuels to renewable energy, these public statements appear simply to be posturing.

Recently, an ExxonMobil executive was caught on tape saying that the reason the company says it supports a carbon tax is that it knows there is a lack of political will to impose one. That is, why not support something you know won't happen? And, of course, the reason for this lack of political will is that corporation-friendly politicians from both parties understand that the fossil fuel industry, and the other industries that revolve around it, have no interest in a meaningful carbon tax. Mike Lee & Corbin Hiar, *Exxon Sting Shakes Up Politics of Carbon Pricing*, E&E ClimateWire (July 6, 2021) (reporting that "Exxon always knew the idea was a nonstarter. Nobody is going to propose a tax on all Americans. But it gives us a talking point. We can say, 'ExxonMobil [is] for a carbon tax' ").

Thus, whatever the outcome of *Citizens United*—whether its repeal by constitutional amendment, its weakening by mandated disclosure, or its diminishment by shareholder activists who compel management to steer clear of overt participation in politics—the power of corporations in government affairs is unlikely to go away. There's just way too much money and a sense of importance to be had by influencing the political process.

2.4.3 *Citizens United*

Business Organizations:
A Contemporary Approach
(3d ed. 2019)
[West Publishers]

Alan Palmiter, Frank Partnoy & Elizabeth Pollman

Chapter 7

Corporation as Political Actor

A. The World Before *Citizens United*

1. Corporations under the Constitution

At the founding of the United States in 1787, most corporations were municipal, religious, or charitable institutions, and very few business corporations existed. The Constitution does not expressly refer to corporations. In 1819, when the Supreme

Court decided one of the earliest cases on corporate rights, the corporation at issue was Dartmouth College and it claimed protection under the contracts clause of the Constitution. Chief Justice Marshall's opinion described the corporation as an "artificial being" and explained that it "possesses only those properties which the charter of its creation confers upon it either expressly or as incidental to its very existence." But, the Court also recognized that a corporate charter is a contract between the state and the private individuals forming the corporation, and once granted it cannot be impaired by the state absent a reservation of authority.

In the late 1800s, as the size and number of business corporations increased in the United States, the Supreme Court expanded the rights of corporations. In a series of headnotes and dicta, the Court stated that a corporation is included in the designation of "person" under the Fourteenth Amendment and has the right to equal protection and due process. By the turn of the century, there was little doubt that corporations could claim constitutional protections related to contract and property interests.

The Court, however, did not extend the same constitutional protections to corporations' non-commercial activities. In the early twentieth century, the Court stated that the liberty protected by the Fourteenth Amendment is "the liberty of natural, not artificial persons." Further, in *Hale v. Henkel*, the Court held that a corporation is not a "person" for purpose of the privilege against self-incrimination because that right "is purely a personal privilege of the witness." But a corporation could claim some Fourth Amendment protections against unreasonable searches and seizures because it "is, after all, but an association of individuals under an assumed name and with a distinct legal entity," And, as the twentieth century continued, the Court displayed a willingness to grant expressive and associational protections to media corporations and nonprofits.

2. Regulation of Corporations as "Political Actors"

The early case law left open the question of how corporations could be regulated as political actors. Before the "progressive era," corporate political contributions, and even bribes, were at the center of allegations of political corruption. Congress responded to these scandals by prohibiting corporations from contributing to or supporting the campaign of any candidate or party in connection with any federal election. President Theodore Roosevelt heralded this legislation as necessary to instill the confidence of "the plain people of small means" in the electoral process and eradicate perceived political corruption. The legislation also prevented corporate managers from using "other people's money" to advance their own political agendas.

Specifically, the Tillman Act of 1907 prohibited corporations from spending "treasury funds" (general corporate assets) on campaign contributions or independent expenditures "advocating the election or defeat of a clearly identified candidate." 2 U.S.C. § 441.

Despite these limits, corporations found other ways to be politically involved. In 1971, Congress passed the Federal Elections Campaign Act (FECA), which allowed corporations and unions to establish "separate segregated funds," popularly called political action committees (PACs). PACs receive voluntary contributions from people with ties to the corporation, not from the corporation's treasury funds. In other words, PAC money comes directly from shareholders, executives, and employees with their consent, instead of coming from the corporation's general funds as determined by the managers who control the corporation.

In addition to using PACs, corporations can pay for communications to their employees and shareholders that expressly support or oppose candidates and pay for "issue ads." Corporations also can donate to charitable and educational organizations, including "think tanks" that advocate political views.

Corporations also can, and do, lobby. Corporate lobbyists must register and disclose any payments they receive if they engage in "direct communications with members of Congress on pending or proposed federal legislation." But many activities that might pass as lobbying—such as TV ads and appearances, congressional testimony, letter-writing campaigns, and comments on government regulations—are not subject to lobbyist disclosure rules.

3. Pre-*Citizens United* Case Law

Citizens United was not written on a blank slate. In several key cases starting in the 1970s, the Supreme Court addressed whether corporations could spend money from their general treasury funds on politics.

First, in 1978, the Court held that the First Amendment limited the ability of states to regulate corporate speech in connection with a referendum. *First National Bank of Boston v. Bellotti*, 435 U.S. 765 (1978) (Powell, J.) The case involved a Massachusetts law that banned corporations from placing political ads for or against pending referenda. A bank that sought to oppose a referendum introducing an individual graduated income tax in the state claimed the legislative ban violated its rights under the First Amendment. The Court agreed and concluded the state had no compelling justifications for targeting the corporate speech at issue in the case. The Court pointed out that if the concern was the use of corporate resources in the political process, the state should also have banned lobbying by corporations. According to the Court, there was no showing "that the relative voice of corporations has been overwhelming or even significant in influencing referenda in Massachusetts." Further, the concern about dissenting shareholders being compelled to fund corporate political speech did not constitute a compelling governmental interest because the "procedures of corporate democracy" already provide sufficient protection and ultimately allow shareholders to decide "whether their corporation should engage in debate on public issues."

Then, in 1986, the Court recognized that not all corporations are the same and held that states could not ban political advocacy by nonprofit corporations. *Federal Election Comm'n v. Massachusetts Citizens for Life, Inc. (MCFL)*, 479 U.S. 238 (1986) (Brennan, J.). The case again arose in Massachusetts where a membership nonprofit corporation that opposed abortion rights sent out a newsletter urging voters to support certain pro-life candidates. The nonprofit used its own funds, not those of a corporate PAC, to finance this voting advocacy. The Court held that the federal ban against independent expenditures by an advocacy nonprofit was unconstitutional, given that such nonprofits are "formed for the express purpose of promoting political ideas" and supported entirely by individuals.

Four years later, the Court reversed direction and upheld the power of states to ban for-profit corporations from spending their general treasury funds for or against political candidates. *Austin v. Michigan Chamber of Commerce*, 494 U.S. 652 (1990) (Marshall, J.). The case involved a Michigan law that banned for-profit corporations from making campaign contributions or expenditures in support or opposition of state candidates. The Michigan Chamber of Commerce, funded in part by for-profit corporations, sought to make expenditures supporting certain candidates in state elections. The Court held that the state law was constitutional. The Court pointed out that corporations are creatures of state law and, given their "unique legal and economic characteristics," regulation was needed to avoid the "the corrosive and distorting effect of immense aggregations of wealth" accumulated through the corporate form. In addition, the Court pointed out that corporate expenditures might not reflect the views of the corporations' shareholders and customers.

Tensions in the Court's jurisprudence on corporate political spending had grown. *MCFL* made sense as an extension of the First Amendment's protection of associational rights. But it was difficult to reconcile *Bellotti* and *Austin*. *Austin* was not a "change in personnel" story: both Justices Blackmun and Stevens were in the majority in each case, though neither wrote an opinion explaining their seemingly inconsistent support for *both* results. Some argued that *Bellotti*'s specific regulation of corporate spending in political referenda was more suspect than *Austin*'s generalized regulation of all corporate spending in state elections. Others said *Bellotti* reflected a belief that the Massachusetts banks may have had a direct interest in maintaining a favorable tax climate so as to attract bank executives, while the Michigan ban on spending by for-profit corporations reflected a concern about the ineluctable "quid pro quo" motives of such spending.

In any event, the two cases stood in stark contrast, until . . .

B. The Court's Decision in *Citizens United*

The Court's various opinions in *Citizens United* span more than 100 pages. Justice Kennedy wrote the majority opinion, which concluded that the federal statute banning corporations from using their general treasury funds to make independent expenditures that expressly advocate for or against a candidate in connection with federal elections, 2 U.S.C. § 441b, could not be read narrowly to avoid constitutional infirmity and held that *Austin* had to be overruled. Nonetheless, the Court upheld certain disclosure and disclaimer requirements of FECA.

Justices Stevens, Ginsburg, Breyer, and Sotomayor dissented from the Court's decision, except the part upholding the disclosure and disclaimer requirements. Justice Thomas joined as to all of Justice Kennedy's opinion, except on upholding the disclosure and disclaimer requirements. Chief Justice Roberts wrote separately to clarify the Court's stance on *stare decisis*, and Justice Scalia wrote in response to the Stevens dissent and articulated the importance of corporate speech at the founding. Justice Alito joined in the Roberts and Scalia opinions.

As you go through the various opinions, ask yourself how the justices seem to view the modern corporation.

(1) **Creature of state law:** The corporation is an artificial entity created by the state, which can regulate its creations when there are "compelling justifications" or simply "reasonable" concerns about corporate participation in political speech.

(2) **Real entity:** The corporation itself is a speaker and the state must provide "compelling reasons" to silence its speech. The corporate person has autonomy and appropriately speaks through management, subject to oversight by shareholders who can replace misguided managers.

(3) **Private voluntary association:** The corporation is an aggregate of its participants who understand that management will speak and act on behalf of their collective interests. Shareholders who don't like this can invest elsewhere or use their corporate governance tools to change corporate decision making.

The story of the case is an interesting one. In January 2008, Citizens United (a political advocacy nonprofit corporation) released a video documentary critical of then-Senator Hillary Clinton, who at the time was the leading candidate for the Democratic nomination for President. Citizens United planned to run TV ads announcing that "Hillary" would be available before the primary elections on cable television through video-on-demand. Citizens United is mostly funded by donations from individuals, but it also accepts a small portion of funds from for-profit corporations. Concerned about possible civil and criminal penalties for violating § 441b, it sued the Federal Election Commission (FEC) seeking declaratory and injunctive relief.

Citizens United argued that § 441b is unconstitutional as applied to "Hillary" and that BCRA's disclaimer, disclosure, and reporting requirements were also unconstitutional as applied to "Hillary" and its proposed TV ads. The District Court granted summary judgment to the FEC.

Citizens United v. Federal Election Commission

558 U.S. 310 (2010)

Justice KENNEDY delivered the opinion of the Court.

Federal law prohibits corporations and unions from using general treasury funds to make independent expenditures for speech expressly advocating the election or defeat of a candidate. *Austin v. Michigan Chamber of Commerce* had held that political speech may be banned based on the speaker's corporate identity.

In this case, we are asked to reconsider *Austin*. We hold that *stare decisis* does not compel the continued acceptance of *Austin*. The Government may regulate corporate political speech through disclaimer and disclosure requirements, but it may not suppress that speech altogether.

Federal law prohibits corporations and unions from using general treasury funds to make *direct contributions* to candidates or independent expenditures that expressly advocate the election or defeat of a candidate, through any form of media, in connection with certain qualified federal elections.

Citizens United asks us to carve out an exception to § 441b's expenditure ban for nonprofit corporate political speech funded overwhelmingly by individuals. In

MCFL, the Court found unconstitutional § 441b's restrictions on corporate expenditures as applied to nonprofit corporations that were formed for the sole purpose of promoting political ideas, did not engage in business activities, and did not accept contributions from for-profit corporations or labor unions. Citizens United does not qualify for the *MCFL* exemption, however, since some funds used to make the movie were donations from for-profit corporations.

We decline to adopt an interpretation that requires intricate (and chilling) case-by-case determinations to verify whether political speech is banned, especially if we are convinced that this corporation has a constitutional right to speak on this subject.

III

The law before us is an outright ban, backed by criminal sanctions. Section 441b makes it a felony for all corporations—including nonprofit advocacy corporations—either to expressly advocate the election or defeat of candidates. These prohibitions are classic examples of censorship.

Section 441b is a ban on corporate speech notwithstanding the fact that a PAC created by a corporation can still speak. A PAC is a separate association from the corporation. So the PAC exemption from § 441b's expenditure ban, § 441(b)(2), does not allow corporations to speak. Even if a PAC could somehow allow a corporation to speak—and it does not—the option to form PACs does not alleviate the First Amendment problems with § 441b. PACs are burdensome alternatives; they are expensive to administer and subject to extensive regulations.

PACs have to comply with these regulations just to speak. This might explain why fewer than 2,000 of the millions of corporations in this country have PACs. Given the onerous restrictions, a corporation may not be able to establish a PAC in time to make its views known regarding candidates and issues in a current campaign.

Section 441b's prohibition on corporate independent expenditures is thus a ban on speech. As a "restriction on the amount of money a person or group can spend on political communication during a campaign," that statute "necessarily reduces the quantity of expression by restricting the number of issues discussed, the depth of their exploration, and the size of the audience reached." *Buckley v. Valeo*, 424 US. 1

Food for Thought

Was Justice Kennedy right that PACs are not a viable option for corporate speech? Consider the rules that apply to corporate PACs.

PACs may contribute to federal election campaigns, up to $5,000 per candidate per election. (By comparison, individual contributions are limited to $2,600 per candidate per election.) PACs, like individuals, can also make unlimited independent expenditures for or against a clearly identified candidate at any time. (But if the PAC coordinates its message with a candidate or campaign, any expenditure is limited as an in-kind campaign contribution.)

PACs are subject to guidelines in soliciting contributions from corporate constituents, with contributions to the PAC limited to $5,000 per person per calendar year.

PACs are also subject to detailed record-keeping and disclosure requirements. In election years, PACs must submit monthly reports to the FEC that disclose, among other things, their total assets, itemized receipts by individual contributors, total contributions itemized by recipient, and operating costs.

Further, for each public communication, whether or not it expressly advocates for or against a candidate, the PAC must include a disclaimer ("I am Citibank PAC and I paid for this message").

(1976). If § 441b applied to individuals, no one would believe that it is merely a time, place, or manner restriction on speech. Its purpose and effect are to silence entities whose voices the Government deems to be suspect.

Speech is an essential mechanism of democracy, for it is the means to hold officials accountable to the people. The right of citizens to inquire, to hear, to speak, and to use information to reach consensus is a precondition to enlightened self-government and a necessary means to protect it. The First Amendment "has its fullest and most urgent application to speech uttered during a campaign for political office."

Premised on mistrust of governmental power, the First Amendment stands against attempts to disfavor certain subjects or viewpoints. Prohibited, too, are restrictions distinguishing among different speakers, allowing speech by some but not others. As instruments to censor, these categories are interrelated: Speech restrictions based on the identity of the speaker are all too often simply a means to control content.

Quite apart from the purpose or effect of regulating content, moreover, the Government may commit a constitutional wrong when by law it identifies certain preferred speakers. By taking the right to speak from some and giving it to others, the Government deprives the disadvantaged person or class of the right to use speech to strive to establish worth, standing, and respect for the speaker's voice. The Government may not by these means deprive the public of the right and privilege to determine for itself what speech and speakers are worthy of consideration. The First Amendment protects speech and speaker, and the ideas that flow from each.

It is inherent in the nature of the political process that voters must be free to obtain information from diverse sources in order to determine how to cast their votes. At least before *Austin*, the Court had not allowed the exclusion of a class of speakers from the general public dialogue.

We find no basis for the proposition that, in the context of political speech, the Government may impose restrictions on certain disfavored speakers. Both history and logic lead us to this conclusion.

The Court has recognized that First Amendment protection extends to corporations. This protection has been extended by explicit holdings to the context of political speech. Under the rationale of these precedents, political speech does not lose First Amendment protection "simply because its source is a corporation." *Bellotti* at 784; *Pacific Gas & Elec. Co. v. Public Util. Comm'n of Cal.*, 475 U.S. 1, 8 (1986) (plurality opinion) ("The identity of the speaker is not decisive in determining whether speech is protected. Corporations and other associations, like individuals, contribute to the 'discussion, debate, and the dissemination of information and ideas' that the First Amendment seeks to foster").

Bellotti struck down a state-law prohibition on corporate independent expenditures related to referenda issues. Thus the law stood until *Austin*, which "upheld a direct restriction on the independent expenditure of funds for political speech for the first time in [this Court's] history." There, the Michigan Chamber of Commerce sought to use general treasury funds to run a newspaper ad supporting a specific candidate. Michigan law, however, prohibited corporate independent expenditures that supported or opposed any candidate for state office. A violation of the law was punishable as a felony. The Court sustained the speech prohibition.

To bypass *Bellotti*, the *Austin* Court identified a new governmental interest in limiting political speech: an antidistortion interest. *Austin* found a compelling governmental interest in preventing "the corrosive and distorting effects of immense aggregations of wealth that are accumulated with the help of the corporate form and that have little or no correlation to the public's support for the corporation's political ideas.

The Court is thus confronted with conflicting lines of precedent: a pre-*Austin* line that forbids restrictions on political speech based on the speaker's corporate identity and a post-*Austin* line that permits them.

In its defense of the corporate-speech restrictions in § 441b, the Government notes the antidistortion rationale on which *Austin* and its progeny rest in part, yet it all but abandons reliance upon it. It argues instead that two other compelling interests support *Austin*'s holding that corporate expenditure restrictions are constitutional: an anticorruption interest, and a shareholder protection interest.

1

As for *Austin*'s antidistortion rationale, the Government does little to defend it. And with good reason, for the rationale cannot support § 441b.

If the First Amendment has any force, it prohibits Congress from fining or jailing citizens, or associations of citizens, for simply engaging in political speech. If the antidistortion rationale were to be accepted, however, it would permit Government to ban political speech simply because the speaker is an association that has taken on the corporation form. The Government contends that *Austin* permits it to ban corporate expenditures for almost all forms of communication stemming from a corporation.

Political speech is "indispensible to decision making in a democracy, and this is no less true because the speech comes from a corporation rather than an individual." *Bellotti* (the worth of speech "does not depend upon the identity of its source, whether corporation, association, union, or individual"). This protection of speech is inconsistent with *Austin*'s anti-distortion rationale. *Austin* sought to defend the antidistortion rationale as a means to prevent corporations from obtaining 'an unfair advantage in the market place' by using 'resources amassed in the economic marketplace.' But *Buckley* rejected the premise that the Government has an interest "in equalizing the relative ability of individuals and groups to influence the outcome of elections." *Buckley* was specific in stating that "the skyrocketing cost of political campaigns could not sustain the governmental prohibition. The First Amendment's protections do not depend on the speaker's financial ability to engage in public discussion."

The *Austin* majority undertook to distinguish wealthy individuals from corporations on the ground that "state law grants corporations special advantages such as limited liability, perpetual life, and favorable treatment of the accumulation and distribution of assets." This does not suffice, however, to allow laws prohibiting speech. "It is rudimentary that the State cannot exact as the price of those special advantages the forfeiture of First Amendment rights."

All speakers, including individuals and the media, use money amassed from the economic marketplace to fund their speech. The First Amendment protects the resulting speech, even if it was enabled by economic transactions with persons or entities who disagree with the speaker's ideas. "Many persons can trace their funds to corporations, if not in the form of donations, then in the form of dividends, interest, or salary."

Austin's antidistortion rationale would produce the dangerous, and unacceptable, consequence that Congress could ban political speech of media corporations. Media corporations are now exempt from § 441b's ban on corporate expenditures. Yet media corporations accumulate wealth with the help of the corporate form, the largest media corporations have "immense aggregations of wealth," and the views expressed by media corporations often "have little or no correlation to the public's support" for those vies. Thus, under the Government's reasoning, wealthy media corporations could have their voices diminished to put them on part with other media entities. There is no precedent for permitting this under the First Amendment.

Austin interferes with the "open marketplace" of ideas protected by the First Amendment. It permits the Government to ban the political speech of millions of associations of citizens. Most of these are small corporations without large amounts of wealth.

When Government seeks to use its full power, including the criminal law, to command where a person may get his or her information or what distrusted source he or she may not hear, it uses censorship to control thought. This is unlawful. The First Amendment confirms the freedom to think for ourselves.

2

The Government falls back on the argument that corporate political speech can be banned in order to prevent corruption or its appearance. In *Buckley*, the Court found this interest "sufficiently important" to allow limits on contributions but did not extend that reasoning to expenditure limits. When *Buckley* examined an expenditure ban, it found "that the governmental interest in preventing corruption and the appearance of corruption [was] inadequate to justify [the ban] on independent expenditures."

With regard to large direct contributions, *Buckley* reasoned that they could be given "to secure a political *quid pro quo*." The Court, in consequence, has noted that restrictions on direct contributions are preventative, because few if any contributions to candidates will involve *quid pro quo* arrangements. The *Buckley* Court, nevertheless, sustained limits on direct contributions in order to ensure against the reality or appearance of corruption. That case did not extend this rationale to independent expenditures, and the Court does not do so here.

The absence of prearrangement and coordination of an expenditure with the candidate or his agent not only undermines the value of the expenditure to the candidate, but also alleviates the danger that expenditures will be given as a *quid pro quo* for improper commitments from the candidate. Limits on independent expenditures, such as § 441b, have a chilling effect extending well beyond the Government's interest in preventing *quid pro quo* corruption. The anticorruption interest is not sufficient to displace the speech here in question.

Independent expenditures do not lead to, or create the appearance of *quid pro quo* corruption. In fact, there is only scant evidence that independent expenditures even ingratiate. Ingratiation and access, in any event, are not corruption. When Congress finds that a problem exists, we must give that finding due deference; but Congress may not choose an unconstitutional remedy. If elected officials succumb to improper influences from independent expenditures; if they surrender their best judgment; and if they put expediency before principle, then surely there is cause for concern. However, an outright ban on corporate political speech during the critical preelection period is not a permissible remedy. Here Congress has created categorical bans on speech that are asymmetrical to preventing *quid pro quo* corruption.

3

The Government contends further that corporate independent expenditures can be limited because of its interest in protecting dissenting shareholders from being compelled to fund corporate political speech. This asserted interest, like *Austin*'s antidistortion rationale, would allow the Government to ban the political speech even of media corporations. Assume, for example that a shareholder of a corporation that owns a newspaper disagrees with the political views the newspaper expresses. Under the Government's view, that potential disagreement could give the Government the authority to restrict the media corporation's political speech. The First Amendment does not allow that power. There is, furthermore, little evidence of abuse that cannot be corrected by shareholders "through the procedures of corporate democracy."

Our Nation's speech dynamic is changing, and informative voices should not have to circumvent onerous restrictions to exercise their First Amendment rights. Speakers have become adept at presenting citizens with sound bites, talking points, and scripted messages that dominate the 24-hour news cycle. Corporations, like individuals, do not have monolithic views. On certain topics corporations may possess valuable expertise, leaving them the best equipped to point out errors or fallacies in speech of all sorts, including the speech of candidates and elected officials.

Rapid changes in technology-and the creative dynamic inherent in the concept of free expression-counsel against upholding a law that restricts political speech in certain media or by certain speakers. Today, 30-second television ads may be the most effective way to convey a political message. Soon, however, it may be that Internet sources such as blogs and social networking Web sites, will provide citizens with significant information about political candidates and issues. Yet, § 441b would seem to ban a blog post expressly advocating the election or defeat of a candidate if that blog were created with corporate funds. The First Amendment does not permit Congress to make these categorical distinctions based on the corporate identity of the speaker and the content of the political speech.

Due consideration leads to this conclusion: *Austin* should be and now is overruled. We return to the principle established in *Buckley* and *Bellotti* that the Government may not suppress political speech on the basis of the speaker's corporate identity. No sufficient governmental interest justifies limits on the political speech of nonprofit or for-profit corporations.

IV.

Citizens United next challenges BCRA's disclaimer and disclosure provisions as applied to *Hillary* and the three advertisements for the movie. Under BCRA § 311, televised electioneering communications funded by anyone other than a candidate must include a disclaimer that "____________ is responsible for the content of this advertising." Under BCRA § 201, any person who spends more than $10,000 on electioneering communications within a calendar year must file a disclosure statement with the FEC. That statement must identify the person making the expenditure, the amount of the expenditure, the election to which the communication was directed, and the names of certain contributors.

Disclaimer and disclosure requirements may burden the ability to speak, but they impose no ceiling on campaign-related activities," and "do not prevent anyone from speaking."

The judgment of the District Court is reversed with respect to the constitutionality of 2 U.S.C. § 441b's restrictions on corporate independent expenditures. The judgment is affirmed with respect to BCRA's disclaimer and disclosure requirements. The case is remanded for further proceedings consistent with this opinion.

Chief Justice ROBERTS, with whom Justice ALITO joins, concurring.

[Justice Roberts explained the Court's decision to overrule *Austin*. He pointed out that the Government's arguments in the case would authorize the Government "to prohibit newspapers from running editorials or opinion pieces supporting or opposing candidates for office, so long as the newspapers were owned by corporations—as the major ones are. First Amendment rights could be confined to individuals, subverting the vibrant public discourse that is at the foundation of our democracy."

Justice Roberts further points out that "*Austin* nowhere relied upon the only arguments the Government now raises to support that decision. In fact, the only opinion in *Austin* endorsing the Government's argument based on the threat of *quid pro quo* corruption was Justice STEVEN's concurrence. Moreover, the Court's only discussion of shareholder protection in *Austin* appeared in a section that sought merely to distinguish *MCFL*. Nowhere did *Austin* suggest that the goal of protecting shareholders is itself a compelling interest authorizing restrictions on First Amendment rights."

Justice Roberts concluded: "Because continued adherence to *Austin* threatens to subvert the "principled and intelligible" development of our First Amendment jurisprudence, I support the Court's determination to overrule that decision."]

Justice SCALIA, concurring.

I write separately to address Justice STEVENS' discussion of the original understanding of the First Amendment. The dissent embarks on a detailed exploration of the Framers' views about the "role of corporations in society." The Framers didn't like corporations, the dissent concludes, and therefore it follows (as night the day) that corporations had no rights of free speech.

To the contrary, colleges, towns, and cities, religious institutions, and guilds had long been organized as corporations at common law and under the King's charter, and the practice of incorporation only expanded in the United States. Both corporations and voluntary associations actively petitioned the Government and expressed their views in newspapers and pamphlets. For example: An antislavery Quaker corporation petitioned the First Congress, distributed pamphlets, and communicated through the press in 1790. The New York Sons of Liberty sent a circular to colonies farther south in 1766. And the Society for the Relief and Instruction of Poor Germans circulated a biweekly paper from 1755 to 1757. The dissent offers no evidence—none whatever—that the First Amendment's unqualified text was originally understood to exclude such associational speech from its protection.

The dissent says that "speech" refers to oral communications of human beings, and since corporations are not human beings they cannot speak. This is sophistry. The authorized spokesman of a corporation is a human being, who speaks on behalf of the human beings who have formed that association—just as the spokesman of an unincorporated association speaks on behalf of its members.

The Amendment is written in terms of "speech," not speakers. Its text offers no foothold for excluding any category of speaker, from single individuals to partnerships of individuals, to unincorporated associations of individuals, to incorporated associations of individuals—and the dissent offers no evidence about the original meaning of the text to support any such exclusion. A documentary film critical of a potential Presidential candidate is core political speech, and its nature as such does not change simply because it was funded by a corporation. Nor does the character of that funding produce any reduction whatever in the "inherent worth of the speech" and "its capacity for informing the public." Indeed, to exclude or impede corporate speech is to muzzle the principal agents of the modern free economy. We should celebrate rather than condemn the addition of this speech to the public debate.

Justice STEVENS, with whom Justice GINSBURG, Justice BREYER, and Justice SOTOMAYOR join, concurring in part and dissenting in part.

The real issue in this case concerns how, not if, the appellant may finance its electioneering. Citizens United is a wealthy nonprofit corporation that runs a political action committee (PAC) with millions of dollars in assets. Under the Bipartisan Campaign Reform Act of 2002 (BCRA), it could have used those assets to televise and promote *Hillary: The Movie* wherever and whenever it wanted to. Neither Citizens United's nor any other corporation's speech has been "banned." All that the parties dispute is whether Citizens United had a right to use the funds in its general treasury to pay for broadcasts. The notion that the First Amendment dictates an affirmative answer to that question is, in my judgment, profoundly misguided. Even more misguided is the notion that the Court must rewrite the law relating to campaign expenditures by *for-profit* corporations and unions to decide this case.

In the context of elections to public office, the distinction between corporate and human speakers is significant. Although they make enormous contributions to our society, corporations are not actually members of it. They cannot vote or run for office. Because they may be managed and controlled by nonresidents, their interests may conflict in fundamental respects with the interests of eligible voters. The financial resources, legal structure, and instrumental orientation of corporations raise legitimate concerns about their role in the electoral process. Our lawmakers have a compelling constitutional basis, if not also a democratic duty, to take measures designed to guard against the potentially deleterious effects of corporate spending in local and national races.

Thomas Jefferson famously fretted that corporations would subvert the Republic. General incorporation statutes, and widespread acceptance of business corporations as socially useful actors, did not emerge until the 1800's.

The Framers thus took it as a given that corporations could be comprehensively regulated in the service of the public welfare. Unlike our colleagues, they had little trouble distinguishing corporations from human beings, and when they constitutionalized the right to free speech in the First Amendment, it was the free speech of individual Americans that they had in mind. While individuals might join together to exercise their speech rights, business corporations, at least, were plainly not seen as facilitating such associational or expressive ends. Even "the notion that business corporations could invoke the First Amendment would probably have been quite a novelty," given that "at the time, the legitimacy of every corporate activity was thought to rest entirely in a concession of the sovereign." In light of these background practices and understandings, it seems to me implausible that the Framers believed "the freedom of speech" would extend equally to all corporate speakers, much less than it would preclude legislatures from taking limited measures to guard against corporate capture of elections.

These basic points help explain why corporate electioneering is not only more likely to impair compelling governmental interests, but also why restrictions on that electioneering are less likely to encroach upon First Amendment freedoms. One fundamental concern of the First Amendment is to "protect the individual's interest in self-expression." Freedom of speech helps "make men free to develop their faculties," it respects their "dignity and choice," and it facilitates the value of "individual self-realization." Corporate speech, however, is derivative speech, speech by proxy. A regulation such as the one challenged here may affect the way in which individuals disseminate certain messages through the corporate form, but it does not prevent anyone from speaking in his or her own voice.

It is an interesting question "who" is even speaking when a business corporation places an advertisement that endorses or attacks a particular candidate. Presumably it is not the customers or employees, who typically have no say in such matters. It cannot realistically be said to be the shareholders, who tend to be far removed from the day-to-day decisions of the firm and whose political preferences may be opaque to management. Perhaps the officers or directors of the corporation have the best claim to be the ones speaking, except their fiduciary duties generally prohibit them from using corporate funds for personal ends. Some individuals associated with the corporation must make the decision to place the ad, but the idea that these individuals are thereby fostering their self expression or cultivating their critical faculties is fanciful. It is entirely possible that the corporation's electoral message will conflict with their personal convictions. Take away the ability to use general treasury funds for some of those ads, and no one's autonomy, dignity, or political equality has been impinged upon in the least.

The majority's unwillingness to distinguish between corporations and humans similarly blinds it to the possibility that corporations' "war chests" and their special "advantages" in the legal realm may translate into special advantages in the market for legislation. Corporations, that is, are uniquely equipped to seek laws that favor their owners, not simply because they have a lot of money but because of their legal and organizational structure. Remove all restrictions on their electioneering, and the door may be opened to a type of rent seeking that is "far more destructive" than what noncorporations are capable of.

The PAC mechanism, by contrast, helps assure that those who pay for an electioneering communication actually support its content and that managers do not use general treasuries to advance personal agendas. It "allows corporate political participation without the temptation to use corporate funds for political influence, quite possibly at odds with the sentiments of some shareholders or members." A rule that privileges the use of PACs thus does more than facilitate the political speech of like-minded shareholders; it also curbs the rent seeking behavior of executives and respects the views of dissenters. *Austin*'s acceptance of restrictions on general treasury spending "simply allows people who have invested in the business corporation for purely economic reasons"—the vast majority of investors, one assumes—"to avoid being taken advantage of, without sacrificing their economic objectives."

Justice THOMAS, concurring in part and dissenting in part.

I join all but Part IV of the Court's opinion.

Congress may not abridge the "right to anonymous speech" based on the "simple interest in providing voters with additional relevant information." In continuing to hold otherwise, the Court misapprehends the import of "recent events" that some *amici* describe "in which donors to certain causes were blacklisted, threatened, or otherwise targeted for retaliation."

The success of such intimidation tactics has apparently spawned a cottage industry that uses forcibly disclosed donor information to pre-empt citizens' exercise of their First Amendment rights. These instances of retaliation sufficiently demonstrate why this Court should invalidate mandatory disclosure and reporting requirements. But amici present evidence of yet another reason to do so—the threat of retaliation from elected officials. My point is not to express any view on the merits of the political controversies I describe. Rather, it is to demonstrate—using real-world, recent examples—the fallacy in the Court's conclusion that "disclaimer and disclosure requirements . . . impose no ceiling on campaign-related activities, and do not prevent anyone from speaking." Of course they do. Disclaimer and disclosure requirements enable private citizens and elected officials to implement political strategies specifically calculated to curtail campaign-related activity and prevent the lawful, peaceful exercise of First Amendment rights.

Points for Discussion

1. Expenditures vs. Contributions

In summary, the Court in *Citizens United* decided:

> (1) the government may not, under the First Amendment, suppress political speech on the basis of the speaker's corporate identity, overruling *Austin v. Michigan Chamber of Commerce*, 494 U.S. 652 (1990).
> (2) the disclaimer and disclosure provisions of Bipartisan Campaign Reform Act of 2002 did not violate the First Amendment, as applied to a nonprofit corporation's documentary and advertisements for the documentary.

Citizens United allows corporations to spend unlimited amounts from their general treasury on independent expenditures. In overruling *Austin* on this point, the Court stated that independent expenditures, uncoordinated with a candidate, do not give rise to corruption or the appearance of corruption. The Court identified the governmental interest in preventing corruption or the appearance of corruption as limited to *quid pro quo* corruption, noting that "appearance of influence or access, furthermore, will not cause the electorate to lose faith in our democracy."

Nonetheless, the Court left standing FECA's *direct contribution* prohibition to prevent the appearance of *quid pro quo* corruption. Also, *Citizens United* did not overturn the BCRA's disclosure and disclaimer requirements. What is the basis for distinguishing so sharply between expenditures and contributions? Do you agree that independent expenditures from corporations do not give rise to compelling concerns about corruption?

2. What kind of person is the corporation?

The Supreme Court (and different justices) have variously viewed the corporation (1) as a creature of state law (a "concession" theory), (2) as a distinct legal entity separate from the incorporating state and its shareholders (a "real entity" theory), and (3) as a voluntary association of participants (an "aggregate" theory).

The "concession" theory is reflected in the *Dartmouth College* case, in which the Supreme Court disallowed states from unilaterally changing the corporate charter, viewing the corporation as an "artificial being" created by the law and a binding contract between two parties—the state and the private individuals who formed the corporation. The "real entity" theory has also appeared in Court decisions, such as when the Court denied "citizen" status to corporations under the privileges and immunities clause, and when it has referred to corporations as having dignity or autonomy interests. In *Citizens United* and other cases granting protections to corporations, the Court has often used the language of the "aggregate" theory, characterizing the corporation as a group of individuals from whom rights can be derived.

Which view best describes the corporation? Does it make sense to determine corporate rights based on these theories of the corporation?

3. Do shareholders have a voice in corporate political activities?

Justice Kennedy pointed out that dissenting shareholders can protect themselves "through the procedures of corporate democracy." How might this happen? The Court did not explain. In the earlier *Bellotti* opinion, the Court referenced state corporate law:

> Acting through their power to elect the board of directors or to insist upon protective provisions in the corporation's charter, shareholders normally are presumed competent to protect their own interests. In addition to intracorporate remedies, minority shareholders generally have access to the judicial remedy of a derivative suit to challenge corporate disbursements alleged to have been made for improper corporate purposes or merely to further the personal interests of management.

Further, the *Bellotti* opinion noted that "the shareholder invests in a corporation of his own volition and is free to withdraw his investment at any time and for any reason."

However, in pointing to the "procedures of corporate democracy" in *Bellotti* and *Citizens United*, the Court did not acknowledge that shareholders often have incomplete information about a corporation's political spending. In addition, many Americans invest indirectly through pension funds and mutual funds, and lack a ready means of exit. And, in any case, selling stock provides a solution only prospectively and does nothing to address the political spending that already occurred.

As a matter of state corporate law, while shareholders elect the board of directors, they generally do not have proxy access to nominate directors. Waging a proxy fight is expensive and it's unclear shareholders would vote to oust directors for approving political spending the directors believed was in the corporation's best interests. Shareholders can also sue the directors for violating their fiduciary duties, but absent fraud or self-dealing, the business judgment rule protects political spending decisions if the board had plausible reasons for its decision.

Shareholders have another avenue for voice—they can propose and vote on precatory (non-binding) resolutions. But many proposals get settled before going to a shareholder vote and even if passed the board is not required to follow the shareholders' recommendations. Nonetheless, since *Citizens United*, shareholder proposals concerning corporate political spending have dramatically increased and resulted in some corporations making voluntary reports about their spending.

Are the "procedures of corporate democracy" sufficient to protect shareholders? Should political expenditures be considered ordinary business decisions subject to business judgment rule protection? Are corporate directors best equipped to make political decisions for the corporation and should they be buffered from special interests and outside forces?

4. What must corporations disclose about political spending?
Corporations have only limited duties under federal law to disclose their political spending. For example, corporations that engage in express advocacy to the public, for the election or defeat of a particular federal candidate, must report to the FEC on a quarterly basis spending of more than $250 per year. Corporations are subject to 48-hour reporting requirements for spending of more than $10,000 in a calendar year on electioneering communications that clearly refer to a federal candidate within a certain period before an election. In addition, disclosure of express advocacy to internal corporate constituencies (employees, shareholders, or management) is required for expenditures above $2,000 per election.

Corporations are also subject to a patchwork of disclosure laws regarding state and local elections. Of particular note, in some states, corporations are allowed to contribute directly to state candidates, and the campaigns will generally disclose the contributions.

Some additional information about corporate political spending is available because some corporations make voluntary disclosures, and some groups such as PACs and Super PACs are required to make disclosures about contributors, including corporations. However, corporations can fund other groups that do not disclose their donors, such as "social welfare" organizations and trade associations that are organized under sections 501(c)(4) and (c)(6) of the tax code. For example, the U.S. Chamber of Commerce, a 501(c)(6) trade association funded by corporations, is one of the top spenders in lobbying for business interests and is not required to disclose its contributors. The lack of transparency of 501(c)(4) and (c)(6) organizations and "dark money" more generally has attracted significant concern and ongoing litigation about disclosure obligations when organizations reach a threshold of election-related activity.

Finally, in the aftermath of *Citizens United*, the Securities and Exchange Commission considered specifically mandating disclosure of corporate political spending, but did not take action. The issue has engendered significant debate.

Citizens United as Corporate Elitism

For many people, *Citizens United* stands for the (shocking) proposition that corporations are "persons." What many don't realize is that corporate personhood has existed from the very beginning of the US corporation. It's an attribute that permits business firms to carry out their commercial purposes, such as entering into contracts, hiring labor, owning property, and suing (and being sued) in court.

Instead, the Supreme Court's decision in *Citizens United* merely held that corporations have the same free speech rights as individuals—to advance "a marketplace of ideas"—unless there are "compelling interests" to treat corporations differently. Second, the Court majority didn't find any compelling interests, rejecting that corporate political speech would "distort" the political discourse, create the impression of a *quid pro quo* corruption, or force captive shareholders to fund political speech by management.

In a scathing dissent, Justice John Paul Stevens did see compelling reasons to regulate the political activities of corporations, but he mustered only four votes. In the end Justice Anthony Kennedy, who wrote for the majority, seemed unwilling to draw lines between nonprofit corporations (which the Court had previously held could be political, if such was the corporation's purpose) and for-profit corporations (which come in all sorts of sizes and flavors).

In *The Meaning of Markets*, Professor Lindblom expanded on some of the points in the Stevens dissent:

> Corporations can be seen as elites who use political messaging to persuade the masses, who come to ask from elites only what elites wish to give them.
>
> This is hardly a novel thesis. Down through history, many of the great minds have been troubled by distortions in thought that bear on social organization and elite manipulation of mass. Plato spoke of shadows in caves rather than reality, Francis Bacon of "idols," Kant of "tutelage," Locke of "insinuations," Rousseau of "capturing volitions," and Marx of "false consciousness." In our time Schumpeter speaks of "manufactured will," Habermas of "distorted communication," and Schattschneider of the "heavenly chorus" that sings "with a strong upperclass accent."
>
> Elites defend their political communications as a contribution to a competition of ideas such as has been prized in liberal and democratic thought. But the competition of ideas works if at all, only when several conditions are met. First, the messages must challenge each other. And, in the contestation, loud voices must not silence others. Third, each of the contesting messages must contain some empirical content. Finally, the contestants must not depart too far from a respect for truth. All of these conditions are in varying degrees violated in elite political messages.
>
> The failure of a competition of ideas on fundamental institutions is a particularly American problem. Ideological homogeneity puts a touch of impropriety on anyone who would question the "American Way," the Constitution, the private enterprise system, the corporation, and equality.

> If genuine democracy requires, by definition, at least a rough equality of political influence or power among citizens in their attempts to control elites, then any significant economic inequality among citizens is an obstruction to democracy. Inequalities in income and wealth create inequalities in opportunity to run for office, in launching candidates, in capacities to use the mass media to influence voters, in lobbying, and in social interchange with party and government officials. Because market systems produce inequality of income and wealth, they obstruct democracy Q.E.D.

Of course, the Supreme Court has not been willing to say that moneyed *individuals* should be limited in how much they spend in advancing their political views—that is, wealth is not a political crime! And the Court in *Citizens United* simply extended this logic to corporations, on the theory (an elitist one, says Professor Lindblom) that the more viewpoints the better.

Mandatory Disclosure of Corporate Political Expenditures

In 2013, the SEC received a rulemaking petition (which attracted over 1.2 million comments) calling on the agency to require public companies to disclose their political spending. The petition sparked a debate among academics, members of the investor and issuer communities, current and former SEC commissioners, and members of Congress. Would disclosure of political spending be counterproductive and lead to more corporate engagement in politics? Would mandatory disclosure be superior to voluntary disclosures by companies? Would an SEC disclosure rule violate the First Amendment? The answer by some law professors (including an SEC commissioner) is no—"the case for keeping political spending under the radar of investors is untenable." Lucian A. Bebchuk, Robert J. Jackson, James David Nelson & Roberto Tallarita, *The Untenable Case for Keeping Investors in the Dark* (2019) [available on SSRN].

One of the reasons for this push for greater transparency about corporate political spending is to allow shareholders and the public to gauge the truthfulness (or insincerity) of corporate political speech. For example, CVS Health (the nation's largest pharmacy chain) has publicly declared its support of LGBTQ rights, while at the same time its PAC has funneled millions of dollars to legislators who either sponsor anti-LGBTQ legislation or oppose non-discrimination laws to protect LGBTQ persons.

> CVS Health received a perfect score from the Human Rights Campaign [the most prominent LGBTQ rights organization in the United States] and changed its Twitter avatar to a rainbow heart in June. The company tweeted that it was "proud to join more than 100 companies that have signed HRC's Business Statement Opposing Anti-LGBTQ State Legislation."
>
> On its corporate website, CVS Health says that it is "proud of our long-standing commitment to eliminating discrimination in health care and health care coverage, including our commitment to support the lesbian, gay, bisexual, and transgender communities."
>
> But, through its corporate PAC, CVS Health has recently supported the sponsors of anti-trans legislation in Texas, North Carolina, and Tennessee, including legislation that would criminalize providing gender-affirming medical care to adults and children.

> In Texas, CVS Health backed co-sponsors of SB1646, a bill that would "change the state's child abuse law" to make it a crime for parents to allow their children to receive gender-affirming medical care. Under the bill, parents that allow their children to receive gender-affirming care could be subject to "the possible removal of the child from their home." Doctors who provide such care could be "accused of child abuse, which would trigger a license investigation by the Texas Medical Board."
>
> In North Carolina, CVS Health backed Senator Ralph Hise (R), the primary sponsor of S514, which The Advocate called "the most repressive anti-transgender health care bill in the nation." The legislation would ban anyone under the age of 21 from receiving gender-affirming treatment, including reversible hormone therapy. It also requires government employees, including teachers, to report children who demonstrate "gender nonconformity" to their parents.
>
> Hise's view on trans issues was not a secret. He was a chief proponent of North Carolina's infamous anti-trans "bathroom bill" in 2016, saying the legislation was necessary "to protect the citizens of the state of North Carolina." Nevertheless, CVS Health donated $1000 to Hise in August 2020.
>
> Since 2019, CVS Health has also donated $259,000 to 54 members of Congress who received a zero rating in HRC's Congressional scorecard for the 116th Congress. In the House, that meant voting against the Equality Act, which would "provide consistent and explicit non-discrimination protections for LGBTQ people across key areas of life."

Judd Legum & Tesnim Zekeria, *These 25 Rainbow Flag-Waving Corporations Donated More than $10 Million to Anti-Gay Politicians in the Last Two Years*, Popular Information (Jun. 14, 2021).

2.4.4 Critiques of *Citizens United*

Citizens United also unleashed a fury of academic criticism. Some pointed out that the Court got First Amendment jurisprudence wrong. Michael Curtis, *Citizens United: Lochner on Steroids and Democracy on Life Support* (2012). Others decried the pernicious effects on political results in elections after the decision. Klumpp, Miailon & Williams, *The Business of American Democracy* (2013). But, for our purposes, the most relevant criticism was that the Supreme Court just didn't quite understand the corporation and the extent to which "corporate democracy" might protect against management (which ultimately makes corporate speech decisions) speaking for unwilling shareholders and other corporate constituents. See Rosenberg, *The Corporate Paradox of Citizens United and Hobby Lobby* (2015).

In a similar vein, Professor Kent Greenfield (who we met in our study of short-termism) has argued that the Supreme Court's conflation of corporations and their shareholders misconceives corporate law. For example, when Arlene's Flowers (a Washington State for-profit corporation) sought an exemption from generally applicable laws based on the religious beliefs of a shareholder, Mrs. Stutzman, the Supreme Court turned to *Burwell v. Hobby Lobby Stores* and *Masterpiece Cakeshop, Ltd. v. Colorado Civil Rights Commission* to conclude that "Arlene's free-exercise rights are synonymous with Mrs. Stutzman's." But Washington corporate law runs counter to this assertion. As stated by the Washington State supreme court: "[a] corporation exists as an organization distinct from the personality of its shareholders." Kent Greenfield, "Brief for Professor Kent Greenfield as Amicus Curiae in Support of Respondents, *State of Washington vs. Arlene's Flowers* and *Ingersoll vs. Arlene's Flowers*" [available on SSRN].

Citizens United Misconceives Nature of US Corporation

Recently, Professor Jonathan Macey (a stalwart defender of the corporation's design) and then Chief Justice Leo Strine (a skeptic of the corporation's design) joined together to argue that *Citizens United* misconceived the nature of the US corporation.

Citizens United as Bad Corporate Law

(2018)

Jonathan Macey & Leo Strine

[available on SSRN]

Citizens United v. FEC, arguably the most important First Amendment case of the new millennium, is predicated on a fundamental misconception about the nature of the corporation. Specifically, the case—which prohibited the government from restricting independent expenditures for corporate communications and held that corporations enjoy the same free speech rights to engage in political spending as human citizens—is grounded on the erroneous theory that corporations are "associations of citizens" rather than what they actually are: independent legal entities distinct from those who own their stock. *Citizens United* is as much a case about corporate law, as it is about the First Amendment.

The major disagreement among the justices in *Citizens United* is about the applicability of settled First Amendment protections to a particular juridical entity, the corporation. Justice Kennedy, writing for the majority, opined that Congress may not take into account the distinctions between corporations and human beings in regulating political speech, and that corporations must be permitted the same freedom to speak as human beings. In dissent, Justice Stevens failed directly to challenge this existential conception of the corporation even though it was at the core of the majority opinion.

The *Citizens United* majority's conception of the corporation as an "associations of citizens" confuses the corporation with the general partnership form of business organization. In fact, the entire point of incorporation is to permit the creation of a legal entity that is not an association of individuals, but rather a discrete legal entity whose rights and obligations are distinct from those of it its creators, investors, managers, and other constituents. Corporations are separate and distinct legal entities, not "associations of citizens" as *Citizens United* asserts. Here are three facts about the corporate form:

> (1) the treatment of corporations as separate legal entities is what distinguishes corporations from general partnerships and sole proprietorships and what justifies the legal notion of "limited liability" and other central characteristics of the corporate form, such as the ability to contract and to sue and be sued;
>
> (2) corporations do not have owners, they have investors who have contract-based, financial interests in the firms and limited management rights; and
>
> (3) corporations are not fiction, but fact only because the law makes them real and distinct entities with a legal identity.

We note a simple, empirical reality that cuts against *Citizens United*'s conception of the corporation as an "association of citizens": stockholders are not owners of the corporation, but rather contract claimants of the corporate entity. In most other areas of its jurisprudence the Supreme Court embraces this traditional entity view of the corporation, and does not treat corporations as associations of citizens. Thus, *Citizens United* and its progeny are outliers, in tension with the Supreme Court's decisional law in key areas like standing, tax law, criminal law, and other areas of constitutional law. In fact, by long tradition, starting under Chief Justice Marshall, corporations are the opposite of Lockean–Jeffersonian human beings endowed with inalienable rights that cannot be taken away by the government. By contrast, corporations have only those rights society gives them by statutory law, and any statutory law may take into account the unique nature of corporations in limiting their ability to act.

Next, we note the stark difference in the Supreme Court's approach when dealing with the free speech of labor unions. In the union context, the Supreme Court's principal concern has been ensuring that no union member has his dues used for political speech without his express authorization, and has held that it is a First Amendment violation to use union dues for political speech. Just this year, in *Janus v. American Federation of State, County, and Municipal Employees, Council 31* the Court went further and held that unions could not even collect fees for the costs due to the core costs of bargaining for higher wages from a workforce member who did not join the union.

In McCain-Feingold, Congress embraced concerns like this and gave corporations the ability to engage in political speech by raising funds voluntarily from stockholders for this purpose. This took into account the corporate law consensus that stockholders' decision to invest in business corporations does not rationally involve any authorization for the corporation to use treasury funds for political speech, and that stockholders are of diverse political viewpoints and only have a shared interest in one thing, getting a good return on their investment. But, applying a starkly different viewpoint than it takes in cases like *Janus*, the Supreme Court struck down McCain-Feingold and trivialized the substantial leeway McCain-Feingold had given for corporations to speak. In analyzing this contradiction, we identify the market realities that make it even less plausible that 21st century American business corporations can be deemed "associations of citizens," especially when most of their stock is owned by institutional shareholders, to whom American investors are in essence compelled to turn over their capital to save for college for their kids and retirement for themselves.

Finally, we comment on the lack of any source for the *Citizens United* majority's view that the corporation is an association of individuals. In particular, we observe that corporations are creatures of state law, not federal law. As the Court observed in *CTS Corp. v. Dynamics Corp.*, "[s]tate regulation of corporate governance is regulation of entities whose very existence and attributes are a product of state law." Therefore, determinations about the nature of the corporation, such as whether the corporation is a distinct juridical entity or an association of individuals, should be made by reference to state law, not federal law.

Congress considered the nature of corporations when enacting McCain-Feingold and took into account that corporations are not associations of citizens, but separate, state-created entities formed for reasons that cannot be rationally attributed to the shared political or philosophical views of their investors. As such, Congress allowed corporations broad freedom to engage in political speech, but only by using funds voluntarily contributed for this purpose by stockholders to a corporate-controlled political action committee (PAC). By this means, Congress left ample room for the corporation to act as a collective vehicle for stockholders who wished to affiliate for that purpose, but protected other stockholders from being forced to subsidize speech that the mere decision to invest cannot plausibly be thought to endorse. By contrast, the Supreme Court ignored, or misunderstood, the traditional corporate law concept of the corporation and thereby subjected millions of American investors to suffer the involuntary use of their entrusted capital for speech that has no rational connection to their decision to buy stock. That is bad corporate law making bad constitutional law.

In a like vein, some research suggests that corporate political spending may sometimes actually be contrary to the corporate purpose to maximize shareholder wealth. For example, soon after *Citizens United*, Professor John Coates (Harvard Law) looked into whether corporate political activities really pay. He found "unobservable political activity is . . . harmful to shareholder interests." See John Coates, *Corporate Governance and Corporate Political Activity: What Effect Will* Citizens United *Have on Shareholder Wealth?* (2010) [available on SSRN]. That is, well-informed shareholders should tend to share the popular moral outrage of corporations becoming over-involved in the political process!

Citizens United Immunizes Corporations from Regulation

Others have lamented the use of the logic of *Citizens United* to invalidate regulation that seeks to diminish corporate activities and speech. For example, Professor John Coates and free-speech advocate Ron Fein have described how the "logic" of *Citizens United* has moved into other areas, beyond corporate spending in support and opposition of candidates to political office. John Coates & Ron Fein, *Courts Are Perverting the Notion of Free Speech*, Newsweek (Aug. 4, 2015). For example, Coates and Fein point out that corporations have flexed their political "personhood" to claim freedom from regulation that requires disclosure of chemicals used in their operations, disclosure of whether the corporation sources minerals from strife-torn countries in Africa, and even corporate discussion about the potential effects of fossil fuels on global climate (and business).

In addition, *Citizens United* emboldened the ongoing corporate campaigns to discredit climate science and "win the global warming war." For example, the Heartland Institute (the think tank launched by ExxonMobil and the Koch Brothers described above) has taken the stance that global warming is good for the planet. See also Aaron Ley, *Mobilizing Doubt: The Legal Mobilization of Climate Denialist Groups* (2018) [available on SSRN]:

> The climate change countermovement (CCCM) deploys a broad repertoire of tactics in its effort to cast doubt on the science of climate change. One tactic is to use open records laws in scientifically uncertain areas to cast doubt on the accuracy of scientific information. This article traces the origin of CCCM groups to the broader conservative legal movement of the 1970s that challenged the dominance of the liberal legal network. It shows how CCCM groups waged an open records campaign against climate scientists in Virginia and Arizona, causing scientists to counter-mobilize by organizing their own legal campaigns. The article provides the first empirical evidence (based on interviews of university researchers) of the effect of CCCM Freedom of Information Act suits on the activities of university researchers. The costs of these tactics are narrowly borne by a concentrated group of scientists whose production of knowledge is a public good that allows us to address climate change.

The power of the corporation to influence the political process and the views of politicians is illustrated by a study finding that politicians don't actually care what their constituents think. Joshua Kalla & Ethan Porter, *Opinion: Politicians Don't Actually Care What Voters Want*, NYT (July 11, 2019). The 2017 study by two political science professors found that regardless of voters' views (based on opinion polls) on such matters as abortion, climate change and gun control, state legislators do not formulate their political views on how corporate constituents view these issues. For an "overwhelming majority" of legislators there is no interest in learning about their constituents' views. When legislators were asked to review a website identifying views in their districts, only 11 percent bothered to look at the website and those who looked at it (like those who did not) were unable to state with any accuracy their constituents' preferences. For example, while 7 of 10 constituents in the average legislative district supported eliminating mandatory minimum sentencing for non-violent crimes, legislators said that fewer than 2 of 10 constituents supported such a policy.

Citizens United Minimizes Human Beings

By elevating corporations to the status of nearly full persons, the Supreme Court in *Citizens United* signaled its respect for corporate Americans, even as in other decisions the Court has reduced the rights of human Americans. Leo Strine again:

> At the beginning of our nation and throughout much of our history, corporations, as the creation of society, were seen as distinctive from human citizens. Human beings were born with certain inalienable rights that government could not take away. By contrast, corporations were the opposite of Lockean-Jeffersonian citizens, in the sense that they had only such rights as society gave them. Under this understanding, society could charter corporations and benefit from their wealth-creating potential while reserving for itself the right to limit corporate activities through externality-reducing legislation and other means so as to protect the public interest.
>
> But, in recent decades, the interactive effect of federal jurisprudence is eroding the ability of society to constrain its own corporate creations. First, recent Supreme Court decisions like *Citizens United* have freed corporations to use treasury funds to make unlimited political expenditures. This is likely to make politicians more responsive to moneyed interests, including both corporations and the economic elites who control them. Corporations have exercised their newfound ability to use treasury funds to influence the political process, often in the form of untraceable "dark money."
>
> Second, the Supreme Court's decisions in other areas have dampened the political influence of minorities and less-affluent citizens. For example, *Shelby County* struck down important elements of the Voting Rights Act, despite the fact that the Act, like the McCain-Feingold Act struck down in Citizens United, had overwhelming bipartisan support. Similarly, the Court has not intervened in cases involving voter identification laws and extreme gerrymandering, legislative action that is likely to diminish the voting power of less affluent voters. And at the same time, as the Court has freed corporations to act on the political process without stockholder consent, it continues to subject labor unions to more election spending restrictions than corporations, diminishing the voice of workers as compared to moneyed interests.
>
> Third, recent Supreme Court decisions like *National Federation of Independent Business v. Sebelius* and *Hobby Lobby* have made it more expensive for Congress to adopt regulatory and social welfare legislation, and have also suggested that expansions of the social security net will be struck down as unconstitutional.
>
> Fourth, although it might be thought that these shifts in jurisprudential direction might result in a more favorable environment for executive branch regulators, who have been able to put in place measures to regulate corporate behavior, the reality has been on balance otherwise. Although there has been lip service to deferential review, federal judges have overturned important corporate regulatory measures, in decisions that can be seen as involving a substitution of the judiciary's own policy views over the judgment made by the regulator selected by Congress. Taken together, the decisions of the Roberts

Court and other like-minded federal judges have had the practical effect of increasing the power of corporations to influence the electoral and regulatory process, diminishing the ability of human citizens to constrain their corporate creations in the public interest, and reducing the practical ability of Congress and executive agencies to adopt and implement externality regulations and new social welfare regulation. The result has been to alter the relationship between society and the corporations that it has created.

Finally, there is the question whether this pattern of decisions is the result of jurists applying precedent and exercising judicial restraint. Because the decisions involve a conscious decision by judges to depart from precedent and to overturn the decisions of the political branches, these decisions are properly regarded as involving judges willing to break new ground, depart from traditional principles of judicial restraint, and move the law in a direction they think better for society.

Leo E. Strine Jr., *Corporate Power Ratchet: The Courts' Role in Eroding "We the People's" Ability to Constrain Our Corporate Creations* (2016) [available on SSRN].

Citizens United Is Antithetical to One-Person/One-Vote

Finally, I invite you to read a thoughtful concurrence by Judge Guido Calabresi, the Yale law-and-economics professor who you may have encountered in your Torts class. (He asserted that tort rules should be designed to minimize the social cost of accidents first by incentivizing risky actors to exercise cost-effective care, and then by spreading the residual risks to minimize insurance costs.) The Calabresi concurrence came in a case challenging New York City's rules prohibiting "pay to play," the practice in which people (including corporations) doing work with the city would contribute lavishly to the campaigns of city politicians as a way to garner their favor on city contracts. Calabresi gives an impassioned argument against corporations receiving free rein to spend money in politics in a democracy built on the notion of one person/one-vote—that is, an egalitarian democracy.

Ognibene v. Parkes

671 F.3d 174 (2d Cir. 2011)

Appellants challenge New York City's "pay to play" rules as an undue burden on political speech and association. They claim the city has improperly limited how much people who have business dealings with the City, including lobbyists, can contribute to political campaigns. They further claim the city lacks evidence of actual pay-to-play corruption in City politics and thus there is no legitimate interest to be protected. Further, they claim that *Citizens United* prohibits all contribution limits based on the source's identity. The district court rejected these arguments and dismissed the claims. We affirm, finding that the city's pay-to-play rules are closely drawn to address the significant governmental interest in reducing corruption or the appearance thereof.

I. Facts

[The majority opinion described how the pay-to-play rules were passed in response to a wave of local scandals in the 1980s. The rules limit how much persons who do business with the City can contribute to campaigns of local politicians and specifically bans all corporate contributions to local candidates. In passing these rules, the City concluded there is "no doubt that these contributions have a negative impact on the public because they promote the perception that one must 'pay-to-play.'" The rules were further tightened in 2006, after the City's election board found that over 120 percent of the contributions in the 2001 and 2005 election cycles were from individuals and entities doing business with the City, who comprised only 5 percent of contributors, and that large contributions came mostly from such donors. The election board stated: "It is important to eradicate this perception and reduce the appearance of undue influence associated with contributions from individuals [and business entities] doing business with the City."]

II. The District Court Decision on Motion for Summary Judgment

[The district court, while not finding recent evidence of actual corruption with respect to campaign contributions, concluded that the public's perception of continuing corruption, fueled by actual pay-to-play scandals in the 1980s, justified the city's "closely drawn" pay-to-play rules. Specifically, the district court upheld the ban on contributions from business entities "to prevent circumvention of the valid contribution limits and the use of business forms to deploy for political ends business assets amassed for business reasons."]

III. Analysis

[The majority opinion explains how the Supreme Court still leaves room for government regulation of campaign contributions where such contributions create actual *quid pro quo* corruption or an appearance of corruption.]

CONCLUSION

For the foregoing reasons, we AFFIRM the judgment of the district court upholding the constitutionality of the contribution limits.

CALABRESI, Circuit Judge, concurring:

> As Jesus looked up, he saw the rich putting their gifts into the temple treasury. He also saw a poor widow put in two very small copper coins. "Truly I tell you," he said, "this poor widow has put in more than all the others. All these people gave their gifts out of their wealth; but she out of her poverty put in all she had to live on."

Luke 21:1–4.

I join the majority opinion because it properly describes and follows the current law of campaign finance. But all is not well with this law, and I believe it appropriate to state in a judicial opinion why I think this is so.

Judge Crotty [for the court] has performed a careful analysis of corruption (actual and its appearance), and only of corruption, as a ground for upholding the regulations at issue in this case. His is the necessary analysis under Supreme Court case law. The High Court has told us that the First Amendment protects the right to speak through the use of money, but that the existence of this right does not prevent governments from enacting campaign finance regulations in furtherance of their interest in limiting actual or apparent corruption. *McConnell v. FEC*, 540 U.S. 93, 143 (2003). "Our cases have made clear that the prevention of corruption or its appearance constitutes a sufficiently important interest to justify political contribution limits.").

At the same time, the Court has rejected the idea that governments may, by campaign finance regulations, pursue what it has rather derisively called "leveling the playing field." *Arizona Free Enterprise Club's Freedom Club PAC v. Bennett*, ___ U.S. ___ (2011). That is, under current Supreme Court doctrine, governments cannot defend campaign finance regulations as a response to the different capacities of the rich and the poor to speak through money. It is with this position that I wish to take issue here.

I agree completely with the Supreme Court that the First Amendment protects each person's right to express political beliefs through money. Where I disagree with the Court is in its repeated insistence that any recognition of the "level playing field" interest (elsewhere referred to as the "antidistortion interest," *Citizens United v. FEC*, 558 U.S. 310 (2010)) is inconsistent with this right. To the contrary, the antidistortion interest promotes this right in two important ways. First, it prevents some speakers from drowning out the speech of others. And second, it safeguards something of fundamental First Amendment importance—the ability to have one's protected expression indicate the intensity of one's political beliefs.

The first benefit of antidistortion measures is not difficult to see. If an external factor, such as wealth, allows some individuals to communicate their political views too powerfully, then persons who lack wealth may, for all intents and purposes, be excluded from the democratic dialogue. In much the same way that anti-noise ordinances help to prevent megaphone users from drowning out all others in the public square, contribution limits can serve to prevent the wealthiest donors from rendering all other donors irrelevant—from, in effect, silencing them. Without restrictions on the size of campaign contributions, the wealthy could flood the campaign coffers of their preferred political candidates, rendering all other contributions negligible by comparison.

The second benefit of antidistortion measures is perhaps more subtle, but of no less importance: it relates to the ability of all persons, rich and poor, to express the intensity of their feelings. In many circumstances, the intensity of a speaker's expression tells us much about the intensity of that speaker's beliefs. Polite applause conveys less enthusiasm than a shouted "Bravo!" Passing criticisms convey weaker disagreement than passionate harangues. And, of course, the tone of a judicial opinion provides some indication of how bleakly a judge views a certain area of the law. But where speech takes the form of a monetary expenditure, the link between intensity of beliefs and intensity of expression, as measured by the amount contributed, can too easily break down. This is a result of the unequal distribution of wealth, which makes the amount of money an individual spends on behalf of a political cause an unreliable measure of the intensity and depth of that individual's support for the cause. "In other words, and crucially, a large contribution by a person of great means may influence an election enormously, and yet may represent a far lesser intensity of desire than a pittance given by a poor person." *Landell v. Sorrell*, 406 F.3d 159, 161 (2d Cir.2005) (Calabresi, J., concurring in the denial of rehearing en banc).

To return to the example of the megaphone in the public square, the problem with its loudness is not just that it drowns out the voices of others, but also that it misrepresents, to an outside observer, the relative intensity of the speaker's views. That is, even if the megaphone user cares little about the issue being discussed, his voice gets heard above all others, while the voices (and intensity of feelings) of those who care passionately about the issue (and shout their beliefs at the top of their lungs) seem small in comparison. The one speaker's relative loudness—along with the other speakers' relative softness—obscures the depth of each speaker's views, thereby degrading the communicative value of everyone's message.

The foregoing example may seem fanciful, but money is not. And there is perhaps no greater a distortive influence on the intensity of expression than wealth differences. The wider the economic disparities in a democratic society, the more difficult it becomes to convey, with financial donations, the intensity of one's political beliefs. People who care a little will, if they are rich, still give a lot. People who care a lot must, if they are poor, give only a little. Jesus's comment about the rich donors and the poor widow says it all.

It is no small irony, then, that in refusing to recognize the existence of a state interest in "leveling the playing field," the Court purports to safeguard "the unfettered interchange of ideas." *Bennett*, 131 S. Ct. at 2826 (quoting *Buckley v. Valeo*, 424 U.S. 1, 14 (1976) (per curiam)). Far from standing in the way of this ideal, the antidistortion interest is vital to its fulfillment. Left unregulated, the "distorting effects of immense aggregations of wealth," *Austin v. Michigan Chamber of Commerce*, 494 U.S. 652 (1990), overruled by *Citizens United*, 130 S. Ct. at 913, will garble the political debate, trumpeting voices that would otherwise be muted and muting voices that would otherwise be trumpeted.

Indeed, if the Court were correct that the level playing field interest does not provide an appropriate reason for regulating campaign contributions, then it becomes difficult to see why the First Amendment does not give individuals the right to pay other individuals to vote for candidates in elections. Such a practice need not raise the specter of quid pro quo corruption; one might still buy votes on behalf of one's preferred candidate even if one could ask nothing from the candidate in return. The critical problem with vote-buying is not corruption; it is rather that allowing the practice would give the wealthiest individuals a huge effect over political elections, making even their relatively minor preferences matter immensely and the possibly intense preferences of the poor matter not much at all.

I am not suggesting that expressing the intensity of one's views is the only thing that matters in campaign finance doctrine, or in election law more generally.[1] Nor am I suggesting that the playing field must be fully level. This is an area of law in which many considerations come into play. But so long as the Supreme Court refuses to recognize the importance of the antidistortion interest, and its connection to the ability

1. If it were, we might expect the ballot to be structured so as to give maximum effect to preference intensity, through such devices as "cumulative voting" or "single-transferrable voting." See Samuel Issacharoff, Pamela S. Karlan & Richard H. Pildes, The Law of Democracy: Legal Structure of the Political Process 1137–75 (3d ed.2007).

to express the intensity of one's feelings, the Court will be ignoring a variable of critical constitutional importance and excluding the most important players—democratically elected legislatures—from their proper role in regard to that variable.

What is at stake here—what everyone knows is at stake here—is what was recognized and expressed so directly, succinctly, and powerfully in the story of the widow's mite. The ability to express one's feelings with all the intensity that one has—and to be heard—is a central element of the right to speak freely. It is, I believe, something that is so fundamental that sooner or later it is going to be recognized. Whether this will happen through a constitutional amendment or through changes in Supreme Court doctrine, I do not know. But it will happen.

It is with that faith in a better future, along with an understanding of the requirements of our flawed present, that I join the majority opinion.

* * *

Concluding Thoughts

Special Risks of Corporate Political Speech

Political speech is a high-risk social phenomenon. While we can often test the truth of other forms of speech—such as whether Honda indeed makes life simpler or whether this book sets you on a personal journey—political speech aims at our primitive, tribal mind and does not come with ready means to test its validity. Is America already great? Or does it have to become great again?

The political theorist Joseph Schumpeter in his 1942 book *Capitalism, Socialism and Democracy* spoke to the dangers of political speech and in particular how easily the public will can be molded by powerful groups:

> The typical citizen drops down to a level of mental performances as soon as he enters the political field. He argues and analyzes in a way that he would readily recognize as infantile in the sphere of his real interest. He becomes a primitive again. There are two ominous consequences.
>
> First, even if there were no political groups trying to influence him, the typical citizen in public matters tends to yield to irrational prejudice and impulse. He is simply "not all there." He will relax his usual moral standards and occasionally give in to the dark urges that the conditions of private life otherwise help them to repress.
>
> Second, the weaker the logical element in the processes of the public mind the greater are the opportunities for groups with an ax to grind. These groups may consist of professional politicians or the exponents of an economic interest. Human Nature in Politics (see point one), being what it is, allows these groups to fashion and, within very wide limits, even to create the will of the people. That is, the analysis of political processes is largely not a genuine but a manufactured will.

> The ways in which issues and the popular will on any issue are being manufactured is exactly analogous to the ways of commercial advertising. We find the same attempts to contact the subconscious. We find the same technique of creating favorable and unfavorable associations which are the more effective the less rational they are. We find the same evasions and reticences and the same trick of producing opinion by reiterated assertion that is successful precisely to the extent to which it avoids rational argument and the danger of awakening the critical faculties of the people. And so on. Only, all these arts have infinitely more scope in the sphere of public affairs than they have in the sphere of private and professional life.
>
> The picture of the prettiest girl that ever lived will in the long run prove powerless to maintain the sales of a bad cigarette. There is no equally effective safeguard in the case of political decisions. Many decisions of fateful importance are of a nature that makes it impossible for the public to experiment with them at its leisure and at moderate cost. Even if that is possible, however, judgment is as a rule not so easy to arrive at as it is in the case of the cigarette, because effects are less easy to interpret.

So, there you have it! Corporate political speech is more dangerous than smoking cigarettes. But we're unlikely to ban either of these addictive behaviors.

UNIT 3

TRIPLE BOTTOM LINE

This third unit looks at recent corporate responses to the corporation's unsustainable design. Using the construct of the "triple bottom line" (planet, people, and profits), this unit considers how corporations have voluntarily sought to be better stewards of the environment, more responsive to societal (human) needs, and more mindful of how they make profits. The triple bottom line, which mirrors the Environmental/Social/Governance movement, invites new understanding of corporate purpose and the metrics by which to measure a corporation's actions.

Another look down the road. Before proceeding on our journey in search of the sustainable corporation, it's useful to get our bearings. For starters, let's consider some terminology. Besides planet, people, and profits (the triple bottom line or TBL), there's "corporate social responsibility" (CSR) and "environmental, social, governance" (ESG)—both of which are often advanced as alternatives to shareholder wealth maximization (SWM). Mathematically, $TBL = CSR \cap SWM \neq SWM$.

As the Spanish poet Antonio Machado said, "we are making our path as we walk it." Here's where we are on the roadmap:

What Is CSR and ESG?

Professor Elizabeth Pollman recently sought to describe the concepts and practices in this fast-evolving area. See Elizabeth Pollman, *Corporate Social Responsibility, ESG, and Compliance*, Cambridge Handbook of Compliance (2020) [available on SSRN]. With calls by leading asset managers, as well as the CEOs of the largest US companies, for a redefined corporate purpose encompassing customers, employees, suppliers, communities and shareholders, Pollman finds there is no consensus on the meaning of CSR, ESG, and even SWM—or the relationship of these concepts to corporate compliance with environmental and emerging sustainability norms. For some, CSR and ESG simply mean full compliance with existing legal norms. For others, these concepts are about extra legal action. And, yet for others, they are meant to identify a new mindset—a new corporate ethos. In short, things are in a state of flux.

Unit 1 Intro to corporation	Unit 2 Unsustainable design	Unit 3 Triple bottom line	Unit 4 Redesign corporation	Unit 5 Rethink corporation
1.1 US law 1.2 US corporation 1.3 US public corp 1.4 US securities reg	2.1 Limited liability 2.2 Short-termism 2.3 Board mono-culture 2.4 Corp in politics	3.1 Planet: environ 3.2 People: CSR 3.3 Profits: SRI	4.1 Benefit corp 4.2 ESG disclosure 4.3 Consortium: Ceres	5.1 Corp as moral system 5.2 Stakeholder capitalism – delusion? 5.3 Personal integrity

Chapter 3.1

Planet: Corporate Environmental Stewardship

This chapter considers the corporation's responsibilities to the "planet"—specifically how corporations have sought to comply with environmental regulations, sometimes voluntarily going beyond them. While corporate limited liability permits corporations to place environmentally-dangerous operations in subsidiaries and thus to externalize environmental costs, environmental law is meant to compel the corporation to internalize these costs.

An animating theme of this chapter and those that follow is why have corporations gone beyond what is required by law, even by what consumer and other markets seem to demand. There seems to be something happening here.

Chapter's Focus

You will want to consider the evolution of corporate responses over the last 50 years to environmental norms and notice how many corporations have come to see environmental compliance not as a cost, but as an opportunity for cost savings and innovation.

You will see that sometimes corporate environmental behavior is regulated, but often not, particularly with respect to sustainability/carbon-footprints in life-cycle processes. You will want to focus on how many corporations comply with environmental laws, even though on a cost-benefit analysis non-compliance might be more profitable.

You should gain an appreciation for a potential new role of government in private-public partnerships, a new kind of "environmental law." Finally, you will want to consider how environmental regulation seeks to overcome the impact of corporate limited liability, though it remains subject to corporate law's profit-oriented assumptions.

Culture Versus Law

This chapter introduces some questions that we will continue to return for the remainder of the book. What is more powerful: law or culture? Which is easier to change? If (corporate) culture is more powerful than (corporate) law, is it enough? Don't we need law to step in—to show the way, to solidify the victories, to hold in place cultural ratcheting up?

Here is a dialogue on this question:

Student reflection: The question of whether the law or culture is easier to change is parallel to the question "can corporations save themselves from themselves?" Culture is the social behavior and norms found in human society. It is closely linked to the beliefs, customs, and capabilities of the individuals in the group or society. It is quite rare to find a group of people who know that their behavior, beliefs, and customs are harmful with no justification. Self-justification is why corporations are not able to save themselves from themselves. It is also the reason that it is easier to change the law than it is to change the culture.

United States history has shown that a change in the law can cause a change in culture. Prior to 1954, "separate but equal" was the law of the land. The separate but equal doctrine set forth in *Plessy v. Ferguson* ruled that racially segregated public schools, if equal, did not violate the Constitution. However, segregated schools were very rarely equal. The standard of education for all-Black schools lagged far behind all-White schools. On May 17, 1954, the Supreme Court issued a landmark ruling in *Brown v. Board of Education of Topeka*. The Court declared that "In the field of public education, the doctrine of 'separate but equal' has no place" and that segregated public schools are "inherently unequal." Chief Justice Earl Warren opined that "[t]o separate [African-American students] from others of similar age and qualifications solely because of their race generates a feeling of inferiority as to their status in the community that may affect their hearts and minds in a way unlikely ever to be undone." This Supreme Court decision was instrumental in changing the culture of the United States. Before this ruling, Black and White children in America had been kept separate during much of their adolescent years. Lack of exposure to those who are different from you has been known to create irrational fears and stereotypes. These fears and stereotypes allowed White Americans to justify their desires to continue a culture of segregation. Without the change in the law that *Brown v. Board of Education of Topeka* brought about, African-Americans and White-Americans would not have been brought together in an educational setting to realize that the only true difference between them is the color of their skin. While America still faces issues of systemic racism, the law helped to break down racial barriers.

Without laws discouraging negative cost externalization, corporations will continue to believe that their support of the economy exceeds the harm of off-loading indirect costs and negative effects on a third-party. Similar to the separate but equal doctrine, the true cost of negative externalization far outweighs its benefit. Negative externalization leads to the collapse of society while corporations realize profits. Corporations have been content to turn a blind eye to the negative effects of externalization so long as the business profits. The law will likely need to step in to save the world from corporations and save corporations from themselves. The culture that has been created around corporations likely will not allow for change unless the belief systems of corporate decision-makers change.

My response. Great job! I agree that this question (law or culture) is at the heart of our search for the sustainable corporation. I also agree that the law is way easier to change than culture. And simply changing law—as happened, for example, in *Brown v. Board of Education*—might have some effect. But think about how deep racism continues to be embedded in much of our society. Think about how people have moved to new neighborhoods, sometimes to new states, to avoid the racial mixing that the Supreme Court thought so important. And even in racially integrated schools, think about how much real socialization of kids across races happens.

That said, to wait for culture to change seems not the answer. Maybe it's thinking about how culture and law can move in tandem. I often think about the almost jaw-dropping way that gay marriage happened in this country. It first happened through changes in attitudes (and a few early court decisions) and then after this happened the law part was easy—including for the US Supreme Court. In short, will just telling corporations to be more ESG be enough?

3.1.1 US Environmental Regulation—a Synopsis

Before looking at how US corporations have responded to environmental norms, it may be useful to understand the nature of the US environmental laws. Here's a synopsis from Wikipedia, Earth Day:

> Earth Day is an annual day on which events are held worldwide to demonstrate support for environmental protection. Earth Day is observed each April 22. The first Earth Day was Wednesday, April 22, 1970 in New York City and around the country. At the time 20 million people took to the streets, parks, and auditoriums to demonstrate for a healthy, sustainable environment.

Politicians of both political parties had never seen anything like it—and they wisely decided to pay heed. By the end of the year, Congress had created the Environmental Protection Agency and passed the Clean Air Act (amended), the Clean Water Act, and the Endangered Species Act. More was to follow. Here is a summary of the major US environmental laws (again from Wikipedia), all of which trace their origins to Earth Day:

(1) The **National Environmental Policy Act (NEPA—1970)** is a United States environmental law that established a U.S. national policy promoting the enhancement of the environment and also established the President's Council on Environmental Quality (CEQ). As one of the most emulated statutes in the world, NEPA has been called the modern-day equivalent of an "environmental Magna Carta."

NEPA's most significant effect was to set up procedural requirements for all federal government agencies to prepare environmental assessments (EAs) and environmental impact statements (EISs). EAs and EISs contain statements of the environmental effects of proposed federal agency actions. NEPA's procedural requirements apply to all federal agencies in the executive branch. NEPA does not apply to the President, to Congress, or to the federal courts.

(2) The **Clean Air Act (CAA – 1970)** is a United States federal law designed to control air pollution on a national level. It requires the Environmental Protection Agency (EPA) to develop and enforce regulations to protect the public from airborne contaminants known to be hazardous to human health. The 1963 version of the legislation established a research program, expanded in 1967. Major amendments to the law, requiring regulatory controls for air pollution, passed in 1970, 1977, and 1990.

The 1970 amendments greatly expanded the federal mandate, requiring comprehensive federal and state regulations for both stationary (industrial) pollution sources and mobile sources. It also significantly expanded federal enforcement.

The 1990 amendments addressed acid rain, ozone depletion and toxic air pollution, established a national permits program for stationary sources, and increased enforcement authority. The amendments also established new auto gasoline reformulation requirements, set Reid vapor pressure (RVP) standards to control evaporative emissions from gasoline, and mandated new gasoline formulations during the summer months.

The Clean Air ActCAA was the first major environmental law in the United States to include a provision for citizen suits. Numerous state and local governments have enacted similar legislation, either implementing federal programs or filling in locally important gaps in federal programs.

(3) The **Clean Water Act (CWA—1972)** is the primary federal law in the United States governing water pollution. Passed in 1972, theThe act established the goals of eliminating releases of high amounts of toxic substances into water, eliminating additional water pollution by 1985, and ensuring that surface waters would meet standards necessary for human sports and recreation by 1983.

The principal body of law in effect is based on the Federal Water Pollution Control Amendments of 1972 and was significantly expanded from the Federal Water Pollution Control Amendments of 1948. Major amendments were enacted in the Clean Water Act of 1977 and the Water Quality Act of 1987.

The Clean Water Act (CWA) does not directly address groundwater contamination. Groundwater protection provisions are included in the Safe Drinking Water Act, Resource Conservation and Recovery Act, and the Superfund act.

(4) The **Safe Drinking Water Act (SDWA—1974)** is the principal federal law in the United States intended to ensure safe drinking water for the public. Pursuant to the act, the Environmental Protection Agency (EPA) is required to set standards for drinking water quality and oversee all states, localities, and water suppliers who implement these standards.

The SDWA applies to every public water system in the United States. There are currently more than 150,000 public water systems providing water to almost all Americans at some time in their lives. These water systems must be analyzed by third-party analytical laboratories. The Act SDWA does not cover private wells.

The SDWA does not apply to bottled water. Bottled water, which is regulated by the Food and Drug Administration (FDA) under the Federal Food, Drug, and Cosmetic Act.

(5) The **Resource Conservation and Recovery Act (RCRA—1976)** is the principal federal law in the United States governing the disposal of solid waste and hazardous waste.

The most notable provisions of the RCRA statute are included in Subtitle C, which directs the EPA to establish controls on the management of hazardous wastes from their point of generation, through their transportation and treatment, storage and/or disposal. Because the RCRA requires controls on hazardous waste generators (i.e., sites that generate hazardous waste in the first place), transporters, and treatment, storage and disposal facilities (i.e., facilities that ultimately treat/dispose of or recycle the hazardous waste), the overall regulatory framework has become known as the "cradle to grave" system. The program exacts stringent recordkeeping and reporting requirements on generators, transporters, and operators of treatment, storage and disposal facilities handling hazardous waste.

(6) The **Comprehensive Environmental Response, Compensation, and Liability Act (CERCLA also known as "Superfund" - 1980)** is aimed at remediating abandoned hazardous waste sites, by establishing legal liability, as well as a trust fund for cleanup activities. In general, CERCLA applies to contaminated sites, while RCRA's focus is on controlling the ongoing generation and management of particular waste streams. RCRA, like CERCLA, has provisions to require cleanup of contaminated sites that occurred in the past.

In 1984, Congress expanded the scope of RCRA with the enactment of Hazardous and Solid Waste Amendments (HSWA). The amendments strengthened the law by covering small quantity generators of hazardous waste and establishing requirements for hazardous waste incinerators, and the closing of substandard landfills.

In 1986, SARA addressed cleanup of leaking underground storage tanks (USTs) and waste storage facilities. The amendments established a trust fund to pay for the cleanup of leaking USTs where responsible parties cannot be identified.

(7) The **Land Disposal Program Flexibility Act (LPDFA - 1996)** is meant to allow some flexibility in the procedures for land disposal of certain wastes. For example, a waste is not subject to land disposal restrictions if it is sent to an industrial wastewater treatment facility, a municipal sewage treatment plant, or is treated in a "zero discharge" facility.

(8) The **Energy Policy Act (EPA—2005)** is an attempt to combat growing energy problems, by changing US energy policy to provide tax incentives and loan guarantees for energy production of various types.

The EPA increaseds the amount of biofuel (usually ethanol) that must be mixed with gasoline sold in the United States to 4 billion US gallons (15,000,000 m3) by 2006, 6.1 billion US gallons (23,000,000 m3) by 2009 and 7.5 billion US gallons (28,000,000 m3) by 2012; two years later, the Energy Independence and Security Act of 2007 extended the target to 36 billion US gallons (140,000,000 m3) by 2022.

The EPA exempts fluids used in the natural gas extraction process of "hydraulic fracturing" from protections under the Clean Air ActCAA, Clean Water ActCWA, Safe Drinking Water ActSDWA, and CERCLA. It also exempts companies drilling for natural gas from disclosing the chemicals involved in fracking operations that would normally be required under federal clean water laws. These exemptions, commonly known as the "Halliburton loophole," refer to former Halliburton CEO Dick Cheney who was reportedly instrumental in the law's passage.

Stop and notice. Basically, all the pro-environmental laws passed by Congress happened between 1968 and 1980. The laws that followed largely cut back on the broad legislative (and largely bipartisan) congressional effort during that remarkable era. Could Congress ever come together again to address climate change and save the environment? Put on your marching boots!

3.1.2 Evolution of Corporate Response to Environmental Regulation

Recently, Professor Daniel Esty (Yale Law) described how the role of business toward the environment has been changing.

New Values: Online Yale Summit to Explore Shift in Corporate Sustainability

(Apr. 14, 2020)

Daniel Esty

[available on environment.yale]

Last summer, the Business Roundtable issued a bold statement redefining the purpose of a corporation. Rather than simply focus on the benefits of shareholders, the statement read, companies should also consider the interests of their employees, customers, suppliers and communities—and should include sustainable practices that protect the environment.

This statement reflects a shift in the corporate sector that has slowly evolved in the decades since the first Earth Day, in 1970

My research over 20 years, during which time I have studied the corporate sustainability efforts of hundreds of companies, suggests that those who bring a systematic approach to environmental issues and make sustainability a core element of their day-to-day business strategy outperform their competition. As I spell out in my book, "Green to Gold," companies that are strategic in their approach to energy and environmental issues often find ways to cut costs, reduce risks, drive growth (both top-line revenues and bottom-line profits), and deliver enhanced intangible value—including strengthened customer loyalty, brand identify, and the ability to attract and retain high-end knowledge workers.

Looking back over the past 50 years, companies have gone through a cycle in their approach to society's environmental needs and the emerging sustainability agenda. Fifty years ago, many companies saw the pressure for higher environmental standards as a burden and an annoyance—and they fought the push for new environmental laws. By the early 1980s, many corporations had come to accept that they had a responsibility to society to manage their waste and control their emissions.

Beginning about 30 years ago, many large companies (and some smaller ones) had developed compliance teams and environmental management strategies—and had become quite proficient in tracking the requirements of laws such as the Clean Air Act and the Clean Water Act. Beginning about 20 years ago, some companies began to see an opportunity to go "beyond compliance" and to use environmental strategies as a way to differentiate themselves in the marketplace.

In the past decade, a large number of businesses have come to recognize that energy and environmental initiatives help to spur innovation, create value, and build competitive advantage. Not that every company is a positive force for a sustainable society, but many now seek to deliver solutions not only in response to their own pollution and natural resource management challenges, but to those of their customers as well.

We have seen in the last few years, a strong shift away from what might have been called "shareholder primacy" and the idea (often attributed to University of Chicago economist Milton Friedman) that the purpose of a corporation should be centered on profit maximization and the best possible returns to shareholders. The Business Roundtable made it clear that in the 21st century, companies should take a broader view—and while continuing to produce attractive returns for their shareholders also be attentive to the needs of other "stakeholders" including customers, employees, suppliers, and the communities in which they operate. I have argued in a similar vein in the recently released volume, "A Better Planet," that we are approaching an "end of externalities" in the business world.

This shift in core values will mean that any company with a business model that depends on imposing harms on society—whether that is pollution up a smokestack, under-paying for natural resources like water, or under-providing for their workers—must expect to be called upon in the next few years to stop their harm-causing behavior or to pay fully for these harms.

I think that the stakeholder vision of corporate purpose is rapidly gaining traction. In January, for example, Larry Fink, the CEO of BlackRock, the world's largest investment manager, declared in a letter to the CEOs of the companies in which BlackRock holds shares that they needed to take action to address critical sustainability issues, such as climate change, and to shift their focus from short-term profitability to "long-term value.

Likewise, a growing number of mainstream investors—not just "impact" or self-identified socially responsible investors—have begun to demand better alignment between the companies in their stock portfolios and their personal values. Thus, there has been a very rapid increase in interest in Environmental/Social/Governance (ESG) metrics so that these investors can better determine which companies are addressing climate change, reducing air and water pollution, improving the diversity of their workforce and management teams, taking seriously the challenge of inequality, practicing good corporate governance, and making progress on a range of other sustainability issues.

Of course, as Todd Cort and I documented in 2016 ["Corporate Sustainability Metrics: What Investors Need and Don't Get," Journal of Environmental Investing] there are still real challenges in getting all companies to move toward sustainable business models. And The New York Times recently reported that a number of companies that had promised to support a "gentler capitalism" have fallen back from that pledge in the face of the Covid-19 crisis.

That said, I believe that moving society onto a sustainable future trajectory requires both behavioral change and broad-based innovation. The creative thinking and breakthroughs that I envision include—but must not be limited to—technology developments such as lower-cost renewable electricity. We also need innovation in finance for sustainable infrastructure—and an expanded flow of capital to renewable power, energy efficiency, and other sustainability-enhancing projects through Green Banks, Green Bonds, and other creative investment vehicles. Likewise, we must find new ways to engage the public in shifting their buying patterns toward more sustainable products and services. And we need new public-private partnerships that help every community, family, and organization in our society to become more sustainable.

3.1.3 Parent Corporation Liability for Pollution by Subsidiaries

Modern regulatory schemes regard the corporation as a "person." Thus, environmental rules that apply to persons apply to corporations. But these regulatory schemes also generally respect the corporate holding-company structures, and thus the separate identity of parent corporations and their subsidiaries. Thus, environmental compliance can be placed exclusively in a subsidiary, even as the parent corporation holds the bulk of the business assets.

Corporate Law Trumps Pro-Environmental Policies

You may remember from Unit 2 the *Bestfoods* case decided by the Supreme Court in 1998. The case resolved whether a parent corporation can be liable for a toxic waste site of a subsidiary. It brought into sharp focus the Court's view that the (federal) environmental laws should not be read as undoing (state) corporate limited liability. Put another way, if corporate management chooses to separate business assets and environmental risks—by placing those risks in subsidiaries, so that the parent corporation and other corporations in the corporate group are shielded from liability—federal environmental law defers to their choice.

The following is a summary of the *Bestfoods* case and the implications of its holding that parent corporations are generally not liable for CERCLA cleanup costs arising from toxic waste sites owned and operated by their subsidiaries.

Corporations: Examples and Explanations

(9th ed. 2021)

Alan R Palmiter

Chapter 33 – Statutory Recognition of Corporation

§ 33.1.2 Corporate Limited Liability Superfund Cases

An important and interesting juxtaposition of limited liability and regulatory policy is the Comprehensive Environmental Response, Compensation, and Liability Act (CERCLA)—the federal Superfund statute, which imposes liability on former and present "owners or operators" of hazardous waste sites. 42 U.S.C. §9607(a).

Since the statute's enactment in 1980, federal courts have taken different tacks in their attempt to reconcile state-based corporate separateness and federal environmental policy. For cases involving parent corporations with wholly-owned subsidiaries that owned or operated waste sites, the Supreme Court resolved more than a decade of conflicting lower court views. *United States v. Bestfoods*, 524 U.S. 51 (1998). According to the Court, the parent corporation can be liable under CERCLA as follows:

- **No "owner" liability.** CERCLA does not abrogate the "ingrained" principle of corporate law that a parent corporation is a separate entity distinct from its subsidiaries. This means that a parent corporation, regardless of its degree of involvement in the subsidiary or its disposal activities, does not legally own the subsidiary's property and cannot be liable as an "owner."
- **Direct "operator" liability.** The parent corporation can be deemed an "operator" if it directs, manages, or conducts the affairs of a "facility"—that is, the subsidiary's hazardous waste site. If, for example, an executive of the parent (who is not also an official of the subsidiary) actively participates in and controls the subsidiary's environmental programs, the parent can become liable as an "operator."
- **Derivative piercing liability.** Even if the parent corporation does not incur "owner" or "operator" liability, it can be charged with "derivative CERCLA liability" when the subsidiary incurs CERCLA liability and the corporate veil may be pierced.

> The Court described piercing as a "fundamental principle of corporate law" that arises when the corporate form "would otherwise be misused to accomplish certain wrongful purposes" on the shareholders' behalf. The Court left open whether piercing factors would be borrowed from state law or would be a matter of federal common law.
>
> The Supreme Court's approach rejects a view adopted by some circuits that CERCLA liability can arise if the parent held the power to control the subsidiary's disposal activities, even though it did not exercise the power. According to *Bestfoods*, control by the parent of the subsidiary's business is not in itself sufficient to create "operator" liability. Moreover, the Court's recognition of direct "operator" liability rejects the view that parent liability under CERCLA can arise only under traditional piercing rules.

Law Makes a Difference

A recent study (also mentioned in Unit 2) identifies how reducing parent liability for subsidiary environmental cleanup costs affects actual corporate behavior—here, industrial pollution. The study looked at how the Supreme Court decision in *Bestfoods* (which strengthened limited liability protection for parent corporations operating through their subsidiaries) affected environmental operations by subsidiaries in jurisdictions where courts had previously adopted veil-piercing standards that imposed parent liability more readily. Using a difference-in-differences framework, the study found that increased liability protection for parents resulted in a 10 percent increase in toxic emissions by subsidiaries—a result not linked to increased production. Rather, subsidiaries after the Supreme Court decision were 12-25 percent *less likely* to engage in pollution abatement activities related to production. The study found that the effects are driven by less-solvent subsidiaries, as well as by parents that are closer to financial distress, a finding consistent with risk-shifting behavior. The authors, two economists, concluded, "our results highlight moral hazard problems associated with limited liability." That is to say, limited liability—by design—makes corporations less responsible. Pat Akey & Ian Appel, *The Limits of Limited Liability: Evidence from Industrial Pollution* (2017) [available on SSRN].

3.1.4 Corporate Liability for Violations of Law

Duty of Obedience

Corporate managers who choose to skirt environmental laws skate on thin ice. Not only do environmental laws often impose personal civil and even criminal liability on executives who order or supervise environmental law violations, but corporate law has something to say here, too. Directors and officers who knowingly (and maybe even recklessly) approve actions that violate non-corporate norms, such as environmental laws, violate their *corporate* "duty of obedience." See Alan R. Palmiter, *Duty of Obedience: The Forgotten Duty* (2010) [available on SSRN]. Thus, even when a directorial decision is fully informed and seeks to advance corporate (not personal) interests, directors breach their fiduciary duties if the decision violates internal or external legal norms. Such corporate officials can be held liable to the corporation in a shareholder's derivative suit for the costs of knowingly or recklessly permitting violations of law. See *In re Caremark Int'l Inc. Derivative Litigation*, 698 A.2d 959 (Del. Ch. 1996) (Chancellor Allen) (holding that directors who knowingly fail to create a corporate monitoring system to prevent Medicare kickbacks violated their fiduciary duties).

While there are only a small handful of cases involving claims of director disobedience that have survived a motion to dismiss—thus, opening the door for director liability—the Delaware courts have sent a clear message that directors are required to follow the law and to establish oversight systems to ensure their corporations follow the law. See Elizabeth Pollman, *Corporate Oversight and Disobedience* (2020) [available on SSRN]. Pollman found that Delaware courts, while prioritizing broad directorial latitude to take business risk, have drawn a line at legal risk. Delaware courts have allowed *Caremark* claims when the board utterly failed to implement a compliance monitoring system or when the directors engaged in disobedience by knowingly managing legal risk or flouting, violating, or ignoring the law. Pollman observes that corporate law's good-faith requirement of fidelity to external law "largely serves a legitimizing role for corporate law."

Board oversight in transition

Recently, the Boeing 737 Max debacle led to a landmark moment in corporate law. Roy Shapira, *Max Oversight Duties: How Boeing Signifies a Shift in Corporate Law* (2022) [available on SSRN]. In 2021, the Delaware chancery court allowed a derivative lawsuit brought by Boeing shareholders to proceed. The suit's theory was that Boeing's directors breached their oversight duties by not doing enough to monitor, prevent, and react to fatal airplane safety issues. The court faulted the Boeing directors for focusing on restoring corporate profitability and image instead of consumer safety. After the case, "mission critical" oversight now includes both compliance meant to protect investors (such as financial reporting) and compliance meant to protect broader societal interests (such as product safety).

Professor Judd Snierson (Southern University Law Center) summarized the relationship between SWM and corporate environmental compliance:

Shareholder Primacy and Corporate Compliance

(2015)

Judd F. Sneirson

[available on SSRN]

Corporations, like the rest of us, must comply with environmental and other laws or suffer the consequences. Unfortunately, these consequences can pale in comparison to the gains to be made from non-compliance. Law-and-economics scholarship recognizes this and sometimes encourages deliberate non-compliance. According to this view, corporate compliance should turn on whether compliance would be profitable to the company.

Corporate law requires directors and officers to ensure that the company complies with applicable laws, and put into place an information-and-control structure to aid in this effort. In addition to this monitoring obligation, corporate fiduciaries must themselves manage the company in accordance with applicable laws. Knowing non-compliance would not only amount to a breach of fiduciary duty, but would also fall outside the business judgment rule and director-exculpation charter provisions.

This rule holds even where non-compliance, after the payment of any fines, would prove profitable: "Under Delaware law, a fiduciary may not choose to manage an entity in an illegal fashion, even if the fiduciary believes that the illegal activity will result in profits for the entity." *Metro Commc'n Corp. BVI v. Advanced Mobilecomm. Technologies*, 854 A.2d 121. 163-64 (Del. Ch. 2004). Directors can be liable for illegal acts under New York law "even though committed to benefit the corporation." *Miller v. Am. Tel. & Telegraph Co.*, 507 F.2d 759, 761 (3d Cir. 1974) (applying New York law).

Consider the following illustration. Suppose a manufacturing facility can save $80,000 a month by switching to a lower-grade fuel, but by making the switch the company would likely violate the Clean Air Act an average of four times a month. If the assessed fine under the Clean Air Act would be $25,000 per violation, a cost-benefit analysis would suggest that compliance is the better, economically efficient choice in that the potential fines ($25,000 times four or $100,000) outweigh the projected fuel-cost savings ($80,000).

However, if there is less than a 100% chance that the authorities will detect the Clean Air Act violations, the cost side of the equation should adjust to reflect this reality. For example, if the likelihood of being caught and paying the full fine is 50%, the average monthly cost of non-compliance drops to $50,000—making lower-grade fuel the more profitable choice. To make matters worse, managers do not run these cost-benefit analyses perfectly and often "underestimate the chances of getting caught, overestimate the potential benefits of breaking the law, and underestimate the potential penalties." Kent Greenfield, THE FAILURE OF CORPORATE LAW: FUNDAMENTAL FLAWS AND PROGRESSIVE POSSIBILITIES 87 & n.46 (2006)

Thus, companies adhering to this law-and-economics view of optional corporate compliance and profit maximization would choose to comply with applicable laws only when cost-benefit analysis would recommend compliance.

Exactly how widespread is this problem of corporate non-compliance? Anecdotal evidence suggests that most companies comply with applicable laws, or at least try to, because the companies' decision-makers view compliance as the "right thing to do." And to the extent companies find themselves out of compliance, it's more a function of not understanding often-complex laws than a conscious choice to flout the law to maximize profits. That is, deliberate corporate non-compliance in the business world seems less pervasive than the law-and-economics scholarship recommends.

Corporate Law as Extension of Environmental Law

All of this has led some to see corporate law as an extension of non-corporate norms, including environmental law:

> A firm is not a black box with a pipe sticking out of it. Firm managers make decisions with environmental consequences long before pollution comes out of a pipe or a smokestack as an externality. Corporate law governs how firms are created and the duties their managers owe to firm stakeholders. Securities regulations govern the information that firms must share with investors. Antitrust law governs how firms behave in the marketplace with respect to competitors and customers. And bankruptcy law governs how firms wind down or are reorganized when they face financial trouble. Each of these fields of positive law governing the firm has significant implications for firm behavior with respect to the environment. Yet they are not ordinarily considered part of the environmental law toolkit. To address fully the most pressing environmental problems of our time, including issues of cumulative harm like climate change, environmental law should embrace these non-traditional levers that are central to its enterprise. The Article sounds a clarion call: the law of the corporation is environmental law.

Sarah R. Light, *The Law of the Corporation as Environmental Law* (2019) [available on SSRN].

3.1.5 Voluntary Corporate Compliance with Environmental Standards

Despite the evidence that limited liability encourages externalization of costs, a growing body of literature suggests that corporations often comply with environmental regulation and even institute *voluntary* environmental standards beyond what current regulation requires. For example, a recent large-sample study that surveyed managers at industrial companies throughout the United States found high levels of compliance with *voluntary* environmental programs and the institution of corporate environmental stewardship practices beyond what regulation requires. The study found that looming regulation explains some of these "beyond-compliance" decisions, but so too do such internal factors as support from top-level management and companies that seek out community input. That is to say, corporate culture matters to the planet! See Jonathan C. Borck & Cary Coglianese, *Beyond Compliance: Explaining Business Participation in Voluntary Environmental Programs* (2011) [available on SSRN].

Reasons for Voluntary Compliance

Why do companies comply voluntarily? Interestingly, financial performance has been shown to be enhanced for companies that engage in environmental compliance. That is, good environmental practices are linked to enhanced financial performance. Not only does this hold true for companies in developed countries, but even more so in developing countries. According to a recent study, "adoption of environmental practices significantly and positively affects the corporate financial performance in developed and developing countries." Sergio Manrique & Carmen-Pilar Marti-Ballester, *Analyzing the Effect of Corporate Environmental Performance on Corporate Financial Performance in Developed and Developing Countries* (2017) [available at MDPI] (based on sample of 2982 large firms from 2008 to 2015).

Moreover, cost of capital is reduced when firms undertake voluntarily to disclose sustainability efforts and focus performance on ESG dimensions. See Anthony C. Ng & Zabihollah Rezaee, *Business Sustainability, Performance, and Cost of Equity Capital* (2015) [available at SSRN] (studying sample of 3,000 firms from 1990-2013 and finding ESG performance reduces equity cost of capital).

Corporate Nudging

In particular, how is it that companies get employees to be more compliant with environmental norms? It turns out that "nudging"—making subtle suggestions or creating almost-invisible incentives–is an effective way to make people more responsible. For example, putting fruit and other healthy foods at eye level in the grocery store is a "nudge," while banning sugary drinks is not.

Should companies use psychological manipulations to induce particular behaviors by employees? According to Professor Todd Haugh (Indiana Kelley School of Business), nudging to get "corporate compliance" is okay, so long as the nudge doesn't take advantage of cognitive irrationality or lead people to do things that they really don't want to do. See Todd Haugh, *Nudging Corporate Compliance* (2017) [available at SSRN].

When companies alter the "situational social factors" to induce ethical behavior, Haugh asserts the end of more compliance (and less *respondeat superior* liability for the company) should not justify any means. Haugh suggests, for example, that subliminally promoting reusable mugs by putting up a poster in the office breakroom that depicts employees drinking from washable coffee mugs, rather than Styrofoam cups, is okay because this doesn't infringe on an employee's personal autonomy, even though the poster operates at a subconscious, emotional level.

But what about a computer warning system that buzzes when an employee (such as a bond trader on Wall Street) is about to make a trade that seems to be unauthorized or based on illegal inside information? This, Haugh says, may go too far—even though rogue traders can cost financial firms billions in losses and fines. What about designing computers that emit a really foul stench whenever a factory supervisor decides to cut corners in environmental compliance?

Shareholder Pressure

Lately, shareholder activism on environmental matters has become more robust. Although we take up the changing attitudes of institutional shareholders to climate change and other environmental concerns in Chapter 3.3, it's useful to understand how calls for corporate voluntary action on climate change is reshaping the corporate landscape.

For example, the following is a press release by Majority Action, a non-profit shareholder advocacy organization, announcing the group's success with a shareholder proposal at JPMorgan Chase's annual shareholders' meeting calling on the bank to align its financing to the Paris agreement goals. The proposal garnered 49.6 percent shareholder support.

> JPMorgan Chase has been increasingly under fire for its role as the world's largest financier of fossil fuels. New York City Comptroller Scott Stringer and the state treasurers of Pennsylvania, Connecticut, Maine, Maryland, Massachusetts, Oregon, Rhode Island, Vermont and Wisconsin called on JPMorgan Chase to align its financing activity with the goals of the Paris Agreement of 2018 and opposed former ExxonMobil CEO Lee Raymond's re-election to the board. New York State Comptroller Thomas DiNapoli, CalPERS and proxy advisor Glass Lewis all opposed Raymond's re-election as well.
>
> Earlier this month, JPMorgan Chase, under pressure from leading shareholders, announced they would remove lead independent director Lee Raymond from his leadership position later this summer—but still has announced no plans for Raymond to retire after 33 years on the board. Instead, Dimon responded to shareholder concerns with praise of Raymond's climate leadership and stated that the "current intent" is to retain Raymond in key committee roles.
>
> BlackRock and Vanguard hold a combined 14.6% of shares in JPM, giving them outsized power to shape the bank's behavior Haugh asserts on climate change. Last year, BlackRock and Vanguard backed 99% of oil and gas and electric power company directors across the S&P 500, and BlackRock and Vanguard voted against all of the U.S. shareholder proposals backed by the Climate Action 100+ investor coalition. As major asset managers have made commitments to center climate change concerns in their voting behavior, their votes at JPM stands as a key test of these promises.

In short, the number of institutional shareholders voting for climate engagement by the bank had doubled in one year, and the bank's board had demoted its independent chair (the former CEO of Exxon Mobil) because of his lackluster leadership on climate change!

Corporate Climate Pledges

Climate pledges have become commonplace. Both governments, such as in the Paris Agreement of, and corporations have increasingly set goals for their responses to the climate crisis. Many corporations frame these pledges in terms of "net zero"—that is, "we'll reduce our carbon footprint, but won't necessarily reach zero carbon emissions, instead we'll do other things (like making donations to tree-planting groups or supporting carbon-capturing agricultural endeavors) that will offset our continued carbon emissions."

Jonathan Foley, executive director of Drawdown, has urged companies to do the following:

(1) Cut your own emissions towards *zero*, not "net zero," as quickly as possible.
(2) Only use carbon removal as a last resort—for *truly* unavoidable emissions.
(3) Pay the "Social Cost of Carbon" for your ongoing pollution.
(4) Don't stop here: Address your *historic* emissions too.
(5) Carefully weigh issues of climate justice in everything you do.

Drawdown is a project of 70 researchers and scientists from 22 countries (along with a 120-person advisory board) who identified, mapped, and modeled the 100 most promising ideas to reduce our GHG emissions and draw down from the atmosphere the GHG emissions (especially CO2 emissions) that threaten the climate. Drawdown has been successful in identifying for many countries how to take on carbon-reduction responsibilities.

3.1.6 Sustainability Practices as "Public Good"

Next you will read a thoughtful article by a law professor who argues that a private-public partnership should be forged so that business firms will undertake "life-cycle analysis" (LCA) of their products and activities. For example, a company like Apple would be asked to investigate the sustainability of its products from design, to manufacture, to shipment, to marketing, to use, and finally to disposal. Such LCA analysis—if viewed as a "public good"—could lead to more widespread and even more *profitable* sustainability practices. This may well require a shift in corporate attitudes, as companies move from viewing environmental compliance as a profit-diminishing expense to seeing LCA analysis as a potential profit center.

Imagining Corporate Sustainability as a Public Good Rather Than a Corporate Bad

(2011)

Wendy E. Wagner

[available at SSRN]

Introduction

Corporations have been criticized for their environmental misdeeds for over a century, so it is not surprising that many view corporate approaches to sustainability with skepticism. Reports of green-washing and other forms of misleading advertising by a handful of corporations only serve to reinforce this negative perception.

Based on this evidence of poor corporate behavior, a number of analysts have concluded that sustainability should be regulated in the same way as other industrial polluting activities. Just as laws require corporations to disclose information on their polluting activities because these activities are wrongs to society, so the thinking goes, corporations should be required to engage in an internal accounting of their unsustainable practices. Specifically, corporations should be required to assess the sustainability of their operations in standardized disclosures and take their resulting, publicly-administered medicine, whether it involves being shamed in the marketplace or subjected to greater regulatory control with respect to resource use or disposal practices

Addressing corporate sustainability by putting the onus on corporations to assess the sustainability of their operations may get the solution exactly backwards, at least at this early stage in advancing sustainability. Rather than view the lack of sustainability efforts as another ***corporate bad*** that individual corporations should be required to redress, corporate sustainability should be treated instead as a ***public good*** that becomes the government's responsibility. Information about an industrial sector's sustainability profile—for example, a life cycle analysis of a typical facility—has clear public good qualities associated with it. This type of assessment allows for cross comparisons between competitors, identifies areas for possible synergies among producing companies, and highlights areas that may ultimately deserve further regulatory oversight. Equally important, if sustainability analyses concerning various production processes and services are produced in the first instance by publicly funded, third-party experts rather than extracted from private actors, the resulting reports are more likely to be reliable, complete, and accessible to a wide-range of stakeholders who can use them in public-benefitting ways.

I. Informed Sustainability

There are multiple avenues for advancing corporate sustainability, but a key component to all of these methods is greater information about corporate practices. Individual corporate decisions about production processes, when amalgamated, yield a global market of goods and services which may be badly inefficient from an ecological point of view. Yet, until the relevant information is gathered and synthesized, the overall impact of corporate practices and the areas for the most promising gains with regard to sustainability are obscured.

A. The State of Information on Corporate Sustainability

Top commentators on corporate sustainability agree that information is not just an important ingredient, but it is also essential to establishing a meaningful sustainability program. At the most basic level, rigorous information on corporate sustainability informs the market—not simply downstream consumers, but also insurers, investors, corporate partners, and others who ultimately keep the corporation in business. Rigorous information on corporate sustainability informs internal practices as well: Enhanced corporate self assessment is touted as one of the primary virtues of mandating information disclosures. Corporate sustainability information also identifies corporate practices that are most likely to benefit from greater regulatory oversight or market intervention.

Yet current regulatory programs provide only limited information on corporate sustainability. The Right-to-Know Act in the United States requires annual disclosures of corporate use and disposal of large amounts of hazardous substances. The resulting Toxic Release Inventory ("TRI") disclosures provide useful information about corporate sustainability with regard to handling and disposal of hazardous substances, but these load estimates offer little insight into meaningful opportunities for a facility to reduce natural resource use, to minimize pollution, or to otherwise decrease a facility's ecological footprint.

The Global Reporting Initiative ("GRI"), established by the United Nations Environment Programme ("UNEP") and the Coalition for Environmentally Responsible Economies ("CERES"), provides a more robust measure of a corporation's ecological footprint because it measures not only outputs, but natural resource use as well. The GRI offers external parties, like investors and customers, an even stronger basis for evaluating a corporation's commitment to and progress toward sustainability as compared with the TRI disclosures. GRI reporting is voluntary, however. Thus, while a number of Fortune 500 companies have conducted self-audits over the last fifteen years, participation in GRI still remains the exception rather than the rule.

GRI and TRI provide useful barometers to measure corporate sustainability, but because both are exclusively input and output focused, they miss opportunities to focus corporations on the ways that production operations can be altered to provide significant sustainability advances. GRI and TRI also allow firms to be self-referencing in benchmarking their progress, a focus that neglects to reward ecologically-innovative business practices.

B. The Unparalleled Virtues of Life Cycle Analysis

Although life cycle analysis is more information-intensive, it offers a substantially improved measure of corporate sustainability relative to the input and output measures embodied in the GRI and TRI reports. Life cycle analysis begins at the "cradle," where raw materials are produced, and follows that production process through transport and manufacturing to the ultimate disposal, often by the consumer. The goal of this analysis is to identify materials and burdens at each stage of the production process that are not recycled in a closed loop, paralleling natural processes. Such a holistic view of the process allows for a greater range of options for minimizing a facility's ecological footprint, including redesigning the process entirely. By focusing on the design of production processes, rather than simply the end-of-the-pipe or output adjustments, much greater environmental gains, as well as cost-savings, are possible.

To the extent that there is proof in the pudding, life cycle analyses boast of concrete victories. A life cycle approach helped Tropicana learn that it was not the transportation of its juice, but the agricultural inputs that led to its larger-than-necessary carbon footprint. As a result, Tropicana focused its primary efforts on reducing fertilizer use rather than dedicating the same resources to increasing the energy efficiency of its vehicles. In a life cycle analysis of coal-fired power plants, Department of Energy ("DOE") consultants compared cleaner coal-fired plants with older plants. This analysis not only quantitatively identified the additional environmental burdens associated with the older plants, but pinpointed those costs to specific features within the life cycle. This analysis also identified design changes that might improve the environmental performance of the older coal-fired systems.

From a regulatory standpoint, life cycle analysis can also pinpoint occasions when adverse environmental impacts are simply shifted within a production process—for example, how end-of-the-pipe controls may reduce one source of pollution only to move the problem elsewhere in the production process where it might be more difficult to address. A life cycle assessment of offshore drilling waste disposal, for example, revealed how strict prohibitions on the discharge of cuttings extracted with certain drilling fluids may have precluded opportunities to identify ways to convert the resulting hazardous waste (disposed in hazardous waste landfills) into a useful product. This internal recycling would have ultimately done much more to limit waste, production costs, and environmental risk than flat prohibitions on the generation of the waste.

II. Impediments to Corporate Self-Assessments of Sustainability

A great deal of the information needed to conduct facility-specific or even industry-wide life cycle assessments lies in the hands of the companies. And, for a variety of reasons, these firms often lack the incentives to collect, analyze, or even share this basic information in a complete or comprehensive way. Much like environmental audits, and even basic TRI and GRI disclosures, corporations may be wary of conducting these assessments and, if they are required, may resist conducting them in a rigorous or comprehensive way.

A. Reliability of Data

A life cycle assessment requires a great deal of data about a large range of inputs (including water usage and various chemicals) and outputs (including pollutant streams and discharges) at each stage of the production process, from natural resource extraction to disposal.

Over time, additional regulatory innovations have helped increase the reliability of some self-produced information from regulated parties. For example, to gather accurate information about the pollutant emissions emanating from large utility stacks, Congress required that continuous monitors be installed on the stacks, and the EPA promulgated supplemental rules that penalize facilities when their continuous monitors break down. Unfortunately, most of the tools developed to collect more reliable information from regulated parties are only useful in a narrow set of circumstances that do not extend to the data-intensive needs of sustainability life cycle assessments.

Compared with GRI, life cycle assessments allow for even more error and bias in extracting basic internal data since there is much greater discretion for the corporation in identifying the types of data to collect, selecting the units of analysis (both in time and scale), and assembling the requisite information from company operations.

B. Disinterested Methods

Beyond problems with ensuring the reliability of the input data, the methods for conducting a life cycle analysis also afford the analyst considerable discretion in how to conduct the assessment. This too presents problems when the company conducting the assessment has a stake in the outcome. For example, there are numerous discretionary points that arise in framing the scope of a life cycle assessment, developing the methods, and interpreting the data. When a company is conducting its own LCA, this remaining methodological discretion raises a risk that it might select the most beneficial assumptions in conducting its assessment and ignore others that might cast the company in a less positive light.

The development of rigorous methods for other types of open-ended assessments, like risk assessments, have posed similar challenges to environmental regulators. For example, there is evidence of sponsor-bias in manufacturers' assessments of the chronic hazards of their products and waste streams. In the biomedical literature, this systemic bias has been dubbed "the Funding Effect" since privately sponsored research is more likely to produce results favorable to the sponsor than research that is financed by disinterested parties, like the federal government. Even more standardized sustainability disclosures, like GRI, have suffered from some of these challenges, since they too provide wiggle room for firms that prefer to highlight successes and downplay failures in applying the GRI indicators.

Unless regulators have substantial resources to scrutinize the models used for self-assessments, significant discretion in a company's life cycle assessment will remain.

C. Comprehensibility

A critical, third feature of a robust life cycle assessment is its comprehensibility to a wide range of users. Because multiple stakeholders will use the assessments, it is important that the assessments be understandable to those outside the life cycle assessment field.

When left to the discretion of an interested party who produces the report, the comprehensibility of life cycle assessments can be controlled or even manipulated. If a corporation conducts a life cycle analysis that reveals embarrassing information, for example, it enjoys considerable discretion to obscure the negative findings by writing the analysis in as technical a way as possible or obfuscating the most incriminating revelations.

GRI reporting would seem immune from this comprehensibility problem given its emphasis on comparable, input and output calculations in generic tables. Yet even GRI reports can be "cluttered with information of little apparent use to readers, while missing out on the big picture risks and opportunities."

III. Corporate Sustainability as a Public Good

Extracting reliable life cycle analyses from corporations is fraught with difficulty, but one simple move can help avoid this impasse: sustainability analysis can be reconceived as a *public good* rather than a responsibility that should be shouldered by corporations. Reconceptualizing life cycle assessments as public information helps sidestep the impediments to collecting reliable and comprehensible information identified in the prior section. It also manages to produce considerably more relevant, accurate, and hopefully path-breaking types of analyses and recommendations in forms that would not occur if individual firms, who have a clear stake in the findings, were the primary source of this information.

Admittedly, a reconceptualization of sustainability assessments as public goods is at odds with conventional wisdom. In most national and international circles, sustainability reporting is understood to be a natural extension of pollution reporting that discloses negative externalities and other bads that a corporation extracts from society. Yet this conception seems to be based more on analogies to TRI reporting and other corporate disclosures than on a thorough analysis of the unique features of sustainability assessments. Such a close analysis reveals a number of ways that life cycle assessments fall closer to the public good side of environmental information than to regulating corporate bads.

There are at least four features of industrial life cycle analyses that are more closely associated with public goods, at least at this early stage in improving corporate sustainability. First, and perhaps most important, it is not clear what a life cycle analysis will reveal for any given industrial sector, and thus a life cycle analysis may not identify the excessive use of natural resources or polluting activities (i.e., negative externalities) in need of intervention.

Second, and along these same lines, conducting life cycle analyses and developing innovative solutions for more sustainable approaches in the future constitutes a type of intellectual property or public good for which a firm is unlikely to be able to capture its investment. Because the methods for LCA are constantly evolving, one corporation's bright idea for how to conduct a life cycle analysis or capture sustainability gains through facility-based innovations may quickly become a good that its competitors can copy. Without patents, copyrights, or other ways to convert these intellectual discoveries into property, sustainability innovations can be co-opted by competitors without compensating the originator of the idea. Firms could even copy and embellish on another facility's life cycle assessment and enjoy reputational gains without doing the initial work associated with conducting the basic assessment.

Ironically, at the same time that first-mover firms who conduct LCAs and identify ways to improve the sustainability of their operations may be providing competitors with a ready template for copying their green advancements, they may also be providing a playbook for competitors to capitalize on their weaknesses. If the life cycle analysis reveals inefficient or excessive waste in a manufacturing system, for example, then this internal self-evaluation can be used against the company before it has had an opportunity to make improvements.

Third, just as the benefits of LCA are broadly dispersed toward public goods, the costs are concentrated on individual firms and can be quite high. Unlike other types of disclosures, like TRI or even Security Exchange Commission ("SEC") disclosures, life cycle assessments can consume considerable resources. Data collection can be extremely costly and applying the models or methods of LCA requires expertise. From the firm's perspective, then, conducting this detailed, introspective sustainability analysis is not a simple or inexpensive exercise.

Utilizing the outputs of LCA also requires an organizational structure that can act on the results, a feature that adds still more costs to the LCA process. Some firms, and perhaps many, lack the internal management structures that allow for the internal cross-fertilization that LCA demands. In one case study, for example, Toyota Motor Sales lacked the internal capacity to conduct the assessment and contracted with UCLA to develop a model for its system. Ultimately, Toyota enjoyed considerable environmental and cost savings by eliminating a particular packaging feature of its process; yet without this investment, the areas for improvement would not have been brought to light.

Last but not least, the large-scale costs associated with developing methods, models, and databases and viewing the problem more synoptically, rather than at an individual level, all favor a public good approach to life cycle analysis. Publicly produced assessments can identify areas for cross-fertilization and better allow for the diffusion of information as compared with private assessments, which might not only lack this broader perspective, but might deliberately avoid sharing internal information since it could undermine a firm's competitive edge.

IV. Reform

Expert, neutral assessments of a manufacturing process are critical ingredients to a rigorous life cycle assessment and help pave the way to the development of sustainable innovations in processes, technologies, and even product lines. Yet it seems naïve to expect corporations will conduct these types of expensive analyses voluntarily, particularly when their own innovations can be easily co-opted by competitors. Even if LCA was mandatory for corporations, the unavoidable discretion afforded to the analyst makes it difficult to ensure that the resulting assessments are reliable and comprehensible. The proposed reform below requires that a public entity should conduct these assessments and describes how this might be done.

A. Step 1: Public Life Cycle Assessments

Since life cycle assessments come closer to being public goods than the straightforward disclosure of negative externalities, a disinterested public organization is the most appropriate entity to produce life cycle assessments. The resulting LCAs would be based on an average firm within a particular industrial sector, much as is currently done by the EPA in setting technology-based air and water pollution standards under the Clean Water and Clean Air Acts. If this generic assessment reveals reasonable areas for improvements, then consumers, investors, shareholders, and even regulators may begin to demand sustainability progress from firms.

Under this public good view of sustainability assessments, life cycle assessments would be done by respected experts who are completely independent of the companies, but have access to internal corporate information. Ideally, much of the analysis would be done cooperatively with firms since the goal is to identify areas for improvement and possibly cost savings. To the extent that the life cycle analysts face opposition from some firms, information extraction tools—like EPA's authority to request information under its various statutory mandates—would be needed to secure internal records or to ensure that the voluntarily provided records are complete. Indeed, because it has legal authority to access private records, the EPA is perhaps best situated to conduct these life cycle assessments, or it could subcontract the work to a respected nonprofit body like CERES. The resulting, industrial-sector life cycle assessments would ideally be peer reviewed and subjected to comments from the affected industry, although the expert assessor group would have complete independence in how to respond to comments. Much like technology-based standards, the life cycle analyses would also be updated at regular intervals or could be subject to more informal updating processes (for example, the expert assessor could post a website that invited comments on revisions over time).

Publicly-prepared life cycle assessments would operate much like penalty defaults: using the worst case assessment as a baseline, corporations would be able to distinguish their processes or boast of accomplishments that go well beyond the laggard facilities in their sector. The corporations can then use this positive comparison in the market to gain a competitive edge with insurers, investors, and the public at large. Unlike a full-blown life cycle analysis, however, this distinguishing effort would limit the opportunities for worrisome discretion since the firm would be forced to compare specific industrial processes against a centralized, detailed model. Nevertheless, a process for validating a corporation's claims in making these positive distinctions should also be established to provide added reliability to the firm's efforts to compare its processes against the publicly produced sustainability assessments.

Ultimately, a more reliable process for benchmarking and validating a corporation's sustainability claims could go a long way towards improving available, environmental information in the current marketplace. One of the difficulties that front-mover firms currently face is the challenge of distinguishing themselves in the marketplace in ways that can be trusted by outsiders. As one leading sustainability consultant notes, "[i]ronically, green marketing has become one of the greatest threats to the success and scale of corporate sustainability practices. Ubiquitous (and often unsubstantiated) green claims have created a green-washed, eco-cluttered and eco-saturated marketplace." The public assessments suggested here should help limit the ability of facilities to exaggerate or "green-wash," since they offer specific baselines against which a firm's boasting can be more readily compared.

There are a variety of other, supplemental LCA tools that could be developed by a centralized expert analyst body to reduce the costs to firms of conducting their own facility-based assessments. For example, a web-based model for a facility-specific LCA could be developed with user-friendly interfaces that allow corporations to insert a few parameters and then run the model. Guides and other learning materials, including workshops and symposia, might also be provided to help firms use the generic, industry-specific LCA for their facility as a springboard to improving sustainability processes. The EPA has already made progress in preparing these types of guidelines, but further outreach and education is needed since "[m]any companies [in the United States] do not see how life-cycle thinking can be applied to their specific operations—or even the benefits of doing so."

B. Step 2: Regulatory Incentives to Do Better

In order to produce meaningful incentives for firms to take sustainability seriously, the life cycle assessment could also be used as a baseline for imposing additional regulatory controls that encourage or even require specific sustainability improvements from corporations. Firms might be "commanded" to reach certain sustainability goals in ways that parallel something like the technology-based standards of the Clean Water and Clean Air Acts. For example, all firms would be required to reach some mid- or best-available level of sustainability within their industrial sector, likely required through legislation.

Alternatively, all firms in a given industrial sector could be charged a sustainability tax based on the total resource use and waste production of the reasonable worst-case life cycle for their industrial sector (perhaps further adjusted by the size or production volume of the facility). Facilities that provide validated accounts of how they accomplish sustainability gains above this baseline could then earn tax credits. Companies that go further and actually pioneer innovations in sustainable technologies or operations might not only enjoy even greater tax credits, but also reputational benefits—for example, being officially certified by the EPA, or another nonprofit, as a corporate leader in sustainable innovation.

It is ultimately possible that some sustainable innovations will be valued as intellectual property due to the high research costs involved in developing the product. At the same time, however, it is counterproductive to reward innovation in sustainable practices with patents that then allow firms to charge others a licensing fee in order to become more sustainable themselves. Since innovations in sustainability should be shared with the larger community, barriers to the diffusion of sustainable innovation due to patents and other forms of corporate intellectual property need to be monitored closely.

C. Information as a Public Good

Traditionally, information disclosures have been used to force firms to disclose their negative externalities; yet this narrow view of information disclosures may be foreclosing opportunities for advances in corporate sustainability. Indeed, a "public good" dimension to environmental information may be a perspective that has been lacking in the design of environmental programs more generally. In drug regulation there appears to be a shift occurring that depends more substantially on the Food and Drug Administration to collect and analyze all publicly available information, including adverse effects reports, and use that information to supplement the research submitted by drug manufacturers. Even historically, the first, often noncontroversial, step toward enacting pollution standards began with an agency like EPA that identifies what the better pollution control technologies could accomplish within various industrial sectors. In these programs, firms were expected to meet publicly established targets but were not required to conduct their own research and development to discover what these targets should be.

This analysis of the public good features of sustainability may only be a start in identifying ways in which reframing some intractable information problems as public goods begins to break up the information logjam that has stalled progress in environmental law. Developing a strong base of public information builds on the expert capabilities of the administrative state and approaches particularly intractable information-based challenges in a more collaborative way. Once information is developed on these environmental practices, complementary political, economic, and related market forces can use the information as a springboard to encourage greater sustainability and related gains in the future.

Conclusion

The United States still "does not have a sustainability strategy." The most promising proposals in the current economically and politically fragile climate are those that can be accomplished without political warfare and that build on progress in incremental ways. The proposal here—to assign to regulators or neutral third-party institutions the task of developing facility-specific life cycle analyses—seems to be a modest first step in this long march towards corporate sustainability. This information-generation approach also develops a partnership with business that is in line with larger goals for enhancing corporate social responsibility in ways that go beyond what specific legal requirements can accomplish standing alone. By producing large amounts of fresh and relevant information about corporate sustainability, consumers, investors, and other actors will be better able to compare and evaluate the sustainability of corporations and, if necessary, demand change.

Sustainability and Antitrust

Whether companies will share such LCA information also raises questions of competition law. As a general matter, information about product LCA is proprietary, even highly proprietary. And its sharing can be seen as anti-competitive. An argument has been made, however, that given the importance of sustainability to society, there should be a "sustainability defense" when companies are charged with collusion, particularly LCA collusion. See Jordan Ellison, *A Fair Share: Time for the Carbon Defence* (2020) [available on SSRN] (arguing that corporate commitments to reduce GHG emissions have sufficient benefit to society so as to justify a non-statutory competition law defense).

Patent-Sharing Initiative

Wagner's idea of a public-private partnership for the sharing of sustainability-related intellectual property has actually been tried without success. In 2008, the World Business Council for Sustainable Development (WBCSD) launched the not-for-profit Eco-Patent Commons. The initiative sought to encourage large multinational companies to provide free access to patents for environmentally beneficial technologies that were not viewed as central to the companies' business. The WBCSD hoped that the initiative would "quickly snowball, encouraging fruitful collaboration between [patent] pledgers and potential users." WIPO Magazine: Special Edition, World Intellectual Property Day (Apr. 2009).

Unfortunately, the Eco-Patent Commons was a flop. The making of green-technology patents accessible royalty-free, studies found, did not result in significant increases in diffusion. See Bronwyn H. Hall & Christian Helmers, *Innovation and Diffusion of Clean/Green Technology: Can Patent Commons Help?* (2013) [available on SSRN]. And in 2016 the Eco-Patent Commons was discontinued. Various explanations were advanced for the Commons not achieving its goals: (1) the patents contributed to the Commons were not valuable to future innovations; (2) the Commons scheme did not offer sufficient incentives to attract valuable patent pledges and thus achieve its goals; (3) patent disclosures alone are insufficient for widespread technology adoption because training and skill are fundamental to the patent's actual value. See Jorge L. Contreras, *Green Technology Diffusion: A Post-Mortem Analysis of the Eco-Patent Commons* (2019) [available on SSRN]

Public-Private Partnership

In connection with calls for a private-public partnership, it's interesting to observe that regulated industries often lobby the government to impose clear, uniform, and effective regulation on their industry—often, it is said, to get ahead of the regulatory game. For example, Bloomberg Environment (Bloomberg has taken the lead in reporting environmental and climate change initiatives in the private sector) recently ran a story on how the US aircraft industry (aircraft manufacturers and airlines) pushed for the government (here the EPA) to expedite the process of the United States joining an international framework for carbon emission standards for aircraft. Likewise, the leading US energy companies came together several years ago to urge Congress to create a carbon tax. Recently, a broad business coalition held a Lawmaker Education & Advocacy Day on Carbon Pricing with members of Congress to pressure for climate legislation. The coalition included 75 businesses, representing a combined market valuation of nearly $2.5 trillion and more than one million US employees. Ultimately, business seems more interested in the will (and wellness) of the people than Congress itself.

An illustration of public-private partnership comes from the recent introduction in the UK of a unique and prescriptive firm-level carbon disclosure law. Although accurate and comparable firm-level information on carbon emissions is important for investors and policymakers to manage climate-related risks, current firm-level carbon emissions disclosure regimes are mostly voluntary and non-prescriptive. The introduction of the UK's mandatory, standardized, and prescriptive disclosure requirements was shown to have a significant effect on corporate GHG emissions. Following the introduction of the UK legislation, UK firms reduced their relative (absolute) GHG emissions by 16 percent (15 percent) more than European firms that were not subject to the disclosure requirements. See Valentin Jouvenot & Philippp Krueger, *Green Technology Diffusion: A Post-Mortem Analysis of the Eco-Patent Commons* (2019) with [available on SSRN] (finding reduction in emissions is particularly pronounced for firms with high levels of tangible assets). The authors point out that these results should inform efforts, such as in the United States, to mandate GHG emissions disclosure for US public corporations (Climate Risk Disclosure Act of 2018).

Consider how US airplane manufacturers and the US airline industry urged the EPA to implement international rules on carbon emissions by airlines. It's disappointing that the regulated industry has to ask to be regulated.

Boeing, GE Seek Quick Takeoff for EPA's Aircraft Climate Rule

(Jan. 26, 2018)

Bloomberg

The EPA is taking steps to adopt international carbon emissions limits for new and in-production aircraft at the urging of industry, the agency's top transportation official said.

"It's a priority," Chris Grundler, director of the Environmental Protection Agency's Office of Transportation and Air Quality, told reporters Jan. 26 on the sidelines of the SAE international conference.

EPA officials, including leadership, have met with representatives from Boeing and General Electric, Grundler said. Those companies stressed the importance of the agency adopting the global carbon dioxide standard agreed to by the International Civil Aviation Organization, he said.

"They're very eager for us to get a proposal out," Grundler said. "I don't have a schedule for you today other than to say we're going to work as quickly as possible now that we understand their certification schedule."

Boeing supports the global standards and designed its new commercial airplanes "to meet the challenging emissions requirements," Katie Perdaris, a company spokesperson, told Bloomberg Environment in a statement.

For example, she said the Boeing 777x, which will come to market in 2020, "will be the world's largest and most fuel-efficient twin-engine jet."

Regulatory Steps

More than 190 nations, including the U.S., reached agreement in 2016 on first-time limits on greenhouse gas emissions from the aircraft sector. The standard—known as the carbon dioxide standard—requires new and in-production aircraft meet specific fuel efficiency and technology requirements.

"Airlines for America and our members join the U.S. airframe and engine manufacturers in supporting adoption of the [International Civil Aviation Organization] fuel efficiency and CO2 certification standard for future aircraft into U.S. law," Vaughn Jennings, a spokesman for Airlines for America, which represents major U.S. airlines, told Bloomberg Environment in a statement.

Despite strong industry support for the standard, the Trump administration hasn't said much publicly about whether it would implement the global agreement. But Grundler said the agency has a team working on the issue, and officials are looking to do an "expedited" rulemaking.

"The administrator decided that we're going to adopt it," Grundler said.

FAA Involvement

He added in comments to reporters that aircraft and engine manufacturers are urging the EPA to move quickly on a rulemaking, so that the Federal Aviation Administration can begin to craft certification requirements based on the new standard.

"They've told us that the U.S. certification process is the gold standard, and they'd rather not have to certify with other international agencies," he said.

The EPA under the Obama administration began the process to adopt the international standard into domestic regulations.

The agency in summer 2016 issued a final finding that greenhouse gases from aircraft endanger public health and welfare, setting the legal foundation for regulation. The Obama EPA also solicited input on the international standard and how the United States would implement it.

The agency's latest regulatory agenda, released Dec. 14, lists proposed aircraft greenhouse gas standards and test procedures as a long-term action and includes no details on when plans might be released.

Adaptive Governance

Some have pointed out that traditional regulation to protect social-ecological systems may be insufficient alone to respond to accelerating environmental change. Barbara A. Cosens, J. B. Ruhl, Niko Soininen & Lance Gunderson, *Designing Law to Enable Adaptive Governance of Modern Wicked Problems*

(2020) [available on SSRN]. To meet the challenges of accelerating environmental change, we need "adaptive governance"—beyond traditional regulatory and market approaches—to address increasing complexity. The state must assist in building adaptive capacity, along with its own capacity to adapt.

Artificial Intelligence may also have a role. As has been pointed out, AI is becoming a new de facto regulator:

> AI systems to control manufacturing operations introduces a new and distinct issue. AI systems are used not just to collect information and provide it to operating personnel, but are also being tasked with using that information to make decisions that were formerly made by real people. This could well lead to more compliance—not only with regulatory norms, but also with private compliance standards. Use of AI systems may also actually make existing pollution limits more restrictive. Many environmental permit limits are expressed in terms of the mass of pollution (such as, pounds per hour or day). When bringing in an AI system, however, the information needs of the system can result in a more frequent or even essentially continuous data sets. This then provides a method to determine compliance status on a much more frequent basis than previously.

David A. Rockman, *Insight: How AI Will Change Environmental Compliance*, Bloomberg Environment (Oct. 29, 2018).

Leap-Frog Government?

This I hold as true:

> That a flower blossoming on a tree is more beautiful than all of man's creation
>
> That the sun rises in the morning, the dawn an eternal promise of renewal
>
> That the sun sets in the evening, the dusk oh so soft and thoughtful
>
> That my wonder only grows, the experience of life washing over me.
>
> *Unknown poet* (circa 2012)

Sometimes private groups have seen it necessary to leap-frog government and undertake initiatives—such as to address the hacking of infrastructure—where government has been ineffective or even complicit in the problem. For example, a consortium of 34 major technology companies put together a 500-page document describing ways to thwart hackers, even those backed by governments, thus "to protect users from cyber attacks on innocent citizens and enterprises, to help customers strengthen their cyber postures, and to partner with other groups to bolster the internet's defenses. See Blake Sobczak, *Tech Giants Vow to Fight State-Sponsored Hacking*, EnergyWire (April 18, 2018).

In fact, private environmental governance may be displacing traditional regulation:

> Environmental law has quietly transformed from a positive law field deeply rooted in administrative law to one that is also heavily rooted in private law and private governance. After two decades (1970–1990) of remarkable activity, more than two decades have now passed without a major federal environmental statute (1991–2012). Whether the appropriate next step is expansion or contraction, reforms to the federal statutory framework have stalled. Federal regulatory activity and state and local measures have filled some of the gap, but private governance efforts—the pursuit of public ends through private standards, monitoring, enforcement, and dispute resolution—now play an im-

> portant role. Corporations report that their toxics use is regulated more by private supply chain contract requirements than the federal toxics statute. The fate of fourteen percent of the temperate forests and seven percent of the fisheries around the world is in the hands of private certification systems. More money is spent on private environmental inspections than on the entire federal EPA enforcement office. The emergence of private governance is hiding in plain view because the conceptual model by which environmental law is viewed and the metrics by which legal activity is measured do not square easily with private governance.

Michael P. Vandenbergh, *Private Environmental Governance* (2013) [available on SSRN]. For example, an unintended consequence of the 1987 Montreal Protocol was to increase demand for hydrofluorocarbons (HFCs), which are potent and increasingly used greenhouse gases. But private initiatives are a promising option because refrigerant loss is often costly to users, and private initiatives can harness a range of motivations to reduce refrigerant emissions without government coercion. See Michael P. Vandenbergh, Shannon Vreeland & Ted Atwood, *Private Governance Response to Climate Change: The Case of Refrigerants* (2019) [available on SSRN].

* * *

Concluding Thoughts

Why Do We Blame Others?

Many of us, me included, tend to blame others for our troubles. This is a common way that people react to environmental calamities, including climate chaos. "That company is just terrible. How could they let that happen? Why did it take them so long to clean up the mess?" Or we blame government. "The EPA should have addressed that issue long ago. Didn't they see that having powerplants clean up their smokestacks would lead to leaching from coal-ash ponds? Can't government do anything right?"

The following is a short essay by a Nigerian physician, Dr. Ojuolape Kuti, who lays out some of the science.

Why Do We Blame Other People?
This is what Psychology has to say.
(July 31, 2021)
Dr. Ojuolape Kuti
[Medium]

When something goes wrong humans seem to need to blame an external outlet. Why do we love to blame everyone else? We do this for multiple reasons but most notable is the need to preserve our sense of esteem.

Think of it this way. Humans are self-preservation creatures (Life Lesson 101). And so, one of the major reasons found for this bias [to blame others] is the need to protect our self-esteem. It's all part of our instinct to be accepted "in the tribe." And you'll agree that constantly beating yourself down isn't going to help that.

This also shows up in the well-studied self serving bias—the tendency for us to attribute *positive* things to internal forces (aka ourselves) while the *negative* is due to the external (aka everyone and everything else).

Probably the most fascinating finding from functional MRI brain scans is the dorsal striatum, which is associated with the reward and motivation neural pathway. So, one theory is that positive attribution is rewarding—in a neurological way—to our sense of self. And this, in turn, further reinforces the behavior of blaming others. Simply put, blaming others and not ourselves makes us feel better.

So, what should we do? On the one hand, blaming ourselves constantly can have adverse effects on our mental well-being. No one should put themselves down always. On the other hand, not taking the blame results in a lack of accountability and a lost opportunity to learn and truly grow.

As with most things in life, balance is key. But a major step is being aware of our tendency to blame others. This is not to make excuses. But perhaps by understanding ourselves (and, indeed, others) better, we can live more productive, compassionate, and peace-with-all-men lives.

Chapter 3.2

People: Corporate Social Responsibility

The next rallying cry in the triple bottom line is People! Specifically, we look at how "corporate social responsibility" (CSR) has sought to make the corporation more responsive to a fuller range of constituents, including employees, customers, workers in the supply chain, and communities. CSR exposes the tension in the triple-bottom-line corporation: Who does the corporation serve primarily? Shareholders or all those who the "corporate system" touches? Is there a hierarchy?

But, first, what is CSR? There are three broad views: (1) CSR is a corporate response to government failure; (2) CSR is a tradeoff between shareholder and stakeholder values; and (3) CSR reflects evolving investor and societal preferences. According to a study that looks at global CSR using firm-level data, CSR is more a function of legal origins than political, social, and even firm-level financial forces. Hao Liang & Luc Renneboog, *Foundations of CSR* (2014) [available on SSRN]. Not surprisingly, the English common law (and its focus on protecting property rights) has the weakest association with CSR and sustainability, while civil law systems are more strongly associated with the corporation's role in social well-being. Finally—and a bit of a spoiler—there is mounting evidence both in the United States and globally that CSR contributes to shareholder value.

Note on chapter

This is a longish chapter. That shouldn't surprise you. A book about "sustainable corporations" had better spend a good deal of time chewing on corporate social responsibility. Thus, the chapter is meant for two class sessions—or a two-stage reading. First is an introduction on how CSR is perceived inside the corporation, the legal attitudes toward CSR, and evolving academic views on CSR. Second are more specific aspects of CSR, such as who in the corporation should be charged with carrying it out, human rights in the corporation, the problem of greenwashing, and finally the arrival of a new form of CSR called environment, social, governance (ESG). Please read on.

Chapter's Focus

This chapter exposes you to a number of voices on the question of corporate social responsibility. You will first want to focus on the voice from within the corporation—an employee with strong, emotional views about trying to be a full person in a corporation. And juxtaposed is the voice of a CEO talking about his company's workforce.

Then we'll turn to the law where you'll hear the voices of judges, who both articulate the centrality of SWM, while at the same time re-stating the BJR. You'll notice that there is a tension in shareholder primacy and unfettered board discretion. Who really calls the shots? This judicial inquiry has led to corporate statutes—non-shareholder constituency statutes—and you will want to listen to the legislative voice on this question.

Then you will also want to focus on some academic voices. The first of these is from a progressive corporate law scholar who identifies that CSR may have at least two faces, each with a different attitude toward people in the corporation. Is CSR a grab for power by non-shareholders in the corporation or a new vision of the corporation? And following this voice you will hear from the leading corporate law academic (perhaps in the world) on the question of CSR and its future. You will find interesting her telling of the CSR story and the place of people in that story. Is CSR a voluntary movement, a mandated corporate responsibility, or something else?

After this will be the voice of an international law scholar who created a set of social-responsibility principles for corporations, particularly with respect to human rights. What are the responsibilities to the people a corporation touches—whether employees, workers in the supply chain, and even those with no formal relationship to the corporation?

And finally, we return to the question left by the first voice, the voice from inside the bowels of the corporation. Is CSR nothing more than cynical window-dressing by corporate management? There are a variety of voices who explain how CSR—especially as displayed in now-ubiquitous corporate CSR reports—often is rife with "greenwashing." The final voices are those of the leading corporate executives in the United States who recently declared their allegiance to CSR, followed by the voice of the leading consulting firms in the world telling corporate executives to wake up to the "value proposition" that is CSR (which they are now calling ESG).

My goodness. What are we to make of all these voices? It's hard to know.

Introductory Voices

Before getting into the question of whether and how "people" are becoming increasingly important in the corporation, the following is a report from the trenches.

Working in the Corporate World Has Taught Me Corporate People Are Mostly Idiots

(July 31, 2021)

Oinotna

[Medium]

[redacted/paraphrased]

I've worked in the corporate world for most of my career. I started as a volunteer in retail. Before I got in, corporate folks seemed smart, even superior to me. They lived in nice houses, drove expensive cars. I wanted that, too.

So, I worked hard to get into the corporate world. But once I got in, after a few jobs, I came to see it's all smoke and mirrors. I was surrounded by selfish idiots.

9–5 Is a Joke

Consider the corporate 9–5 lifestyle. It's fine if you put your job before your personal life. Working 9–5 means you can't accept deliveries at home, do your banking at a bank, or see a doctor—unless you take time off.

9–5 means being stuck to a desk for long hours with people you probably don't like. And there's not much you can do about it.

Everyone's on a Path to Nowhere

Most in the corporate world are going nowhere. They think they've got goals, but it's a lie meant to make everyone work harder. Or it's a way to cope with the truth you're wasting your life.

Management keeps certain people from succeeding no matter what. Basically, if you're not white and of a certain class, you don't have much of a chance.

It's All Image

If you give it all at any job to get ahead, you know what you get instead? More work. If you work hard in a corporate job, they're more likely to take advantage of you.

If you work hard but can't fake a smile or don't want to go out for drinks, you don't stand a chance. That is, unless you threaten people. That's how incompetent, mean bosses get ahead. They make a scene, and the company figures it's easier to just promote them.

Corporate People Are Manipulable

Humans are generally easy to manipulate, but corporate people are pushovers. Give a rousing speech over some sappy music and they'll pay you good money to tell them how to live.

Companies can treat their employees like dirt, but when they donate to some charity those very same employees think their company is amazing. It's nuts. Like, do oil companies really care about the environment?

Most Employees Are Lazy

Lots of people in the corporate world are too lazy to sit at a desk. They complain about being burnt out. They never had to lift a finger and when asked to do something they say they need some R&R in Mexico.

They Constantly Take Advantage of You

For the most part, work is just the company taking advantage of you. But if you give a little, they'll take everything. If you're willing to go above and beyond, they'll expect it all the time.

It's gotten worse during COVID. The managers are all still working from home, drinking on the job, while everyone else picks up the slack. Risking getting sick at the office.

Be Confident and Succeed

Corporate employees are not rewarded for hard work. That's mostly why I despise the corporate world. You're rewarded for sucking up and being confident. Everyone should try doing that. But rarely are the confident best for the job.

People overestimate their abilities and think they're great if they can finish all their tasks for one day. But completing all your tasks just means you're competent. It's the bare minimum.

There's Usually No Company Structure

It's shocking, but many companies have a poor structure. There are too many managers, not enough people who can handle the important jobs, and the wrong people in the wrong jobs.

It's a Feeble, Spineless Culture

I could go on and on. To sum up, the corporate world is for submissive [expletive deleted]. To go anywhere, you have to give into a bukkake of bullshit just to survive. Unless you're at the top, you've gotta be an idiot to want to be part of the corporate world.

No offence.

That was pretty raw. So, in all fairness, let's hear from management. The following is a CEO's view on employees at his company.

Letter from Jim Goodnight, CEO, SAS

(2014)

The three pillars of sustainability—economic, environmental and social—are cornerstones of the SAS business model, fueling both decisions and practices to support our world and our people. SAS's commitment to a sustainable future is evident through according to indeed.com our corporate responsibility efforts to prepare employees and our business.

Our interactions, thoughts and activities are driven by data—data that is doubling almost every other year within the digital universe. Knowledge gleaned from our company data helps us serve as environmental stewards, spanning efforts across numerous global offices. From incorporating the best design, engineering, materials and technology available to recycling and energy usage, we follow green building standards for our design, construction and renovation projects. Protecting our planet is as important to us as we know it is to our community.

SAS continues to invest in our greatest asset—our people. Through better employee health, well-being and work-life balance, we help our employees perform and excel. SAS continues to rank at the top of a variety of best places to work lists in the US and around the world. Happy employees help us maintain an exceptional retention rate, far above the industry average. That loyalty translates into satisfied customers who benefit from long relationships with experienced, committed employees.

As one of the world's best workplaces, we can attract and retain superb people who are inspired to develop great software. Our business grew from managing and analyzing large amounts of data, and even today SAS still leads the ever-expanding analytics market. In 2014, we experienced a record 39th consecutive year of growth and profitability, with approximately US$3.09 billion in worldwide revenues.

We are passionate about our responsibility in preparing the next generation of innovators, which is why education is our primary philanthropic initiative. To support that effort, in 2014 we introduced SAS® Analytics U, which provides students and teachers free and low-cost options for accessing SAS Analytics software and training. Additionally, SAS supports a host of education initiatives promoting science, technology, engineering and math.

As our world expands and evolves, I am proud and excited about our company's future and the opportunities we all have to contribute to a strong community and a sustainable planet.

Jim Goodnight

CEO of SAS

[SAS is the largest privately-owned data analytics company in the world and widely regarded as one of the most profitable tech companies, though according to indeed.com employee reviews are middling.]

3.2.1 Corporate Law and Corporate Social Responsibility (CSR)

Dodge v. Ford Motor Co.

We begin our formal look at CSR with *Dodge v. Ford Motor Co.*—one of the most cited cases in US corporate law, at least among academics, though not by courts. You may remember that we encountered the case in Leo Strine's article on *The For-Profit Corporation* (Chapter 1.3). The case articulates a principle that the purpose of the corporation is shareholder wealth maximization, but also accepts that corporate boards deserve business judgment deference when planning for the long-term. That is to say, the case expounds a fundamental conundrum.

Dodge v. Ford Motor Co.

(Mich. 1919)

[available on Casetext]

[The Ford Motor Company was founded in 1903 by a number of investors, including Henry Ford and brothers John F. Dodge and Horace E. Dodge ("the Dodge brothers"). Henry Ford, who held a 58% interest in Ford Motor, was also Ford Motor's President and a director on its board. The Dodge brothers held a 10% interest, were not on the board of directors nor employed by Ford Motor. But their company would later supply Ford Motor with the chassis and motors used in the assembly of its cars.

Ford Motor's business strategy was focused on cars that were low-priced and appealed to a large group of potential customers. To do this, Ford Motor focused on mass production of cars and vertical integration (owning the businesses that produced the raw materials needed to produce cars). These strategies allowed it to continuously reduce the cost of its cars, and the lower costs allowed selling the car at a lower price, making its cars affordable to customers who were previously priced-out. For example, according to Wikipedia, the standard Model T 4-seat open tourer of 1909 cost $850 (equivalent to $20,513 today). The price dropped to $550 in 1913 (equivalent to $12,067 today) to $440 in 1915 (equivalent to $9,431 today) and to $290 (equivalent to $3,258 today) in the 1920s.

Beginning in 1911, regular annual dividends were $1.2M. In addition, between 1913 and 1915 the company paid special dividends of $10-11M each year. Then, in 1916, Henry Ford announced that Ford Motor would no longer pay special dividends and that profits would be retained to pay for the new River Rouge plant, which would allow Ford Motor to expand its production capacity, to double employees' salaries, and to cut the price of its cars.]

The Dodge brothers sued: (1) for a decree requiring Ford Motor to distribute to stockholders at least 75% of the accumulated cash surplus, and to distribute in the future all of its earnings "except such as may be reasonably required for emergency purposes"; and (2) to enjoin the construction of the River Rouge plant.]

* * *

As we regard the testimony as failing to prove any violation of anti-trust laws or that the alleged policy of the company, if successfully carried out, will involve a monopoly other than such as accrues to a concern which makes what the public demands and sells it at a price which the public regards as cheap or reasonable, the case for plaintiffs must rest upon the claim, and the proof in support of it, that the proposed expansion of the business of the corporation, involving the further use of profits as capital, ought to be enjoined because inimical to the best interests of the company and its shareholders, and upon the further claim that in any event the withholding of the special dividend asked for by plaintiffs is arbitrary action of the directors requiring judicial interference.

The rule which will govern courts in deciding these questions is not in dispute. This court, in *Hunter v. Roberts, Throp & Co.*, recognized the rule in the following language:

> It is a well-recognized principle of law that the directors of a corporation, and they alone, have the power to declare a dividend of the earnings of the corporation, and to determine its amount. Courts of equity will not interfere in the management of the directors unless it is clearly made to appear that they are guilty of fraud or misappropriation of the corporate funds, or refuse to declare a dividend when the corporation has a surplus of net profits which it can, without detriment to its business, divide among its stockholders, and when a refusal to do so would amount to such an abuse of discretion as would constitute a fraud, or breach of that good faith which they are bound to exercise towards the stockholders.

When plaintiffs made their complaint and demand for further dividends, the Ford Motor Company had concluded its most prosperous year of business. The demand for its cars at the price of the preceding year continued. It could make and could market in the year beginning August 1, 1916, more than 500,000 cars. It had declared no special dividend during the business year except the October 1915, dividend.

It had been the practice, under similar circumstances, to declare larger dividends. Considering only these facts, a refusal to declare and pay further dividends appears to be not an exercise of discretion on the part of the directors, but an arbitrary refusal to do what the circumstances required to be done. These facts and others call upon the directors to justify their action, or failure or refusal to act.

In justification, the defendants have offered testimony tending to prove, and which does prove, the following facts: As early as in June 1915, a general plan for the expansion of the productive capacity of the concern by a practical duplication of its [manufacturing] plant [and the building of a smelting plant] had been talked over by the executive officers and directors and agreed upon. It is hoped, by Mr. Ford, that eventually 1,000,000 cars will be annually produced.

The contemplated changes will permit the increased output. The plan calls for a reduction in the selling price of the cars. The plan does not call for and is not intended to produce immediately a more profitable business, but a less profitable one; not only less profitable than formerly, but less profitable than it is admitted it might be made.

It is the contention of plaintiffs that the apparent effect of the plan is to continue the corporation henceforth as a semi-eleemosynary institution and not as a business institution. In support of this contention, they point to the attitude and to the expressions of Mr. Henry Ford.

Mr. Henry Ford is the dominant force in the business of the Ford Motor Company. No plan of operations could be adopted unless he consented, and no board of directors can be elected whom he does not favor. "My ambition," said Mr. Ford, "is to employ still more men, to spread the benefits of this industrial system to the greatest possible number, to help them build up their lives and their homes. To do this we are putting the greatest share of our profits back in the business."

The record, and especially the testimony of Mr. Ford, convinces that he has to some extent the attitude towards shareholders of one who has dispensed and distributed to them large gains and that they should be content to take what he chooses to give. His testimony creates the impression, also, that, although large profits might be still earned, a sharing of them with the public, by reducing the price of the output of the company, ought to be undertaken.

There should be no confusion (of which there is evidence) of the duties which Mr. Ford conceives that he and the stockholders owe to the general public and the duties which in law he and his codirectors owe to protesting, minority stockholders. A business corporation is organized and carried on primarily for the profit of the stockholders. The powers of the directors are to be employed for that end. The discretion of directors is to be exercised in the choice of means to attain that end, and does not extend to a change in the end itself, to the reduction of profits, or to the nondistribution of profits among stockholders in order to devote them to other purposes.

As we have pointed out, it is not within the lawful powers of a board of directors to shape and conduct the affairs of a corporation for the merely incidental benefit of shareholders and for the primary purpose of benefiting others. . . .

We are not, however, persuaded that we should interfere with the proposed expansion of the business of the Ford Motor Company. The ultimate results of the larger business cannot be certainly estimated. The judges are not business experts. It is recognized that plans must often be made for a long future, for expected competition, for a continuing as well as an immediately profitable venture. The experience of the Ford Motor Company is evidence of capable management of its affairs.

[The court then upheld the lower court's decree that a dividend must be paid, but reversed the lower court's injunction against building the smelting plant.]

What Was the Case About?

The contradiction is glaring—no? The Michigan court first decided that Ford Motor's board of directors could not change the company's dividend policy to finance Henry Ford's expansion plans. Then the court said it would not interfere with that very expansion plan approved by the same board. Go figure!

At first blush, the case seemed to turn on Ford's stated view that his company "has made too much money, has had too large profits . . . and sharing them with the public, by reducing the price of the output of the company, ought to be undertaken." Nonetheless, more was below the surface. The plaintiff Dodge brothers (former suppliers of car chassis and motors to Ford Motor) hoped to use the special dividend to finance their own start-up car manufacturing company, and Henry Ford's dividend cutback may have been intended to forestall this competition.

The court's decision to second-guess perhaps the most successful industrialist ever is at odds with the general judicial deference to management, as well as with the Michigan court's specific observation that Ford Motor's great success had resulted from its "capable management." Perhaps the court was concerned about Ford Motor gaining to much economic (and even political) power and sought to ensure a more pluralistic auto industry.

That is, the Michigan court may have used corporate law to advance a social agenda. Fixing on snippets from Henry Ford's public relations posturing, the court labeled him an anti-shareholder altruist. This justified the court's order that Ford Motor help fund the Dodge brothers' new car company, thus injecting some balance into the expanding auto industry and ultimately into Michigan politics. Soon after, the Dodge brothers parlayed their court victory into a lucrative buyout of their Ford Motor holdings. (It is worth noting that no other minority shareholders participated in the case, though Henry Ford eventually bought them out, too.)

Ironically, the case so often cited as declaring a philosophy of shareholder wealth maximization may best be understood—on closer examination—to have been about a squabble between two competitors where the stakes were consumer prices, product choice, employee wages, industry competition, and political pluralism. That is, the case was about corporate social responsibility.

"Other Constituency" Statutes

Over the past several decades, beginning during the takeover wave of the 1980s, many states have enacted "other constituency" statutes that permit, but do not require, directors to consider nonshareholder constituents (or stakeholders). Pennsylvania's statute is typical:

> In discharging [their] duties, the . . . directors of a business corporation may, in considering the best interests of the corporation, consider to the extent they deem appropriate: . . . shareholders, employees, suppliers, customers and creditors of the corporation . . . communities in which offices or other establishments of the corporation are located . . . [and] the short-term and long-term interests of the corporation. . . .

See Pa. BCL §1715. The statutes have been controversial. Some commentators have praised them as signaling a new era of corporate social responsibility; others have criticized them as a ruse for incumbent entrenchment and fecklessness. By permitting directors to rationalize corporate decisions on such open-ended concepts as "long-term interests" and "communities where the corporation operates," the statutes appear to dilute director accountability.

Although (remarkably) very few cases have confronted the meaning of the "other constituency" statutes, most cases give mixed signals about directorial deference to nonshareholder stakeholders. Some cases suggest directors can take stakeholders into account only if rationally related to promoting shareholder interests. See *Revlon v. MacAndrews & Forbes Holding*, 506 A.2d 173 (Del. 1986). Yet others suggest directors have significant latitude to consider "corporate culture," not just immediate shareholder returns, when responding to takeover threats. See *Paramount Communications, Inc. v. Time, Inc.*, 571 A.2d 1142 (Del. 1990).

3.2.2 Different Understandings of CSR

As you're beginning to notice, CSR is like nuclear fusion. It's hard to put it into a container. Just as soon as you pressure it one side, it pops out on the other.

Next is an article by a self-declared progressive corporate law scholar, Professor David Millon (Washington & Lee). He identifies two different CSR models—one in which CSR is inconsistent with SWM, and the other in which it is consistent. The first model, the conventional one, views CSR as existing in a "zero sum" game in which shareholders are asked to make concessions to other non-shareholder constituents. This model has had a good deal of academic buy-in. See Einer Elhauge, *Sacrificing Corporate Profits for the Public Good* (2004) [available at NYU Law Review]. The second model identified by Millon, one that is lately ascendant, sees the CSR movement not as a cost but as a benefit that creates a larger set of opportunities for business where both shareholders and other constituents gain from management's growing awareness of the financial value of sustainability.

Two Models of Corporate Social Responsibility

(2011)

David Millon

[available on Wake Forest Law Review]

There are two basic ways to think about business corporations: as mere aggregations of natural persons or as entities in their own right. As entities, they have been described as either natural or artificial, and the idea of the corporation as a person is itself fraught with ambiguity. This Article focuses on two perspectives and traces their respective implications for notions of corporate social responsibility ("CSR"). One is familiar and has impeded efforts to argue that corporations should be managed with attention to their obligations to society. The other, less familiar perspective draws on the concept of sustainability and offers potentially more promising prospects for those concerned about CSR.

The first perspective focuses on the corporation's constituent elements: senior management, shareholders, employees, creditors, consumers, and communities in which the corporation operates. Each of these constituencies has its own interests and these interests often conflict with those of other constituencies. For example, shareholders' desire for profit may be at odds with workers' desire for high wages. Here the primary normative question is the amount of weight that should be given to constituency interests and whose interests should take priority.

The second approach focuses on the corporation as an entity existing in time. Rather than an aggregation of numerous constituencies, the corporation is itself a distinct person. The primary emphasis then is on the various external relationships that determine its long-term survival. Here the key question is how the corporation should interact with its various stakeholders to ensure its long-run viability.

The structural approach ignores this temporal dimension and attends to the immediate impact of favoring the interests of one constituency over those of others, without reference to possible long-term considerations. So, for example, economic benefits to the corporation accruing in the future will not necessarily justify expenditures that reduce profits in the short term.

These different ways of thinking about the corporation support two different ways of thinking about CSR. The first model speaks in structural terms, emphasizing the broad range of interests that the corporation's management should take into account and balance—subordinating the shareholders' desire for profit maximization to the claims of nonshareholder stakeholders. This view might be referred to as the "constituency" model of CSR.

The second model is temporal in focus, with the key question being the corporation's success over the long run. Long-run sustainability depends crucially on the viability of the various corporate stakeholders: workers, suppliers, and customers, as well as investors, and even the environment. Decisions of corporate management often affect the well-being of these stakeholders in positive or negative ways. If the corporation's long-run sustainability is a serious objective, management must cultivate and nurture these relationships. My main point in this Article is that a long-run orientation to corporate management – that considers both profits and the well-being of nonshareholder constituents—will achieve many of the objectives favored by CSR advocates. This model might therefore be referred to as the "sustainability" model of CSR.

I. The Constituency Model of CSR

A. The Model

The constituency model of CSR sees the corporation as an organization consisting of a number of different groups of people, in which the members within each group share common interests. Shareholders, for example, generally seek maximal return on their investments. Employees want rewarding work, satisfactory working conditions, and good wages. Creditors expect to be paid according to the terms of their contracts. Often, conflicts exist among these and other constituencies' interests. High returns for shareholders can mean low wages for workers. Increased leverage may be good for shareholders but bad for bondholders. Conflicts like these mean that those in charge must make trade-off judgments. These choices are assumed to be zero-sum games.

According to this view of the corporation, CSR requires management to balance shareholder and nonshareholder interests. For example, shareholder profit maximization, even when pursued within the boundaries of the law, can lead to plant closings that harm workers and local communities, environmental damage, and human rights violations in developing countries. Socially responsible leadership therefore necessitates that management temper its pursuit of profit with regard for such considerations.

The constituency model of CSR largely takes for granted the trade-off or zero-sum assumption that sees benefit to nonshareholders coming at the expense of shareholders. Proponents must therefore rely on moral or ethical arguments, conceding the economic critique. Thus, for example, so-called corporate law progressives justify the balancing approach to CSR on fairness grounds, arguing that nonshareholders should not be required to rely on their own contractual bargaining capabilities to protect their interests. For the most part, however, the constituency model of CSR—which has long been the standard way of thinking about CSR—makes no effort to appeal to shareholder interests.

B. Current Legal Status

Corporate law endorses the constituency model of CSR, although only permissively. As of 2003, forty-one states had enacted "constituency statutes" that authorize management to take into consideration a range of nonshareholder interests in addition to those of shareholders. Importantly, however, these statutes only permit balancing of interests rather than requiring it. Corporate boards would thus be free to pursue CSR policies but cannot be sanctioned for choosing not to do so.

Delaware—the state of incorporation for nearly two-thirds of U.S. publicly traded companies—has not enacted a constituency statute. Nevertheless, Delaware law is not committed to shareholder primacy. Management's duties are owed to "the corporation and its stockholders," rather than to the shareholders alone. Moreover, the Delaware courts have never stated plainly that management's fiduciary responsibilities—the duties of care and loyalty—imply a general duty to maximize profits without regard to competing nonshareholder considerations. Thus, in the face of management policies to favor nonshareholder constituencies over shareholders, the shareholders lack the ability to challenge such policies even if the result is reduction of profits. Under the business judgment rule, courts will not second-guess decisions—including decisions that appear to benefit nonshareholders at the expense of shareholders—as long as management can assert some plausible connection with the corporation's long-run best interests.

C. Current Practice

Although not required to do so by law, management of U.S. corporations typically pursues short-term profit maximization as measured by investors looking to quarter-to-quarter earnings. The objective is enhancement of share price, which depends on a reliable stream of regular earnings; failure to meet earnings targets usually results in immediate share price decline. Because the constituency model of CSR envisions expenditures—in the form of cash outlays or foregone revenues—that are designed to benefit non-shareholders, such policies would mean lower net income and therefore would conflict with management's emphasis on the currently accepted short-term conception of shareholder value. In other words, current practice generally embraces shareholder primacy and rejects CSR.

There are several explanations for current practice, which as explained above, is not required by law. Today's shareholders typically adopt a short-term perspective that manifests itself in a strong preference for immediate results measured in terms of current share price. Management thus finds itself under scrutiny to deliver results on a quarter-to-quarter basis and goes to great lengths to achieve accounting results that meet or exceed earnings targets.

Management compensation also encourages concentration on current share price. Stock and stock option grants are significant elements of senior officer compensation at most U.S. corporations. The justification is alignment of shareholder and management interests in order to reduce agency costs. The effect is to encourage a short-term focus on profits in order to boost the value of shares and options awarded to executives of the corporation.

Social norms shape an environment in which management tends to understand its role in terms of maximization of current share prices. Business schools, apparently misapprehending the law, preach this ethic at the expense of a richer, more complex conception of responsibility. Corporate lawyers charged with advising boards on their responsibilities typically take shareholder primacy for granted. The business press insists on the same idea, and prominent corporate law academics—most of whom tend to embrace a conservative law-and-economics agenda—likewise assume that shareholder primacy rather than CSR is legally mandated.

II. The Sustainability Model of CSR

A. The Model

The sustainability approach to CSR posits that the corporate entity should remain economically viable over the long run. The corporation must generate profits because survival requires it, but survival most emphatically does not require short-term profit maximization. In fact, a short-term time horizon may impede the corporation's long-run sustainability because it can result in policies that sacrifice future earnings for current net income.

The connection between sustainability and CSR is simply the realization that the corporation's long-run prosperity depends on the well-being of its various stakeholders, including workers, suppliers, and customers. Sustainability also requires ongoing availability of natural resources and a natural environment in which the corporation and its various constituencies can survive and flourish. Well-functioning markets and stable and supportive governments are also essential. Because the corporation itself has a significant role to play in determining the welfare of these stakeholders and in nurturing productive, reliable relations with them, a sustainability approach to business success has the potential to achieve many of the goals that CSR proponents advocate.

The sustainability model of CSR differs from the constituency model in a fundamental way. The constituency approach sees attention to nonshareholder interests as a trade-off cost that comes at the expense of profit and therefore of shareholder value. In contrast, the sustainability perspective sees attention to nonshareholders—including investment in their well-being—as essential to the viability of the firm and therefore also to the enhancement of shareholder value. The key difference is the relevant time horizon.

B. Illustrations

The sustainability approach to corporate management accommodates CSR expenditures because it takes into account long-term payoffs that benefit the corporation and thereby its shareholders as well. For transnational corporations doing business in developing countries, sustainability may require investment in community-level infrastructure development projects, technological innovation, education, and health care. An example is Nestlé's entry into milk production in the Moga district of India. Investments in refrigeration, well drilling, veterinary medicine, and training have vastly increased output; enhanced product quality has allowed Nestlé to pay higher prices to farmers. The result is higher incomes for farmers and their employees, and the region now has a significantly better standard of living compared to neighboring communities.

By spending money on projects like these, corporations incur immediate costs that reduce current profits. Longer-run benefits, however, have the potential to generate net gains in the form of enhanced productivity, greater skills and knowledge, commitment, increased consumer demand, political and social stability, and long-run viability. The corporation and its shareholders benefit—but so too do the local communities in which its workers and producers live. In contrast, a narrow, short-term orientation seeks simply to locate production in developing countries in order to take advantage of low wages and lax regulations. Current expenses are reduced, but long-run productivity and sustainability considerations are ignored.

C. "Strategic" versus "Philanthropic" CSR

A strategic emphasis on investments that serve the interests of key stakeholders can bolster the corporation's long-term sustainability. Because such policies are justified in economic terms—in terms of the corporation's long-run profitability—there is no need to resort to moral or ethical arguments, as is the case with the constituency model of CSR. The whole point is to generate net gains in the future from expenditures incurred in the present—benefits to nonshareholders come not at the expense of shareholders but rather are deployed for their ultimate advantage.

For this reason, this approach to CSR objectives can be labeled "strategic." In contrast, the notion that CSR requires firms to forego profits—and therefore reduce shareholder wealth—in order to spend corporate funds to benefit nonshareholder constituencies might be termed "philanthropic" CSR. An example would be refusal to immediately close a plant generating subnormal returns because of concerns about the harsh impact the closure would have on the labor force, the local community, and perhaps also on the company's reputation among consumers, investors, and the general public. Such a decision could be characterized as "philanthropic" in the sense that corporate management has chosen voluntarily to forego profits in order to benefit nonshareholder constituencies. These benefits come at the expense of the shareholders. From that perspective, the decision is analogous to a charitable donation to a nonprofit organization.

III. The Prospects for Sustainability CSR

The economic argument for sustainability CSR ought to have broad appeal. Because it is not based on purely moral or ethical considerations, it avoids standard objections raised against the constituency CSR model based on the interests of shareholders and their claims of privilege vis-à-vis the corporation's various nonshareholder groups. Further, unless blinded by short-term myopia, corporate executives should appreciate the importance of the corporation's long-run viability. They therefore should be receptive to the idea that investment in the well-being of key stakeholders can generate significant financial returns. Indeed, the many examples of strategic CSR indicate that many executives understand this point and are incorporating it into their business strategy. Nonetheless, there are significant impediments to its widespread adoption.

A. Sustainability CSR's Problematic Appeal

As discussed above, CSR policies based on a commitment to sustainable profits are a casualty of the current obsession with short-termism embraced by shareholders. And management compensation practices that typically include stock-based pay further encourage a short-term focus. So too do business norms that focus on quarterly earnings as the relevant metric by which management is to be evaluated. As long as corporate executives prioritize short-term results over long-run value, sustainability considerations will be of only secondary importance.

B. Accounting Conventions

Current accounting conventions generally do not express the future value of strategic investments in the well-being of nonshareholder constituencies. Thus, an investor who seeks information about the potential future payoffs of current expenditures that are designed to generate sustainable profits by promoting the interests of nonshareholders will find it difficult to obtain that information from the corporation's financial disclosure. Similarly, corporate executives who approve expenditures benefiting nonshareholders may be frustrated at their inability to express the future value of those expenditures in the corporation's financial statements.

According to Generally Accepted Accounting Principles, expenditures designed to benefit nonshareholders so as to create future value typically must be reported as expenses that reduce net income in the accounting period in which they are paid. The fact that they are supposed to generate future profits potentially extending over many years is not reflected on the income statement or balance sheet—instead they are accounted for as current expenses just as are, say, rent or salary or interest payments. So, for example, a corporation that spends money training farmers in more productive, less environmentally damaging agricultural practices or encouraging its employees to pursue healthier life choices will have to account for those costs on its income statement when the expenditures are made, reducing net income by the amount of the expenditure, even though the goal is to produce value in the future. Although these might better be thought of as investments rather than expenses, their value is not expressed on the balance sheet.

Compare in this regard expenditures made to acquire fixed assets, that is, assets that are expected to contribute value to the corporation over a number of years. The cost of these assets is allocated over their useful lives, rather than treated as an expense to be assigned entirely to the period in which they are purchased. The theory is that the cost of these assets should be accounted for over the entire period during which they generate value. Further, the value of fixed assets is included on the balance sheet, expressed in terms of historical cost.

Conclusion

The orthodox model of CSR—which I have termed the "constituency" model—envisions the corporation as composed of a number of constituencies whose interests often conflict. Policies designed to benefit a nonshareholder constituency are assumed to reduce profits and therefore affect shareholder interests adversely. As management attempts to mediate among these conflicting interests, zero-sum trade-offs are assumed to be inevitable. Seen in this light, CSR has enjoyed limited traction among business leaders, academics, lawyers, and policymakers because it is widely taken for granted that shareholder primacy is the relevant benchmark.

The "sustainability" model of CSR rejects the zero-sum trade-off assumption of the constituency model and instead embraces the idea that the corporation's long-run sustainability depends in part on the long-run viability of key stakeholders. The corporation has a role to play in ensuring that viability. Investment in the well-being of key nonshareholder constituencies—even though costly in the short run—can generate payoffs in the future that justify those expenditures. Indeed, failure to attend to such considerations may threaten the corporation's long-run competitiveness.

The sustainability model of CSR avoids the standard objections to the constituency model based on shareholder primacy. Long-run sustainability requires economic success over time. Strategic investments beneficial to nonshareholders are thus designed ultimately to enhance profits. The long-run perspective facilitates appreciation of the relevance of future returns on current investments and their potential to promote shareholder value.

Conceived in this way, CSR grounded in sustainability concerns can produce real benefits for nonshareholders. It is nevertheless important to bear in mind that it still may not do enough to satisfy fully the corporation's responsibilities to society. Because it is grounded on cost-benefit analysis, sustainability CSR may not go far enough.

David Millon is the J.B. Stombock Professor of Law, Washington and Lee University. An earlier version of this Article was presented at the symposium on "The Sustainable Corporation" held at Wake Forest University School of Law in April 2011.

ALI Principles of Corporate Governance

The question of CSR has been part of the "corporate purpose" debate for many decades. In the 1980s when the American Law Institute attempted to identify the fundamental principles of corporate law, the divided ALI drafters came up with this description of the corporation's purpose:

> **§ 2.01 The Objective and Conduct of the Corporation**
> (a) Subject to the provisions of Subsection (b), a corporation should have as its objective the conduct of business activities with a view to enhancing corporate profit and shareholder gain.
> (b) Even if corporate profit and shareholder gain are not thereby enhanced, the corporation, in the conduct of its business:
> (1) Is obliged, to the same extent as a natural person, to act within the boundaries set by law;
> (2) May take into account ethical considerations that are reasonably regarded as appropriate to the responsible conduct of business; and
> (3) May devote a reasonable amount of resources to public welfare, humanitarian, educational, and philanthropic purposes.

Hardly anyone cites to the ALI Principles on Corporate Governance, except a handful of corporate law scholars. Others have criticized the ALI Principles for coming from a "tainted process." See Charles Elson & Michael L. Shakman, *The ALI Principles of Corporate Governance: A Tainted Process and Flawed Product,* 49 Bus. Law. 1761 (1994). But more fundamentally, the statement of the corporate purpose has been criticized as employing the language of "law and economics"—thus cabining the corporation as a private phenomenon, not a social institution with public responsibility. See James Boyd White, *How Should We Talk About Corporations? The Languages of Economics and Citizenship*, 94 Yale L. J. 1416 (1985):

> The language of section 2.01 [of the ALI Principles of Corporate Governance] creates a false opposition between the economic goals of a corporation (expressed as an ultimately self-interested duty to enhance "corporate profit and shareholder gain") and certain other corporate aims or activities, which are conceived of as public-spirited or philanthropic (including its obligation to obey the law). This opposition is, I think, inconsistent with the basic conception of the corporation expressed in the best tradition of American corporate law and practice. What is worse, it invites thought and discussion of a clashing and unproductive kind about these important matters. . . . To say that a corporation's only goal is to make money would be to define the business corporation-for the first time in American or English law as I understand it-as a kind of shark that lives off the community rather than as an important agency in the construction, maintenance, and transformation of our shared lives.

The Recent Trajectory (and Future) of CSR

Next is a masterful summary of the issues, evidence, and arguments regarding the current state of CSR. Professor Cynthia Williams (Osgoode Hall Law School, York University, Toronto) touches on and brings together many themes we have been considering. (It is worth noting that Professor Williams's 1999 article *The SEC and Corporate Social Transparency* in the Harvard Law Review was a seminal piece in the legal literature on CSR.) What is CSR? Is it a matter of reporting or of substantive action? Is CSR voluntary or mandatory? Does CSR lead to better firm financial performance and among what firms? What have been the arguments for and against CSR by those who espouse shareholder primacy and by those who advance a stakeholder theory of the corporation? Can CSR be the cure to the ills of capitalism?

Corporate Social Responsibility and Corporate Governance

(2015)

Cynthia A. Williams

[available on SSRN]

I. Introduction

Corporate social responsibility (CSR) has been given increased attention in the last two decades in practice and in theory, both in management and law. An influential 1970's article defined it as "the firm's considerations of, and response to, issues beyond the . . . economic, technical, and legal requirements of the firm to accomplish social benefits along with the traditional economic gains which the firm seeks." In 2011 the European Commission went beyond this definition and explained "[e]nterprises should have in place a process to integrate social, environmental, ethical, human rights and consumer concerns into their business operations and core strategy in close collaboration with their stakeholders." Thus, the emphasis has shifted from philanthropy and attention to corporate action "beyond law," to how a company conducts its business.

Evidence of this developing norm of CSR is that nearly all global companies today highlight their social initiatives and performance on their websites, while over 90% of the Global 250 companies voluntarily disclose more environmental, social and governance (ESG) information than required by law—many with associated certification schemes and requirements for third-party attestation or auditing. These voluntary initiatives are increasingly being supplemented by domestic and multilateral government actions to encourage, or in some cases require, companies to pay closer attention to the social and environmental consequences of their actions and to disclose more information about those consequences.

Investors as well have become more attentive in recent years to environmental and social risks in portfolio companies, and therefore more concerned with CSR. Global assets under management with sustainability screens have risen 61% since 2012, to

US$ 21.4 trillion at the start of 2014. Institutions managing US$ 45 trillion of invested capital have committed to the U.N. Environment Program's Principles for Responsible Investment (PRI), which require investors to incorporate ESG issues into investment practices across their asset classes. And, as of 2015, over US$ 92 trillion of the world's invested capital backs the Carbon Disclosure Project (CDP) 's work with 2,000 companies around the world to gather data on those companies' greenhouse gas emissions. Indeed, CSR itself has become an industry "awash with PR consultants, social auditors, firms providing verification or 'assurance' for companies' social and environmental reports, and investment analysts all vying for business."

While these trends indicate that CSR has achieved some place within mainstream corporate and investor activities, in important respects CSR is both too strong and too weak: too strong an assertion of a social role for the corporation and its management to coexist comfortably with the view of the purely economic role of the corporation within shareholder-focused corporate governance systems, and yet too weak for academics taking a stakeholder view of the corporation who are concerned with global problems they view companies as having helped to create, including climate change, environmental degradation, exploitative labor conditions and worsening economic inequality.

II. Voluntary CSR Initiatives

A. CSR Reporting

The most comprehensive source of data on ESG reporting is that done by KPMG in the Netherlands. KPMG published its first ESG report in 1993, and its most recent in 2013. In 1993, 12% of the top 100 companies in the OECD countries (ex. Japan) published an environmental or social report. By 2013, 76% of the top 100 companies in the Americas publish a separate CSR report, as do 73% of top 100 companies in Europe and 71% in Asia. Of the largest 250 companies globally, reporting rates are 93%.

In addition to the quantity of CSR reporting, KPMG also evaluates the quality of reporting. Here, European companies generally do substantially better than those in Asia or the Americas (average quality scores of 71 out of 100 in Europe versus 54 in the Americas and 50 in Asia Pacific). Within the Global 250, 87% identify climate change, material resource scarcity and trends in energy and fuel as "megatrends" that will affect their business. Ultimately KPMG concludes that "[m]any companies no longer see CSR as a moral issue, but as core business risks and opportunities [relevant to the company's competitive position]."

B. Substantive CSR Initiatives

1. Private Initiatives

The focus on expanded ESG disclosure has occurred concomitantly with the proliferation of transnational, voluntary standards for what constitutes responsible corporate action. Thus, over the past two decades such standards have been developed—in just about every industry and sometimes across industries—by governments; public/private partnerships; multi-stakeholder negotiation processes; specific industries and companies; institutional investors; functional groups such as accountancy firms and social assurance consulting groups (many of which did not exist more than ten years ago); NGOs; and non-financial ratings agencies. And many companies have engaged third-party certifiers to ensure that their suppliers and subsidiaries are meeting those standards.

2. Multilateral Initiatives

A number of significant multilateral instruments have also been developed or recently strengthened by multilateral international organizations. While these instruments do not establish binding treaty obligations, they do articulate governments' expectations of responsible corporate action—including the OECD's Guidelines for Multinational Enterprises; the ISO 26,000 CSR standards; the U.N.'s Global Compact; and the U.N.'s more recent "Protect, Respect and Remedy" framework articulating states' and companies' human rights responsibilities.

The OECD's Guidelines, initially promulgated in 1976 and most recently amended in 2011, encourage companies to promote sustainable development, and include standards based on ILO and U.N. treaty obligations, including standards of transparency, labor protection, international human rights protection, responsible supply chain management, environmental protection, anti-bribery standards and fair tax contributions (added in 2011 and unique among international CSR standards).

The International Standards Organization (ISO), which has developed thousands of technical standards since its establishment after World War II, developed the ISO 26,000 standard for CSR in 2010, after five years of consultation among standards bodies from 90 countries and 40 international or regional organizations. ISO 26,0000 defines general principles of accountability, transparency, ethical behavior, respect for stakeholder interests, for rule of law, for international norms and human rights as the field of CSR; and core subjects include governance, human rights, labor practices, the environment, fair operating practices, consumer issues, and community involvement.

Among multilateral frameworks, the U.N.'s Guiding Principles on Business and Human Rights, adopted by the U.N. Human Rights Council in 2011, seems to have the greatest potential to develop into a baseline global legal framework for companies' social responsibilities. (The OECD Principles only apply to companies in or from adhering countries.) The U.N. Guiding Principles set out the core spheres of obligation for states and companies with respect to human rights: states have the duty to *protect* their citizens from violations by third parties, including companies, by promulgating laws and regulations; companies have the responsibility to act with due diligence to *respect* citizens' human rights; and both have the duty to provide access to *remedies* for victims. Developed after the failure in 2004 of the U.N. Human Right's Commission's Draft Norms on the Responsibilities of Transnational Corporations and Other Business Enterprises with Regard to Human Rights, which "business vehemently opposed," the Protect, Respect, and Remedy framework was developed in a six-year process led by Prof. John Ruggie of Harvard University.

III. Significant Legal Requirements

For the most part, CSR standards are voluntary, with the exception of new legislation in India, which as of 2014 has required companies to establish a CSR committee of the board and contribute 2% of net profits to CSR initiatives. That said, many of the topics that CSR addresses are subject to domestic regulation, such as labor rights, environmental protection, consumer protection, anti-discrimination, or anti-bribery.

As of 2015, many European countries or their stock exchanges, and the EU itself, require some environmental or social disclosure, to varying degrees of specificity. The EU's requirement is a directive that entered into force in 2014, giving member states two years to transpose the directive into national law. The directive requires approximately 6,000 large companies and "public interest organizations," such as banks and insurance companies, to "prepare a non-financial statement containing information relating to at least environmental matters, social and employee-related matters, respect for human rights, anti-corruption and bribery matters."

Notably missing from any of these lists of comprehensive ESG disclosure is the United States, which does have specific disclosure requirements in certain regulatory contexts but no general ESG disclosure framework. Since 1986, the Environmental Protection Agency has required facility-by-facility disclosure concerning the release into the environment and/or management through recycling of over 650 chemicals through the Toxic Release Inventory. The U.S. Securities and Exchange Commission (SEC) requires substantial corporate governance disclosure from its publicly-listed companies, as do most countries. Yet, generalized requirements for environmental or social disclosure tend to be narrower than those described above.

IV. Empirical Findings

The topic of CSR has been given increasing academic attention in the past decades, as this table prepared by Timothy Devinney, University Professor of International Business at the University of Leeds, indicates. This table shows the number of published articles on CSR within various fields.

Area	< 1990	1991 - 1995	1996 - 2000	2001 - 2005	2006 - 2010
Environmental Sciences	2	0	2	13	61
Economics	19	6	9	46	174
Management	189	149	217	604	1460
Sociology	14	4	10	105	295
Psychology	3	0	2	6	17
Law	23	3	11	50	153

A. CSR and Financial Performance

One of the perennial debates in this field is whether CSR initiatives lead to better firm-level financial performance, the "business case" for CSR. There are two primary issues here: (1) whether CSR initiatives pay off or whether they are a waste of money? and (2) if higher-CSR firms exhibit better financial performance, which way does causation go? Do better-performing firms invest in CSR because they have more resources, or do CSR investments come first and the better financial results follow?

Results are emerging that CSR investments can pay off:

- superior CSR performance from companies in countries with a Scandinavian legal origin, and then German and French legal origins, and the superiority of all three in comparison to the common law countries [Hao Liang and Luc Renneboog – SSRN]
- companies with a strategic focus on ESG issues show financial outperformance, and stock market and accounting value premiums, based on 18 years of observations of 90 matched pairs of high-sustainability versus low-sustainability companies [Bob Eccles, Ioannis Ioannou and George Serafeim]
- management attention to material sustainability risks yields financial outperformance of 3% to 8%, evaluated within industries using specific concepts of industry-relevant materiality being developed in the United States by the Sustainability Accounting Standards Board (SASB) [George Serafeim, Mozaffar Khan and Aaron Yoon - SSRN].
- companies with a longer-term management focus or a stakeholder orientation promote innovation within the firm and higher levels of trust of the firm among various external stakeholders [Caroline Flammer and Aleksandra Kacperczk]
- increase in firm value after the firms adopted longer-term management compensation plans, and also found improved operating performance on each of three metrics (return on assets, net profit margin, and sales growth) [Caroline Flammer and Pratima Bansal]
- CSR strategies and operating procedures positively influence intangibles of innovation, human capital improvements, reputation and corporate culture, and that these intangibles are significantly related to corporate financial performance [Jodi Surroca, Josep Tribó and Sandra Waddock]

A comprehensive review in 2014 of empirical studies of the financial results of CSR by Gordon Clark, Andreas Feiner and Michael Viehs found that 90% of studies show that sound sustainability standards lower firms' cost of capital; 80% of studies show that the stock price performance of companies is positively influenced by good sustainability practices; and 88% of studies show that better E, S, or G practices result in better operational performance.

B. Board Composition and Committees

One structural feature that would seem to indicate a seriousness of purpose about CSR, or at least the potential for a connection between a governance mechanism and corporate social performance, would be a board committee dedicated to the topic. Yet the empirical evidence is mixed on this point. The authors of one study found two noteworthy effects regarding the board. First, the existence of a specialized environmental board committee was related to both better and worse environmental performance, suggesting that board committees could be established either to promote better environmental performance or as a reaction to environmental problems. Second, more independent, larger, and less diverse boards were associated with worse environmental outcomes, possibly because of a lack of in-depth knowledge of environmental risks to the company.

When in doubt, remember Warren Buffett's rule of thumb:

> I want employees to ask themselves whether they are willing to have any contemplated act appear the next day on the front page of their local paper—to be read by their spouses, children and friends– with the reporting done by an informed and critical reporter. [From a Berkshire Hathaway CSR report, which are the only such reports that have no pictures.]

But that even Alibaba, a Chinese internet sales company incorporated in the Cayman Islands and being investigated for selling counterfeit products on its website, includes a "sustainability" page on its website. This suggests at least two things: global companies feel pressure from social actors to be seen to embrace positive social and environmental values; and companies' disclosure is not an unambiguous signal of actual CSR.

C. Patterns of Shareholder Ownership

There is evidence that some institutional shareholders are paying more attention to ESG issues, and this is one source of pressure on companies to also pay more attention. Trillions of dollars of invested capital supporting initiatives such as the U.N. Environment Program's Principles of Responsible Investment or backing the Carbon Disclosure Project's efforts to get better data on company's management of GHG emissions sends a signal to companies that at least some investors care about these topics. Of potentially greater significance, since 2009 Bloomberg has included 79 environmental and social data points in the information it sells to brokers and dealers throughout the world – presumably because there's a market for it.

A 1999 study (and follow-up 2006 study) show that firms with higher percentages of long term, pension fund investors had significantly better performance on social issues and environmental issues than firms with lower percentages.

D. CSR, Legal Origins and Corporate Governance Systems

Consistent with what one might predict, empirical evidence shows that both country-level sustainability ratings and company-level CSR ratings are higher in countries with a stakeholder-oriented corporate governance system than in countries with a shareholder-oriented corporate governance system. A 2013 study using data from MSCI's Risk Metrics found that:

> Among different legal origins, the English common law—widely believed to be mostly shareholder oriented—fosters CSR the least; within the civil law countries, firms of countries with German legal origin outperform their French counterparts in terms of ecological and environmental policy, but the French legal origin firms outperform German legal origin companies in social issues and labor relations. Companies under the Scandinavian legal origin score highest on CSR (and all its subfields).

In the common law system, the state's role in the economy is understood to be more limited in addressing economic inequality or promoting and protecting labor or environmental interests. In Scandinavian countries and those based on civil law legal families, there is more legal pressure for voluntary CSR initiatives to address these issues.

V. Implications and Analysis

Whether attention to CSR does lead to financial outperformance in some cases, and what those cases are, does not settle the "case of CSR," for there is a much deeper disagreement. That is the perennial (even religious) debate over the purpose of the firm. Is it "simply" to produce products and services that create economic rents to be distributed to rights' holders according to pre-existing contractual, statutory and (possibly) normative obligations? Or does the firm also have a social obligation to minimize harm to people and the natural environment in its pursuits of profits, or even a positive duty to promote social welfare beyond its creation of economic rents?

A. Shareholder Primacy

Milton Friedman's articulation of firms' responsibilities is the iconic expression of a predominantly economic perspective on the nature of the firm:

> There is one and only one social responsibility of business—to use its resources and engage in activities designed to increase profits so long as it stays within the rules of the game, which is to say, engages in open and free competition without deception or fraud.

This statement was part of a *New York Times* article in which Friedman contributed to a vigorous debate that was then on-going within the business community. Some academics and members of the U.S. business community had begun to argue that companies had responsibilities to respond to civil rights and anti-war unrest, as well as strategic interests in providing an attractive alternative to collectivist social movements like Marxism, socialism and organized labor, by paying greater attention to making a positive social contribution.

Later writers, including Professors Hansmann and Kraakman, would later assert that a deviation from honest profit-making within the confines of law would dilute management's focus, thus undermining economic performance and ultimately social welfare.

From the shareholder-oriented perspective, CSR is too much responsibility to impose on directors. Advancing social policy goals is the job of government, not business. In contrast, directors are elected by the shareholders to run the firm in the shareholders' interests. Balancing other constituents interests' by making "tradeoffs between the welfare of shareholders and that of non shareholder constituencies" is problematic because it is inconsistent with the proper exercise of directors' power to advance shareholders' interests, and because it risks undermining accountability by allowing directors to act in their own self-interest while claiming to act in other constituents' interests.

In short, CSR is too strong a concept: it risks economic underperformance, it usurps government's policy roles, and it is beyond the boundaries of directors' and managers' legitimate exercise of power by seeking to advance non-shareholder interests.

B. Stakeholder Theory

In contrast, to some academic critics, CSR is still too weak. The stakeholder theory—generally attributed to Ed Freeman but part of "a very old tradition that sees business as an integral part of society rather than an institution separate and purely economic in nature"—posits that economic value is created by voluntary relationships among many parties who cooperate to create successful businesses. It is an ethical theory about the values of management in relationships with those parties:

> Capitalism works because entrepreneurs and managers put together and sustain deals or relationships among customers, suppliers, employees, financiers, and communities.

This theory does not deny that shareholders are important stakeholders in the firm, but does reject the view that shareholders' interests are the only interests that managers and directors should consider in managing a successful firm.

To these theorists, CSR is too modest, given its emphasis on disclosure and voluntarism. For example, Andy Crane has shown that "modern slavery" (traditional slavery, bonded labor, human trafficking and forced labor) is endemic in some industries (agriculture, mining, extraction, construction, brickmaking, carpet weaving, domestic work and sex work)—with global estimates range from 12 million to 30 million people enslaved throughout the world.

Despite voluntary CSR initiatives in various industries (such as the West African cocoa industry), modern slavery persists. For example, Barrick Gold settled claims in 2015 that its security personnel had raped 137 women in Papua New Guinea over a period of decades; and the Rana Plaza factory that produced clothes for 29 global clothing companies collapse in Bangladesh in 2013 and killed 1,134 people.

Thus, from both the stakeholder and the sociological perspective CSR is both too weak and too strong. It is an insufficient constraint on how companies do business in the world, yet it effectively undermines calls for more substantive regulation.

C. Evaluating the Arguments

Today the argument that CSR requires companies and the board to take on an essentially political role for which they are ill-suited rings hollow, given the extensive involvement of American companies in law-making, lobbying, litigation to narrow regulation, and constitutionally-protected electoral politics. But two arguments for shareholder primacy remain important to address: balancing multiple stakeholders' interests will undermine management accountability; and because boards and managers must act in the interests of shareholders only, CSR initiatives could be a breach of fiduciary duty.

Two points are relevant to both issues. First, the data do not support the view that CSR initiatives inevitably cause financial losses—in fact, as we've seen, to the contrary. Second, arguments against CSR ignore what large companies are saying they are doing, around the world. Unless one considers *everything* that a company says about its social responsibilities to be unsubstantiated public relations, then judges and law professors should consider these facts.

1. *Shareholder versus stakeholder theory*

Corporate boards' legal obligations regarding CSR has been vigorously debate in the United States. Lynn Stout's short polemic, written for a popular audience, entitled "The Shareholder Value Myth: How Putting Shareholders First Harms Investors, Corporations and the Public" inspired multiple, equally polemical reactions by respected scholars, including Leo Strine who rejects that "the business judgment rule [cloaks directors with the ability] to act for any reason they deem appropriate."

Lately, the problem has not been CSR, but the tight coupling of managers and markets, which has allowed managerial rent extraction in the U.S. to an historically unprecedented degree. Moreover, today's concern is that shareholders are putting short-term pressure on companies in ways that are unproductive for the future success of the corporate enterprise. As Bill Bratton and Michael Wachter have shown, activist investors seek that (1) more money be given back to shareholders, (2) the company sell itself or its premium assets, (3) the company increase leverage, or (4) the company cut costs. The first three, and sometimes the fourth, destroy longer-term value, such as putting off needed maintenance of plant and equipment, delaying marketing campaigns, cutting back on research and development, or even engaging in financial reporting fraud or value-destroying mergers and acquisitions—concerns identified by none other than Michael Jensen.

2. CSR Reconciliation

In conclusion, perhaps the competing views of CSR as simultaneously too strong and too weak can be reconciled. Even Friedman believed that business has an obligation to conform "to the basic rules of the society, both those embodied in law and those embodied in ethical custom."

There is a range of regulatory approaches that might facilitate effective, voluntary initiatives. Regulatory approaches to deal with human rights abuses, labor exploitation, climate change and declining natural resources (including fresh water) are in place in some parts of the world. These approaches can be canvassed for best practices and further learning. Moreover, the accounting industry has developed and is continuing to develop approaches to integrated financial and non-financial reporting, and true-value accounting to incorporate the cost of negative externalities.

VI. Conclusion

Can CSR be a cure for the ills of capitalism? Certainly, some CSR initiatives have improved the conditions of employment for some around the world. And some CSR initiatives have brought more attention to environmental problems and have motivated companies to develop innovative products and solutions to address those problems. Empirical evidence is even starting to show that CSR can even be a smart business strategy.

But CSR is no panacea. It can be used to dissuade governments from taking regulatory action, making problems worse. It leaves gaping holes, such as its failure to establish "no go" zones. For example, how can there be "responsible tar sands mining"? Just as whiskey has been said to be the "nicest of cures" that don't work for the common cold, CSR may be the nicest of cures to our modern capitalism.

Cynthia A. Williams is Osler Chair in Business Law, Osgoode Hall Law School, York Univ, Toronto, Canada

3.2.3 CSR and Employee Rights

So, what is the place of employees in the corporation—a critical constituent for the CSR corporation? The idea that employees should have a greater role in the corporation recently has gotten a good deal of traction. At many corporations, there is a trend to include employees in decision-making in order to improve productivity and to give employees a greater sense of empowerment and ownership. It has even been suggested that employees be given a non-binding vote on the pay of the top executives, just as shareholders already have a "say on pay." See Robert Rhee, *Intra-Firm Monitoring of Executive Compensation* (2015) [available at SSRN] (arguing that employees—unlike diffuse, diversified and short-term shareholders—have a corporate and social role in monitoring senior executives, thus to legitimate executive pay at firm and political levels).

Although a bit dated, the following is a view on what the role of employees should be in the corporation. It's a view that has achieved much ascendance—namely, that the HR department should be leading the corporation's CSR charge. What do you think?

Why HR Needs to Take a Leadership Role in CSR

Forbes (Jan. 6, 2014)

Karen Higginbottom

[redacted/paraphrased]

Companies are spending a lot on corporate social responsibility (CSR). One reason has been to restore trust among shareholders, employees, and customers—another to improve company reputations. But what role has HR played in CSR and should HR take a more leading role in guiding corporate CSR strategies?

"CSR" emerged in the 1960s and went mainstream in the 1990s, especially after reports on poor working conditions in global supply chains. Although CSR has its skeptics as well as advocates, its defining feature is that companies do it voluntarily. CSR is separate from legal compliance.

Attitudes to CSR are changing. Jonny Gifford, a researcher at the Chartered Institute of Personnel and Development, commented, "The more we talk about responsible business practices the better. There are two broad aspects to corporate responsibility: one is the traditional focus on CSR which is what the organization does with the local communities in which it operates and environmental policies and then activities which are core to the business and how they make their money."

Further, it's people who create value in business. As Gifford pointed out. "For example, how you treat your customers and how you treat suppliers ethically affects business value creation. If you define your value creation only in narrow financial terms while maintaining disregarding social responsibility, you can take this only so far. But a triple bottom line view focuses on long-term value creation and brings this together with a much wider stakeholder view. This leads organizations to look at what is socially and environmentally sustainable and ethics is integrally linked to value creation."

With this in mind, HR professionals have three roles in CSR. First, to make sure HR practices are ethical. Second, to embed corporate responsibility through support and training. Third, to inculcate ethics into the organizational culture, beginning at the board level.

One of the challenges facing corporations with respect to CSR is measuring its impact. CSR involves issues like environmental pollution, child labor and product safety—which are often seen as outside the traditional boundaries of a business. CSR performance is hard to measure using traditional business indicators such as return on investment. CSR must consider economic, social and environmental impact.

Given that embedding corporate responsibility into a business is about integrating it into corporate culture, HR is ideally situated to assess the organizational culture and change it.

Nonetheless, research shows that HR is rarely involved in devising CSR strategy. A recent report, which surveyed 353 HR professionals and 523 middle and senior managers, found that only 13% of companies make HR responsible for setting CSR strategy. As for implementing CSR strategy, only 26% of companies make HR responsible for its implementation. The report found that the biggest driver for an organization's focusing on CSR was regulatory pressure.

It's time for HR professionals to take an active role in CSR strategy. Often CSR strategy involves people, and the HR profession should grasp this opportunity.

Human Capital Management

When an idea has gone mainstream, it starts getting discussed using MBA-babble. Rather than describing the importance of corporate employees as "people in the triple bottom line," they are now part of "human capital management." That is to say, humans become a factor of production, just like debt or equity capital. MBA folks are special, aren't they?

The leading thinker about this is Professor George Georgiev (Emory Law).

The Human Capital Management Movement in US Corporate Law

(2021)

George S. Georgiev

[available on SSRN]

Corporations cannot exist without workers, yet workers are not part of the formal or informal governance structures established by U.S. corporate law. Commentators and policymakers have bemoaned this state of affairs for decades, to little avail. Since the mid-2010s, however, a concept related to workers, human capital management (HCM), has become an increasingly prominent part of U.S. corporate governance. HCM is premised on the notion that workers can be viewed as "assets" and ought to be managed just as carefully as firms manage physical and capital assets. In practice, HCM is an expansive concept that has been used to refer to workforce training, compensation and retention issues, gender pay equity, diversity and inclusion, health and safety, matters related to corporate culture, employees' ability to participate in stock purchase programs, and various other matters.

The speed with which HCM has emerged and the depth and breadth of its reach have been surprising. While broadly fitting within the rubric of environmental, social, and governance (ESG) factors, HCM has quickly surpassed more traditional ESG topics in terms of prominence and uptake. Boards of directors have started to focus on HCM as part of their monitoring and oversight responsibilities, including by amending committee charters to cover HCM matters, identifying HCM as a desirable qualification for director nominees, and incorporating HCM metrics into executive compensation plans. Investors are now actively engaging with management and boards on questions pertaining to HCM. In August 2020, the Securities and Exchange Commission (SEC) adopted a new rule requiring HCM disclosure by public companies. A variety of private standard-setting organizations have already developed detailed HCM reporting standards, which firms have started to adopt. Taken together, these developments represent a powerful and heretofore unprecedented push to incorporate worker-related concerns in corporate governance—a phenomenon I describe as an "HCM movement." This Article presents a comprehensive analysis of the origins, impact, and normative desirability of the HCM movement with reference to the broader transformation of U.S. corporate governance and the often-ignored historical and comparative context.

Subject to certain qualifications, HCM would seem a broadly positive and much-overdue corporate governance development: HCM disclosure contributes to more accurate firm valuation by shining a spotlight on a key driver of success in the modern knowledge-based economy; HCM oversight at the board level ensures that firms focus appropriately on the management of what has come to be referred to as a "mission-critical asset." To realize HCM's full promise, however, participants in the HCM movement should seek to disambiguate the HCM concept by breaking it down into its appropriate constitutive elements, and, to the extent possible, focusing the relevant discussions on those specific elements. In addition, boards should resist isomorphic approaches, particularly ones developed by organizations such as large asset managers that are lacking in regulatory legitimacy, accountability, and HCM expertise. The SEC can and should serve as a nexus for coordination among the various participants in the HCM movement. As an initial step, the SEC should revisit the HCM disclosure rulemaking process and reject the unstructured, "principles-based" approach reflected in the 2020 HCM disclosure rule, which is based on an impoverished understanding of the important concept of materiality. In its final part, the Article considers HCM's limits as a solution to problems beyond the core concerns of corporate law and suggests that the rapid rise of the corporate governance HCM movement has in fact highlighted the need for a governmental human capital agenda aimed at the active development and protection of human capital, not just its management.

Corporate Responsibilities Under International Law

Maybe you are willing to accept that employees should have a greater role in the corporation. What should be the rights of these more-empowered employees? The rights given them under their employment contracts? Some special rights assigned to them in the corporation's governance structure? Or maybe simply basic human rights, as recognized under international law?

Now, that's an interesting question. Are corporations obligated to respect human rights? The United Nations Guiding Principles on Business and Human Rights (the so-called Ruggie Principles), which were also described in Cynthia Williams's article, answer this question by defining (1) the duties of states to protect human rights; (2) the duties of states to ensure that corporations observe human rights; and (3) the duties of corporations to have internal processes to safeguard human rights.

The UN Guiding Principles on Business and Human Rights "The UN Protect, Respect and Remedy Framework"

(2016)

Shift Project

In June 2011, in an unprecedented step, the United Nations Human Rights Council unanimously endorsed a set of **Guiding Principles on Business and Human Rights**. The Guiding Principles establish an authoritative global standard on the respective roles of businesses and governments in helping ensure that companies respect human rights in their own operations and through their business relationships.

The Guiding Principles were developed by the Special Representative of the UN Secretary-General for Business and Human Rights, Professor John Ruggie of Harvard Kennedy School, over the six years of his UN mandate from 2005 to 2011. They elaborate on the three pillars of the UN "Protect, Respect and Remedy" Framework that Prof. Ruggie proposed to the Human Rights Council in 2008:

- The state duty to protect against human rights abuses by third parties, including business, through appropriate policies, regulation, and adjudication;
- The corporate responsibility to respect human rights, that is, to act with due diligence to avoid infringing on the rights of others and address adverse impacts with which they are involved; and
- The need for greater access by victims to effective remedy, both judicial and non-judicial.

As Prof. Ruggie stated when presenting the Guiding Principles to the UN Human Rights Council:

> Each pillar is an essential component in an inter-related and dynamic system of preventative and remedial measures: the State duty to protect because it lies at the very core of the international human rights regime; the corporate responsibility to respect because it is the basic expectation society has of business in relation to human rights; and access to remedy because even the most concerted efforts cannot prevent all abuse.

Note

UN Guiding Principles on Business and Human Rights

The State duty to protect human rights

A. Foundational principles

1. States must protect against human rights abuse within their territory and/or jurisdiction by third parties, including business enterprises. This requires taking appropriate steps to prevent, investigate, punish and redress such abuse through effective policies, legislation, regulations and adjudication.

2. States should set out clearly the expectation that all business enterprises domiciled in their territory and/or jurisdiction respect human rights throughout their operations.

B. Operational principles

General State regulatory and policy functions

> 3. In meeting their duty to protect, States should: (a) Enforce laws that are aimed at, or have the effect of, requiring business enterprises to respect human rights, and periodically to assess the adequacy of such laws and address any gaps; (b) Ensure that other laws and policies governing the creation and ongoing operation of business enterprises, such as corporate law, do not constrain but enable business respect for human rights; (c) Provide effective guidance to business enterprises on how to respect human rights throughout their operations; (d) Encourage, and where appropriate require, business enterprises to communicate how they address their human rights impacts.

. . .

II. The corporate responsibility to respect human rights

A. Foundational principles

11. Business enterprises should respect human rights. This means that they should avoid infringing on the human rights of others and should address adverse human rights impacts with which they are involved.

12. The responsibility of business enterprises to respect human rights refers to internationally recognized human rights – understood, at a minimum, as those expressed in the International Bill of Human Rights and the principles concerning fundamental rights set out in the International Labour Organization's Declaration on Fundamental Principles and Rights at Work.

13. The responsibility to respect human rights requires that business enterprises: (a) Avoid causing or contributing to adverse human rights impacts through their own activities, and address such impacts when they occur; (b) Seek to prevent or mitigate adverse human rights impacts that are directly linked to their operations, products or services by their business relationships, even if they have not contributed to those impacts.

14. The responsibility of business enterprises to respect human rights applies to all enterprises regardless of their size, sector, operational context, ownership and structure. Nevertheless, the scale and complexity of the means through which enterprises meet that responsibility may vary according to these factors and with the severity of the enterprise's adverse human rights impacts.

15. In order to meet their responsibility to respect human rights, business enterprises should have in place policies and processes appropriate to their size and circumstances, including: 16 (a) A policy commitment to meet their responsibility to respect human rights; (b) A human rights due diligence process to identify, prevent, mitigate and account for how they address their impacts on human rights; (c) Processes to enable the remediation of any adverse human rights impacts they cause or to which they contribute.

. . .

III. Access to remedy

A. Foundational principle

25. As part of their duty to protect against business-related human rights abuse, States must take appropriate steps to ensure, through judicial, administrative, legislative or other appropriate means, that when such abuses occur within their territory and/or jurisdiction those affected have access to effective remedy

State-based judicial mechanisms

26. States should take appropriate steps to ensure the effectiveness of domestic judicial mechanisms when addressing business-related human rights abuses, including considering ways to reduce legal, practical and other relevant barriers that could lead to a denial of access to remedy

Well, that was pretty much a punt. Ruggie concludes that corporations are not actors under international law, so they can't be obligated to do anything under international law. But states (the subjects of international law) are obligated to make sure their corporations behave decently toward human beings. Of course, who's going to enforce that? To date, no one—that is, no state or international body has stepped up to tell a state how to have its corporations respect human rights.

But maybe the UN Guiding Principles have some utility. They suggest what "best practices" are for corporations and provide a blueprint for corporations treating people humanely. In fact, as you've been noticing, CSR initiatives in some companies—at least based on their CSR reports and letters written by the CEO—are broader than those laid out in the Ruggie Principles. This leads to a question: What has become of the state/government in CSR? Some have asserted that we are entering into a new period in which markets and private corporate codes are displacing the state. See Larry Catá Backer, A Lex Mercatoria for Corporate Social Responsibility Codes Without the State?: On the Regulatory Character of Private Corporate Codes (2016) [available on SSRN] (arguing that "globalization and its re-situating of the state" has resulted in "rule systems being developed by private actors, primarily corporations and NGOs, and public actors, most recently the Organization for Economic Cooperation and Development and the apparatus of the UN Human Rights Council").

Thus, according to Professor Backer, there has been an evolution in the legalization and legitimacy in governance, from "its twentieth century formalist rigidity into something of a bridge between the political and social sphere." This threatens the underlying foundations of the current law-state and moves us toward a "love of ancient custom" (or *lex mercatoria*) that creates a new meaning for legalization and legitimacy "in a new world order that has yet to be revealed."

3.2.4 CSR: New Ethos or Smokescreen?

Perhaps you have browsed a corporate CSR report. Are these reports real or fiction? Read a typical CSR report and see what you find. I often ask students to read the executive summary of Cisco's CSR report for 2012, a typical CSR report of the 2010s. Cisco is a US-based multinational that makes and sells the networking hardware and software on which the Internet runs. Its 147-page report (and 29-page executive summary) describe the company's sustainability efforts for the year and its future sustainability plans. The report describes how the company's sustainability performance measured up under the Global Reporting Initiative on environmental, labor, human rights, society, and product responsibility measures. It's interesting, but the company's 10-K (its annual financial report filed with the SEC) for that same year touched on virtually none of these topics.

Summary
Cisco—Corporate Social Responsibility Report
(2012)

Typical of CSR reports, Cisco's 2012 CSR report (and executive summary) begins with a letter from the company's CEO. The letter describes the company's "foundational priorities" for promoting the growth of computer networks and the Internet.

The CEO states his belief that "education and the Internet are the two great equalizers in life." The letter seeks to explain the formula that "you + networks = impact[x]"—a quite catchy equation, as equations go.

Next in the CSR report (and the executive summary) is a letter from the company's senior VP for corporate affairs, the office responsible for CSR reporting. The letter describes the company's five CSR pillars: (1) governance and ethics; (2) supply chain; (3) people; (4) society; and (5) environment.

The CSR executive summary details the company's CSR purposes and the results in these five areas:

1. **Governance and Ethics.** "Cisco's commitment to ethical conduct and strong corporate governance has helped us build a robust company with a recognized CSR program." The CSR executive summary sets out the company's three main CSR objectives with respect to governance and ethics, all of which the CSR report declares the company had achieved: (1) to continue to undertake robust stakeholder engagement on all CSR issues; (2) to use credible research firms and indices, to benchmark the company against its peers; and (3) to create issues-based working groups to inform the company's responses on CSR developments, including the UN's Guiding Principles on Business and Human Rights.
2. **Supply Chain.** "We expect our suppliers to meet the same high standards on ethics, labor rights, health and safety, and the environment that we apply to our own people and operations." The CSR executive summary describes how the company communicated its expectations to its more than 600 suppliers through a "Supplier Code of Conduct." The report lays out seven CSR objectives with respect to suppliers for the year, six of which the company said it had achieved. These included sustainability questions in supplier scorecards, a new supplier appreciation award, training for employees that engage with suppliers, acknowledgement by suppliers of the "Supplier Code of Conduct," compliance processes to meet supply-chain reporting under federal and state law, and working with industry groups to address global sustainability. The one objective that was not achieved was partnering with suppliers to realize sustainability improvements.
3. **People.** "We work hard to inspire and engage our employees. We want them to feel that working at Cisco is more than just a job." The CSR executive summary shows that 82% of employees said "Cisco is a great place to work," down from 87% in 2008. The percentage of female employees was 22%, down from 24% in 2008. The objectives in this area included a leadership commitment to have senior leaders invite employees to build "the Next Cisco," compensating employees more than at peer companies, and focusing on employee engagement through programs for movement and promotion. The company said the first two objectives were met, but not the third.
4. **Society.** "Information and communications technology (ICT) brings people together to spur innovation and improve livelihoods." The CSR executive summary summarizes performance in this area, describing corporate giving ($294 million, up from $92 million in 2008), employee volunteer hours (107,150,

up from 88,870 in 2008), and students taking a course on Cisco networking (1,000,000, up from 700,000 in 2008). The executive summary identifies six objectives in this area, of which three were achieved. The objectives achieved: launching a new global volunteer effort, complying with US law on accessibility, working with partners on Palestinian entrepreneurship. The objectives not achieved: maintaining strategic relationships with the World Economic Forum, helping poverty-focused programs measure social impact, and enhancing veterans programs within Cisco.

5. **Environment.** "We believe information and communications technology (ICT) can both improve living standards and reduce resource waste including energy." The CSR executive summary says that "energy and GHG emissions are the most important and complex issues for Cisco"—though this was said on page 26 of the 29-page executive summary, and the company's 10-K report for 2012 does not mention GHG emissions. The executive summary states that total "contractual emissions" (a term not defined) were 251,672 metric tons of CO2, down from 429,411 in 2008. Air-travel GHGF emissions were 139,431 metric tons of CO2, down from 205,796 in 2008. Of the five objectives in this area, only two were achieved: including CDP (carbon emissions reporting) in supplier scorecards and investing in the development of Sector 3 standards (emissions by Cisco customers). Otherwise, the other objectives in this area were not achieved: to have suppliers report GHG emissions, to move GHG and other sustainability data to a company-wide information system, to roll out power distribution units in the company's engineering labs, and to expand EV charging stations at the company's headquarters.

Greenwashing

There has been a good deal of talk about "greenwashing" by corporations—that is, companies overstating their CSR claims. For example, Volkswagen spent $77 million in 2014 on a US ad campaign touting its "clean diesel" technology, while it was also programming 11 million of its cars to cheat on emission tests and show much lower emissions than the cars actually produced on the road. See *Social Responsibility that Rubs Right Off*, New York Times (Oct. 17, 2015). Many companies find it attractive to overstate their companies' commitment to CSR for a number of reasons: (1) to attract consumers and lately shareholders, (2) to enhance their public image, and (3) to make company executives, and perhaps some employees, feel better about themselves.

A study in the early 2010s found that nearly all large companies engage in "greenwashing." See Delmas & Burbano, *Drivers of Greenwashing* (2011) [available on SSRN]. Some companies focus on narrow product attributes (not their overall environmental or social impact); others rely on weak or non-existent data (such as the percentage of recycled material in a product); others equate "natural" (including toxic chemicals that occur in nature) as "green," making irrelevant and misleading claims (such as stating a product is CFC-free, even though the chemical is banned by law). Other companies distract consumers from a product's dangers (such as by touting "organic cigarettes"), falsely claiming a product meets a standard (such as false EnergyStar ratings), or simply inventing bogus certifications. There is little legal enforcement in this area, given that false CSR claims may be no more than "puffing," a form of commercial free speech protected by the First Amendment.

Next is an explanation of "greenwashing" by a group that seeks to assist businesses in making credible claims that their products and services are environmentally-friendly and sustainable. The group describes the "seven deadly sins of greenwashing" and then offers its services (as part of the Underwriters Laboratory) to help businesses avoid the appearance of greenwashing. That is, there are now firms to help corporations greenwash their greenwashing!

Sins of Greenwashing

(2010)

TerraChoice

[TerraChoice is part of the Underwriters Laboratories global network providing environmental services to companies around the world. UL Environment works to advance global sustainability, environmental health, and safety by supporting the growth and development of environmentally-preferable products, services, and organizations.]

[redacted/paraphrased]

The world has been awakening to false and misleading environmental claims. We at TerraChoice hope to see more reporting on this. Scrutiny of environmental claims can make a difference if it both discourages greenwashing and encourages more green product innovation and commercialization. Our Sins of Greenwashing research seeks to focus attention on home and family products, and to add a constructive perspective to the debate.

Our research finds more "green" home and family products and less greenwashing over the past several years. In the 24 stores we visited in both 2007 and 2010 (same brand, same location, same size), the number of products claiming to be "green" increased by 73%. Yet over 95% of "greener" products commit one or more of the seven "Sins of Greenwashing." Nonetheless, the proportion of sin free products has gone from less than 1% in 2007 to almost 4.5% in 2010. Categories of products with more "greening" history have less greenwashing and more reliable "green" certification.

Eco-Labeling has been useful. Of products certified by an ISO 14024-based program, more than 30% were sin-free (compared to 4.4% overall). Good eco-labeling helps prevent (but doesn't eliminate) greenwashing. That said, the use of fake labels (a sin we dubbed the "Sin of Worshiping False Labels") has increased dramatically.

Here are the Seven Sins of Greenwashing:

1. **Sin of Hidden Trade-Off.** Products are said to be "green" using a narrow set of attributes, ignoring other important environmental issues. For example, paper from a sustainability-harvested forest does not mean the paper was manufactured in a high-GHG-emission process or bleached with chlorine.

2. **Sin of No Proof.** Products are said to be "green" but without easily accessible supporting proof or reliable third-party verification. For example, facial tissues that claim various percentages of post-consumer recycled content often fail to provide any evidence of this.
3. **Sin of Vagueness.** Products are said to be "green" using terms that have no meaning or are easily misunderstood by consumers. For example, "all natural" means nothing. Arsenic, mercury, and formaldehyde are all naturally occurring—and toxic.
4. **Sin of Worshiping False Labels.** Products are said to be "green" based on third-party endorsements that do not exist. For example, a seal of the Best Fishery Practices Council on fish labeled "sustaintably fished" is misleading, given that no such council exists.
5. **Sin of Irrelevance.** Products are said to be "green" based on unimportant or unhelpful information. For example, plastics that are said to be "CFC-free" is meaningless, because CFCs are banned by law.
6. **Sin of Lesser of Two Evils.** Products are said to be "green," which may be true, but masks other environmental or health concerns. For example, organic cigarettes may come from organically grown tobacco leaves, but remain a cancer risk.
7. **Sin of Fibbing.** Products are said to be "green" based on a claim that is false. For example, appliances might be labeled Energy Star certified, even though they are not.

Is CSR Elitist?

Reflect for a second. Isn't CSR essentially a bunch of corporate executives and law/management professors describing how companies say they're doing the right thing. But is that what people in corporations also see? Here is a comment on a Listserv for corporate law professors that suggests we law professors are out of touch with the world so many others inhabit:

> If you teach out of the Smith & Williams Bus Orgs text, you may teach *Case Farms*, which centers on whether an organization Case Farms hired to recruit workers for its chicken processing plant was acting under its authority when it promised workers in Texas and other Southern states transportation, housing, wages, and benefits that turned out to be false and in violation of the law. The first time I taught it, students didn't understand why workers would get on a bus from Texas to Ohio without any money or connections because of what the recruiter promised. The next semester, I found a volunteer in the class who had been on a callback interview to NYC. I asked that student a lot of questions about what he did to ensure that he would not get to NYC without any money, cab fare, hotel, and a way back, and of course he had done nothing. I pointed out that in our industry, we trust that the person on the phone/email promising to reimburse us if we go to an interview or conference, but other industries don't have the same norms and traditions of trusting authority.

3.2.5 Business Roundtable Shifts Course, Maybe

But hold the presses! In a remarkable about-face the Business Roundtable (BRT) recently declared last year that the purpose of the corporation is not to maximize shareholder wealth, but instead to consider all corporate stakeholders (listing shareholders behind customers, employees, suppliers, and communities).

Press Release

(Aug. 19, 2019)

Business Roundtable Redefines the Purpose of a Corporation to Promote "An Economy That Serves All Americans"

Updated Statement Moves Away from Shareholder Primacy, Includes Commitment to All Stakeholders

WASHINGTON – Business Roundtable today announced the release of a new Statement on the Purpose of a Corporation signed by 181 CEOs who commit to lead their companies for the benefit of all stakeholders—customers, employees, suppliers, communities and shareholders.

Since 1978, Business Roundtable has periodically issued Principles of Corporate Governance. Each version of the document issued since 1997 has endorsed principles of shareholder primacy– that corporations exist principally to serve shareholders. With today's announcement, the new Statement supersedes previous statements and outlines a modern standard for corporate responsibility.

"The American dream is alive, but fraying," said Jamie Dimon, Chairman and CEO of JPMorgan Chase & Co. and Chairman of Business Roundtable. "Major employers are investing in their workers and communities because they know it is the only way to be successful over the long term. These modernized principles reflect the business community's unwavering commitment to continue to push for an economy that serves all Americans."

"This new statement better reflects the way corporations can and should operate today," added Alex Gorsky, Chairman of the Board and Chief Executive Officer of Johnson & Johnson and Chair of the Business Roundtable Corporate Governance Committee. "It affirms the essential role corporations can play in improving our society when CEOs are truly committed to meeting the needs of all stakeholders."

Industry leaders also lent their support for the updated Business Roundtable Statement, citing the positive impact this commitment will have on long-term value creation:

"I welcome this thoughtful statement by Business Roundtable CEOs on the Purpose of a Corporation. By taking a broader, more complete view of corporate purpose, boards can focus on creating long-term value, better serving everyone—investors, employees, communities, suppliers and customers," said Bill McNabb, former CEO of Vanguard.

"CEOs work to generate profits and return value to shareholders, but the best-run companies do more. They put the customer first and invest in their employees and communities. In the end, it's the most promising way to build long-term value," said Tricia Griffith, President and CEO of Progressive Corporation.

"This is tremendous news because it is more critical than ever that businesses in the 21st century are focused on generating long-term value for all stakeholders and addressing the challenges we face, which will result in shared prosperity and sustainability for both business and society," said Darren Walker, President of the Ford Foundation.

* * *

Business Roundtable Statement on the Purpose of a Corporation
Americans deserve an economy that allows each person to succeed through hard work and creativity and to lead a life of meaning and dignity. We believe the free-market system is the best means of generating good jobs, a strong and sustainable economy, innovation, a healthy environment and economic opportunity for all.

Businesses play a vital role in the economy by creating jobs, fostering innovation and providing essential goods and services. Businesses make and sell consumer products; manufacture equipment and vehicles; support the national defense; grow and produce food; provide health care; generate and deliver energy; and offer financial, communications and other services that underpin economic growth.

While each of our individual companies serves its own corporate purpose, we share a fundamental commitment to all of our stakeholders. We commit to:

- Delivering value to our customers. We will further the tradition of American companies leading the way in meeting or exceeding customer expectations.
- Investing in our employees. This starts with compensating them fairly and providing important benefits. It also includes supporting them through training and education that help develop new skills for a rapidly changing world. We foster diversity and inclusion, dignity and respect.
- Dealing fairly and ethically with our suppliers. We are dedicated to serving as good partners to the other companies, large and small, that help us meet our missions.
- Supporting the communities in which we work. We respect the people in our communities and protect the environment by embracing sustainable practices across our businesses.
- Generating long-term value for shareholders, who provide the capital that allows companies to invest, grow and innovate. We are committed to transparency and effective engagement with shareholders.

Each of our stakeholders is essential. We commit to deliver value to all of them, for the future success of our companies, our communities and our country.

Aftermath of BRT Statement

As you might guess, the reaction to the BRT statement in business, academic, and government circles was immediate. Some questioned the sincerity of the BRT statement; others said that a vague, non-mandatory stakeholder focus would simply give corporate managers even more discretion ("a servant who seeks to serve many masters is a servant to none"); and some saw the declaration as a revision to capitalism and thus anti-American. As Bloomberg reported:

> The shift in corporate priorities comes as some politicians and critics question whether the fundamental premise of American capitalism should be revamped. Some executives also have complained that an outsize focus on share prices and quarterly results hamper their ability to build businesses for the long term.
>
> The group's statement offers scant detail on how the commitments will be converted into action and presents no road map for getting there. Many companies vow to do good things but often resist releasing data to let others independently verify such promises. And it will fall on CEOs, who on average last no longer than six years, to convince fickle investors, including powerful activists, that shifting resources will pay off in the long term.
>
> The idea that businesses exist primarily to benefit shareholders—also known as shareholder primacy—took hold in corporate America in the 1980s. In 1997, the Business Roundtable embraced the idea in a document outlining governance principles.
>
> The concept has been criticized for leading to a fixation on short-term results and helping fuel the rapid increase in executive pay. Last year, public companies in the U.S. began disclosing the difference between their CEOs' compensation and that of their median workers. At S&P 500 firms, the average ratio is about 280-to-1, according to data compiled by Bloomberg.

JPMorgan's Dimon Among CEOs Rejecting Investor-Centric Model, Bloomberg Law (Aug. 19, 2019).

Lack of Board Approval of BRT Statement

While some have greeted the BRT statement with enthusiasm, others are less sanguine. Here's an op-ed by Lucian Bebchuk and Roberto Tallarita, two Harvard law professors who head Harvard's Corporate Governance Center:

> By putting American workers through months of turmoil, the Covid-19 crisis has heightened expectations that large companies will serve the interests of all "stakeholders," not only shareholders. The Business Roundtable raised such expectations last summer by issuing a statement on corporate purpose, in which the CEOs of more than 180 major companies committed to "deliver value to all stakeholders." Although the Roundtable described the statement as a radical departure from shareholder primacy, observers have been debating whether it signaled a significant shift in how business operates or was a mere public-relations move. We have set out to obtain evidence to resolve this question.
>
> To probe what corporate leaders have in mind, we sought to examine whether they treated joining the Business Roundtable statement as an important corporate decision. Major decisions are

typically made by boards of directors. If the commitment expressed in the statement was supposed to produce major changes in how companies treat stakeholders, the boards of the companies should have been expected to approve or at least ratify it.

We contacted the companies whose CEOs signed the Business Roundtable statement and asked who was the highest-level decision maker to approve the decision. Of the 48 companies that responded, only one said the decision was approved by the board of directors. The other 47 indicated that the decision to sign the statement, supposedly adopting a major change in corporate purpose, was not approved by the board of directors.

We received responses from only about three-tenths of the signatories. Yet there is no reason to expect that these companies are less likely than companies electing not to respond to have obtained board approval for joining the statement.

What can explain a CEO's decision to join the Business Roundtable statement without board approval? Even "imperial" CEOs tend to push major decisions through the board rather than disregard it. Similarly, it is implausible that CEOs didn't seek board approval because they viewed the statement as reflecting a personal belief rather than a commitment made in their "official" capacity. In fact, the Business Roundtable presented the statement as a commitment by CEOs "to lead their companies for the benefit of all stakeholders," thus reflecting a pledge regarding the goals of the companies led by these CEOs.

The most plausible explanation for the lack of board approval is that CEOs didn't regard the statement as a commitment to make a major change in how their companies treat stakeholders. That may be because they believe their companies are already meeting the standard for taking care of stakeholders. But it still implies that they believed signing the statement wasn't a major step for their businesses.

We supplemented the evidence above with a review of the board-approved corporate governance guidelines of the companies whose CEOs joined the statement. We found that these guidelines, including the many that have been updated since the issuance of the Business Roundtable statement, mostly reflect a clear "shareholder primacy" approach.

Take the corporate governance guidelines of JPMorgan Chase, whose CEO, Jamie Dimon, chaired the Business Roundtable at the time the statement was issued. These guidelines state that "the Board as a whole is responsible for the oversight of management on behalf of the Firm's shareholders."

The corporate governance guidelines of Johnson & Johnson—whose CEO, Alex Gorsky, served as chairman of the Business Roundtable Corporate Governance Committee—indicate in clear terms that "the business judgment of the Board must be exercised . . . in the long-term interests of our shareholders."

Further, about 70% of the U.S. companies that joined the statement are incorporated in Delaware, which is widely viewed as a state with shareholder-centric corporate laws. In a 2015 law-review article, Delaware Chief Justice Leo Strine stated that "a clear-eyed look" at Delaware law "reveals that . . . directors must make stockholder welfare their sole end."

Nonetheless, the Business Roundtable, and the numerous Delaware companies endorsing its statement, didn't address the potential constraints imposed by Delaware law. This disregard of the issue is consistent with the view that corporate leaders don't contemplate a significant change in corporate strategy.

The evidence is clear: Notwithstanding statements to the contrary, corporate leaders are generally still focused on shareholder value. They can be expected to protect other stakeholders only to the extent that doing so would not hurt share value. That conclusion will be greatly disappointing to some and welcome to others. But all should be clear-eyed about what corporate leaders are focused on and what they intend to deliver.

Lucian Bebchuk and Roberto Tallarita, *'Stakeholder' Capitalism Seems Mostly for Show*, The Wall Street Journal (Aug. 6, 2020).

McKinsey Joins the ESG Movement

Yet the BRT statement comes at a time when there is a growing recognition that companies adopting an ESG "value proposition" are stronger, more resilient, and ultimately more profitable. By doing good, you do well! Here is a recent article by McKinsey & Company on "Five Ways that ESG Creates Value." (McKinsey is the oldest and largest of the "Big Three" managemnt consulting firms in the world; it offers professional services to corporations, governments, and other organizations.) When I started putting together matierals for this book nine years ago, I expected that CSR (and now ESG) would creep into corporate America in a generation or so. But things are happening faster than I imagined possible.

Five Ways that ESG Creates Value

McKinsey Quarterly (Nov. 14, 2019)

Witold Henisz, Tim Koller, and Robin Nuttall

Your business, like every business, is deeply intertwined with environmental, social, and governance (ESG) concerns. It makes sense, therefore, that a strong ESG proposition can create value—and in this article, we provide a framework for understanding the five key ways it can do so. But first, let's briefly consider the individual elements of ESG:

- The E in ESG, environmental criteria, includes the energy your company takes in and the waste it discharges, the resources it needs, and the consequences for living beings as a result. (McKinsey is the oldest and largest of the "Big Three" management consulting firms in the world; it offers professional services to corporations, governments, and other organizations.) Not least, E encompasses carbon emissions and climate change. Every company uses energy and resources; every company affects, and is affected by, the environment.
- S, social criteria, addresses the relationships your company has and the reputation it fosters with people and institutions in the communities where you do business. S

includes labor relations and diversity and inclusion. Every company operates within a broader, diverse society.

- G, governance, is the internal system of practices, controls, and procedures your company adopts in order to govern itself, make effective decisions, comply with the law, and meet the needs of external stakeholders. Every company, which is itself a legal creation, requires governance.

Just as ESG is an inextricable part of how you do business, its individual elements are themselves intertwined. For example, social criteria overlaps with environmental criteria and governance when companies seek to comply with environmental laws and broader concerns about sustainability. Our focus is mostly on environmental and social criteria, but, as every leader knows, governance can never be hermetically separate. Indeed, excelling in governance calls for mastering not just the letter of laws but also their spirit—such as getting in front of violations before they occur, or ensuring transparency and dialogue with regulators instead of formalistically submitting a report and letting the results speak for themselves.

ESG Oriented Investing Has Experienced a Meteoric Rise—Global Sustainable Investments Now Top $30 Trillion

Thinking and acting on ESG in a proactive way has lately become even more pressing. The US Business Roundtable released a new statement in August 2019 strongly affirming business's commitment to a broad range of stakeholders, including customers, employees, suppliers, communities, and, of course, shareholders. Of a piece with that emerging zeitgeist, ESG-oriented investing has experienced a meteoric rise. Global sustainable investment now tops $30 trillion—up 68 percent since 2014 and tenfold since 2004. The acceleration has been driven by heightened social, governmental, and consumer attention on the broader impact of corporations, as well as by the investors and executives who realize that a strong ESG proposition can safeguard a company's long-term success. The magnitude of investment flow suggests that ESG is much more than a fad or a feel-good exercise.

So does the level of business performance. The overwhelming weight of accumulated research finds that companies that pay attention to environmental, social, and governance concerns do not experience a drag on value creation—in fact, quite the opposite (Exhibit 1). A strong ESG proposition correlates with higher equity returns, from both a tilt and momentum perspective. Better performance in ESG also corresponds with a reduction in downside risk, as evidenced, among other ways, by lower loan and credit default swap spreads and higher credit ratings.

A 2015 study in the Journal of Sustainable Finance found that of the more than 2000 studies that looked at "the impact of ESG propositions on equity returns," 63 percent of the studies had "positive findings" and only 8 percent had "negative findings."

But even as the case for a strong ESG proposition becomes more compelling, an understanding of why these criteria link to value creation is less comprehensive. How exactly does a strong ESG proposition make financial sense? From our experience and research, ESG links to cash flow in five important ways: (1) facilitating top-line growth, (2) reducing costs, (3) minimizing regulatory and legal interventions, (4) increasing employee productivity, and (5) optimizing investment and capital expenditures (Exhibit 2). Each of these five levers should be part of a leader's mental checklist when approaching ESG opportunities—and so should be an understanding of the "softer," more personal dynamics needed for the levers to accomplish their heaviest lifting.

A strong ESG proposition is linked to value creation in five essential ways:

(1) **Top-line growth.** A strong ESG proposition attracts B2B and B2C customers with more sustainable products and achieves better access to resources with stronger community and government relations. A weak proposition (poor sustainability practices—human rights, supply chain, unsafe products) leads to loss of customers and lack of access to resources.

(2) **Cost reductions.** A strong ESG proposition results in lower energy consumption and reduced water intake. A weak ESG proposition generates unnecessary waste and high waste-disposal costs, as well as packaging costs.

(3) **Regulatory and legal interventions.** A strong ESG proposition achieves greater strategic freedom through deregulation and earns government subsidies and support. A weak ESG proposition leads to advertising restrictions and results in fines and enforcement actions.

(4) **Productivity uplift.** A strong ESG proposition boosts employee motivation and attracts talent because of social credibility. A weak ESG proposition forces dealing with "social stigma" that restricts talent pool and loss of talent because of weak purpose.

(5) **Investment and asset optimization.** A strong ESG proposition enhances investment returns by allocating capital for the long term (such as sustainable plant equipment) and avoids longer-term environmental issues. A weak ESG proposition results in stranded assets and write-downs, and falling behind competitors that are more energy-efficient.

Five Links to Value Creation

The five links are a way to think of ESG systematically, not an assurance that each link will apply, or apply to the same degree, in every instance. Some are more likely to arise in certain industries or sectors; others will be more frequent in given geographies. Still, all five should be considered regardless of a company's business model or location. The potential for value creation is too great to leave any of them unexplored.

1. Top-line growth

A strong ESG proposition helps companies tap new markets and expand into existing ones. When governing authorities trust corporate actors, they are more likely to award them the access, approvals, and licenses that afford fresh opportunities for growth. For example, in a recent, massive public–private infrastructure project in Long Beach, California, the for-profit companies selected to participate were screened based on their prior performance in sustainability. Superior ESG execution has demonstrably paid off in mining, as well. Consider gold, a commodity (albeit an expensive one) that should, all else being equal, generate the same rents for the companies that mine it regardless of their ESG propositions. Yet one major study found that companies with social-engagement activities that were perceived to be beneficial by public and social stakeholders had an easier go at extracting those resources, without extensive planning or operational delays. These companies achieved demonstrably higher valuations than competitors with lower social capital.

ESG can also drive consumer preference. McKinsey research has shown that customers say they are willing to pay to "go green." Although there can be wide discrepancies in practice, including customers who refuse to pay even 1 percent more, we've found that upward of 70 percent of consumers surveyed on purchases in multiple industries, including the automotive, building, electronics, and packaging categories, said they would pay an additional 5 percent for a green product if it met the same performance standards as a nongreen alternative. In another study, nearly half (44 percent) of the companies we surveyed identified business and growth opportunities as the impetus for starting their sustainability programs.

The payoffs are real. When Unilever developed Sunlight, a brand of dishwashing liquid that used much less water than its other brands, sales of Sunlight and Unilever's other watersaving products proceeded to outpace category growth by more than 20 percent in a number of water-scarce markets. And Finland's Neste, founded as a traditional petroleum-refining company more than 70 years ago, now generates more than two-thirds of its profits from renewable fuels and sustainability-related products.

2. Cost reductions

ESG can also reduce costs substantially. Among other advantages, executing ESG effectively can help combat rising operating expenses (such as raw-material costs and the true cost of water or carbon), which McKinsey research has found can affect operating profits by as much as 60 percent. In the same report, our colleagues created a metric (the amount of energy, water, and waste used in relation to revenue) to analyze the relative resource efficiency of companies within various sectors and found a significant correlation between resource efficiency and financial performance. The study also identified a number of companies across sectors that did particularly well—precisely the companies that had taken their sustainability strategies the furthest.

As with each of the five links to ESG value creation, the first step to realizing value begins with recognizing the opportunity. Consider 3M, which has long understood that being proactive about environmental risk can be a source of competitive advantage. The company has saved $2.2 billion since introducing its "pollution prevention pays" (3Ps) program, in 1975, preventing pollution up front by reformulating products, improving manufacturing processes, redesigning equipment, and recycling and reusing waste from production. Another enterprise, a major water utility, achieved cost savings of almost $180 million per year thanks to lean initiatives aimed at improving preventive maintenance, refining spare-part inventory management, and tackling energy consumption and recovery from sludge. FedEx, for its part, aims to convert its entire 35,000-vehicle fleet to electric or hybrid engines; to date, 20 percent have been converted, which has already reduced fuel consumption by more than 50 million gallons.

3. Reduced regulatory and legal interventions
A stronger external-value proposition can enable companies to achieve greater strategic freedom, easing regulatory pressure. In fact, in case after case across sectors and geographies, we've seen that strength in ESG helps reduce companies' risk of adverse government action. It can also engender government support.

The value at stake may be higher than you think. By our analysis, typically one-third of corporate profits are at risk from state intervention. Regulation's impact, of course, varies by industry. For pharmaceuticals and healthcare, the profits at stake are about 25 to 30 percent. In banking, where provisions on capital requirements, "too big to fail," and consumer protection are so critical, the value at stake is typically 50 to 60 percent. For the automotive, aerospace and defense, and tech sectors, where government subsidies (among other forms of intervention) are prevalent, the value at stake can reach 60 percent as well.

In many industries, corporate profits are at stake because of external engagement. Consider theshare of EBITDA at stake in the following industries:

- Banks (50-60%) – capital requirements, systemic ("too big to fail" regulation, consumer protection
- Automotive, aerospace, defense (50-60%) – government subsidies, renewable energy regulation, GHG regulation
- Transport, logistics, infrastructure (45-55%) – pricing regulation, liberalization of sector
- Telecom, media (40-50%) – tariff regulation, interconnection, fiber deployment, spectrum, data privacy
- Energy and materials (35-45%) – tariff regulation, renewables subsidies, interconnectionb, access rights
- Consumer goods (25-30%) – obesity, sustainability, food safety, health and wellness, labeling
- Pharma and healthcare (25-30%) – market access, generic drugs, pricing, innovation, clinical trials

4. Employee productivity uplift
A strong ESG proposition can help companies attract and retain quality employees, enhance employee motivation by instilling a sense of purpose, and increase productivity overall. Employee satisfaction is positively correlated with shareholder returns. For example, the London Business School's Alex Edmans found that the companies that made Fortune's "100 Best Companies to Work For" list generated 2.3 percent to 3.8 percent higher stock returns per year than their peers over a greater than 25-year horizon. Moreover, it's long been observed that employees with a sense not just of satisfaction but also of connection perform better. The stronger an employee's perception of impact on the beneficiaries of their work, the greater the employee's motivation to act in a "prosocial" way.

Recent studies have also shown that positive social impact correlates with higher job satisfaction, and field experiments suggest that when companies "give back," employees react with enthusiasm. For instance, randomly selected employees at one Australian bank who received bonuses in the form of company payments to local charities reported greater and more immediate job satisfaction than their colleagues who were not selected for the donation program.

Just as a sense of higher purpose can inspire your employees to perform better, a weaker ESG proposition can drag productivity down. The most glaring examples are strikes, worker slowdowns, and other labor actions within your organization. But it's worth remembering that productivity constraints can also manifest outside of your company's four walls, across the supply chain. Primary suppliers often subcontract portions of large orders to other firms or rely on purchasing agents, and subcontractors are typically managed loosely, sometimes with little oversight of workers' health and safety.

Farsighted companies pay heed. Consider General Mills, which works to ensure that its ESG principles apply "from farm to fork to landfill." Walmart, for its part, tracks the work conditions of its suppliers, including those with extensive factory floors in China, according to a proprietary company scorecard. And Mars seeks opportunities where it can deliver what it calls "wins-wins-wins" for the company, its suppliers, and the environment. Mars has developed model farms that not only introduce new technological initiatives to farmers in its supply chains, but also increase farmers' access to capital so that they are able to obtain a financial stake in those initiatives.

5. Investment and asset optimization

A strong ESG proposition can enhance investment returns by allocating capital to more promising and more sustainable opportunities (for example, renewables, waste reduction, and scrubbers). It can also help companies avoid stranded investments that may not pay off because of longer-term environmental issues (such as massive write-downs in the value of oil tankers). Remember, taking proper account of investment returns requires that you start from the proper baseline. When it comes to ESG, it's important to bear in mind that a do-nothing approach is usually an eroding line, not a straight line. Continuing to rely on energy-hungry plants and equipment, for example, can drain cash going forward. While the investments required to update your operations may be substantial, choosing to wait it out can be the most expensive option of all. The rules of the game are shifting: regulatory responses to emissions will likely affect energy costs and could especially affect balance sheets in carbon-intense industries. And bans or limitations on such things as single-use plastics or diesel-fueled cars in city centers will introduce new constraints on multiple businesses, many of which could find themselves having to catch up. One way to get ahead of the future curve is to consider repurposing assets right now—for instance, converting failing parking garages into uses with higher demand, such as residences or day-care facilities, a trend we're beginning to see in reviving cities.

Foresight flows to the bottom line, and leaning into the tailwinds of sustainability presents new opportunities to enhance investment returns. Tailwinds blow strongly in China, for example. The country's imperative to combat air pollution is forecast to create more than $3 trillion in investment opportunities through 2030, ranging across industries from air-quality monitoring to indoor air purification and even cement mixing.

The personal dynamic

The five links to value creation are grounded in hard numbers, but, as always, a softer side is in play. For leaders seeking out new ESG opportunities or trying to nudge an organization in directions that may feel orthogonal to its traditional business model, here are a few personal points to keep in mind.

Get specific

It's important to understand the multiple ways that environmental, social, and governmental factors can create value, but when it comes to inspiring those around you, what will you really be talking about? Surprisingly, that depends. The individual causes that may inspire any one of us are precisely that—individual. That means that the issues most important to executives on your team could incline in different directions. Large companies can have dozens of social, community, or environmental projects in motion at any time. Too many at once can be a muddle; some may even work at cross-purposes.

In our experience, priority initiatives should be clearly articulated, and the number should be no more than five. To decide on which ones and to get the most out of them, let the company be your lodestar. For one leading agribusiness, that means channeling its capabilities into ameliorating hunger. The company taps its well-honed competencies to work with farmers in emerging regions to diversify their crops and adopt new technologies, which increases production and strengthens the company's ties with different countries and communities.

Even within the same industry, different companies will have different ESG profiles depending on their position in the corporate life cycle. Attackers typically have high upside potential to drive growth from ESG initiatives (for instance, the craft brewer BrewDog donates 20 percent of its annual profits), while longer-established competitors simply don't have that choice. For some companies, such as coal businesses or tobacco manufacturers, ESG will be more effectively geared to maintaining community ties and prioritizing risk avoidance. Regardless of your company's circumstances, it will be the CEO's role to rally support around the initiatives that best map to its mission.

Get practical

Value creation should be the CEO's core message. Anything else could sound off-key.

Managers, especially more senior ones, are usually assessed based on performance targets. Under those conditions, top-down ESG pronouncements can seem distracting or too vague to be of much use; "save the planet" won't cut it. To get everyone on board, make the case that your company's ESG priorities do link to value, and show leaders how, ideally with hard metrics that feed into the business model (for example, output per baseline electricity use, waste cost in a given plant or location per employee, or revenue per calorie for a food-and-beverage business).

The case will be simpler if you've done the hard work to analyze what matters along your value chain, where the greatest potential lies, and which areas have the most impact for your company. Proactive companies carefully research potential initiatives, including by tapping thought leaders and industry experts, iterate their findings with internal and external stakeholders, and then publish the results. Making the case publicly—not least to investors—enforces rigor and helps ensure that practical actions will follow.

Get real

An honest appraisal of ESG includes a frank acknowledgment that getting it wrong can result in massive value destruction. Being perceived as "overdoing it" can sap a leader's time and focus. Underdoing it is even worse. Companies that perform poorly in environmental, social, and governance criteria are more likely to endure materially adverse events. Just in the past few years, multiple companies with a weak ESG proposition saw double-digit declines in market capitalization in the days and weeks after their missteps came to light. Leaders should vigilantly assess the value at stake from external engagement (in our experience, poor external engagement can typically destroy about 30 percent of value) and plan scenarios for potential hits to operating profits. These days, the tail events can seem to come out of nowhere, even from a single tweet. Playing fast and loose with ESG is playing to lose, and failure to confront downside risk forthrightly can be disastrous.

Conversely, being thoughtful and transparent about ESG risk enhances long-term value—even if doing so can feel uncomfortable and engender some short-term pain. Ed Stack, the CEO of North American retailer Dick's Sporting Goods, said he expected that the company's 2018 announcement to restrict gun sales would alienate some customers, and he was right: by his own estimate, the announcement cost the company $150 million in lost sales, or slightly less than 2 percent of yearly revenue. Yet the company's stock climbed 14 percent in a little over a year following the shift.

ESG for the Long Term

Who says that a strong environmental, social, and governance (ESG) proposition cannot create value for companies and their shareholders? Not Milton Friedman. "It may well be in the long-run interest of a corporation," the economist wrote a half-century ago, "to devote resources to providing amenities to [its] community or to improving its government. That may make it easier to attract desirable employees, it may reduce the wage bill . . . or have other worthwhile effects."

Shareholders and stakeholders do not compete in a zero-sum game. Quite the opposite: building a strong connection with broad elements of society creates value, not least because it builds resilience into the business model. Compromising your connections with stakeholders simply to make earnings targets, on the other hand, destroys value. It's the essence of short-termism, measurably and overwhelmingly harmful to most shareholders' economic interests. Research shows that firms that make significant investments for longer term payoffs have future cash flows that are discounted less by investors than the cash flows of firms that allocate a smaller portion of their cash for the long term; immediate-minded fixes such as share repurchases (which arguably divert cash from investments that generate longer-term returns) correlate with increased discounting as well. Businesses need to play the long game. That means they need to satisfy the needs of their customers, employees, and communities—these days, often a global community—in order to maximize value creation. Thriving businesses concerned with long-term horizons fuel a virtuous cycle. They create jobs, increase tax revenue, and raise standards of living. ESG helps generate wealth, and wealth is not a fixed pie.

But just as it's wrong to assume that shareholders' interests must perforce come at stakeholders' expense, one should not assume that shareholders' and stakeholders' interests cannot conflict. Of course they can! Should companies pay employees more than is necessary to keep them engaged and productive, even if doing so would place employee interests above those of the company as a whole and its shareholders in particular?

The question isn't theoretical—shareholders have sued management on that very issue. While US courts have typically looked to the business-judgment rule, which affords directors wide discretion to decide such matters, judges have even weighed in about shareholder value maximization. For example, in 2010, when the directors of classifieds site Craigslist admittedly sought to run their business without a shareholder-maximization objective, putting the interests of the community above "the business of stockholder wealth maximization, now or in the future," the Delaware courts—the most important jurisdiction in the United States for matters of corporate law—insisted that corporations exist to promote value for shareholders. ("The 'Inc.' after the company name," the deciding court said, "has to mean at least that.") The ruling thus proceeded to invalidate a poison pill that would have allowed Craigslist's board to execute "a business strategy that openly eschews stockholder wealth maximization."

Different countries come to different conclusions about the purpose of business. But across legal systems, maximizing wealth for the long term demands that managers consider tradeoffs. In a system such as that of the United States, where shareholder wealth maximization can have the force of law, executives can meet their shareholder-minded mission through an approach that economist Michael Jensen calls an "enlightened value maximization." Under that framework, managers "spend an additional dollar on any constituency provided the long-term value added to the firm from such expenditure is a dollar or more." That enforces a cost-benefit analysis for ESG investments, just as companies would do when allocating capital for any other purpose and keeping long-term value creation in mind.

One reason for the resilience of Dick's Sporting Goods may be that gun sales were already a declining part of the company's portfolio. Another reason was that it remained stubbornly committed to its sense of purpose. Researchers have found that the market capitalization of firms increases with stakeholder support, particularly in times when peer stakeholders criticize or attack firm operations. Holding to your company's central values is particularly essential today as polarized forces widen the social gyre. "Fueled in part by social media, public pressures on corporations build faster and reach further than ever before," BlackRock's Larry Fink observed in his highly influential 2019 letter to CEOs. Fink argued that "[a]s divisions continue to deepen, companies must demonstrate their commitment to the countries, regions, and communities where they operate." Walking the talk on purpose strengthens the company and its community. "Profits," Fink notably concluded, "are in no way inconsistent with purpose—in fact, profits and purpose are inextricably linked."

* * *

Concluding Thoughts

Stand By Me

Adapted from a story by Elizabeth Gilbert

Some years ago, I was stuck on a crosstown bus in New York City during rush hour. The bus was filled with cold, tired people. Many were irritated—with one another, with the sleety weather, with the world itself. Two men barked at each other about what might have been a shove. A pregnant woman got on, but nobody offered her a seat. Rage, not mercy, was in the air.

As the bus approached Seventh Avenue, the driver got on the intercom. "Folks," he said, "I know you've had a rough day. I can't do anything about the weather or traffic, but here's what I can do. As each of you gets off the bus, I will reach out my hand. As you walk by, drop your troubles into the palm of my hand, okay? Don't take your problems home to your families tonight—just leave 'em with me. My route goes right by the Hudson, and when I drive by there later, I'll open the window and throw your troubles in the river. Sound good?"

A spell was lifted. We burst out laughing. Faces gleamed with delight. People who'd been pretending not to notice each other began grinning at each other. "Is this guy serious?"

Oh, he was.

At the next stop—as promised—the driver reached out his hand, palm up, and waited. One by one, the exiting commuters placed their hand just above his and mimed dropping something into his palm. Some laughed as they did this, some teared up—but everyone did it. The driver repeated the ritual at the next stop, too. And the next. All the way to the river.

Sometimes it's tough to be human. Sometimes we have a bad day. Sometimes they last for years. We struggle and fail. We lose jobs, money, friends, faith, and love. We witness horrible things; we watch the news; and we become fearful and withdraw. We long for the light but don't know where to find it.

But maybe each of us can be the light.

That's what this bus driver taught me—that anyone can be the light, at any moment. This guy wasn't some big power player. He wasn't a spiritual leader. He wasn't some media-savvy "influencer." He was a bus driver—an invisible worker. But he possessed real power. And he used it beautifully for our benefit.

When life feels especially grim, or when I feel particularly powerless, I think of this man and ask myself, "What can I do, right now, to be the light?"

No matter who you are, or where you are, or how mundane or tough your situation may seem, I believe you can illuminate our world. In fact, I believe this is the only way the world will ever be illuminated. One bright act of grace at a time . . . all the way to the river.

Chapter 3.3

Profits: Socially Responsible Investing

Over the last decade, socially-responsible investing—often called ESG investing—is on a tear. What explains this meteoric rise? As with corporate environmental stewardship (Planet) and corporate social responsibility (People), ESG investing (Profits) reflects new ways in which the corporation is being harnessed to meet the expectations of the triple bottom line.

Sustainable Investing in the United States 1995–2020

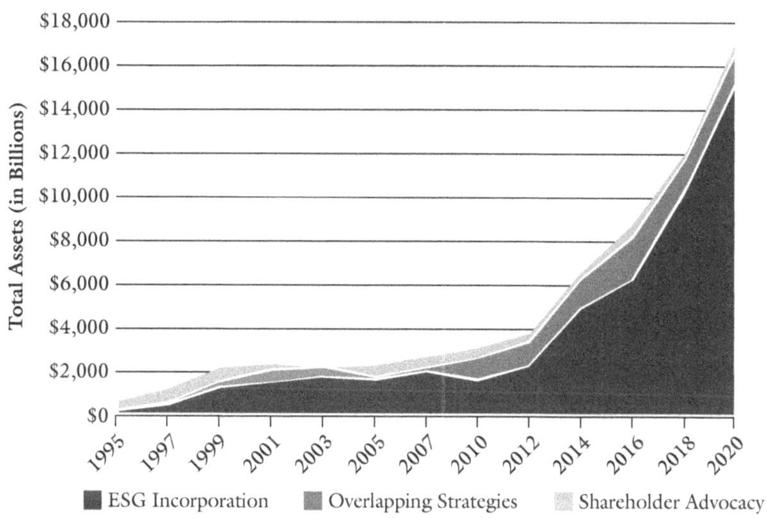

Source: US SIF Foundation

Notice that ESG investing is not a remaking of the corporation's DNA. The corporation remains an externalizing, short-termist, inward-focused, politically-manipulative machine—but less so.

And like Planet and People, the Profits component of the triple bottom line has been voluntary. There is no government regulation (at least, in the United States) that has told investors to become more aware of the corporation's environmental, social, and governance footprint. Rather, it turns out, doing this is simply a smart investment strategy.

Chapter's Focus

You will want to focus on what socially responsible investing is. It comes in many different flavors. You'll find it interesting to see what such investing means from the perspective of Fidelity, one of the leading *managed* mutual fund groups.

After this overview, you'll want to focus—yet again—on the debate whether the corporation is "primarily" for its shareholders (a property model) or for other stakeholders (a social model). As you can tell, the social model is becoming ascendant.

You'll then want to consider the important and quickly growing SRI movement, now usually described as ESG investing. You'll want to consider its theoretical underpinnings and its recent success in attracting institutional shareholders, as well as retail investors.

Next, you'll want to consider how institutional shareholder activism has been playing out lately. You'll want to focus on how the SEC shareholder proposal rule has been harnessed to put pressure on corporate managers to consider and act on ESG matters. You'll also be interested to see how proxy activism led to a soft palace coup at . . . ExxonMobil!

Finally, you'll want to consider how duties of institutional shareholders are shifting. Modern portfolio theory calls on institutional shareholders to not only include but make ESG the focus of their investment strategies. That is to say, what began as a niche is now going mainstream.

3.3.1 Overview of ESG Investing

So, the graph above shows that ESG "incorporated" into investing decisions is taking off. This describes investing decisions in *managed* investment portfolios, which increasingly take into account such factors as a company's carbon footprint, its use of scarce natural resources (like water or clean air), its production of products and services that fit into a "circular economy," its treatment of employees and other workers in the supply chain, and the diversity and incentives in its governance structure. The graph also describes how some institutional shareholders are picking up their "advocacy" game, especially by advancing and supporting shareholder ESG proposals.

But sometimes ESG investing means that investors (most often institutional shareholders) are really focused on the ESG performance of companies in their portfolios. That is, institutional shareholders are not just taking ESG into account in their investing decisions, but have made ESG the driver of portfolio construction.

How has sustainable investing played out – and what are the key drivers? Fidelity, the second largest mutual fund group in the world, recently laid this out for its investors. Fidelity International, Sustainable investing is the "new normal" – here are its four key drivers (accessed 8/6/2022).

As Fidelity explains, modern portfolio theory posits that the core purpose of investing is to "deploy capital in search of positive risk-adjusted returns." But things are changing. Beyond the financial risks of the traditional model, there are now "external factors such as climate change" and increased awareness of social and governance issues – in short, there are now ESG risks.

Fidelity International
Sustainable Investing Is the "New Normal"

(2021)

[redacted/paraphrased]

The acceleration toward ESG investing – a term coined in a 2004 study "Who Cares Wins" by the UN Global Compact – has caught the eye of both retail and institutional investors.

The sustainable surge
Consider the rise of ESG-focused funds, which in June 2020 reached $1 trillion because of record inflows during the pandemic.

Assets Under Management in ESG Funds

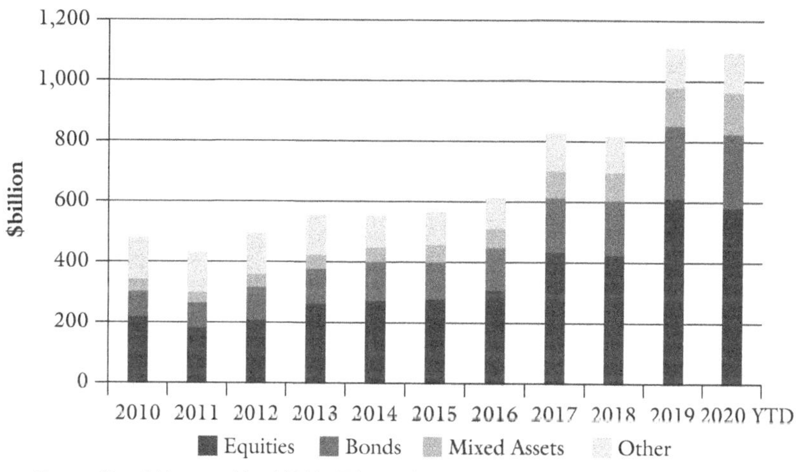

Source: Broadridge as at May 2020 in USD. Includes all domicilles ex North America. Includes ETFs but excludes fund of funds. Excludes Islamic funds.

Although global AUM is over $90 trillion, this figure only measures the AUM at funds explicitly focused on ESG. Globally, institutional investors are applying ESG criteria—for example:

- Japan's Government Pension Investment Fund (GPIF), with AUM over $1.5 trillion, announced that new investments will only go to managers with ESG credentials and in 2020 launched a program to promote ESG factors in fixed income investments.
- Denmark's public pension funds (with $100 billion in AUM) have been divesting "negative ESG" companies from their portfolios and will soon offer members climate-focused, carbon-neutral investments.

- In September 2019, a group of 30 institutional investors – part of the UN-convened Net-Zero Asset Owner Alliance with $5 trillion AUM – committed to transition their investment portfolios to net-zero GHG emissions by 2050.

Once "indirect" ESG assets are included, estimates of total ESG AUM are $41 trillion –closer to 50% of global AUM. What are the drivers of these trends? Fidelity identified four:

Driver #1 – Awareness and expectations
We are more aware of ESG and expect more from our investment portfolios. Besides more media coverage and dissemination of scientific advances, international accords such as the Paris Agreement have captured a rising recognition (especially among the younger generations) that our future must be a sustainable, low-carbon one. Demands by younger investors of all political stripes has translated into commitments by companies, as well as asset managers.

According to a 2019 study, 73% of investors believe companies have a duty to behave more ethically, 65% believe ethical business will deliver better investment returns, and 47% of their portfolios would be invested specifically "according to ESG principles." How much of your portfolio would you so invest?

Driver #2 – Outperforming returns
Although many people once assumed that sustainable investing meant sacrificing returns, the data now show otherwise. Sustainable investing is today outperforming the wider market.

Consider what happened during the pandemic-induced market selloff in early 2020. Companies with high ESG ratings outperformed the benchmark S&P 500. According to Fidelity, higher ESG ratings—among a sample of 2,689 equity issuers and 1,398 bond issuers—meant both better stock returns and reduced credit declines:

Fidelity ESG rating	Stock return (%)	Stock return vs S&P 500 (%)	Credit decline (%)
A	–23.1	+3.8%	–9.2
B	–25.7	+1.2	–13.1
C	–27.7	–0.8	–16.9
D	–30.7	–3.8	–20.7
E	–34.3	–7.4	–20.0

Nor is this a recent phenomenon. Morningstar has found that, over the last ten years, almost 60% of sustainable funds both outperformed their "conventional" peers and had better survivorship rates (72% compared to 46% for 'traditional' funds). Predictably, as evidence grows that sustainable investing is superior to traditional investing, so too will its popularity and demand.

Driver #3 – Long-term resilience
Resilience – the ability of companies to weather uncertainty – is another driver of ESG investing. Companies that were already resilient score highly on ESG measures.

Simply put, resilient companies are better across such areas as culture, supply chain management, and customer relations. Furthermore, they have fewer scandals.

Given that future crises will likely arise from ESG issues like climate change, companies will be rewarded if they strengthen their sustainability by building long-term resilience.

Notice that awareness and expectations, outperforming returns, and long-term resilience are "organic" forces within companies that spur ESG investing. On the "inorganic" side is the final driver – regulations.

Driver #4 – Regulation

For many governments, sustainability is central to post-Covid recovery plans. Even before the pandemic, industry regulators were encouraging companies to focus on sustainability.

For example, the EU Non-Financial Reporting Directive mandates that large EU companies disclose certain ESG factors. And this will soon extend to sustainability-related disclosure regulations for investment firms, requiring that they show how they are integrating ESG risks into investment decisions. Likewise European bank regulators are planning "climate stress tests" to assess banks' exposure to the potential economic impacts of climate change.

Other regulations have focused on sustainability in the supply chain. For example, the California Transparency in Supply Chains Act and the UK's Modern Slavery Act anticipate that company transparency will pressure companies to ensure the ethicality of their supply chains, particularly with respect to human trafficking and slavery. Ignorance is no longer an excuse.

Sustainable investing – just normal

Fidelity summarized where things stand:

> The powerful drivers behind sustainable investing are only getting stronger. Not only is sustainable investing here to stay, it eventually could be the predominant engine of capitalism. It may be the "new normal" today, but soon just the "normal" of tomorrow.

SRI Investing—The Early Days

In 2007, a groundbreaking article in the SRI literature surveyed the emergence of SRI funds, which began to grow exponentially beginning in the early 2000s. Luc Renneboog, Jenke ter Horst & Chendi Zhang, *Socially Responsible Investments: Methodology, Risk Exposure and Performance* (2007) [available on SSRN]. SRI funds seek explicitly to have the best of both worlds: both financial returns comparable (or better) than available in the market, and social objectives that strengthen good corporate management, sound environmental standards, and good stakeholder relations. SRI funds are designed to be instruments of triple-bottom-line investing. The article identified that SRI funds come in many different flavors: some with "negative" investment standards (no tobacco, no child-labor, no fossil fuel) and some with "positive" investment standards (diversified boards, strong environmental compliance, focus on renewable energy). The article found that "negative" SRI funds tended to under-perform comparable non-SRI funds, while "positive" SRI funds out-performed comparable non-SRI funds.

An SRI Fund

An example of an SRI fund is Vanguard's FTSE Social Index Fund, with about $7.5 billion in assets. The Fund, which Vanguard has offered since 2000, invests in large-cap US stocks screened for "social, human rights, and environmental criteria." Recently, the Fund announced it would be screening its investments ***not to include*** any companies in the fossil-fuel businesses.

Interestingly, the Vanguard FTSE Social Index Fund lists JP Morgan Chase as its fifth largest holding, even though the financial firm is the world's largest lender to the fossil-fuel industry, with total financial commitments for oil, gas, and coal exploration, drilling, and extraction of about $200 billion. To give you a sense of the enormity of this financial commitment, ExxonMobil spends about $3 billion each year on oil and gas exploration and R&D.

Different SRI Filters

There are so many ways for an SRI investor to seek to have its portfolio conform to criteria. A great place to get an overview of SRI investing is the Forum for Sustainable and Responsible Investing—a non-profit that collects information, provides guidance to institutional shareholders (particularly smaller SRI funds), and generally has led the way for the SRI community. The Forum identifies different kinds of ESG strategies:

ESG Strategies and Terms

Negative/Exclusionary: the exclusion from a fund or plan of certain sectors or companies based on specific ESG criteria—for example, no tobacco or fossil-fuel companies

ESG Integration: the systematic and explicit inclusion by investment managers of ESG risks and opportunities into traditional financial analysis—or example, how exposed is the company to climate change risks

Positive/Best in Class: investment in sectors, companies or projects selected for positive ESG performance relative to industry peers—for example, the renewable energy sector or agricultural companies focused on carbon-capture farming methods

Impact Investing: targeted investments, typically made in private markets, aimed at solving social or environmental problems—for example, companies focused on greater workplace diversity or banks lending to green start-ups

Sustainability Themed Investing: the selection of assets specifically related to sustainability in single- or multi-themed funds—for example, a "climate change" fund that combines some of the strategies mentioned above with a focus on climate change risk and opportunity

ESG Investing as Private Initiative

ESG investing, which is mostly institutional, seems to arise as a result of private initiative. For example, "green bonds" are a form of debt financing whose proceeds are specifically dedicated to environmentally-friendly "green" projects. This market has emerged as an integral response to the threat of climate change. Missing, however, from the still-nascent green bond market are government regulators. Instead, governance of the market is decentralized and primarily shaped by private governance regimes (such as investment standards, certification schemes, ratings, and third-party assessment), which compete or collaborate with each other for market adoption. See Stephen Park, *Investors as Regulators: Green Bonds and the Governance Challenges of the Sustainable Finance Revolution* (2018) [available on SSRN].

ESG Investing Is Global

More remarkable, perhaps, is that the SRI movement is global. Although it once varied according to the "country of origin," with most SRI in Europe and far fewer in the United States and Asia, the search for superior returns through ESG investing has gone global.

International money management firms, motivated by both financial and social returns, put pressure on companies to increase their environmental and social (E&S) performace—when the firms come from countries where there is a "strong community belief" in the importance of E&S. That is, institutional investors transplant their social norms around the world. See I. J. Alexander Dyck, Karl V. Lins & Lukas Roth, *Do Institutional Investors Drive Corporate Social Responsibility? International Evidence* (2018) [available on SSRN] (looking at SRI activities in 41 countries).

SRI Principles Extend Into Other Financial Markets

The principles of SRI also extend to other financial markets. For example, major European insurers have now stopped insuring companies and their operations that increase climate risk. *Allianz to Stop Insuring Coal Industry Amid Climate Concerns*, ClimateAction (May 4, 2018). For example, Allianz—a German insurer with €1.9 trillion of assets under management—announced it will no longer insure the coal industry in a move designed to support the transition to a low-carbon economy; specifically, the company announced it would no longer sell insurance to coal-fired power plants or coal mines. Insurance companies in the United States, however, have been slower to respond. Of the nine largest insurance companies headquartered in the United States, none has committed to discontinuing underwriting of coal assets or divesting their coal investments. See *US Insurers Are Sticking with Coal,* ClimateWire (Dec. 5, 2018) (noting that 19 major global insurance companies, accounting for one-fifth of the industry, have taken action to divest from coal).

3.3.2 A Return to the Question of Corporate Purpose

One of the givens in the financial literature (and implicit in Fidelity's description of the ESG investing phenomenon) is that SRI must be measured according to the SWM principle. But is this right? A path-breaking article from the early 2000s by Professor Lynn Stout asserted that shareholder primacy is a misinterpretation of the law, a misstatement of actual practice, and a theoretical mistake. Lynn A. Stout, *The Problem of Corporate Purpose*, Brooking Institute—Issues in Corporate Governance (2012). Instead, Stout pointed out that the corporation is more valuable and robust for all of its constituents if the board is seen (and acts) as a "mediator" of the different constituent interests, thus placing employees and others on par with investors.

Support for the notion that the board has long acted as a mediator comes from Canada, where after a decision by the country's highest court that directors should consider stakeholder interests led to . . . well, a big yawn. Brue Tingle & Eldon Spackman, *Do Corporate Fiduciary Duties Matter?* (2019) [available on SSRN]. The move from SWM to a "stakeholder regime" by the court did "not have an impact on litigation patterns, takeover premiums, equity asset values, and equity risk premiums." In other words, as measured by corporate litigation behavior and stock prices, the change in stated directorial fiduciary duties had no apparent impact on perceptions of the corporation.

But, to be clear, SWM has hardly been discarded. Economists point out that adopting some enlightened form of SWM (with objectives other than "wealth creation") has economic consequences, and "competing social objectives" should come within the "purview of politics." Richard M. Frankel, SP Kotharri & Luo Zuo, *Why Shareholder Wealth Maximization Despite Other Objectives* (2018) [available on SSRN].

Despite clunks in the armor of SWM, others question the move of policymakers to refashion corporate governance and its "guiding principle" of shareholder primacy. For example, Professor Jill Fisch asserted:

> The effort to employ shareholders as agents of public values and, thereby, to inculcate corporate decisions with an increased public responsibility is misguided. The incorporation of "publicness" into corporate governance mistakenly assumes that shareholders' interests are aligned with those of nonshareholder stakeholders. Because this alignment is imperfect, corporate governance is a poor tool for addressing the role of the corporation as a public actor.

Jill E. Fisch, *The Mess at Morgan: Risk, Incentives and Shareholder Empowerment* (2016) [available on SSRN] (Fisch argued that "improved corporate governance" in the form of shareholder empowerment, rather than functioning as a solution, may exacerbate corporate governance problems, such as the trading scandal at JP Morgan; as a result, regulatory approaches such as the Volcker rule may be warranted).

3.3.3 Shareholder Activism on ESG Issues

Shareholder ESG Proposals

Lately, the shareholder proposal rule—an SEC rule that permits shareholders to put proposals on the the company's proxy ballot at company expense—has been used as a mechanism for ESG reforms. Shareholder proponents today submit as many proposals on environmental, social, and political matters as on straight-line corporate governance matters. Lately, there have been as many proposals put to shareholder vote on matters such as climate risk reporting, political expenditures, and workplace equity as on such things as proxy access, poison pills, and staggered boards. And overall shareholder support for such ESG proposals has been growing on average from less than 20 percent to close to 30 percent, with a handful of proposals getting majority shareholder support. *Early Look at 2019 Shareholder Proposals*, Harvard Corporate Governance Blog (Mar. 5, 2019). Nonetheless, whether an ESG proposal survives SEC no-action review is often the result of political pressures on SEC staff and even depends on which individual staff member decides the issue—that is, the no-action process can be hit or miss. See Gregory Burke, *SEC Rule 14a-8 Shareholder Proposals: No-Action Requests, Determinants, and the Role of SEC Staff* (2021) [available on SSRN].

Not only have ESG proposals become more common, but so too the breadth of support for them. In 2018, continuing a trend that began in 2017, more than two-thirds of the shareholder proposals put to vote at Russell 3000 companies covered environmental and social matters, rather than governance-related subjects such as proxy access or executive pay. According to Institutional Shareholder Services (the largest proxy advisory firm, which gives institutional shareholders recommendations for how to vote), this is "part of a recent shift in the kind of issues shareholder advocates are raising and how mainstream investors are reacting." For the first time E&S submissions outnumbered governance proposals. And for the first time, BlackRock and Vanguard (the world's two biggest investment managers) voted for climate change proposals, and State Street (the third largest investment fund) voted against companies without any women on their boards. For the year, the top topics were corporate lobbying and political spending disclosures, followed by proposals urging companies to set goals for cutting their climate impact or to report on climate-related risks. See Andrea Vittorio, *Climate, Gender Concerns Part of Investor Advocacy's New Look* Bloomberg Environmental News (Feb. 27, 2018).

Although voting on ESG proposals is undergoing a Renaissance, there are limits on how effective such voting can be. The problem is that some institutional shareholders are not really designed to engage in full-throated SRI activism. Professor John Morley (Yale Law) commented that even though big investment management firms (like Vanguard and Fidelity) now have enough corporate votes to control huge swaths of American industry, we should not expect them to do much in terms of ESG activism. See John Morley, *Too Big to Be Activist* (2018) [available on SSRN]. For example, Morley pointed out, no large asset manager has ever started an activist hedge fund, even as the market for activism by smaller hedge fund managers has been booming. Big funds are simply too big to be activists; they manage hundreds of different funds and other investment vehicles for many different clients, creating intense horizontal conflicts of interest. For example, if one BlackRock fund invests in a company's debt and another in the company's equity, then any attempt by BlackRock to influence the company's capitalization will inevitably harm the interests of one group of clients. At most, big funds "can sometimes support the activist efforts of a smaller manager or practice gentle forms of activism on its own—but almost never seek to control a company directly."

Engagement by Institutional Shareholders

But, if not "open" activism, what about "passive" activism by voting in support of those who engage with management? Do institutional shareholders have an incentive to do this? One answer is not really, because of the free-riding problem—that is, value-creating activism is a cost borne by only the activist, but the value is shared by all. Economic theory suggests that the "rational response" to free-riding is to be apathetic. But institutional intermediaries, in fact, often seek to obtain information on portfolio companies and vote "actively"—thus, cooperating with like-minded firms. Luca Enriques & Alessandro Romano, *Institutional Investor Voting Behavior—A Network Theory Perspective* (2018) [available on SSRN].

Conferences bringing together institutional shareholders, corporate leaders, academics, and policymakers are now underway globally. See Dionysia Katelouzou & Henning Jacobsen, *Global Shareholder Stewardship: A Conference Report* (2020) [available on SSRN] (reporting on conference co-hosted by academic institutions, government groups, and institutional shareholders—"to share experiences, enhance dialogue, disseminate good practice, guide scholarship, and shape future stewardship policy through evidence-based recommendations").

3.3.4 Duties of Institutional Shareholders

Traditionally, shareholders owe no fiduciary duties to the corporation. They are, instead, independent and free agents, able to exercise their rights to "vote, sell, and sue" according to their own perceived best interests. The only exception has been when a shareholder (or group of shareholders) holds a controlling interest in the corporation, and then this position of power comes with responsibilities. Under established corporate law, controlling shareholders (such as a parent corporation that holds a partially-owned subsidiary) has duties of loyalty to the corporation not to engage in transactions unfair to the corporation, and thus to minority shareholders.

Duties to the Corporation

But things may be in a state of flux. There have been calls by academics for non-controlling shareholders (such as hedge funds) to owe duties to the corporation when they are in a position to use that position to undermine corporate interests. And, recently, the Delaware Supreme Court has intimated that such duties may exist as a matter of law.

In the most downloaded "forum" piece on corporate governance in the 2010s, two law professors argued that institutional shareholders in US public corporations ***should have*** fiduciary duties when they vote. We know that corporate managers have fiduciary duties when they manage "other people's money," so why not the intermediary institutional shareholders, too? Notice, however, that the fiduciary duties that the article advocates are not CSR duties, but duties of institutional shareholders to fellow shareholders and to the corporation. Iman Anabtawi & Lynn Stout, Fiduciary Duties For Activist Shareholders (2008) [available on SSRN]. Their focus is on activism by hedge funds and the support such company-damaging activity receives from other institutional shareholders:

> Power in public corporations is dispersed among three key groups: shareholders; the board of directors; and the company's executive officers, including its Chief Executive Officer (CEO). Each group has rights and privileges. Each also has duties and responsibilities.
>
> Contemporary corporate case law and scholarship, however, pay far more attention to corporate officers' and directors' duties than to those of shareholders. Officers and directors are understood to owe fiduciary duties of loyalty and care that are broad and deep, constraining their every material business decision. Shareholders, in contrast, are thought to have far more limited obligations. In fact, outside the narrow contexts of closely-held companies and self-dealing by majority shareholders, many commentators assume shareholders have no duties at all. Minority stockholders in public companies are often viewed as free agents, at liberty to try to influence corporate policy as they see fit—including trying to influence corporate policy in ways that favor their own interests over those of the corporation and other shareholders.
>
> Why has the possibility that minority shareholders in public firms might use their power in self-serving ways attracted so little attention? First, until recently minority shareholders have played a largely passive role in public companies. The second reason is that, even when minority shareholders become active, it has been generally believed that their primary goal is to improve the firm's overall economic performance—presumably a beneficial influence.
>
> Both of these assumptions are becoming increasingly inaccurate. The economic and legal contexts in which American public corporations do business are changing swiftly in ways that create a pressing need to reexamine conventional notions of shareholder duties. As a result of recent developments in the financial markets, in business practices, and in corporate law, minority shareholders are finding it economically rational to try to influence corporate decisionmak-

> ing. Meanwhile, even as shareholders are becoming more powerful, their interests are becoming more heterogeneous. Increasingly, the economic interests of one shareholder or shareholder group conflict with the economic interests of others. The result is that some activist shareholders are using their growing influence not to improve overall firm performance, as has generally been assumed, but to profit at other shareholders' and at the firm's expense.
>
> We believe fiduciary duty doctrine can and should be interpreted in a new way that takes into account changes in the corporate landscape and reaches such opportunistic behavior. Indeed, we believe that the law of fiduciary duty is uniquely suited to address the growing problem that opportunistic shareholder activism poses for corporate governance.

The Anabtawi and Stout article is part of the increasing academic attention to whether institutional shareholders (both wholesale funds and retail funds) owe duties to their beneficiaries. See Richardson, ***Fiduciary Responsibility in Retail Funds: Clarifying the Prospects for SRI*** (2013) [available on SSRN]. And the attention is global. Andreas Kahn, *The Shareholders' Fiduciary Duty in German Company* (2017) [available on SSRN] (concluding that "shareholders may not exercise their membership rights in a manner that would be prejudicial to the interests of the company and their fellow shareholders").

In fact, both the law and management academy are pointing out that institutional shareholders should be managing their indexed portfolios not on a company-by-company basis, but taking into account overall portfolio returns and risk. It's pretty obvious. Thus, if there are companies in the portfolio that are dragging down the whole portfolio, they should either be disciplined and brought into line. For example, if ExxonMobil and its fossil-fuel fetish is causing losses to other companies—by imposing its externalities on insurance companies (which face liabilities for climate-change induced damage) or agricultural companies (which also are struggling with droughts and flooding from climate change or . . . you get the picture—then ExxonMobil should get shoved back into line.

You can do a Google search and discover at least 100 articles since 2020 making this point.

Case Study: The Palace Coup at ExxonMobil

If ExxonMobil is hurting investment portfolios by its externalization of fossil-fuel costs onto other companies in the portfolio, what are institutional shareholders to do? If you have an indexed portfolio, you can't sell ExxonMobil. And even if you have a managed portfolio, it might be better to "reform" ExxonMobil than to dump it. That's what happened when an activist hedge fund—looking for some quick financial returns—sought to place three new directors on the 12-member ExxonMobil board. The hope was that these new directors might convince the other directors to turn the company away from the cliff toward which it was heading—not because of some altruistic purpose, but to make money when ExxonMobil undertook this turnaround.

The hedge fund was simply fulfilling its fiduciary duty to its investors to maximize the returns of the fund. It's a story of how capitalism might save itself from itself.

Boardroom coup at ExxonMobil is a global governance earthquake

Board Agenda: Governance (Jun. 17, 2021)

Neil Boom

A tiny activist hedge fund's success in reshaping the board at ExxonMobil is the most important corporate governance development in decades.

In the end money talks, like it always does. If you skip through the financial and business pages of the newspapers as you head for the sport, or are still half asleep when Dominic O'Connell gives us the daily business news at 6.15am on the Today programme, a couple of weeks ago you might have missed a piece of financial news of genuine world-changing significance.

And what was this news of such import? It was that the board of ExxonMobil, the biggest of Big Oil & Gas, was forced against its will by a six-month-old tiddler activist hedge fund called Engine No.1, to appoint at least three new directors onto its board who are strong advocates in favour of introducing an urgent carbon reduction strategy at the lumbering oil giant.

Somehow this little hedge fund, with its own miniscule 0.02% shareholding in ExxonMobil and a paltry $240m funds under management, corralled some of the largest global institutional investors including BlackRock and the Vanguard Group, Exxon's largest single shareholder worth $7tn, to vote in fresh blood onto the board.

The new board directors all have a track record in lowering carbon emissions in the industry

The new board directors all have a track record in lowering carbon emissions in the industry and a commitment to bringing in a low-carbon future, and therefore have the wherewithal to help steer the company in a new direction. This a matter of ESG policy with teeth in action and credible governance leadership.

In short, these aren't just directors with a brief to tackle climate change or say nice things about worthy environmental stewardship—they have real experience where it counts in renewable energy and will be on a mission to find ways of generating long-term, sustainable profits in the sector.

Commitment to renewables

BlackRock's role in the board reshuffle has been pivotal. It was an early backer of Engine No.1's boardroom coup to force in new blood. Once BlackRock was onside, it was much easier for other large investors to follow suit. Larry Fink, BlackRock's CEO, has made a public commitment to wanting all the companies it invests in to become net carbon zero by 2050.

So while it would be nice to believe that altruism played its part in shaping the new board, and perhaps it did a bit, the more likely reality was that the oil majors have been bleeding value for the last decade and the rot needed to stop.

Powerful institutional investors like BlackRock want to see the oil and gas majors make a much stronger commitment to renewable energy

Bluntly put, pumping oil and gas is no longer the exciting investment it once was. Last year, ExxonMobil was already struggling, and had in just one day surrendered a $225bn market valuation advantage it had over Chevron, as investors feared its future was beginning to look less than rosy. While the company recovered much of that lost value it went on to post over $20bn of losses in 2020, although admittedly much of this was driven by the loss of economic activity caused by Covid.

Going forward, powerful institutional investors like BlackRock want to see the oil and gas majors make a much stronger commitment to renewable energy and believe that sustainable energy sources such as wind, solar, and to a lesser extent hydroelectricity, are the future. Simply put, this is where the new big money will be made, and the oil and gas majors could and should be leading players in this growth sector.

No more greenwashing

With their powerful backing for Engine No. 1's boardroom putsch, we can see that global institutional investors have finally lost patience and are no longer prepared to listen to the oil majors spout greenwashing platitudes about their commitments to the environment. They want visible action now, and they want to see ExxonMobil, and the other oil and gas companies they invest in, compete successfully while decarbonising over the long-term.

After decades of talk about shareholder activism, it has finally arrived

And with Joe Biden in the power seat in the US, and the country once again a signatory to the Paris Climate Accord, he is expected to be an important player in November's 26th UN Climate Change Conference of the Parties (COP 26) and has given his strong political commitment to cutting global carbon emissions and controlling rising temperatures.

So, after decades of talk about shareholder activism, it has finally arrived. The new board of ExxonMobil is the most important development in corporate governance in decades.

With this news announced on the same day as the Dutch court verdict ordering oil giant Royal Dutch Shell to cut its carbon emissions by 45% by the end of 2030 in response to pressure from climate activists, it is hoped, for all our sakes, that such movements are the sign of much more to come.

The Delaware Approach

Taking the lead from the law academy and anticipating the storms on the horizon, the Delaware Supreme Court recently intimated that an activist shareholder has duties to the corporation. *In re PLX Technology Inc. Stockholders Litigation*, 211 A.3d 137 (2019), *aff'g*, 2018 WL 5018535 (Del. Ch. Oct. 16, 2018). In that case, the trial court found that (1) an activist stockholder had aided and abetted a board's breaches of fiduciary duties, but (2) there was insufficient proof that this breach resulted in damages to the corporation.

The case arose when an activist hedge fund, Potomac Capital Partners II, acquired a stake in PLX Technology for the purpose of inducing (ultimately successfully) PLX to sell itself to a company called Avago. When a co-managing member of Potomac, Eric Singer, who had attained a position on the PLX board of directors, received an insider tip about Avago's interest in acquiring PLX, Singer failed to disclose this tip to the rest of the PLX board (or the PLX stockholders). The trial court held that failing to disclose the tip amounted to a breach of Singer's duty of disclosure as a director, and that Potomac had aided and abetted the breach because of Singer's actions as an agent of Potomac. But the trial court also found that the plaintiffs had not proven any damages, given that the company was sold for a fair price despite the flaws in the sale process. Although the Delaware Supreme Court affirmed the finding on damages—and therefore declined to reach the issue of breach of fiduciary duties—the court intimated that the hedge fund did indeed have a duty to the corporation by virtue of Singer's board position.

Big 3 → Giant 3 → Problem of 12

According to Professors Bebchuk and Hirst (Harvard Law), the Big Three institutional shareholders (BlackRock, Vanguard, and State Street) hold 25 percent of the votes at S&P 500 companies. See Lucian Bebchuk & Scott Hirst, *The Specter of the Giant Three* (2020) [available on SSRN]. And, given the Big Three's past growth and current status, they assert that the Big Three will likely grow into the Giant Three with 40 percent of voting power in the next couple decades. In addition, Professor John Coates (Harvard Law) asserts that three ongoing mega-trends — indexing, private equity, and globalization — are reshaping corporate governance. John C. Coates, IV, *The Future of Corporate Governance Part I: The Problem of Twelve* (2019) [available on SSRN]. According to Professor Coates, indexation has progressed farther than most realize, because of foreign ownership, institutional indexation, and "closet" indexation. Thus, in the near future roughly 12 individuals will have practical power over the majority of US public companies.

Engagement by Indexed Funds

As more and more of common stock is held by indexed funds (whether mutual funds or other passively-managed portfolios), the question arises: What is the role of the index fund managers in voting portfolio shares? On one hand, the idea of a low-cost, indexed fund is to keep costs low, including the information-gathering, collective-action, and other costs associated with voting shares. On the other hand, most indexed funds are held for beneficiaries who have long-term objectives, which include both financial performance and ESG issues. See Sean J. Griffith & Dorothy S. Lund, *Conflicted Mutual Fund Voting in Corporate Law* (2019) [available on SSRN]. Professors Sean Griffith (Fordham Law) and Dorothy Lund (USC Law) assert that the so-called "disinterested vote of shareholders" does not reflect true investor interests, given that most shareholders are intermediaries often with non-convergent interests on both sides of a shareholder vote or conflicting interests in currying favor with the corporation's managers.

Thus far, the performance of the large index-fund managers has not matched their sustainability rhetoric. The big three index-fund asset managers—BlackRock, Vanguard and State Street, which together control about 25 percent of the voting power in US public corporations—have remained relatively unfocused on sustainability issues. It's been pointed out that the Big Three face incentives not to be engaged, thus placing oligopolistic power in the hands of just a few (indifferent) human decision makers. These indexed-fund asset managers are inclined to under-invest in their oversight and governance roles with the result that there is inadequate engagement with portfolio companies. In fact, it's reported that except for the 200 largest US corporations, most public companies cannot expect to have meaningful engagement with these three large shareholders.

An Assessment of the Big Three's Activism

As described by Professor Caleb Griffin (Arkansas Law):

> By voting one-quarter of shares at large public companies, just three index funds increasingly control American corporate governance. Nowhere is this control more acute than in the case of environmental and social ("E&S") voting. The "Big Three" funds—Vanguard, BlackRock, and State Street—have the power to determine the fate of the bulk of E&S proposals.

Caleb N. Griffin *Environmental & Social Voting at Index Funds* (2020) [available on SSRN]. The overall support for E&S proposals is low for the Big Three. In the 2018-2019 proxy season, Vanguard's largest funds supported 7.5 percent of unique shareholder E&S proposals, while State Street's largest funds supported 22.7 percent of such proposals and BlackRock's largest funds supported 7.1 percent of such proposals. "Only by blind luck could these funds, who seek no input from their investors and make no serious attempts to discern investor preferences, be accurately reflecting investors' interests with their voting behaviors."

Even though the Big Three have said that climate change is a significant global risk, critics point out that the biggest money managers historically have refrained from taking action. Instead, the big institutional shareholders have usually backed the positions of hesitant corporate managers—and downplayed investor alarm about the financial consequences of a warming world. See Avery Ellfeldt, *3 Wall Street giants can force action on climate. Will they?*, ClimateWire (May 4, 2020) (describing report that found of 41 "climate-critical" proposals in 2019, BlackRock only voted in favor of five, while Vanguard backed only four); see also Emily Chasan & Annie Massa, BlackRock, *Vanguard Faces Shareholder Rebuke Over Climate Votes*, Bloomberg Green (Dec. 13, 2019) (reporting on study by ShareAction of 65 climate-related resolutions that BlackRock and Vanguard lag behind their European counterparts).

Do institutional shareholders vote responsibly?

A recent study looks at the voting records of 133 institutional shareholders on a large sample of sustainability proposals, comparing how the shareholders voted to the voting recommendations of ISS and Glass Lewis. The study found a large difference among shareholders, with European institutions more socially responsible compared to US institutions. The study found that the Big Three were "unwilling to openly support sustainability initiatives." Both conclusions assumed, of course, that ISS and Glass Lewis know better than the institutions what it means to be socially responsible. Anne LaFarre, *Do Institutional Investors Vote Responsibly?* (2021) [available on SSRN]. For example, BlackRock's current stated policy is to vote against any shareholder proposal that calls for a membership quota for board membership based on gender, race, or ethnicity. Yet BlackRock regularly votes for directors who would add board diversity. How should one score BlackRock?

Nonetheless, despite the lackadaisical attitudes of the Big Three on sustainability/environmental issues, the Big Three have actually proven effective in addressing fraud and misconduct by corporate managers. See Alexander I. Platt, *Index Fund Enforcement* (2020) [available on SSRN]. Based on a study of actual engagement by the Big Three and personal interviews, Professor Alexander Pratt (Tulsa Law) found that the Big Three have "pro-enforcement" incentives and have used their power for "engagement, voting, and litigation to discipline culpable companies and managers."

This observation is consistent with the view, among some academics, that the Big Three have limited financial incentives to become involved in corporate governance, given their style and scope. See Edward B. Rock & Marcel Kahan, *Index Funds and Corporate Governance: Let Shareholders be Shareholders* (2021) [available on SSRN]. Professors Ed Rock and Marcel Kahan (NYU Law) acknowledge that the Big Three's capacity to engage in general monitoring of portfolio companies may be limited because of their low-cost business model. Instead, they conclude that hedge funds and actively-managed mutual funds that seek out underperforming companies are better positioned to identify firm-specific problems, with the Big Three playing a collaborative role.

Others point out that index-fund managers, particularly the Big Three, face legal uncertainties if they collaborate, given that such activism might subject their funds to regulation as a "group" under the Securities Exchange Act of 1934. See Gaia Balp & Giovanni Strampelli, *Collective Engagements* (2020) [available on SSRN] (calling on SEC to provide "greater clarity"). Professor Gaia Balp and Giovanni Strampelli (Bocconi Law) point out that coordinated engagement by non-activist shareholders—though potentially beneficial by allowing cost-sharing and lowering free-rider problems—faces the regulatory risk of the collaboration being subject to 13D group disclosures and Regulation FD.

Institutional Shareholders Taking the Lead From Their Investors

One solution to the problem that index funds are naturally disinclined to engage in cost-added corporate governance oversight is to have them identify their "bespoke governance" preferences to investors and let fund investors choose the funds whose voting/engagement commitments that match their investor preferences. See Buyung Hyuun Ahn, Jill E. Fisch, Panos N. Patatoukas & Steven Davidoff Solomon, *Synthetic Governance* (2020) [available on SSRN] (recommending that asset managers identify positions on such corporate governance matters as dual class voting structures, staggered boards, and separating CEO-chair; investors' fund choice would also create a market-based tool for evaluating the relationship between corporate governance and stock returns).

There have been other calls for reform. One is to have indexed fund managers survey their beneficiaries on how portfolio shares should be voted. For example, "Do you want us to vote to have investor-owned utilities move from high-carbon electricity to non-carbon solar/wind renewables?" See Jill E. Fisch, *The Uncertain Stewardship Potential of Index Funds* (2020) [available on SSRN] (recommending institutional shareholders holding indexed assets to engage in stewardship with respect to their portfolio companies). It might well be that investors whose money is held in indexed funds would prefer what some call "non-economic" values like a healthy planet and happier people. Perhaps we should give direct corporate democracy a try!

3.3.5 Emerging Duties of Institutional Shareholders to Society

BlackRock Fink's 2018 Letter to CEOs

The history of global capitalism has some black-letter dates, moments when small events marked major changes. There was the publication of Luca Pacioli's *Summa de Arithmetica*, the birth of modern double-entry accounting. There were the sermons by John Calvin, collected in the *Institutes of the Christian Religion*, which in 1536 declared the value of savings, hard work, and commerce. There was the rise of mercantilism and the middle class in The Netherlands, memorialized in Vermeer's 1658 painting *The Little Street*, the depiction of a tranquil city scene. There was the 1792 agreement signed under a buttonwood tree by 24 stockbrokers for their trading of stocks, the ownership interests in the nascent private business firms called corporations. There was the crash of stock prices on the New York Stock Exchange on Tuesday, October 29, 1929, an event that catapulted the United States and the world into a great economic depression, leading to a world war—but from which arose a global financial system, as well as national and now global securities regulation.

And in February 2018 there was a letter written by Lawrence Fink, the CEO of BlackRock (the world's largest institutional shareholder, with more than $6 trillion in assets then under management—today close to $10 trillion). In the letter, addressed to CEOs in the BlackRock's portfolio—which means all the CEOs of all the public companies in the world—Fink called on them to ensure their companies have a social purpose. It's a watershed moment in world capitalism, I believe. Those who know Fink say the letter was heartfelt and actually represented a turnabout in his views on the value of SRI, which just a few years before he had disparaged as a misguided idea.

Larry Fink's Annual Letter to CEOs

Laurence D. Fink is Founder, Chairman and Chief Executive Officer of BlackRock, Inc. He also leads the firm's Global Executive Committee

BlackRock Investor Relations

A Sense of Purpose

Dear CEO,

As BlackRock approaches its 30th anniversary this year, I have had the opportunity to reflect on the most pressing issues facing investors today and how BlackRock must adapt to serve our clients more effectively. It is a great privilege and responsibility to manage the assets clients have entrusted to us, most of which are invested for long-term goals such as retirement. As a fiduciary, BlackRock engages with companies to drive the sustainable, long-term growth that our clients need to meet their goals.

In 2017, equities enjoyed an extraordinary run—with record highs across a wide range of sectors—and yet popular frustration and apprehension about the future simultaneously reached new heights. We are seeing a paradox of high returns and high anxiety. Since the financial crisis, those with capital have reaped enormous benefits. At the same time, many individuals across the world are facing a combination of low rates, low wage growth, and inadequate retirement systems. Many don't have the financial capacity, the resources, or the tools to save effectively; those who are invested are too often over-allocated to cash. For millions, the prospect of a secure retirement is slipping further and further away—especially among workers with less education, whose job security is increasingly tenuous. I believe these trends are a major source of the anxiety and polarization that we see across the world today.

We also see many governments failing to prepare for the future, on issues ranging from retirement and infrastructure to automation and worker retraining. As a result, society increasingly is turning to the private sector and asking that companies respond to broader societal challenges. Indeed, the public expectations of your company have never been greater. Society is demanding that companies, both public and private, serve a social purpose. To prosper over time, every company must not only deliver financial performance, but also show how it makes a positive contribution to society. Companies must benefit all of their stakeholders, including shareholders, employees, customers, and the communities in which they operate.

Without a sense of purpose, no company, either public or private, can achieve its full potential. It will ultimately lose the license to operate from key stakeholders. It will succumb to short-term pressures to distribute earnings, and, in the process, sacrifice investments in employee development, innovation, and capital expenditures that are necessary for long-term growth. It will remain exposed to activist campaigns that articulate a clearer goal, even if that goal serves only the shortest and narrowest of objectives. And ultimately, that company will provide subpar returns to the investors who depend on it to finance their retirement, home purchases, or higher education.

A New Model for Corporate Governance

Globally, investors' increasing use of index funds is driving a transformation in BlackRock's fiduciary responsibility and the wider landscape of corporate governance. In the $1.7 trillion in active funds we manage, BlackRock can choose to sell the securities of a company if we are doubtful about its strategic direction or long-term growth. In managing our index funds, however, BlackRock cannot express its disapproval by selling the company's securities as long as that company remains in the relevant index. As a result, our responsibility to engage and vote is more important than ever. In this sense, index investors are the ultimate long-term investors—providing patient capital for companies to grow and prosper.

Just as the responsibilities your company faces have grown, so too have the responsibilities of asset managers. We must be active, engaged agents on behalf of the clients invested with BlackRock, who are the true owners of your company. This responsibility goes beyond casting proxy votes at annual meetings – it means investing the time and resources necessary to foster long-term value.

The time has come for a new model of shareholder engagement—one that strengthens and deepens communication between shareholders and the companies that they own. I have written before that companies have been too focused on quarterly results; similarly, shareholder engagement has been too focused on annual meetings and proxy votes. If engagement is to be meaningful and productive—if we collectively are going to focus on benefitting shareholders instead of wasting time and money in proxy fights—then engagement needs to be a year-round conversation about improving long-term value.

BlackRock recognizes and embraces our responsibility to help drive this change. Over the past several years, we have undertaken a concentrated effort to evolve our approach, led by Michelle Edkins, our global head of investment stewardship. Since 2011, Michelle has helped transform our practice from one predominantly focused on proxy voting towards an approach based on engagement with companies.

The growth of indexing demands that we now take this function to a new level. Reflecting the growing importance of investment stewardship, I have asked Barbara Novick, Vice Chairman and a co-founder of BlackRock, to oversee the firm's efforts. Michelle will continue to lead the global investment stewardship group day-to-day. We also intend to double the size of the investment stewardship team over the next three years. The growth of our team will help foster even more effective engagement with your company by building a framework for deeper, more frequent, and more productive conversations.

Your Strategy, Your Board, and Your Purpose

In order to make engagement with shareholders as productive as possible, companies must be able to describe their strategy for long-term growth. I want to reiterate our request, outlined in past letters, that you publicly articulate your company's strategic framework for long-term value creation and explicitly affirm that it has been reviewed by your board of directors. This demonstrates to investors that your board is engaged with the strategic direction of the company. When we meet with directors, we also expect them to describe the Board process for overseeing your strategy.

The statement of long-term strategy is essential to understanding a company's actions and policies, its preparation for potential challenges, and the context of its shorter-term decisions. Your company's strategy must articulate a path to achieve financial performance. To sustain that performance, however, you must also understand the societal impact of your business as well as the ways that broad, structural trends – from slow wage growth to rising automation to climate change—affect your potential for growth.

These strategy statements are not meant to be set in stone—rather, they should continue to evolve along with the business environment and explicitly recognize possible areas of investor dissatisfaction. Of course, we recognize that the market is far more comfortable with 10Qs and colored proxy cards than complex strategy discussions. But a central reason for the rise of activism—and wasteful proxy fights—is that companies have not been explicit enough about their long-term strategies.

In the United States, for example, companies should explain to investors how the significant changes to tax law fit into their long-term strategy. What will you do with increased after-tax cash flow, and how will you use it to create long-term value? This is a particularly critical moment for companies to explain their long-term plans to investors. Tax changes will embolden those activists with a short-term focus to demand answers on the use of increased cash flows, and companies who have not already developed and explained their plans will find it difficult to defend against these campaigns. The U.S. tax bill is only one such example—regardless of a company's jurisdiction, it is your responsibility to explain to shareholders how major legislative or regulatory changes will impact not just next year's balance sheet, but also your long-term strategy for growth.

Where activists do offer valuable ideas—which is more often than some detractors suggest—we encourage companies to begin discussions early, to engage with shareholders like BlackRock, and to bring other critical stakeholders to the table. But when a company waits until a proxy proposal to engage or fails to express its long-term strategy in a compelling manner, we believe the opportunity for meaningful dialogue has often already been missed.

The board's engagement in developing your long-term strategy is essential because an engaged board and a long-term approach are valuable indicators of a company's ability to create long-term value for shareholders. Just as we seek deeper conversation between companies and shareholders, we also ask that directors assume deeper involvement with a firm's long-term strategy. Boards meet only periodically, but their responsibility is continuous. Directors whose knowledge is derived only from sporadic meetings are not fulfilling their duty to shareholders. Likewise, executives who view boards as a nuisance only undermine themselves and the company's prospects for long-term growth.

We also will continue to emphasize the importance of a diverse board. Boards with a diverse mix of genders, ethnicities, career experiences, and ways of thinking have, as a result, a more diverse and aware mindset. They are less likely to succumb to groupthink or miss new threats to a company's business model. And they are better able to identify opportunities that promote long-term growth.

Furthermore, the board is essential to helping a company articulate and pursue its purpose, as well as respond to the questions that are increasingly important to its investors, its consumers, and the communities in which it operates. In the current environment, these stakeholders are demanding that companies exercise leadership on a broader range of issues. And they are right to: a company's ability to manage environmental, social, and governance matters demonstrates the leadership and good governance that is so essential to sustainable growth, which is why we are increasingly integrating these issues into our investment process.

Companies must ask themselves: What role do we play in the community? How are we managing our impact on the environment? Are we working to create a diverse workforce? Are we adapting to technological change? Are we providing the retraining and opportunities that our employees and our business will need to adjust to an increasingly automated world? Are we using behavioral finance and other tools to prepare workers for retirement, so that they invest in a way that that will help them achieve their goals?

As we enter 2018, BlackRock is eager to participate in discussions about long-term value creation and work to build a better framework for serving all your stakeholders. Today, our clients—who are your company's owners—are asking you to demonstrate the leadership and clarity that will drive not only their own investment returns, but also the prosperity and security of their fellow citizens. We look forward to engaging with you on these issues.

Fink's letter sent shock waves through the investment world, including at The Wall Street Journal, which immediately carried an op-ed piece pooh-poohing the letter, offering up a variety of false and misleading statements:

> Wall Street considers it a truism that money sloshes around the globe seeking the highest return. But there are countless investors, believe it or not, who are willing to accept lower returns. P.T. Barnum supposedly said there's a sucker born every minute. Many of them go into so-called socially responsible investing. Laurence Fink of BlackRock, which manages $6 trillion in assets, is only the latest to evangelize this fad. But the basic idea is to throw money away. In reality there is no trade-off of Vice vs. Nice. There are only returns.
>
> "Corporate social responsibility" fails under the same halo. Reread Milton Friedman's 1970 article "The Social Responsibility of Business Is to Increase Its Profits." For stockholders to push their view of social responsibility, Friedman wrote, is simply to force others "to contribute against their will to 'social' causes favored by the activists."
>
> Profits are the best measure of a business's value to consumers—and to society. No one holds a gun to the customer's head. If

> the buyer weren't glad to pay the free-market price, he would make the product or perform the service himself. Yet this idea is questioned all the time.
>
> Don't be fooled by the word "sustainable." Al Gore and Goldman Sachs alum David Blood set up Generation Investment Management to pair sustainability research with traditional investing rigor. A few leaks of Generation's returns have shown pretty good numbers. But it depends on what the meaning of "sustainable" is.
>
> Master investor Charlie Munger [Warren Buffet's right-hand man at Berkshire Hathaway] summed it up last year: "Gore hired a staff to find people who didn't put CO2 in the air, and of course that put him into services. Microsoft, and all these service companies were just ideally located, and this value investor picked the best service companies, so all of a sudden the clients are making hundreds of millions of dollars . . . and he's an idiot."
>
> The bottom line is this: Do whatever you want with your money. Feel virtuous. But if you think you're being charitable for "responsible" investing, you are, but not in the way you think. If you don't put your money where the returns are, someone else will. By passing up gains, you're just making guys like George Soros and Steven Cohen richer so they can buy more bad art. Let the money slosh.

Andy Kessler, *Inside View: Stocks Weren't Made for Social Climbing*, Wall St. J. (Jan. 22, 2018). But what if The Wall Street Journal's editorial board is actually wrong and SRI actually produces better financial returns? Just because there have been instances of "good deeders" not beating the market (the op-ed piece cites to Etsy and CalPERS as firms that let "doing good" impede making money) doesn't mean that SRI is a failed investment technique. In the end, who would you put your money with—Kessler or Fink?

The stock markets went with Fink. Not cautiously, not half-heartedly, but all in! Again, here is the chart that shows the rise in ESG investing—the new moniker given to SRI investing:

Sustainable Investing in the United States 1995–2020

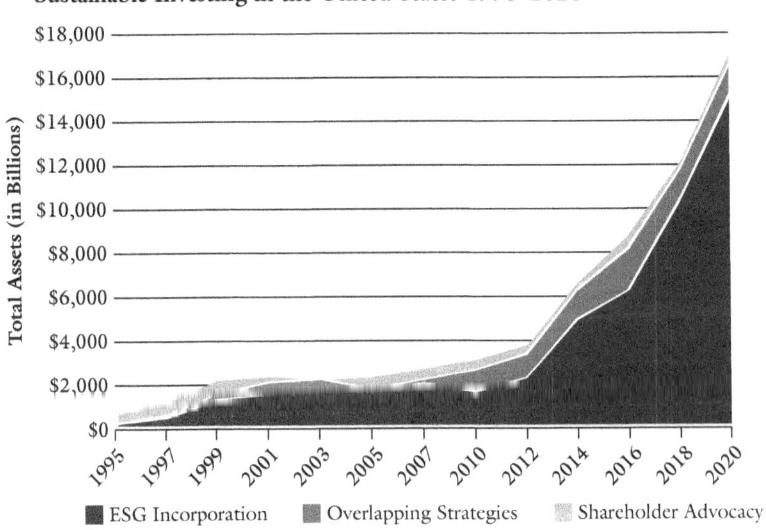

Source: US SIF Foundation

A Quick Epilogue

Two years later, Fink followed up with another letter in which he issued a strong warning to business leaders on the climate crisis, describing steps companies should be taking. See Alan Mirabella & Annie Massa, *BlackRock Puts Climate at Center of $7 Trillion Strategy* Bloomberg (Jan. 14, 2020). In the annual letter to CEOs, Fink made clear that climate change would upend global finance sooner than we might think.

Fink's letter may have come in response to protestors from groups such as Amazon Watch and the Sunrise Project, who have been trailing Fink and other financial leaders to work, to speaking engagements, and to formal events and have decried BlackRock's inaction on global warming and other issues. "Climate change has become a defining factor in companies' long-term prospects," Fink wrote. "Awareness is rapidly changing, and I believe we are on the edge of a fundamental reshaping of finance."

The letter outlined the following changes at BlackRock: making sustainability integral to portfolio construction and risk management; exiting investments that present a high sustainability-related risk; launching new investment products that screen fossil fuels; and strengthening the firm's commitment to sustainability and transparency in its investment stewardship activities.

Specifically, BlackRock committed to exit both debt and equity investments in thermal coal producers in its active portfolios ($1.8 trillion). As for its passive/indexed funds, Fink said BlackRock would take steps to bring climate considerations to portfolio companies, double its lineup of sustainable ETFs to about 150, and pressure index providers to create sustainable versions of their flagship indexes.

Nonetheless, despite BlackRock's stated intentions to address climate risk, an analysis of the 2019 proxy voting records of BlackRock and its peer Vanguard Group by non-profit Majority Action found the two firms voted against at least 16 climate-related shareholder proposals where their support could have given the measures majority support.

As governments continue to flail at the climate crisis, can the financial and business community fill the vacuum and meet the challenge? In January 2020, BlackRock joined Climate Action 100+, a group of more than 370 investment managers with a combined $41 trillion in assets that pressures greenhouse gas emitters to reform. Perhaps, we are at a turning point.

* * *

Concluding Thoughts

Purpose of Market Capitalism

What is the purpose of market capitalism? Is it just to make money for capitalists? Or is it something bigger? Perhaps the purpose of market capitalism has been—and is becoming even more—to free us of suffering.

Think about what you feel when you go to your favorite grocery store or spend a weekend morning at the local farmers' market. The produce, glistening under the store lights or in the sunlight, was brought to you through the forces of market capitalism. The shelves with their neatly arranged boxes, the ingredient labels reminding you that every decision we make about food is a moral decision. The baskets of homemade breads and jams, each telling you how many people were involved in their production. The food is there to relieve our hunger, our thirst, our suffering.

That the food in the store or in the market may have some elements of badness, even evil, does not change its essential character. Its essential goodness. Inescapable is its great inter-connectedness with all that we are and all the planet on which we live offers us.

Should we begin to think of capitalism as humanism? As collective action, but with a unified purpose – a unified voice? Its anthem Giuseppe Verdi's *Va, pensiero?* It is not a crazy idea.

UNIT 4

REDESIGNING CORPORATION

In this unit we look at proposals for the fundamental redesign of the corporation—that is, proposed modifications to its DNA. These modifications seek to mandate new "firm commitments"—that is, business attitudes focused on protecting our environment, addressing social problems, and creating new sources of entrepreneurship and innovation.

Another look down the road. In this unit, we start by looking at benefit corporations. Then we examine the use of public-company disclosure to encourage management to think "sustainably." Finally, we look at how institutional shareholders, business executives, and thought leaders are coming together to form new "consortia" that seek to move the corporation toward sustainability.

Unit 4 sets up Unit 5, the book's final unit. There we consider how the corporation can be seen as a system with multiple inputs and outputs, all of which have moral dimensions. We next ask whether stakeholder capitalism is real or delusional. And, finally, we turn the corporation inside-out and look at how we function in a business organization—are we true to ourselves?

Unit 1 **Intro to corporation**	Unit 2 **Unsustainable design**	Unit 3 **Triple bottom line**	Unit 4 **Redesign corporation**	Unit 5 **Rethink corporation**
1.1 US law 1.2 US corporation 1.3 US public corp 1.4 US securities reg	2.1 Limited liability 2.2 Short-termism 2.3 Board mono-culture 2.4 Corp in politics	3.1 Planet: environ 3.2 People: CSR 3.3 Profits: SRI	4.1 Benefit corp 4.2 ESG disclosure 4.3 Consortium: Ceres	5.1 Corp as moral system 5.2 Stakeholder capitalism–delusion? 5.3 Personal integrity

Chapter 4.1

Social Enterprise (Benefit Corporations)

This chapter looks at efforts to re-think and re-formulate the for-profit corporations as a "social enterprise"—one that balances *both* financial profits and environmental/social good. Specifically, we'll look at the benefit corporation. What is a benefit corporation? What has been its story during its first decade of existence? What does its future hold?

Chapter's Focus

We start with a look at neo-liberal economics, the foundation of the modern SWM corporation. You will want to consider its assumptions—market efficiency, price is equal to value, and humans are selfish, rational maximizers. Does this seem right? You will want to consider ways to re-frame our understanding of the corporation.

Then you will want to focus (actually re-focus) on the debate on whether shareholder primacy is the appropriate way to frame the corporate purpose, compared to a model of multiple stakeholders.

You will then want to focus on the emergence of benefit corporations in the United States, a hybrid entity that mixes social purposes and shareholder profits. Also, whether a mixed-purpose corporation can function, both in a culture in which shareholders expect profits and managers are told to make space for social/environmental goals?

Finally, you will want to consider whether when we as humans are "instructed" to do the right thing, we actually tend to do the opposite. But when we "believe" we are doing the right thing, our behavior is different. That is, how is goodness best incentivized?

4.1.1 Rethinking Neoliberal Economics

Before we get started on re-designing the corporation, let's re-consider its current philosophical underpinning—namely, neoliberal economics. The corporation, the essential mechanism for the functioning of our market capitalism, can be seen as being built on a philosophical justification—namely, that shareholder wealth maximization will raise all ships, thus producing a state of bliss for all. But what if neoliberal economics is wrong? What if the corporation, rather than a means toward wealth-enhancing, externality-shedding competition, is better seen as a collaborative social enterprise? What if sharing wealth actually creates more wealth?

To get you thinking about the place of the corporation in our economy, consider a recent *TED* Talk by Rick Hanauer, an early investor in Amazon and after a series of business successes, the founder of a lucrative venture capital firm:

The Dirty Secret of Capitalism – and a New Way Forward

(July 2019)

Rick Hanauer

TED Talk – TED Summit

I am a capitalist, and after a 30-year career in capitalism spanning three dozen companies, generating tens of billions of dollars in market value, I'm not just in the top one percent, I'm in the top .01 percent of all earners.

Today, I have come to share the secrets of our success, because rich capitalists like me have never been richer. So, the question is, how do we do it? How do we manage to grab an ever-increasing share of the economic pie every year? Is it that rich people are smarter than we were 30 years ago? Is it that we're working harder than we once did? Are we taller, better looking?

Neoliberal Economics Works for the Wealthy Elites

Sadly, no. It all comes down to just one thing: economics. Because here's the dirty secret. There was a time in which the economics profession worked in the public interest, but in the neoliberal era, today, they work only for big corporations and billionaires, and that is creating a little bit of a problem. We could choose to enact economic policies that raise taxes on the rich, regulate powerful corporations or raise wages for workers.

We have done it before. But neoliberal economists would warn that all these policies would be a terrible mistake, because raising taxes always kills economic growth, and any form of government regulation is inefficient, and raising wages always kills jobs. Well, because of that thinking, over the last 30 years, in the USA alone, the top one percent has grown 21 trillion dollars richer while the bottom 50 percent have grown 900 billion dollars poorer, a pattern of widening inequality that has largely repeated itself across the world.

And yet, as middle-class families struggle to get by on wages that have not budged in about 40 years, neoliberal economists continue to warn that the only reasonable response to the painful dislocations of austerity and globalization is even more austerity and globalization.

What Is the New Economics?

So, what is a society to do? Well, it's super clear to me what we need to do. We need a new economics. So, economics has been described as the dismal science, and for good reason, because as much as it is taught today, it isn't a science at all, despite all the dazzling mathematics. In fact, a growing number of academics and practitioners have concluded that neoliberal economic theory is dangerously wrong and that today's growing crises of rising inequality and growing political instability are the direct result of decades of bad economic theory.

What we now know is that the economics that made me so rich isn't just wrong, it's backwards, because it turns out it isn't capital that creates economic growth, it's people; and it isn't self-interest that promotes the public good, it's reciprocity; and it isn't competition that produces our prosperity, it's cooperation.

What we can now see is that an economics that is neither just nor inclusive can never sustain the high levels of social cooperation necessary to enable a modern society to thrive.

So where did we go wrong? Well, it turns out that it's become painfully obvious that the fundamental assumptions that undergird neoliberal economic theory are just objectively false, and so today first I want to take you through some of those mistaken assumptions and then after describe where the science suggests prosperity actually comes from.

False Assumption #1: The Market Is Efficient and in Equilibrium

So, neoliberal economic assumption number one is that the market is an efficient equilibrium system, which basically means that if one thing in the economy, like wages, goes up, another thing in the economy, like jobs, must go down.

So, for example, in Seattle, where I live, when in 2014 we passed our nation's first 15 dollar minimum wage, the neoliberals freaked out over their precious equilibrium. "If you raise the price of labor," they warned, "businesses will purchase less of it. Thousands of low-wage workers will lose their jobs. The restaurants will close." Except . . . they didn't. The unemployment rate fell dramatically. The restaurant business in Seattle boomed. Why? Because there is no equilibrium. Because raising wages doesn't kill jobs, it creates them; because, for instance, when restaurant owners are suddenly required to pay restaurant workers enough so that now even they can afford to eat in restaurants, it doesn't shrink the restaurant business, it grows it, obviously. (Applause)

False Assumption #2: Price and Value Are the Same

The second assumption is that the price of something is always equal to its value, which basically means that if you earn 50,000 dollars a year and I earn 50 million dollars a year, that's because I produce a thousand times as much value as you.

Now, it will not surprise you to learn that this is a very comforting assumption if you're a CEO paying yourself 50 million dollars a year but paying your workers poverty wages. But please, take it from somebody who has run dozens of businesses: this is nonsense.

People are not paid what they are worth. They are paid what they have the power to negotiate, and wages' falling share of GDP is not because workers have become less productive but because employers have become more powerful. And by pretending that the giant imbalance in power between capital and labor doesn't exist, neoliberal economic theory became essentially a protection racket for the rich.

False Assumption #3: Humans Are Selfish, Rational Maximizers

The third assumption, and by far the most pernicious, is a behavioral model that describes human beings as something called "*homo economicus*," which basically means that we are all perfectly selfish, perfectly rational, and relentlessly self-maximizing. But just ask yourselves, is it plausible that every single time for your entire life, when you did something nice for somebody else, all you were doing was maximizing your own utility?

Is it plausible that when a soldier jumps on a grenade to defend fellow soldiers, they're just promoting their narrow self-interest? If you think that's nuts, contrary to any reasonable moral intuition, that's because it is, according to the latest science, not true.

But it is this behavioral model, which is at the cold, cruel heart of neoliberal economics. And it is as morally corrosive as it is scientifically wrong because, if we accept at face value that humans are fundamentally selfish, and then we look around the world at all the unambiguous prosperity in it, then it follows logically, then it must be true by definition, that billions of individual acts of selfishness magically transubstantiate into prosperity and the common good.

If we humans are merely selfish maximizers, then selfishness is the cause of our prosperity. Under this economic logic, greed is good, widening inequality is efficient, and the only purpose of the corporation can be to enrich shareholders, because to do otherwise would be to slow economic growth and harm the economy overall.

And it is this gospel of selfishness which forms the ideological cornerstone of neoliberal economics, a way of thinking which has produced economic policies which have enabled me and my rich buddies in the top one percent to grab virtually all the benefits of growth over the last 40 years.

But, if instead we accept the latest empirical research, real science, which correctly describes human beings as highly cooperative, reciprocal and intuitively moral creatures, then it follows logically that it must be cooperation and not selfishness that is the cause of our prosperity, and it isn't our self-interest but rather our inherent reciprocity that is humanity's economic superpower. So, at the heart of this new economics is a story about ourselves that grants us permission to be our best selves, and, unlike the old economics, this is a story that is virtuous and also has the virtue of being true.

The New Economics Is in Search of New Textbooks

Now, I want to emphasize that this new economics is not something I have personally imagined or invented. Its theories and models are being developed and refined in universities around the world building on some of the best new research in economics, complexity theory, evolutionary theory, psychology, anthropology, and other disciplines. And although this new economics does not yet have its own textbook or even a commonly agreed upon name, in broad strokes its explanation of where prosperity comes from goes something like this.

So, market capitalism is an evolutionary system in which prosperity emerges through a positive feedback loop between increasing amounts of innovation and increasing amounts of consumer demand. Innovation is the process by which we solve human problems, consumer demand is the mechanism through which the market selects for useful innovations, and as we solve more problems, we become more prosperous. But as we become more prosperous, our problems and solutions become more complex, and this increasing technical complexity requires ever higher levels of social and economic cooperation in order to produce the more highly specialized products that define a modern economy.

Now, the old economics is correct, of course, that competition plays a crucial role in how markets work, but what it fails to see is that it is largely a competition between highly cooperative groups—competition between firms, competition between networks of firms, competition between nations—and anyone who has ever run a successful business knows that building a cooperative team by including the talents of everyone is almost always a better strategy than just a bunch of selfish jerks.

The New Economics Creates a More Prosperous and More Equitable Society

So how do we leave neoliberalism behind and build a more sustainable, more prosperous, and more equitable society?

The new economics suggests just five rules of thumb.

- **Jungles → gardens.** First is that successful economies are not jungles, they're gardens, which is to say that markets, like gardens, must be tended, that the market is the greatest social technology ever invented for solving human problems, but unconstrained by social norms or democratic regulation, markets inevitably create more problems than they solve. Climate change, the great financial crisis of 2008 are two easy examples.
- **Inclusion → growth.** The second rule is that inclusion creates economic growth. So, the neoliberal idea that inclusion is this fancy luxury to be afforded if and when we have growth is both wrong and backwards. The economy is people. Including more people in more ways is what causes economic growth in market economies.
- **Shareholders → stakeholders.** The third principle is the purpose of the corporation is not merely to enrich shareholders. The greatest grift in contemporary economic life is the neoliberal idea that the only purpose of the corporation and the only responsibility of executives is to enrich themselves and shareholders. The new economics must and can insist that the purpose of the corporation is to improve the welfare of all stakeholders: customers, workers, community, and shareholders alike.
- **Rapacious greed → cooperation.** Rule four: greed is not good. Being rapacious doesn't make you a capitalist, it makes you a sociopath. (Laughter) (Applause) And in an economy as dependent upon cooperation at scale as ours, sociopathy is as bad for business as it is for society.
- **Unchangeable → new narratives.** And fifth and finally, unlike the laws of physics, the laws of economics are a choice. Now, neoliberal economic theory has sold itself

to you as unchangeable natural law, when in fact it's social norms and constructed narratives based on pseudoscience.

If we truly want a more equitable, more prosperous, and more sustainable economy, if we want high-functioning democracies and civil society, we must have a new economics. And here's the good news: if we want a new economics, all we have to do is choose to have it.

Thank you.

4.1.2 Imagining Corporations Without SWM

Classic Debate of Serving More Than One Master

What if nonshareholder constituents had corporate law rights? Consider the nonshareholder constituency statutes (which we saw in Chapter 3.2 when we looked at *Dodge v. Ford Motor*) that give directors leeway to consider the nonshareholder effects of their decisions. Then imagine, as did the progressive corporate law scholar Larry Mitchell, that such statutes can be enforced in court by employees, creditors, communities, and other nonshareholder corporate constituents. Lawrence E. Mitchell, *A Theoretical and Practical Framework for Enforcing Corporate Constituency Statutes* (1992) [available on HeinOnline]. In cases of vertical conflicts—that is, conflicts between stakeholders, as opposed to horizontal conflicts between shareholders and management—courts would balance their interests and decide what outcome would be in the "best interests of the corporation." Would this work?

Then consider the classic "too many masters" defense of shareholder primacy by the law-and-economics scholar Jonathan Macey. *An Economic Analysis of the Various Rationales for Making Shareholders the Exclusive Beneficiaries of Corporate Fiduciary Duties* (1991) [available on OpenYLS]. Management, if permitted to justify any decision based on stakeholder interests, would be answerable to no one. Shareholders, who paid for their "ownership" rights, would lose the fruits of their voting prerogatives and their claim to fiduciary protection. Does invoking the New Testament edict that you cannot serve two masters work?

Nonshareholder-Constituency Statutes in Practice

A recent study looks at how the nonshareholder-constituency statutes have played out over the last 40 years. Three Harvard law professors examined the performance of the nonshareholder-constituency statutes adopted in over 30 US states, looking at a large sample of acquisitions that were governed by the statutes. They found that when companies were acquired (mostly by private equity firms) corporate managers used their bargaining power to obtain gains for shareholders and themselves—but hardly at all for other constituents.

> Corporate leaders made very little use of their power to negotiate for protection of any stakeholders. Despite the risks that private equity acquisitions posed for stakeholders, corporate leaders made very little use of their power to negotiate for stakeholder protections. In the cases in which some such provisions were included, they were largely practically inconsequential or cosmetic. We conclude that constituency statutes failed to deliver the benefits to stakeholders that they were supposed to produce.

Lucian A. Bebchuk, Kobi Kastiel & Roberto Tallarita, *For Whom Corporate Leaders Bargain* (2020) [available on SSRN]. As the authors explained, "the statutes failed because of corporate leaders' incentives not to benefit stakeholders beyond what would serve shareholder value."

Reconsidering the Ecology of Commerce

The 1994 release of Paul Hawken's book *The Ecology of Commerce*, marked an important milestone in rethinking business. The book laid down a gauntlet for business to reconsider its design—especially its externalization of costs. The book went well beyond suggesting rights be allocated to particular stakeholders or imagining that all can be made well under a long-termist shareholder umbrella. The book—considered the "father" of the social enterprise movement—imagined that business culture must change so that responsible use of our ecological resources is as "natural as falling off a log."

The Ecology of Commerce: A Declaration of Sustainability

(1994)

Paul Hawken

Every natural system in the world today is in decline. The loss of habitat and of biodiversity is not only continuing, but is in fact accelerating. Multinational corporations have become so large and so successful at exploiting the earth's natural resources that we are witnessing the physical limits being reached.

A large array of toxic waste products are being released into the environment where they will never be broken down—chemical compounds such as chlorinated hydrocarbons have no counterparts in nature, and therefore there are no natural processes to assimilate them. They include the CFCs that are depleting the ozone layer, as well as the millions of gallons of herbicides that are applied annually to North American lawns. The current method of increasing profits for corporations and their shareholders is to eliminate employees. In California, PacBell has told its telephone operators that they can no longer use the word "please." This will save enough time to allow them to lay off enough operators to save 5 million dollars per year.

At the turn of the century, the total number of human beings that inhabited the planet was 1.5 billion. Today, the problems to be faced are vast and complex, but come down to this: 5.5 billion people are breeding exponentially. The process of fulfilling their wants and needs is stripping the earth of its biotic capacity to produce life; a climactic bust of consumption by a single species is overwhelming the skies, earth, waters, and fauna. Making matter worse, we are in the middle of a once-in-a-billion-year blowout sale of hydrocarbons. They are being combusted at a rate that will effectively double-glaze the planet within the next fifty years.

To reverse the current trend and live on current solar income instead of spending our capital, we need to reduce the throughput of energy and resources per person by 80 percent. Recently, a Swiss research group has come up with a figure that is closer to 90 per cent. We are all stressed out, in debt, and working long hours. This is it. This is as fast as it gets. We've reached the limit.

Business is the only entity with the resources and skills to implement such a large undertaking. Business must:

1. Reduce absolute consumption of energy and natural resources in the North by 80 percent within the next half century.
2. Provide secure, stable, and meaningful employment for people everywhere.
3. Be self-actuating as opposed to regulated or morally mandated.
4. Honor market principles.
5. Lead to a way of life that is more rewarding than our present one.
6. Exceed sustainability be restoring degraded habitats and ecosystems to their fullest biological capacity.
7. Rely on current income.
8. Be fun and engaging, and strive for an aesthetic outcome.

An even more radical change is currently being discussed in Sweden and is in fact agreed on by all political parties. It is known as the "tax shift." This will eventually become the economic model here in North America. It involves a complete restructuring of the tax system. Taxes will be taken off of income and profits, and placed instead on emissions, energy, resources, and pollution.

An example of how this would work in the United States is as follows: to minimize economic dislocation, the tax change is phased in over 20 years. This allows companies to write off existing investments in plant and equipment. The tax is made revenue neutral for low and middle-income earners. So, for example, a 3.00 dollar per gallon carbon tax is added to gasoline to more accurately reflect the true costs associated with consuming it. This would mean an increase of 2,400 dollars per year in the gasoline bill for the average American. To make it revenue neutral, the average income tax is reduced by a corresponding 2,400 dollars. Therefore, it doesn't cost you one penny extra to run your car. However, you are now living in an economy that is giving you more accurate information about the impact of your actions on the environment. You have a lot more incentive to buy an energy efficient car, and the auto industry has more incentive to design and build one.

SWM as Response to Populism

An interesting defense of the theory of SWM comes from Professor Stephen Bainbridge (UCLA Law), who suggests that "board primacy" is one way to advance shareholder interests. Bainbridge asserts that in the wake of the 2016 US presidential election and similar populist movements in Europe, there has arisen on both the political right and left a deep suspicion of big business. According to Bainbridge, SWM should be seen as a refuge from the political storms:

> Left of center corporate social responsibility campaigners have long advocated the use of "boycotts, shareholder activism, negative publicity, and so on" to pressure corporate managers to act in ways those campaigners deem socially responsible. Right of center populists could use the same tactics to induce corporate directors to make decisions they favor.
>
> Would modifying the SWM norms to give managers more discretion to take the social effects of their decisions into account lead to outcomes populists would view as desirable? Populists historically have viewed corporate directors and managers as elites opposed to the best interests of the people. Today, right of center populists find themselves increasingly at odds with an emergent class of social justice warrior CEOs, whose views on a variety of critical issues are increasingly closer to those of blue state elites than those of red state populists.
>
> This article reverses field by suggesting that the case for Delaware's rule of SWM becomes even stronger when right-wing populists have significant political power. A resurgent right-wing populism may impose alternative constraints on corporate political power sufficient to revitalize the argument for leaving regulation of corporate externalities to general welfare legislation.

Stephen M. Bainbridge, *Corporate Purpose in a Populist Era* (2018) [available on SSRN].

4.1.3 Emergence of Benefit Corporation

The corporation can be seen as a continuum. On one end (let's go toward our right) is a strict SWM in which the corporation exists for the profit of its shareholders, subject to legal norms that seek to ameliorate inevitable externalities. On the other end (let's go toward our left) is a mandated CSR in which the corporation must take into account all constituents, particularly vulnerable stakeholders. In between is the reality of corporations, which varies depending on their history, their line of business, and their composition (especially the nature of their investors and management). Corporations have tendencies toward both SWM and CSR. Is a legal structure that recognizes, even mandates, this duality feasible? Is it worthwhile?

As we have seen before, the corporation (as it exists in law and practice) might already provide a framework for sustainable management and business practices. That is, the ample BJR and the doubtful normative meaning of SWM suggest that corporate participants already seem to agree that a for-profit corporation can take into account nonshareholder interests. We may not really need a new legal structure, given the malleability of the existing one—at least in the United States.

Other hybrid social enterprises

Even though we may already have the legal tools for a corporation that is ESG-leaning or even ESG-focused, corporate statutes in many states over the past decade have sought to make explicit that the corporation need not be only SWM. Since 2008, about half of the states in the United States have passed enabling legislation for "social enterprises"—that is, hybrid business forms that combine social purpose and investor profitability. Some of these social enterprises, such as "low-profit limited liability companies" (L3C) have been modeled on similar enterprises formed under laws in Europe. Others, such as the "benefit corporation" (or sometimes called the "public benefit corporation") are uniquely American.

Nature of the Benefit Corporation

The following article by Professor Dana Brakman Reiser (Brooklyn Law), a pioneer in the study of the benefit corporation, describes and critiques this new structure. You'll want to ask yourself why business managers and investors would migrate to a "benefit corporation," given what we know about the dynamic flexibility of the regular for-profit business corporation. You'll also want to consider whether the expectations of investors in a benefit corporation—who presumably seek not only a return on investment, but also a commitment to the firm's CSR mission—are adequately protected. Finally, doesn't the benefit corporation detract from reforming the traditional corporation, creating the false impression that for a business to have a social mission the only viable option is to reincorporate as a benefit corporation?

Benefit Corporations—A Sustainable Form of Organization?

(2011)

Dana Brakman Reiser

[available on SSRN]

Founders of social enterprises believe profits and social good can be produced in tandem and wish to form organizations that will pursue these dual missions. They will, however, encounter obstacles to articulating and enforcing such dual missions if they adopt either a traditional nonprofit or for-profit form of organization. Nonprofit forms bar profit distribution and for-profit forms will create practical, if not legal, pressure to favor profit maximization over social good when the two come into conflict.

Social entrepreneurs believe social good can be produced along with profits and desire hybrid forms of organization to smooth a single enterprise's path to realizing both goals.

A mounting number of jurisdictions have attempted to meet this demand by enabling new hybrid organizational forms: low-profit limited liability company ("L3C") available in nine U.S. states and the "B Corp," a private certification for U.S. for-profits that demonstrate their commitment to a dual mission of making profits and promoting social good.

This Article examines another recent entrant into the hybrid form category: the benefit corporation and evaluates whether the innovations in the benefit corporation form can meet the goals social entrepreneurs have for hybrid organizational forms, ultimately concluding it will fall short.

I. The Benefit Corporation

Before delving into the details of the new benefit corporation form, it is useful to describe the dynamic scene onto which it enters. When social entrepreneurs' frustration with traditional nonprofit and for-profit forms became apparent, jurisdictions began to respond with new hybrid forms. An early mover here was the United Kingdom, which established the community interest company (CIC) in 2004. The CIC is a company formed for community benefit purposes, which may offer investors limited dividends, but must lock its assets and earnings beyond these limited disbursements into the community benefit stream.

Innovation began stateside with the L3C, first adopted by statute in Vermont in 2008. The L3C is a limited liability company formed to "significantly further the accomplishment of one or more charitable or educational purposes" and for whom neither income production nor property appreciation may be a significant purpose. An L3C may have investor members who can receive unlimited disbursements during the L3C's existence or upon dissolution, and if the L3C ceases to pursue its educational and charitable purposes it transforms into an ordinary LLC.

In addition, companies have been able to obtain private certification as a "B Corps" since 2006. B Corps must provide in their formative documents that fiduciaries must consider the impact of their decisions on various nonshareholder constituencies, including the environment and the local, state, and national economy. A private nonprofit organization, B Lab, vets aspiring B Corps to confirm that these governance structures have been established and conducts an extensive survey to determine how well an applicant uses "the power of business to solve social and environmental problems." Those applicants meeting B Lab's standards may license the B Corp mark and are subject to audit by B Lab on an ongoing basis.

In 2010, Maryland became the first state to establish a "benefit corporation"—a form of organization distinct from the standard corporate form. Although it exists under a separate statutory framework, "benefit corporation" status is available both to newly forming corporations that may use the form from their inception and to existing for profit corporations that adopt benefit corporation form by amending their charters, only after special notice and a supermajority two-thirds vote of shareholders.

Public Benefit

The main thrust of benefit corporation statutes is to require these entities to pursue purposes beyond profit-making. A benefit corporation must be formed for a "general public benefit," meaning a "material, positive impact on society and the environment." All statutes permit the benefit corporation to pursue more "specific public benefits," including:

- Providing [low income or underserved] individuals or communities with beneficial products or services;
- Promoting economic opportunity for individuals or communities beyond the creation of jobs in the normal course of business;
- Preserving [or improving] the environment;
- Improving human health;
- Promoting the arts, sciences, or advancement of knowledge; Increasing the flow of capital to entities with a public benefit;
- Accomplishing any other particular [identifiable] benefit for society or the environment.

The statutes all declare that the general or specific public benefits that benefit corporations pursue "are in the best interests of the corporation," seemingly conclusively. In addition, the benefit corporation statutes define how directors ought to make decisions and provide additional liability shields.

Directorial Obligations and Protections

Each statute explains the obligations of benefit corporation directors. They are *required* to consider the impact of their decisions on shareholders, employees of the corporation, subsidiaries, and suppliers, "customers [to the extent they are] beneficiaries of the general or specific public benefit purposes of the benefit corporation," the community, society, and the local and global environment. Unless the benefit corporation's charter specifies otherwise, directors may base their decisions on any one or combination of these groups or interests.

The statutes also specifically provide directors of benefit corporations with immunity from liability for performance of their duties within the broad discretion given to them by statute and provide that no duty of such a director runs to the corporations' beneficiaries.

This broad discretion—modeled on nonshareholder constituency statutes for business corporations—can be faulted for giving directors unbridled discretion, with which they might pursue social good or might pursue foolish or self-serving practices. Some later-enacted statutes suggest specific concerns about protecting benefit directors in the takeover context, requiring directors to consider "the short-term and long-term interests of the benefit corporation, including benefits that may accrue to the benefit corporation from its long-term plans and the possibility that these interests may be best served by the continued independence of the benefit corporation." Thus, directors of benefit corporations appear protected from personal liability on claims that they have insufficiently produced public benefits or inadequately pursued profits for shareholders, whether in the context of ordinary business decisions or control transactions.

Third-Party Standard-Setters

To distinguish corporate purposes and directorial obligations in business corporations and benefit corporations, only corporations pursuing a general (and perhaps also specific) public benefit can qualify as benefit corporations. To make these initial determinations, the benefit corporation statutes delegate this responsibility to third-party standard-setters. All the statutes anticipate that such third parties will make available standards "for defining, reporting, and assessing" the social and environmental performance of aspiring benefit corporations – though without specifying minimum content for such standards. Instead, the statutes simply mandate that standard-setters be independent and transparent.

B Lab—an independent non-profit—has been deeply committed to and involved with the passage of benefit corporation statutes. Its survey and audit processes are described online to fit the transparency requirements. B Lab evaluates potential B corporations using the B Impact Assessment, which looks at issues of corporate accountability, employee policy, products' benefit to consumers, the company's relationship with its community, and its impact on the environment. The assessment contains a total of two-hundred points, and companies must score eighty points to be certified and granted access to the B Corp mark. B Lab also audits twenty percent of those companies who qualify for B Corp certification every two years.

Enforcement

Whether or not B Lab is joined by other standard-setters, the benefit corporation is also subject to self-enforcement. The statutes impose disclosure obligations upon benefit corporations, requiring them to provide annual benefit reports to their shareholders and to post them on their public websites—and sometimes to file them with a state office. The statutes describe the contents of this report differently, but all require timely benefit reports including elements of description and assessment. Assessment requires each benefit corporation to consider and report how well it performed in accordance with its third-party standard as compared with prior performance.

In addition, benefit corporation statutes create a special right of action often called a "benefit enforcement proceeding" to enforce the special duties of benefit corporation directors and officers and the public benefit purposes of the corporation. The statutes limit potential plaintiffs in benefit enforcement proceedings to shareholders entitled to bring derivative actions and, in some cases other groups, if specified in a corporation's charter.

As yet, there is no case law addressing the obligations of benefit corporation fiduciaries, and the statutes do not speak to how courts should analyze such claims. One commentator argues that "the core duty of the benefit corporation can be defined as the duty to secure profits for the shareholders while considering the socially beneficial purposes of the corporation." But without greater legislative explanation or judicial interpretation, it remains difficult to provide guidance to fiduciaries in situations where profit and social benefit goals conflict.

Conclusion

The benefit corporation is thus significantly different from both traditional nonprofit and for-profit business forms and from other hybrid forms. By retaining traditional business purposes and adding the requirement of pursuing general public benefit, the benefit corporation allows entities to pursue a dual mission of both profit and social good.

The benefit corporation also differs in substantial ways from other hybrids currently available. Unlike the United Kingdom's CIC, the benefit corporation may offer investors unlimited midstream and residual returns and is subject to no government regulation of its purposes or activities. These attributes are shared by L3Cs, but the benefit corporation has more rigid governance structures than the almost fully flexible governance by contract in an L3C. The benefit corporation also requires greater disclosure than the L3C. These disclosure and fiduciary authorization mandates also represent a divergence from the B Corp structure, though B Corps and benefit corporations share the fundamental idea of third-party review of public benefit purposes – and an idea not found in either the CIC or L3C.

II. Assessing The Benefit Corporation

Fundamentally, founders and operators of social enterprises unsatisfied with traditional nonprofit or for-profit forms seek a type of organization that will legally establish their sense of a dual profit-making and social mission and enforce it over time. They would also like a hybrid form to expand the range of funding streams they can effectively access. Further, they seek to use the hybrid form as part of their effort to brand their social enterprises to enable them to market their products and services to consumers, business partners, and others as special and different from those offered by typical nonprofit charities and for-profit businesses. Will benefit corporations accomplish these goals?

Articulating and Enforcing a Dual Mission

The Limitations of Traditional Forms. One might think social entrepreneurs could use traditional nonprofit or for-profit forms to house their dual mission enterprises. After all, nonprofit forms do not bar profit-making. These forms do, however, dramatically cabin profit distribution under the nondistribution constraint, which is imposed by state law (and tax-exemption rules) and prevents distributing net profits to shareholders, other investors, directors, and officers. Therefore, if a social entrepreneur wishes to distribute profits to investors, a nonprofit form is a nonstarter.

The problems with adopting a traditional for-profit form for social enterprise are more complex and arise from both legal and nonlegal sources. At inception, it appears permissible to include charitable or social goals as part of a corporation's purposes. Yet, anecdotal reports suggest that in some states, inclusion of such goals as a major component of corporate purposes may stall or block acceptance of articles by the secretary of state. Typically, LLC law will be flexible enough to allow adoption of both profit and social purposes, though partnership statutes requiring a "business purpose" may create barriers to social enterprises in that form.

Still, there are concerns that in a social enterprise formed as a traditional for-profit, fiduciaries will be hemmed in by their responsibilities to pursue profits for owners. There is considerable debate about the degree to which for-profit fiduciaries may properly pursue other purposes without breaching their duties. Even those who argue that for-profits possess substantial leeway to pursue social goals seem to be arguing about the edges of for-profit activity, not its core.

If a for-profit social enterprise wants to draw market-rate investors, its dual mission will be squarely put at risk. Consensus favoring a dual mission can easily break down and market-rate investors may refuse to invest or quickly or detrimentally sell off their ownership stakes. Rather than fearing litigation, the founder of a for-profit social enterprise may instead worry about locking in a dual mission legacy, about sufficient access to capital, or both. Dual mission is not easily embedded in traditional for-profit forms.

Ideally, a hybrid organization would offer a solution to this dual mission dilemma. To solve it, a hybrid form of organization should provide guidance on which goal, profit maximization or social good production, has priority and in what situations this priority must be given. This does not necessarily mean that either profit maximization or social good production must be prioritized every time the two come into conflict. Instead, the structure must work predictably and relatively transparently, and there must be some method for enforcing it.

The Benefit Corporation and Dual Mission Articulation. When one thinks more deeply about how a dual mission will be articulated in a benefit corporation doubts emerge. The requirement of general public benefit is vague and undefined. The determination of whether a particular organization's goals pursue a general public benefit is left to an unregulated third-party standard-setter. Moreover, the statutes provide no baseline or guidance for the standards these third parties should use to make this determination; they require only transparency and independence. If a standard-setter clearly and transparently sets low standards, it may qualify unrelated entities to form as benefit corporations just as would a standard-setter with higher standards, leaving the door open to greenwashing or even fraud. At the moment, benefit corporations require only formal articulation of a dual mission, and oversight over the genuineness of these statements is lacking.

The Benefit Corporation and Dual Mission Enforcement. Third-party standard-setters, fiduciaries, and shareholders all play enforcement roles in the benefit corporation. Although standard-setters are initial gatekeepers, their role in ongoing enforcement is less clear. For example, while the statutes envision public benefit assessments in annual benefit reports made with reference to the third-party standard, none specifies whether or how standard-setters should be involved in vetting public-benefit provision after incorporation.

As for shareholders, outside the context of transformation to fully for-profit status, the statutes offer little guidance to shareholders or fiduciaries on the thorny issue of how profit and social good should be balanced. They allow directors to forego profit maximization in favor of social good production or vice versa, but they do not instruct directors on how to exercise this broad discretion. Thus, the statutes impose no clear framework for directorial decision making. Without one, it is difficult to identify a metric by which shareholders might enforce fiduciaries' compliance with dual mission.

Shareholders of all benefit corporations retain the informational, voting, and litigation rights of ordinary shareholders. Any of these rights could, theoretically, be used to enforce dual mission. Benefit corporation shareholders may demand to inspect corporate books and records beyond the benefit report to determine how a particular mission conflict was resolved. They may vote out directors who fail to sufficiently pursue their favored balance of profits and mission. They may even sue directors for a failure to meet their special fiduciary obligations under the statute, and the later-enacted statutes also provide for the benefit enforcement proceeding.

Still, shareholders are unlikely to be assiduous and consistent enforcers. Their ability to obtain damages to redress faulty directorial decisions is significantly limited by ordinary fiduciary liability concepts like the business judgment rule and will be further frustrated by benefit directors' broad and unguided discretion and immunity. Moreover, benefit corporation shareholders have an additional reason not to engage in enforcement of dual mission—or at least a serious potential bias toward one-half of it. If a benefit corporation begins veering away from its dual mission to achieve greater profits, shareholders stand to gain financially from this decision.

The statutes uniformly exclude other potential parties from engaging in enforcement through litigation. Beneficiaries and the public will not have standing to challenge actions by benefit corporation directors. This position resonates with the traditionally extremely limited standing to challenge actions by nonprofit corporate directors. This policy is justified as necessary in order to recruit directors, which are most often uncompensated, to serve on nonprofit boards. However, the nonprofit context provides for government enforcement by state attorneys general and, for exempt nonprofits, the IRS. There is no regulatory role for any public official in the benefit corporation.

The Benefit Corporation's Disclosure Model

The benefit corporation form relies significantly on disclosure, both to amplify dual mission articulation and to lubricate enforcement. The benefit report gives shareholders and the public an opportunity to view how the entity reacts to situations in which profit and social mission conflict. Whether these recipients of disclosure will actively enforce is not yet known.

In terms of disclosure, benefit corporations occupy a sort of middle ground between the situations of traditional nonprofit and for-profit entities. On the one hand, benefit corporations must issue self-styled disclosures about public benefit provision to shareholders and allow for public review, a different kind of transparency than would be required of a nonprofit. Nonprofits must provide standardized annual reports on their charitable activities to state attorneys general and, if they are tax-exempt, they must submit annual informational tax returns to the IRS and make them public. The level and contents of required disclosures for benefit corporations should provide greater transparency on how a dual mission is being managed than would be available from a standard for-profit corporation, partnership, or LLC. Benefit corporation disclosures are thus fairly robust and are certainly more closely tailored to address dual mission performance than either nonprofit or for-profit disclosures.

Conclusion. In sum, the benefit corporation form is effective in allowing social enterprises formally to articulate a dual mission. In terms of enforcement, the benefit corporation usefully limits movement in and out of dual mission status by its shareholder vote requirements but gives little guidance on enforcing dual mission outside of the ultimate exit question. Third-party standard-setters could take a more active role here, but they need not do so under the statutes. Benefit corporation statutes expressly permit, but do not require, the pursuit of social goals over profit, and bend over backwards to protect fiduciaries from liability for their decisions. In this context, shareholder enforcement will be challenging and shareholders themselves may become biased toward profit goals or be bought out by others seeking financial over social gains.

Expanding Funding Streams

Founders or operators of social enterprises can opt to form their entities as traditional nonprofit corporations or as one of various for-profit organizational forms. Yet, any of these choices will limit the funding streams available to their enterprises.

Due to the nondistribution constraint, equity capital will not be available to social enterprises formed as nonprofits, but they can obtain capital through donations, income earned on investments, or sales of goods and services, and borrowing. Further, although nonprofits may borrow, banks and other lenders may be less willing to lend to nonprofits or require more onerous terms from them due to an accurate or mistaken impression of the organization's financial risk or its lack of an equity cushion.

Organizing as a traditional for-profit entity will give social entrepreneurs access to equity and debt, but a social entrepreneur using a for-profit form may find it difficult to convince arms-length investors to take equity positions, and it may be hard to obtain loans without offering personal guarantees or collateral. Using traditional business forms may avoid some concerns among investors or lenders about the incentives of the entity and its leaders to succeed financially and to repay its debts.

A for-profit form also limits access to donated funds. Adopting a traditional business form bars tax-exemption and eligibility for deductible contributions. This is so regardless of whether an entity pursues social purposes or charitable activity. Of course, forming as a for-profit will not necessarily preclude all socially-motivated sources of revenue. Cause-related marketing campaigns—like the RED campaign to combat AIDS in Africa—have raised millions of dollars through sales by purely for-profit corporations. If hybrid forms can ease access to donations and other socially-motivated funding sources, social entrepreneurs will prefer them to traditional for- profit forms.

The benefit corporation statutes do not speak expressly to the question of financing, but adopters of this form would certainly be ineligible to receive deductible contributions. Rater, benefit corporations can pursue the funding sources available to traditional for-profits. In this pursuit, the dual mission embedded in the form may or may not prove advantageous. The benefit corporation form seems likely to draw potential investors and lenders' attention to the dual mission of the organization. On the one hand, this may make those motivated purely by profit even more hesitant to invest or lend to a benefit corporation than to a for profit social enterprise. On the other hand, it may attract potential investors or lenders who are interested in combining their financial contributions with a purchase of social good.

The indeterminate ability of the benefit corporation form to expand funding streams is not unusual in the hybrid space. None of the other current hybrid forms can offer tax deductions to donors. Likewise, none of the hybrids appear much more likely to attract market-rate investors. CICs offer only capped dividends and lock remaining assets into the community benefit stream; thus, its investments are simply not on par with market-rate products. The L3C is amenable to tranched investment, which some believe will enable it to draw investors seeking market-rate returns. But without providing governance or other guarantees to market-rate investors, I am skeptical that they will view L3C investment as a substitute for market-rate products. Thus, to my mind, the L3C, like the CIC, the B Corp, and the benefit corporation, is likely to draw in new investment capital only from the socially-motivated category of investors.

Sustainability

Finally, social entrepreneurs may also see a hybrid form as providing their enterprises with greater sustainability than traditional nonprofit or for-profit forms can offer. Of course, sustainability can mean many different things. When thinking about sustainable development, the UN Brundtland commission defined it as "meeting the needs of the present without compromising the ability of future generations to meet their own needs." When researching sustainable corporations, one quickly runs across ideas like the triple bottom line (economic, social, and environmental outcomes) or the 3-P model (People, Profit, Planet). These ideas clearly resonate with the fundamental ideas of a social enterprise, melding pursuit of profits with social good, often including environmental goals. But the benefit corporation form is not there yet. This new hybrid form must allow social enterprises to articulate and enforce dual missions, to obtain greater access to capital, and to brand themselves to consumers and partners as distinct and special entities offering distinct and special products, in order to truly embody the sustainable corporation.

Conclusion

The benefit corporation will not yet achieve all of the goals social enterprises desire from a hybrid form. Benefit corporation statutes have opened up a place for social enterprises to legally articulate their dual mission, and have guarded the ultimate exit from the hybrid form with significant shareholder voting requirements. Leaving all content to unregulated standard-setters and providing little guidance or enforcement apparatus for midstream decision making, however, does not do enough to ensure benefit corporations can enforce a dual mission over time. Thoughtful founders and leaders of social enterprises considering the benefit corporation form will consider whether investors, consumers, partners, and employees will find this balance and brand appealing. Until a hybrid form is created that clearly and powerfully enforces dual mission, though, I believe access to expanded capital and sustainability will remain elusive.

Widespread Adoption and B-Lab

Maryland enacted the first benefit-corporation statute in 2008. Since then, more than 40 states have adopted these statutes. See B-Lab, Benefit Corporation 101.

In addition, a certifying organization B-Lab has arisen. B-Lab, a nonprofit corporation, certifies the structural and operational "public benefit" attributes of benefit corporations. Benefit corporations, once organized under state corporate statutes, that are certified by B-Lab are referred to as "B-corporations."

Benefit corporations not certified by B-Lab are often referred to simply as "registered benefit corporations" – that is, corporations incorporated (registered) as a benefit corporation.

A recent book extols the B-Lab model:

> B Lab's strategy is to build and organize a network of private companies on the foundation of parity between profit and purpose. It works toward two central goals: (1) to organize a community of B economy leaders and practitioners, and (2) to create the legal basis, state by state and nation by nation, for B corporations that commit irreversibly to the dual roles of business.
>
> Today, B Lab reports that more than 50,000 nonprofit and for-profit companies in at least 60 nations are using its assessment tool to measure progress toward the dual goals of performance and purpose. They include international brands, such as Dannon (yogurt), Patagonia (outdoor clothing and gear), and Eileen Fisher (women's clothing); prominent social enterprises, such as Ben & Jerry's (ice cream) and Kickstarter (online fundraising); and many other smaller ventures. They also include progressive financial institutions, such as Amalgamated Bank, Virginia Community Capital, and Beneficial State Bank.
>
> One other thing makes B Lab different: its success at passing benefit corporation statutes in 34 states with broad bipartisan support. The laws offer systemic, state-specific ways to set up and run for-profit businesses without favoring investors over all others. B Corporations meet requirements in their legal documents that commit them to producing positive impacts on society, workers, their communities, and the environment. By embedding benefit obligations, they are telling investors, lenders, employees, customers, and others that their responsibility is not solely to produce profits for investors.

Keith Mestrich & Mark A. Pinsky, *Why Thousands of Companies Are Turning Their Backs on a Business Doctrine That's Been Accepted for Decades*, Inc. Magazine (Nov. 2019).

Model Benefit Corporation Law

In addition, model benefit-corporation legislation has been drafted to create greater uniformity. See Model Benefit Corporation Legislation (with Explanatory Notes) (2017). Some have argued for using benefit corporations in settings such as health care where the profit-motive is at odds with the nature of the enterprise. See Yaniv Heled, Liza Vertinsky & Cassady V. Brewer, *Why Healthcare Companies Should Be(Come) Benefit Corporations* (2019) [available on SSRN] (arguing that "our broken health care system"—in which the United States spends more on healthcare per capita than any other country, yet has relatively poor health outcomes—arises from "the inherent problem with relying on profit-focused corporations to drive healthcare innovation and provide healthcare services and products; instead, the benefit-corporation form would more closely align private incentives with public need").

Delaware's "Public Benefit Corporation"

Delaware has also gotten on the benefit corporation bandwagon. In 2013, Delaware surprised the corporate sustainability movement by amending its corporate statute to allow entities to incorporate as a "public benefit corporation." Like benefit corporations elsewhere, Delaware's benefit corporations are a new hybrid corporate form that requires managers to balance shareholders' financial interests with the best interests of stakeholders materially affected by the corporation's conduct—and to produce a public benefit. What has been the early experience in Delaware with this new business form? According to a study, during the first 90 days of the Delaware statute, 55 public benefit corporations were incorporated or converted in Delaware as follows:

- 74 percent of these new corporations were in early stages of operation
- 31 percent provided professional services (such as consulting, legal, financial, architectural design); 11peercent were in the technology and education sectors; 10 percent produced consumer retail products; 9 percent were in the healthcare sector
- 35 percent of these corporations could have alternatively incorporated as a charitable nonprofit exempt from federal income tax.

Role of corporate lawyer

It has been pointed out that lawyers for social enterprises face particular challenges. Not only are the types of such entities in flux, but so too are the business/investment expectations. Lawyers must be aware of the differences that arise in social enterprise not only when the entity is formed, but also during its ongoing internal governance. The "complex and novel set of [social enterprise] laws" calls on corporate lawyers to use their "contextual reasoning skills." Joan Macleod Heminway, *Lawyering for Social Enterprise* (2019) [available on SSRN].

A Look to Europe

In a similar vein, governments in Europe have been a major driver of "institutionalized CSR"—that is, getting corporations to implement triple-bottom line concepts—precisely because governments have been explicit about what they expect from corporations. European success in the CSR movement is largely due to explicit legislative standards and encouragement of businesses to meet the standards through their reporting on CSR. Studies have found that greater government concern with reporting and verifying CSR leads to better results in these areas.

But a recent study from Italy suggests that hybrid forms, such as benefit corporations, may be less effective in creating a broad CSR focus. Instead, such forms simply create a more customer-focused company.

> Lawmakers from all over the world are increasingly looking at new ways to foster socially and environmentally responsible conduct on the part of corporations and other for-profit enterprises. New hybrid entities have emerged that rely on corporate governance rules to combine profit and social goals without prioritizing either of the two—including the US benefit corporation and its Italian counterpart, the società benefit. The extent to which they improve the existing tools to foster corporate social responsibility varies depending on the legal system. Under both systems, however, hybrid organizational forms may do more to help consumers, users, and clients, than to support other non-shareholder constituencies.

Chiara Picciau, *Fostering Corporate Social Responsibility Through Hybrid Organizational Forms: A Comparison Between the United States and Italy* (2019) [available on SSRN].

4.1.4 Assessments of Emergent Benefit Corporation

As you can see, there is a lively debate on whether benefit corporations accomplish what they are meant to accomplish. Some have argued that in its current form the benefit corporation is not a panacea, but with some more oversight and financial engineering (such as the use of convertible debt instruments), it has potential. Others question whether benefit corporations, which are voluntary, can be the answer to corporate irresponsibility—arguing for a "bolder approach" to structural corporate reform.

Soon after Delaware's "public benefit corporation" statute was enacted, then-Chief Justice Leo Strine of the Delaware Supreme Court concluded that benefit corporations (particularly in Delaware) may create a structure for business managers to "do the right thing," compared to the "current corporate accountability structure" in which shareholders are the only constituency given enforceable corporate rights. Strine found benefit corporations to represent an "incremental change" in corporate accountability. Looking at the Delaware benefit corporation statute, he saw a meaningful shift in the balance of power toward a structure in which corporate managers become subject to enforceable duties to "do the right thing." Leo Strine, *Making It Easier for Directors to "Do the Right Thing"?* (2014) [available on SSRN].

Securities offer or charitable solicitation?

Benefit corporations, which occupy a space between the for-profit business firm and the nonprofit organization, raise several novel issues. For example, when a benefit corporation raises money, is it subject to the capital formation rules applicable to for-profit firms (such as federal securities regulation) or to the charitable solicitation rules applicable to nonprofit charities—or both? Specifically, are social enterprises "charitable organizations" whose fundraising constitute the "solicitation" of charitable contributions or are they exempted from the solicitation rules as "commercial co-venturers"? Among other things, subjecting social enterprises to the charitable solicitation rules would require an enforcement mechanism to hold such enterprises accountable to their stated social and environmental goals. See Robert Esposito, *Charitable Solicitation Acts : Maslow's Hammer for Regulating Social Enterprise* (2015) [available on SSRN] (arguing that social enterprises should be seen as *sui generis* and regulated as a new "animal").

Thus, the benefit-corporation movement raises a number of questions. First, have the early benefit corporations been credible— that is, has the initial wave of entrepreneurs who chose the benefit-corporation form been genuinely committed to CSR? Second, have benefit corporation shareholders (the only constituency with enforceable rights) voted their long-term social/environmental consciences instead of insisting on short-term financial gains? Third, will benefit corporations pass the "going public" test by convincing public investors of their long-term financial viability?

Mixed Early Evidence on Benefit Corporations

In looking at the first decade of US benefit corporations, Professor Ronald Colombo (Hofstra Law) concludes that the "benefit corporation statutes do not materially change the rules of corporate governance. Rather, they simply explicitly permit benefit corporations to conduct themselves according to standards of conduct that traditional corporate law statutes already implicitly permit." Ronald Colombo, *Taking Stock of the Benefit Corporation* (2019) [available on SSRN] (appendix chart compares benefit corporation statutes in 34 adopting states). In short, changes in Corporate America's views on the corporation's purpose may have resulted in "a normative shift in corporate decision making . . . on a far broader scale."

Despite Chief Justice Strine's hopeful assessment of the Delaware benefit corporation, a recent article questions whether the benefit corporation is positioned to accept investment dollars from investors seeking a "warm glow" when they make social-purpose investments, whether helping the homeless like ArtLifting, PBC or helping the environment like Patagonia, Inc. The author, a business school professor, asserts that "benefit corporations are being held back by one serious flaw: a patchwork of unworkable [state-by-state] disclosure rules."

> The existing rules fail to inform investors what their financial and social return will be (and thus have the perverse impact of discouraging investment by socially conscious investors), and likewise fail to inform the broader public whether the corporation is living up to its stated benefit purpose.
>
> Instead, there should be a uniform disclosure regime that applies to all benefit corporations. The regime would standardize disclosure, and thus allows stakeholders (both investors and the broader public) to compare and contrast competing firms. Further, the proposed regime would have an enforcement mechanism that would allow both investors and the broader public to ensure that benefit corporations are providing the required disclosure.

Brent J. Horton, *Rising to Their Full Potential: How a Uniform Disclosure Regime Will Empower Benefit Corporations* (2019) [available on SSRN].

Others have questioned whether the benefit corporation structure is actually needed, given the fulsome capacity of the for-profit corporation. Why bother with a benefit corporation when a for-profit corporation can provide a comparable, if not identical, structure in its articles? See Joseph Yockey, *Does Social Enterprise Law Matter?* (2015) [available on SSRN]. For this reason, some states have not adopted benefit corporation legislation—North Carolina among them.

So, as you can see, there is a swirling debate on whether benefit corporations are a new hope for reforming capitalism or a thinly disguised ruse for exploiting investors and customers. What sort of investment is occurring in benefit corporation? Is it different from ordinary early-stage investment? A recent study finds:

> Benefit corporations are receiving investment at significant rates, and that investment is coming from typical sources of venture capital including traditional, profit-seeking VC firms such as Sequoia Capital, Andreessen Horowitz, and others. We also find that venture capital funds are investing in more consumer-facing industries, as well as investing smaller amounts than traditional investments.

Michael B. Dorff, James Hicks & Steven Davidoff Solomon, *The Future of Fancy? An Empirical Study of Public Benefit Corporations* (2019)[available on SSRN].

The study's authors conclude that benefit corporations are in their infancy and until there is more experience with this new business form "investment in [benefit corporations] is likely to remain siloed in smaller, newly formed firms."

A recent study by Professor Ellen Berrey, a sociologist at the University of Toronto, throws cold water on the benefit-corporation party. As of 2018, Berrey counted 7,704 benefit corporations that had been formed in the United States since 2010—with Oregon, New York, Nevada, Delaware, and Colorado leading the way. Ellen Berrey, *Social Enterprise Law in Action: Organization Characteristics of U.S. Benefit Corporations* (2018) [available on SSRN]. She found, however, "a lot of inactivity and that a substantial portion of benefit corporations are not evidently delivering any social or environmental benefits." Of the firms with an online presence, she found that 71 percent did not even describe themselves as benefit corporations. In short, given the lack of oversight, the benefit-corporation movement "would seem to have fallen short of its transformative promise to upend the prevailing model of shareholder supremacy."

Social Enterprise "Platforms"

The benefit corporation is not the only game in town for bringing those committed to sustainability together. Lately, beyond the privately-held social enterprise is the emergence of "platforms" that facilitate and coordinate connections among users committed to social responsibility. Here's an explanation:

> A significant development in the global economy over the last two decades has been the emergence of "platform businesses" that use digital and emerging technologies to facilitate connections between groups of users. Think Amazon (connecting buyers and sellers), Facebook (connecting friends and family), or Uber (connecting service providers and service users). These companies have become the largest in the world, leading other companies to consider integrating platform ideas into their operations.
>
> We identify the distinctive features of a "platform business model" and introduce the concept of a "sustainable platform"—a platform-style business that is both innovative and socially responsible. We, however, find a "disconnect" between the current business needs and values of sustainable platforms and contemporary policies and regulation—particularly their corporate governance.

Mark Fenwick & Erik P.M. Vermeulen, *A Sustainable Platform Economy & the Future of Corporate Governance* (2019) [available on SSRN].

4.1.5 Effect of "Social Focus" Directives on Manager Behavior

As you may have noticed, an underlying assumption of the social enterprise movement is that we do the right thing when instructed to do the right thing. But is this true? How do people behave when they are asked to do good? That is, after reading a CSR mission statement for a social enterprise (like a benefit corporation), do business people actually engage in meaningful CSR?

To answer this question, a study from Germany looked at whether human subjects (German college students) changed their "sharing" propensities when presented with a "stakeholder norm" (a statement similar to the "other constituency" statutes described before) or were they more moved by incentives (the possibility of being allowed to continue in a game in which they made money).

The study's findings are both expected and surprising. First, when a person (as principal) gives away their own money, they are somewhat generous. Second, when an agent/manager gives away another's money (the principal's money), the agent/manager is generally even more generous than the principal. Third, the agent/manager becomes comparatively stingy when they know the "principal" might replace them for being too generous. Fourth, and this might be surprising, the agent/manager actually gives away even less money when they are read instructions about being generous to others—whether or not they can be replaced by the principal.

Here's how the German management professors explained the results of their study:

> How do barely incentivized norms impact incentive-rich environments? We look at social enterprise legislation that establishes rules on behalf of constituencies that have no institutionalized means of enforcing them. By relying primarily on managers' other-regarding concerns whilst leaving corporate incentive structures unaltered, how effective can such legislation be? This question is vital for the ongoing debate about social enterprise forms, as recently introduced in several US states and in British Columbia, Canada.
>
> We ran a laboratory experiment with a framing likened to German corporate law, which traditionally includes social standards. Our results show that a stakeholder provision, as found in both Germany and the US, cannot overcome material incentives. However, even absent incentives the stakeholder norm does not foster other-regarding behavior, but slightly inhibits it instead. Our experiment thus illustrates the paramount importance of taking into account both incentives and framing effects when designing institutions.

Sven Fischer, Sebastian J. Goerg & Hanjo Hamann, *Cui Bono, Benefit Corporation? An Experiment Inspired by Social Enterprise Legislation in Germany & US* (2015) [available on SSRN].

Based on the findings in this study, it seems benefit corporations might not accomplish what they are meant to. Just because benefit-corporation directors are told to "do good" does not necessarily mean they will—and, in fact, it might lead them to do less good than if told nothing.

Alter brain chemistry?

According to a recent study, "sharing" can be induced by changing the chemistry of subjects' brains. That is, law may not be the only way to induce a greater sense of "otherness." The chemical? Dopamine—the chemical that causes our brain to believe in conspiracy theories.

* * *

Concluding Thoughts

Is Past Prologue?

One day a young man walked into a village. He noticed an old woman hanging clothes on a clothesline in front of her house. He approached her and asked, "Excuse me, ma'am. I have a question." The woman looked up from her work. "Yes, please tell me. What is your question?" The young man said, "Well, I'm thinking of moving to this village, and I wanted to know what it's like." The woman answered, "Tell me about the village where you now live." The young man said, "It's really not that nice. People treat each other unkindly. It's a difficult place to live. I'm ready to get out." The woman paused and looked at the young man, "I think that you'll find this village to be quite the same."

Later that day, another young man walked into the village. Seeing the woman on her porch knitting, he approached her and asked, "Ma'am, excuse me. May I ask you a question?" The woman looked up from her knitting, "Yes, what is your question?" The young man said, "I'm thinking of moving to this village, and I'm wondering what it's like." The woman asked, "And what is the village like that you're now living in?" The man said, "Well, it's quite nice. The people are friendly. Everyone gets along. But I think it's time for me to make a change." The woman paused and looked at the young man, "I think that you'll find this village to be quite the same."

* * *

You see, our past experiences and even our disposition (think SWM corporation) are likely to color our perception of present experiences (think benefit corporation). That is, our experiences in a village in which we once lived—whether not so nice or actually quite good—may lead us to view a new village in the same way.

Maybe the goal should not be benefit corporations, but instead maybe the goal should be to inculcate attitudes of otherness in shareholder capitalism—so that it takes on the feel of stakeholder capitalism.

Chapter 4.2

ESG Disclosure

This chapter continues our look at proposals and some initial steps to redesign the legal contours of the corporation to be more sustainable. We consider how and whether disclosure mandates might be used to focus management attention on ESG matters, thus leaning on the business maxim that "what gets measured gets managed."

We start by looking at a 2010 interpretive guidance by the SEC directing public companies to identify when the risks and opportunities of climate change are "material" to investors, thus requiring disclosure in SEC filings. But, soon after, the SEC exited the fray, failing to follow-up on enforcing the disclosure standards identified in the guidance.

Nonetheless, many institutional shareholders became increasingly interested in having their portfolio companies describe not only climate risks faced by the company, but also other ESG factors. In fact, the Institutional Shareholder Services (the world's largest proxy advisory firm) answered the call of institutional clients by creating multi-factor "scores" of ESG disclosures by companies. And, putting the heat on institutional shareholders, an initiative by Ceres (the NGO focused on corporate sustainability—see Chapter 4.3) and others sought to measure how well institutional shareholders consider and act upon ESG factors in their investing and voting decisions. That is, while the SEC and its leadership on disclosure stumbled, actors in the financial markets have picked up the slack.

Then, in 2022, the SEC again entered the arena with a proposal to mandate climate-related information. The proposal, which deals only with climate-related risks, would require publicly traded companies to describe: (1) the company's governance of climate-related risk and related risk-management processes; (2) how climate-related risks might affect the company's business and financial performance in the short-, medium-, and long-term; (3) how climate-related risks are likely to affect the company's strategy and business model; and (4) how climate events (storms, droughts, rising temperatures, and so on) and company transition activities are likely to affect the company's finances. Companies would also be required to describe their direct GHG emissions (Scope 1), their indirect GHG emissions (Scope 2), and their GHG emissions from downstream-suppliers and upstream-customers (Scope 3). The rule, if adopted, would go into effect fully in 2024.

Large institutional shareholders, as might be expected, seem not interested in waiting that long. Many are pressuring companies in their portfolios to begin full-fledged, climate-related, and other ESG disclosure immediately. And many companies, feeling this pressure, have begun "integrated reporting"—that is, single reports that combine the financial-type reporting required by current SEC rules (such as the annual Form 10-K) and ESG-type reporting that once was relegated to corporate social responsibility (CSR) reports. Investors view both sets of information as critical to evaluating a company's earnings potential and risk profile.

In short, the financial markets are now ahead of government in moving corporations toward sustainability. It's a new era.

Chapter's Focus

You should become familiar with the arguments for and against using corporate disclosure as a corporate governance tool—that is, as a tool to change behavior.

You will then learn about the 2010 SEC guidance on climate risk disclosure, which gave US public companies obligations with respect to disclosing regulatory, international treaty, product/service market, and operational risks related to climate change. You will want to focus on how some securities lawyers viewed the SEC guidance as a "new day" in corporate ESG disclosure, and how corporations failed to respond to the SEC guidance, continuing their practice of either not discussing climate risks or giving them cursory "boilerplate" treatment.

Next, you will want to consider how and why institutional shareholders—and the proxy advisory firms on which many rely for voting recommendations—have sought to have companies disclose their ESG practices and risks. This has led to an SEC proposal—somewhat similar to a rule already adopted by the EU for listed companies in Europe—that would mandate climate-related disclosures that until now have not been seen as relevant to "corporate finances."

Finally, you will want to consider the arguments for and against this SEC proposal and whether the financial markets (often using AI) are making SEC disclosure mandates somewhat irrelevant.

4.2.1 Disclosure as Corporate Governance Tool

Disclosure has long been used as a governance tool by the SEC to "cajole" management into new habits of corporate behavior. For example, disclosure requirements on the "independence" of directors compelled companies to be mindful and thus more proactive in putting non-management directors on the board. Other disclosure-based reform initiatives, such as those to address the upward spiral in executive pay and to determine the sourcing of "conflicts minerals" in Africa (especially the Congo) have had less success and have produced unintended consequences.

Consider the attempt in the Dodd-Frank Act of 2010 to rein in executive pay, which is far higher in the United States than any other developed country. Among other things, Dodd-Frank required public companies to the ratio of the CEO's pay package and that of the average worker. A recent article concluded that the "level of anger" of laypersons (leading them to want that someone "do something" about executive pay) "is determined exclusively by absolute levels of pay and by the median pay ratio disclosure, not by firm performance." Minor Myers & Justin Sevier, *The Paradox of Executive Compensation Regulation* (2019) [available on SSRN] (the authors assumed, perhaps naively, that "views of lay persons shape policy because politicians will be responsive to public opinion," rather than the attitudes of stock market participants who believe executive pay should be aligned with firm performance). Thus, the authors concluded that executive pay disclosure creates a paradox in which "the pay ratio disclosure [mandated by Dodd-Frank] undermines the policy goal of aligning pay with performance." Who is the corporation for, after all — the execs who run it or the people who work in it and who consume its products?

Beware of unintended consequences

The story of the unanticipated effects of the SEC disclosure rules on executive pay provide a reminder that sometimes the results of well-intentioned action are different from (even the opposite of) what was intended. The SEC's 1992 rules requiring greater details and discussion of corporate pay resulted not in a "chilling effect" on out-sized executive pay, but instead an upward spiral in such pay as corporate boards (now armed with data on how executives at "peer companies" were being compensated) sought to show that their executives—and by extension the directors themselves—were above average! Some called it the "Lake Wobegon" effect, referring to the fictional town created by Garrison Keillor where "all the children are above average." Aren't corporate execs sometimes like children?

4.2.2 SEC Climate Change Guidance (2010)

SEC Guidance

In 2010, the SEC issued a Guidance on Climate Change Disclosure. It described the growing importance of climate change (and the regulatory initiatives to control carbon emissions) on the assets and business operations of US public companies. It also identified the types of "forward looking" disclosures required of US companies, where management is asked to anticipate what the future holds for the company and its investors - in particular with respect to climate change.

A number of US law firms took notice of the SEC guidance and the impact it would have on company disclosure obligations. In addition, NGOs pointed out ways in which companies should be reporting climate change risk and opportunity noting that climate change in not only a risk, but also as a potential opportunity for business.

Company-by-company disclosure

Although the 2010 SEC guidance proved to be a flop, it nonetheless put the question of climate change disclosure on the corporate radar screen. For example, the failure of ExxonMobil to disclose the company's 1970s ground-breaking research (and knowledge) about the effect of GHG emissions on climate change has garnered much attention, including an investigation by the NY Attorney General into whether the company engaged in securities fraud by seeking to lead investors to believe the "science is unsettled." And, in 2017, a widely-followed shareholder proposal urging the company to prepare a report on company-specific climate risks garnered more than 60 percent shareholder support.

Assessment of SEC Guidance

After the SEC's 2010 guidance, Ceres kept tabs on how company disclosures were measuring up to expectations. In the decade after the guidance,

Climate disclosure boilerplate

The ExxonMobil 10-K annual report for 2014 identified the following two risk factors (of 17) related to climate change—the only discussion in the 10-K on the subject. Do you notice anything that investors didn't already know?

Climate change and greenhouse gas restrictions.
"Due to concern over the risk of climate change, a number of countries have adopted, or are considering the adoption of, regulatory frameworks to reduce greenhouse gas emissions. These include adoption of cap and trade regimes, carbon taxes, restrictive permitting, increased efficiency standards, and incentives or mandates for renewable energy. These requirements could make our products more expensive, lengthen project implementation times and reduce demand for hydrocarbons, as well as shifting hydrocarbon demand toward relatively lower-carbon sources such as natural gas. Current and pending greenhouse gas regulations may also increase our compliance costs, such as for monitoring or sequestering emissions."

Government sponsorship of alternative energy.
"Many governments are providing tax advantages and other subsidies and mandates to make alternative energy sources more competitive against oil and gas. Governments are also promoting research into new technologies to reduce the cost and increase the scalability of alternative energy sources. We are conducting our own research efforts into alternative energy, such as through sponsorship of the Global Climate and Energy Project at Stanford University and research into hydrogen fuel cells and fuel-producing algae. Our future results may depend in part on the success of our research efforts and our ability to adapt and apply the strengths of our current business model to providing the competitive energy products of the future."

companies did not take the SEC initiative seriously and most climate risk disclosures remained perfunctory, mostly boilerplate.

A scathing 88-page article written in 2015—which Ceres asked the author not to publish—described the failure of the SEC guidance and speculated on why it had flopped:

> In 2010 the SEC issued an interpretive guidance calling on public companies to take seriously their disclosure responsibilities with respect to climate risk. The guidance identified the SEC line-item rules that required discussion and analysis of how (1) climate change regulation, (2) international treaties, (3) shifting consumer and supplier demand, and (4) severe weather events could affect the company's bottom line. The guidance was met with great fanfare, with more than 50 corporate law firms sending special alerts to their clients describing the new disclosure initiative, with socially-focused investor groups declaring victory in putting climate change on the corporate agenda, and with the SEC announcing plans to intensify its focus on the issue.
>
> Then it all unraveled. Although corporate disclosure ticked up in the months after the guidance, it remained mostly boilerplate (with statements like "concerns about climate change could lead to additional regulations that could affect our business"). During the first years after the SEC guidance, fewer than three-fifths of companies in the S&P 500 mentioned climate change in their 10-K annual reports, most of these including only a short one-paragraph risk factor. Yet these same companies (more than 95%) provided extensive disclosure about the importance of climate change in their glossy CSR reports and many offered extensive CO2 emissions data in voluntary reports to various NGO clearinghouses.
>
> Why has climate change disclosure been anathema to corporate management in SEC filings, while becoming a mainstay of public relations and even voluntary environmental compliance? Rather than being treated as a business risk similar to compliance risk, climate change seems to have been cabined into a public relations hole.
>
> Why is this? Here are seven hypotheses: (1) SEC disclosure mandates on moral/ethical matters, such as response to climate change, engender management resentment; (2) the impact on a particular company of climate change, given its unprecedented

> nature, is nearly impossible to predict; (3) SEC filings (compared to voluntary CSR disclosures) carry liability risks; (4) voluntary climate disclosures, typically limited to specific activities (like carbon emissions), are more rewarding to corporate management; (5) company assessment of climate risk and opportunity is highly proprietary, perhaps even a key to business survival in many sectors; (6) sustainability issues, including those related to climate change, are not woven into the governance and operational fabric of modern business, making them hard to quantify, analyze and report; and (7) the SEC recognized that mandating a corporate focus on climate change is beyond its regulatory competence or its statutory mandate to regulate financial disclosures.
>
> The failure of the SEC Guidance makes clear that for climate change disclosure to be meaningful it must be an element of integrated corporate engagement with the issue. Like financial disclosure, climate change disclosure must arise from a systemic approach that includes identification, recognition, measurement, assessment, and auditing. Given the ongoing gridlock in our national regulatory system, it is unlikely climate change will receive systemic governmental attention. Instead, the real engine for abatement and adaptation will come from the private sector—and specifically from consortia of institutional shareholders and corporate management. How to engage corporate management and move climate change from the glossy back burner to the hot front burner is a great question of our time—perhaps the greatest. The SEC Guidance and its denouement make clear that regulatory mandates for disclosure of climate risk may be a necessary part of new structures of corporate engagement with climate change, but mandates alone cannot be sufficient.

Alan R. Palmiter, *Climate Change Disclosure: A Failed SEC Mandate* (2015) [available on SSRN].

Others have also questioned whether regulation of corporate governance (through disclosure mandates) can be effective. See Barnali Choudhury & Martin Petrin, *Corporate Governance that "Works for Everyone": Promoting Public Policies Through Corporate Governance Mechanisms* (2018) [available on SSRN] (concluding that "overreliance" on corporate governance disclosure requirements "to address societal issues is misguided," and arguing instead that corporate governance mechanisms should be seen as a "complementary strategy" with direct external regulation to equalise wealth distribution, promote labour equality, and pursue environmental goals).

SEC Foot-Dragging

During the 2010s, the SEC not only dragged its feet on climate change disclosure, but also "resisted reform or impeded shareholders' access to sought-after ESG information." Donna M. Nagy & Cynthia A. Williams, *ESG and Climate Change Blind Spots: Turning the Corner on SEC Disclosure* (2021) [available on SSRN]. Here's their list:

(1) the SEC's refusal to act on several rulemaking petitions submitted during the years 2009 to 2018, which called for expanded ESG disclosure;

(2) the SEC's grudging promulgation of rules concerning social disclosures as required by Congress in the Dodd-Frank Act of 2010;
(3) the SEC's 2020 revisions to SEC Rule 14a-8, which make the submission of shareholder proposals more difficult, thereby thwarting investor efforts to raise ESG concerns; and
(4) an SEC commitment beginning in 2016 to move away from line-item disclosure to a more principled-based system.

Why this foot-dragging in the face of "clear trends among investors reflecting the importance of ESG information"?

> The SEC either mistakenly assumed issuers already operate under an affirmative disclosure obligation when ESG information is material or more generally resisted the concept that much ESG information is material, decision-useful information using traditional definitions of "materiality." Specifically, many SEC officials adhered to an unduly narrow construction of the SEC's tripartite mission—to protect investors; maintain fair, orderly, and efficient capital markets; and facilitate capital formation—and they thereby regarded disclosure to effectuate social or political change as outside the scope of the agency's mission.

The authors then questioned the SEC's assumptions:

> In adopting the federal securities laws in the 1930s, Congress had a much broader understanding of the purposes of disclosure, which included giving shareholders information on how America's public companies were being managed and how companies and banks were exercising power—power that had profound effects on the American economy. Fundamentally, Congress sought mechanisms of corporate accountability, which is precisely what it sought to achieve in the Dodd-Frank ESG provisions, and what current investors are demanding through the shareholder-proposal process and through ESG-rulemaking petitions.

Doesn't the SEC understand its mission? It makes you wonder why even bother with the SEC to get climate risk and ESG disclosure right?

Climate Risk Disclosure in Europe

Interestingly, regulatory initiatives requiring ESG disclosure by public companies have fared somewhat better in other countries—especially in Europe, where a collapse of the Gulf Stream would be catastrophic to the continent.

For example, the "much debated and criticized" Section 172(1) of the UK Companies Act, which recognized a duty of directors to consider various stakeholders' interests and needs within the public company, has led UK courts to interpret the provision as creating a directorial duty to disclose non-financial CSR matters. See Sabrina Bruno, *The "Enlightened Shareholder Value" in UK Companies Ten Years Later: What the European Directive N. 2014/95/EC Can Do* (2015) [available on SSRN].

Further, this duty in UK companies was "brought to new life" by European Directive [2014/95/EU] (adopted in 2014 and applicable in 2017), which seeks to coordinate disclosure of non-financial information by having companies prepare non-financial statements on environmental, social and employee-related matters, respects for human rights, and anti-corruption/bribery matters. Large companies in Europe have heeded the Directive's call, with 95 percent of such companies producing "sustainability reports" containing information on ESG factors. Thus, the European directive (through its disclosure mandates) has been seen as "bringing ESG factors into companies' internal policies and procedures."

You can feast your eyes on how the EU keeps its directives short and sweet. Here's the operative article from the ESG disclosure directive:

> [Companies with more than 500 employees] shall include . . . a non-financial statement containing information to the extent necessary for an understanding of the [company's] development, performance, position and impact of its activity, relating to, as a minimum, environmental, social and employee matters, respect for human rights, anti-corruption and bribery matters, including: (a) [the company's] business model; (b) [the company's] policies pursued in relation to those matters, including due diligence processes implemented; (c) the outcome of those policies; (d) the principal risks related to those matters linked to the [company's] operations . . . and how the undertaking manages those risks; (e) non-financial key performance indicators relevant to the particular business.

By comparison, the SEC proposal to require ESG disclosure of public companies runs 490 pages—and its request for comments doesn't even propose an actual rule. But then, unlike the EU directive which was issued in 24 official languages, the SEC only used English.

4.2.3 Pressure on Companies to Disclose

ISS Scores on ESG Metrics

Even as the SEC's 2010 climate change guidance floundered, there arose a flurry of activity by institutional shareholders demanding *voluntary* corporate ESG disclosures—whatever the "corporate disclosure" regulator might or might not say. Below is a 2018 press release (and Q&A) from Institutional Shareholder Services describing the proxy advisory firm's initiative to score company disclosures on topics like climate change and human rights.

The ISS explains that the new ESG scores respond to growing institutional shareholder demand for assessments beyond company disclosures on executive pay and

ISS role in corporate governance

The ISS is a big deal in US and global corporate governance. Its voting recommendations typically swing corporate voting by about 25 percent—that is, a 60-40 vote "against" a corporate voting matter becomes a 53-47 vote in favor of the matter if the ISS issues a "for" recommendation. James Cotter, Alan Palmiter & Randall Thomas, *ISS Recommendations and Mutual Fund Voting on Proxy Proposals* (2010) [available on SSRN].

other governance issues. The ISS anticipates that shareholder clients will use its ESG scores to evaluate company transparency and how to vote on pay packages, director elections, and shareholder proposals. Initially, ISS said it would score about 1,500 companies in energy, materials, and other industries most exposed to ESG risks, with plans to expand coverage to more than 5,000 companies globally. See Bloomberg, BNA Corporate Law & Accountability Report (2/6/18).

Environmental, Social, and Governance Quality Scores to be Reflected in ISS Proxy Research Reports

(Feb. 5, 2018)

ROCKVILLE, M.D.—Institutional Shareholder Services Inc. (ISS), a leading provider of governance and responsible investment solutions to the global financial community, today announced the launch of Environmental & Social QualityScore, a new component of ISS' industry leading corporate profiling and scoring solution for institutional investors.

E&S QualityScore represents a data driven approach to measuring the quality of corporate disclosures on environmental and social issues, including sustainability governance, and to identify key disclosure omissions. Expectations regarding disclosure practices are defined by industry groups, based on the specific environmental and social risks identified in industry and multi-stakeholder initiatives and reflected in authoritative standards and recommendations from groups such as the Global Reporting Initiative, the Sustainability Accounting Standards Board and the Task Force on Climate-related Financial Disclosures.

Today's launch covers an initial set of 1,500 companies across industries viewed as being most exposed to E&S risks, including: Energy, Materials, Capital Goods, Transportation, Automobiles & Components, and Consumer Durables & Apparel. An additional 3,500 companies spanning 18 industries will be added later in 2018, bringing the total coverage universe to more than 5,000 companies, globally.

"With this launch, we are extremely pleased to respond to the growing demand from our institutional investor clients for high-quality data and analytics covering environmental and social topics," said ISS Chief Operating Officer, Stephen Harvey. "Investment professionals, who increasingly rely on extra-financial data and research for investment decision-making and portfolio risk mitigation, will benefit greatly when screening for companies where risks in operations, business, and supply lines are often latent."

Underpinning E&S QualityScore are more than 380 unique environmental and social factors under analysis of which at least 240 apply to each industry group. Like its governance counterpart, E&S QualityScore provides a score for each company in its coverage universe that measures the company's level of environmental and social governance disclosure risk, both overall and within eight broad categories. Broad topical areas under the E&S QualityScore methodology for environmental disclosures include: Management of Environmental Risks and Opportunities; Carbon and Climate; Natural Resources; and Waste and Toxicity. Meanwhile, Human Rights; Labor, Health, and Safety; Stakeholder and Society; and Product Safety, Quality, and Brand comprise topical areas for social-related disclosures.

An analysis of initial data underlying E&S QualityScore shows significant disparities in environmental and social disclosures by region, with European companies generally scoring far better on environmental factors compared with their peers in the Americas and Australasia.

"The launch of E&S QualityScore is an important milestone for institutions that turn to ISS for a fully integrated, global solution to aid in responsible investment portfolio construction," said Marija Kramer, Head of ISS-Ethix, the responsible investment arm of ISS. "Clients will now enjoy access to timely and accurate data on portfolio companies alongside robust solutions and services, including policy development, screening, research, and engagement."

Later this month, ISS' benchmark policy proxy research reports will include the subject company's top level scores under the E&S scoring methodology in addition to that for the company's corporate governance.

To learn more about E&S QualityScore, download a set of FAQs here and a companion Key Issues document here.

* * *

Environmental and Social QualityScore FAQ

SCORING OVERVIEW

What is E&S QualityScore Disclosure & Transparency Signal?
A data driven approach to measure the quality of corporate disclosure on environmental and social issues, including sustainability governance, and identify key disclosure omissions. Expectations regarding disclosure practices are defined by industry groups, based on the specific environmental and social risks identified in industry and multi-stakeholder initiatives and reflected in authoritative standards such as the Global Reporting Initiative (GRI), the Sustainability Accounting Standards Board (SASB) standards and the Task Force on Climate-related Financial Disclosures (TCFD) recommendations.

What are the E & S 1–10 scores based upon?
Consistent with the scoring for Governance QualityScore the decile scores, 1–10, represent a relative measure based on the raw score calculations of peer companies within a specific industry group. This process is conducted at each pillar category and at the overall pillar score level. Each category as well as the overall pillar score generates an independent range of scores and the resulting decile rankings. A score in the 1st decile indicates relatively higher quality disclosure and transparency practices and relatively fewer disclosure omissions, and conversely, a score in the 10th decile indicates key

disclosure omissions and relatively lower quality disclosure and transparence practices. What does the score measure? Scores measure the depth and extent of disclosure. This showcases the company's understanding of its environmental and social risks, along with its preparedness to face and mitigate them, and drastically increasing its responsibility and accountability. An additional measure is company participation in multistakeholder initiatives. This provides a risk-management framework supported by stakeholders, gives access to shared learning on best practice from industry peers, and confirms the company's commitment to expected standards. Disclosure is core to shareholder expectations as it informs investment decisions and several initiatives have converged around thematic disclosure. The E&S Quality Score Disclosure & Transparency Signal provides a rounded measure across environmental and social issues.

Where is the information in the reports sourced?
Data is collected from company publications including mainstream filings, Sustainability and CSR reports, Integrated Reports, publicly available company policies and information on company websites. Confirmation of company participation in or formal endorsement of authoritative multi-stakeholder initiatives is collected from websites or member list made available by the relevant initiatives. Issuers are invited to review and verify their data through routine data verification.

What data points are captured?
More than 380 factors across the environmental and social pillars are analyzed. The specific factors under analysis—around 240—vary by industry group. The factor selection and sector allocation has been informed by the recent developments in disclosure standards and frameworks, such as the Global Reporting Initiative (GRI), the Sustainability Accounting Standards Board (SASB) standards and the Task Force on Climate-related Financial Disclosures (TCFD). Section 2 below outlines in more detail the Pillars and Categories covered by E&S QualityScore Disclosure & Transparency Signal.

Why is there no overall score like there is in the Governance QualityScore?
The E & S Pillar scores stand alone as does the G Pillar overall score. Coverage What are the Environmental Pillar categories? Management of Environmental Risks and Opportunities; Carbon & Climate; Waste & Toxicity; and Natural Resources. Under the categories there are 12 subcategories in total.

What are the Social Pillar categories?
Product Safety, Quality & Brand; Stakeholders & Society; Labor Health & Safety; and Human Rights. Under the pillars there are 25 subcategories in total.

What industry groups are covered in the initial launch?
At launch six industry groups are covered: Energy, Materials, Capital Goods, Transportation, Automobiles & Components, and Consumer Durables & Apparel. Initial sectors selected based on industries most exposed to E&S risks.

What additional industry groups will be covered?
ISS will add 18 additional industry groups in Q2 2018 including: Commercial & Professional Services, Consumer Services, Media, Retailing, Food & Staples Retailing, Food, Beverage & Tobacco, Household & Personal Products, Healthcare

Equipment & Services, Pharmaceuticals, Biotech & Life Sciences, Banks, Diversified Financials, Insurance, Software & Services, Real Estate, Utilities, Telecom Services, Semiconductors & Equipment, and Tech Hardware & Equipment.

How many companies are covered in the initial launch?
Approximately 1,500 from the US, Canada, EMEA, and Australasia. How many companies will be covered in the additional coverage? Approximately 3,500 will be added bringing the universe total to approximately 5,000 companies.

Where does the data collection occur?
All data is collected by ISS Data Collection Teams which span the globe. ISS E&S QualityScore Disclosure and Transparency Signal leverages ISS' industry leading global footprint, which includes deep legal and language expertise across key global capital markets

How often is data updated?
Potentially daily.

Companies within the ISS QualityScore coverage universe are invited to review, verify and provide feedback on the data used to determine their scores via a complementary Data Verification tool accessed through ISS Corporate Solutions' Governance Analytics platform. Submissions of corrected or updated data factors can be made online through the platform. Online QualityScore profiles are updated once daily, at approximately 0500 Eastern. Aside from issuer data verification, company data is updated annually on a rolling basis, based roughly on the timing of their annual general meeting which is the typical time of filing annual reports and sustainability reports, issuing updates on company policies and introducing other significant changes to corporate disclosures.

METHODOLOGY

What is the broad approach to the methodology?
The methodology focuses on quantitative and qualitative aspects of disclosure practices, including global disclosure standards and key industry initiatives. A top-level environmental score is presented in parallel to a top-level social score; these scores are equivalent to the GQS company-level score. Each top-level score is supported by four categories and supporting sub-categories. Only factors relevant to a company's Global Industry Classification Standard (GICS)1 industry group are incorporated within a model.

Will the methodology change?
Annual review ensures the methodology remains in step with disclosure standards as they adapt to reflect developments in company practice and stakeholder expectations. How does the methodology reflect the differences companies face across industries? The methodology identifies the range of practices that issuers adopt in each industry on disclosure practices for each factor, and categorizes these to reflect industry good practice. 1 https://marketintelligence.spglobal.com/documents/products/GICS-Mapbook-Brochure.pdf

How are GRI, SASB, and TCFD incorporated into the methodology?
These standards were used in both selecting the factors that made it into the ultimate methodology and the weighting of those questions relative to the overall score. Said

another way, factors that are related to these standards are more heavily weighted than other factors.

How does the E&S Quality Score relate to the ISS-Ethix Norm-Based Research signal?
E&S QualityScore measures the company's depth of understanding of its environmental and social risks, whereas Norm-Based Research (NBR) signals how a company is managing the specific environmental and social controversies it faces. A company's robust understanding of environmental and social risks provides the foundation for avoiding, managing or mitigating controversies. ISS-Ethix's NBR analyses reported allegations of adverse impacts by business on society and the environment in line with business principles on human rights, labor rights, environmental protection and anti-corruption as recognized under the UN Global Compact. NBR findings inform investors about prospective reputational risks and potential long-term financial risks linked to the identified adverse impacts of their investments on society and the environment.

Does the focus on pure disclosure provide meaningful insights?
Investors report that company disclosure is a meaningful signal in its own right—i.e. limited disclosure is often a sign that further investigation is needed to rule out the presence of poor practice—and a prerequisite to an effective comparison of company performance against peers.

ISSUER SPECIFIC QUESTIONS

How can my company access my E&S Quality Score?
Issuers will be able to verify the data that has been collected via Data Verification tool on the ICS Governance Analytics platform. If you need an account to log into the Governance Analytics platform, please email contactus@isscorporatesolutions.com. Please note, if you already have a login to the Governance Analytics platform, your current login will provide access to the E&S QualityScore Data Verification tool.

Will the E&S QualityScore be on the ISS Proxy Analysis?
Yes, just as the Governance Quality Score appears, the Environmental and Social scores will be on the ISS Benchmark Proxy Analysis.

How will the E&S QualityScore affect ISS' vote recommendations on the proxy analysis research report?
Just like the Governance Quality Score, the Environmental and Social scores will have no impact on ISS' proxy voting recommendations.

Who do I contact if I think something is incorrectly profiled?
The first step to attempt to change the way something is profiled is through the Data Verification process. If the suggested change is not made and additional clarification is needed please email ESGHelpdesk@issethix.com. Is there a specific period for data verification? The initial launch will have data verification open from December 18, 2017–January 14, 2018. Following the blackout period for preparing the initial data for launch on January 22, 2018, data verification will reopen and remain open throughout the year. Additional blackout periods are anticipated in one week cycles with the launch of the additional industry groups and after annual methodology changes. Unlike with Governance QualityScore, there will be no blackout period related to filing Def14a and the AGM.

How does ISS anticipate investors will use the scores and underlying data? Institutional investors can be expected to use the scores and data to facilitate identifying and targeting portfolio companies with poor environmental and social disclosure and transparency, construct portfolios around environmental and social disclosure and transparency, and consider environmental and social disclosure factors in investment decisions. The additional E&S pillars provide a new metric to use alongside the Governance pillar to provide more holistic ESG evaluation.

How is the ISS scoring methodology similar or different from other ESG ratings? ISS E&S QualityScore Disclosure & Transparency Signal has a robust methodology. Methodology focuses on quantitative and qualitative aspects of disclosure practices, including global disclosure standards and key industry initiatives. The methodology is made transparent through the QualityScore Key Issues Tech Doc. Annual review ensures the methodology remains in step with disclosure standards as they adapt to reflect developments in company practice and stakeholder expectations.

Will the scores be included on Yahoo! Finance or other financial platforms? ISS E&S QualityScore Disclosure & Transparency Signal will not immediately be presented on external sites. Once the full universe is completed ISS intends to distribute the scores through the same channels as Governance QualityScore.

Institutional Shareholders and "Other People's Money"

You might ask, "who guards the guards?" That is, who makes sure that institutional shareholders are responding to pressures from their investors—namely, the savers, the pensioners, and the insured who actually invest their money—to be more socially aware and responsive?

In 2017, Ceres and a hodge-podge of other organizations launched an initiative to "grade" institutional shareholders on how well they were incorporating ESG into their investment and voting activities. See *Investor Agenda* (developed by Asia Investor Group on Climate Change, CDP, Ceres, Investor Group on Climate Change, Institutional Investors Group on Climate Change, Principles for Responsible Investment, and UNEP Finance Initiative). The report they produced—the first in a series in annual reports on how institutional shareholder are tackling climate change and achieving the goals of the Paris Agreement—looked at four areas: (1) investment, (2) corporate engagement, (3) investor disclosure, and (4) policy advocacy toward a low-carbon future, phasing out thermal coal, and energy efficiency.

The Investor Agenda put out a report card in 2019. It stated that as of September 2019:

- 262 investors are taking action in line with one or more Investment actions of The Investor Agenda, thus demonstrating a clear commitment to (1) scaling up low-carbon investments, (2) phasing out thermal

Report on countries' climate change policies

The Investor Agenda's annual report cards for institutional shareholders didn't happen in 2020, 2021, or 2022. Instead, The Investor Agenda group decided to re-direct its attention and point its finger at countries, instead of companies. It issued a report in October 2021 that said:

> AIGCC, Ceres and IGCC [not all The Investor Agenda members] have assessed the climate policies of G20 countries against the five policy recommendations in the Investor Agenda's 2021 Global Investor Statement to Governments on the Climate Crisis. The Report Card found that most G20 countries have a lot of work to do to attract the trillions of dollars of investment needed in solutions to the climate crisis.

The report card identified whether each country was on track with respect to (1) "nationally-determined contributions" by 2030; (2) "net zero" decarbonization targets; (3) credible policies to meet these targets; (4) COVID spending; (5) climate-risk disclosures. Any countries with a passing grade? Any countries with a failing grade? How did your favorite G20 country do on its report card?

	2030 GHG target	Net zero target	Credible policies	COVID spending	Climate disclosure
Argentina	o	★	o	o	o
Australia	o	o	o	o	☆
Brazil	o	☆	o	☆	☆
Canada	☆	☆	o	★	☆
China	o	☆	o	o	☆
E.U.	☆	★	☆	n/a	★
France	☆	★	☆	★	☆
Germany	☆	★	☆	★	★
Indonesia	o	o	o	o	o
India	o	o	☆	o	o
Italy	☆	★	☆	o	★
Japan	☆	☆	☆	☆	☆
Mexico	o	o	o	o	☆
Russia	o	o	o	o	o
Saudi Arabia	o	o	o	o	o
South Africa	o	☆	☆	o	☆
South Korea	n/a	☆	o	☆	o
Turkey	o	o	n/a	★	o
U.K..	★	☆	☆	☆	★
U.S.A.	☆	☆	o	o	☆

Legend:

★ acceptable
☆ not yet acceptable
o unacceptable

coal investments and/or (3) integrating climate change into portfolio analysis and decision making. [The report pointed out that the IPCC had estimated that $2.4 trillion annual investments in clean energy were needed through 2035 to prevent dangerous global temperature increases. Yet only $332 billion (about 12 percent of this amount) had been invested in clean energy in 2019. It also noted that 1,001 investors with $8.8 trillion (about 10 percent of all global AUM) had committed to divest from oil and gas; the others had not.]

- 759 investors are acting in line with the Corporate Engagement focus of The Investor Agenda by (1) requesting that portfolio companies measure and manage their environmental impacts [over 560 investors with $96 trillion in AUM]; (2) collecting environmental data from more than 7,000 companies worldwide and feeding that data back into the market for investor use; (3) actively targeting companies that are persistent non-responders to CDP's Disclosure Request, with a focus on the 100 systemically important emitters, accounting for two-thirds of annual global industrial emissions [more than 360 investors with $34 trillion AUM did this].

- 403 investors are providing climate-related financial disclosure, thus enabling clients, beneficiaries and other stakeholders to understand how climate change-related risks and opportunities are being assessed and managed by investors; it was said that these disclosures increase the demand for more consistent, comparable and reliable disclosure of climate-related information by companies [overall support for climate-related financial disclosures grew to 824 organizations in 2019 (from 513 in 2018) and includes the world's largest banks, asset managers and pension funds, responsible for assets of $118 trillion].
- 515 investors (with $35 trillion AUM) have signed a statement calling for government action to tackle climate change, with the seven founding partners of The Investor Agenda sending an open letter to governments of the world to strengthen their Nationally Determined Contributions under the Paris Agreement by 2020.

It's a bit like law school. The professors grade the students, the students evaluate the professors, and then US News ranks the law schools. Everyone gets a score! Is the cause of justice advanced?

4.2.4 SEC's ESG Disclosure Rulemakings

SEC Rulemaking Petition Seeking ESG Disclosures

After the 2020 election, the Biden Administration named Gary Gensler to be SEC chair. Soon after being confirmed, Gensler said he thought investors were concerned about climate risk and the SEC should be, too. And, suddenly, climate change disclosure was back on the table.

So in 2021, a group of law professors (joined by institutional shareholders, mostly state pension funds, with $5 trillion in assets under management) submitted a formal rulemaking petition to the SEC asking the agency to "develop a comprehensive framework for clearer, more consistent, more complete, and more easily comparable information relevant to companies' long-term risks and performance" to provide "clarity to America's public companies on providing relevant, auditable, and decision-useful information to investors." The petition explained:

> Today, investors, including retail investors, are demanding and using a wide range of information designed to understand the long-term performance and risk management strategies of public-reporting companies. In response to changing business norms and pressure from investors, most of America's largest public companies are attempting to provide additional information to meet these changing needs and to address worldwide investor preferences and regulatory requirements. Without adequate standards, more and more public companies are voluntarily producing "sustainability reports" designed to explain how they are creating long-term value. There are substantial problems with the nature, timing, and extent of these voluntary disclosures.

Bolstering the petition was a 2018 survey of 542 institutional asset owners and investment consultants world-wide, who stated that they are mostly displeased with ESG disclosures by public companies, especially the ESG disclosures by Asian, UK, and US companies (compared to those in Canada and Europe). In addition, companies had become increasingly more willing than ever before to negotiate with shareholders advocating on issues such as climate change and boardroom diversity.

Rather than pushing back, companies such as Amazon and Citigroup were instead reaching agreements with shareholder activists to change the company's board diversity policies or commit to more climate disclosure, as several energy companies have done. As a result, in 2018 investors ended up withdrawing a record 44 percent of the ESG proposals they submitted after reaching negotiated settlements with management. In part, this shift at the negotiation table happened because BlackRock and Vanguard, for the first time, voted for climate proposals and State Street voted against all-male boards—leading to a domino effect among other institutional shareholders and portfolio companies. See *Companies, Activists Find Common Ground on Climate, Diversity*, Bloomberg News (July 6, 2018).

Thus, the question of whether the US corporation's nature should be re-made by changing the legal requirements for public company disclosure had become ripe.

SEC Proposal on Climate Change Disclosure

In March 2022, the SEC (by a 3-1 vote) sought comments on a proposal to require public companies (including foreign private issuers) to include climate-related information in their SEC filings (registration statements in public offerings, and quarterly and annual reports). As proposed by the SEC, the required information would include:

(1) oversight and governance by the company's board and management related to climate risks;
(2) likely material impacts of climate risks on the company's operations, finances, and business strategies;
(3) how the company identifies, assesses, and manages climate risks; and
(4) GHG emissions directly by the company directly (Scope 1), indirectly by its purchase of energy (Scope 2) and from upstream-supplier and downstream-customer activities (Scope 3).

The global regulatory winds are shifting

The SEC's proposed climate-related disclosure rule follows actions by other regulators worldwide (such as the UK, EU, and Hong Kong) to shift from voluntary to mandatory climate disclosure, following recommendations of the Task Force on Climate-Related Financial Disclosures (TCFD).

The TCFD has pointed out that investors, consumers, and other market participants are clamoring for a global climate disclosure standard—both to obtain consistent information and to identify company greenwashing. Thus, as part of its climate-related rulemaking, the SEC, along with other members of the International Organization of Securities Commissions (IOSCO), plans to review proposed climate disclosure standards from the International Sustainability Standards Board (ISSB).

Further, there would be enhanced disclosure requirements on companies that had set public climate-related targets or had adopted climate-related transition plans. The new requirements, if adopted, would be phased in and become fully applicable to all SEC filings in 2024.

Many have seen the SEC climate disclosure proposal as a big deal. Proponents of the rule and SEC in its release accompanying the proposed rule changes pointed out that many investors are seeking information about climate-related risks because of their "present financial consequences"—thus making them relevant to investment and voting decisions. Critics argued that the rule, if adopted, would be a significant regulatory overreach that would constitute substantive environmental policymaking and impose lots of unwarranted burdens on public companies.

In some respects, an SEC rule on climate change disclosure is less significant than you might think. Whatever the outcome of the SEC rulemaking, investors and other corporate stakeholders continue to seek relevant climate risk information—whether produced by the company, trade groups, government organizations, or NGOs. For example, many companies already reveal their GHG emissions voluntarily and such disclosure is subject to the securities antifraud rules.

(1) *Climate-Risk Oversight and Governance*

Although the SEC proposal anticipates disclosure on board climate-related oversight and governance, already investors are asking boards to appoint members with climate expertise or to enhance climate knowledge among existing board members. In addition, many companies are providing extensive climate-related data in sustainability reports, as to which existing disclosure and financial controls and procedures apply. Companies also face significant pressures from shareholders and auditors to increase internal talent and their climate capacity across business functions.

(2) *Potential Company-Specific Climate Impacts*

Companies are also being asked by shareholders to describe actual and potential impacts of material climate-related risks as part of the company's business strategy, financial planning, and capital allocation. Many consulting firms are conducting physical climate risk assessments of a company's assets, supply-chain vulnerabilities, and shifting customer preferences. Some companies are engaging in "scenario analysis" to assess potential climate impacts, such as those developed by the Intergovernmental Panel on Climate Change or the International Energy Agency.

(3) *Processes to Manage Climate Risks*

Many companies—often at the behest of investors –have begun to identify, assess, and manage material climate-related risks, including physical and transition risks. Among the processes would be to require climate-related

Liability and litigation risk of climate-risk disclosure?

Climate-related information in SEC filings is subject to SEC enforcement actions (and potential fines) and, under the proposed SEC rule and current rules, subject to officer certifications regarding disclosure and internal controls. That is, misstating your company's carbon footprint could get your company and you in hot water.

Although the proposed SEC rule would create a safe harbor for disclosure of Scope 3 emissions and forward-looking climate disclosures, litigation risk for false or misleading climate-related disclosures would continue. Though it might be less if the rule is promulgated, given that the current amorphous "materiality" standards for climate-risk disclosures and omissions would be replaced by "rule-based" standards. In the end, it's hard to know whether the SEC rule would increase or decrease "climate washing."

information from a public company's suppliers and customers, especially those that are privately-held. For example, a public company dependent on certain suppliers, which themselves face climate risks, is required to disclose those risks if material to the company's financial prospects.

(4) *Disclosure of GHG Emissions*

Not all companies disclose their Scope 1 (company) emissions and Scope 2 (purchased energy) emissions, and very few companies disclose their Scope 3 (supplychain, employee commuting, waste disposal, customer) emissions. Nonetheless, many consultants are assisting companies to disclose under the GHG Protocol (a widely-accepted GHG accounting standard) and calculate their emissions. For financial companies, calculating "financed emissions" (a category of Scope 3 emissions) is a challenge, but one described in standards adopted by the Partnership for Carbon Accounting Financials.

Many companies, because of pressure from investors and the public, have stated climate-related targets and goals—such as, "we will be net-zero by 2040." Others have adopted transition plans or started internal carbon pricing. The SEC proposed rule would have companies that set such targets and goals to provide enhanced disclosure, though it is unclear whether this would be any greater than the current SEC disclosure requirements that pubic companies disclose "material" information related to the company's financial prospects.

SEC Authority to Require Climate-Related Disclosures

Ideological battle at the SEC

The SEC proposal to require climate-related disclosures led to sharp words by the SEC commissioners.

Commissioner Peirce (a Trump appointee) said such a rule would prevent companies from disclosing "their performance through their own eyes"—as opposed to the eyes of investors, it would seem. Her dissenting statement was titled, *We are Not the Securities and Environment Commission—At Least Not Yet*. Peirce said, "existing disclosure requirements already capture material risks relating to climate change." In short, let the courts under existing materiality standards, not the SEC, decide what climate-related information is "likely to be considered important" to investors.

Commissioner Herren Lee (also a Trump appointee) described climate risk as the "elephant in the room . . . the single most momentous risk to face the financial markets since the financial crisis. In [being conspicuously silent], we [put] US companies at risk globally."

And each camp has its political allies!

In the end, whether the SEC has authority to promulgate a rule requiring climate-related disclosure will be decided by the federal courts. And, as in many matters before the federal courts, the question will likely be whether corporations and big financial firms support the rule or are against it. That is, the rule's validity will likely depend on how the Business Roundtable, the Council of Institutional Investors, and the US Chamber of Commerce weigh in on the issue.

As you might guess, the SEC's climate-disclosure proposal unleashed a torrent of comments—15,000 in all from a variety of quarters. Besides thousands of form letters (a total of 30 different forms), detailed and often nuanced comments came from individual investors (1,000), public companies (200), institutional shareholders (150), university professors and think-tank scholars (85), industry trade groups (45), commercial trade groups (35), environmental activists (35), elected officials (30), international NGOs (30), law and accounting firms (30), investment firms (15), director and accounting professional associations (10), and citizen advocacy groups (10).

Comments from law professors were split. Some argued that the SEC has no authority to regulate disclosures that are not "material" to investors. These critics asserted that no reasonable investor would be interested in knowing the carbon footprint of a company, its governance practices related to climate risks, or the impact of the climate on the company's business. See Bernard S. Sharfman, *Comment Letter to the SEC on Climate Change Disclosures* (3 Nov 2021) [available on sec.gov] (arguing that the SEC's "statutory authority does not allow the SEC to stray far from" an approach that focuses on whether climate change risks "are reasonably likely to have a material effect on a public company's financial condition or operating performance"). That is, unless climate-related disclosure is likely to affect a company's security's price, then the SEC lacks authority to promulgate any disclosure rules even under statutes that permit the SEC to mandate disclosure "in the public interest." Further, some argued that the SEC proposal likely fails a cost/benefit analysis. Even if the investment markets are hungry for company-specific climate-related information, an SEC rule mandating climate-related disclosure would be just too costly for companies. It would be better for the investment markets to expend their own resources to try to figure out and then price the climate risks at a particular company.

Other academics, however, see a broader role for the SEC. For example, Professor George Georgiev (Emory Law) concluded, "A close review of the [SEC climate-related disclosure proposal] suggests that it is firmly grounded within the traditional SEC disclosure framework that has been in place for close to nine decades. The proposal is in keeping with longstanding regulatory practice." George S. Georgiev, *The SEC's Climate Disclosure Proposal: Critiquing the Critics* (2022) [available on SSRN]. Georgiev then offered a statutory analysis, a story of regulatory practice, a walk-through of Supreme Court precedent, and a look at the First Amendment—all enough to delight the heart of any administrative law professor. In the end, Congress authorized the SEC to require disclosures "in the public interest or for the protection of investors"—without mentioning "materiality" as the linchpin of the SEC's disclosure-setting authority. But aside from this, Professor Georgiev also addressed the meta-question whether disclosure useful to investors, and at the same time to non-investors, is legitimate:

> The SEC's climate disclosure proposal immediately prompts the well-worn question: Is this disclosure intended for shareholders or for stakeholders? But posing this as a binary choice automatically shifts the terms of the debate in favor of opponents of climate-related disclosure, regardless of the actual content of the proposal. Since climate

Investors push for more climate data

In 2021, Goldman Sachs' $2.5 trillion asset-management arm took a harder line in voting against directors, often on the audit committee, at companies that were lax in disclosing their GHG emissions and other climate-impact data.

Goldman said its investment team needs the information. "We want this so we don't have to rely on third-party data, which is often wrong," said Catherine Winner, global head of stewardship at Goldman Sachs Asset Management. "We're not going to wait for the SEC [climate disclosure] rule to kick in," Winner said.

Goldman began treating climate-impact data on par with boardroom diversity, a topic that had led Goldman in 2020 to vote against 7,661 directors worldwide, or about 15 percent of the time. In 2021, Goldman engaged with 271 companies whose emissions disclosures were seen as insufficient, and in about 100 companies the directors became vulnerable for failing to increase the company's climate-related disclosures.

Meanwhile, like other big banks, Goldman itself faced shareholder pressure to end new fossil fuel financing. Curiously, Goldman has opposed shareholder resolutions calling for such action, saying it would not cut emissions or demand for fossil fuels.

AI to the rescue

A Google search in April 2022 revealed the following. Notice the dates are all before 2022. It seems, at some point, firms employing AI to figure out ESG stopped talking to journalists.

- AI can help sustainable investors process mountains of data that hold essential information. for ESG investing. S&P Global (2/25/20).
- AI and machine learning enable finance teams to detect and analyze unstructured data and automate the manual research and extraction processes. Forbes (3/30/20)
- Companies such as Idaciti, Datamaran and TruValue Labs are harnessing AI algorithms in an effort to optimize ESG analysis and thus accountability. Greenbiz (4/21/21)
- The use of Machine Learning in relation to ESG factors is still poorly explored and is a topic that has undoubtedly experienced a surge in popularity. Adjourn (10/26/21)
- AI could provide more accurate and timelier ESG-related data, which could in . . . (AI) but there is no shortage of ways companies can use. The Choice (6/9/21)

change has society-wide implications, information about it will inevitably resonate beyond the boundaries of the disclosing firm and the capital markets, even when the focus is on financially-material disclosure relying on investor- and issuer-generated disclosure frameworks.

As Bill Weihl said, "[An SEC rule on climate-related disclosures] will make it possible for all interested stakeholders, including shareholders, to then push companies to take real action." (Weihl is the head of Climate Voice—and the former "green energy" czar at Google and director of sustainability at Facebook.)

Government Role in ESG Disclosure

Is an SEC climate disclosure rule really needed? Already big institutional shareholders are using the "tools at hand" (engagement and shareholder proposals) to get companies to provide better climate data. And AI is being used to process large amounts of data to understand what is happening at individual companies. Some have pointed out that the current SEC rulemaking might actually be counter-productive given its slow implementation timeline, a signaling to companies that the government is okay with them going slow on ESG disclosure. Others have pointed out that the big banks, which have not liked being scolded about their own ESG foot-dragging particularly on financing new oil and gas ventures, were on the task force on which the SEC relied in its rulemaking. But most companies may not be paying attention to what the SEC thinks the big investors want, rather they are responding to what their big investors are demanding.

4.2.5 Future of Sustainability Disclosure and Corporate Governance

Just as financial reporting has come to turn on the Management Discussion & Analysis of the company's annual report—think Warren Buffett's famous "letters to shareholders"—it has been argued that sustainability-focused companies should provide a Sustainability Discussion & Analysis in the annual report. See Jill E. Fisch, *Making Sustainability Disclosure Sustainable* (2019) [available on SSRN] (arguing that the relationship between issuer sustainability practices and risk management, business plan and economic vulnerability, as well as the need for investors and regulators to evaluate those claims, warrant incorporating sustainability information into SEC-mandated financial reporting).

Disclosure Without Engagement

In the end, the question remains whether greater ESG disclosure will lead to greater corporate attention to ESG issues and thus meaningful corporate sustainability. That is, does mandatory disclosure—but without real engagement by both management and shareholders—offer just a new form of deeper-level corporate greenwashing. Recently, Ceres commented on this:

> Today, many of the world's largest companies are starting to integrate sustainability into their board governance systems, but too often board systems are still rudimentary and do not focus on material issues. In many cases, board governance for sustainability does not drive performance. In other words, it is ineffective. However, companies with the right board governance systems, including formal board mandates for sustainability, board expertise on sustainability, and executive compensation linked to sustainability, are more likely to have established strong sustainability commitments and are better positioned to deliver sustainability performance.

Use of ESG Metrics in Setting Executive Pay

ESG metrics and scores can be used for all sorts of things. One of the most controversial is using ESG metrics in setting executive pay. Some like the idea. [quote from Ceres Roadmap]

Some think it will distract corporate executives from the task at hand to maximize shareholder wealth. See Lucian A. Bebchuk & Roberto Tallarita, *The Perils and Questionable Promise of ESG-Based Compensation* (2021) [available on SSRN]. Here's a critique:

> With the rising support for stakeholder capitalism and at the urging of its advocates, companies have been increasingly using environmental, social, and governance (ESG) performance metrics for CEO compensation. The use of ESG-based compensation, we show, has at best a questionable promise and poses significant perils.
>
> Based partly on an empirical analysis of the use of ESG compensation metrics in S&P 100 companies, we identify two structural problems. First, ESG metrics commonly attempt to tie CEO pay to limited dimensions of the welfare of a limited subset of stakeholders. Therefore, even if these pay arrangements were to provide a meaningful incentive to improve the given dimensions, the economics of multitasking indicates that the use of these metrics could well ultimately hurt, not serve, aggregate stakeholder welfare.
>
> Second, the push for ESG metrics overlooks and exacerbates the agency problem of executive pay, which both scholars and corporate governance rules have paid close attention. To ensure that they are

What about the G in ESG?

As the SEC begins to consider new ESG disclosure rules that cover environmental and social (E&S) matters beyond climate change, some have questioned whether disclosure of E&S risks is enough to protect investors. Jennifer O'Hare, *Don't Forget the "G" in ESG: The SEC and Corporate Governance Disclosure* (2022) [available on SSRN]. She argues that any ESG disclosure rule should also require information on (1) how the board manages E&S risks, and (2) shareholder governance rights—all laid out in a new Summary Corporate Governance Table in the company's proxy statement. This would "cause public companies to adopt better corporate governance practices and, in turn, strengthen the ability of shareholders to hold boards accountable if they fail to address E&S risks."

> designed to provide effective incentives rather than serve the interests of executives, pay arrangements need to be subject to effective scrutiny by outsiders. However, our empirical analysis shows that in almost all cases in which S&P 100 companies use ESG metrics, it is difficult if not impossible for outside observers to assess whether this use provides valuable incentives or rather merely lines CEO's pockets with performance-insensitive pay.
>
> The current use of ESG metrics, we conclude, likely serves the interests of executives, not of stakeholders. Expansion of ESG metrics should not be supported even by those who care deeply about stakeholder welfare.

We are in transition. Will there come the day, as Paul Hawken urged, that "sustainability thinking" in business is as natural as falling off a log?

* * *

Concluding Thoughts

Apology

When corporations issue "corrective disclosures"—whether to restate earnings or to clean up their greenwashing—such disclosures are a form of apology. Sometimes the apology works, and investors and regulators choose not to sue. Sometimes the apology rings hollow, and a securities fraud lawsuit can follow.

What makes an apology effective? Here's an open letter (somewhat edited and paraphrased) that illustrates the importance and the power of apology. Notice the elements of a true apology.

* * *

An Open Letter
9 February 2021
[redacted / paraphrased]

to the families of students, teachers, crew members of *Ehime Maru* [a teaching fishing boat] from Former Captain Scott Waddle of the *USS Greenville* [a US Navy submarine]

Today marks the 20th anniversary of the collision between the USS *Greenville* and the *Ehime Maru*. On February 9, 2001, the submarine I commanded performed a (training) emergency surfacing maneuver, collided with the *Ehime Maru* from underneath, and sank the vessel within 10 minutes. The collision caused the loss of life of four students, two instructors, and three crewmen.

The purpose of this letter is to apologize to the families who lost loved ones. As the former captain of the *Greenville*, I alone am solely responsible for the accident. The collision was avoidable, and I failed in my duties to prevent it. This letter is not intended to solicit empathy or sympathy. The families of those who died and the survivors of the accident warrant that and not me.

An hour after the US Coast Guard rescued the survivors, I would learn nine people had perished. Hearing that report was the most devastating thing I have ever experienced. When families arrived in Honolulu on Sunday the 11th. I asked the Commander of the Pacific Fleet to meet with the family members face-to-face for me to offer an apology. My request was denied. I was told that I was the last person the families would want to see.

I am truly sorry I did not try harder. The first apology I gave was via a press release drafted by my Navy and civilian attorneys. Although I questioned the word "regret" in the release, instead of "apologize," I was counseled this was the best word to use. In my heart, I knew it was wrong. I should have said, "I apologize and am sorry." This press release caused more anger and emotional distress to the victims' families.

After weeks of search and rescue efforts failed to locate the missing, the families returned to Japan. The first week in March the first group of family members would return to Honolulu to witness the court of inquiry considering the accident and my conduct. On March 9, I met with families for the first time. I bowed before them and, with the help of an interpreter, I apologized, listened to them, and answered questions.

At the end of our meeting, Mrs. Naoko Nakata, the widow of Jun Nakata, gave me a personal letter. It was reprinted that afternoon in the local newspaper and began: "Dear captain, I was meant to share every sadness and suffering with my husband. Your submarine sank him. You will share the burden of the accident. You said you will bring your sorrows to your grave. But my husband was sent to the grave without knowing what happened to him."

I share the burden. My actions took your husband from you and your children. I am truly sorry. Mrs. Nakata continued: "Don't judge the demerits and the merits, and please explain why it happened. Figure out what you should have done and what you didn't do. Please reveal the cause of the accident, make an effort to prevent it from happening again, and make proposals to that effect."

The Court of Inquiry was thorough and identified mistakes that were made. In the end, it was my fault and mine alone. [Waddle was later reprimanded and honorably discharged.] For the past 20 years, the US Navy has taught those responsible for the safe navigation of US submarines the details of the accident. And for the past 20 years, I have shared the story of this accident and my shortcomings to many different audiences around the globe.

Mrs. Nakata concluded: "I'd like to tell my son and daughter someday that daddy's accident was a sad incident but that it made the Hawaiian ocean a safe place for all people and ships around the world. Before my husband Jun departed for his fifth voyage, he told his father Kazuo, "If something happens to the ship, Dad, I would let all the students go first. I would never escape before the students."

In closing this letter, I ask that you pray for the families of the *Ehime Maru* and that the soul of Takeshi Mizuguchi [whose body was never recovered] will continue to protect mariners that sail on top of and below the surface of the Hawaiian waters and that his soul will rest in peace.

Sincerely and very respectfully,

Scott Waddle, Commander USN (Retired)

Chapter 4.3

Shareholder-Manager Consortia (Ceres)

This chapter looks at an emerging phenomenon: consortia of sustainability-focused institutional shareholders and corporate managers. It is a formal, more permanent version of the ad hoc "engagement" between ESG-focused institutional shareholders and corporate executives at their portfolio companies.

While the previous chapters in this unit have involved hard law—new corporate norms (4.1 Benefit corporations) and revised disclosure rules (4.2 ESG disclosure)—this chapter moves us back toward soft law. No shareholders or corporate managers are compelled to engage with each other, much less to engage on a regular ongoing basis. But this is what has been happening at Ceres, an NGO founded in 1989 in response to the Exxon Valdez oil spill in Alaskan waters. Today Ceres is the leader in identifying and promoting the business structures for transitioning to sustainable corporations—and thus a more just and sustainable global economy.

Yes, we finally reached it: the sustainable corporation. In this our journey in search of the sustainable corporation, this chapter gives you a chance finally to observe and evaluate the contours of this elusive creature. Perhaps the most remarkable thing is that it was in 2010 that Ceres laid out "The 21st Century Corporation: A Roadmap for Sustainability." Hardly anyone paid attention. There were no law review articles, no management studies, no academic symposia. In the academy, very few recognized the NGO's existence, even among those committed to saving the planet. It was, I guess, unfathomable that a corporation could have a roadmap toward sustainability.

We have come a long way. We began our course with a look at the nature of the US corporation—in particular, the US public corporation and securities regulation. We then moved to consider the corporation's unsustainable design—corporate limited liability, the BJR and short-termism, board monoculture, and the corporation's political "personhood" and influence.

Sustainable business law

Sustainable business law—some call it ESG law—has emerged as a distinct area of academic inquiry and curricular reform at the intersection of sustainability, business, and law—with an emphasis on finance and corporate governance. See Colin Myers & Jason J. Czarnecki, *Sustainable Business Law? The Key Role of Corporate Governance and Finance* (2022) [available on SSRN]. This could be a pernicious development. As law and business schools begin to offer courses on the subject, there is the risk that faculties will assume that the "hot topic" of ESG is covered—and nothing more need be done.

Thank goodness some younger lawyers get it. As Charlie Wowk (Duke Law '21) explained, "Climate change is the issue of my generation. If it's farmland, think of the impact that it has on the crops, if it's in a dense city, the impact that it has on infrastructure and hospitals, if it's a coastal city, the impact that it has on housing. Some places are just going to become unlivable, so you're going to have a swath of climate refugees. . . . I don't think any of my peers will have a choice. We will all have to be 'ESG lawyers' in some way or another, because these issues are going to impact pretty much every sector." See Jeannie Naujeck, *How The Environmental, Social, and Governance Movement Is Gaining Ground in Boardrooms, Law Firms, and Legal Scholarship*, Duke Law Magazine (Fall 2021) (noting new courses at Duke Law on Corporate Social Responsibility and Social Entrepreneurship).

We then looked at the emerging "triple bottom line" responses to these unsustainable attributes—mandated and voluntary environmental compliance, increased focus on CSR, and socially-responsible investing and the new shareholder ESG activism. In short, we considered the essence of the corporation's DNA and how recent adaptations have sought to make the corporate organism more responsive to its environment.

This unit has considered ways in which the corporate DNA is being modified – after all, the corporation is an organism that is regularly being genetically modified. We started with a look at a fundamental redesign of the corporation—specifically, stakeholder "rights" in benefit corporations. Then we moved to looking at how corporate disclosures are being re-formulated to explicitly consider ESG. And now we focus on new engagement (a consortium) of institutional shareholders and corporate management.

This unit is a precursor to our final unit in which we look at the corporation as a "moral system," where we consider whether stakeholder capitalism is a delusion, and then whether "outside" pressures on corporate decision makers are enough. Our search for the sustainable corporation has made clear that sustainability is a moral issue—a question of discerning right and wrong. Is the new ESG-driven focus on stakeholders enough? And, even more relevant, is the prevalent focus on "incentives" misguided? That is, perhaps we should also be looking to the moral "fiber" of the corporation, to what the corporation is really made of, and thus "inside" the individuals (all of us) who constitute this figment of the human imagination. This thing we call "the corporation."

Chapter's Focus

You will want to focus on the elements of a developed model of the "sustainable corporation"—a model created by Ceres, a non-profit that brings together socially-minded shareholders and corporate executives.

You will notice that the Ceres Roadmap for a sustainable corporation identifies four building blocks: governance, stakeholder engagement, disclosure, and performance evaluation. However, the Ceres roadmap does not anticipate a significant role for government, either in defining corporate law norms or even in creating systems of sustainability regulation (such as carbon pricing, GHG emission standards, environmental treaties, or new disclosure regimes).

You will want to focus on how corporate sustainability under the Ceres Roadmap goes well beyond thinking of the corporation as shareholder-centric or stakeholder-driven, but instead as a system of interconnected sub-systems. You should be left with the question: Why would investment managers and corporate executives engage with the Ceres Roadmap? What are their incentives?

Finally, you will want to consider whether corporate sustainability can be entrusted to a private consortia or whether the coercive power of law must play a role – that is, we are back to our original question about the nature of the corporation. Is it private or public? (Maybe you are starting to see that it's both.)

Note about chapter's format: As you'll notice, much of this chapter is not the usual textual presentation, but often a series of guiding questions about Ceres and its 2010 Roadmap for the sustainable "21st Century corporation" [accessible on the Ceres website, requiring a simple log-in]. That is, the chapter is more a series of scavenger hunts than a set of textual readings. Why this way? Rather than present the 88-page Ceres Roadmap and ask that you slog through it, the chapter asks you specific questions about the report (identifying the page number) and invites you to explore it at your leisure – with me as your guide. Please, as is the custom, remember to leave a tip for your tour guide!

4.3.1 Remarkable Ceres

We begin by looking specifically at Ceres – a non-profit organization that we already encountered when considering the nature of the ESG movement, the SEC guidance on climate change disclosure, and more recently the SEC proposed climate disclosure rule. (Ceres, as you may remember, was the organization that first asked the SEC to issue its guidance and then identified the failure of the guidance to change the way companies described climate change risk in their SEC filings; Ceres has also been a principal proponent of the SEC's initiatives to require more uniform and comprehensive ESG disclosure by corporations, including on climate change.)

Scavenger hunt – Ceres

To introduce you to Ceres, I ask you to "surf" the organization's website and answer seven "scavenger hunt" questions about Ceres.

Scavenger Hunt – Ceres

1. Go to ceres.org. What is Ceres? How would you describe the organization to a family member? Click here or https://www.ceres.org/about-us.
2. There's a video that describes Ceres and its first 20 years that might interest you. What did you find surprising in learning about the Ceres story? Click here or http://vimeo.com/4417955 [6:49].
3. What is the history of Ceres? How was it founded? What have been some of its achievements? What do you find most impressive? Click here or https://www.ceres.org/about-us → History.
4. Who is part of the Ceres "consortium"? What are the Ceres "networks"? Would you say there is more interest in Ceres from institutional shareholders or large companies or policy wonks? Click Ceres home page → "Our Networks" tab / here for Investor Network / here for Company Network / here for Policy Network.
5. If you headed a large institutional shareholder, would you want to be part of the Ceres coalition? What might be your reasons for joining? Click / here for Investor Network.
6. Ceres regularly issues press releases. Click here or https://www.ceres.org/news-center/press-releases. As you browse the press releases, how often is government action mentioned? How often are private investors and companies (or business groups) mentioned?

7. Ceres is hiring – for both internships and full-time jobs. Would you be interested in working at Ceres? Click here or https://www.ceres.org/careers.

The Ceres Mission

Founded in 1989, Ceres has undertaken to identify global problems and then to call on corporations to make the changes necessary to prevent future social and environmental harm. The Ceres mission, displayed on its home page, states that the organization "advances leadership among investors, companies and capital market influencers to drive solutions and take action on the world's most pressing sustainability issues" Ceres does this by issuing reports covering a wide range of disciplines, including economic, social, and environmental concerns. It measures its effect by conducting progress reports for corporations that have pledged to implement change.

Ceres as "Soft Law"

In some respects, the Ceres expectations represent a new "soft law" for corporations. They create a new "corporate regulatory framework" – supplementing and even supplanting the usual "rules of the road" that come from state corporate law, federal securities regulation, and the panoply of regulation affecting business behavior (such as environmental, land use, public utility, and climate change regulation). Although Ceres has been around for nearly 30 years, its role in creating a framework for engagement and action by institutional shareholders and corporate management on sustainability issues is relatively new – an initiative only in the last decade.

Ceres's History

Ceres started its mission in 1989 after the Exxon Valdez oil spill devastated Prince William Sound, Alaska. Before the Deepwater Horizon oil spill in 2010, this was the largest oil spill that occurred within U.S. territory. The event was the catalyst for Ceres' founder, Joan Bavaria, to create an organization of environmentalists and investors that sought to encourage a new vision for corporations. Bavaria and her group "redefined the role and responsibility of companies as stewards of the environment and agents of economic and social change."

Academics Mostly Fail to Notice Ceres

Surprisingly, little has been written about Ceres in the academic literature. A search in SSRN for articles that mention Ceres in their titles results in a big zero. There are only seven articles that mention Ceres in their abstracts—with only one (the next reading) that focuses on the Ceres mission to create a new framework for shareholder-management collaboration on sustainability issues.

Some of the more recent articles that mention Ceres address the NGO's role in creating usedful data on a variety of corporate sustainability topics:

(1) **Climate-related disclosure in SEC filings.** Christine Chou & Steven O. Kimbrough, *Talking about Climate Change: What Are Enterprises Saying in Their SEC filings?* (Dec. 2019) [available on SSRN] (unpublished study examines 16 climate-related terms in 19,739 SEC filings from 2003-2016 for "preeminent firms" in nine industries, finding "significant increase of use in their annual reports (10-Ks) from the 2003--2009 period compared to the 2010--2016 period, though the pattern for such terms in current reports (8-Ks) is much weaker; the results were compared to "well-regarded content analysis report done by a prominent nonprofit organization, CERES" and the authors found the two studies are complementary and together yield a more nuanced picture of SEC reporting).

(2) **Value of formal ESG mandates for corporate boards.** Veena Ramani & Bronagh Ward, *How Board Oversight Can Drive Climate and Sustainability Performance* (2019) [available on SSRN] (published in peer-reviewed journal, study presents evidence that board leadership is essential for solving critical sustainability issues like climate change and, drawing on a report by Ceres and KKS Advisors, study concludes that creation of formal board mandates for sustainability is an important "best practice" –finding that when such governance features are put in place, "sustainability performance improves notably" at companies).

(3) **Most US directors are indifferent to ESG.** Tensie Whelan, *U.S. Corporate Boards Suffer From Inadequate Expertise in Financially Material ESG Matters* (2021) [available on SSRN] (report by director of NYU Stern Center for Sustainable Business, finding that many US public company boards "have little [ESG-related] oversight or expertise; based on PWC's Annual Corporate Directors Survey only 38 percent of board members think ESG issues have a financial impact on the company and some 56 percent of directors complain that investors are giving too much focus to ESG–nearly twice those with that viewpoint in 2018; only 34 percent said there needed to be more racial/ethnic diversity on their boards; citing to Ceres study on the board credentials of the top 475 of the Fortune 2000 companies, which found that most board members do not have demonstrable sustainability credentials (only 17 percent qualified) and just 13 percent of boards have robust oversight of ESG issues,

One person

Before starting Ceres, Joan Bavaria had created Trillum Asset Management in 1982 after graduating from Harvard Business School. Today, Trillum was the first firm to focus exclusively on SRI. Its website honors its founder: "[Joan] is often referred to as the "Founding Mother" of Socially Responsible Investing (SRI). Under [her] visionary leadership, Trillium grew to become one of the largest SRI investment firms in the United States."

Bavaria's first experience in corporate finance gave her insights into ways corporations can become more sustainable. Understanding the nature and the inner-workings of an investment firm, Bavaria identified ways such firms are not working. This, with her frustration over the Exxon Valdez oil spill, inspired Bavaria to dedicate herself to making corporations the solution. She noticed a culture of silence that maintains the status quo in the business world. Bavaria actively spoke out against this silence and encouraged business innovation. As Harvard Business School noted, "Bavaria argued that investment houses could use their funds to promote corporate social responsibility and that such investments could be profitable. This was considered extremely unorthodox in the industry at the time."

and only 10% of the boards regularly reviewed relevant sustainability issues at board meetings).

(4) **Institutional shareholders drive global sustainable investing.** Gordon L. Clark Tessa Hebb, *Why Do They Care? The Market for Corporate Global Responsibility and the Role of Institutional Investors* (2005) [available on SSRN] (published in peer-reviewed journal, finding that institutional investors, primarily pension funds, drive global financial markets, noting that CalPERS screens investments in companies in emerging markets using "both the CERES and Sullivan Principles to monitor corporate behaviour").

The handful of other articles and essays on SSRN that mention Ceres in their abstracts deal with such questions as the statistical "least squared method" and business "human rights guidelines after Brundtland." It's remarkable – at least to me – that such a significant new trend in corporate governance is almost off the academic radar screen.

Despite this lack of academic attention to Ceres, quite a bit of academic attention has been given to how institutional shareholders have been driving the ESG movement – or, as some call it, "stakeholder capitalism." For example, looking at hand-collected data from companies in the S&P 1500, Professor Cathy Hwang (Virginia Law) and Professor Yaron Nili (Wisconsin Law) conclude that shareholders (not management) have been the driving force behind new ESG principles. See Cathy Hwang & Yaron Nili, *Shareholder-Driven Stakeholderism* (2020) [available on SSRN] (identifying shareholder activism as behind the ESG movement, in particular resulting in the Business Roundtable statement on revised purpose of corporation). In particular, the authors conclude, "institutional shareholders and proxy advisory firms have taken the lead [on] pushing ESG policies on management."

Curiously, the authors state their article provides "public companies *a roadmap* to engage in policies that better promote diversity, sustainability, and community stewardship" – without mentioning Ceres. We law professors tend to live in ivory silos.

Science Based Target Initiative

Ceres is not the only game in town. The Science Based Target Initiative is also at the intersection of private actions being taken by companies to reduce GHG emissions, aligned with the criteria set by existing U.S. government programs. The goal of SBTI is to "incentivize and further legitimize the actions of the business community [by driving] ambitious climate action in the private sector by enabling companies to set science-based emissions reduction targets." SBTI was established in 2015 by the World Resources Institute, CDP, World Wide Fund for Nature, and the UN Global Compact.

Professors Michael Vandenbergh and Jonathan Gilligan (both Vanderbilt University) were among the first to recognize the potential for aggregate company GHG reductions as a meaningful proportion of needed global cuts. They described this potential reduction as the "private governance wedge." *Beyond Gridlock* (2015) [available on SSRN].

In the end, though, the goals and scope of the SBTI pale next to their bigger, much older sister.

4.3.2 Ceres *Roadmap* for 21st Century Sustainable Corporation

Comprehensive Vision for Sustainable Corporation

We now turn to a fundamental Ceres document, perhaps the only of its kind, that sets out a comprehensive vision for the "sustainable corporation" – in some ways, it is the culmination of our journey. The document titled *The 21st Century Corporation: The Ceres Roadmap for Sustainability* was drafted in 2010 and picks up on most of the themes of this book: the governance structure of the corporation; the corporation's tendency toward externalization of risk/harm; the importance of management/board culture; and the relevance of performance criteria.

Scavenger Hunt – Ceres Roadmap

Rather than reproduce the full 85-page/147-footnote Ceres *Roadmap*, it seems more useful to offer a "scavenger hunt" of its main points. The hunt begins with a look at the *Roadmap's* overview, next reviews its executive summary, and then turns to various performance areas (governance, stakeholder engagement, disclosures, and specific topics). You'll notice that the *Roadmap* is laced with short summaries, quick-read stories, and lots of graphics. It's meant to be read by business and finance folks!

Scavenger Hunt – Ceres *Roadmap*

In 2010, Ceres released *The 21st Century Corporation: The Ceres Roadmap for Sustainability*. This scavenger hunt asks you to look at the *Roadmap* and answer some questions. The *Roadmap* itself can be downloaded from the Ceres website: https://www.ceres.org/resources/reports/21st-century-corporation-ceres-roadmap-sustainability [you must register, but this is a way to get their newsletters].

Overview

1. Let's first look at the Ceres website, which offers an overview of the *Roadmap*. According to this overview, how does the *Roadmap* serve as a vision and a practical guide? Click here https://www.ceres.org/resources/reports/21st-century-corporation-ceres-roadmap-sustainability
2. Let's turn now to the *Roadmap* (P6) and an introductory letter that includes four "key pillars" for achieving global sustainability. What are they? Where does the *Roadmap* fit in?
3. The *Roadmap* (PP14-15) lays out four broad areas that companies should focus on: governance, stakeholder engagement, disclosure and performance. What are the 20 key expectations in these four areas?

4. OK. You've downloaded the *Roadmap*. Let's start exploring it. On P2 you'll see the Table of Contents. After the foreword, letter from the Ceres president, and thought leader perspectives, there's a 6-page introduction that we'll go through carefully. What are the four main sections of the report?
5. Done looking at the Table of Contents. Let's turn to the Foreword (P3), which is written by an investment manager. What is Generation Investment Management? Click here. Is the investment firm broadly diversified? Who is on its board of advisors? Who are its clients?
6. That was an interesting glimpse into the world of "sustainability investment." Let's go back to the *Roadmap* (P3), and see what David Blood has to say about the "sustainable corporation." Does he imagine that corporations will be restructured as new business entities? How does he see sustainability fitting into existing business models focused on "growth, profitability, competitive position and shareholder returns"? How does Blood define sustainability for business? How does Blood see the *Roadmap* fitting into the corporation of the 21st Century?
7. Next, let's turn to the introductory letter (P4) from Mindy Lubber, the president of Ceres. She begins with a quick summary of the Ceres story, and then the importance of integrating sustainability thinking into all aspects of a business. She explains that Ceres has identified in a 20-20 vision statement four "key pillars" to achieve global sustainability by 2020. What are they? Do you agree with these pillars? She then goes on to explain how the *Roadmap* focuses on the second pillar, "new standards and expectations for business leadership." The *Roadmap* has 20 "key expectations" arising from its main topics – governance, stakeholder engagement, disclosure, and performance. What do you think of these expectations? Are they realistic?
8. We're getting a feel for what the *Roadmap* is up to. On P5 there are some "thought leader perspectives." Notice who is at the table: an environmental NGO, a big institutional investor, a couple corporate managers. Who is not at the table? What parties in the sustainability movement do not seem to be part of the Ceres dialogue?

Executive Summary

9. Now the introduction to the report – really, the executive summary (P6). The introduction lays out "new imperatives for [corporate] leadership" – what are they? Why is "business as usual" no longer acceptable? The introduction then identifies big changes (trillion dollar changes) that must be made. What industry is targeted? What opportunities are mentioned? Do business executives view sustain-

ability as a priority – what do recent surveys show? See The Economist, *Managing for sustainability* (Feb. 2010) [available on Enel_WEB].

10. The introduction then describes the four broad areas that companies should focus on: governance, stakeholder engagement, disclosure and performance. What are building blocks in each of these areas? You might want to jump forward to PP12-13, where these four areas are broken down.
11. Ah, notice that the introduction (P13) offers a widely cited definition of sustainability. How do you like the Brundtland definition? Does the *Roadmap* seem more focused on "essential needs of the world's poor" or "the ability of future generations to meet their own needs"?
12. The introduction (P8) then identifies the drivers of sustainability (I guess, the reasons for the *Roadmap*). What if global resources weren't strained and climate change were not happening, would sustainability be an issue? Would "business as usual" be acceptable? Is sustainability really driven by "the world being flat" (economic globalization and connectivity), or are these simply the circumstances in which resource limits and climate change must be addressed?
13. The introduction (P9) then identifies how various stakeholders have a role in the sustainability movement. Why aren't governments part of Ceres? Where do labor unions, consumers, employees fit into Ceres? Are they (or their representatives) at the Ceres table?
14. The introduction (P10) next focuses on the "investor perspective" – notice how the perspectives of other stakeholders on the previous page don't get special attention! Why is the investor perspective important? Who is this *Roadmap* really written to? There's some interesting information here: What is the Investor Network on Climate Risk? What are "sustainability investment products"? How do these products relate to sustainability financial indices? Check out the MSCI Global Climate Index. How is sustainability factored into lending practices of major banks? Remember during our look at SRI investing the Principles of Responsible Investment (http://www.unpri.org/)? (There are six, and signatories to the Principles have $45 trillion in assets under management.)
15. We're getting a bit afield. Let's get back to the *Roadmap*. Here's a graphic from P11 that gives you a visual for the *Roadmap*:

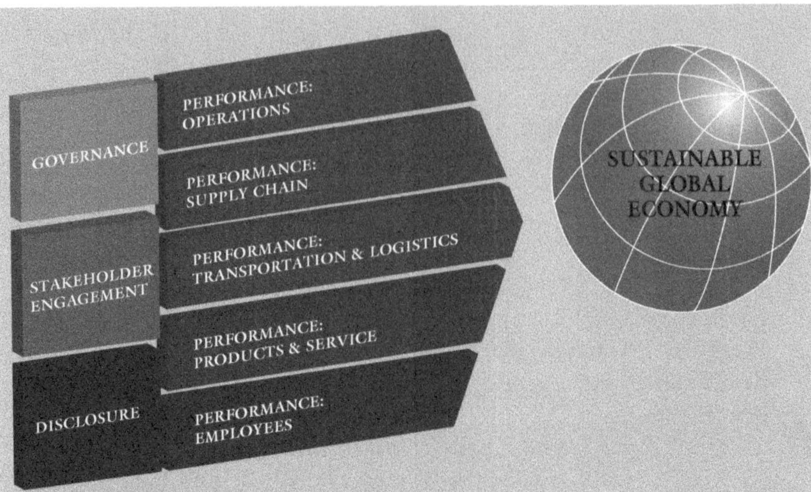

How are the chapters in the *Roadmap* laid out? Does "vision → business rationale → expectations → examples" make sense?

16. Let's turn to the introduction's description of Governance (P12) and then focus on how the *Roadmap* describes this area. If you were a corporate CEO (or board chair), what reasons would there be for you to implement the governance reforms advocated by the *Roadmap*? How much of a change are these governance reforms from current governance practices?

Reasons for joining Ceres *Roadmap*

17. If you were a corporate CEO (or board chair), what reasons would there be for you to implement the governance reforms advocated by the *Roadmap* (P14)?

18. If you were the head of a mutual fund's "voting policy group," what reasons would there be for you to become involved in the stakeholder dialogue advocated by the *Roadmap* (P14)?

19. If you were the General Counsel of a public company, responsible for disclosure of company information, what reasons would there be for you to have your company engage in the sustainability reporting advocated by the *Roadmap* (P14)?

Performance areas

20. The report lays out five "performance" areas that companies in the Ceres network are supposed to achieve according to the *Roadmap* (P15). Which areas seem achievable?

21. The green part of the *Roadmap* (PP14-23) deals with governance. What is the vision? What are the five expectations? Do you agree directors are legally required to assess risk – including social, environmental and political risks? If you were advising a board of directors about sustainability issues, what would you say? What aspects of the *Roadmap*'s section on governance would you highlight? What recommendations would you make to the board? Do you think a board should set executive performance standards based on sustainability performance measures? Would you recommend that the board create a Chief Sustainability Officer? What about recommending a sustainability committee of the board – what specific things might you recommend (P19)?

22. There's an interesting case study (P20) that identifies how Ceres measures and benchmarks climate risk and corporate governance at different companies. What are the items on the "scorecard"? Do you think that these are the right things to be measuring and scoring? What about the significant weight place on Strategic Planning and Performance?
23. Turn next to how the *Roadmap* (P21) recommends that companies should have policies on such issues as human rights and biodiversity. Isn't this asking companies to become "states" – with mission statements that look like a political "declarations of human rights" and policies that read like a constitutional "bill of rights"?
24. The brown part of the *Roadmap* (PP24-31) deals with stakeholder engagement. What is the vision? What are the four expectations? Who are inside the company and who are outside? See Figure S-1 (P27). What does the chart (P26) on shareholder proposals on sustainability issues indicate? Consider the "Vodafone Material Issues" chart (Figure S1-2 P27), does it make sense for a company to be concerned about stakeholder concerns? Where does investor engagement fit in? See P30. Are you convinced that stakeholder engagement pays off? Consider the companies highlighted in the *Roadmap* – GE and Dell. By the way, Timberland's quarterly stakeholder calls became a thing of the past in 2012 when the company was bought by VF Corp. Click here to hear one of those earlier calls.
25. Again, if you were the head of a mutual fund group's "voting policy group," what reasons would there be for you to become involved in the stakeholder dialogue advocated by the *Roadmap* (P30)? Would you want to join Ceres?
26. The blue part of the *Roadmap* (PP32-43) deals with disclosure. What is the vision? What are the six expectations? If you were the general counsel of a public company, responsible for disclosure of your company's financial information, what reasons would there be for you to have your company engage in the sustainability reporting advocated by the *Roadmap* (P36)? What do you think of the examples given in the *Roadmap* – such as Suncor's GHG performance data ({37)? What's in it for companies to disclose GHG information? See Box at P38. How does the reporting that the *Roadmap* advocates differ from legally required reporting under government regulations? Consider whether CSR reports are actionable – or protected under the First Amendment as commercial speech. See *Kasky v. Nike* (Cal. 2002)
27. If you were the head of public relations of a retailer, like Walmart, would you want to label your products with a sustainability index? Should such labeling be mandatory or voluntary, or subject to

oversight by some non-profit organization? What has happened to the Walmart Sustainability Index Initiative? See Walmart THESIS Index (formerly Sustainability Index), Walmart Sustainability Hub.

Performance Expectations

28. Finally, the red section of the *Roadmap* (PP44-75) deals with performance. What is the vision? What are the five expectations? Notice that each expectation comes with multiple parts. The section begins with a quote from Jeff Immelt, CEO of GE, to focus all of the company's innovative powers on energy use and environmental stewardship." Would you invest in GE?

29. Let's look at the five performance expectations. The first (PP46-52) deals with putting money into measuring "environmental neutrality" and "respect for human rights," as well improving and measuring performance on GHG emissions, energy efficiency, facilities and buildings, water, waste, and (last, but not least) human rights. In looking at the specific, sub-expectations, what are the GHG emission, energy efficiency, power use, and renewable energy expectations? See P47. What about expectations for facilities and buildings? P48-49. Then there's water management: what are the targets? P50. The next is to eliminate waste – are there profits in them there hills? P51. Finally, as for human rights, what's to be measured? Would you invest in a company that joined Ceres and committed itself to these *Roadmap* performance standards?

30. The next performance expectation (PP53-59) deals with the supply chain. Notice the quote (P53) by John Ruggie, the Harvard politics professor who wrote the UNI Guiding Principles for Business and Human Rights. We saw him and his Ruggie Principles when we looked at CSR and its incorporation of "salient" human rights. Consider the EPA's Green Supplier Network (P53). Are you impressed with the savings? Why is the trend for companies to create and impose supplier codes of conduct? See Trends (P53) and McDonald's soya story (P54). The expectation (P55) also extends to companies purchasing from "women and minority owned businesses." Isn't this an invitation – without government rules – an invitation to fraud and abuse? This expectation (P56) does have some specific performance goals with respect to suppliers meeting the company's standards for sustainability performance. Do these seem attainable or, perhaps, too low? The expectation (P59) also anticipates that companies will disclose their suppliers' sustainability performance. Does this open up companies to legal liability for commercial disparagement?

31. The next performance expectation (PP60-63) deals with transportation and logistics. Notice that in the Trends (P60) that freight represents half of GHG emissions attributed to US transportation. When gasoline/diesel prices fall, does it make sense to be concerned about GHG emissions? Is the *Roadmap* really adding anything by urging businesses to be more efficiency in minimizing transportation costs?

Or perhaps the *Roadmap* (and follow-up reports) serve as a clearinghouse of information on sustainability "good practices." Notice in Figure P3.2 (P62) how much more efficient ocean transport is compared to truck transport. What does this suggest about how companies should move goods? Finally, what do you think about more tele-commuting and public transit? Consider the Google policy (P63) of giving employees who bike into work access to a car for errands.

32. The next performance expectation – they just keep coming – deals with product and services. Isn't this again something that can happen only as the market demand exists for "green" products and services? For example, if consumers are already demanding green products and want assurances their products are green (Trends - P64), won't companies meet the demand? The *Roadmap* says companies will transition to sustainable product and services. What are these? For example, how sustainable is the computer you're using right now? Does anybody know? Same question for sustainable R&D (P66). For example, Whirpool (P66) is making appliances that can interact with the smart grid, thus lowering electric use. Does that make the appliances sustainable?

33. It's interesting: the *Roadmap* began talking about how the $6 trillion energy industry had to transition away from carbon-based energy and how opportunities exist for companies that aim at the $5 trillion in developing markets. We finally get to that idea. But won't the companies aiming at developing markets and identified in the *Roadmap* (P67) and many more like them go after this new demand anyway? And what reason is there to satisfy the developing-market demand with green products and services – isn't price (regardless of sustainability) even more important in a developing market? Then there's life cycle assessment (P68). Notice the example of Canon (P68) developing a new line of office devices that have less bad stuff and more good stuff, but what motivated Canon to do this?

34. Next the *Roadmap* (P69) mentions sustainable design – finally, we get to real innovation and creativity. What do you think about glasses made from wine bottles – upcycling? And to wrap up this part on products and services, the *Roadmap* urges companies to "do no harm." How is it possible for companies to keep their existing business models – like Coca-Cola, a company that makes most of its money selling toxic sugar water – to be engaged in sustainability? And then this part finishes with collaboration, such as "open sourcing." With all the stories of goodness and sharing, I feel like I'm in church. But isn't that the idea?

35. The final, and also the shortest, performance expectation (PP72-75) deals with employees. So in the triumvirate of profits, people, and planet, it looks like the *Roadmap* relegates people to last place. The *Roadmap* talks about human rights, diversity, and company culture. But maybe this is the aspect of the sustainability movement that is already underway. While "old school" investors and managers may remain wedded to the paradigm of "shareholder primacy," it seems that young people get it. See Trends (P72). That is, perhaps CSR is the green-washed story that companies use to attract young talent, and then that young talent changes the washing to green.

36. Finally, it's worth browsing the footnotes. As you went through the *Roadmap*, you may have noticed how many stories were footnoted —and also how many were not. I often clicked on the links, more often than not discovering that the link was dead. Notice that the footnotes are also mostly from sources with a URL. How many are dead links? I did some quick sampling: most lead to "error" pages.

Wow! That was a long read, even by grueling law school standards.

Ceres *Roadmap* Progress Reports

After the *Roadmap*, there were a series of biannual "progress reports" by Ceres on how well companies (as of 2012, 2014, 2016, 2018) had followed the *Roadmap*. The results, as you might guess, were somewhat disappointing.

In 2012, Ceres reminded companies that sustainability requires the collaboration of shareholders, management, non-governmental organizations, and other stakeholders—though apparently not government. In 2014, Ceres identified among the 600 largest US corporations some progress along various sustainability metrics, but with lots of room for improvement. In 2016, Ceres decided not enough was being done and tinkered with the *Roadmap*, though its essential four-pillar structure remained intact.

Then, in 2018, Ceres undertook a major initiative to re-invigorate the *Roadmap*—seeing 2018 as a turning point when corporations really began to take seriously sustainability. In the eight years since the *Roadmap*, Ceres identified that real progress had been made. But it's worth asking whether the Ceres vision of the corporation represents the future for the corporation? And was the corporation really at a turning point in 2018? And, even if so, are corporations moving toward Ceres's vision of the sustainable corporation fast enough?

Here are the key findings from the 2018 progress report:

#1 Materiality matters, but its role in decision-making remains unclear

Driven by investor calls to disclose the most material sustainability risks—including climate change, natural resource scarcity, diversity and inclusion, among others—more companies are taking steps to prioritize the environmental and social issues of greatest importance. By defining what is critically important, companies can direct more time and resources to the issues that matter most to their businesses and stakeholders. Companies increasingly understand that materiality assessments matter—but how they use this information to guide strategic planning and decisionmaking remains unclear.

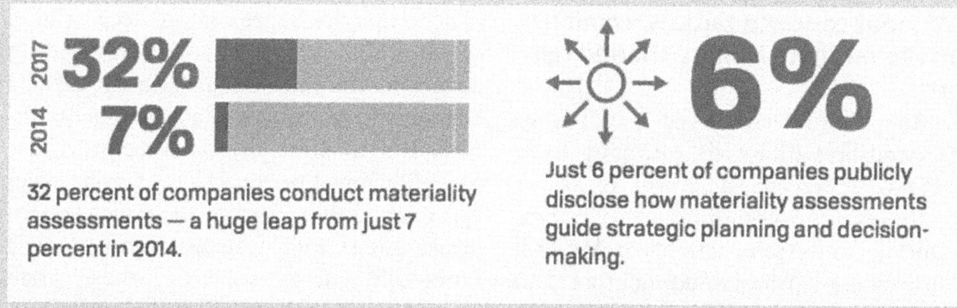

#2 Executive-level sustainability oversight improves, while board oversight plateaus.

Climate change, global water security, human rights abuses, and inequality present new and evolving challenges that both executives and corporate boards must consider as part of their fiduciary duty. Although accountability for these material issues has increased among senior executives, oversight among corporate boards has not kept pace.

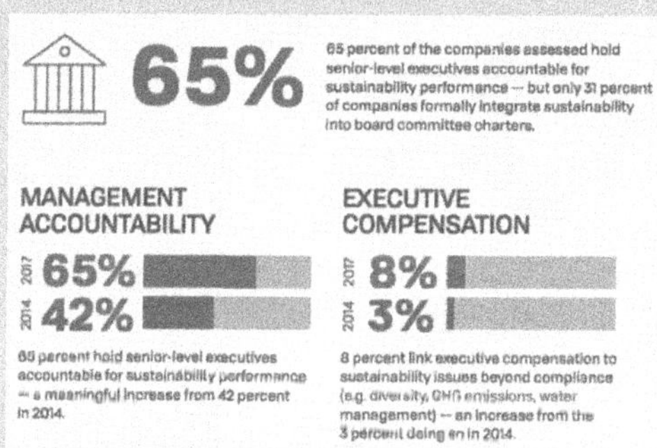

#3 Employee engagement can unlock sustainable innovation and drive talent retention, but not enough companies recognize training as the key.

Employees are an under-utilized sustainability resource. Every day, they make decisions that affect corporate sustainability performance, and often have the most successful and innovative ideas for improving sustainability. Employee training builds skills and changes behaviors, and the potential for sustainability innovation and impact can be compounded by job-specific training.

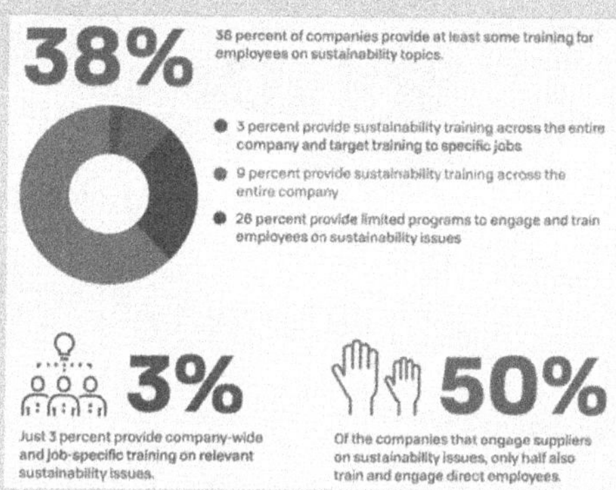

#4 Financial risk disclosure improves, but lacks detail and nuance.

Robust disclosure provides investors information needed to make better decisions. As the financial implications of a changing climate, increasing resource scarcity, data privacy violations and human rights abuses become ever more tangible, investors expect more transparency about actions companies are taking to address these risks. While more companies disclose sustainability risks in annual financial disclosures, most stick to boilerplate language, failing to provide investors decision-useful information.

#5 Without concrete targets, commitments to mitigate climate change fall short.

With the announcement of the Trump administration's intent to withdraw from the Paris Agreement, a chorus of voices from the business community spoke their resounding objections. The "We Are Still In" movement—now including more than 2,500 government, business, investor and university leaders; 127 million Americans; and companies representing $6.2 trillion of the U.S. economy—demonstrates a collective commitment to address climate change and transition to a clean energy future. But to limit global temperature rise to well below 2 degrees Celsius, companies must not only set goals to reduce greenhouse gas (GHG) emissions and increase renewable energy sourcing, those goals must be concrete, measurable, ambitious, and science-based.

32%

RENEWABLE ENERGY

32 percent of companies commit to increase renewable energy sourcing, but just 10 percent set time-bound targets and **only half** of those targets are science-based in line with the Ceres Roadmap.

64%

GHG EMISSIONS

64 percent have commitments to reduce greenhouse gas (GHG) emissions.

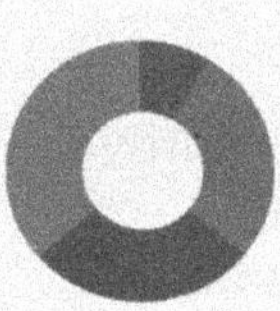

- 9 percent set science-based targets in line with the Ceres Roadmap
- 27 percent set time-bound, quantitative targets to reduce GHG emissions, but are not in line with the Ceres Roadmap
- 28 percent have general commitments to reduce GHG emissions, but no time-bound targets

55%

WATER MANAGEMENT

55 percent commit to managing water use.

- 14 percent set targets that prioritize action in the parts of the value chain with highest risk to water resources
- 6 percent set time-bound, quantitative targets to manage water impacts, but do not prioritize highest-risk operations
- 35 percent have general commitments to manage water impacts, but no time-bound targets

81%

81 percent of the companies in water-dependent sectors — including food and beverage, footwear and apparel, and semiconductors — have water stewardship programs, but just 29 percent of companies set quantitative targets focused on prioritizing action in the parts of value chain that pose the highest risk to water resources.

#6 More companies commit to water stewardship, but few prioritize areas most at risk.

Access to clean water and global water variability—resulting in increasingly severe droughts and flooding—are among the most significant climate impacts facing communities around the world. Today, more than 40% of the world's population suffers from water scarcity, undermining health, economy, environment and security. Despite the global scope of the water crisis, companies must not only understand impacts to water resources across the value chain, but also develop and prioritize specific local responses.

#7 Human rights commitments increase—but systems to protect workers remain scarce.

Human rights are everyone's business, and every business has a critical role to play in ensuring fair, safe and equitable workplaces. A growing number of companies are formalizing commitments to protect the basic human rights of workers across their global supply chains. Surprisingly, these companies do not always extend the same protections to employees within their own corporate walls, nor do they put in place systems needed to ensure those commitments translate into action.

15% Just 47 percent of companies with formal human rights policies have basic systems in place to ensure those policies are carried out, and only 15 percent conduct human rights impact assessments of operations and global supply chains.

67% 67 percent of human rights policies explicitly prohibit the use of forced and child labor, a significant increase from the 42 percent doing so in 2014.

2017 **49%**

2014 **31%**

49 percent have formal policies protecting the human rights of direct employees — up from 31 percent in 2014.

#8 Building sustainable global supply chains is underway, but it will take more than just words on paper.

Supplier codes that guide environmental and social performance have become commonplace for multinational corporations, and are a critical first step for extending sustainability commitments deep into the value chain. Unfortunately, only a small group of industry leaders translate these commitments into action, by proactively engaging and incentivizing suppliers toward improved performance. Those companies with formal audit programs are, however, significantly more likely to deploy a range of meaningful engagement tactics in order to improve the lives of workers and the communities they live in.

2017 **69%**

2014 **58%**

69 percent of companies assessed set sustainability performance requirements for their suppliers — an increase from 58 percent in Ceres' 2014 assessment.

34% While 69 percent call on their suppliers to effectively manage their environmental and social impacts, only **34 percent** engage suppliers through training, capacity building and incentivies.

36% The 36 percent of companies assessed that formally audit suppliers are **over three times more likely** to integrate environmental and social criteria into procurement decision-making and **over five times more likely** to proactively engage suppliers on sustainability issues through training, capacity building and other incentive programs.

#9 More companies commit to diversity, but don't yet incentivize change.

As tensions over race, gender, and sexual orientation increase, so does the value investors, companies, and employees place on diverse and inclusive workplaces. In the 2017 proxy season, nearly 100 shareholder resolutions asked companies to examine gender pay equity, improve diversity on boards of directors and management, and prepare diversity and non-discrimination reports—all considerable increases from 2016. But although more companies formalized diversity and inclusion commitments, few actually link compensation to diversity performance metrics, missing a key opportunity to incentivize change.

66% 66 percent implement formal trainings or employee resource groups focused on diversity and inclusion.

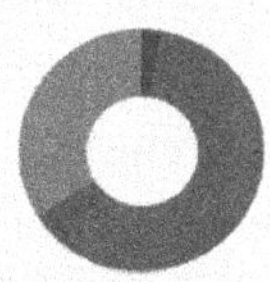

- 3 percent link executive compensation to diversity performance metrics
- 58 percent hold a senior executive accountable for diversity, but no links made to compensation
- 5 percent provide only basic training and/or resource groups on diversity and inclusion

#10 Accountability at the top drives business integration and stronger ambition—but sustainability needs to hit paychecks.

Holding the most senior decision-makers in the company—including the C-suite and board of directors—accountable for sustainability performance leads to more ambitious commitments. And connecting accountability to compensation drives even higher levels of business integration.

98% 98 percent of the companies with time-bound and company-wide targets to reduce greenhouse gas emissions hold senior executives accountable for sustainability.

97% 97 percent of companies with targets to address water impacts hold senior executives accountable for sustainability, compared to the average of 65 percent.

2x Companies with board oversight, who also link executive compensation to sustainability oversight, are **over two times more likely** to have company-wide time-bound targets to reduce GHG emissions and to formally protect the human rights of employees, than those who do not.

How Does Ceres Compare to Other ESG Initiatives?

A research paper prepared by Rylan Brooks (Brooklyn Law '20) looked at corporate transparency initiatives beyond Ceres in the fashion industry.

Transparency Initiatives in Fashion Industry

(Dec. 2019)

Rylan Brooks

[redacted/paraphrased]

In the fashion industry, beyond Ceres, several transparency initiatives exist, including: the Fashion Transparency Index, Good on You, Stand.Earth, Pulse of the Fashion Industry (published by Global Fashion Agenda, Boston Consulting Group and Sustainable Apparel Coalition), as well as certifications like Cradle to Cradle and certified LEED sustainable factory, amongst many others.

Ceres offers by far the most extensive and comprehensive assessment of corporate performance by utilizing 63 core indicators mapped to align with the 20 Roadmap expectations, and it provides companies with practical guidelines to implement sustainability practices (an important factor that many initiatives lack).

For example, Ceres uses scorecards to rank 613 companies (15 of which are in the footwear and apparel industry) on their governance, stakeholder engagement, and disclosure, as well as their performance (including operations, supply chain, transportation and logistics, and employees. In contrast, the Fashion Transparency Index, which reviews 200 of the biggest global fashion brands and retailers, ranks fashion companies on the following:

- policy & commitments (including a brand's social and environmental policies), whether the brand is putting its policies into practice, how the brand decides which issues to prioritize, the brand's future goals for improving its impacts
- governance (including whether there is board level responsibility for the company's social and environmental impacts), whether a relevant department or individual be easily contacted with questions, and whether the brand links human rights and environmental issues to its employee and supplier's performance

- traceability (including whether the brand publishes a list of suppliers from manufacturing to raw material level, and, if so, how much detail the brand shares), know, show & fix (including whether the brand assesses the implementation of its supplier policies; whether the brand fixes problems when found in its supplier facilities
- whether the brand discloses assessment findings (and how workers can report grievances); and spotlight issues (including what the brand is doing to address gender equality and female empowerment, what the brand is doing to support freedom of association and the payment of living wages, and what the brand is doing to tackle waste and recycling, sustainable production and climate change).

While the Fashion Transparency Index does not provide comprehensive guidelines to implement corporate sustainability, an admitted weakness, its strength lies in its depth of data-points and the fact it is the largest compilation of data on transparency and corporate disclosures in the fashion industry.

While Ceres and the Fashion Transparency Index both conclude that brands are increasingly taking greater strides to disclose more about their ESG policies, practices, and impacts, their corporate scorecards significantly differ. For instance, where Ceres ranks Foot Locker as generally exceeding the universe average (the highest score available) in terms of its supply chain, Foot Locker fares poorly when ranked by the Fashion Transparency Index: there, it gets a 6% overall, and under traceability (which speaks to supply chain transparency) Foot Locker scores a measly 0%, whereas the 3 highest scoring brands ranked in the Fashion Transparency Index received a 64%.

To conclude, despite confusion caused by significant differences in findings, it still feels like having seemingly conflicting information is better than having no information at all. So for now, this information, albeit conflicting, will have to be good enough because it does increase transparency and inform consumer choice.

4.3.3 Assessment of Voluntary Efforts Toward Corporate Sustainability

Shareholder Reaction to Voluntary ESG Programs

Are voluntary "sustainability" efforts by corporations likely to be viable? A 2010 study found that shareholders reacted poorly to announcements by companies that had joined a voluntary EPA program called Climate Leaders. Yet, companies that announced they had joined Ceres received a yawn from shareholders – no price change! That is, voluntary compliance and new "soft law" – at least, as of 2010 – were not yet something that the then SWM-driven financial markets recognized as creating corporate value. Karen Fisher-Vanden [Penn State Business School] & Karin S. Thorburn [Norwegian School of Economics and Business Administration], *Voluntary Corporate Environmental Initiatives and Shareholder Wealth* (2010) [available on SSRN]. Here are the study's conclusions:

> Researchers debate whether environmental investments reduce firm value or actually improve financial performance. We provide compelling evidence on shareholder wealth effects of membership in voluntary

environmental programs (VEPs). Companies announcing membership in EPA's Climate Leaders, a program targeting reductions in greenhouse gas emissions, experience significantly negative abnormal stock returns. The price decline is larger in firms with poor corporate governance structures, and for high market-to-book (i.e., high growth) firms.

However, firms joining Ceres, a program involving more general environmental commitments, have insignificant announcement returns, as do portfolios of industry rivals. Overall, corporate commitments to reduce greenhouse gas emissions appear to conflict with firm value-maximization. This has important implications for policies that rely on voluntary initiatives to address climate change. Further, we find that firms tend to join Climate Leaders either in response to climate-related shareholder resolutions or due to weak corporate governance standards, which give managers the discretion to make such voluntary environmentally responsible investment decisions—decisions that may result in lower firm value.

Phases of Grieving: Pathway to Corporate Sustainability

As you noticed, the Ceres *21st Century Corporation Roadmap* views corporate sustainability as a system. In a 2014 book, a group of Australian business and law academics took the same approach and identified how corporations as they move toward a sustainable model go through various stages of metamorphosis. You may find it interesting to cogitate on where corporations currently fall?

Organizational Change for Corporate Sustainability

(Routledge 3d ed. 2014)

Suzanne Benn, Dexter Dunphy, Andrew Griffiths

Human Sustainability: Inside the Corporation

The sustaining corporation "contributes to a society where human capabilities are enhanced rather than degraded and this process of continuous up-skilling improves the quality of life in society as a whole" (p. 294). It seeks to become an employer of choice. We propose a phase model for corporations progressing toward greater sustainability. The model focuses on environmental sustainability as well as human sustainability. The quotations below summarize the progression toward greater human sustainability. It addresses human systems within the corporation; that is, employees.

Phase 1: Rejection

"Employees and subcontractors are regarded as a resource to be exploited. Health and safety features are ignored or paid 'lip service'. Disadvantages stemming from ethnicity, gender, social class, intellectual ability and language proficiency are systematically exploited to advantage the organization and further disadvantage employees and subcontractors. Force, threats of force and abuse are used to maintain compliance and workforce subjection. Training costs are kept to a minimum necessary to operate the business; expenditure on personal and professional development is avoided. The organization does not take responsibility for the health, welfare and future career prospects of its employees nor for the community of which it is a part. Community concerns are rejected outright" (p. 28).

Phase 2: Non-Responsiveness

"Financial and technological factors dominate business strategies to the exclusion of most aspects of human resource management. 'Industrial relations' (IR) or 'employee relations' (ER) strategies dominate the human agenda, with 'labour' viewed as a cost to be minimized. Apart from cost minimization, IR/ER strategies are directed at developing a compliant workforce responsive to managerial control. The training agenda, if there is one, centres on technical and supervisory training. Broader human resource strategies and policies are ignored, as are issues of wider social responsibility and community concern" (pp. 28-29).

Phase 3: Compliance

"Financial and technological factors still dominate business strategies but senior management views the firm as a 'decent employer'. The emphasis is on compliance with legal requirements in industrial relations, safety, workplace standards and so on. Human resource functions such as training, IR, organization development, total quality management (TQM) are instituted but there is little integration between them. Basically the organization pursues a policy of benevolent paternalism with the expectation of employee loyalty in response. Community concerns are addressed only when the company faces the risk of prosecution or where negative publicity may have a damaging impact on the company's financial bottom line. Compliance is undertaken mainly as a risk-reduction exercise" (p. 29).

Phase 4: Efficiency

"There is a systematic attempt to integrate human resource functions into a coherent HR system to reduce costs and increase efficiency. People are viewed as a significant source of expenditure to be used as productively as possible. Technical and supervisory training is augmented with human relations (interpersonal skills) training. The organization may institute programmes of teamwork around significant business functions and generally pursues a value-adding rather than an exclusively cost reduction strategy. There is careful calculation of cost-benefit ratios for human resource expenditure to ensure that efficiencies are achieved. Community projects are undertaken where funds are available and where a cost benefit to the company can be demonstrated" (p. 30).

Phase5: Strategic Proactivity

"The workforce skills mix and diversity are seen as integral and vitally important aspects of corporate and business strategies. Intellectual and social capital are used to develop strategic advantage through innovation in products/services. Programmes are instituted to recruit the best talent to the organization and to develop high levels of competence in individuals and groups. IN addition, skills are systematized to form the basis of corporate competences so that the organization is less vulnerable to the loss of key individuals. Emphasis is placed on product and service innovation and speed of response to emerging market demands. Flexible workplace practices are strong features of workplace culture and contribute to the workforce leading more balanced lives. Communities affected by the organization's operations are taken into account and initiatives to address adverse impacts on communities are integrated into corporate strategy. Furthermore, the corporation views itself as a member of the community and as a result contributes to community betterment by offering sponsorship or employee time to participate in projects aimed at promoting community cohesion and well-being" (pp. 30-31).

Phase 6: The Sustainable Corporation

"The organization accepts responsibility for contributing to the process of renewing and upgrading human knowledge and skill formation in the community and society generally, and is a strong promoter of equal opportunity, workplace diversity and work-life balance as workplace principles. It adopts a strong and clearly defined corporate ethical position based on multiple stakeholder perspectives and seeks to exert influence on the key participants in the industry and in society in general to pursue human welfare, equitable and just social practices and the fulfillment of human potential of all. People are seen as valuable in their own right" (pp. 31-32).

Is Voluntary Action Enough?

In the end, perhaps voluntary change is not enough – or not realistic. The corporation after all is a legal construct. And perhaps we need the steely, exigent hand of government to modify the corporate DNA. Consider an update on how big corporations are (and aren't) fighting global warming:

Consider How Global Corporations Are—and Aren't—Fighting Global Warming

(June 23, 2018)

Ben German

[available on Axious]
[redacted/paraphrased]

Major companies in the U.S. and worldwide are increasingly taking steps to lower the carbon footprint of what they produce, how they ship goods, and the energy they buy.

They're driven by market signals, government mandates, reputational interests, investor pressure and other factors. Here's a few snapshots of how some major industries are approaching the topic.

Big oil: A number of the world's biggest oil-and-gas companies are ramping up their investments in low-carbon technologies like renewables and electric vehicle infrastructure. For instance . . .

- Shell: In late 2017, the company pledged to cut the "net carbon footprint of its energy products by around half by 2050," with an interim reduction goal of 20% by 2035. The company also said spending on its alternative energies division would reach $2 billion per year by 2020.
- BP: The company this year made a high-profile pledge to lower emissions of methane, a potent greenhouse gas, from its operations. Like Shell and some other

majors—led by European firms—the company is boosting investment in renewables and batteries. Recent moves include a three-year, $200 million investment to gain a 43 percent stake in the solar power company Lightsource, and May's announcement that BP's venture arm is investing $20 million in the EV battery firm StoreDot.

Yes, but: These investments represent a very small part of the industry's overall spending. Consider that last year's Shell's overall capital spending was $24 billion.

And critics say the industry has, at best, a split personality, noting for instance that companies are members of trade associations that have lobbied against U.S. carbon emissions regulations.

Power purchasing: In late May the International Renewable Energy Agency, in its first global tally of corporate renewable power sourcing, said that last year companies bought around 465 terawatt-hours of renewable energy, such as from solar and wind facilities. This is almost the equivalent of France's power demand.

Big Tech has emerged as an important player in the trend. Apple and Google both say their operations—including power-thirsty data centers—are now powered completely by renewables, and companies like Microsoft and Amazon also have major initiatives.

But, due to rising global electricity demand largely in emerging economies, the share of fossil fuels in the worldwide power mix has remained constant over the last 20 years, despite the surge in renewables, a recent BP report on global energy data noted.

In particular, coal, which is the most carbon intensive energy source, has retained a 38 percent share in the worldwide electricity mix for the last two decades.

The bottom line: Absent stronger national policies worldwide, the role of the corporate moves, alongside sub-national actors like U.S. states, won't stem global emissions enough to prevent high levels of warming.

4.3.4 Ceres *Roadmap 2030*

The Vision

In 2020, Ceres released its *Roadmap 2030*: 10-Year Action Plan for Sustainable Business Leadership. This update to its 2010 *Roadmap* identified a variety of issues and solutions for corporations to implement – all organized around three intertwined themes: critical impact actions, business integration actions, and system change actions. As Ceres explained, "As people are mistreated and denied the resources to thrive, survival outweighs environmental stewardship. Failure to address one issue exacerbates the risk of another." In short, the *2030 Roadmap* recognizes the importance of building "just and inclusive" corporate governance while protecting our climate and natural resources.

Goal 1: Critical Impact Actions

The *2030 Roadmap* identified "the private sector impacts that are most material across economic sectors and have the greatest potential to disrupt our planet, communities, and economy. To help companies transition from commitment to impact at scale, the actions detail specific performance milestones for today, 2025 and finally, 2030." The three subcategories are intended to stabilize the climate, protect water and natural resources, and build a just and inclusive economy.

Need to act. The *2030 Roadmap* begins by describing the need to stabilize the climate and how our planet is threatened. In 2020, deforestation, greenhouse gas emissions, and global temperatures reached record-breaking numbers; meanwhile, only two percent of the largest corporations have taken action to control climate change by 2030. Ceres calls on companies to engage with GHG emission reductions, carbon removal, zero to low emission transportation, deforestation elimination, land restoration, and 100% reliance on renewable energy. Later in the report, Ceres gives specific instruction on how to implement these actions.

Protection of water and natural resources. Ceres points to rising population and scarcity of resources. Broadening its approach, the *2030 Roadmap* calls for improving water quality by reducing pollution and adapting water use to high-water stress situations. It calls on corporations to "protect and contribute to the restoration of natural ecosystems and biodiversity by achieving resource positivity for key raw materials, sharply reducing demand for renewable and non-renewable resources and bringing circular economy business solutions to scale throughout the value chain." Corporations must undertake additional (though unspecified) research to achieve these goals.

Human rights concerns. Looking to the past and future, Ceres calls on corporations to guarantee people a just and inclusive economy. Although in recent years we have made strides in addressing the injustices that indigenous people, people of color, and women face, these issues persist today. "Our fellow citizens continue to face systematic racism and sexism in the workforce that prevents them from having the financial and bodily security that many white men have in America. Devastatingly, modern-day slavery still exists hidden under a veil of low-wage labor and human trafficking.

And many human trafficking cases go unreported. Corporations that knowingly create or ignore human rights violations need to be exposed, and thus to change these inhumane industry standards.

Four-part solution. To create a just and inclusive economy, the *2030 Roadmap* lays our four solutions: First, corporations must address human rights by creating opportunities that further social progress for underrepresented groups like minorities and women. Second, a company's workforce should mirror the diversity of the community and engage in anti-discriminatory practices. Third, wage and benefit equity must be addressed across all positions in the workplace, so that all employees make at least a livable wage. Fourth, during a company's transition, corporations must avoid the business model disruption that creates adverse impact and look instead to models that support workers and the community. Some goals - like wage equity – can be achieved quickly. Others – like hiring a diverse staff – may take some time.

Goal 2: Business Integration Actions

The *2030 Roadmap* next mapped out concrete steps that companies should take "to re-engineer corporate systems and business models for a more sustainable future, providing a clear pathway for improving . . . business accountability, strategic planning and execution, and transparency and disclosure. That is, it's not enough to change manufacturing practices, but rather business structures.

Strategic planning and execution. To bridge the gap between maximizing profits and planning for the future, corporations typically function with a short-term mindset, racing to increase profit margins on an annual or even quarterly basis. The *2030 Roadmap* brings to the attention of companies the benefits of long-term investment, suggesting integrating this initiative into the company's mission statement—the corporation's role in society, the relevance of sustainability impacts to financial risks and strategic planning, and the value of inviting other stakeholders to the conversation. Here, Ceres provides specific ways of reaching this goal—almost immediately by expanding the metrics companies use to identify risk or by calling a meeting to promulgate a new mission statement.

Business accountability. The *2030 Roadmap* explains that "in the face of a crisis, strong governance, accountability and management can be the difference between success and failure. For decades, forward-looking investors have viewed formal accountability for sustainability performance as a proxy for good governance overall and a signal of greater corporate resilience." For a strong and effective corporate governance, Ceres tells corporations to integrate sustainability into board discussions on risks and revenues, to require C-Suite executives to oversee sustainability efforts, and to train its workforce to consider these issues – again with clear actions that corporations can easily implement.

Transparency and disclosure. In an age when corporate transparency is expected, corporations must seek to disclose their sustainable actions to the public – thus to improve consumer attitudes toward the business and hold the corporation accountable and incentivize further efforts. If not, society will expose corporate lapses – for example, the boycott of Wendy's because of the company's unsustainable human rights violations. "The Ceres Roadmap 2030 challenges companies to create and maintain disclosures that are goal- and metric-driven, consistent, comparable, decision-useful, accessible and stakeholder relevant." Ceres calls on companies to create uniform metrics to allow accurate reporting on the progress the corporation has or has not made.

Goal 3: Systems Change Actions

The *2030 Roadmap* also "recognizes that no one company alone can create a more equitable, just and sustainable economy.' The *2030 Roadmap* thus calls for companies "to proactively communicate, advocate and collaborate within and across industries and sectors, in order to positively influence customers, suppliers, industry groups and policymakers to create the Systems Change needed to support and enable sustainable business practices."

There are no subcategories in this action category. But a good example of this goal is for companies to join the Business for Innovative Climate and

Energy Policy (BICEP), also known as the Ceres Policy Network. This is an initiative for US companies, now more than 75, including McDonalds, Nike, and Microsoft. As the *2030 Roadmap* explains, the BICEP Network "helps companies voice their support for the policies our economy urgently needs to prevent the dire financial and material risks of the climate crisis while unleashing new industries, jobs, and growth as part of the solution. These companies are respected leaders in their industries, and they recognize that transitioning to a just and inclusive clean energy economy is win-win for the planet and for business." This innovative network, one of Ceres's key triumphs, puts corporations in the driver's seat and encourages trust and understanding between sustainability advocates and business leaders.

Looking at issues from a public-policy perspective, this goal calls on corporations to notice the increasing need to use their power to influence regulatory policy. Rather lobbying against such things as environmental protection and labor rights, companies (and investors) are called on to do their homework and see the connection between sustainability and long-term profitability. Finally, Ceres mentions the need to meet with the community and other organizations to encourage multi-stakeholder collaboration.

The *2030 Roadmap* explains this new direction for US corporate political action:

> Over the years, Ceres BICEP Network members have advocated for policies across all levels of government to advance renewable energy and fuel efficiency standards, implement sustainable transportation policies, invest in clean power sources, and achieve the goals of the Paris Agreement. At the state level, members have played a critical role in passing some of the most ambitious climate laws in the country. And the BICEP Network's influential and respected voice is credible across the political spectrum—helping achieve key bipartisan climate victories in states across the country. (Ceres: BICEP)

Thus, the Ceres BICEP Network complements work by NGOs and others dedicated to specific issues like renewable energy. The BICEP Network becomes an essential part of the political efforts for sustainability in law and policy.

Changes in Demographics

Although not listed as an action item, the *2030 Roadmap* focused on new demographics. New employees are demanding that their corporations increase social responsibility for workers within the corporation and up and down the supply chain. Ceres estimates that 55% of the workforce will be composed of Gen Z and Millennials by 2025. With access to the internet that illuminates shortcomings in corporations' treatment, these generations are equipped with the knowledge and compassion to effectuate change. The Boston Consulting Group, for example, has said that "more than two-thirds of Millennials expect their employers to have a purpose-driven mission and their individual jobs to have a positive societal impact." Even if the incumbent predominately white, male business leaders hang around for a while longer, they will have to take into account future employees' interests if they want to employ young and innovative thinkers.

* * *

Concluding Thoughts

Live Life Fully

So, apparently, this is a true story.

There was a restaurant manager in New York City named George. He was beloved by patrons who would come to his restaurant just to see him. When anybody asked him, "George, how are you?" he would answer, "If I were any happier, I would be two persons."

When people came to the restaurant where George worked, they always wanted to talk to him. When he moved from one restaurant to another, the wait staff moved with him to the new restaurant. They, too, wanted to be around George.

One day George made a mistake. He forgot to lock the back door of the restaurant, and some robbers got into the restaurant. At gunpoint, they told him to open the safe. But he was so nervous that his sweaty fingers slipped on the safe's combination lock. The robbers got flustered, and one of them shot him.

Fortunately, somebody heard the gunshot and was able to call 911 right away. George was rushed by ambulance to the hospital. When he arrived at the hospital, he was wheeled immediately into the surgery room. There, he saw the look in the eyes of the doctors and the nurses. They had almost given up on him. Their eyes said that they thought he would die.

So, before the anesthesiologist put him under, a nurse asked George whether he was allergic to anything. He paused – to make sure everyone was paying attention. "I'm allergic to bullets. I want to live. Please, save my life."

The surgical team did. Then, after a difficult recovery, George returned to the restaurant where he worked. He still had some bullet fragments in him and still was in pain. When people came to the restaurant, they asked him, "George, how are you?" He looked at them and said, "If I were any happier, I would be two persons."

* * *

Live life fully! Maybe that's what some of the investment managers and business executives who have joined the Ceres networks are trying to do. No?

UNIT 5

RETHINKING CORPORATION

In this our final unit, we consider how the corporation can be seen as a system with multiple inputs and multiple outputs, all of which have moral dimensions. We also consider whether awakening capitalism—sometimes called stakeholder capitalism—is real or delusional. And we conclude by turning the corporation inside-out and look at how we as humans function in a business organization—are we true to others and to ourselves?

Reaching the end of the road. We've come a long way. We started by looking at the basic attributes of the US corporation (Unit 1) and then its unsustainable design (Unit 2). It was often easy to become discouraged. Although the US corporation is characterized by its adaptability in responding to social, economic, and technological changes, much of its design seemed incompatible with meeting current human needs while not jeopardizing the needs of future generations.

The Triple Bottom Line (Unit 3) told the story of recent, voluntary actions to address the corporation's unsustainable design. Environmental stewardship, the CSR (or more recently the ESG) movement, and the rise of socially responsible investing all provided some reason for hope. And recent reforms of the corporation (Unit 4) suggested even more fundamental redesign of the corporation's DNA—benefit corporations, mandatory ESG disclosure, and the remarkable Ceres.

But even if the modern business/financial system—that is, capitalism—is beginning to awaken to the challenges faced by humanity, there are lingering questions. Is the corporation capable of being moral (Ch 5.1)? Is awakening capitalism really happening, or is it a delusion (Ch 5.2)? And, even if the corporation is awakening to our inter connected world, is the corporation as a set of incentives (carrots and sticks) capable of adapting to carry out its new role (Ch 5.3)? These are the questions of this our final unit.

Unit 1 **Intro to corporation**	**Unit 2** **Unsustainable design**	**Unit 3** **Triple bottom line**	**Unit 4** **Redesign corporation**	**Unit 5** **Rethink corporation**
1.1 US law 1.2 US corporation 1.3 US public corp 1.4 US securities reg	2.1 Limited liability 2.2 Short-termism 2.3 Board mono-culture 2.4 Corp in politics	3.1 Planet: environ 3.2 People: CSR 3.3 Profits: SRI	4.1 Benefit corp 4.2 ESG disclosure 4.3 Consortium: Ceres	5.1 Corp as moral system 5.2 Stakeholder capitalism–delusion? 5.3 Personal integrity

Chapter 5.1

Corporation as Moral System

This chapter offers you a deeper perspective on the questions we've addressed thus far: What is the purpose of the corporation? What is its essential nature—private or public? How might the corporation be redesigned to become more sustainable?

But perhaps we have framed these questions incorrectly. Rather than search for a single (or hybrid) corporate purpose, it may be that the corporation is best understood as having multiple purposes—that is, the essential nature of the corporation may best be understood as a "system." If so, systems thinking and analysis may be a more fruitful approach as we search for the sustainable corporation. Seeing the corporation as a system, much like the human body, avoids the "duality thinking" of either/or, up/down, shareholder/stakeholder—all of which may be false binaries.

Instead, perhaps the corporation is neither a legal creature nor an economic phenomenon, but instead a "moral system" constantly called on to distinguish right from wrong. Treating the corporation as a set of financial incentives misses the point that implicit moral values may be even more important in corporate decision-making. Seeing the corporation as a "moral being—a "person" imbued with a moral character, rather than a chameleon that changes colors according to the prevailing economic, financial, and market conditions—may be more explanatory than current approaches. And in observing corporate culture as having personhood, we can gain insights from nature.

Perhaps, the corporation is best seen as a super-organism with a moral character.

Chapter's Focus

You will want to focus on the notion that the corporation is a multi-purpose system and that no single, overarching purpose explains how it does or should function. You will see the argument that the shareholder primacy norm—even as articulated in terms of long-term shareholder value—lacks objective content. You will want to consider how a multi-purpose corporation's outputs might be measured and thus managed—such as customer satisfaction, employee well-being, and sustainable-resource use—and notice the echoes of the Triple Bottom Line.

You will want to consider how the largest investor-owned utilities (IOUs) in the United States responded in various settings to the EPA's proposal to regulate CO_2 emissions through state-by-state emission goals—a moral response by corporate organisms. You will also want to consider how "moral psychology" has identified that we make moral decisions intuitively, instantly, and largely invisibly. In this regard, you will want to consider why IOUs in responding to the EPA's proposed Clean Power Plan used the rhetoric of progressives (in their CSR reports), conservatives (in their EPA comments), and libertarians (in their SEC filings).

Finally, you will want to focus on how US corporations are taking moral stands on issues, such as civil rights, workplace discrimination climate change, and recently the Russian invasion of Ukraine, even when the government has been sometimes more cautious. The question you should consider is not whether the corporation is a moral system, but rather what kind of moral system it is and what it is becoming.

5.1.1 Corporation as Multi-Purpose System

The debate on the nature of the corporate purpose is at a crossroads.

Next is an article by Professors Tamara Belinfanti (New York Law) and Lynn Stout (Cornell Law). It offers "a unifying approach to understanding corporations—that of systems thinking—in which public companies can be viewed as complex systems in which multiple inputs (including resource capital, human capital, and financial capital) interact with each other to perform a variety of useful and desirable outputs (providing goods and services, employment opportunities, investor returns, and tax revenues) under uncertain conditions and over time." Belinfanti and Stout assert that a corporation viewed in this way is more sustainable—read on!

Contested Visions: The Value of Systems Theory for Corporate Law

(2018)

Tamara Belinfanti & Lynn Stout

[available on SSRN]

Introduction

Any attempt to answer the question "what is a corporation?" is an exercise in negotiating contested visions of the nature and purpose of the corporate form:

- the corporation is a grantee of the state and should serve a public purpose (concession theory)
- the corporation as a separate legal entity with the ability to hold property and enter contracts in its own name (entity theory)

- the corporation is not "real" but rather is a nexus of privately-negotiated contracts (nexus of contract theory)
- the corporation is an aggregation of natural persons (aggregate theory) or, relatedly, an aggregation of shareholder property (property theory)
- the corporation is an aggregation of specific assets, whose use is mediated by a centralized board (team production)

The recent twin U.S. Supreme Court cases of *Citizens United v. FEC* (2010) and *Burwell v. Hobby Lobby Stores, Inc.* (2014) bring these contested visions into sharp focus. In *Citizens United*, Justice Kennedy's opinion for the majority described corporations as "associations of citizens," while Justice Steven's dissent insisted that are legal entities that "have no consciences, no beliefs, no feelings, no thoughts, no desires." In *Hobby Lobby*, Justice Alito repeatedly described a corporation's shareholders as its "owners," implying that a corporation is its shareholders' property, while Justice Ginsberg's dissent maintained that corporations were "artificial persons" separate from any individual and noted that, besides shareholders, workers "sustain the operations of" corporations.

Meanwhile, Anglo-American corporate scholarship and corporate governance practice for most of the past three decades have assumed a "standard" economic account that shareholders own and ultimately ought to control corporations; that shareholders' principal interest is increasing their wealth; that the interests of other corporate constituencies, like employees and customers, should be protected primarily by contract and regulation; and that the market price of a public company's shares is the principal measure of shareholders' wealth. But, as the *Citizens United* and *Hobby Lobby* opinions illustrate, this consensus seems to be falling apart. The Anglo-American model ignores the significance of corporate legal personhood; it does not fit with the very limited control granted shareholders under actual corporate law; the standard model leads to social inefficiency when, as may often be the case, contracts are incomplete and regulation is imperfect; and that stock market prices often fail to capture long-term economic value.

In this Article, we suggest a new and more unifying approach to understanding corporations—that of systems thinking. We argue that public companies in particular can be viewed as complex systems in which multiple inputs (e.g., financial capital, physical capital, and human capital) interact with each other to perform a variety of useful and desirable outputs (e.g., providing goods and services, employment opportunities, investor returns, and tax revenues) under uncertain conditions and over time.

We conclude that, especially in light of the close correspondence between systems thinking and traditional corporate law and practice, systems theory offers an intriguing and indeed compelling approach for understanding the nature of corporations, their proper purpose, and the best way to hold their managers accountable. In the process, it offers to integrate and sometimes reconcile the many competing visions of the corporation being debated today.

I. Contested Visions and the Role of Shareholder Value Theory

A. Contested Visions

Scholars, judges, regulators, and practitioners have long debated the questions of what corporations are and what their purpose should be. Thus the corporation has been described as: (1) an entity; (2) an aggregate of people; (3) a web of contracts; (4) a government concession or "franchise government"; (5) a collection of specific investments; and (6) the property of its shareholders. Each model offers its own particular vision of how best to describe the corporation, given its semiautonomous, perpetual nature, legal personhood, and the interwoven web of human relationships and interactions that often present in the corporate form.

B. The Rise and Evolution of Shareholder Value Theory

For the past quarter-century, the dominant narrative of corporate purpose in the Anglo-American world has been that business corporations have but one goal: to maximize shareholder wealth or "shareholder value." It is difficult to overstate just how much shareholder value theory has influenced contemporary corporate governance, especially in the United States.

Yet it is only relatively recently that the idea that public corporations exist to maximize shareholder wealth has acquired such power. Why did this occur? In part, shareholder value theory gained traction because it served the purposes of powerful interest groups, including newly-emerging "activist" investors and executives whose compensation, due to 1993 changes in the tax code, increasingly was based on share price. Shareholder value theory has been justified on three grounds: first, that shareholders "own" corporations; second, that shareholders are the residual claimants in corporations; and third, that shareholder value provides the single quantifiable metric that is essential to constrain agency costs and hold corporate directors and executives accountable.

The notion that shareholders "own" corporations is demonstrably incorrect. Corporations are legal persons with rights, which means that, just as a natural person cannot be owned by another, a corporation cannot be owned by its shareholders. What shareholders do own are shares, a set of limited rights from the corporate entity. One such right is the right to elect and remove directors. But, since at least the days of Berle and Means, this right carries almost no real influence in the context of a public corporation with dispersed share ownership.

The second claim that shareholders are the residual claimants entitled to all profits left over after the business has met its contractual and legal obligations (e.g., interest due creditors, wages due employees, and taxes due governments) is also incorrect. Again, experts increasingly recognize that, for several reasons, shareholders are not the sole residual claimants of corporations—at least not of operating companies. First, corporations are their own residual claimants. The corporation's profits are the property of the corporate entity and not the property of its shareholders. Second, modern options theory teaches that once a corporation has issued debt, its debtholders also have a residual interest in how the company is run. Third, when important corporate "stakeholders" make specific investments in a corporation's continued operation (for example, when employees acquire skills uniquely valuable to the company as an employer, or customers become dependent on its products), these stakeholders also acquire a residual interest in the company's operations. Fourth, if social norms and government regulation cannot perfectly control corporate behavior—a likely scenario—directors' and executives' managerial decisions can generate external costs and benefits for third parties. These externalities give third parties an interest in how the company is managed.

These flaws in the first two claims traditionally used to defend shareholder value theory have led contemporary commentators to rely ever more heavily on a third justification: that shareholder value is necessary to ensure managerial accountability—that is, the only way to ensure managerial accountability is to hold managers' collective feet to the fire by demanding they maximize a single quantifiable metric. As influential economist Michael Jensen has put it, "telling the manager to maximize current profits, market share, future growth profits, and anything else one pleases will leave the manager with no way to make a reasoned decision. In effect it leaves the manager with no objective." Jensen concluded that a "true (single dimensional) score" was essential.

But asking managers to maximize "shareholder value" generates a host of corporate pathologies, including excessive risk-taking, underinvestment, reduced innovation, increasing disparities between executive and rank-and-file pay, and a general focus on short term results at the expense of long-term performance. An unhealthy managerial focus on immediate results has been accused of driving companies like Motorola and Hewlett-Packard to sacrifice their resilience and long-term performance by restructuring, selling assets, and cutting "expenses" for marketing, R&D, and employee development in order to boost the bottom line. It was suspected of encouraging companies like BP to cut safety and regulatory corners. It has also been identified as a root cause of the 2008 financial crisis, when it drove banks to make risky mortgage loans and to leverage themselves to the brink of insolvency and beyond.

In response, many supporters of shareholder value have adjusted their stance yet again. They now emphasize that what they mean is "long-term shareholder value." For example, in a 2015 opinion piece Steven Bainbridge wrote that "the law requires corporate directors and managers to pursue long-term, sustainable shareholder wealth maximization." In the 2009 case of *In Re Citigroup Inc. Shareholder Derivative Litigation*, which arose from the 2008 financial crisis, Delaware Chancellor William B. Chandler opined that "[u]ltimately, the discretion granted directors and managers allows them to maximize shareholder value in the long term." But can long term shareholder value provide the single quantifiable metric needed to constrain agency costs and hold corporate managers accountable? We think not.

C. Why Long-Term Shareholder Value Cannot be Used to Hold Managers Accountable: The Problem of Uncertainty

On first inspection, the idea of defining "shareholder value" in terms of the long term seems eminently sensible. Corporations, after all, are perpetual entities, capable of earning profits and paying dividends into an indefinite future. Throughout history they have pursued projects that lasted years, decades, or even centuries. In the Middle

Ages, corporate entities constructed monasteries, cathedrals and universities. In the seventeenth century they opened continents for trade. In the eighteenth, nineteenth, and twentieth centuries they built canals, railroads, and electrical grids. Today they are developing self-driving cars and commercial space transport.

Yet once we shift from defining "shareholder value" in terms of stock price or similar short term metrics, to an amorphous concept like long term shareholder value, the claim that shareholder value theory offers a superior way to hold managers accountable begins to collapse. This is because, once we abandon the fundamental-efficient-markets presumption that today's stock price perfectly captures intrinsic value, the corporate entity's perpetual nature raises insoluble barriers to objectively quantifying "long-term value." Over time, a successful business corporation provides shareholders with a stream of financial returns in the form of share appreciation and dividends paid. Shareholder value theory blithely presumes this stream of future returns can be observed, neatly summed up, and discounted to present value, so as to reach a single agreed-upon number. This presumption unrealistically assumes away one of the business world's most endemic challenges: the problem of uncertainty.

Investors, analysts, and finance professors can employ a number of comfortably familiar mathematical techniques to value economic ventures that are merely risky. But they have not yet figured out how to deal with uncertainty. Uncertainty allows subjective disagreement. Rational people cannot disagree on the probable results of a coin toss, but they can disagree about whether Apple will thrive or fail without Steve Jobs. Uncertainty and disagreement make the task of valuing an ongoing business venture notoriously difficult and subjective.

The reality of uncertainty undermines the claim that demanding corporate directors and executives to maximize long-term shareholder value somehow adds clarity or rigor to the messy business of gauging whether managers are doing a good job. Once we attempt to attach any number other than today's market price to a company's shares, the number becomes subject to disagreement and manipulation. The CEO claims her chosen business strategy will maximize shareholder value "in the long run;" the activist hedge fund manager argues his proposed restructuring will better "unlock shareholder value." There is no way to prove who is correct. Both claims are unfalsifiable until the future arrives.

This means that, far from supplying an objective metric for holding corporate managers accountable, "long-term shareholder value" may provide no observable metric at all. The concept simply cannot perform the function that supposedly justifies it as a theory of corporate purpose. It cannot provide a way to objectively assess managerial performance. Which raises the question: what is left of the case for shareholder value theory?

A diehard defender of shareholder value as the corporate maximand might reply that, whatever its weaknesses, long-term shareholder value remains the best possible corporate objective because it is better to use an imperfect tool than no tool at all. We argue that an alternative tool for assessing corporate performance—one that honors the complexities of corporations and board decisionmaking, and allows for better managerial accountability and monitoring—is indeed available. That alternative is systems thinking.

II. The Systems Alternative

A. What is Systems Theory?

Systems theory is a design and performance assessment methodology routinely used in many fields, including engineering, biology, computer science, and (significantly) management science.

What, then, is a "system"? A system has been defined as any set of distinct but interconnected elements or parts that operate as a unified whole to serve a function or purpose. Consider, for example, the humble coffee machine. Its different parts—filter, water reservoir, heating element, coffee pot—are distinct, but operate together for the purpose of brewing coffee. The human body also is a system. Its elements include lungs, circulatory system, musculature, skeletal frame, etc. Each is distinct, but the elements interact with each other to function as a unified organism. In contrast, pebbles randomly scattered along the street do not constitute a system. They are not interconnected, nor do they form a cohesive whole that serves a particular function or purpose.

Systems accordingly have certain core characteristics: (1) they consist of distinct elements (2) these elements are coordinated and interconnected; and (3) the elements operate as a unified whole to serve a given function or purpose. In addition, a fourth core characteristic of systems implicit in the literature, and of critical importance for our discussion, is (4) systems perform their function or purpose over time. The coffee machine, it is hoped, will brew coffee not only today, but tomorrow.

Systems take many forms. Some systems, such as the coffee machine, are designed. Other systems, like organisms, evolve. Still other systems are hybrids that are both designed and evolved. Examples of hybrid systems include business corporations.

Business corporations consist of separate yet interconnected elements, including human capital (employees, executives, directors), financial capital (funds raised from operations and from equity and debt investors), and physical capital (plant and equipment, inventory). Each element is distinct and serves a distinct purpose. For example, directors and officers supply managerial expertise; employees supply labor; the physical plant produces goods for sale; and financial capital purchases the labor and raw materials needed to produce more goods. These elements do not exist in isolation vis-à-vis each other. They are interconnected, influencing each other in ways that allow them to operate as a unified whole, separate and apart from their individual selves. This unified whole performs several useful functions: generating goods and services, investment returns, and tax revenues. Finally, it performs these functions over time. Indeed, an incorporated entity in theory can operate in perpetuity.

B. Systems Theory and The Nature of the Corporation

Perhaps the first and most fundamental principle in systems theory is that systems are more than the sum of their parts. The individual pieces of a coffee machine, left lying about, do nothing. It is only when these pieces are connected and fitted together properly, and interact with and affect each other, that the machine can brew coffee.

This principle applies straightforwardly to business corporations. The individual elements that comprise the corporation—physical assets, intellectual capital, financial resources, labor—perform quite differently when disconnected and disaggregated from each other, than when they are coordinated with each other through the corporate entity. A pile of money, sitting alone, does nothing. It is only when investors' money is combined and coordinated with intellectual capital, physical capital, and human capital, that the money can generate additional wealth for investors (along with goods, services, employment opportunities, and innovations). The firm, like the coffee machine and other systems, operates as an integrated whole to perform functions that its individual parts cannot perform in isolation.

A second fundamental principle of systems thinking is that systems are fractal, in the sense that it is useful to think of systems as comprised of subsystems, which in turn are comprised of other subsystems, and so on, ad infinitum. Conversely a system typically can also be described as a subsystem of another larger system. Thus a human being is comprised of organs, which are comprised of cells, which are comprised of protein molecules, etc. At the same time, an individual can be viewed as part of a family, which is part of a community, which is part of a nation, and so forth. To keep the amount of information needed to make decisions within manageable bounds, systems thinkers typically order systems into hierarchies. Any system can be broken down into component subsystems, or viewed as a subsystem of a larger system.

Again, this lesson applies to corporations. A corporation can be viewed as comprised of a number of different subsystems, such as its managerial team; its production process and facilities; its marketing team; and its financial operations. Each subsystem is comprised of elements that interact with each other to perform some subpurpose (raising financing, manufacturing products, generating sales). Conversely, a corporation can be viewed as part of a larger system (e.g., a corporate conglomerate, or a nation's economy). For present purposes—that is, for analyzing the nature, purpose, and best way of monitoring the performance of business corporations—we treat the corporate entity as the system of interest and the appropriate level of analysis.

A third general principle of systems theory that flows from the first and second principles is that the overall health and continued functioning of a system depends on the continued health and functioning of each of its essential subsystems. Each subsystem must work for the whole system to work properly, and changes in the elements or relationships of a subsystem can affect the system as a whole. If a coffee machine's heating element breaks, for example, the coffee machine can no longer brew coffee.

Corporations similarly depend on all their subsystems to function. If equity or debt investors refuse to supply funds; if employees stop manning the production facilities; if executives mismanage; the entire corporation may soon cease to function.

Finally, a fourth important lesson from systems theory is that, to fulfill its purpose or function, a system must survive. Recall that a basic characteristic of systems is that they perform purposes or functions over time. The time period necessary to fulfill the system's purpose or function may be quite short (consider the fruit fly or the hand grenade). But it may also be quite long. This is especially likely to be true in the case of business firms organized as perpetual corporate entities. For example, the Hudson Bay Company has been operating continuously since 1670; General Electric (a corporate adolescent by comparison) was founded in 1892. When systems must operate over long periods of time to perform their functions or purposes, system survivability—or, to use a more common label, sustainability—becomes a desideratum.

Systems thinkers accordingly devote considerable attention to questions of sustainability. This focus is apparent in the systems literature, which identifies multiple strategies to improve the odds a system will survive long enough to achieve its intended purpose. Because sustainability may be a particularly desirable attribute for perpetual entities like corporations, we conclude this section by exploring some common sustainability strategies in greater detail.

One straightforward sustainability mechanism found in many systems is redundancy—that is, devoting more resources to some purpose than necessary under current conditions. Redundancy is often seen, for example, in engineering, where it is common practice to employ backup systems, or make structures stronger than they need to be. Redundancy is inefficient in a narrow sense, as redundant resources seem "wasted" as long as conditions remain stable. In an uncertain world, however, conditions may change, and redundant resources prove essential for the system's survival. This explains why redundancy is often seen in organisms. (If efficiency were all evolution cared about, people would not become overweight, or have two kidneys.)

A second sustainability mechanism found in many systems is homeostasis—that is, information and control feedback loops that allow the system to adjust to disturbances in its external environment, and stay within the parameters necessary for continued functioning. For example, the dihedral ("V"-shaped) wings of aircraft provide homeostasis. When a wing dips in flight, it tends to rebound. Organisms similarly use feedback loops to achieve homeostasis; hunger is a feedback mechanism that prompts an organism to eat when running short on calories. Systems theorists have something of an obsession with feedback loops, which can be stabilizing or destabilizing ("runaway" feedback loops), and may have limits or breakdown points. (Dihedral wings alone are unlikely to save an aircraft turned upside down.)

Finally, a third sustainability mechanism found in some systems is the capacity for self-organization—the ability for the system itself to change ("to learn, diversify, complexify, evolve") in response to shifts in the external environment that might otherwise overwhelm the system's feedback loops, and threaten the system's survival. For example, birds are warm-blooded, but many species do not rely only on homeostasis to avoid freezing; they have also evolved the ability to fly south for winter.

Business firms can, and often do, exhibit redundancy, homeostasis, and self-organization. For example, it is common for corporations to employ redundancy by maintaining an "equity cushion" (holding more assets than necessary to meet liabilities). Financial controls that document rising inventories or declining sales figures are homeostatic information feedback loops that alert companies when they must reduce production to remain profitable. Finally, firms can self-organize by merging, moving to other jurisdictions, or amending bylaws and charters to evolve new governance structures (e.g., adopting a classified board or a dual class share structure) in response to changes in the regulatory or market environment. In effect, their legal form "evolves."

Companies that embrace these sorts of sustainability mechanisms exhibit resilience: the ability to recover and continue functioning after encountering a destabilizing and potentially destructive force. Citibank, BP, and JPMorgan were each able to recover after unforeseen destabilizing events—the subprime mortgage crisis, Gulf oil spill, and "London whale" fiasco, respectively. Enron and Lehman Brothers proved too fragile for the shocks they encountered.

In sum, at least four basic principles from systems theory apply to corporate entities if we think of them as systems: (1) the whole of the corporate system is more than the sum of its parts; (2) the corporate system can be viewed as composed of subsystems and also as part of a larger system, making it essential to choose the appropriate level of analysis in decisionmaking; (3) the health of the corporate system depends on the health of each of its critical subsystems; and (4) to perform over time, the corporate system must be sustainable.

C. Systems Theory and The Question of Corporate Purpose

As we have described, systems theory offers a variety of insights to benefit our understanding of the nature of corporate entities. But some of the most valuable lessons systems thinking offers corporate law scholarship lies in what it teaches about how we might think about corporate purpose.

Consider again the coffee machine. One purpose of a coffee machine is, obviously, to brew coffee. But anyone designing a coffee machine is likely to have other goals in mind as well. In addition to being able to brew coffee, the coffee machine also should be energy efficient; have a beautiful design; not be too expensive; and not occupy too much counter space. Finally but fundamentally, the machine should be durable. (As systems-thinker Meadows puts it, "[a]n important function of almost every system is to ensure its own perpetuation.")

Multiple purposes are the rule, not the exception, in systems. Indeed, it is hard to think of any designed system whose designer would not have had more than one goal in mind. This naturally raises the question: if even a simple coffee machine has multiple purposes, is it not reasonable to believe that a system as complex as a corporation also might serve more than one purpose?

Corporations provide investment returns to shareholders. They also make interest payments to debtholders; pay salaries to employees; provide revenues to suppliers; pay taxes to governments; provide goods and services to consumers; and make technological breakthroughs that benefit future generations. These are all legitimate and beneficial outcomes of corporate activity. Systems theory accordingly challenges shareholder value theory's fundamental assumption of a singular, uniform corporate goal, and instead supports the view that corporate purpose need not be homogenous.

At the same time, it inevitably raises the question: how, then, should we determine a corporate entity's purpose? One obvious way to think about the purposes of a designed system is in terms of the intentions of the person or persons who designed it. The coffee machine, for example might be designed to brew coffee quickly and efficiently while looking attractive and occupying minimal counter space. The intentions of the coffee machine's designer delineate its purposes.

Who "designs" corporations? Perhaps most fundamentally, corporate entities are designed and created by the states whose laws make incorporation possible. In this sense systems thinking reinforces the concession/state franchise model of the corporation. Beyond the state, however, one might also say the corporation is designed by the entrepreneur who drafts and files the corporate charter (often with the aid of lawyers). In addition, one could say the corporation is designed by the individuals who serve as its board of directors and executive team, and even its employees. Finally, creating a business corporation usually requires investment capital, which comes from equity and debt investors. To the extent the corporation is organized to appeal to potential creditors and shareholders, both debt and equity investors might be said to participate in its design. It should be apparent at this point that the shareholder class is only one, and not necessarily the most important, of the many different groups that "design" a corporation and participate in it on a voluntary basis; each of which has its own objectives in mind.

But inquiring into designers' intentions may not be the end of the inquiry into a designed system's purpose. A third lesson of systems thinking is that even a designed system may surprise us by exhibiting behaviors and performing functions that were not intended or anticipated by its designers; automobiles are designed for transportation, but also prove unfortunately effective at causing injury. When we observe a system, we may find the functions it actually performs to be quite different from what its designers intended.

This insight is consonant with the entity approach to thinking about corporations. It recommends that we look at what corporations do, not only at what academics, judges, or executives say they do or ought to do. Despite the rhetoric of shareholder value, business corporations continue to pursue strategies that seem clearly inconsistent with maximizing accounting profits or share price: rejecting premium takeover bids, adopting poison pills and dual class share structures, resisting activist shareholders' demands. Systems theory, without answering whether the gap between shareholder value theory and actual corporate behavior is good or bad, cautions us to pay close attention to the difference.

Finally, systems theory teaches that what we observe about a system's apparent purpose will depend on our level of analysis—what level in the system hierarchy and subpurpose are we looking at? The purpose of the human circulatory system is to move blood; the purpose of the human skin is to contain the other organs of the body. If the skin is breached and the circulatory system continues to move blood, you might bleed to death. It is important not to focus only on promoting the purpose of a single subsystem, if we care about the functioning of the system as a whole. When a single subsystem's goals dominate, overall system function can suffer.

Thus a fourth and, we believe, critical lesson that systems thinking offers on corporate purpose is that the overall purpose or goal of the corporate system should not be subordinated to the goals of one of its subsystems. This observation cautions against placing exclusive emphasis on the goals of shareholders, as shareholder value theory recommends. There are other corporate subsystems that matter, including the subsystems that produce the goods and services the corporation sells, the subsystems that market these goods and services to customers, the subsystems that manage the corporation's employees, and so forth. For the systems thinker, "[k]eeping subpurposes and overall system purposes in harmony is an essential function of successful systems."

In exploring systems theory's implications, we do not claim to offer a definitive answer to the difficult question of corporate purpose. Different corporations can have different sets of purposes, and perceptions of purpose can vary depending on the perspective of the participant in the system and on the level of analysis. In other words, systems theory treats system purpose as complex, fluid, and to some degree dependent on the observer's perspective.

Systems theory accordingly carries several obvious and important implications for contemporary corporate governance scholarship. First, shareholder value theory demands corporations pursue a single, uniform objective, but systems thinking embraces the possibility of multiple objectives. Second, shareholder value theory presumes the desires of the corporation's current shareholders should determine what corporations are designed to do, but systems theory acknowledges that corporate purpose can be viewed from different perspectives, including the desires of the state whose laws made incorporation possible in the first place. Third, shareholder value theory conflicts with much observed corporate behavior, but systems thinking explains why companies often eschew opportunities to "maximize" current profits or share price. Finally, shareholder value theory focuses obsessively on promoting the goals of the shareholding subsystem, while ignoring the goals of the corporate system as a whole.

D. Systems Theory and The Problem of Measuring Corporate Performance

Systems thinking may offer a more promising solution to the problem of measuring corporate performance. This idea may seem counterintuitive, for systems theory acknowledges that corporate purpose need not be monolithic and that different companies may have different purposes. Systems thinking allows us to gauge current performance and sustainability reasonably well, without risking the damage that can follow from emphasizing share price or accounting profits to the exclusion of all other corporate concerns.

Systems thinking strongly cautions outside observers, like courts and government agencies, to exercise restraint in drawing conclusions about whether or not a particular company is performing well. One cannot simply assume what goal or business strategy is "best" for any particular company. The company's purpose depends to some extent on the observer: shareholders might think the company should pay more dividends; creditors might think the company should build more equity to reduce risk; executives might think the company should invest more in developing new products; the state might think the business should pay more taxes. When different groups hold different views of company purpose, there is room for subjective disagreement about how well the company is being managed. Systems thinking accepts this disagreement, counseling against a rigid, "top-down" strategy that attempts to impose a single objective on all business corporations.

But who or what can hold managers accountable? In part, the answer lies in recognizing that like many systems, companies have homeostatic feedback loops that provide managers with information and incentive to keep the firm and its essential subsystems operating within the parameters necessary to ensure continued functioning. To survive, a business firm must be able to please customers well enough to keep sales stable or growing; satisfy employees enough to keep turnover within reasonable bounds; satisfy debt and equity investors enough to raise financing at a reasonable cost when needed; satisfy talented executives enough to retain them; and satisfy taxing authorities and regulatory enough to avoid costly sanctions. And, of course, it must make sufficient profits to do all these things and stay in business.

So, where does this leave us? How would a systems thinker address the problem of measuring firm performance?

First, it is important to recognize that companies typically generate a wealth of potentially useful feedback information: sales trends, employee and executives and employees (who may have invested significantly in firm-specific human capital, turnover, investment expenditures, borrowing costs, inventory changes, and customer satisfaction surveys, along with accounting profits and (for public companies) stock price.

Second, when perpetuation is an important system goal, systems theorists pay close attention to what they call "constraints:" the limits beyond which the system's sustainability mechanisms can no longer protect the system. Typically this involves identifying the parameters that the system and its essential subsystems must stay within to function. For example, a coffee machine's heating element must receive a certain minimum amount of electrical current but not excessive voltage. Just like other systems, companies must operate within constraints to survive: to remain functioning, the typical company must retain a certain number of employees, must invest a certain amount in marketing and developing new products, and must provide returns to debt and equity investors sufficient to keep them happy without disgorging so much cash that it cannot pay its employees or develop new products. Sustainability requires that the company stay within these constraints, even if the external environment changes.

Third, systems thinkers have devised a wide range of analytical and mathematical techniques to try to identify ways to improve system performance while keeping the system within its constraints. This process is sometimes called "optimization," a phrase that accepts the possibility of multiple objectives in a way that "maximization" cannot. For example, nonlinear programming is a staple of systems analysis that acknowledges the importance of protecting resilience by keeping the system within relevant constraints. The use of multiobjective functions is also common. Such techniques can be combined with scenario analysis, queuing theory, stochastic analysis, network analysis, time graphs, and other arcana of operational research to identify ways to measure and improve a company's ability to achieve its intended objectives while preserving sustainability. And in fact, corporate managers routinely apply these techniques when making decisions about financing, manufacturing, and supply chain management.

Systems thinking counsels against focusing on any single metric. Raising next quarter's profits by cutting valuable employees or eliminating customer support can lead to long-term disaster. Profits are not so much an objective as a constraint the firm must meet to stay in business. In this sense, systems theory incorporates elements of shareholder value theory by recognizing profitability as an essential constraint to be considered in corporate decision-making. In contrast to shareholder value theory, however, the systems approach does not focus on profits alone, and does not direct managers to try to maximize them. Metrics like profits, employee turnover, customer satisfaction surveys, supplier costs, research budgets, and so forth are not ends in themselves. Rather, they are sources of information about whether the company is healthy and resilient, and likely to continue to generate multiple benefits into the future. It is to this goal, first and foremost, we may wish to hold managers "accountable."

A second important lesson from systems thinking is that, given multiple purposes and the complexity inherent in systems analysis, courts and regulators will rarely be well-positioned to judge whether a company is performing well or poorly. It is those involved in the business, such as customers, employees, investors, and executives, who are in the far better position to make such an assessment, and whose behavior is likely to provide the most useful feedback. This observation provides additional support for a contractarian approach to corporate governance and state corporate law's business judgment doctrine. It also suggests that it will be difficult for academics, lawmakers, or corporate governance advisors to identify reforms that can reliably improve the performance of all companies. Attempts to impose generic silver-bullet solutions are more likely to result in what Roberta Romano has pithily described as "quack corporate governance" that does more harm than good.

Systems theory counsels that to remain resilient, companies must maintain harmony between overarching system goals and subsystem goals. There is danger in focusing too much on improving one subsystem's performance at the expense of another's. Maximizing a coffee machine's output leads to system failure if it causes the machine to overheat and break down, while maximizing the machine's energy efficiency by turning off the heating element leads to system failure in the form of cold, weak coffee. Similarly, maximizing a company's current profits by cutting research and development expenditures can eventually cause the firm to fail for lack of new products, just as maximizing R&D expenditures at the expense of profitability can lead to a different kind of failure. Systems theory treats the health and functioning of a system's essential subsystems' elements as incommensurables. Constraints must be respected if the system is to survive.

III. Systems Thinking in Corporate Practice and Corporate Law

A. Systems Thinking in Corporate Management

Systems thinking offers methods for measuring corporate performance—methods with arguably more rigor, and greater potential for truly holding managers accountable, than the much-lauded but essentially subjective mirage of "long-term shareholder value."

This tension can easily be heard, for example, in the way founders, directors and executives of successful corporations talk about their business objectives. When companies publish statements describing their purpose or mission, they typically describe it far more broadly than shareholder wealth maximization, instead in terms of providing quality goods or services, or serving multiple corporate stakeholders. (The Johnson & Johnson credo begins "We believe our first responsibility is to the doctors, nurses, and patients, to mothers and fathers and all others who use our products and services . . .") This embrace of multiple objectives is far more consistent with the systems approach, than with shareholder value thinking.

Moreover, even executives who publicly espouse shareholder value as their ultimate objective pay close attention to the company's sales trends, employee morale, customer satisfaction, supply chain, and reinvestment initiatives. In line with systems thinking, they intuitively recognize that the best strategy for enhancing future performance in the face of uncertainty is to ensure that each of the company's essential subsystems remains healthy and resilient. This philosophy was captured in a 2009 Financial Times interview with iconic CEO Jack Welch, a leading champion of the shareholder value theory of corporate purpose. According to Welch, "on the face of it, shareholder value was the dumbest idea in the world. Shareholder value is a result, not a strategy . . . Your main constituencies are your employees, your customers, and your products."

B. Systems Thinking in Corporate Law

The consonance between the principles of systems thinking, and the ways successful corporate managers talk about and do their jobs, provides compelling evidence of the relevance of systems thinking to business corporations. Still more evidence can be seen in the striking way the systems approach fits with traditional state corporate law.

Corporate law typically is found in three places; corporate codes; case law; and the "internal" law of corporate articles and bylaws. None of the three meshes well with shareholder value thinking. Starting with state corporate codes, these notably do not require corporations to pursue shareholder value. The Delaware General Corporate Law provides, for example, that "[a] corporation may be incorporated or organized under this chapter to conduct or promote any lawful business or purpose[s]." This enabling language implicitly contradicts the notion that corporations must adopt shareholder wealth maximization (or anything else) as their singular goal.

Indeed, the majority of states go even further than Delaware, and explicitly reject shareholder value theory in their codes by providing that directors may serve the interests not only of shareholders but other constituencies like employees, customers, suppliers, and the community as a whole.

Turning to case law, some opinions at first glance seem to provide support for shareholder value theory. Closer inspection reveals, however, the support is more apparent than real. Recall Justice Alito's 2014 opinion for the majority in *Burwell v. Hobby Lobby Stores, Inc.*, declaring that "modern corporate law does not require for-profit corporations to pursue profit at the expense of everything else, and many do not do so."

Finally, let us consider the internal law of corporate charters and bylaws. Here, the conflict between shareholder value theory and corporate law reality becomes still more evident. The overwhelming majority of charters describe the corporation's purpose in the same flexible terms as corporate codes, as "anything lawful." This is telling. If a shareholder value maximand were such a superior business strategy, and so important to attract equity investors, we should expect to see companies trumpet shareholder value as their purpose in their charters, both at formation and when going public. They do not.

Indeed, corporations are taking advantage of the enabling nature of state codes to evolve in the opposite direction. Many are responding by going public with staggered boards and classified share structures that deliberately insulate managers from such demands. (Snap Inc., which sells the app Snapchat, recently filed documents revealing a plan to go public by offering common shares with no voting rights at all.)

C. On the Risks of Ignoring Systems

Could policy interventions driven by the dominant vision of shareholder value thinking—interventions that often ignore, or even contradict, the lessons of systems theory—do more harm than good?

The question is not merely academic. Over the past three decades the Anglo-American corporate landscape has shifted significantly. Public companies today face increasing pressure to become more "shareholder-centric," and to focus on raising share price or reported earnings per share in the near future through strategies like leveraging; repurchasing shares; selling off assets; or cutting accounting expenses for payroll, customer support, and research and development.

This trend has been driven largely by external forces. These include innumerable federal regulatory initiatives, especially changes in tax rules, securities law, and Department of Labor regulations. To give only a few examples, with the passage of the Employee Retirement Income Security Act (ERISA) in 1974, federal rules encouraged the growth of institutional investors (tax-favored pension and mutual funds) which now collectively control nearly half of all shares traded on U.S. exchanges. In 2003 the SEC furthered the shift to a shareholder-centric model by adopting rules requiring exchange-listed companies to have a majority of independent directors on their boards (independent directors are more responsive to shareholder demands than "inside" directors who are also employees) and requiring mutual funds to publicly disclose how they vote shares held in their portfolios. This last rule change spurred the growth of the remarkably powerful—and remarkably unaccountable—"proxy advisory" service known as Institutional Shareholder Services (ISS), which has added substantially to the pressure public companies feel to pursue shareholder value as their dominant objective.

There is theoretical reason to question whether policy interventions springing from such sources are always, or even often, wise or efficient. State corporate law is mostly common law or derived from common law principles; as a number of scholars have noted, the common law tends to evolve to favor efficient rules. In contrast, federal regulation tends toward a rigid, "one-size-fits-all" approach that threatens the resilience of companies by limiting their ability to self-organize in response to changes in the market environment, and that insulates incorporators from the competitive pressures that otherwise might encourage them to select efficient rules.

Conclusion

Despite the dominant role corporations play in our economy, culture, and politics, the nature and purpose of corporations remains hotly contested. This conflict was brought to the fore in the recent Supreme Court opinions in *Citizens United* and *Hobby Lobby*. Although the dominant narrative for the past quarter-century has been that corporations belong to shareholders and should pursue shareholder value, support for this approach, which has been justified as assuring managerial accountability, is eroding. It persists today primarily in the form of the argument that corporations should seek "long-term" shareholder value. Yet, when shareholder value is interpreted to mean "long-term" shareholder value, it no longer offers that desired managerial accountability.

What can? Systems theory offers an answer. It provides an approach to understanding the nature and purpose of corporate entities that is not only consistent with elements of many otherwise-conflicting visions of the firm, but also with important features of corporate law and practice. It offers proven methods for measuring corporate performance that recognize the possibility of multiple goals and the importance of sustainability. And it cautions that, by ignoring the lessons of systems theory, shareholder value thinking may have encouraged regulatory and policy interventions into corporate governance that are not only ineffective, but destructive.

Corporations are perpetual entities designed to operate into an uncertain future. They are comprised of elements and subsystems, each of which has an individual purpose that may at times come into conflict with the overarching purpose of the corporation. Systems thinking accepts, rather than dismisses, these realities. It honors the corporation as its own separate legal entity, while recognizing the state's part in its creation. It respects the important roles played by shareholders and other stakeholders, while also explaining the board's function in mediating among these interests to keep the system in check.

Echoes of the "public corporation as private corporation." Recall the thesis in Chapter 1.3 that the US public corporation shares the essential structure of US republican government. The "public corporation as private constitution"suggests that the corporation, like our republican government, operates as a system with multiple purposes. Consider the corporate analogues to the republican objectives of "life, liberty and the pursuit of happiness." Certainly, the corporation must satisfy customers by providing goods and services of value to society or, at least, goods and services that society perceives as having value. Further, the corporation, except in some new bizarre cyber-corporation forms, must have human agents/employees who carry out the business and themselves depend on the business for everything from wages to health care insurance to matrimonial opportunities. And the corporation is also an intermediary between resources and resource use, sometimes for good and sometimes for less than good.

The blossoming of systems thinking on corporate governance. I am not alone in these musings. Others have used a systems framework to explain and understand corporate governance, which has been described as a legal system that serves as a "cognitive resource" to stabilize normative expectations and reduce transaction costs—thus enhancing cooperation. Corporate governance and its default rules, like other legal systems, must adapt to external economic conditions, while ensuring legal continuity and certainty. Simon Deakin & Fabio Carvalho, *System and Evolution in Corporate Governance* (2010) [available on SSRN].

Professor Stephen Healey (Western Sydney University) points out that the deepening ecological crisis (alongside a half century of widening inequality and economic instability) makes clear that "business as usual" cannot go on. Stephen Healey, *Corporate Enterprise as Commonwealth* (2018) [available on SSRN[. Arguing that transformation is necessary, Healey asserts that shareholders primacy is a "powerful social norm that constrains transformation." He reviews "critical legal theory" and suggests it might be more appropriate to think of the corporation as a commons managed for the benefit of multiple parties—a viewpoint found in enterprise traditions, such as cooperatives in Italy and elsewhere.

An integrative/systems approach, though more complex, explains the corporation better than the reductionist SWM, which reduces the corporate purpose to a single animating goal—the maximization of shareholder profits. See Paul B. Miller, *Corporations* (2019) [available on SSRN]. The "dominant reductive analyses distorts the corporate form by treating it as a mere extension of various singular forms of interaction found in contract, property, and fiduciary law." Instead, an integrative approach reinterprets "the core elements of the corporate form—corporate personality, purpose, agency and fiduciary administration."

Further, it was a systems approach that animated the Sustainable Market Actors for Responsible Trade (SMART) project, an interdisciplinary project at the University of Oslo to identify how market actors can contribute to sustainable development within planetary boundaries. See Beate Sjåfjell & Hanna Ahlstrom, *Facilitating Interdisciplinary Corporate Sustainability Research: The SMART Research Guide* (2020) [available on SSRN]. The authors identify the centrality of "systems thinking, as the methodological overarching approach employed" in their SMART project. They propose a "regulatory ecology"to facilitate their interdisciplinary and comparative regulatory analysis to identify barriers to and possibilities for corporate sustainability. That is, the corporation and corporate regulation should be understood as operating as complementary systems.

What is driving this move toward systems thinking? Perhaps, institutional shareholders—who themselves are imbedded in multi-factor systems. See Ann Lipton, *What We Talk About When We Talk About Shareholder Primacy* (2019) [available on SSRN] The shift away from SWM is "due to the changing nature of the shareholder base" from "docile and silent" to "institutional investors [that have] made it known that their actual preferred outcomes often diverged from the ones predicted by corporate theory."

It's worth pointing out that, the corporation we are mostly talking about is the multinational corporation, one that transcends national (and regulatory) boundaries. Thus, as we think about the corporation as legal system, we should see it also as a global phenomenon—after all, the relevant stakeholders (workers, consumers, communities, suppliers, shareholders, and even government regulators) are not defined by any particular national system. See Dionysia Katelouzou & Peer C. Zumbansen, *The New Geographies of Corporate Law Production* (2020) [available on SSRN]. Corporate governance has become "a transnational regulatory field of law production, contestation and policy conflict."

> As the societal role of corporations expands beyond an essentially financial role, corporate governance norm production mirrors the diversification of regulatory concerns associated with the firm's place in society. From a sociological perspective, we argue that the transnationalization of present-day corporate governance regimes constitutes not so much a categorically different state of corporate law in an age of "globalization", but a continuation of the corporate law's inherent legal pluralism in terms of co-existing public and private, hard and soft, formal and informal norms.

In the words of John Lennon, "Imagine there's no countries / It isn't hard to do / Nothing to kill or die for / And no religion, too." Well, except for the religion of market capitalism—the corporation's abiding essence.

Role of Directors in Multi-Purpose Corporation

As we begin to leave behind the theory of the corporation as a structure for minimizing conflicts between shareholders and managers—namely, agency theory—we are left with the question of the role for the board of directors in a multi-purpose corporation. What is the role of directors in a system of multiple inputs and multiple outputs?

Already there are some indications that directors sense their new role, which requires a greater understanding and integration of the many aspects of the corporate system. As the board moves from a "monitoring" function aimed at addressing the vertical conflicts between shareholders and corporate executives to a "systemic" function aimed at identifying and resolving the horizontal tensions between corporate stakeholders, including shareholders and executives, directors have been called on to assimilate more information than ever before. For example, what is a board to make of hedge fund activism seeking strategic change, customer demands for more sustainable products, or social pressures to be more politically responsive?

A provocative answer to these questions comes in an article by Professors Faith Stevelman (New York Law) and Sarah Haan (Washington & Lee Law), who observe that practices in corporate governance have moved from a paradigm in which the corporation inhabits a "private" sphere, shaped by "public" government regulation, to a new paradigm in which corporation inhabits both a private and public sphere. As a result of this paradigm shift, the new "active board" looks beyond stock prices to firm-wide information and communications systems. See Faith Stevelman & Sarah C. Haan, *Boards in Information Governance* (2020) [available on SSRN]. The active board—catalyzed by legal requirements on board monitoring, industry best practices, and increased shareholder pressure—has sought to address risk management, legal compliance, and ESG matters. That is, as the corporation has undertaken a new identity, the board is compelled to invest in data gathering, far-flung deliberations, and reporting processes that reflect the shift in corporate purpose. Directors are further called on to re-assess their own roles and then to communicate this new collective identity to the various corporate constituents, through different channels.

In a similar vein, the move from the profit-maximizing corporation to a "sustainable corporation" has meant a focus "ranging from environment and climate, to diversity and other workplace concerns, to privacy and supply chain management." Stavros Gadinis & Amelia Miazad, *Corporate Law and Social Risk* (2020) [available on SSRN] (based on interviews with over 300 roundtable participants, including "leading public and private companies, large asset managers, investors and pension funds, shareholder advisory firms, and sustainability standard-setters and data providers"). Further, rather than seeing sustainability as addressing "downside risks," the sustainable corporation "encourages intervention even when laws have not caught up. Rather than dwelling in the past, sustainability builds a new vision for the future hoping to inspire and gain trust." Broad and growing investor "support for sustainability is precisely because [mitigating social risk] helps fight risks that are otherwise hard to diversify." The authors point out that this re-imagined corporation calls for a reexamination of boards' duties in risk oversight beyond averting crises to establishing "a well-running sustainability function with proper board oversight that reaches out to stakeholders relevant to the company's business."

What about executive pay? The rubber hits the road when we begin to think about compensation in a multi-purpose corporation. Rather than executive pay tied to stock-price metrics, a systemic approach to the corporation calls on multiple metrics for executive pay. See Leo Strine & Kirby Smith, *Toward Fair Gainsharing and a Quality Workplace for Employees: How a Reconceived Compensation Committee Might Help Make Corporations More Responsible Employers and Restore Faith in American Capitalism* (2020) [available on SSRN]. As Strine asserts, although after WWII workers and stockholders shared equitably in the nation's growing wealth, this "fair gainsharing" has declined as most gains from increased corporate profitability and productivity have gone to stockholders and top management, much less to employees. To address the income gap and the economic insecurity it creates, corporate governance must change to give greater weight the interests of workers –specifically, by reconceiving the compensation committee.

> A reconceived comp committee would focus on the company's entire workforce, not just senior management. The committee would become charged with understanding "the nation's, the industry's, and the company's traditional gainsharing practices" thus to more rationally establish metrics for top management and key personnel involved in gatekeeping functions tied to good EESG practices (including worker safety, racial and gender equality, sexual harassment and inclusion, and training and promotion policies) and not just to stock price. Not only that, the reconceived compensation committee should monitor company practices in its supply chain to ensure that the company's adopted policies regarding fair treatment of workers extend to those workers who work for company contractors. By this evolutionary means that builds on the existing American corporate governance system, important strides can be taken toward making our capitalist system work better for the people most critical to its success: workers.

A global trend. Already in other common-law jurisdictions, directors' duties are shifting from ShWM to StWM—that is, from shareholder wealth maximization to stakeholder wealth maximization. See Jean Du Plessis, *Directors' Duty to Act in the Best Interests of the Corporation: "Hard Cases Make Bad Law"* (2019) [available on SSRN]. The duty of directors "to exercise their powers 'in the best interests of the corporation as a whole' and 'the shareholders as a general body' creates "considerable complexity and legal uncertainty." Instead, directors "can no longer prioritize shareholder interests" unless these interests align with the best interests of the corporation as a separate legal entity, taking into account third party stakeholder interests). See also Beate Sjåfjell & Mark B. Yalor, *Clash of Norms: Shareholder Primacy vs. Sustainable Corporate Purpose* (2019) [available on SSRN] (arguing that "shareholder primacy as legal purpose for the corporation is incorrect and must give way to the legal purpose of the corporation on a socially and environmentally sustainable footing").

Of course, with new director responsibilities come potential new liabilities. Will corporate directors face liability for not addressing or addressing inadequately a multi-purpose corporation—for example, as corporations take on climate change? See Rolf H. Weber & Andreas Hoesli, *Climate Change Liability—Increasing Risks for Directors? Perspectives From Common and Civil Law Jurisdictions* (2020) [available on SSRN]. Businesses "are increasingly expected to consider the environmental and social impacts of their undertakings," resulting in climate change litigation against corporations. Questions of director liability for corporate climate responses "has received considerable attention from common law commentators" but less so in the civil law world.

Move toward the "networked corporation." In all of this, a couple corporate theorists from Australia have observed that agency theory and shareholder primacy are simply stepping stones toward a "networked corporation"—one in which trust among the networked members is the critical, even defining, attribute of the corporation. (Recall the earlier readings on Blockchain, the much-discussed and fashionable "trust creation" methodology.) Not only may the networked corporation offer a better explanation of what is happening, such a network approach also gives life to a corporation that recognizes the salience and roles of the corporation's many stakeholders. See Roman Tomasic & Folarin Akinbami, *Trust and Public Companies: Beginning to Reconceptualise Corporate Law in a Networked World* (2013) [available on SSRN].

Super-wicked problem

As we saw in our look at short-termism, the climate crisis presents a "super-wicked" problem. That's because it's a problem that will happen in the future and, meanwhile, financial markets discount future costs—especially those costs that lay far in the future. That is, why bother to pay now to save the future planet, if the discounted value today of saving the planet is miniscule compared to the present price tag of changing course.

But maybe we're seeing this the wrong way. Maybe we must, in the words of Charles Lindblom, "muddle through." The climate is a system, the corporation is a system, and when the two meet we'll just have to experiment with new laws and policies—and corporate governance techniques—to address the impending climate catastrophe. What? You expected a single silver bullet? See Jonathan M. Gilligan & Michael P. Vandenbergh, *Beyond Wickedness: Managing Complex Systems and Climate Change* (2020) [available on SSRN].

5.1.2 Corporation as Moral System

So, you might be thinking, that's all fine and good, but how does a networked corporation operating as a multi-purpose system really work? To be honest, I'm not entirely sure. The next reading offers a tentative answer. It's an essay that I prepared for the annual Abraham L. Pomerantz lecture at Brooklyn Law School.

The essay describes responses by US electric utility companies to the moral dilemma of how to reduce CO_2 emissions while continuing to provide reliable, affordable electric power to their utility customers and ensuring financial returns for their investors. Specifically, the essay describes how investor-owned utilities (the publicly-traded corporations that supply most of the nation's electricity) responded in various documents to the EPA's 2014 proposed Clean Power Plan to regulate CO_2 emissions in the power sector.

> During the year following the EPA's proposed Clean Power Plan to regulate CO_2 emissions in the power sector, the largest investor-owned electric utilities engaged in a curious triplespeak. Employing the moral language of political conservatives, the utilities focused on whether and how the EPA had transgressed its "traditional" regulatory role, thus altering the "structure" of energy federalism and potentially "degrading" orderly power supplies. In their disclosure filings with the SEC, the utilities used the moral language of political libertarians, focusing on the "financial risks" that federal government "intervention" poses to efficient power "markets" and to the "freedom" of utilities to match energy supplies and customer demand. Meanwhile, in their CSR reports, the utilities used the moral language of political progressives, highlighting their concern for the "well-being" of their customers and other stakeholders, their desire to "protect" the environment from the "threat" of climate change, and their "ongoing voluntary efforts" to shift away from fossil fuels toward renewables. In many instances the same utility company took all of these seemingly inconsistent stances at about the same time.
>
> In some respects, this triplespeak is unremarkable. Utility companies understandably would take different views on the EPA's proposal to revamp the power sector's fuel mix, depending on where the utility operated and whether it was coal-dependent or had a portfolio of non-carbon nuclear and renewables. Moreover, within a utility company's organizational chart, the existence of different viewpoints—reflecting the audience to which the organizational unit is supposed to cater—is not surprising. Investors tend to believe in free markets and are more libertarian; regulators tend to believe in the status quo and are more conservative; and the socially-attuned public is more concerned about consumer welfare and environmental damage and thus is more progressive. But these explanations are incomplete. Some utilities were more progressive in their responses to the EPA proposal than regional politics and their fuel mix might suggest; some utilities were more libertarian than others when presenting their story in CSR reports; and some utilities were less conservative than others in their comments to the federal regulator. And nearly all the utilities were internally a hodge-podge of political viewpoints.
>
> This essay suggests an answer: the utilities engaged in triplespeak as an adaptive measure. Faced with unprecedented business, regulatory, and technological change—not to mention the changes to climate wrought by carbon-generated electricity—the utilities used triplespeak as a way to begin a process of self-transformation. The utilities' different moral takes on the EPA proposal—each a moral mutation—prepare the industry to respond to an uncertain, volatile future. Whether the power sector's future is market-based, regulation-dependent, or ecology-driven (or even, and more likely, a combination of these forces), the large utilities responded to the EPA's proposal by honing their vocabulary to explain their moral choices –whatever they might be.

In identifying the moral positions of the electric utilities, the *Corporate Triplespeak* essay draws on the nascent field of "moral psychology." Next is an excerpt from the essay that explores the notion that we make moral decisions according to our often unperceived group identity and that these decisions are driven by equally invisible moral foundations or vectors that lead us to conclusions that we immediately rationalize to ourselves and to others. Thus, our moral decisions—that is, decisions involving right and wrong—are implicit, intuitive, instinctive, invisible, and instantaneous. This notion is contrary to the Western philosophical tradition beginning with Socrates, through the Enlightenment, to modern "law and economics"—a tradition that assumes we are rational when making moral decisions.

Corporate Triplespeak: Responses by Investor-Owned Utilities to the EPA's Proposed Clean Power Plan

(2018)

Alan R. Palmiter

[available on SSRN]

* * *

III. A Dalliance in Moral Psychology

To better understand "corporate triplespeak"—perhaps a characteristic of modern corporate personhood that extends well beyond the investor-owned utility industry—it is useful to turn to moral structures that have been identified by social psychology and its relatively nascent sub-field of moral psychology.

A. Haidt's Moral Foundations

Over the past couple decades, studies and experiments have revealed that our moral judgments and discourse arise from a moral matrix, different for each person that mixes and matches fundamental moral values that can be expressed as opposites, each along a separate axis:

1. care / loyalty
2. fairness / cheating
3. liberty / oppression
4. loyalty / betrayal
5. authority / subversion
6. sanctity / degradation

Hume had gotten it

The Scottish essayist David Hume was among the few philosophers (or proto-psychologists) to notice we actually make our moral judgments and take action on the basis of "passions" that we don't really recognize, then use our "reason" to rationalize what we have done.

Hume was a good friend of Adam Smith. Although Smith was an upright establishment figure and Hume held radical ideas, including an open skepticism about religion, their 25-year friendship was a source of strength to both.

Adam Smith, who is widely seen as the father of economics and modern capitalism, celebrated free markets and free trade. But his adherence to market capitalism was not absolutist—Smith, after all, was the chair at the University of Glasgow in *moral philosophy*. His book *The Theory of Moral Sentiments*—published 17 years before his "The Wealth of Nations"—asserted that "our moral ideas and actions are the product of our very nature as social creatures." His book on moral sentiments was deeply influenced by his friend David Hume, who had an international reputation as one of the greatest philosophers ever to write in English. (Einstein would later credit Hume with inspiring his theory of relativity.) Today, Hume is seen by some as the father of modern cognitive science.

According to these studies, we humans weight these values in different ways—often based on the social or political group with which we identify. In this country, self-identified political liberals are moved almost exclusively by the values of caring/compassion and fairness/equality, with adherents feeling strong (even visceral) reactions against narratives of harm and inequality. Meanwhile, political conservatives are moved by the additional values of loyalty, authority/order, and sanctity, with adherents experiencing strong reactions against narratives involving disloyalty, disrespect, and desecration. And, political libertarians are moved primarily by the value of liberty/freedom, with strong reactions against government (or other) coercion that restricts individual freedom and collective free markets.

The following schematics from Haidt's *The Righteous Mind* identify the different weights these moral values hold for American progressives, conservatives, and libertarians:

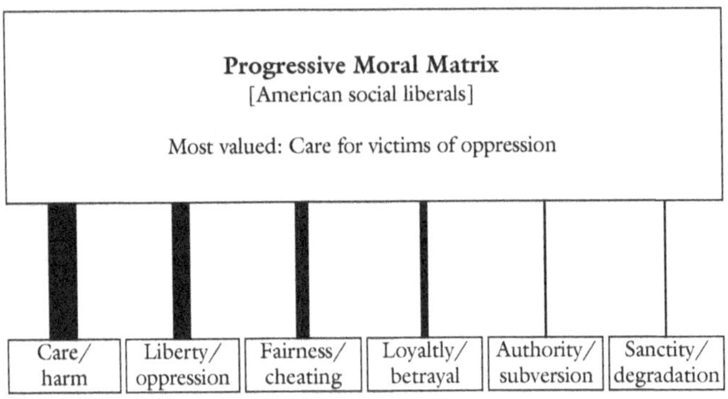

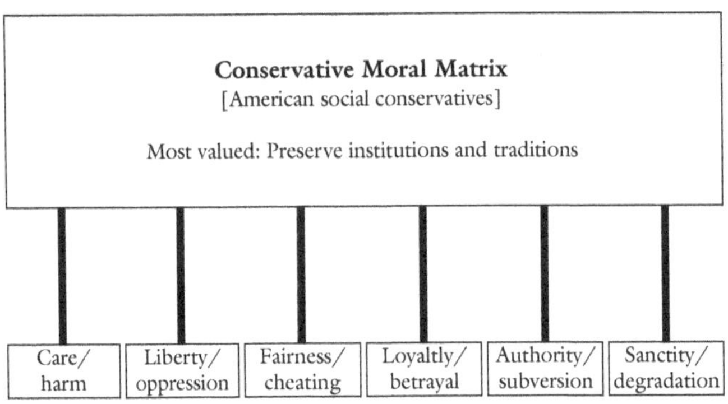

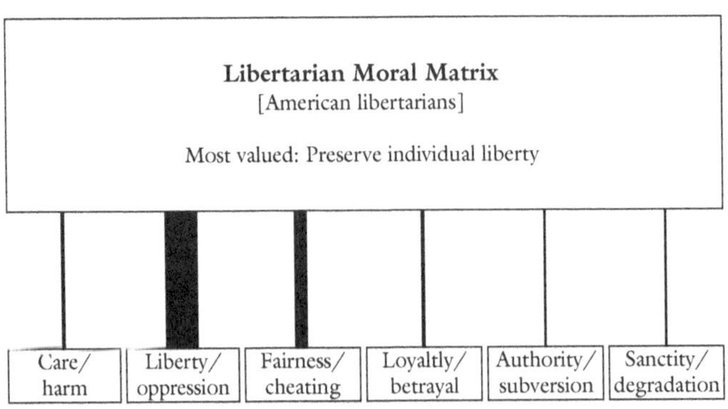

Further, as each political group self-reinforces its own value matrix, the group's views are purified and harden as the group members "bind" together and then become "blind" to the other. Thus, each political camp—which for the past fifty years has become more compartmentalized and purer—is built upon a set of "moral foundations" that constitute the camp's moral matrix. For progressives, the defining account is "oppressed versus protected," using narratives that value compassion and fairness in a struggle against hatred and inequality. For conservatives, the defining account is "traditional versus radical," built on narratives that value ordered authority built on deeply-held (often religious) views. For libertarians, the defining account is "free markets versus regulatory intervention," using narratives of individual and collective liberty struggling against the tyranny of regulatory (public and private) intrusion and coercion.

Using different narratives, moral psychologists have conducted experiments that gauge the responses to different moral narratives given by adherents to each group. Members of different groups react strongly to different narratives:

Political group	Narrative Evoking Strongest Response	Values Triggered
Progressive	A man walks down a sidewalk and kicks a dog sleeping on the side of the sidewalk.	Caring, fairness
Conservative	A woman finds an old American flag in her attic and cuts it into rags to clean the toilet.	Loyalty, authority, sanctity
Libertarian	A parent, whose gambling hurts their family, is jailed for being a compulsive gambler.	Individual freedom

The studies on how people react to these and similar stories reveal that our moral views are mostly emotive, even instinctual—and happen almost instantly, often subconsciously. These studies find that human decision-making appears to arise from two cognitive systems: System One is quick and intuitive, and System Two is slow and considered. The studies indicate that our moral positions and actions arise through System One and then are explained and defended by System Two, which seems to engage in motivated reasoning (like that of a zealous, close-minded defense lawyer) rather than constructive reasoning (like that of an objective, fair-minded judge).

Motivated reasoning. That is, our moral explanations (rationalizations) come only after arriving at a moral conclusion about a given situation. Thus, these studies address and answer the age-old question of whether we are essentially rational beings who sometimes must tame our emotions, or whether we are emotional beings who use reason to justify our actions and beliefs. The resounding answer from the studies is that, at least with respect to moral judgments on how we respond to other humans, we are emotional beings who come to moral views based on a moral matrix that we are often unaware of and that we often take from the moral group to which we are aligned. And only after coming to a moral conclusion do we then rationalize our view by resorting to the language sets provided by each of the fundamental moral values.

The studies also suggest that value matrices tend to harden into psychological (perhaps even neurologically-based) attitudes. For example, conservatives tend to like order and predictability (both attributes of tradition and authority), while liberals tend to like variety and diversity (both attributes of tolerance and liberty). Thus, when shown dots moving on a screen, conservatives prefer the images of dots moving in lock step, while liberals prefer random movement.

In addition, liberals tend to be universalists who view people everywhere in the world as relevant to their moral equation, sometimes even more than people nearby, while conservatives are more parochial staying focused on people in their country or their self-defined communities. Thus, political policies aimed to improve the lives of people generally in the world resonate with liberals, while those same policies when presented to conservatives both have less salience and suggest disloyalty to one's own.

Likewise, the studies suggest liberals are more open to new experiences, while conservatives have trouble assimilating to modernity. That is, liberals exhibit the trait of being willing to accept and accommodate to change, while conservatives remain cautious and prefer the predictability of tradition.

Moving beyond one's moral matrix. Change is not easy. This is particularly true when we do not see how our context drives our views. Thus, "facts" often don't matter—we will have a compendium of rationalizations to avoid, explain, or simply avoid uncomfortable truths. That is, expounding a message is not the road to change. Instead, given that our moral views arise from the context of our social surroundings, change will happen only if the messenger changes.

Even though some studies suggest that techniques such as "debiasing" stereotypes can make constructive reasoning possible, there is an axis we tend to automatically turn to without thinking. If we actually think, it can be different, but as Daniel Kahneman persuasively argues in *Thinking, Fast and Slow*, we do this far less often than we realize.

Reflecting on our ability to recognize our own intuitive, emotional thinking (System One thinking) and change ourselves, Daniel Kahneman is not optimistic:

> Well, what is disappearing, or seems to be disappearing, is a culture of debates between diverse opinions. . . . What can be done is superficial . . . so teaching statistics to the young would be useful, teaching economics to the young would be useful, teaching self-critical thinking, or better yet, how to criticize other people, because this is more pleasant and more interesting. . . . But those are very marginal improvements. When it comes to the big issues, I'm not very optimistic.

And change in others may be even harder. In fact, presenting facts to someone who does not share your views may even be counterproductive. According to recent studies, when people are presented with evidence that goes against their deeply held beliefs, they are not swayed by the evidence. Instead, they invent more reasons to justify their prior position as correct. In fact, smarter people exhibit greater ability to rationalize and reinterpret information at odds with their beliefs, thus "the greater the polarizing boomerang effect is likely to be."

Developments in Electric Utility Industry

Since my look at how the US electric utility industry responded to the EPA's proposed Clean Power Plan, the industry continues to undergo change—even radical change. As one industry participant noted of the traditional power-generation/transmission/distribution model, "What you see here is a slow train wreck."

Increasingly, the industry and its public utility regulators have "formulated, used, and applied" an evolutionary stakeholder theory in which "rules arise out of the ongoing search for cooperative solutions among all stakeholders. William Kline & Karl McDermott, *Evolutionary Stakeholder Theory and Public Utility Regulation* (2019) [available on SSRN].

5.1.3 Corporation as Super-Organism

The notion of the corporation as "person" has been a thread that has wended its way through this book—sometimes explicitly, often implicitly. Perhaps if we think of the corporation in biological terms, we can better understand its networks of trust and cooperation (and cheating) in a more useful and organic way.

Corporation as Larger Than Individual

The following is a blog that muses on human evolution and the rise of corporate super-organisms.

Human Evolution and the Rise of the Corporate Super-Organisms

Medium (2018)

Christian Filli

Our prehuman ancestors, like today's great apes, were able to solve problems by thinking. But they were almost entirely competitive, aiming only at their individual goals. As changes in their ecosystem forced them to put their heads together and pursue shared goals, early humans developed the ability to cohere, coordinate their actions, transcend self-interest and outcompete other groups.

Social psychologist Jonathan Haidt [whose studies and insights about "moral psychology" form the basis for my study on corporate triplespeak in the electric utility industry] has called this ability the hive switch, observing that we may very well resemble chimpanzees in the way we are shaped by individual competition, but at the same time we are like bees in the way we can "lose ourselves in something larger than ourselves".

If we are to understand the full picture of our own survival, we must explore the inherent balance between individual subsistence and the cohesion of the group as a greater unity that encompasses the individual.

Multilevel Selection Theory

In 1998 David Sloan Wilson and Elliott Sober proposed a framework called multilevel selection theory. The theory asserts that, while there's no question that individual organisms with favorable traits are more likely to pass along their genes to the next generation, similar processes could operate at other levels of the biological spectrum, thus perpetuating traits that are favorable not only to a gene, cell or individual, but to a social unit such as a flock or a colony, or to an entire species, or even to an ecosystem made up of many species.

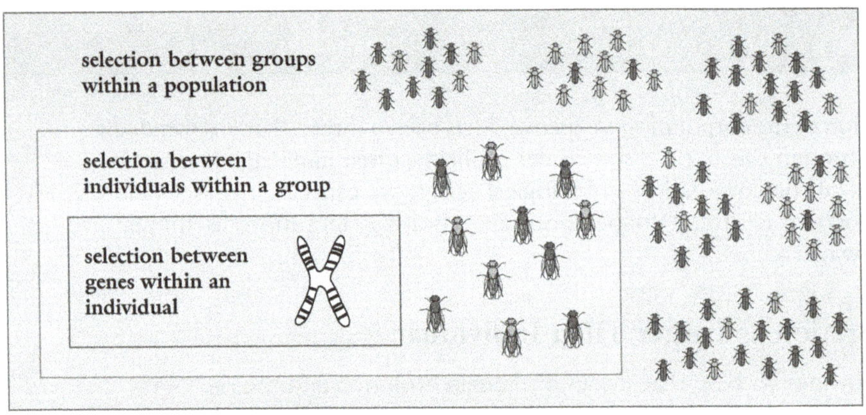

While this may still be part of the human (and corporate) experience today, there is a broader idea unfolding around us, and that is the phenomenon of super-organisms.

A super-organism is an organized society that has achieved critical mass and functions as an organic whole. Critical mass is only one aspect of what defines a super-organism. Another, and arguably more significant, is that it holds itself together organically and naturally by invested relationships, without the need for an artificial shell to force organization and cooperation.

Corporation as Super Organism

The majority of corporations, regardless of how big they are, would probably collapse if you removed traditional hierarchies, bureaucratic structures, as well as carrot-and-stick mechanisms. Why? Because these elements maintain an artificial model that vastly ignores intrinsic human motivations — including our social instinct — that power behavior. Paul Herr, author of Primal Management, sums it up this way:

> We don't think of ourselves as tribal people because we abandoned that lifestyle long ago, yet it still affects every aspect of our minds, emotions, personalities, and organizations. The motivational mechanism is a distinctively tribal apparatus that often malfunctions within the context of modern complex societies. Hierarchically organized corporations are not united or tribal and do not take full advantage of nature's motivational mechanism. Rather, they starve the social appetites and end up with motivationally malnourished employees.

Thus, "survival of the fittest" is mostly about preservation (survival) of the system, whether it is a single cell or an entire species. One of the key principles of evolution is that increasing levels of complexity require increasingly complex interactions, which are designed to sustain the entire system.

Consider planet Earth itself, which has evolved over billions of years to contain a large variety of self-regulating and interdependent systems — such as atmosphere composition, ocean salinity and surface temperature — acting in unison, constantly seeking a physical and chemical environment that is optimal for life.

The corporate super-organism cannot survive without the broader economic environment of which it is a part, and vice-versa. Interestingly enough, the financial machinery that has governed our way of life for the past couple of centuries — a super-organism in its own right — is on the verge of a historic shake-up. So the question we face is: how can we create a more sustainable system?

Advent of Networked Intelligence

The much anticipated linkage [think about Blockchain, for starters] of 9 billion minds (7 billion in the short-term) represents not only a technological milestone but a transcendental leap for our civilization, as it will launch human evolution into a new era — one that may not bring as many changes in our bodies but certainly in our perception, our attitudes, our consciousness, and our work.

Prominent thinkers have referred to this new outlook of the world as networked intelligence, which is characterized by a massive shift away from centralized top-down hierarchies and towards decentralized interdependent networks.

Because corporate super-organisms tend to be more efficient in comparison to silo organizational structures (for perspective, Apple generates $233 billion in annual revenue with 115,000 employees, while GM produces $152 billion and employs 216,000 people), a growing portion of the workforce is expected to reside within a mega-scale internet-enabled open marketplace.

While nobody really knows the full repercussions of this new model down the road, it's probably fair to say that we've only seen the tip of the iceberg so far. As the constellation of interdependent networks continues to evolve, people may start taking full advantage of it by developing a great variety of skills and experiences that can be assembled and reassembled creatively — much as kids play with Legos.

Market dynamics are ceasing to revolve around the zero-sum game of winning and losing. In many ways, we are in the early stages of understanding the world as a multi-layered web of life, as opposed to the limiting predator-versus-prey framework.

Surely, as everything else in evolution, changes don't happen overnight. But in this new ecosystem that's being created, the best fitted organism, whether an individual or group, is the one that becomes a beacon for ideas, connecting itself to the web of life, as an active agent for innovation and growth.

Our networked intelligence carries great promise of elevating the potential of humanity, and advancing the notion that we are one planet with one common destiny.

Triple Bottom Line Organism

So, what kind of super-organism is the corporation? Well, the question is a loaded one, because it assumes that the corporation comes in just one size just one flavor. If nothing else, this book has introduced you to the myriad ways in which the modern corporation has adapted to its financial, social, and resource environments.

We thus return to imagining the ideal corporation that balances profits, people and planet—where all three align. In astronomy the alignment of three celestial bodies is called "syzygy" [**siz**-i-jee].

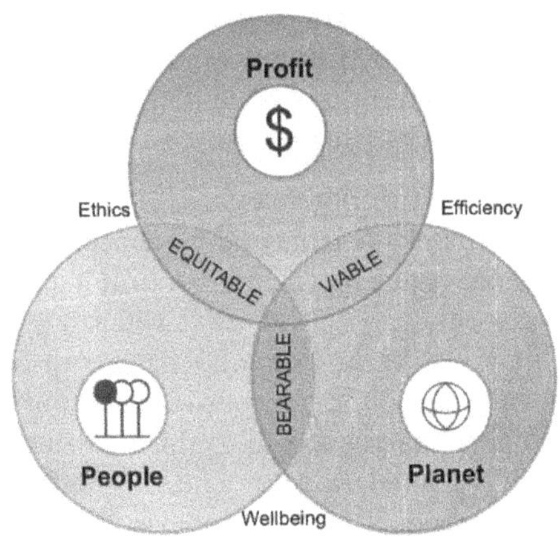

John Elkington—the management guru who coined the term *triple bottom line*—argued that for corporations to become sustainable, corporate intelligence had to evolve from the destructive "locust" horde to the sustainable "honey bee" hive. Elkington explained: "Ours [today] is a caterpillar economy, often destructive of natural, social, and other forms of capital." Yet caterpillars can evolve into butterflies, creatures with low environmental impact and graceful, regenerative qualities.

From an Aristotelian perspective, corporate locusts are immoral because they do not facilitate the "good life." Instead, locusts swarm with a high burn rate and an inability to foresee the negative impact they have upon global systems. When Volkswagen manipulated the emission systems of its diesel cars, it showed itself to have a degenerative, high-impact "locust" intelligence.

Although corporate caterpillars have unsustainable business models, they (unlike corporate locusts) have evolutionary potential. In 2002, Elkington claimed that 3M resembled a "caterpillar" intelligence. Since then, 3M has rethought its operations by embracing, then abandoning, and finally refining the Six Sigma processing system—and, as part of Six Sigma, an extensive sustainability effort. Perhaps 3M has evolved to embody a "butterfly" intelligence.

Corporate butterflies, therefore, are an improvement on the locust and caterpillar intelligences. Further, they are graceful media darlings with highly-touted sustainable business models, though carrying a significant risk of reversion. Despite their self-congratulatory comparisons to their locust and caterpillar peers, the butterflies lack sufficient impact to bring about any sort of change in other companies and society. Elkington argued that Ben & Jerry's, for example, resembles butterfly intelligence. But while butterflies are sustainable, they are far too dainty to inspire the "good life" within society.

Instead, the moral, sustainable corporation has "honeybee" intelligence. The honeybee is hyper-connected and regenerative; the honeybee is a good steward of its surroundings; and its honeycomb is ultra-clean. In short, the honeybee improves everything it touches. While a true honeybee corporation may be rare, candidates include Zespri or Novo Nordisk.

In a student paper for this course, Mike Garrigan first offered these insights about Elkington and locusts/caterpillar-butterflies/honeybees—and then looked at where the curriculum of US business schools fell as of 2018. His conclusion was that US business schools are, at best, training caterpillars. While the top-tier MBA schools have a curricular focus on the triple bottom line, mid-tier schools give the topic only desultory attention, and low-tier MBA schools are oblivious to the corporate sustainability movement. The Financial Times also noticed this about the top-tier schools. *US Business Schools Realize ESG Is No Fad But Part of Long-Term Trend*, Financial Times (Oct 20, 2019).

In a reflection on the corporation as a system, Emily Melvin wrote in a student reflection paper on this unit:

> As a former beekeeper (for s short period of time), It helps me to think about this issue in terms of a beehive. A beehive is the quintessential example of a super-organism. Each bee's task is essential to the survival of all the bees. A queen can't get big and fat enough to produce eggs/larvae without the drone bees, and drone bees can't feed and mate with the queen bee without worker bees collecting pollen and nectar. And the eggs won't turn into viable bees without enough honey produced from the pollen and nectar. But enough honey must be stored to feed all the bees over winter. If the larvae get all the honey, then the queen and other bees die off and the beehive eventually dies. The larvae can be compared to shareholders. If shareholders are always placed above all other interests, then the other stakeholders slowly lose out. Moreover, when bees run out of pollen in the immediate vicinity, they are forced to travel further and further to feed the hive. Once the distance becomes too far, worker bees can't keep

pace and the hive collapses. Similarly, as corporations use up natural resources, they are forced to search farther and dig deeper—once the resources becomes too scarce, the company collapses and leaves environmental destruction in its wake.

5.1.4 Corporation as Moral Force

A few years ago, the New York Times ran a story noticing the moral voice of corporate America—namely, that corporations have assumed a social/public consciousness that was once reserved exclusively for government. David Gelles, *The Moral Voice of Corporate America (*Aug. 19, 2017) (describing the nation as "split into political tribes" and the emergence of "a surprising group of Americans its moral voice more forcefully than ever: CEOs").

This transformation has gained momentum as the country continues to engage in heated debates over everything from immigration, to climate change, to responding to the pandemic, to answering Russian aggression in Ukraine. The following are two accounts of how corporations have taken moral stances when, first, government seemed to balk and, second, in tandem with government action.

Corporate moral indignation about Charlottesville

adapted from David Gelles,
The Moral Voice of Corporate America
New York Times (Aug. 19, 2017)
[available on nytimes.com]

On August 17, 2017, Nazi-saluting white supremacists rioted in Charlottesville, Virginia. One of them drove his car into a crowd of protestors, murdering one and injuring 35 others. When President Trump dithered in his response, a chorus of business leaders rose up to condemn hate groups and to espouse tolerance and inclusion. CEOs suddenly became the conscience of America:

- Mary T. Barra (the CEO of GM): People should "come together as a country and reinforce values and ideals that unite us—tolerance, inclusion and diversity."
- Jamie Dimon (CEO of JPMorgan): "The equal treatment of all people is one of our nation's bedrock principles."
- Howard Schultz (chairman of Starbucks): "The reason people are speaking up is that we are fighting for what we love and believe in, and that is the idealism and the aspiration of America, the promise of America, the America that we all know and hold so true."

- Doug McMillon (CEO of Walmart): "As we watched the events and the response from President Trump over the weekend, we too felt that he missed a critical opportunity to help bring our country together by unequivocally rejecting the appalling actions of white supremacists."
- Kenneth Frazier (CEO of Merck): "As a matter of personal conscience, I feel a responsibility to take a stand against intolerance and extremism."

In a further rebuke to the president, who had said there were "good people" on both sides at Charlottesville, a wave of CEOs (including Elon Musk of Tesla) resigned from the president's business advisory councils, leading to their disbandment. In short, CEOs spoke truth to power—risking customers being offended and government relations suffering.

So why this transformation? There has been pressure from employees, who increasingly want their companies to take positions on social or economic causes. Board members have become worried about company reputation. And shareholders (especially institutional shareholders) increasingly understand the value of companies meeting social and political expectations.

The battle lines are drawn

James Murdoch (CEO of 21st Century Fox and son of Rupert Murdoch, a staunch supporter of Mr. Trump) said:

> What we watched this last week in Charlottesville and the reaction to it by the President of the United States concern all of us as Americans and free people. There are no good Nazis. Or Klansmen, Or terrorists.

In response, John Carney (business editor for Breitbart News, the conservative news site) wrote:

> Corporate America is now part of the opposition. The confederacy of the media institutions, the American left, and Corporate America has aligned itself against the populist uprising that brought Trump to the White House. The battle lines are clear.

All this is not completely new. Companies have faced issues of race, class, and gender for generations.

- In 1960, after four black college students sat down at the segregated lunch counter at a Woolworth's store in Greensboro, NorthCarolina, the civil rights sit-in movement was born—and five months later, Woolworth's desegregated.
- In the 1980s, activists called on US companies to divest from apartheid South Africa—and many big companies, including GM and Pepsi did.
- In the 1990s, many companies (including Apple, Disney, and Xerox) extended health care benefits to partners of gay and lesbian employees—and this led to broader acceptance of gay rights, including by the US Supreme Court.
- In 2015, Indiana passed a law making it easier for religious conservatives to refuse service to gay people—and many employers threatened to leave the state and the legislature watered down the law.

But this is not to say corporate leaders are now beacons of morality. Sexual abuse scandals remain an engrained part of the C-suite. And greenwashing, such as happened at VW before "dieselgate," remains widespread. And, lately, the corporate establishment has railed against the "woke" movement. As one executive said, "We all recognize that with every decision we make, there is a group of people that are not going to agree

Which companies left and which stayed?

After Russia's invasion of Ukraine, two Yale management professors created a scorecard of the corporate exodus from Russia:

Leaving Russia - 253 companies [30.3%], including Accenture, Alcoa, American Airlines, Bain & Company, Ball, BCG, BlackRock, BP, Carnival, Deloitte, Delta, eBay, EY, KPMG, McKinsey & Company, Nasdaq, PwC, Reebok, Salesforce, Shell, Stanley Black & Decker, Take-Two Interactive, Uber

Suspending activity - 248 companies [29.7%], including Adidas, ADP, American Express, Burger King, Chanel, Coca-Cola, Dell, Disney, Estée Lauder, GM, Hendrick & Struggles, Hewlett Packard Enterprise, Honeywell, HP, Hyundai, IBM, Levi's, MasterCard, McDonald's, Nike, Oracle, Paramount, PayPal, Starbucks, ThermoFisher Scientific, Trane Technologies, UPS, Visa, Xerox

Scaling back activity - 75 companies [9.0%], including Bacardí, Caterpillar, Coinbase, John Deere, Dow, GW, Goldman Sachs, J.P. Morgan, Kellogg's, Mars, PepsiCo, PPG, Whirlpool, Yum! Brands

Halting investments - 96 companies [11.5%], including Abbot, AmerisourceBergen, Baker Hughes, Cargill, Colgate-Palmolive, Credit Suisse, Danone, Johnson & Johnson, P&G, Mondelez International, Siemens, Unilever

Staying the course - 162 companies [19.4%], including Acer, Alibaba, Asus, Cloudflare, International Paper, Koch, Lenovo

Jeffrey A. Sonnenfeld & Steven Tian, *Some of the Biggest Brands Are Leaving Russia. Others Just Can't Quit Putin* Yale_Insights (Apr. 7, 2022).

with us, But you must define your core purpose for being. We stand in the interest of something greater than just making money."

* * *

Corporate support for Ukraine

adapted from Belinda Luscombe,

Hundreds of CEOs Came Out Against Russia - Their Involvement Could Change War Forever

Time Magazine (Mar. 11, 2022)
[available on time.com]

Traditionally, corporations that do business with countries seen as international pariahs draw a line between matters of trade and matters of state. As some CEOs explain, "Even if I don't much like a particular government—and there are plenty to choose from—we couldn't do business anywhere. After all, we're a cog of capitalism that spreads investment and jobs. And investment is often correlated with prosperity and thus political freedom."

This changed when Russia invaded Ukraine in February 2022. While NATO countries imposed unprecedented financial and economic penalties on Russia, a wave of corporations unilaterally announced they would join in the sanction effort and suspend or terminate business dealings with Russia. The business community has thrown itself into "a geopolitical conflict with a whole new force, which could have a significant impact on how wars are fought—and peace is negotiated—in the future."

Not only did energy companies, credit card companies, media companies, management firms, and tech giants leave Russia, they did it with bravado:

- Al Kelly (CEO of VISA): "We are compelled to act following Russia's unprovoked invasion of Ukraine, and the unacceptable events that we have witnessed."
- Chris Kempczinski (CEO of McDanalds) in temporarily closing its restaurants in Russia: "We cannot ignore the needless human suffering unfolding in Ukraine."

- Xxx (CEO of TMF): "It's that sense of crossing a line. We wanted to show that integrity was one of the company's core values and "why are we wasting our time waiting for sanctions?"

What has surprised sanctions experts is how many corporations imposed restrictions on their own and how quickly they moved. Even before the full suite of government sanctions kicked in, the private sector decided to divest, to withdraw investments, and to minimize exposure to Russia.

The most remarkable exits were by energy companies, who had significant investments in Russia and were among the first to announce their exits. Although the bottom lines of many companies is not affected by exiting Russia, Shell's LNG joint venture with Gazprom was considered a crown jewel. The same for other energy companies including BP and ExxonMobil.

What is the future of global warfare with private companies opting to add their poor to the engines of war? Compliance experts are confused: how do you advise clients on whether to sanction or not? As a consultant to multinational tech companies with operations in Russia said, "This playbook is being written as we're speaking."

Companies have accelerated the isolation of Russia, a major global economy, unknown in modern history. These moves have also forced Russian enterprises to seek trading partners elsewhere, especially China. For example, Russian banks are turning to using credit cards powered by China's UnionPay system rather than Mastercard and Visa, both of which removed access to their services.

In addition, as the business world flexes its diplomatic muscles, government diplomats and statesmen are discovering that some levers of power have been transferred to a different operator, with different priorities. For example, after the US negotiated a deal to lift sanction on Iran, then-secretary of State John Kerry had to go on a global tour trying to persuade banks to start doing business there again. They all declined, making impossible for other businesses to renew business in the country. Iran accused the West of not living up to its bargain.

The same is likely to happen with Russia. The abrupt and undiplomatic way many corporations announced their exits—with dismay and disgust rather than the usual excuses about operational difficulties—may make Russian less than eager to welcome them back. And the corporations may also decide that the risks of another Russian "adventurism" are too great to justify returning.

Have corporations taken on a new role as moral arbiters of national policies and actions? Where does the corporate role begin and where does it end? And, now, rather than turning to the United Nations or other diplomatic channels will people oppressed in different parts fo the world turn to corporations for support?

As Charlottesville and the Russian invasion of Ukraine illustrate, the private sector (the corporation) seems to be leading rather than following the public sector (government and the law). For example, while sexual harassment in the workplace has led to "the corporate sector taking really firm, hard stands on this, we see zero movement in the government and politicians. And we see the corporate sector really questioning their tolerance for the bombastic, raging, shut-people-down." Interview of Brene Brown, On Being (2018).

How Does Culture Change?

So, one of the deep questions about this shift in corporate culture is the question, "How does culture change?" This is a deep philosophical and sociological question, but one that business law academics have begun to ask. Consider this critique by a management school professor of how corporate culture must change to respond to the climate crisis:

> Today, we have made climate change trivial by making its solutions easy—generally framed in the language of commerce. In the long run, this won't work. There is no technological or political silver bullet to solving our environmental problems. While important in the short term, Elon Musk and the power of the market alone will not save us in the long term. In the long term, we will have to change the way we think. Without systemic changes in our culture and values, we will never recover from the destructive path on which we are embarked. We find ourselves facing a new scale of environmental problems in the Anthropocene, an era that requires a fundamental change in the intellectual, cultural and psychological conceptions of who we are as humans, what is the world around us, and how the two are intertwined. And to that end, solutions must be found in religion and philosophy. If we can connect the teachings of the Bible, Torah, Quran, Bhagavad-gītā, Tripitaka, and oral traditions of indigenous peoples, and the philosophies of Aurelius, Locke, Voltaire, Madison, Wordsworth, Thoreau, and Russell, then the world can change on its axis. It has happened before. But it will involve a culture shift as grand and sweeping as the Enlightenment, Reformation, or Scientific Revolution.

Andrew John Hoffman, *Our Emerging Cultural Shift: Regaining the Moral Case to Address Climate Change, Behavioral Scientist* (2019) [available on SSRN]. Interestingly, the urgency of a fundamental social rethinking—even awakening—is not widely acknowledged. While many acknowledge that we have the technology to move to renewable energy and avert climate catastrophe, the stumbling block lies in "the realm of the social sciences." This is largely unacknowledged, with the social sciences receiving only 0.12 percent of the $1.3 trillion in funding for climate-related research. See Indra Overland & Benjamin K. Sovacool, *The Misallocation of Climate Research Funding* (2020) [available on SSRN].

* * *

Concluding Thoughts

Focusing the System

adapted from Emily PG Erickson,
The Cocktail Party in Your Head
(Jan 27, 2022)
[elemental.medium.com]

One Sunday afternoon, while walking along the river path near where I live in St. Paul, I wandered off the pavement to a clearing where the bluffs swing out over the Mississippi. I watched as the wind pushed a pocket of snow perched in an oak to the ground below. During its descent through a slant of sunlight, the snow sparkled.

In the wintertime, a serene stillness settles over the land. But my brain doesn't get the memo. When everything outside of me is quiet, my mind's chatter revs up.

The voices inside of me berate me and repeat themselves. Frankly, they're downright rude. The details are boring. They feature my personal bugaboos—namely, that I'm a failure, with all the ubiquitous castigation that implies. It can get uncomfortably crowded in my head.

But if my head were a crowded room, it might not be quite so bad. Why? The cocktail party effect—the psychological phenomenon whereby we can selectively attend to particular auditory stimuli and ignore others, just as we do at the eponymous party. It's like a biological mute button.

When I made this connection recently, I decided to see if I could apply the cocktail party effect internally. I was surprised by what I found. I began by noticing the different thoughts in my head. Then I practiced tuning in to specific thoughts while letting others fade into the background.

When I examined the content of my thoughts one by one, I noticed a pattern. My first thoughts are often the wisest. The rest are frequently an attempt to muscle my way toward logical narrative coherence, which sometimes fails to account for important information for which I don't yet have the words.

Noticing this pattern has freed me to apply the cocktail party effect to even greater benefit. When the crowd in my head begins to feel overwhelming, I ask myself, "Who do I want to seek out and hear from right now?" My answer is often my wisest self. Now that I know she tends to arrive early, I can seek her out right away.

When I take time to listen—really listen—I feel better. I feel settled. I feel still. I feel something like that snowy scene I encountered by the Mississippi.

Chapter 5.2

Stakeholder Capitalism: A Delusion?

This chapter looks at whether stakeholder capitalism is up to the challenge of confronting the environmental and social troubles that ail us.

What if capitalism—even modified stakeholder capitalism—lacks the incentives to save itself? What if the ESG movement is just a massive marketing ploy—greenwashing of monumental proportions? What if the rush to ESG investing is simply a postponement of the inevitable?

Consider the rise in ESG investing and the trajectory of GHG emissions in the United States over the last several years. While ESG investing has more than quadrupled in the last decade, GHG emissions have fallen by only 10 percent. Almost no bang for the buck.

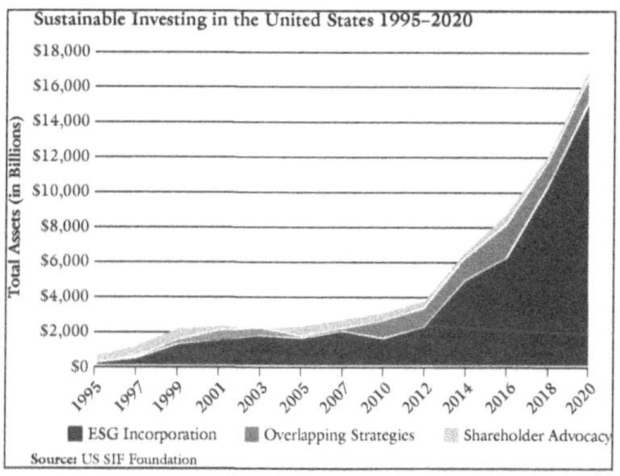

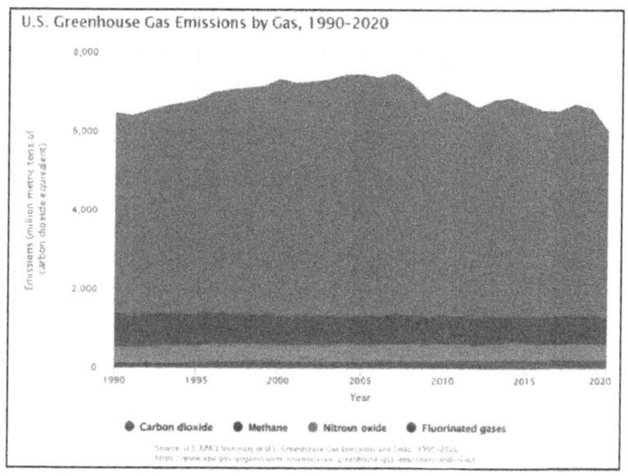

This chapter considers whether stakeholder capitalism is a delusion. If the corporation's design is to externalize harm, to focus only on the short-term, to be a mono-culture, and to exercise political clout to stay this way, then counting on the corporation to save the planet and its people would seem a fool's errand.

Chapter's Focus

You will want to first consider the assertion that capitalism is awakening. Perhaps the ESG movement is creating incentives that change the corporation's design—thus to begin internalizing environmental and social harm, to consider more than the short term, to include in corporate decision-making a more diverse set of leaders, and to view the political process as a tool to advance the corporation's sustainability goals. What a change!

Next, you will want to consider the assertions that the corporation remains as it has been—an internalizing, short-termist, myopic, and politically manipulative machine focused on shareholder wealth. That is to say, stakeholder capitalism is a mirage. We cannot count on the system that brought us here to get us out of the mess it's created.

5.2.1 The Problem: The Corporation?

Systemic challenges require systemic solutions. If our environmental and social challenges inhere in our economic institutions and our cultural attitudes, then tweaking capitalism – or, specifically, the corporation – would seem a losing strategy. Thus far, we have assumed that capitalism can save itself from itself only if there are fundamental, systemic changes.

Perhaps, in our search for the sustainable corporation, we have been wasting our time imagining that voluntary corporate and investment actions—given the pervasive, animating power of the shareholder profit motive—can confront our environmental and social challenges on the timeline that the challenges present us. The Covid pandemic illustrates the point. Without the coercive "command and control" power of government, would there have been travel restrictions and lockdowns, would facemask mandates have worked, would vaccine rollouts have occurred? Perhaps, but probably not enough to have pushed down the Covid curve.

The same questions now present themselves as rising climate urgency and racial/economic inequalities demand action. Perhaps most telling is that as ESG investing has taken off, its impact on actual CO2 emissions, racial injustice, and income disparities have been negligible. There is a disconnect between purported motives and actual results. What we are observing seems to be a massive greenwashing.

Nobody's Coming to Save Us, Especially Not the Government. We Have to Save Each Other

Medium (Feb. 3, 2022)

Jessica Wildfire

Post-it notes.

That's what Alberta's Health Services offered survivors dealing with brain damage from Long Covid. Instead of treatment and therapy, they described a bunch of life hacks that would help them get back to their "normal" productivity, because that's what matters.

In case you're wondering, it didn't go over very well. Their Twitter feed blew up with sarcastic comments from Covid long haulers, who said they needed more than listicles. Alberta Health Services responded by taking down the tweet, and scrubbing the story.

Critics have pointed out the irony of health agencies in wealthy countries sitting back and tacitly encouraging everyone to put themselves at risk with a "mild" variant of a dangerous virus. They've done nothing while op-ed columnists fill up newspapers with verbal snake oil about "super immunity" and the "relief" people feel after catching Omicron.

Turns out, it was all garbage.

Our governments are bathing in wishful thinking.

It's not just Canada.

The U.S. and Britain have also been trying to sell the public a fiction that once they get vaccinated and boosted, the pandemic is over. The CDC has dragged its feet for a year now when it comes to delivering accurate, honest information about how to protect ourselves. Britain's health officials plan to stop publishing daily Covid data in April, despite a recent surge in deaths that came right after they dropped restrictions.

Here's how that's going:

> A tweet: "My nephew got Covid twice within a month. And "recovered." Maybe re-infecting kids every 6 months, without a single peer-reviewed study on LT conseuqences of frequesnt pediatric reinfections is short succession, was not a brilliant idea."

That's the story of millions. Aided by the media, our governments misled us on issues that were critical to our health and well-being. Now people are suffering. Those public officials so eager for everyone to get back to normal are now trying to cover up their enormous mistakes.

It's not just the pandemic.

The pandemic is the most obvious, glaring example of our government's total incompetence. It's getting worse.

We've got real problems staring right at us. Housing prices are going up, and I hate to break it to you, but they're never coming down again. Ever. Climate change has crippled our lumber supply, and it's driving prices up a cliff. On top of that, wages and purchasing power are flat lined against inflation.

Our food supply is in danger.

We've been relying on fertilizer and monoculture crops for decades now, stripping the soil bare for future generations. Severe drought has been devastating farmland. We still waste a third of what we produce. We chuck it straight into dumpsters, when it could be directed to food banks and homeless shelters, or even just used for compost.

All of that's the real reason why food prices are going up, that and reckless profiteering. Big Agriculture doesn't want change.

It's profitable to let people starve.

Nobody's coming to save us.

Our governments don't serve us anymore. They don't protect us. Our leaders are preoccupied with Twitter spats and drone strikes. They're catering to hateful minorities, and nurturing our worst traits. When they're not doing that, they're selling our natural resources to billionaires.

Politics won't get us out of this mess. We don't enjoy a choice at the polls anymore. One side wants a neo-fascist dictatorship that crams the Bible down everyone's throats. The other wants to let things fall apart at a more gradual pace, while they sit back and eat ice cream.

We've got to save ourselves.
Here's how:

Inform yourself. It's pretty clear by now that we can't trust our major institutions anymore, not at face value. We've all got to get better at evaluating where our information comes from and whether we can trust it.

Simplify your life. Sustainability is the key to the future. The less you can live on and be happy, the better. The endless push for convenience has ingrained a sense of dependence in us. Relying on robots will make us helpless when the power goes out, and our appliances break down, and we can't afford replacements.

Learn first aid and basic healthcare. The anti-vaxxers and wishful thinkers have broken our hospitals. They're not going to recover in our lifetimes. Hundreds of thousands of experienced doctors and nurses have quit. There's only one solution here. Wherever we can, we've got to learn how to treat our own injuries and emergencies. Do you know how to administer CPR? Do you know how to take someone's blood pressure? Do you know how to sew stitches, or disinfect and dress a wound? Do you know how to set a broken bone?

Grow your own food. We're not always going to be able to rely on grocery stores. Some of us already can't. It takes a long time to learn how to grow, harvest, and preserve your own food Learn what foods you can grow in your local climate. Learn what foods grow during what seasons. Build structures where they can survive extreme weather.

Teach your own kids. Public schools are falling apart. You know it's bad when substitutes make less than starting wage at Starbucks. Even full-time teachers can't make ends meet anymore. There's simply no incentive for bright, intelligent, caring people to enter the profession. When they do, they burn out in a few years. They leave. If kids aren't shot at or infected with a deadly virus, they're persecuted and bullied all day. They're fed right wing propaganda. They spend their days doing shooter drills and filling out worksheets.

Build communities. None of us are going to survive this dystopian future on our own, hunkering down in bunkers with beans and rifles. Even if we could, that's no way to live. Who wants that? Society is clearly unraveling. If we want a shot at a meaningful, fulfilling life, we've got to form smaller sustainable communities where we can depend on our neighbors in times of crisis. We're going to need people who can grow food, who can set bones, who can fix plumbing, who can build greenhouses and windmills, mend clothes, and teach our kids.

Change the way you think. Most of us have been trapped in limited trains of thought for the last year. Half of us have wrapped ourselves up in fake hope and wishful thinking. The other half watched the world fall apart on their phones, feeling helpless to do anything but doomscroll and panic.

***

If we can't get timber for houses, we'll have to use bamboo. If we can't rely on supply chains, we'll have to reinvest in local production. If we can't rely on fossil fuels, we'll have to ditch our cars for bicycles. If we can't rely on schools, we'll have to teach our own kids. If our bosses won't pay us living wages, we'll have to learn to live without wages. It's time to develop true resilience now. We've got to learn how to live with less and be happy. We've got to learn practical skills and build robust communities.

That's what a true revolution looks like. It's not about overthrowing the government. It's about living differently.

It's the only way.

5.2.2 Is Capitalism Healing Itself?

Here's an essay that I wrote in the fall of 2021. In some ways, it's the culmination of my own search for the sustainable corporation—though it leaves open the question of what is happening to the usual incentive structures in the corporation. That question is the subject of Chapter 5.3, the book's final chapter on "personal integrity"—basically, keeping one's word. It's hard to imagine a sustainable corporation not founded and steeped in human trust.

Capitalism, Heal Thyself

(Nov. 25, 2021)

Alan R. Palmiter

[available on SSRN]

A paradigm shift is underway. The corporation—much reviled as an externalizing, short termist, inward-focused, politically manipulative machine—is undergoing a radical change. A real metamorphosis.

The driver has been the financial community's recognition that ESG produces company value—and lots of it. This has resulted, beginning about five years ago, in widespread ESG investing—which has gone exponential. Portfolio companies have seen their stock price rewarded by pursuing such environmental practices as reducing their carbon footprint (E), focusing on customer, employee, and social well-being (S), and revamping firm governance to become more aware of the world's interconnectedness (G). The communication and information revolutions wrought by the Internet have also contributed.

There are also powerful feedback loops that only accelerate these phenomena. Companies that infuse real ESG into their operations—not the fake stuff that the financial markets are getting better and better at ferreting out—attract money from the big investment firms engaged in ESG investing. And with additional capital, these real ESG companies increase their (presumably still real) ESG operations, attracting further ESG investing.

Everything Is Connected

Before explaining this, it's useful to consider how everything is connected—that's the essence of ESG. I do so with a plastic bottle sitting in front of me:

> So, it turns out that animals and fungi split from living organisms called protists about 1.54 billion years ago, while plants split from protists a bit earlier, about 1.55 billion years ago. That means that 1.55 billion years ago, there was a Mama protist that had some offspring. One of them was a mutant—the first plant. Then about 10 million years later one of her offspring had another mutant—that was the first animal.
>
> Stop and think about this. That means that plants are related to me (as an animal) going back some countable generations. That is, we can go back and are both related—plants and I—to our great-great-great . . . grandmother, the Mama protist who was a progenitor for both of us. How many generations back? Well, I'm not sure. You'd have to ask a biologist. But it's probably in the range of a few billion generations, not much more.
>
> It also means, as I contemplate this plastic bottle on the table, that we're cousins—me and the bottle. Well, cousins several times removed. The bottle is made from petroleum, which was once plant life that became muck and then—with the help of fungi—that muck got deposited underground. And there my cousin, the plant, stayed for 10 to 180 million years. Until she was processed and joined me today at this table.
>
> Here we are reunited after so many years, my cousin the bottle and me. Not in some poetic or metaphoric sense, but rather in a biological, DNA, chemical sense. Really.
>
> And here's our family tree:

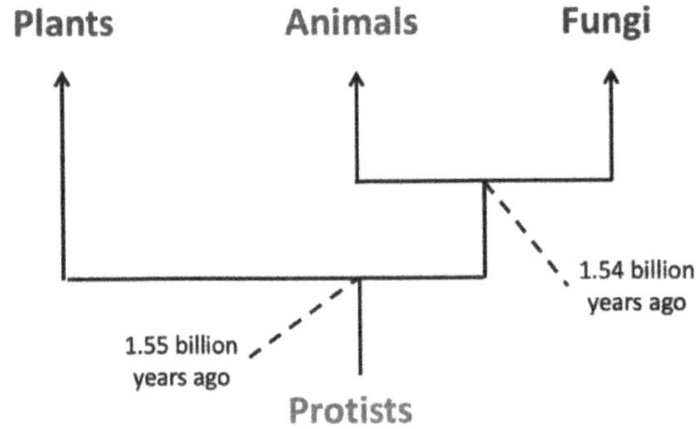

Source: Bright Hub Education

Look at ExxonMobil

So, when I think about plastic bottles, I think about ExxonMobil. It turns out that the financial community has also been noticing how everything is connected with respect to the company. As a result, the financial community seems to have decided that ExxonMobil's oil and gas business has a dismal future. The company is sitting astride a massive wasting asset—$336.7 billion as of September 2021. (The company's market cap is $275.3 billion—go figure.)

Although the recent palace coup led by Little Engine No. 1 (the "little engine that could" placed a couple of renewable energy folks on the company board) may be improving the odds that ExxonMobil will awaken before it digs deeper and goes down the drain, the data are stunning.

In the last five years, the stock price of ExxonMobil (the world's largest oil and gas company) has fallen 27%, while the S&P 500 (even though dragged down by ExxonMobil, the rest of the fossil-fuel sector, and the non-ESG companies that haven't gotten the message) has risen 112%.

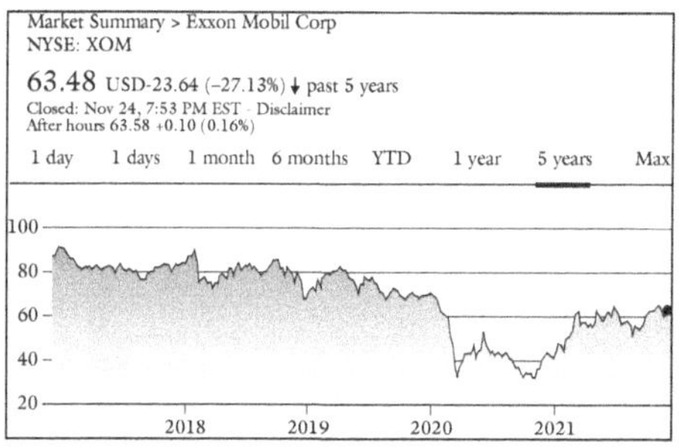

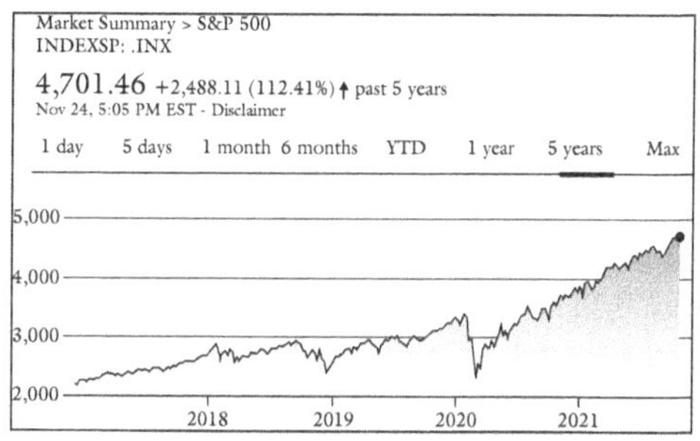

In some ways, I need say no more.

In short, the market has looked into its crystal ball—which gives a blurry picture of the future, about 7 to 10 years out. And using "time value of money" concepts (discounting), the market has arrived at a present value of what ExxonMobil's future financial prospects look like, including (lately) what the company's social costs are likely to be.

ExxonMobil's recent stock prices reveal that the market thinks the company's future is bleak. Not only is the company's stock price trending downward, but it's also way more downward compared to the market. Notice that the overall market—whose price is also a bunch of discounted guesses about companies' future prospects—seems somewhat hopeful and lately even more hopeful about the global financial future.

Follow the Money

Capitalism is in the process of saving itself from itself. And it's not as though Capitalism had to reconceptualize itself. It is still mesmerized by the profit motive. It's still about shareholder returns. It's just that Capitalism is realizing that shareholder returns that are built on lousy wages, dumping GHG gases into the atmosphere, and selling shoddy and dangerous products are . . . well . . . not sustainable. Financially.

Because everything's connected, that's why. The easiest way to see this is again to use our punching bag ExxonMobil. If ExxonMobil is creating a product that leads to so-called Level 3 GHG emissions that cause storm surges, droughts, floods, fires, and so on, the company's activities hurt a bunch of other companies' profits because of storm surges, droughts, floods, fires, and so on.

For those investors—that is, all the big institutional shareholders in the world, with about 80 percent of all financial assets under management—who have both ExxonMobil and these other victimized companies in their managed portfolios, they want to get rid of ExxonMobil. Some have—see the price chart. But if they hold ExxonMobil in an indexed portfolio, one that tracks the market and thus includes ExxonMobil and other fossil-fuel companies, they can't sell ExxonMobil. So, what have these institutional shareholders done? They've used their enormous voting power, held in both their managed portfolios and indexed portfolios, to communicate to ExxonMobil to stop ruining their overall investment returns.

And this story is being played out across all financial markets. And it's gone exponential.

Exponential Growth in ESG Investing

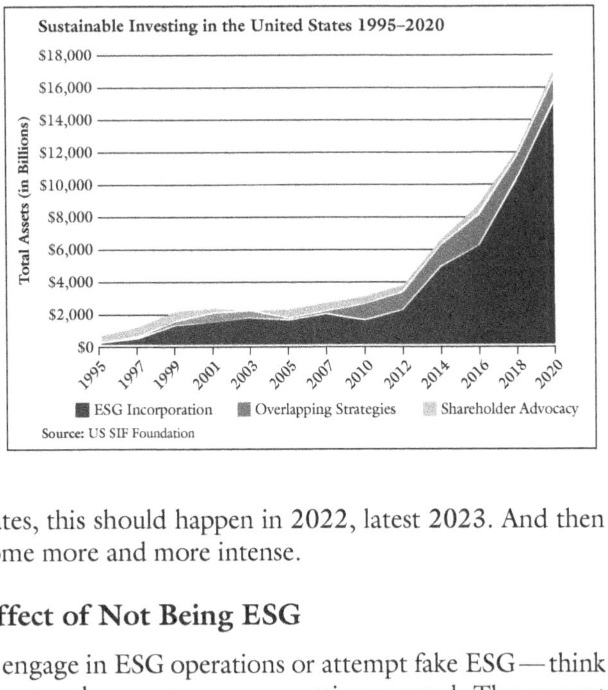

Here is the growth in "managed portfolios" that have embraced ESG by incorporating it into their investment models—as of 2020:

Something happened in about 2012, and there's no indication it's going to end soon. In fact, there's every reason to believe that nearly all AUM globally will soon have some form of ESG flavor—whether ESG-incorporated, ESG-focused, ESG-activist, or ESG-impact investing. At current exponential growth rates, this should happen in 2022, latest 2023. And then the ESG flavors will only become more and more intense.

Effect of Not Being ESG

Companies that either do not engage in ESG operations or attempt fake ESG—think ExxonMobil and its claims about carbon capture—are getting reamed. The current global oil and gas crisis, for example, seems to have been caused by the oil and gas industry starting to run out of investment dollars. Or that's what The Economist concluded. But think about it. Why would anyone today invest (or insure) an oil and gas operation, especially given that renewable energy is increasingly cheaper and more available? In the end the Koch Brothers have only so much money to prop up a bygone energy model.

Look back to the last decade. All the major coal companies in the United States went bankrupt in the 2010s. For example, Peabody (the largest U.S. coal company) went from $900 per share to $2 per share in five short years, before giving up and declaring bankruptcy. The rest of the fossil fuel industry is now standing in line, waiting for its bell to be tolled.

Here's what coal looked like and what one might guess oil and gas will look like. The question is not really whether, just when.

You gotta feel sorry for the fossil-fuel industry. It has no chance. Solar power and wind power, which almost every day make strides in efficiency and materials innovation, continue to come down in price. And, once installed, they're essentially free. (Despite calls by the fossil-fuel industry to tax sunlight, it remains free.) Meanwhile, mining and drilling are only getting more expensive—and both are so non-ESG. For these companies, reality is what happens whatever your beliefs otherwise – including the beliefs of those (like climate deniers) who so want to believe it isn't happening.

Effect of Being ESG

It turns out that EVs are better than internal combustion engine (ICE) vehicles. Or, at least, that's the view of the stock markets. Tesla's current market cap of $1,040 billion is greater than the combined market cap of the next eight vehicle manufacturers: Toyota, Rivian (a recent arrival), VW, BYD (an EV maker), Daimler, GM, Lucid (more EV), Ford. And all these others have solemnly declared their commitment to EVs. What about the legacy automakers: real ESG or fake ESG? The stock markets aren't sure; they're sorting it out.

Here's what pursuing ESG looks like. Did you catch how much Tesla went up? More than 28 times in five years.

Tesla is not alone. Other companies have experienced a big stock market "pat on the back" when they pursue real ESG. Just Google, "best ESG companies and stock price performance." But I warn you, some of these may be companies trying fake ESG (commonly called greenwashing).

Everyone seems to be trying to figure it out, many asking AI for help. And everyone's getting better, because real ESG gives you those golden long-term returns (and a stock price bonanza) and fake ESG just fizzles. But, looking at the number of Teslas and other EVs sold, you can run the numbers on how much less net CO2 these EVs emit—and the graph you get, like EV sales, will be exponential. (Remember EV sales are today miniscule; that will be changing—at least according to the stock market.)

What's clear is that companies that look to maximize shareholder welfare (which may mean more than just maximizing the current stock price) will be rewarded eventually . . . in the stock market.

What Is ESG?

OK, you've been wondering. What is ESG? ESG is when a company pays attention to environment, social, and governance in its decision-making and operations. (Some think of it as sustainability, social justice, and leadership—but ESG rolls off the tongue more easily.) There are still lots of way that ESG is being defined. But here's a quick sampling of what companies pursuing ESG may be saying:

> We're taking climate change seriously, trying to be conscious of water use, adopting sustainable farming methods—that's the E (for environment) in ESG.
>
> We're trying to be good to people by focusing on fair wages, safe products for our customers, no products made using child or slave labor—that's the S (for social) in ESG.
>
> We're adding diversity on our leadership team, aligning pay to encourage environmental stewardship and corporate social responsibility, and giving useful disclosure to investors—that's the G (for governance) in ESG.

By the way, ESG used to be called corporate social responsibility (CSR), but the CSR brand got a bad name because it sounded like giving away shareholders' money. So now it's just called ESG. Same thing happened to socially responsible investing (SRI), which sounds too altruistic, and it's now called ESG investing.

Let's be clear. There is no perfect ESG company, not even Patagonia. Some of its organic cotton will come from unsustainable farming; some of its employees will feel useless, and some people in the supply chain will feel exploited; and power will go to the heads of some on the board. So there never will be a completely "real ESG" company. We are human; we all fall from grace.

And some companies will struggle to get the E, and the S, and the G all aligned and correct. Sometimes it may be that they just can't do it. Think Coca-Cola. It might do great on water usage, on reducing its carbon footprint, on contributing to sustainable farming. And it might be OK on diversity, equity, and inclusion (DEI) in the workplace and company governance. But how can selling something some call "toxic sugar water" be socially OK?

Other times companies might be trying to hit on all three cylinders, but simply don't have the EQ. They need help. They need modeling. They need guidance. The big consulting firms say they can help—advising on ESG has become a big part of their business. And there's always the stock market and the world of shareholder proposals (advisory votes by shareholders) giving companies gentle nudges—and sometimes shoves.

At best, companies can be on an ESG trajectory—and the various markets in which the company operates will make comparisons. That is what is happening. Think about the recent jury award that would have Tesla pay an employee $137 million because he had endured a hostile work environment and racist abuse while working at the company. That's real money. But Tesla's stock price likely will take a hit only if the company shows it doesn't really care about treating employees with dignity. And looking at employee ratings of the company, compared to those at other auto makers, suggests Tesla is in a pickle. Failing to get work-life balance, pay and benefits, job security and advancement, management, and corporate culture right could well lead to a hit to the stock price. Yes, the stock price.

That's why Tesla's most recent shareholders' meeting was so interesting—and so telling. At the meeting, Tesla shareholders signaled their displeasure with the two directors up for election by giving them lackluster support; they voted for annual director elections; and they approved a strongly worded DEI proposal—even though CEO Elon Musk, who then held 22% of the company's voting stock, seemed unhappy with this shareholder insouciance.

And now, much more than before, it's hard to externalize costs. When Tesla developed its latest battery, the so-called 4680, it was important that it be sourced from non-toxic materials (almost all lithium and phosphate), that it be recyclable (so say the geeky blogs), that it be quickly rechargeable (the YouTubers will soon report on this), and that it have greater power density (the quarterly financials will reveal this). Failing to see how everything is connected—as it seems happened for GM when its batteries started to self-combust—can be devastating. Including to the stock price.

Relationship Between ESG and Financial Performance

So, we've seen the exponential growth in ESG investing—that is, the growth of investment portfolios that incorporate ESG. Is there reason for this? Do companies' ESG activities really lead to better financial performance?

Let's look at the data.

A recent NYU Stern School of Business meta-study collected and analyzed more than 1,000 mostly academic studies from 2015-2020 on the correlation between ESG operations and company financial performance. The findings:

> We found a positive relationship between ESG and financial performance for 58% of the "corporate" studies focused on operational metrics such as ROE, ROA, or stock price with 13% showing neutral impact, 21% mixed results (the same study finding a positive, neutral, or negative results) and only 8% showing a negative relationship.

The NYU study also looked at the correlation between ESG investing and financial returns:

> For investment studies typically focused on risk-adjusted attributes such as alpha or the Sharpe ratio on a portfolio of stocks, 59% showed similar or better performance relative to conventional investment approaches while only 14% found negative results.

There were two other meta-studies identified by the NYU study on the correlation between ESG investing and financial returns. They found that ESG investing had generally not produced better returns than the market. But all that this means is that the market is absorbing the value produced by ESG companies and their strong financial performance. That is, in the jargon of the investment community, "alpha is being absorbed into beta." And fast.

$$\text{Return(fund)} = \alpha + \beta^{*}\text{Return(mkt)}$$

For any of you who attend to details, what's happening is that modern portfolio theory is recognizing that the composition of the portfolio affects the portfolio's overall returns. And some are noticing that there is fleeting alpha when you identify real ESG happening—or at least, when you identify more real ESG than fake ESG. (And, if you're really attentive to details, you would have noticed that the formula should have included something called the risk-free rate, but it's not important—particularly when beta is one, that is when you're talking about overall market returns.)

Problems with the Studies

Of course, there are problems with almost all these studies. For one, most are in peer-reviewed management publications, which means there is a two-year or so lag between the time the studies gather data and the time they are published. For example, a 2020 study is likely to use ESG and performance data from 2018 and before. That is the studies aren't capturing what has happened in the last two to three years—see the sustainable investing chart above.

Further, as the NYU study points out, there's lots of "inconsistent terminology, insufficient emphasis on 'material' ESG issues, ESG data shortcomings, and confusion regarding different ESG investing strategies." That's the academy! We academics have trouble getting things straight.

But not the markets. They're grinding away separating the wheat from the chaff, the real ESG from the fake ESG. And unlike academics doing their marvelous studies, the folks who inhabit the financial markets have huge financial incentives to separate the real and the fake—and to do so correctly and to do so fast. That is, for example, financial analysts have big incentives to figure out whether ExxonMobil's CSR report and its stated commitments to get to net zero by 2050 are real or just more BS—and then act on this before other analysts come to the same conclusion.

The NYU study makes the point that an area that's woefully under-researched is "the causal factors for improved financial performance by corporates with robust sustainability strategies." That is, what aspects of ESG are the real drivers of financial performance? Good question. As the NYU study asks, are the drivers "sustainability-driven innovation, employee relations, supplier loyalty, customer demand, risk mitigation, operational efficiency," or maybe eyes-wide-open governance practices? Could be a little of each.

Some studies, highlighted recently by The Financial Times, suggest that good leadership teams—that is, well-run companies—are the drivers of financial performance. But whatever the answer, the financial markets will be figuring it out long before the academics complete and publish their studies. To understand the correlation between ESG and financial performance, simply follow the money.

ESG-Induced Investment Returns

What does ESG-induced stock performance look like? Here's a chart from Morgan Stanley Capital Investment (MSCI).

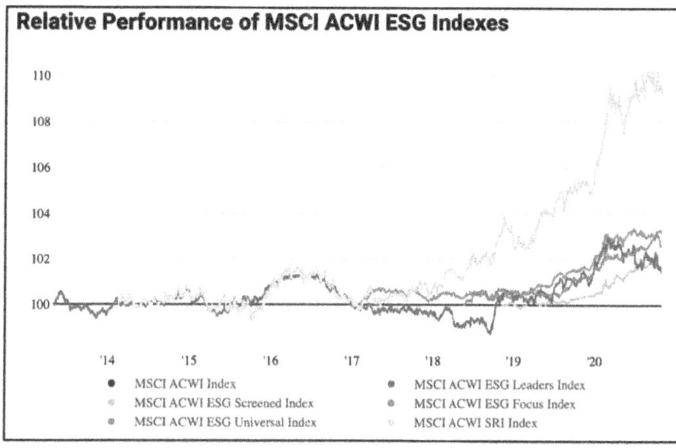

According to this MSCI data, if you had invested in a global index of companies designated as ESG Leaders during any period after 2019, you would have outperformed the global index of all companies — by a few percentage points. If you had invested in an SRI index (25% best-in-class sector approach), you would have handily beat the global index of all companies for each year beginning in 2018.

Notice that according to this chart the "ESG advantage" is about two percentage points. Beating an index by two percentage points is a big deal. Over 20 years, for example, the difference between 8% annual returns and 10% annual returns is the difference between $100,000 becoming $466,096 (assuming 8%) and $672,750 (assuming 10%).

In all of this, however, causation is still not for sure. Does investing in ESG companies lead to better investment returns because everyone is chasing these companies or because ESG companies are actually producing better financial returns? Early evidence points to the latter.

There are all kinds of other charts. But remember, once a company is identified as pursuing real ESG, it gets blessed by the stock market. And companies faking ESG get sent on a downward spiral. At least, this has been quite clear since about 2012.

Oh, by the way, there's another feedback loop that only enhances ESG performance. It's one involving "managed" funds and "indexed" funds. So, we know the managed funds are buying and selling, looking for ESG alpha. Meanwhile the indexed funds—denied the luxury of buying and selling stocks in their portfolio—are engaging with companies, using their leverage and voting power. It's a good-cop/ bad-cop play. The weak or fake ESG companies can't hide.

What About Making People Better?

Political progressives have been convinced that we can't count on the corporation. Capitalism is too corrupt, corrupted, corruptible. We need to have government tell boards of directors to do the right things. We have to read them the riot act about the doughnut of sustainability. Inside the doughnut hole we fail to meet humanity's current needs, outside the doughnut we overstress our planet and her resources. Like Goldilocks, we should aim to be just right.

I believe the progressives were once right. I've been one of them. We were right until about 2012. The corporation—and the financial markets—had been living under the false impression (a delusion) that externalities caused by companies were absorbed by someone else besides other companies. Perhaps this delusion had some validity, given that indexing was only coming into its own . . . at around 2012. But things have been changing. It was in 2012 that indexed funds began to grow faster than managed funds, reaching and passing them in 2019.

Role for Government

Government has played a role, an important one, in the ESG movement. It has insisted on transparency about companies' financial performance—not to mention the financial performance of many of the institutional shareholders. And it has also been quite good at disciplining both companies and investment firms that lie—or are reckless—in their financial disclosures.

And government has insisted on some environmental compliance, some workplace safety, some human dignity in the workplace. It has supplemented health care coverage when companies dropped the ball. And this is all important, but there's still a lot of play in the joints—that is, a lot that the government has not done. Like a carbon tax or caps on CO2 emissions.

But government has also done some damage—like subsidizing some loser sectors, particularly the fossil-fuel industry. But even with these subsidies, these ESG laggards have a dismal future, perhaps no future. The bell will soon toll for them—though, because of the subsidies, perhaps it will toll a bit later than it would otherwise. Congress can only subsidize so much—it would have to empty the national treasury to beat back the markets.

Role for Nonprofits and NGOs

Nonprofits (including foundations) and other NGOs also have an important role to play in the ESG movement. Nonprofits are mostly funded by wealthy elites—and this goes without saying for foundations, too. NGOs (especially international NGOs) get their funding from a combination of sources, including governments and for-profit corporations—again organizations who owe their allegiance to the elites.

The result is that the nonprofits and NGOs, recognizing that the world is inter-connected, look to fill the gaps where government and corporations have failed to advance the ESG agenda. Why have governments failed? Mostly because of their delusional belief that pursuing ESG is not in the best interests of the elites and corporations to whom they answer. Likewise, the corporations targeted by the non-profits and NGOs are those that live in la-la land continuing to believe that the world is not inter-connected and that they can make money by externalizing their costs.

So, nonprofits and NGOs pursue environmental and social activism, catalyzing real action on such things as climate change and social justice—because that is what their funders want. They seek to remind government and sometimes corporations of the importance of climate action and of the value of human dignity—both important matters for the funder elites.

Think about 350.org. Although a lot of the work is done by volunteers, the funding comes from certain elites. And their agenda is clear: tell government and corporations to wake up to the value of confronting climate change. Sometimes, for example, that means telling corporations to wake up out of their stupor and decarbonize—fast. The "divest movement" is nothing more than these elites working to get corporations to notice what the markets are also telling them. Boy, are corporations dense. The delusion in which they've been living—that the world is not inter-connected and externalizing costs is the way to go—is a powerful one.

A final point. Of course, there are some elites who believe that they can make even more money—a desire of most elites—by investing in corporations that make profits in good part by externalizing costs. Think of brownwashing in the oil and gas industry where publicly-held companies sell their CO2 emitting units to privately-held companies. This business strategy reminds me of Charles Prince's famous statement, which he made before Citibank was hit by the Financial Crisis of 2008, "As long as the music is playing, you've got to get up and dance." Externalizing costs may have once been a successful business strategy. But, beginning in about 2012, it is increasingly not.

Being Good

One other thing. We don't need to ask corporations to be good. We have only to ask them, in the words of Paul Hawken, to do what is as easy and natural as falling off a log: to make profits in an inter-connected world. This is a critical point. This is not about changing the corporation's DNA, but rather understanding (a paradigm shift) that it is now being re-purposed to focus on the value of pursuing real ESG.

For example, we don't really need benefit corporations, those corporations that have a hybrid profit and social/environmental purpose. All the companies that are doing big ESG—world-changing ESG—are your garden-variety for-profit (for-shareholder-profit) corporations. Maybe there are some benefit corporations, like my friend Patagonia, who like the label. But Patagonia didn't have to be a benefit corporation to do what it's doing.

That said, there's a problem with fake benefit corporations, the ones pretending to do ESG. Because many are small- and medium-sized enterprises (SMEs), the stock market is not there to put them into line—though these companies live in other financial markets, including banking and insurance. And thank goodness for the Internet. Customers, employees, and bloggers can make a difference. If only Amazon would stop allowing fake reviews of the SME products it sells. Ah, but Amazon's public, it will get put into line if it lets fake info overrun its website.

So, it turns out that awakened Capitalism may be all we need. Some call it enlightened Capitalism, but that suggests it's some new form of Capitalism. Some call it stakeholder Capitalism, but that doesn't fully capture what's happening. These other terms make it sound as though companies and investors must first have had some sort of existential epiphany to do the right thing. Nope, just good old-fashioned, profit-loving Capitalism—awakened and repurposed to notice that everything is inter-connected. That's all we have, and that's all we need. Awakened Capitalism supported by perceptive government and guided by full-hearted NGOs.

What About the Time Horizon?

This worries me. Mother Nature has begun her own feedback loops. The fires this summer in Siberia-which make the US West Coast fires (as devastating as they've been) look like a kid playing with matches—are thawing the tundra and unleashing ungodly amounts of methane. Next year will probably be worse. And this is just one of many feedback loops. Think also about the storm surges, the droughts, the floods. It's sometimes hard to take it all in.

Can Capitalism catch up? The race is on, and Capitalism started late and is behind. But Capitalism, unlike Mother Nature, does not work on an annual, solar cycle. It works on at least a quarterly cycle—that's when companies file their financial 10-Qs. And, given the way that financial analysts have every incentive to know as much about big public companies as the companies themselves, Capitalism is really working on an almost day-to-day, minute-to-minute cycle. Look at what happened to energy stock prices when the current oil and gas shortages hit.

That said, the timing question—some call it the transition question—seems to invite better research, particularly on Capitalism's feedback loops. You see if we're going to catch up, those feedback loops will have to be faster and more powerful than Mother Nature's. There's a Nobel Prize in Economics (or whatever it's called) for someone who digs into and quantifies alpha moving into beta and (especially) the operation of the feedback loops.

Back to Government

So, we've got a big problem—if government gets in the way. It might say, for example, you must disclose your ESG stuff not according to some minimum baseline but "our way or no way." That could deny the market the ESG information it so thirsts for. Or the fake ESG companies might go to government and say, "Protect us from our real ESG rivals. Like, leave subsidies for us or give us new ones, but make things tough for them." That's a problem. The infrastructure bills still wending their way through Congress have had some of this.

Ah, but thank goodness. Congress is in the pocket of the elites and the corporations. How much so? A study of public opinion polls from 1981-2002 (a massive data set) found that policy preference held *only* by the poor and middle-class (think a wealth tax or better Medicare coverage) never became federal law. That is, only public policy preferences of the elites and corporations have a chance. The Princeton political scientist and Northwestern sociologist who put together the study concluded that maybe we don't have a functioning democracy. I agree with them. What we have is market Capitalism.

So, what will the elites and the corporations ask Congress? Will fake ESG or real ESG carry the day? If Congress listens to folks in the financial markets, we're probably OK—because the financial markets have figured out that real ESG presents a better investment strategy than fake ESG. Who will Congress listen to? Remember that all the big institutional shareholders call the shots, they're the boss. In fact, just three of them (the Big Three of BlackRock, Vanguard, State Street) control 25% of voting in US public companies. Add another few on the conference call (the Big Twelve), and they control 51% of this voting. And these big institutional shareholders seem to really want—and certainly say they want—real ESG.

Oh, maybe you're worried about pro-ESG legislation and regulations getting past the US Supreme Court. You can rest assured. The Supremes apply a long-standing rule of law in cases involving corporations: "The corporation is almost always right." According to a regular stream of articles by The Wall Street Journal, this is the Roberts Court's rule in nearly all cases when a corporation goes up against the state, a government agency, or an individual. And based on what I've observed, when big investors show up before the Court, they win even more often than the corporations. Those guys and gals on the Supreme Court, after all, are capitalists—and those who might have socialist sentiments, they're now in the distinct minority.

My dear friend Jack Bogle was worried about the Big Three and the Big Twelve. Jack, who is in heaven, I tell you this, "It's OK." The big institutional shareholders have every reason to heal Capitalism, to save the world. And, if any of them got out of line and slipped back into old habits of making money by looking for companies that externalize costs (non-ESG companies), those institutional shareholders would see investors flee from them. Yes, it's in the financial best interests of the big institutional shareholders to save the world—and that's becoming (exponentially) clearer and clearer.

Why It's So Hard to Get It

All of this is about guessing the future. Companies that pursue ESG are hoping that they're doing the right thing. Investors using ESG investing techniques are hoping that these will identify the companies that are doing ESG—at least better than other companies. And in both cases, the companies and the investors are working with exponential change.

We humans don't perceive and grasp exponential change very well. Our brains don't seem well designed to handle it. We are linear thinkers—extrapolate from past, draw a straight line. Some of us notice the tangent—the rate of change at a specific moment. But we can't really imagine that the future—our future—is being written by the second derivative.

Here's a great graphic on this that I've adapted from waitbutwhy.com. I thank my son for having told me about Tim Urban. And I thank Tim Urban for helping me understand why it is that we are often delusional about what's happening to our reality—specifically, for me, my misunderstanding of what's been happening to Capitalism.

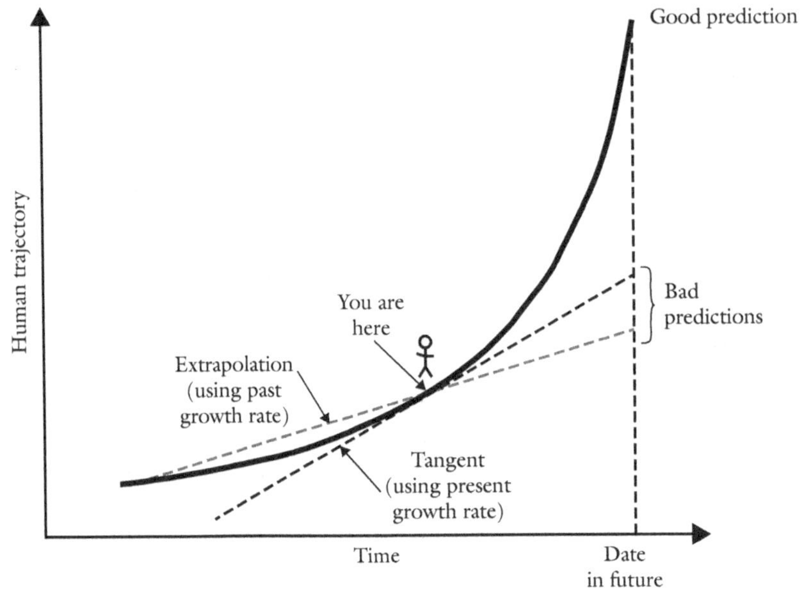

So, here we are. When we think about the future, we tend to extrapolate from the past—and some of us are tempted to extrapolate from the recent past, thinking about the harm that Capitalism has been causing and continues to cause. Some of us, more astute, try to guess the future by thinking about the current rate of change—which gives some reason for hope, given that Capitalism seems to be more and more focused on ESG. But it's almost incomprehensible to believe that Capitalism and real ESG are together on an exponential curve—and with it our economies and even our planet.

In short, the combination of market portfolios, ESG performance, and the Internet appear to have come together in such a way that Capitalism—an awakening Capitalism—is now beginning to position itself to heal itself. With help from each of us—focused, data-driven, change-embracing, and present and caring. We each have a role, and we can't afford to dally.

Not one day.

5.2.3 Voices of Caution

Is capitalism indeed healing itself? Some look at the evidence—and also the models on which modern neo-liberal economics is based—and say, "No. Can't be. The evidence is lacking. And our models don't allow this to happen."

Why should indexed-fund managers bother with ESG? For one, some have questioned that portfolio managers of indexed funds have undertaken to become stewards of the environment. What's in it for them?

The Limits of Portfolio Primacy

(2022)

Roberto Tallarita

[available on SSRN]

According to a theory that is gaining increasing support, we should expect large asset managers (and, in particular, index fund managers) to become "climate stewards" and force companies to reduce their impact on climate change. According to this theory, by maximizing the value of their entire portfolio (portfolio primacy) rather than the value of the individual company (shareholder primacy), index fund managers are incentivized to reduce climate externalities and therefore to steer companies toward decarbonization.

This Article offers the first systematic critique of this theory and identifies four crucial limits that undermine its practical impact: mispricing of climate mitigation, portfolio biases, fiduciary conflicts, and insulation from index funds stewardship.

First, the stock market underestimates the social benefits of climate mitigation. In particular, stock prices do not accurately incorporate climate risk, and private investors discount the distant future at a much higher rate than the social discount rate.

Second, index funds are not real "universal owners"; rather, they invest in subsets of the economy that are relatively less vulnerable to climate change. Many of the Big Three index funds with the largest holdings in the top U.S. oil companies have incentives to oppose aggressive carbon mitigation measures, and even index funds with the broadest market bases internalize global climate externalities in a very limited way.

Third, climate stewardship would create unsolvable fiduciary conflicts on multiple levels: between fund managers and fund investors; between large asset managers and undiversified shareholders; and between corporate directors and the individual company.

Fourth, even if index fund managers undertook the role of climate stewards, most firms across the world would be partially or totally insulated from index fund stewardship, because they are privately held, are owned by state governments, or have a controlling or influential shareholder.

The analysis of this Article reveals the serious limits of portfolio primacy and shows that this approach offers no adequate answer to the crucial threat of climate change. Policymakers should not rely on portfolio primacy as an effective substitute for climate regulation.

Sustainability verification liability

Critical to ESG investing (sometimes called sustainability finance) are sustainability verifiers. These are the professional service providers who review an issuer's alignment with established "green financing" frameworks, thus assuring the accuracy and completeness of this information to investors.

It's a new industry, and there are weaknesses in the current verification model, including conflicts of interest and low quality. The solution? Strict *ex ante* regulation has flaws, including the risk of erecting entry barriers, privileging incumbents, and sacrificing information quality. Instead, as Professor Paul Rose (Ohio State Law) argues, regulators could best protect investors against greenwashing by creating *ex post* securities liability for verifiers. Such liability could drive verifiers to protect their "reputational capital" and thus create a vibrant, effective market in sustainability verification. Paul Rose, *Sustainability Verification* (2022) [available on SSRN] (making recommendations based on experience with credit rating agencies and proxy advisors).

Has the corporation's nature really changed? Further, Professor Joel Bakan, whose documentary *The Corporation* (2006) case identified the corporation as a "psychopathic externalizing machine," doesn't see much difference after the corporation's ESG makeover. A pig is a pig is a pig.

Don't Be Fooled by the Corporation's "Makeover," Documentary Warns

University of British Columbia News, Q&A: Joel Bakan (Sept. 10, 2020)

[available at UBC_News]

In 2003, a Canadian documentary called The Corporation helped audiences understand that the law treats a corporation just like a person—and if it were a person, it would fit the description of a psychopath.

The New Corporation: The Unfortunately Necessary Sequel premieres on Sunday at the Toronto International Film Festival. It's based on Joel Bakan's new book, *The New Corporation: How "Good" Corporations are Bad for Democracy*. Bakan is a professor at the Peter A. Allard School of Law and executive producer of the new film, which he co-directed. We spoke with him about the project.

To what degree did your original version of The Corporation achieve its goals?
The idea of the first project was to develop a critical awareness of the corporation and hopefully have that percolate into policy and governance structures to contain the power of these institutions, which we had revealed as too powerful, too threatening to democracy, and dangerous to society and the environment.

About 10 years after the film and book I looked around and thought, "Wow, we tried to slay the dragon of corporate capitalism but it has actually become much more powerful, and the fire it's breathing is much more dangerous. We really need to go back to the drawing board." And I started thinking about a sequel.

What were corporations doing during that time to increase their power?
After the film and book came out, I spoke to a lot of business groups. People would say to me, "You know, Joel, you're right. The corporation was problematic. We were acting in bad ways, but we've cleaned up our act now."

That's why I called this one The New Corporation, because corporations did a substantial makeover and started to position themselves as providers of solutions to world problems, rather than creators of those problems. If you go to the website of any major corporation, you'll think you've accidentally landed at an activist group's website. It's all about solving poverty, solving climate change, solving social and environmental problems.

I was struck by this disjunction that on one hand, things seemed to be getting worse on all fronts—climate change, workers' rights, human rights—and on the other hand, corporations were saying, "We've become better." That tension is what drives the narrative in both the book and the film.

We hear a lot about "corporate social responsibility" these days, but I take it you're skeptical?
The way the corporation is constructed does not allow it to ever put social and environmental values as fundamental goals. No matter how goodhearted and well-

intentioned a CEO might be, he can't say to his shareholders, "You know what, I'm going to pursue these environmental values and it's going to cost you money." That is simply not within the rules of what a CEO can do and what a corporation can do.

It's been 17 years since The Corporation. If the new film has the impact you hope, what will things look like in another 17 years?
We'll have a much deeper, more social, more environmental democracy. We will have corporations in their rightful place of being governed by democratic institutions rather than governing democratic institutions. We will have democracy operating in robust ways at the local, regional, state and federal levels.

It's not that we won't have corporations and markets, but we will have them contained to doing the things they do well. Markets are a good way to organize production. They're not necessarily a good way to run a school or a water system or a social welfare service.

In both the book and the film, we look at places where democracy is actually starting to evolve in interesting and more robust ways that aren't beholden to corporate power. I don't know if I'm optimistic, but I'm hopeful.

Can ESG go it alone? But perhaps the most damning critique of the ESG corporation comes from Tariq Fancy, the former chief investment officer for sustainability at BlackRock. Although it's unclear why he left this position, it's clear that he's on the lecture, interview, and writing circuit questioning the ESG movement. He formed a nonprofit, the Rumie Foundation, "a global movement of motivated learners, volunteers and organizations to create and share insightful and authentic learning through an innovative technology ecosystem." It's hard not to wonder, though, whether this is all a whirling dervish?

The following story from *The Economist* identifies greenwashing as a fundamental danger created by ESG investing, which the story asserts must be addressed with government regulation. After this is an op-ed piece in USA Today by Tariq Fancy himself, also cautioning about greenwashing and the need for government regulation. Both pieces come from early 2021. Are you persuaded? Persuaded of what?

The Dangers of Greenwashing

The One-handed Economist (May 4, 2021)

David Zetland

In March 2021 Tariq Fancy, the previous chief investment officer in the department of ESG investing at BlackRock (the largest asset manager in the world), published an opinion article in which he essentially stated that ESG investing is "little more than a marketing hype." (ESG stands for "Environment, Sustainability and Governance.")

He exposed parts of the industry by claiming that some companies who label themselves as ESG actually do not act sustainably, and some even invest in fossil fuel companies and other polluting industries. His piece caused a flare-up in discussions around ESG investing and the greenwashing that it has caused.

Greenwashing happens when funds present themselves to be sustainable when they are not to attract more investors. The rise of greenwashing amongst funds has risen because of the rising profits in the ESG market. ESG funds and ETFs are becoming increasingly profitable, reaching record-breaking heights last year. This increased attractiveness of ESG is reflected by a large increase in funds rebranding themselves as ESG. However some of these rebranded funds are not as green as they want others to think. Firms are able to greenwash without repercussions because concrete rules and checks are lacking, allowing them to publish incorrect or manipulated data.

One might think that because there are no current regulations, greenwashing can't be that harmful. However this is a dangerous assumption considering we are nearing a point of no return with climate change. Greenwashing presents a problem because of two reasons: First, it causes a barrier for investors to integrate an ESG framework into their decisions, meaning that the potential that ESG investing has in changing consumption goes lost. Second, it puts up the façade of a positive change happening in big firms, when realistically they are still irresponsible producers. Fancy emphasizes the last issue in a call for action addressed to the government, as we are running out of time to take climate action, and we cannot afford to not take action.

The solution to greenwashing seems obvious: a clear set of regulations for what is defined as sustainable and what is not. Luckily it seems that governments and multigovernmental institutions like the EU have also been noticing the issues with the current rules around ESG investment and sustainability labels. On March 10th the EU issued a new set of rules to help define the difference between sustainable and non-sustainable products. The US government also took notice and announced the creation of a Climate and ESG taskforce, which will "proactively identify ESG-related misconduct." Hopefully the implementation of these regulations will be effective so that ESG investment can keep on expanding in a way that actually makes progress rather than standing still.

Bottom Line: Greenwashing is presenting itself as an big issue in ESG investing. This issue needs to be solved as soon as possible, and the best solution seems to be government regulations.

* * *

Financial World Greenwashing the Public with Deadly Distraction in Sustainable Investing Practices

Opinion, USA Today (Mar. 16, 2021)

Tariq Fancy

[available at USA_Today]

Wall Street is greenwashing the financial world, making sustainable investing merely PR, which is a distraction from the problem of climate change.

The financial services industry is duping the American public with its pro-environment, sustainable investing practices. This multitrillion dollar arena of socially conscious investing is being presented as something it's not. In essence, Wall Street is greenwashing the economic system and, in the process, creating a deadly distraction. I should know; I was at the heart of it.

As the former chief investment officer of Sustainable Investing at BlackRock, the largest asset manager in the world with $8.7 trillion in assets, I led the charge to incorporate environmental, social and governance (ESG) into our global investments. In fact, our messaging helped mainstream the concept that pursuing social good was also good for the bottom line. Sadly, that's all it is, a hopeful idea. In truth, sustainable investing boils down to little more than marketing hype, PR spin and disingenuous promises from the investment community.

SEC Looking to "Proactively Identify ESG-Related Misconduct"

In many instances across the industry, existing mutual funds are cynically rebranded as "green"—with no discernible change to the fund itself or its underlying strategies—simply for the sake of appearances and marketing purposes. In other cases, ESG products contain irresponsible companies such as petroleum majors and other large polluters like "fast fashion" manufacturing to boost the fund's performance. There are even portfolio managers who actively mine ESG data to bet against environmentally responsible companies in the name of profit, a short-selling strategy. Risk managers are focused on protecting their investment portfolios from potential damages done by a worsening climate rather than helping prevent that damage from occurring in the first place.

As disheartening as this reality is, claiming to be environmentally responsible is profitable. Last year alone, ESG mutual funds and exchange-traded funds nearly doubled. The investment community understandably reacted to this with cheers. But those cheers were only for fund managers and their bottom lines. No matter what they tout as green investing, portfolio managers are legally bound (as well as financially incentivized) to do nothing that compromises profits. To advance real change in the environment simply doesn't yield the same return.

In early March, my sentiments were echoed by the U.S. Securities and Exchange Commission (SEC), which announced it was creating a Climate and ESG Task Force to "proactively identify ESG-related misconduct" such as inaccurate or incomplete disclosures by funds and companies—an unprecedented move that suggests there might be abuses that have gone unaddressed.

Ironically, the COVID-19 pandemic has forced us to learn some painful lessons. The initial response of rosy forecasts, loose half-measures and group denial boosted morale, but it also lulled the public into a false sense of security that prolonged and worsened the crisis.

We need to fix the system before disaster strikes

While how we fight a pandemic and climate change are very different, one aspect is clear. Both threats can only be won through the combined efforts of science and policy. In response to the pandemic, we've learned that only top-down government action, such as forcing the closure of high-risk venues and mandating masks indoors, makes a real difference. A "free market" will not correct itself or fix the problem by its own accord.

Imagine the planet is a cancer patient, and climate change is the cancer. Wall Street is prescribing wheatgrass: A well-marketed, profitable idea that has no chance of curing or even slowing down the cancer. In this scenario, wheatgrass is the deadly distraction, misleading the public and delaying lifesaving measures like chemotherapy. But like giving false hope to unproven cures in the midst of a pandemic, the consequences of such irresponsibility are all too obvious. And motivation for why the industry continues to greenwash is all too obvious.

When I left the industry in late 2019, due to family business obligations following the passing of my father-in-law, I was frustrated by the lack of any real change. But I took some comfort in believing that if we weren't doing as much as we could, at least we weren't doing any harm. Since my departure, I have had a lot of time to think about this issue, and I've reassessed my opinion. I believe we are doing irreversible harm by stalling and greenwashing. And all in the name of profits.

We're running out of time and need to accept the truth: To fix our system and curb a growing disaster, we need government to fix the rules.

* * *

Concluding Thoughts

Law and Economics

This is a story told by Armen Alchian, an economist who taught at UCLA in the 1940s through the 1980s. Many believe he should have won a Nobel prize in economics. His work on institutional economics and property rights is widely viewed as groundbreaking.

One day Professor Alchian arrived late for his introductory economics class at UCLA. He said the following to his students:

> I'm sorry for being a few minutes late to class. There was an accident on the freeway. So, I stopped and there was a car that was really banged up. Then I noticed there was a woman inside the car, and she seemed to be badly hurt. I thought she needed to go to the hospital right away.
>
> So, I was about to get her in my car and take her to the hospital when I remembered that this would cause me to be late to class. And I realized that my tardiness would be an imposition on all of you. So, I thought about how much you would be put off by me starting class 15 to 20 minutes late and maybe rushing through the lecture.
>
> Now I assumed that many of you would be OK with this if I paid you $10. So, I did some quick calculations. There are 120 of you. Assuming you would value the inconvenience of me being tardy at $10 per student, I should pay you a total of $1200 for showing up late for our class.

So, I told the woman that I would take her to the hospital but only if she could give me $1200. She was losing consciousness and did not answer. So, I continued on my way.

* * *

What do you think of this story? Maybe you're appalled. What sort of human being was this economist Armen Alchian? His economic analysis seems so flawed—so morally wrong. Or maybe you thought he did the right thing. After all, students were counting on him to start class on time. Everything in life has a price.

Or does it? Well, it turns out that Armen Alchian was a teacher of mine. He told this story, which he had dreamt up, to make the point that economic analysis doesn't work for everything. I met him at a one-week teach-in for law professors who had gathered to learn how to use economic analysis in our scholarship and classroom teaching.

At the end of the conference, Alchian took me aside and said about our week of law and economics: "Don't believe any of the stuff that we talked about this week. It's all made up."

Perhaps the committee that in the 1980s decided on the Nobel prize in economics knew this about Professor Alchian and was worried what he might say during his acceptance speech.

Chapter 5.3

Personal Integrity

This final chapter takes a fresh look at the corporation and offers a fundamental rethinking of the nature of the corporation. Rather than viewing the corporation exclusively as something that shapes incentives for people in business—through a system of rewards and punishments or "carrots and sticks"—perhaps we should also see the corporation as a human organization in which we all bring our own sets of values, perspectives, and concerns. That is, perhaps we should view the corporation both as a place where "external" conflicts arise and are ameliorated, and as a place where the "internal" ones that we all carry with us must also be addressed.

This chapter invites you to turn your understanding of the corporation inside out. In the process, our search for the sustainable corporation takes on a new meaning. Thus far, we have been asking the question, "What should others do to make the corporation—this most powerful of all human institutions, this moral super-organism—into something that might be sustainable, thus to meet the needs of humanity without exhausting our planetary resources?" Notice that the question, as phrased, removes us as participants in this endeavor. We become observers, not actors. But this is not the reason I wrote this book or the reason that you have read this far.

Borrowing the famous words of John F. Kennedy, this chapter invites each of us to ask, "What can I do for humanity?"

Chapter's Focus

You will want to consider whether the "nexus of contracts" corporation is incomplete. That is, viewing the corporation merely as a set of relationships (and mediations) between various corporate participants may not tell the whole story. You will want to think beyond the shareholder-versus-stakeholder debate. You will notice that the many corporate governance mechanisms touted as ways to solve the corporation's failings (independent directors, performance-based pay, shareholder empowerment, more transparency, and so on) seem not to work as promised.

You will want to focus on whether the conflicts in the corporation go beyond external "agency conflicts," but also include (in significant ways) internal "personal integrity" conflicts. You will want to consider whether "business ethics"—that is, sets of norms for appropriate business behavior—is the answer to misbehavior and compliance issues in the corporation. You will want to consider how individuals in business might come to have a sense of autonomy, competency/mastery, and purpose/relatedness—powerful predictors of learning, performance, and psychological health.

Finally, you will want to focus on whether the notion of "personal integrity" (keeping one's word) may be key to engendering trust in the corporation. You will want to consider the importance of trust in hierarchical human organizations—particularly the corporation—and how trust can be created and lost. In this vein, you will want to consider how personal integrity (as a linchpin for self-determination) can be inculcated in the corporation—thus to make the corporation sustainable. That is, you will want to ask whether "sustainable corporations" can exist.

5.3.1 Cracks in "Agency Theory"

Peter Tunjic, the Australian commentator on corporate governance who we encountered before in Ch 2.2 when we considered "groupthink" in the boardroom, has observed that we are living in a new age of Copernicus. It seems that most everyone believes the Sun (the corporation) revolves around the Earth (its shareholders), and we have constructed complex geometric and mathematical systems (corporate governance) to explain this "reality." Yet, as history teaches us, it is much easier to understand cosmological phenomena by saying the Earth revolves around the Sun. And, so too with corporate governance, Tunjic asserts that the elaborate system of agency-cost controls should be fundamentally rethought and jettisoned. They don't comport with our observations of corporate reality.

A Copernican Revolution in Corporate Governance

(April 7, 2016)

Peter Tunjic

[available on OnDirectorship]

2016 feels a lot like 1543.

In the time before Nicholas Copernicus: "Astronomy's complexity was increasing far more rapidly than its accuracy and that a discrepancy corrected in one place was likely to show up in another." (Kuhn 1972)

In an age and a discipline far removed from medieval astronomy, history is repeating. Despite no empirical connection between "best practice" and performance, good governance grows more complicated each year.

At present, corporate governance has no broadly held theoretical base (Tricker, 2009). Rather, it is overwhelmed by multiple and polarizing theories (Letza and Sun, 2002) and whilst a number of broad or even global theories have been proposed (e.g. Hilb, 2006; Hillman and Dalzeil 2003; Nicholson and Kiel, 2004) to date none have gained universal acceptance. More importantly, agency theory, widely recognized as the dominant theoretical perspective of corporate governance (Durisin and Puzone, 2009) continues to suffer from empirical research unable to validate its claims or accurately predict outcomes (Daily, Dalton and Cannella, 2003).

The only thing academics can predict with any certainty is that the solution to one governance problem will become the next.

In 1976 the biggest problem facing capitalism was aligning the interest of managers and shareholders. Solved when Jensen and Meckling came up with the idea of paying managers in securities. But this led to exorbitant executive remuneration, financial engineering and artificial ratio manipulation. Solved by ensuring that there are more independent directors. Which in turn has lead to Boards lacking sufficient industry knowledge and experience to provide sufficient directorship and assurance which in part led to the global financial crisis. Solved by greater oversight. Which in turn has produced greater levels of distrust between boards and managers.

Corporate governance has become a "Copernican Monster"

In the preface to his most famous book the Revolutions of the Heavenly Spheres, Copernicus (though there is some argument whether he said this or the publisher) comments of his contemporaries:

> "Nor have they been able thereby to discern or deduce the principal thing—namely the shape of the universe, and the unchangeable symmetry of its parts. Within them it is though an artist were to gather the hands and feet head and other members for his images from diverse models, each part excellently drawn, but not related to a single body, and since they in no way match each other, the result would be a monster and not a man."

Copernicus thought that an honest appraisal of contemporary astronomy showed the earth centered approach to the problem of the planets was hopeless. Traditional techniques had and would never solve the problem; instead they produced a monster (Kuhn, 1957).

It takes little imagination, to see a Copernican Monster lurking within corporate governance codes and guidelines than share no common theoretical foundation other than to force the shareholder into the centre of the corporate universe.

Ironically, Copernicus' contemporaries papered over the flaws in their theory with things called epicycles. Patches (that look a lot like piecemeal governance reforms) that worked for a time but were fundamentally flawed. More independent directors, more committees, more rules will not solve the problems of corporate existence whilst academics, regulators and even directors labor under the impression that corporations exist to maximize the wealth of shareholders. These will become the next problem.

Epicycle on Epicycle. Reform on Reform until, as we saw in 2008, the system almost collapses.

The solution to the mess is to follow the astronomer's lead

Substitute the corporation for the shareholder at the centre of the corporate universe encircled by stakeholders. Each held in an elliptical orbit by the ever changing gravitational pull of both the corporation and the stakeholders self interest rightly understood.

It's not hard to observe this principle in practice.

Watch a healthy company and you may notice that interests (defined as all the capitals - human, intellectual, financial, natural, produced and social) are prioritized in a way that contributes to the strength, resilience and ultimate longevity of the corporation as a sovereign legal entity. Financial and non-financial capital constantly being traded for all things that are needed to sustain a company into perpetuity. And, as promised by Adam Smith, the interests of stakeholders are obliquely met in proportion to their contribution to the corporation's self interest.

But why has it taken so long to notice?
Another ancient astronomer may have the answer. Johannes Kepler, who went on to perfect the laws of planetary motion, understood his discipline's blind spot. When questioning why Copernicus had not seen that the planets moved in ellipses he responded, "Copernicus did not know how rich he was, and tried more to interpret Ptolemy than nature." Likewise, to understand the nature of the firm, it is far more productive to study what real corporations do and not what economists or law professors say.

But the last word goes to Copernicus, whose advice to his deniers applies equally to those who would deny corporate personhood as the organising principle of the corporation: "The hypothesis of this book need not be true, nor even probable. It suffices if they make possible calculations which fit with observations. We may confidently place them alongside older hypothesis which are no more probable."

* * *

Based on Peter Tunjic, *Directorship Theory: Kuhn, the Copernican Monster and the Crisis in Capitalism*, presented at "Corporate Governance and the Global Financial Crisis," The Wharton School, Philadelphia (Sep. 24-25, 2010).

Agency Theory as Subterfuge
Others have also noticed that agency theory may be frayed. For example, some have observed that the corporation, rather than a hierarchical structure with a purpose of SWM, is best explained as a locus of managerialism—the unstated understanding that the corporation is a fiefdom for, by, and of corporate executives. Consider this critique of managerial hubris and the "cult of agency" by JB Heaton, a financial polygot:

> Agency theory—as applied to debates in corporate governance—rests on a myth of separated ownership and control. The true separation, however, is between ownership and ownership: ownership of shares by shareholders and ownership of assets by the corporation. Shareholders are not principals; directors, officers, and managers are not shareholders' agents. Shareholders do elect directors, but directors then act according to corporate law, which rarely requires maximizing current shareholder value. To the contrary, corporate law allows - even encourages - directors to work for corporate longevity so long

as directors have a plausible argument that their actions are in shareholders' "long-run" interests.

Agency theory ignores this reality. Instead, much as early civilizations interpreted real-world phenomena by reference to their relationship with unseen deities, agency theorists tell tales of shareholders who struggle to keep peace with sacrifices (paying monitoring expenditures), managers make divine promises to behave (incurring bonding costs), but shareholders in the end are left to deal with the gods' uncontrolled whim (remaining managerial discretion).

Yet despite thousands of articles, there is no evidence this battle is real. Managers are usually loyal, probably because so much of the focus of existing corporate law is on the control of managerial disloyalty and because the business world is far more competitive than most agency-cost models assume, leaving little scope for managerial slack. What evidence shows instead is that managers suffer from cognitive biases; most importantly, they are too optimistic. Managerial optimism and the flexibility of corporate law explain most arguable failures to maximize current shareholder value. Scholarship in both economics and law would improve if researchers faced these realities and left the cult of agency behind.

J.B. Heaton, *Corporate Governance and the Cult of Agency* (2018) [available on SSRN].

5.3.2 Agency Theory and "Incentivized" Managers

Agency theory depends at its core on the assumption that corporate managers work for shareholders. It posits that corporate structures and law seek to reduce—through various devices and incentives—the tendency of managers to engage in shirking and cheating. But do the incentives work?

Next is an article by Professor Jaap Winter (Vrije Universiteit Amsterdam Law), a Dutch law professor and an expert on executive compensation in modern public corporations. He points out that much of the contemporary design of executive compensation, which to date has largely involved fine-tuning "performance" incentives, may actually misconceive how people (including corporate executives) are motivated. He points out that there are psychological phenomena that indicate that when others create "incentives" for us, we sometimes do exactly the opposite of what we are "incentivized" to do. (Think of when you were a kid, and you were told to clean the dishes to earn your allowance. How many dishes did you allow to fall to the floor?) He argues that we must break down the myths of what motivates people, particularly executives in corporations, and replace them with new (or perhaps ancient) understandings of what deeply moves us.

Corporate Governance Going Astray: Executive Remuneration Built to Fail

(2012)

Jaap Winter

[available on SSRN]

I. Bonuses of Contention

Most of the modern academic thinking on corporate governance starts from the understanding that in public companies with dispersed ownership an agency relation exists between the managers as agents whose decisions affect the shareholders as principals. Corporate governance and underlying company law mechanisms are very much about addressing the issues triggered by this relationship, seeking to ensure that managers act in the interests of shareholders.

A relatively new corporate governance mechanism, introduced in the 1990s, is to align the interests of managers with the interests of shareholders through the remuneration of executives. This was done by making executive pay dependent upon meeting performance targets and by paying executives in stock options and shares of the company. Scholars in the US claimed that the problem of executive remuneration was not that CEOs received too much pay, but that their pay was not related to the performance of companies (Jensen, Murphy 1990).

Performance based pay in the US [encouraged by US tax laws] primarily took the form of stock options, based on the belief that stock options did not present a cost to the company. Europe was quick to catch up with performance-based pay. Large cash bonuses, stock option and share awards have become common pay features for executives of EU listed companies.

Performance pay, popularly captured under the now ominous term "bonuses," in the meantime has become highly contentious in the wake of the financial crisis. Many believe extreme variable pay schemes have led executives, managers and traders of financial institutions to excessive risk taking with short term private benefits for themselves and the risks shifted to the institutions.

Public outrage has been triggered even more by the continuation of excessive bonus payments by some financial institutions while they and other institutions with which they trade have received billions and billions of aid from governments, paid for by tax payers' money (Sandel 2009). Although performance-based pay did receive criticism before the financial crisis (Bebchuk, Fried 2004, Jensen, Murphy 2004), the public and political outrage after the crisis go way beyond such criticism and cause a major rift between financial institutions, and perhaps the business community at large, and the rest of society.

Both the public outrage and the lack of responsiveness from the industry preclude a sensible debate about the effectiveness of performance-based pay. My sense is that we can only return to normal if both sides of the debate would focus on what performance-based pay is actually doing.

This article seeks to contribute to such a debate. The key argument is that performance-based pay for executives not only suffers from the original criticism of bad governance and poor design, but that it cannot be made to work because people behave differently than performance-based pay assumes. I think we have shot ourselves in the foot with a governance mechanism that was supposed to mitigate the agency problem but has aggravated it instead. My argument is not of a legal nature but is concerned primarily with the reality of being human that underlies our rules and practices.

This article is about performance-based pay for executive directors of listed companies, as a governance response to the perceived agency problem of well-informed managers who are in control and may not always act in the interest of less or uninformed dispersed shareholders. I am not making the claim that performance-based pay never works in any setting, although I do believe the evidence presented here may also be relevant for the effectiveness of performance-based pay in other settings.

II. Initial Criticism: The Governance and Design of Executive Renumeration

Criticism of performance-based pay systems to reward executives is not new. In 2004 Bebchuk and Fried published their book "Pay without Performance, the Unfulfilled Promise of Executive Compensation" (Bebchuk, Fried 2004). The core element of their argument is that performance-based pay for executives assumes that a company's board of directors negotiates pay arrangements at arm's length from executives, which does not happen in reality.

> Directors have had various economic incentives to support, or at least go along with, arrangements favorable to the company's top executives. Various social and psychological factors—collegiality, team spirit, a natural desire to avoid conflict within the board team, and sometimes friendship and loyalty – have also pulled board members in that direction. Although many directors own shares in their firms, their financial incentives to avoid arrangements favorable to executives have been too weak to induce them to take the personally costly, or at the very least unpleasant, route of haggling with their CEOs. Finally, limitations on time and resources have made it difficult for even well-intentioned directors to do their pay-setting job properly.

Bebchuk and Fried suggest a number of improvements both to pay schemes (for example, reducing windfall profits) and to the governance and transparency of performance based pay schemes, including requiring shareholder approval of equity based plans.

After having promoted performance-based pay as a means to mitigate the principal-agent problem, Jensen and Murphy have reviewed actual pay practices in 2004, concluding that the design is often poor (for example on performance targets) and that boards typically simply ratify executive's remuneration initiatives (Jensen, Murphy 2004).

Regulation of executive remuneration until now also primarily focuses on the governance of remuneration: the role of independent non-executive directors, shareholder vote on remuneration policy or remuneration reports and on share-based schemes of remuneration, independence of remuneration consultants, disclosure of individual director pay etc. Regulation, as the initial criticism, assumes that performance-based pay can be made to work if only it would be designed and governed better.

III. Can We Handle Executive Performance Based Pay?

Research from a wider field of cognitive sciences seriously questions whether performance-based pay for executives can ever be made to work. The nature of the challenges has everything to do with who and how we are as human beings. The evidence provided comes from new research into how we make decisions and choices, our biases, our blind spots, our self-serving nature and our perceptions of fairness. Somehow little of the findings of this research has found its way to the debate on performance-based pay for executives.

In the following paragraphs I will discuss what we know about incentives, target setting and benchmarking and why this, at least for me, destroys the validity of our assumptions underlying performance-based pay for executives. It appears that we as humans simply cannot handle performance-based pay.

IV. Incentives and Behavior

Economic theory has long held that monetary incentives improve performance. Since the governance crisis at the start of this millennium it has been recognized that in particular. stock options as the mechanism that was introduced to reward executives may provide perverse incentives. Coffee explained how the surge in stock option schemes in the 1990s has led to a proportionate surge in restatements of annual accounts by listed companies in the US (Coffee 2003). Shares acquired under stock option schemes could be sold immediately, which lead executives to drive up the stock price through aggressive earnings forecasts, which they then satisfied by premature earnings recognition thus sustaining higher market valuations.

But the problem with monetary incentives lies much deeper. A growing body of psychological research raises serious questions about the effects of monetary incentives. An important phenomenon that is now widely evidenced is *crowding out.* Monetary incentives appear to have the effect that the intrinsic motivation of people to perform a certain task well is moved aside by the extrinsic monetary incentive. This often has the effect that people actually perform less than without the monetary incentive.

An often cited example of the "crowding out" effect are fines that a day care center in Israel imposed on parents who arrived late to pick up their children, which resulted into more parents coming late. Parents perceived the fine as a price to be paid for additional services, which substituted the feeling of guilt or obligation parents may have towards their children and their care-takers (Gneezy, Rustichini 2000).

Once an explicit incentive is introduced the perception may shift to the understanding that effort is only required because of and according to the incentive, and the social norms as a basis for providing effort are forgotten. Ariely offers a variety of examples, including one of lawyers who generally refuse to offer services for retirees at a very low rate of $30 an hour, but overwhelmingly agree to offer those services for free (Ariely 2008). The low fee signals that the activity is governed by market norms with sharp-edged exchanges and no place for pro-social behavior. Without the fee being offered the perception is that the activity is governed by social norms, based on our need for community and mutual help.

The crowding out effect is not all. A different strand of research indicates that monetary incentives have a negative impact on creative, non-mechanical tasks. In 1945 Duncker conducted an experiment, giving participants a candle, a box of thumbtacks and a book of matches and asking them to fix the candle to the wall so that it would not drip on the table below. Many participants try to fix the candle to the wall with the thumbtacks, or to glue it to the wall by melting it, which all does not work. Only a few find the solution to empty the box of the thumbtacks and fix the box to the wall with the tacks as a platform for the candle to stand on.

Glucksberg reported in 1962 that participants who are told they will receive a reward for solving the candle problem faster actually are slower in solving the problem than participants who are only told they are being timed in order to find out how fast people can solve the problem (Glucksberg 1962). The reward narrows the cognitive focus, blocking creativity. In other words, the carrot in front of our eyes blinds us, in particular when we need to perform complex tasks, requiring assessment of complex information. This is a cognitive analogy to limitations in our visual perception called inattentional blindness. We have a tendency to only see what we are looking for and to miss what we are not looking for, even when we are staring directly at it.

Perverse incentives, crowding out and narrowing of cognitive focus—the evidence from modern research is that the effect of monetary incentives on the performance of complex cognitive jobs is likely to be negative. The job of an executive is complex, requiring not only strong analytical skills but also an awareness of and an openness to yet unknown or uncertain factors and information and the ability to weigh opportunities and risks in light of these uncertainties. The alignment theory as a justification for performance-based pay in itself is a strong signal that the performance contingent incentive is intended to be controlling, seeking to ensure that the executives as agents perform in the interests of shareholders as principals, which they, apparently, would not do otherwise. The insistence by shareholders that executives should only be paid if there is clear, measurable performance gives the same signal. The variable part of total pay of the executive has increased substantially over the last decade and a half. This has enforced the crowding out effect and at the same time has narrowed the cognitive focus of executives to ensuring that targets will be met and the performance-based pay is actually paid.

V. Target Setting, Gaming, and Cheating

A crucial element of performance-based pay for executives is setting targets in advance and measuring if and to what extent these targets have been met. The pay-out is then related to the actual achievement in relation to the pre-set targets. Based partly on experience and partly on perception, shareholders and code regulators have insisted that the targets to be set should be objective and measurable and should be disclosed to the extent not competition sensitive.

I leave aside here that the targets often used in performance-based pay systems offer only a one-sided, often short term perspective on performance that is to be rewarded, typically produced by financial performance indicators that happen to be available. Regulation attempts to deal with this by insisting that longer term targets and non-financial targets should be used to measure performance that is to be rewarded. But target setting has a number of negative side effects that are completely ignored in the discussion on executive remuneration.

As Ordonez, Schweitzer, Galinsky and Bazerman write on the basis of a study of literature on goals setting and performance, target setting can narrow focus, motivate risk-taking, lure people into unethical behaviour, inhibit learning, increase competition, and decrease intrinsic motivation (Ordonez, Schweitzer, Galinsky, Bazerman 2009). Jensen describes the same phenomenon for the other example of goal setting we are so completely accustomed to: budgeting. Jensen calls budgeting a game that pays people to lie twice, both at the setting of the budget and when measuring whether the budget has been met or not. "Tell a manager that he or she will get a bonus when targets are realised and two things are sure to happen. First, managers will attempt to set targets that are easily reachable, and once the targets are set, they will do their best to see that the targets are met even if it damages the company to do so." (Jensen 2003)

The cheating that goes on in target-setting and measurement in business is ubiquitous and at the same time accepted as a matter of fact. Paradoxically, most people engaged in this process do not see themselves as being dishonest. In corporate life this cheating has become very much the norm when it comes to target setting for budgeting purposes, in particular when performance-based pay is related to such targets, with very little or no attention at all to standards of honesty and integrity. The result is that target setting defeats its purpose of ensuring that only real and objectively measurable performance is rewarded.

VI. (Bad) Luck

Another, related problem with performance-based pay is that it tends to reward windfall profits, increases in performance which are just a result of general market developments rather than real performance of executives. The solution is to try to single out the individual performance of a company as compared to general market trends.

The tendency to overestimate our performance fits into a pattern in which we generally view ourselves in a more positive light than is objectively accurate. The basis for this tendency is our motive to affirm self-worth. People react to negative information about themselves by making more self-serving attributions that affirm their worth. We look for reasons outside our own performance to explain the failure to reach targets. To preserve our self-worth we then explain that we worked very hard in a difficult market, which justifies that we receive our bonus. Or we start to cheat to ensure that targets will be met, to the possible detriment of the company, or to show that targets have indeed been met while in reality they have not.

VII. Benchmarking for Fairness and Status

A final essential feature of modern executive remuneration schemes is the benchmarking of the performance of the company to the performance of other companies in a peer group. Similar to the insistence on objective and measurable targets, benchmarking was introduced to provide for a more objective standard of the company's performance and, possibly, to exclude windfall profits. And as with performance targets, the composition of peer groups has been widely manipulated in order to ensure that executive remuneration would go up regardless of performance. But the heart of the problem is much more pervasive. Benchmarking is an expression of the human reality that we perceive the fairness of our income in relative terms, relative to what others make for similar or different jobs.

One particular element of the benchmarking of executive remuneration warrants special attention. Remuneration policies typically provide that the company will reward its executives above the median, or sometimes in the top quartile of the peer group. The argument for this has generally been that a company with an ambition to be successful cannot afford to pay its executives only in the lower 50% of the companies it compares itself with. The result is well known: the remuneration of executives of all companies will spiral up. If a company is not yet paying its executives in the upper half, it will have to increase remuneration to get there. As a result another company will drop from the upper half and will have to increase its executive remuneration to get back above the median—and so on and so forth.

Many blame the disclosure of individual directors pay, which has been made mandatory in many EU member states in the last few years (Ferrarini, Moloney, Ungureanu 2009), as the root cause for this effect on executive pay. I do not think it is the main cause. Benchmarking would have taken place also without disclosure of individual director pay. It is the core business of remuneration consultants advising companies and their non-executive directors on pay levels and structures.

The fairness of executive remuneration as executives perceive it themselves is closely related to social status. In our world of financial capitalism, remuneration has become the key measure for the status of executives. It is the same with fund managers, investment bankers, management consultants, doctors and lawyers. High remuneration signals high social status among peers. The problem with social status is that it is a zero sum game: if you have more status than I have, then I should get more by receiving even higher pay, after which your status will have been reduced and you need to get paid more in order to get more status etc (Layard 2005).

The Russian peasant, whose neighbor has a cow, when asked by God how He can help, answered: "Kill the cow." (Layard 2005) We all continuously need to *keep up with the Joneses* and executives are no different. The status factor probably is even more important than the actual income derived from pay schemes as such. Most executives when asked admit that they do not need the high income they receive and would be willing to cut back but only when others accept a cut-back too.

VIII. Regulation Will Not Help

The research described here indicates that the difficulties with executive remuneration are much more fundamental than previously discussed. Financial incentives often work counterproductive, in particular when the incentives are large and the job to be done is cognitively complex. Performance based pay on the basis of pre-set targets induces manipulation and cheating, while our self-serving nature allows us to maintain that we are honest, deserve the pay and ignore the cost of lack of integrity. With remuneration as the key indicator of status for executives, they are all trapped in an upward spiraling race that no one can ever win.

I very much doubt that any new design or better governance of executive pay schemes can solve these fundamental problems of performance-based pay for executives. Additional design elements are likely to enhance the control-nature of the incentives, targets and wider conditions of performance-based pay. They will have precisely the unintended effect of crowding out executives' intrinsic motivation to perform well and will provide ever more incentives to cheat and manipulate and to not feel bad about it.

A typical response in such a situation would be to regulate executive remuneration, prohibit performance-based pay or at least restrict it substantially. The prospects of such regulation however are dim. Moreover, regulation will never be realistic if we do not fundamentally reconsider the pros and cons of performance-based pay. Also, the problem of ineffective and counterproductive executive pay in essence is a private problem, the consequences of which are suffered by companies and shareholders in the first place.

In all likelihood regulation will have precisely the opposite effect. The more we regulate, the more our responsibility focuses on compliance rather than on the effect of our behavior. The more rules we make the more we only care about following the rules and think that within the rules we are free to do whatever suits us best, regardless of the consequences for others (Winter 2010).

Companies and their shareholders will have to come to their senses: performance-based pay for executives is not a solution for the alignment problem, not because of the design or governance but because of who we are.

IX. A Paradigm Change

Coming to our senses is easier said than done. The business community and the financial industry within it have created a strong belief that performance-based pay is the right way to remunerate executives. With executives being on the bonus drip for almost two decades and remuneration consultants depending on creating benchmarks and designing complex performance-based pay systems there are powerful vested interests to maintain the current remuneration paradigm. So what should we do? I offer three things: deconstruct the myths surrounding performance-based pay, building a new narrative and some lessons for the key actors: shareholders, non-executives and executives. None of this is rule or incentive based. And none of this is of a quick-fix nature.

Deconstructing Myth

The business community (companies and their shareholders) has created a cascade of myths surrounding performance-based pay that its members have massively started to believe in. The myths include:

- performance based pay for executives actually enhances overall performance of companies
- the more performance based pay the better the performance of the company
- executives personally create success for their companies
- when executives lead companies to higher performance they are entitled to receive part of the gains
- executives only perform well when they have "skin in the game"
- substantial performance-based pay is essential to retain first class managers in an international market for executive talent
- financial rewards are the key indicators of personal success.

The combination of these myths leads to worldviews and frames of reference that have come to dominate the business community and how it behaves. Erhard, Jensen, Zaffron and Granger describe worldviews and frames of reference as "the network of unexamined ideas, beliefs, biases, prejudices, social and cultural embeddedness and taken for granted assumptions through which an individual interprets and interacts with the world, other people and himself or herself or with a given specific something in his or her world". (Erhard, Jensen, Zaffron, Granger 2010)

The pattern of action that follows may not be consistent at all with what is actually there. Here is an example of how it works. David de Cremer, a Rotterdam based professor of Behavioural Business Ethics, recently interviewed fifteen executives of Dutch banks, with some revealing results (De Cremer 2010). They all believed that others in the banking world find bonuses more important for performing well than they themselves do. De Cremer continues with asking the executives to make a choice between two types of bankers to manage their personal wealth. Type A banker only works for his personal financial incentive, type B banker has a genuine interest in banking matters and wants to provide service to customers. All executives said they would bring their money to banker B. The self-created myth about what sort of remuneration is needed to retain talent leads banking executives to hire the people they would not entrust with their own money. Who is fooling whom?

Our standard legal (i.e. rules prohibiting or prescribing behaviour) and economic (i.e. incentives determining the behavior of rational subjects) approaches will not challenge the myths surrounding performance based pay, they are based on these myths. They need to be fundamentally innovated with the input of modern cognitive sciences.

Building a New Narrative

Deconstructing the myths surrounding executive performance-based pay will also require that an alternative remuneration narrative is built. The new narrative should include a few key elements:

- *Make remuneration less significant:* rather than using remuneration as a primary instrument to steer executive behavior we should reduce the importance of remuneration. Money is a threshold motivator: it motivates only up to a baseline, beyond that it does not do much and likely more harm than good.
- *Benchmark internally instead of externally:* the crucial factor that can move remuneration off the table is fairness. Fairness here is relative fairness, compared to what others receive for similar or different jobs. As long as people perceive that their remuneration is unfair in light of what others receive remuneration will remain an issue. Our current model is set to focus excessively on external fairness, in relation to peers in the industry. At the same time internal fairness is often ignored completely, with executive remuneration becoming ever higher multiples of average employee pay. Refocusing benchmarks on internal fairness will help to stop the upward spiraling that is the result of automatic benchmarking with external peers, pushing remuneration up without any connection to underlying performance. Most companies need executives who are committed more to the company's future than to their own remuneration.

Self-determination in the workplace

Business consulting firms have understood the importance to business of motivating people in business to grow and change. According to McKinsey, for example, this can happen when "three innate psychological needs—autonomy, competence, and relatedness or connection—are fulfilled." See *Self-Determination Theory*, Int'l Encyclopedia of the Social & Behavioral Sciences (2d ed. 2015). Thus, for companies to retain talent, "serious attention" must be paid (as is happening) to mental-health issues. The stresses of COVID-19—leading to workers' feelings of isolation and burnout—have given rise to a slew of employer-sponsored mental-health programs and flexible work arrangements. In the end, having a sense of collective purpose is critical to workplace functioning.

- *Reduce variable pay substantially and use a wide set of collective targets:* executive variable pay today often doubles or triples fixed pay. This triggers the cognitive focus on everything that can ensure the desired outcome regardless of the risks or costs involved. Variable pay should be reduced substantially as part of overall compensation. And as long as performance-based pay systems are used, the target setting should include a wide set of measures, indicating the company's performance in a number of areas that are critical for its success in the future, including non-financial indicators.
- *Our real motivation:* remuneration should not be allowed to destroy our real motivation to do well at our jobs. Pink has researched extensively what truly motivates us and three factors stand out: autonomy, mastery and purpose (Pink 2010). A sense of autonomy—willful choice, and the opposite of control—has a powerful effect on individual performance as a number of behavioral studies indicate (Csikszentmihalyi 1975). Autonomy requires trust both from the person who does the job and from the person who assesses the performance. Autonomy leads to engagement, which enhances the ability of people to take responsibility for the job they should perform. Performance based pay is precisely doing the opposite as it seeks to exercise control over performance by rewarding achievement of pre-established targets and takes distrust as its starting point. The second element is striving for mastery, which appears to be a strong predictor of productivity. If the challenges are set right, not too high when the fear of failing creates anxiety, or too low when we get bored, people can get into flow, continuously improving their mastery. Work becomes play and self-fulfilling: the activity is its own reward. The third element, is purpose. People become particularly motivated if they can contribute to something that is larger than themselves. Chasing personal profit goals and reaching them does not satisfy us, while striving to reach purposes beyond ourselves has a lasting effect on our happiness. Modern happiness studies all indicate that finding purpose in something larger than ourselves is a crucial factor contributing to happiness. Seligman describes transcendence as one of the six virtues endorsed by almost all religious and philosophical traditions (Seligman 2008). Haidt describes the elevation that stirs a warm emotion in us when we witness moral beauty (Haidt 2006). It is also the source of power and passion that leaders need (Erhard, Jensen, Zaffron, Granger 2010). And again, performance-based pay is doing precisely the opposite: it makes our own direct pay off the driving force of our actions, rather than the larger purposes we could be striving for.

Lessons for Shareholders, Executives and Non-Executives
What are the lessons? Performance based pay for executives in its current form does not reduce the agency problem, but exacerbates it. Substantial performance-based pay increases the focus of executives on their personal interests to the detriment of all other interests, including the interests of shareholders. Alignment of financial interests has proven to be an illusion.

So what is the alternative? The idea that executives of public companies cannot be trusted to take the interests of shareholders sufficiently into account is deeply rooted. But one of the core reasons for the lack of trust between shareholders and executives may be a lack of engagement between the two. Working toward engagement is a much more promising avenue for shareholders to secure the value of their investments than relying on performance-based pay for executives to create an illusory alignment of financial interests.

Seeing our worldviews and frames of reference that guide our perception and actions is difficult for all of us. If you also have a strong material interest in maintaining them, like executives have with performance-based pay, it becomes all the more difficult. It is therefore no surprise to see that executives struggle to listen, understand and appreciate the criticism on their remuneration and not dismiss it outright, there is simply too much worldview and self-interest in the way. More regulation restricting remuneration in form and scope will not help executives to see their self-created myths on remuneration, it will only confirm them in their view that the politicians, media, trade unions and the public in general don't know what they are talking about. Many theories about leadership have been developed over time, but a crucial commonality is that leadership is not about the success of the leader but of the organization he leads. It is precisely this shift of attention from oneself to the purpose beyond oneself that also gives the leader access to a much deeper level of enduring satisfaction and happiness. This finding is so basic and yet so easy to ignore, certainly in the face of large personal gains that can be made. "You only see it when you get it," is how Johan Cruijff, the famous Dutch soccer player, describes it (Winsemius 2005). It takes courageous leaders to acknowledge that the focus on personal income has not worked well and to develop new, truly motivating stories.

Solving the Candle Problem

An interesting TED Talk by Dan Pink, a best-selling author on behavioral economics in business and a law graduate who never practiced law, echoes Professor Winter's thesis. Pink describes how when subjects are offered incentives to solve problems (such as the famous "candle problem") they perform less well than when not rewarded. And when offered larger rewards, they perform even worse! Carrots and sticks don't seem to work as well as the sheer pleasure of accomplishing something—"intense autonomy" is what Pink calls it. In short, business doesn't seem to understand human motivation! Paying for performance actually leads to less performance. Instead, intrinsic motivation, autonomy, mastery, and a sense of larger purpose—the key elements of human happiness—are what produce results. See Dan Pink, TED Talk (2009).

When We Are in Business Mode

Furthermore, when we are motivated to act like automatons in a business setting, we put our moral compasses to one side. Consider, for example, a recent study that found that employees in a large Swiss bank are more prone to lie when they are in their "work mode." The study asked the employees to guess how a coin flip would come out—but to reveal their guess *after* the flip. That's right: the experiment tested the participants' honesty When the employees were not in work mode—after answering benign non-work-laden questions like "how much TV do you watch"—they tended to report that their guesses were about 50/50 correct. That is, they were being honest. But when prompted subliminally to think about work—"fill in the word __oker" (and they said "broker" instead of "smoker" or "poker")—they became quite dishonest, with some reporting 100 percent success in guessing the coin flip. Thus, when we are in "work mode," we become immoral! (The same results happened when employees at manufacturing and telecommunications firms were put into work mode. Of course, the results would be different in law schools where everybody is morally above reproach.)

5.3.3 Business Ethics as a Smokescreen

How does one create more business ethics? The typical answer: more rules! Consider, for example, the international campaign to get financial regulators to commit to "creating consistent global ethical standards for financial institutions. The campaign assumes away differences in industry structure and national cultures in the service of a vision of a consistent financial regulatory regime applied to banks and non-bank financial firms across the world." David Zaring, *The International Campaign to Create Ethical Bankers* (2017) [available on ideas.repec.org]. One has to wonder how this really will or can work.

Lately, large US companies have begun using compliance management systems (CMSs) to address compliance issues in a variety of areas: environment, workplace health and safety, finance, health care, and aviation. CMSs establish systematic, checklist-like processes meant to improve organizational compliance with government regulation. They can help managers identify compliance obligations, assign responsibility for meeting them, track progress, and take corrective action as needed. In effect, CMSs internalize inspection and enforcement responsibilities. Recognizing their potential benefits, some government policymakers and regulators have started to require certain firms to adopt CMSs.

Do CMSs work to foster a culture of business ethics? Or are they a smokescreen that hides self- or other-delusion? In a recent, comprehensive look at CMSs, an MBA and a law professor conclude that "firms with certain types of CMSs in place experience fewer compliance violations and show improvements in risk management. But these effects appear to be rather modest. Compliance in large organizations generally requires more than just a CMS; it also demands appropriate managerial attitudes, organizational cultures, and information technologies that extend beyond the systematic, checklist processes characteristic of CMSs." Cary Coglianese & Jennifer Nash, *Com-*

pliance Management Systems: Do They Make a Difference? (2020) [available on SSRN].

An expert in corporate compliance (and the first person to consult with the Department of Justice on corporate compliance under the US sentencing guidelines) identified seven ways in which corporate compliance programs mask festering ethical problems. Hui Chen, *Compliance: Seven Signs of Ineffective Compliance Programs*, Bloomberg Law (Mar. 21, 2018). Basically, corporate compliance has become a way to "do just the bare minimum"—a cynical attitude that invites a disregard for the spirit of the law. The author points to seven symptoms: lackadaisical financial reporting, legalistic posturing (and hiding behind the attorney-client privilege), a focus on avoiding jail, empty metrics, one-time (rather than continuous) monitoring, a narrow focus on single-statute compliance (such as the FCPA), and an obsession with minutia (like travel budgets, not million-dollar pay packages).

Instead, ethics and morality seem to be contextual. Many studies look at the important influence that "tone at the top" has on organizational ethics. See Mark Penno, *A Theory of Assurance: Balancing Costly Formal Control with Tone at the Top* (2018) [available on SSRN] (concluding that informal "tone at the top" and formal corporate controls may be complementary); Dov Fischer & Hershey H. Friedman, *Tone-at-The-Top Lessons from Abrahamic Justice* (2017) [available on SSRN] (identifying Abraham's "leadership by example" as a template for business ethics, as applied to whether business leaders violate duties to shareholders by engaging in legal tax avoidance).

Interestingly, it turns out that "tone in the city" may also be relevant. A recent study looks at how misconduct rates in financial firms vary widely (sometimes by a factor of three) depending on where the firm's headquarters are located. Christopher A. Parsons, Johan Sulaeman & Sheridan Titman, *The Geography of Financial Misconduct* (2018) [available on SSRN]. The study identified that in 20 US cities, average rates of financial-firm misconduct are three times higher in high-misconduct cities (Miami and Dallas) compared to low-misconduct cities (Minneapolis and Indianapolis). The study used as proxies for social misconduct such measurable factors as political corruption, financial advisor fraud, options backdating, spousal infidelity, and rent-seeking physicians. The authors pointed out that while spatial differences in enforcement or firm characteristics do not account for these patterns, city-level norms appear to be very important. For example, social misconduct rates are strongly also related to unethical behavior in the city among its politicians, doctors, and (potentially unfaithful) spouses. Where do you think you should live?

5.3.4 "Integrity" as a Principle of Human (and Thus Corporate) Behavior

Retreat from Agency Theory

Finally, we consider whether agency theory is an adequate description of the corporation. The idea that the corporation is meant to ameliorate shareholder-management conflicts comes from Professor Michael Jensen (Harvard Business), who we've come across in numerous instances in this book. He wrote the influential 1976 article on "agency costs," identifying the corporation as a principal-agent relationship and corporate law as a set of rules to reduce the conflicts between shareholders (the principal/owners) and corporate managers (the agents). The article is the most cited article in the history of corporate law—more than 10,000 citations in Westlaw JLR, and more than 140,000 downloads on SSRN. Michael C. Jensen & William H. Meckling, *A Theory of the Firm: Governance, Residual Claims and Organizational Forms*, 3 J. Fin. Econ. 305 (1976) [available on SSRN]. (Jensen is also the founder of SSRN.)

Much has happened since Jensen's 1976 article. For one thing, most economics (and law) academics have accepted as "truth" that the corporation—as well as the many instruments of corporate governance—is mostly about getting managers to act for the benefit of shareholders. That is, the Jensen "agency theory" model accepts shareholder wealth maximization as an unquestioned norm and then identifies the ways in which corporate law and business norms can be employed to move managers to be "shareholder thinking." For another thing, nearly all academic writing on corporate governance both in law and management—and thus nearly all corporate policy—has sought to identify and ameliorate the manager-shareholder conflict. Corporate contracts, stock markets, securities regulation, and even business norms all point toward this one vision of the corporation.

Agency theory, however, has not lived up to its promise. This has been a principal theme of this book, brought to a head with the readings that began this unit. While some corporate governance mechanisms have reduced agency costs, others have had untoward effects. For example, rules that fostered markets in corporate control resulted in the leveraging of companies in ways that were not sustainable; stock option compensation created incentives for managers to manipulate stock prices; and risk management by so-called independent directors resulted in disastrous group-think. In short, agency theory has not anchored the corporation in a "purpose" that people can fully believe in.

In fact, the financial literature seems to be abandoning the notion that the conventional, rational *homo economicus* model explains human behavior in business and financial settings. Remember the TED Talk from Ch 4.1 by Nick Hanauer in which he described economics as "the dirty secret of capitalism." The academic literature is also turning against the neo-liberal conception of human business/finance motivations:

> Research in behavioral corporate finance has accumulated to the point that it may now be a viable contender as an alternative to traditional corporate finance. First, I discuss the foundations behind these two competing theories. I clarify concepts such as rational versus irrational behaviors of managers contrasted with those of the investors. Second, I make side-by-side comparisons and a critical examination of the two theories in the main topic areas of dividends, capital structure, and investments. Part three gives practical suggestions on how practitioners may use behavioral finance in their dealings as well as avoid known behavioral biases.

James S. Ang, *Behavioral vs. Traditional Corporate Finance: An Unabashed Critical Review* (2018) [available on SSRN].

Jensen's "Integrity Project"

The data thus raise doubts about the assumptions of "agency theory." The right "carrots and sticks" do not necessarily lead human actors to think and to act as expected. Perhaps there is something more—some "dark matter" in the corporation—that explains how we really think and behave in a business organization.

This has been on Professor Jensen's mind. Here is a redacted summary of his "integrity model"—one in which a necessary condition to full workability and productivity in any human/social setting is that individuals and organizations "keep their word."

> We present a positive model that distinguishes four phenomena—integrity, morality, ethics, and legality. Integrity exists in a positive realm devoid of normative content—it is not about good or bad, right or wrong, what should or should not be. Morality, ethics, and legality exist in a normative realm of virtues—that is, they are about good and bad, right and wrong, and what should or should not be.
>
> Thus, integrity is the objective state or condition of an object, system, person, group, or organizational entity. This is consistent with the first two of the three definitions in Webster's dictionary, which defines integrity as a state or condition of being whole, complete, unbroken, unimpaired, sound, perfect condition.
>
> We assert that integrity (the condition of being whole and complete) is a necessary condition for workability, and that the resultant level of workability determines for an individual, group, or organization the available opportunity set for performance.
>
> For an individual, integrity is that person's word being whole and complete. For a group or organizational entity, integrity is that group or organization's word being whole and complete. In both contexts, integrity is honoring one's word.
>
> We define "honoring your word" to mean that you either keep your word or, as soon as you know that you will not, you say that you will not and clean up any mess you caused by not keeping your word. By "keeping your word" we mean doing what you said you would do and doing it by the time you said you would.
>
> Honoring your word is also the route to creating whole and complete social and working relationships. In addition, it provides an actionable pathway to earning the trust of others. Perhaps most importantly, it provides an actionable pathway to being whole and complete with oneself—that is, to being an integrated person.

Werner H. Erhard, Michael C. Jensen & Steve Zaffron, *Integrity: A Positive Model that Incorporates the Normative Phenomena of Morality, Ethics, and Legality—Abridged* (2010) [available on SSRN].

The following interview of Michael Jensen lays out his "integrity project."

Integrity: Without It Nothing Works

Interview with Michael C. Jensen by Karen Christensen
Rotman Magazine (Fall 2009), *revised* 2014 (M. C. Jensen)
[available on SSRN]
[redacted/paraphrased]

There is some confusion between the terms integrity, morality, and ethics. How do you differentiate them?

> We understand these three phenomena as providing standards of "correct" behaviour. But we often confuse them. For me, integrity is a purely positive proposition—nothing to do with good versus bad. It's like the Law of Gravity: there is no such thing as "good" or "bad" gravity; like integrity, it just "is." For me, morality and ethics are normative concepts that deal with good or bad. Morality is a set of social standards of right and wrong. Ethics is a set of normative values that apply to all members of a group or organization.

You define integrity as "what it takes for a person to be whole and complete." What does this look like in daily life?

> We are whole and complete when our word is whole and complete—that is, when we honor our word. We do this, first, by keeping our word and on time. And, second, when we know that we won't keep our word, we let everyone know who is counting on us and we clean up any mess that we've caused. By doing this, this, we have honored our word and we have maintained our integrity.
>
> This means, we should be careful before giving your word to anyone. When we cannot or will not keep our word, this is sure to lead to out-of-integrity behavior.
>
> Integrity is important to individuals, groups, organizations, and society because it creates workability. Without integrity, things don't work. Therefore, integrity is necessary for maximum performance. It's how others trust us.

"One's Word." Defined

A person's word consists of each of the following:

What you said: whatever you say you will do or not do—and when.

What you know: whatever you know to do or not to do—and as it's meant to be done and on time.

What is expected: whatever you are (explicitly or not) expected to do or not do—and on time.

What you say is so: whenever you have given your word to others about something, your word includes being held accountable that the otherswho rely on you.

What you say you stand for: What you stand for (as you declare to others or yourself) is a part of your word.

Social moral standards, group ethical standards, and governmental legal norms, are all part of one's word unless (a) you have explicitly and publicly said you do not intend to not abide by one or more of these standards, and (b) you are willing to bear the costs of your refusal to conform.

You've said that integrity involves the relationship one has with oneself. Can you explain this?

> Our word to ourselves is critical to integrity. To be a person of integrity you must give your word to yourself and declare the following: "Who I am is my word" and "I give my word to myself that I am a person of integrity."

If we fail to honor our word to ourselves, we both undermine ourselves and diminish who we are as a person. Without this aspect of integrity, we create "unworkability" in our lives. Others see us as inconsistent, unreliable, and unpredictable. This happens too much. We often point to external causes of the mess in our lives and have trouble acknowledging that the mess comes from our own out-of-integrity behavior.

Your Ontological Law of Integrity says that integrity is critical to business performance. How does integrity translate into performance?

So, integrity is a necessary for maximum performance. Only if something is in integrity – is whole, complete, unbroken—can it have maximum workability. Although workability (a product of integrity) is not sufficient for maximum performance, it is necessary. If you respect the Law of Integrity, you will experience increases in performance, both in your organization and in your life.

You have said that out-of-integrity behavior causes much more damage than most people know. Can you explain?

We often view integrity as a virtue that is "nice to have," not as something directly related to performance. We fail to link difficulties in our lives or in our organizations to being out of integrity. But the potential increases in output and productivity by focusing on integrity are huge. Not 10%, but more like 100% to 500%. At my organization [the Social Science Research Network (SSRN)] after three years of implementing these notions, we've seen more than a 300% increase in output, with essentially no increase in inputs. And our people are happier.

How is integrity related to "cost-benefit analysis"?

Every business school I know teaches students the importance of cost/benefit analysis in everything they do. This is often useful—but not when it comes to integrity. In fact, viewing integrity (honoring your word) as a matter of cost/benefit analysis nearly guarantees you will be out of integrity. When you apply a cost/benefit analysis to honoring your word by stating the cost/benefit contingency is part of your word, you are really saying: "I will choose to honor my word if on a cost-benefit analysis I decide it is expedient." Once you have said this, your word means nothing.

We should make clear to our business school students that that cost/benefit analysis is important—but not with respect to honoring one's word. In my view, our failure to do this is a major root cause of the current economic crisis.

Trust in the business community has plummeted. How can it be restored?

Integrity of an Organization, Defined

An organization (or any human system) is in integrity when:

It is whole and complete with respect to its word. Nothing is hidden, there is no deception, there are no untruths, contracts and property rights are respected, etc.

The organization keeps its word internally (between its members) and externally (with those it deals with). This includes what the organization says both to its members and to outsiders.

Consider the subprime mortgage crisis. Each aspect of the system evolved in a way that left it out-of-integrity. The system rewarded people for creating and selling mortgages and mortgage-backed securities, with no expectation they would be paid.

How to put the system back in order? It's simple: people have to start honoring their word. If they do, trust will materialize almost instantly. It's curious, but you actually can create trust more rapidly if you fail to keep your word, but then you honor it. For example, I might say: "I said that I would give you the report next week, but now I realize I can't get it to you then. I apologize. I'll get it to you in 10 days, instead. Please, let me clean up the mess I've caused for you." If I get the report to you in 10 days, our relationship will be strengthened. But if I simply don't keep my original word, you won't trust me.

Michael Jensen is the Jesse Isidor Straus Professor of Business Administration, Emeritus at Harvard Business School. He was the founder of the Social Science Research Network, which brings "Tomorrow's Research Today" to people worldwide. This interview is based on his paper, *Integrity: A Positive Model that Incorporates the Normative Phenomena of Morality, Ethics and Legality* (co-written with Werner Erhard and Steve Zaffron) [available on SSRN].

The "Integrity" Corporation

Others are also thinking along these lines. Consider the place of trust in the modern corporation. If the "nexus of contracts" corporation that agency theory posits is incomplete, what replaces it? Some modern theorists find agency theory and shareholder primacy as stepping stones toward a "networked corporation"—one in which trust among members of the network is critical, even the defining attribute. In looking at the move toward CSR and SRI, perhaps this metamorphosis is already underway. Not only may the "networked corporation" better represent what is happening, but such a network approach also gives life to a CSR corporation that recognizes the salience and roles of the corporation's many stakeholders. See Roman Tomasic & Folarin Akinbami, *Trust and Public Companies: Beginning to Reconceptualise Corporate Law in a Networked World* (2013) [available at SSRN].

What is the purpose of the corporation? Professor Eli Bukspan (Reichman University Law, Israel) offers an important answer as we move toward what he describes as "stakeholderism." Eli Bukspan, *Corporate Purpose and Stakeholder Fairness Through the Lens of Behavioral Economics* (2022) [available on SSRN]. With many participants in the corporation, including regulators and judges, now attempting to turn ideological statements into practical initiatives, a paradigm change is in progress. Bukspan bridges the gap between the idealism of stakeholder capitalism and the shareholder-focused history of corporate law.

> The new view of corporate purpose and stakeholder capitalism is closely related to the concept of fairness. Thus, certain foundational concepts developed in behavioral economics, rather than traditional economic theory, can help describe and justify the newfound prominence of the stakeholder approach and the rejuvenated discourse on corporate purpose.
>
> Critical in human decision-making is the idea of fairness, something which contradicts several basic assumptions of neoclassical economics. Not only are the basic doctrines of corporate law evolving (legal personality, piercing the corporate veil, and directors' oversight duties) but so too are non-corporate fields (such as specific legislation, contract law principles of good faith and public policy, class actions, and taxes). Overall, the law is in the process of recognizing new obligations towards stakeholders, as well as liability for failing to meet those obligations.
>
> It is possible to observe that fair corporate behavior has advantaged "early adopters"—a natural consequence of the fall of "will theory" in modern contract law and the related weakening of the "nexus of contracts" conception of the corporation. To recognize the fairness bias, guided by behavioral economics research, the law should consider fairness to be part of the modern corporation's DNA. This results, for example, in a reframing of the underlying approach towards the UK Companies Law, the primary legislation which regulates business sector activities.
>
> Reframing the corporate purpose as one based on fair consideration of stakeholder interests, along with profit-maximizing shareholder interests, harnesses the expressive function of the law by integrating desired social and business norms. It produces an alternative culture of fairness and trust, thus moving towards an intrinsic implementation of fairness and loyalty in the most crucial economic (and social) institution of our time.

In short, fairness and trust in the evolving corporation are becoming and should become like falling off a log.

Individualism Versus Collectivism

The integrated, networked corporation exposes a tension between individualism (the basis of the classic agency theory) and collectivism (where trust underlies intra-corporate interactions). Can such an organization exist? Isn't it contrary to human nature? Here's a story of a company (from the author who described the corporation as a super-organism) that seems to strike a healthy balance between individualism and collectivism—that is, between the chimpanzee and the honey bee:

> Semco S.A. is a large and diversified company headquartered in Brazil that manufactures more than 2,000 products including high volume industrial dishwashers, rocket-fuel-propellant mixers and cooling units for air conditioners. Ricardo Semler, President & CEO, is known around the world for championing the concept of employee

empowered leadership. Shortly after taking over the small family engineering firm in the mid-80's, he dismantled managerial structure to eliminate "corporate oppression" and encourage core business values of employee participation, profit sharing and free flow of information. Named as a "Global Leader of Tomorrow" by the World Economic Forum, and twice as Brazil's "Business Leader of the Year", Semler has worked hard to get out of the way.

At Semco, teams set their own production quotas, decide among themselves the best time to come to work, and design their own work environments. Each division in the company is allowed to set its own salary structure. Job candidates have to interview with dozens of potential direct reports before being offered a position. All financial information is discussed openly and freely. There are no secretaries or personal assistants, no executive dining rooms and no personalized parking spaces. There are now six co-CEOs who rotate every six months, allowing Semler to function at the highest levels of leadership and not make decisions. Instead, he is free to ask questions, cast vision, and work with others to build the future of the company. The result has been a resounding success over the past three decades, with a 25% annual growth rate and an employee turnover of just 1%.

Although Semco has remained relatively low-profile, and in a league of its own for quite some time, it is being joined by the likes of Alphabet (Google), Alibaba, Facebook, Apple and Netflix, among others. All of these companies continue to expand into new domains, focus on purpose and foster a sustainable culture.

The ultimate goal of corporate super-organisms isn't to build volume, but rather to create value. They will strive to be more than the sum of their parts. They will have low tolerance for members that don't contribute to the whole, regardless of rank. They will evaluate team effectiveness rather than individual performance. And they will reward a very different set of virtues than the ones currently being taught in most business schools, and worshiped across C-suites.

Christian Filli, *Human Evolution and the Rise of the Corporate Super-Organisms*, Medium (2018).

5.3.5 New Vocabulary of Integrity

Responsible Citizenship

Sometimes the truth has been right in front of our eyes for a long time. It's just a matter of waking up. Back in the 1980s, as agency theory became imbedded in our vocabulary and the corporation separated from its social purposes to become a maximizer of shareholder value, Professor James B. White (Michigan Law) observed that the corporation was losing its bearings:

> My immediate subject in this Comment is section 2.01 of the American Law Institute's proposed *Principles of Corporate Governance*

(Tentative Draft No. 2), which defines in general terms the proper objectives and conduct of a business corporation. My larger subject has to do with the adequacy and inadequacy of various languages in which corporate purposes and limits might be expressed, and especially with the limits of the economic language used in the ALI Draft.

What can serve as a sensible conception by which to organize corporate life? Not a conception of return, I believe, but a conception of intellectual and ethical attitude, of character. Our best goal is to be a certain kind of person, or company, or nation: the kind that can tolerate uncertainty, adapt to shifts in understanding, recognize the unknowability of the complex webs of causation in which we are caught, yet remain true to a sense of self and relation to others. Our best businessmen have always known this, for these are the qualities they have sought in their managers and leaders.

The real question is what language we should use to describe and constitute our business enterprises. The language of making money is wholly inadequate, even in the most conservative view—*especially* in the most conservative view—as to what goes on and should go on in the business world. In my view, the proper way to talk about this is to subordinate economic language to a language of citizenship, in a formula such as the following: "The business corporation should always endeavor to act as a responsible citizen in its economic and other activities."

This is at least where I would begin, leaving it in the first instance to corporate actors and critics, and to the courts, to give meaning to this standard as cases arise. I think the discourse that would arise on such a foundation would be clear enough to provide adequate guidance to private and public actors. They should certainly understand how to frame the essential questions for themselves. And this discus-

How to Activate Social Change

How might law induce changes in behavior when individuals view costs to them as outweighing social benefits—assuming there is no close-knit community to impose sanctions for failure to change? Professor Michael Vandenbergh (Vanderbilt Law) pondered this question. Michael P. Vandenbergh, *Order Without Social Norms: How Personal Norm Activation Can Protect the Environment* (2005) [available on SSRN]. Here is his answer on how to induce individuals to adopt pro-environment behaviors:

> Internalized personal norms, rather than social norms, should be the first "target of opportunity" for influencing behavioral change. Drawing on social psychology literature, a theory of environmental norm activation suggests the contours of an "innovative regulatory reform" that could enable the norm-activation process. Starting with existing reporting schemes, originally developed for industrial polluters, publication of an annual profile of toxic releases by individuals and households would address negative-payoff, loose-knit group situations by activating norms that affect behavior directly. Further, it would generate civic support for government investments that make individual behavior change less expensive and more convenient for individuals to adopt.

Assuming the government would have the gall to report your household's individual pollution footprint, would publication of this information lead you to change your anti-environmental ways?

> sion should at least not collapse into the endless reassertions of a false dichotomy of the kind the present formulation invites.
>
> Of course, this change in language would not provide automatic answers to particular questions; indeed, it would make many of them seem harder than they now do, for who is to decide what citizenship should mean, and how should they do so? But whatever we may pretend, the corporation is in fact a social institution as well as an economic one, and we should welcome, rather than reject, difficulties attendant upon the recognition of that fact. To do otherwise would be to choose one set of social consequences—those implicit in the 'economic' model—without knowing what we were doing or why.
>
> If more specificity were sought in the standard itself, it could be of two kinds. First, certain specified activities, such as partisan politics or campaign financing, could be restricted or eliminated, on the ground that the corporation's citizenship role ought not extend to electoral politics (for to do so would bias the electoral process even further in favor of the rich and politicize internal corporate life in an inappropriate way). Or one might specify the criteria of citizenship more fully, saying for example that the corporation should attempt to produce useful products and services, to provide adequate returns to investors and fair rewards to employees, to maintain its own health as a social and economic institution, and to do so with proper regard for the interests of other members of the larger community.
>
> Whatever formulation is ultimately chosen, my main point remains this: that the language of economics is inadequate to what business corporations do and ought to do. This point extends far beyond corporation law.

James B. White, *How Should We Talk About Corporations? The Language of Economics and of Citizenship* (1985) [available on UM_Law_Repository]. In short, those who constitute the corporation—all of us—will be more integral and thus richer together if we speak of ourselves as forming part of a body politic—as part of the whole.

Lessons from Trees

Or, better yet, we might want to learn from the trees and their forests. Richard Rohr (a Catholic theologian) described how Robin Wall Kimmerer (a botanist, professor, and member of the Citizen Potawatomi Nation) observed in her book *Braiding Sweetgrass* that science is finally validating the wisdom of Native American elders:

> In the old times, our elders say, the trees talked to each other. They'd stand in their own council and craft a plan. But scientists decided long ago that plants were deaf and mute, locked in isolation without communication. The possibility of conversation was summarily dismissed. Science pretends to be purely rational, completely neutral, a system of knowledge-making in which the observation is independent of the observer. And yet the conclusion was drawn that plants cannot communicate because they lack the mechanisms that animals use to

> speak. . . . But pollen has been carried reliably on the wind for eons, communicated by males to receptive females to make . . . nuts. If the wind can be trusted with that fecund responsibility, why not with messages?
>
> There is now compelling evidence that our elders were right—the trees are talking to one another. They communicate via pheromones, hormonelike compounds that are wafted on the breeze, laden with meaning. Scientists have identified specific compounds that one tree will release when it is under the stress of insect attack—gypsy moths gorging on its leaves or bark beetles under its skin. The tree sends out a distress call: "Hey, you guys over there? I'm under attack here. You might want to raise the drawbridge and arm yourselves for what is coming your way." The downwind trees catch the drift, sensing those few molecules of alarm, the whiff of danger. This gives them time to manufacture defensive chemicals. . . . The individual benefits, and so does the entire grove. Trees appear to be talking about mutual defense. . . . There is so much we cannot yet understand with our limited human capacity. Tree conversations are still far above our heads.
>
> Some studies of mast fruiting have suggested that the mechanism for synchrony comes not through the air, but underground. The trees in a forest are often interconnected by subterranean networks of mycorrhizae, fungal strands that inhabit tree roots. The mycorrhizal symbiosis enables the fungus to forage for mineral nutrients in the soil and deliver them to the tree in exchange for carbohydrates. The mycorrhizae may form fungal bridges between individual trees, so that all the trees in a forest are connected. These fungal networks appear to redistribute the wealth of carbohydrates from tree to tree. A kind of Robin Hood, they take from the rich and give to the poor so that all the trees arrive at the same carbon surplus at the same time. They weave a web of reciprocity, of giving and taking. In this way, the trees all act as one because the fungi have connected them. Through unity, survival. All flourishing is mutual.

We are all connected. Through unity, survival. All flourishing is mutual.

* * *

Concluding Thoughts

Little League (and About the Author)

Not many people know that I played Little League baseball for one spring. It was 1966. I was in sixth grade in Toledo, Ohio. Marty Ball's dad was the coach. We had uniforms and baseball caps, and we played other sixth-grade teams.

Most of our games were at the field behind Christ the King church on Sylvania Road. We practiced behind Jackman Elementary School. I rode my bike, as I remember, to practice and to the games. That was when kids were allowed to roam free.

I was absolutely the worst player on the team. But Mr. Ball let me practice and put me into many of the games. I played second base and right field, the positions where the weakest players on any Little League team were put, including mine.

In the whole season that I played Little League, I did not have one base hit. I made contact only once with the ball, tapping a lazy pop fly to the first baseman. Otherwise, nothing. I swung a few times, but except that once I never made contact.

In practice, Mr. Ball would throw me soft pitches, and once I hit the ball out of the infield and it landed in left field. A real hit. But that was because, trying to build my confidence, his pitches were slow and big. Not the blazing fastballs I faced during real games.

This does not mean I was not a success. I single-handedly won at least one game, maybe two. The reason that I never made contact with the ball as a hitter was that I swung my bat menacingly at the plate and then, as the pitch arrived, crouched down.

I was walked a lot. In fact, I may have had an OBP that rivaled Jeff Rediger, the most imposing player on our team. Jeff was a big kid, a bit paunchy. He could hit home runs. He was a friend. Some kids called him names. I hated them.

So, once on base, I was a devastating base runner. Not that I was that fast, but because I was astute and fearless. As soon as a hitter made contact, I knew to run. I would throw my body at the second baseman on an infield hit. The ball would pop out of his mitt.

And then I would scream around third base on the way to home. I looked straight into the eyes of the catcher, saying to him, "I'm going to hurt you if you get close to me." The catcher would often signal to the outfielder to throw to the shortstop.

I scored many runs, as I remember. I wasn't the biggest scorer. But once I was on base, there was a good chance I would score. And Mr. Ball knew that about me. Even though I was the worst player on the team, I may have had the biggest heart.

In the field I was not that good, either. I could scoop up the ball at second base and sometimes get it to first base in time for an out. Remember, I had never really thrown balls in Bolivia, where I grew up. There, I was the worst soccer player on my third-grade team.

But in Little League I would sacrifice my body lunging for the ball at second base. Or diving or sliding or doing whatever it took to catch a ball in right field. Once in the bottom of the seventh (the last inning in Little League), I slid and caught a fly ball. We won!

So, the reason for this story was to say that I hope you will play with even more intensity than I do. When I believe in something—as I did our Little League team—I bring myself into the game. I do not leave my soul at the door. Nor should you.

Index

C

Q

R